Third Edition

Law in Society

Canadian Readings

Edited by

Nick Larsen
Chapman University

Brian Burtch
Simon Fraser University

D0882384

NELSON / EDUCATION

NELSON / EDUCATION

Law in Society: Canadian Readings, Third Edition

by Nick Larsen and Brian Burtch

Vice President, Editorial Director:
Evelyn Veitch

Editor-in-Chief, Higher Education:
Anne Williams

Senior Acquisitions Editor:
Lenore Taylor-Atkins

Senior Marketing Manager:
David Tonen

Developmental Editor:
Katherine Goodes

Permissions Coordinator:
Nicola Winstanley

Production Service:
MPS Limited

Copy Editor:
Colleen Ste. Marie

Proofreader:
Barbara Storey

Manufacturing Manager:
Joanne McNeil

Design Director:
Ken Phipps

Managing Designer:
Franca Amore

Interior Design:
Tammy Gay

Cover Design:
Katherine Strain

Cover Image:
Michael Burtch—Artist
"Matin", 1999—Title
polyester resin and fibreglass

Cover Photographer:
Faye Smedley

Compositor:
MPS Limited

Printer:
RR Donnelley

COPYRIGHT © 2010, 2006 by Nelson Education Ltd.

Printed and bound in the United States
1 2 3 4 12 11 10 09

For more information contact Nelson Education Ltd., 1120 Birchmount Road, Toronto, Ontario, M1K 5G4. Or you can visit our Internet site at http://www.nelson.com

ALL RIGHTS RESERVED. No part of this work covered by the copyright herein may be reproduced, transcribed, or used in any form or by any means—graphic, electronic, or mechanical, including photocopying, recording, taping, Web distribution, or information storage and retrieval systems—without the written permission of the publisher.

For permission to use material from this text or product, submit all requests online at www.cengage.com/permissions. Further questions about permissions can be emailed to permissionrequest@cengage.com

Every effort has been made to trace ownership of all copyrighted material and to secure permission from copyright holders. In the event of any question arising as to the use of any material, we will be pleased to make the necessary corrections in future printings.

Library and Archives Canada Cataloguing in Publication

Law in society : Canadian readings/edited by Nick Larsen, Brian Burtch,. —3rd ed.

Includes bibliographical references.
ISBN 978-0-17-650020-7

1. Sociological jurisprudence—Textbooks.
2. Law—Canada—Textbooks.
I. Burtch, Brian E., 1949- II. Larsen, Nick, 1948-

KE3098.L38 2009   340'.1150971
C2009-902423-3

ISBN-13: 978-0-17-650020-7
ISBN-10: 0-17-650020-0

For mentors and friends:
Simon Verdun-Jones and Phil Wichern—Nick Larsen

To R.S. Ratner and the memory of Richard V. Ericson, graduate school mentors, and to the memory of Brodie Osborne-Campbell ("Not forgotten")—Brian Burtch

Contents

Lesbian and Gay Rights
Chapter Eight
Douglas Victor Janoff

Part Three: Women and the Law. 215
Partner-Abuse Claims
Chapter Nine
Linda C. Neilson

Women and Religious Arbitration
Chapter Ten
Natasha Bakht

Charter-based Litigation
Chapter Eleven
Diana Majury

Domestic Violence
Chapter Twelve
Jennifer Koshan and Wanda Wiegers

Part Four: Future Directions in Law and Society 319
Addressing Homophobic and Transphobic Bullying in Schools
Chapter Thirteen
Rebecca Haskell and Brian Burtch

Canadian Responses to 9/11
Chapter Fourteen
Reg Whitaker

Environmental Law
Chapter Fifteen
David R. Boyd

Preface

This third edition of essays covers a range of topics, including racism, censorship, the so-called war on drugs, regulation of gambling, the aftermath of the Westray mining tragedy in Nova Scotia, homophobic violence and legal responses to it, equality rights for women, environmental law, the debate over euthanasia, Aboriginal treaty rights, debates over family law, and anti-terrorism measures since 9/11. We have included many of the most topical works from the second edition and have added eight new chapters.

This reader brings forward a distinctly Canadian perspective on law making and legal conflicts. While we do draw on international parallels—for example, the war on drugs, or comparative studies of gambling legislation and anti-terrorism measures—for the most part we focus on Canadian examples. This focus allows us to consider examples that are closer to home and to examine how major theoretical perspectives may apply, or not apply, when we consider Canadian circumstances. As editors, we are interested in the overlap between the legal system and the wider society, and how the two interact as societies change along with their legal structures.

Increasingly, social scientists are exploring the impact of specific legislation and key legal decisions as part of their exploration of power and stratification in our society. Similarly, there is a noticeable increase in critical legal scholarship from law students and law professors and practitioners. The authors in this collection are some of the leading scholars in law in society studies. We have edited some works for clarity, but for the most part you will be accessing many key works in their entirety. As you will see, some works are firmly planted in sociological or philosophical paradigms whereas others are drawn from jurisprudence and have a more legally based outlook. Critical discussions of gender, race, and class have become inescapable in most discussions of law; indeed, we were hard-pressed to find scholarship with an unvarnished liberal or conservative outlook on legal questions. That said, given the deepening debate over same-sex marriage in Canada and the United States, for example, liberal and conservative values are very much part of Canadian political life, of culture, and certainly of the spirit of law making and dispute resolution.

The essays in this collection draw on the complexity and vitality of rights struggles in Canada. Issues of warfare, poverty, human dignity, racial and ethnic hatred, terrorism, civil liberties, and social justice are evident in this century, and there is much at stake on a local, national, and international scale. We hope that you will reflect on instances whereby law has excluded as well as included people, and where it has denied or affirmed legal protections for various groups and individuals. Readers will learn from specific facts and cases taken from historical and contemporary cases, and will come to recognize how there are no settled questions, no definite answers to the impact of laws on our social framework. We know there will be continued emphasis on legal decisions and also on the social context in which legal decisions are made. While there are no definitive conclusions about law in society, we believe that using jurisprudence and social science evidence enriches our theoretical and practical understanding of formal social control measures and the informal forces that constantly influence legal structures.

ACKNOWLEDGMENTS

We have been fortunate to work with the editorial team at Nelson Education Limited, especially Bram Sepers, acquisitions editor; and Susan Calvert, director of content and media production; as well as Katherine Goodes, developmental editor at My Editor Inc., and Colleen Ste. Marie, copy editor. Their support and professionalism were instrumental in bringing this project to fruition. We thank Hal Harder for encouraging us to undertake this project several years ago, and for helping us develop the original proposal. We are grateful to the contributors to this edition for their responsiveness and for working with us under a tight deadline.

Reference librarians at Simon Fraser University assisted with database searches and other information. We wish to thank the staff, faculty, and students in the School of Criminology and the Department of Women's Studies at Simon Fraser University. We are grateful to Carol Hird, Leora Burtch, and Joe Lelay for their support throughout this project, and to our parents for their encouragement in our academic pursuits.

Nick Larsen

Brian Burtch

Introduction

Legal conflicts and debates surround us. In the media, legal disputes are an important staple of coverage by television, radio, newspapers and magazines, and, increasingly, the World Wide Web. Politicians, lawyers, judges, and the public are drawn into debates over such issues as national standards of child support after marriage breakdown, Aboriginal rights, abortion, firearms possession, same-sex marriage, and the possible secession of Quebec. Statistics are presented and principles are outlined as different groups try to advocate their particular approach on numerous law and society issues. Law has thus become a vital institution in Canadian society, flanked and pressured by an array of social values and economic interests as legislators and legal officials seek to re-create a sense of justice and purpose in Canada. While this process is enormously complex, it is essential to the smooth functioning of a democratic society.

Even while legal debates surround us, it is difficult to assess particular laws or determine the overall meaning of legal regulation. One way of expanding our understanding is to study patterns of legal decisions systematically and conduct theoretical analyses of the issues. These tactics will help us explore how power, social inequality, and social change play a part in legal decision making. While our space here is limited, we believe it is appropriate to review some key theoretical frameworks in understanding law and society.

Liberal political theory rests heavily on the notion of individual freedoms and individual rights protected through law by the doctrine of the rule of law. Citizens are thus free to pursue activities, unless these activities are deemed so harmful to other individuals or to society as a whole that they must be prohibited or regulated. Liberalism appeals to many people since it is built around a concept of pluralistic diversity, with the state and other institutions ideally working to preserve our freedoms. Liberalism does not present a revolutionary focus on social and legal change, opting instead for gradual reforms of specific statutes, policies, and cultural life.

The law has also been influenced by conservative political traditions. In some circumstances, Conservatives tend to emphasize social order as a higher priority than individual freedoms, which they sometimes see as destructive forms of licence. Examples of conservative influences in the law include barriers to liberalized divorce, opposition to spousal benefits, and marriage for same-sex couples. The conservative influence is also evident in calls for more severe sanctions against young offenders and against criminals generally. Conservatives may also borrow from liberal discourse on individual freedoms, an approach that is obvious, for example, in protests against what is seen as undue interference through gun control and gun registration legislation. Although rarely discussed in academic circles, and often dismissed as reactionary by some scholars and activists, conservative influences are nevertheless extremely influential among politicians, law enforcement officials, the judiciary and legal profession, as well as the public. These actors exert enormous influence on the operation of the legal system, and thus conservative theories cannot be ignored by academics.

Feminist theory must also be considered in the study of law and society. Although feminism is a diversified perspective, all feminists generally share the assumption that women are disadvantaged in many, if not all, spheres of society, and feminists are committed to improving the condition of women. However, beyond this, feminists differ greatly in terms of their analyses of the causes of women's subordination and the best strategies for achieving equality. In broad terms, feminists can be subdivided into liberal, socialist, and radical camps. Liberal feminists tend to be the most willing to use the existing legal system to rectify many of the inequalities that beset women. They argue that reforms to achieve formal legal equality will ultimately lead to substantive social and economic equality for women. Therefore, they focus on minor changes, such as equal pay for equal work, or the gender-neutral enforcement of prostitution laws against female prostitutes and male customers. Liberal feminists are less likely, however, to question the illegality of prostitution on the grounds that such laws increase the subordination of women by male pimps and customers.

Socialist feminists, on the other hand, are much more skeptical that superficial legal changes will necessarily achieve substantive equality for women. They argue that the roots of female subordination can be traced to long-established patterns of patriarchal and economic oppression, and that these patterns must be overturned before legal reforms will have the desired effect. In particular, socialist feminists argue that economic power is essential to achieving equality in other areas, and will empower women in their struggle to overcome patriarchy. Thus, socialist feminists would argue that counteracting violence against women, as well as achieving justice in family and reproductive law (e.g., abortion), are dependent on women's achieving economic power. For this reason, socialist feminists focus on combating economic discrimination and workplace inequities. They argue that once women gain economic power, they will be able to overcome many of the non-economic aspects of patriarchal relationships.

Radical feminists argue that radical changes to all areas of society, including the legal system, are necessary to overcome the entrenched discrimination that affects all areas of women's existence. They attribute women's subordination to patriarchal oppression, which they argue existed long before the development of modern economic systems. Thus, while economic power is important, it will not overcome discrimination in all other areas of women's lives. (For example, sexual assault and spousal abuse also affect women from higher economic classes.) Radical feminists also caution that there are risks inherent in relying on existing legal structures to further women's interests. This concern stems in part from what they argue is a patriarchal legacy in law, reflected in the dominance of men in virtually all aspects of law making and law enforcement, including the judiciary, the legal profession, and the legislatures. Radical feminists argue that it is impossible for these institutions to represent fairly the interests of women because they are riddled with chauvinist biases. This approach is in stark contrast to the liberal and socialist feminists, who favour using legal institutions as part of a broader effort to change society. In this collection, contributors explore the impact of measures in the areas of domestic violence, religious arbitration, employment equity initiatives, and *Charter*-related cases and equality rights

The Marxist and neo-Marxist traditions have been often applied to legal issues. Drawing on the Marxist emphasis on the impact of broad economic forces in capitalist, class-divided societies, some Marxists view the law as merely an instrument of the dominant class, and as a means of disguising social inequality and legal injustices through the mantle of individual liberties and the non-partisan nature of law. In this view, legal officials tend to support the dominant class, repressing other classes through criminal law, labour law, and a host of other measures. As with feminism, the Marxist approach generates considerable disagreement over social change, the nature of oppression, and whether law is inherently antagonistic to a movement toward socialism or communism. The issue of social class appears throughout this collection, exemplified in essays that combine social class analysis with issues of race and gender, such as Natasha Bakht's work on religious arbitration and women's rights. Toothless legislation directed at corporate offences contrasts with punitive law enforcement that is often directed toward an underclass. John McMullan's chapter on miners' deaths at the Westray mine explores many elements of state powers and workers' safety. This approach is also developed in Barry Sneiderman's critique of the war on drugs and David Boyd's closing chapter on environmental law and policy in Canada.

With gender and social class issues, there has been considerable work in the critical race studies tradition. This tradition explores ways in which people are categorized into racial or ethnic groups and are subjected to stereotypes, social inequalities, and discriminatory legal treatment. Here, often with the focus on gender and class noted above, there is great attention to ways in which race and ethnicity become the grounds for discriminatory treatment. From analyses of harassment of people of colour, to hiring barriers and myriad forms of discrimination in housing and welfare, theorists bring race and ethnicity into the foreground. Some analysts challenge assumptions of a common Canadian cultural tradition and shared language by pointing to linguistic differences and clashing cultural approaches to dispute resolution. Other scholars explore the subjective experiences of being treated as a visible minority, as well as ways in which laws are unfairly applied to such minorities. Constance Backhouse's account of the Viola Desmond case in Nova Scotia shows how racism has been embedded in Canadian society and how it has been challenged through the courts and through other measures. The over-representation of African-Americans in prisons in the United States and the over-representation of Aboriginal peoples in Canadian prisons are two examples. Legal scholars have also documented how women and racial and ethno-cultural minorities have been discriminated against by law schools and legal practices (Kay & Brockman, 2000; Kay, Masuch, & Curry 2006; Pruitt, 2002).

Postmodern influences are also evident in law in society studies. Postmodernism generally takes a pessimistic or at least a cautious stance against the Enlightenment ideals of rationality and progress, including how these concepts are fixed in legal ideology. Postmodernists thus contest taken-for-granted assumptions about the desirability of the rule of law, or the steady progress of liberal pluralist policies. Such challenges have led to what has been called postmodern legality, where the effects of law and social control are examined, and new forms of dispute resolution are developed to empower minority groups. Postmodernism is thus linked with attempts to deepen democratic relationships with the "new social movements" surrounding issues of disability or "ableism," sexual orientation, multinational politics, race and ethnicity, and environmental and peace movements, to name a few (Anyon, 2005; Rosenau, 1992).

The scholarly study of law and social change has matured dramatically in the past generation. We now have specialized journals, texts, and associations exploring how legislation is formed and applied. Specific topics are discussed in considerable detail by some commentators. The rich tradition of sociological approaches to law continues to deepen, with incisive theoretical commentaries on Marxist, feminist, and postmodernist approaches to the law (see, for example, Hunt, 1993). We now have the benefit of descriptions of how legislation is created, accounts of specific legal decisions on a wide range of issues, and socio-legal theories of law, power, and social change (Burtch, 2003; Vago, 2009). This volume brings forward ongoing concerns about law and the treatment of women, racial minorities, gays and lesbians, and people who are generally disadvantaged.

The growing body of texts and resources helps us to approach several key questions about law in society. For example, what is the impact of law on social values and human behaviour? The chicken-and-egg question of whether specific laws can produce social change or whether legislation emerges from changing values and interests in society is very much alive. Some legal scholars (Barnett, 1993) argue that legal change tends to lag behind changing social values, exemplified by such topics as euthanasia and abortion. Others argue that law can constitute an effective tool for instigating social change, citing the benefits of seat-belt legislation, occupational health and safety requirements, and stricter firearms regulations. On a broader scale, one can hardly discount the positive impact that the extremely unpopular desegregation laws exerted on racism and discrimination in the United States. In this respect, many legal scholars assert that it is important for the law to demonstrate leadership on the many critical social-legal issues facing contemporary societies, rather than simply following public opinion.

In the years since the publication of the first and second editions of this book, Canadian courts have emerged as much more activist players in a changing legal landscape. One of the most dramatic and controversial examples of recent social change was instigated by the courts when both the Ontario and British Columbia Supreme Courts ruled that the prohibition of same-sex marriage was unconstitutional. The federal government's subsequent decision to legalize same-sex marriage was affirmed by the Supreme Court of Canada, and legislation was drafted to revise the federal definition of marriage to include same-sex couples. Although the Conservative Party opposes same-sex marriage, and initially promised to introduce legislation to reinstate the traditional definition of marriage once elected, it subsequently announced that it would not revisit the issue. In retrospect, this decision to change the definition of marriage to include same-sex couples has engendered relatively little public debate in Canada and is now a non-issue, except among conservative religious groups. This stands in stark contrast to the situation in the United States, where many states have enacted binding propositions limiting the definition of marriage to "a union between one man and one woman." This contrast raises the question of whether public opinion differs so drastically between the United States and Canada. It is at least arguable that the legalization of same-sex marriage has positively influenced the degree to which the Canadian public accepts same-sex relationships, but it is difficult to predict its effect on American public opinion. Regardless, it appears that Canadian judicial activism is becoming increasingly important with respect to controversial issues, at least in part because politicians are frequently reluctant to tackle such issues head on. Note, however, that judicial activism has not been uniform across the legal spectrum, as the courts have been much more reluctant to overturn laws against euthanasia on constitutional grounds.

A final question that recurs in the following chapters is whether legal regulation is desirable. For liberals, state regulation through law and other institutions is essential, ideally giving individuals a balance of security and freedom of expression. For conservatives, these same ideals may be sought, but often with a greater emphasis on tradition and what is generally called social order. More critical theorists challenge the legitimacy of the legal order, seeing it as a form of overt or covert domination over citizens, especially people with limited economic means, visible minorities, women, or gays and lesbians. Powerful contributions in the Marxist and feminist traditions have been joined by postmodernist interpretations of law in society. The overall effect of these challenges is to leave an unsettled quality to the legal order, with complex arguments advanced regarding various issues. This collection of essays seeks to present a variety of theoretical perspectives, even though our selection, like the field of sociology of law in general, is weighted toward more critical outlooks. As you read and discuss these chapters, it is important to remain skeptical regarding the value of legal regulation, and to consider whether many of these issues would resolve themselves more equitably without legal regulation.

REFERENCES

Anyon, J. (2005). *Radical possibilities: Public policy, urban education, and a new social movement*. London: Taylor and Francis.

Barnett, L. (1993). *Legal construct, social concept: A macrosocial perspective on law*. New York: Aldine de Gruyter.

Burtch, B. (2003). *The sociology of law: Critical approaches to social control* (2nd ed.). Toronto: Thomson Nelson.

Hunt, A. (1993). *Explorations in law and society*. London: Routledge.

Kay, F., & Brockman, J. (2000). Barriers to gender equality in the Canadian legal establishment. *Feminist Legal Studies*, 8(2), 169–198.

Kay, F., Masuch, C., & Curry, P. (2006). Growing diversity and emergent change: Gender and diversity in the legal profession. In E. Sheehy and S. McIntyre (Eds.), *Calling for change: Women, law, and the legal profession* (pp. 203–236). Ottawa: University of Ottawa Press.

Pruitt, L. (2002). No black names on the letterhead? Efficient discrimination and the South African legal profession. *Michigan Journal of International Law 23*, 545–676.

Rosenau, P. (1992). *Post-modernism and the social sciences*. Princeton, NJ: Princeton University Press.

Vago, S. (2009). *Law and society* (9th ed.). Upper Saddle River, NJ: Prentice-Hall.

Part One

Morality and the Criminal Law

The criminal law represents a society's most formal attempt to control the behaviour of its citizens. Although all types of law are ultimately forms of social control, the imposition of criminal sanctions is specifically designed to deal with activities that are considered a threat to the entire society. Although there is agreement that murder, robbery, and assault clearly fit this criterion, the criminal law is also used to control activities that do not constitute so clear a threat.

The first three chapters in this part focus on the application of Canadian criminal law to activities that are frequently classed as victimless crimes: gambling, drug use, and euthanasia. Many people argue that these activities involve moral choices and that the application of the criminal law enforces moral values that may not be shared by the participants or by society generally. The fourth chapter included in this section deals with corporate harms. Although this topic is not usually included in academic discussions of morality and the law, it is included here because many members of the public consider it a type of victimless crime. Much of the public debate about crime focuses on activities such as drug use, gang-linked violence, prostitution, and pornography, and excludes all but the most sensational examples of corporate crime. Because so many people are unaware of the nature and extent of corporate crime, it is important to understand the damage associated with it and to contrast it with the other crimes discussed in this section.

The first chapter presents a critical analysis of legislation and social policies related to gambling in Canada. Colin Campbell, Timothy Hartnagel, and Garry Smith provide a comprehensive account of the changing nature of legislation, policies, and public perceptions of various gambling enterprises, comparing the Canadian situation with that in a number of other countries.

The second chapter is Barney Sneiderman's discussion of drug-enforcement policies. In his work, "Just Say No to the War on Drugs," Sneiderman analyzes the failure of the current drug-prohibitionist policies employed in Canada and the United States. He begins by outlining the origins of the war on drugs in the aftermath of the Vietnam War and traces the development of that policy into a volatile political issue that has seen the United States imprison a greater proportion of its citizens than South Africa did during the apartheid era. Using a satirical style that takes the form of conversations between a visiting alien and various Canadian drug experts, Sneiderman critically discusses many of the myths and misconceptions that motivate present-day drug-enforcement policies in Canada and the United States. Besides questioning the link between drugs and crime, he also criticizes the hypocrisy implicit in the contradiction between the legality of alcohol and tobacco and the criminal status of marijuana. He argues that during the 1920s, prohibition of alcohol in the United States was unsuccessful and that our current prohibitionist approach to marijuana and other drugs is also doomed to fail. Sneiderman concludes by arguing for the decriminalization of marijuana, combined with the adoption of a health model to deal with other forms of drug abuse.

The third chapter deals with issues associated with euthanasia and assisted suicide. These issues have become increasingly important in Canada over the past two decades. Michael Cormack notes that recent polls indicate that most Canadians favour assisted suicide for people suffering from an incurable disease. Despite this public support and the ambivalence within the medical profession, numerous attempts to codify Canadian jurisprudence on end-of-life decision making have failed. Cormack compares this situation to that of Australia, where some states experimented with assisted suicide and voluntary euthanasia before the federal government outlawed the practice, as well as to developments in the United States and the Netherlands.

The fourth and final chapter in Part One involves corporate wrongdoing and accountability in Canadian society. In "Lost Lives at Westray: Official Discourse, Public Truth and Controversial Death," John McMullan addresses harms caused by corporate deviance. Building on established work in criminology that explains how corporate deviance constitutes a de facto victimless crime where wrongdoers are rarely censured or stigmatized to the same degree as street criminals, McMullan offers a detailed look at events leading up to the Westray tragedy and responses by officials, corporate stakeholders, and the public.

Chapter One

The Legalization of Gambling in Canada

Colin S. Campbell, Timothy F. Hartnagel, and Garry J. Smith

Editors' Note: Damon Runyan famously concluded that "all life is 6 to 5 against" (Partington, 1997), a wry comment on how life itself can be seen as a risk, one in which we must reckon with the odds. This chapter addresses legislation and social policies related to gambling in Canada. Campbell, Hartnagel, and Smith present a historical background to this topic, tracing the evolution of legal regulations and public opinion concerning gambling. This work emerged from a Law Commission of Canada initiative focused on determining "What Is a Crime?"

Today, with a more liberal outlook on what was once cast as vice, Canadians are more tolerant of such activities. We can readily access various forms of gambling: lottery tickets; betting on sports events, including professional sports (hockey, baseball, etc.), betting horserace tracks; online gambling; and casinos. Restrictions were eased on many forms of gambling with amendments to the Criminal Code in 1969 and again in 1985. Moreover, provincial governments became key players in the regulation of gambling, developing a fine line "between regulation and prohibition." In the process, gambling has proven to be profitable for the private sector and also for government bodies, with provincial governments receiving an appreciable percentage of their annual revenue from gambling-related activities. In a play on words, the authors contend that "governments had become addicted to the money generated from gambling" and that they continue to depend on gambling-related revenues.

This chapter covers a wide range of issues, including ongoing concerns over what might be called problem or compulsive gambling and public concern over video lottery terminals (VLTs) and Internet-based betting sites. The chapter also addresses the somewhat murky issue of how authority to operate gambling organizations can be delegated, particularly in the context of the Criminal Code. Later, the chapter presents information from other countries—the United States, Great Britain, and Australia—to help put the Canadian situation in a comparative context. The chapter also includes a discussion of key social science theoretical frameworks, including functionalism and more critical approaches to neoliberal government policies and other parties who profit from the gambling industry.

INTRODUCTION[1]

This chapter reviews the transformation of the social control of gambling[2] in Canada and some of the consequences of this transformation. In Canada, there has not been a dramatic contraction of the scope of criminal law regarding gambling. Criminal prohibitions remain firmly in place. However, what has been undeniably transformed is the extent to which provincial governments can now grant exemptions to the general prohibitions pertaining to gambling contained in the *Criminal Code of Canada*. Provincial exemptions have culminated in the emergence of a multi-billion-dollar legal gambling industry. We identify and discuss not only the nature and extent of legal gambling within Canada but also the contentious legal, behavioural, and public-policy issues that have arisen. In addition, we contrast Canada's experiences in regard to

Source: Colin S. Campbell, Timothy F. Hartnagel, and Garry J. Smith, "The Legalization of Gambling in Canada." Paper presented at the annual meeting of the American Society of Criminology, Royal York, Toronto, ON. Reprinted with permission from Colin Campbell and UBC Press.

gambling with that of Australia, Great Britain, and the United States. The chapter concludes with a consideration of theoretical perspectives that provide insight into the sources and effects of the transformation in the social control of gambling in Canada.

Until several decades ago, most forms of gambling in Canada were illegal, while permissible gambling (for example, on track betting at horse races) was greatly restricted. This situation was transformed with *Criminal Code* amendments in 1969 and 1985, which spurred a proliferation of legal gambling formats that were licensed, operated, and regulated by provincial governments over the past 30 years. Many gambling activities and behaviours have been transformed from a status of being criminal and prohibited to a status of being legal and licensed. Given the current provisions of the *Criminal Code*, it is our view that modern criminal law in Canada has not been deployed for the purpose of controlling or preventing either the operation of or participation in gambling activities. Rather, existing provisions have facilitated a widespread expansion of a variety of gambling activities, provided they are conducted and managed under provincial jurisdiction.

As provincial governments have moved to legalize and exploit gambling's economic potential, regulatory systems have been constructed to investigate, monitor, inspect, license, audit, and control gambling in the interest of sustaining gambling's integrity as a government revenue source. However, *gambling* remains an elusive term in Canada because, depending upon the format and circumstances surrounding it, a variety of legal statuses are possible. Legalization has thus tended to blur public perceptions about the status of gambling with some forms of legal gambling, such as electronic gambling machines (EGMs), singled out for continuing social censure.[3] Furthermore, crime and gambling remain linked in numerous ways and new forms of "deviance" associated with gambling (e.g., "excessive" or "problem" gambling) have emerged (Campbell & Smith, 2003; Smith & Wynne, 1999; 2004).

For the majority of participants, gambling may be a harmless amusement; however, because of the potential for chicanery,[4] exploitation, and overindulgence, "the law has historically taken a stern view toward gambling" (Bowal & Carrasco, 1997, p. 29). Despite its drawbacks, gambling appears here to stay. History has taught us that complete suppression is virtually unachievable (Dixon, 1991). Given this reality, modern legislators have tried generally to strike a balance between regulation and prohibition. Inevitably, efforts to control gambling result in policies stipulating where, when, and under what conditions the activity is permissible. Consequently, gambling can be legal or illegal depending on the context, circumstances, and the operators of the game. For example, the *Criminal Code of Canada* contains provisions that dictate when gambling is an indictable offence and outlines the range of sanctioned gambling formats that provincial governments can license or operate if they so choose.

THE EVOLUTION OF THE CRIMINAL CODE'S GAMBLING PROVISIONS

When the Canadian *Criminal Code* was first enacted in 1892, under a section titled "Offences against Religion, Morals and Public Convenience," a series of gambling offences that had been created by acts of Parliament in 1886 and 1888 were simply incorporated therein. From 1892 to 1969 there were a series of ad hoc, seemingly minor amendments to the sections of the Code on gambling. Taken together, these early amendments facilitated a very gradual expansion of legal gambling in Canada. While there was some public lobbying, beginning in the 1930s, in favour of reform and a gradual shift in public opinion toward more liberal attitudes (Morton, 2003), these *Criminal Code* amendments were typically made in the absence of any significant public debate. Indeed, the last public review of the gambling sections of the *Criminal Code* took place in 1954–55 when a Special Joint Committee of the House of Commons and Senate examined the issues of lotteries (Campbell & Smith, 1998; Canada, 1956).

The work of the Special Joint Committee on lotteries had its genesis in 1949 when the government of Canada established a Royal Commission with a mandate to systematically review and update the provisions of the *Criminal Code* for the first time since codification in 1892. The Royal Commission reported in 1954 but chose not to address the gaming provisions of the Code due to their controversial nature. Subsequently, the task of reviewing the lottery provisions fell to the 1954 Joint Committee (Campbell, 1994, p. 228; Osborne, 1989, pp. 48–49).

When the Joint Committee tendered its report, it noted that lotteries and other games of chance, such as bingo, were extensively carried out by non-profit, community-based organizations in Canada despite their formal prohibition under the existing law (Campbell, 1994, p. 229). The committee observed that the police were often reluctant to enforce laws against well-intentioned community organizations. This, according to the committee, caused two problems: contempt for the law and ineffective control (Osborne, 1989, p. 50). Accordingly, the Joint Committee recommended new legislation that would provide workable laws capable of effective enforcement. The committee also called for some relaxation of existing prohibitions in line with reforms introduced with respect to the control, sale, and consumption of alcohol. The Joint Committee concluded, however, that there should be no state lotteries in Canada (Campbell, 1994, p. 234). The recommendations would not be acted on until late 1967 (Osborne & Campbell, 1988, p. 23).

Table 1.1 condenses the key amendments and notable developments in the history of gambling in Canada.

Table 1.1 Chronology of Amendments and Developments Regarding the Legal Status of Gambling in Canada

Date	Amendment or Development
1892	*Criminal Code of Canada* first enacted.
1901	Exemption for raffles at any bazaar held for charitable and religious objects.
1906	The phrase "lottery scheme"[5] inserted into the *Code*.
1909–10	Select Committee of House of Commons convened to inquire into horse-race betting.
1910	Betting limited to horse-race tracks.
1917	Order-in-council suspends betting as "incommensurate" with war effort.
1919–20	Royal Commission in [sic] Racing Inquiry convened to examine horse-race betting.
1920	Racetrack betting reinstated using pari-mutuel system.
1922	Offence created for betting on dice games, shell games, punchboards, coin tables, or wheels of fortune.
1925	Select games of chance, including wheels of fortune, permitted at agricultural fairs and exhibitions.
1938	Gambling on the premises of bona fide social clubs permitted if operators did not exact a percentage of the stakes.
1954	Game of Three-card Monte added to the list of prohibited games.
1954	Special Joint Committee of House of Commons & Senate convened to examine need for law reform in regard to lotteries. Recommends no state lotteries but calls for greater clarity in existing provisions.
1969	Federal & provincial governments allowed to conduct lotteries; broadening of charitable gambling under provincial licence; continuation of exemption for fairs and exhibitions.
1973–85	Federal–provincial conflict over authority to conduct lotteries.
1985	Provinces delegated exclusive authority to manage and conduct lotteries and lottery schemes, including games conducted via computer, video device, or slot machines. Betting on horse races via telephone permitted.
1998	Prohibitions against dice games removed from *Code*.

The Process of Legalization: The Modern Context

The liberalization of gambling under state regulation began in 1967 when then Minister of Justice Pierre Trudeau introduced an omnibus bill to amend several aspects of the *Criminal Code*. The proposed amendments included the following:

- Removing criminal sanctions for abortion, homosexual practices between consenting adults, and lottery schemes
- Allowing federal and provincial governments the option of conducting state lotteries
- Broadening charity gambling
- Continuing the existing exemption for agricultural fairs and exhibitions
- Creating a new exemption for gambling at public places of amusement under provincial licence (Osborne, 1989, p. 59)

In 1968, when Parliament was dissolved for a general election, the bill was abandoned. However, when the Liberal Party was re-elected under Trudeau as prime minister, the House of Commons passed an identical bill in 1969. Thus began the transformation of gambling from federal prohibition to provincial regulation.

From the mid-1970s to the mid-1980s, the federal and provincial levels of government embroiled themselves in an acrimonious legal battle with respect to jurisdiction over lotteries and lottery schemes, the details of which are beyond the scope of this discussion.[6] Suffice to say, however, that court actions were halted when the provinces and the federal government reached a contractual agreement to amend the *Criminal Code* in such a manner that the federal government would concede exclusive control over lotteries and lottery schemes to the provincial level of government. The amendment took effect in 1985 and permitted provinces alone or in partnership with other provinces to operate lotteries and lottery schemes through a computer, video device, or slot machine.

The current provisions of the *Criminal Code* dealing with gambling are set out in Part VII: Disorderly Houses, Gaming and Betting. Part VII provides definitions of the following terms: *disorderly houses, bawdy houses, betting houses, gaming houses, gaming, betting,* and *lotteries*. The section also presents a number of presumptions with respect to disorderly houses and establishes a series of prohibitions related to betting, gaming, lotteries, and games of chance. Part VII also lists exemptions from these prohibitions that have facilitated the expansion of legal gambling under provincial operation and regulation.

Most germane to an understanding of permitted gambling in Canada are (1) section 204, which, in addition to exempting private betting between individuals, also, since 1920, permits betting on horse racing via a pari-mutuel system[7] operated under the auspices of the federal Minister of Agriculture and Agri-Food; and (2) section 207, subtitled Permitted Lotteries. It is under section 207 that the transformation and expansion of gambling in Canada over the past 35 years has occurred. Section 207 legalizes the creation and operation of lotteries run by any of the bodies specified in s.207(1) (a) to (d). (See Figure 1.1.) As well, section 207 provides for the regulation of such schemes under provincial laws and under terms and conditions of licences that may be granted pursuant to provincial authority. In other words, section 207(1) permits lotteries to be created and operated by a province, or under licence by charitable or religious organizations, by a board of a fair or exhibition or by any other person to whom a licence has been issued if the ticket cost does not exceed $2.00 and the prize does not exceed $500 (Martin's Annual *Criminal Code*, 2005, p. 397).

It is under these *Criminal Code* provisions that provinces have been granted exclusive authority to operate and/or license particular forms of gambling. As a consequence, all Canadian provinces and territories conduct or permit gambling to some extent.

Figure 1.1   Permitted Gambling Under Part VII of the *Criminal Code*

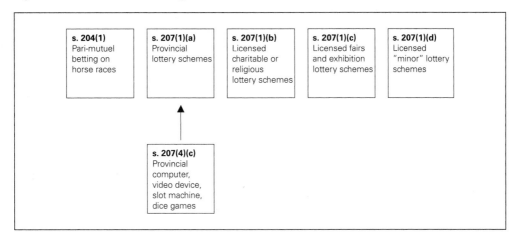

The two formats that now dominate Canadian gambling are (a) electronic gaming machines (EGMs), such as video lottery terminals (VLTs) and slot machines, and (b) casino gambling, which, in addition to the traditional green felt table games, now offers a variety of electronic gaming devices, such as slot machines. Lotteries—once the primary source of government gambling revenues—have now been eclipsed by revenues derived from electronic gaming machines and casinos.

In the over two decades since the 1985 amendment, legal gambling in Canada has become a big business. There are currently over 145 000 venues and/or opportunities to gamble legally in Canada. In 2004, there were over 87 000 electronic gambling machines (EGMs) in casinos, bars, lounges, and racetracks; 33 000 lottery ticket centres; 25 000 licensed charitable events; 60 permanent casinos with 1700 gambling tables; and 250 racetracks and tele-theatres (Azmier, 2005).

According to recent data developed by the Canada West Foundation, government-run gambling (bingo, EGMs, table games, and lotteries) generated a gross profit of $12.7 billion in 2003–04. After paying costs of $6.4 billion associated with generating gambling revenues, government-run gambling produced a net profit of $6.3 billion with virtually a 50/50 split of the gross profit between provincial governments and private sector gaming service providers.[8] Compared to 1992–94, the net profit from government-run gambling rose by 275 percent in 2003–04 (Azmier, 2005, pp. 4–5).

In addition to government-run gambling, other gambling formats licensed by provincial governments (charitable bingos, raffles, casinos, horse racing, and several First Nation venues) together generate another $1.8 billion in gross profits. Thus, in 2003–04, a total of approximately $14.5 billion in gross gambling profits was generated in Canada. The per adult loss in Canada in 2003–04 averaged $596 (or almost $50 per month) and ranged from a low of $369 in Prince Edward Island to a high of $886 in Alberta (Azmier, 2005, p. 6).

As a proportion of provincial government revenue, gambling constituted 3.8 percent of all revenue raised by government and ranged from a low of 2.9 percent in British Columbia to a high of 5.5 percent in Manitoba (Azmier, 2005, p. 7). While provincial governments are the single largest beneficiary of gambling revenues, it is to be noted that other levels of government also garner a share of gambling revenues, albeit much smaller. More specifically, under the terms of the agreement that resulted in the 1985 amendment to the *Criminal Code*, an amount is paid annually (adjusted according to the Consumer Price Index) to the federal government. Each province contributes a share calculated proportionally to its lottery sales. In 2003, the amount contributed by the provinces under this agreement amounted to approximately $60 million and represented about 0.93 percent of net profits (Canada, 2004, Proceedings of the Standing Senate Committee on Legal and Constitutional Affairs, Dec. 1 & 2; Canadian Partnership for Responsible Gambling, 2004). In British Columbia, Alberta, Manitoba, and Ontario, revenue-sharing agreements have been negotiated with some municipalities. Under these relatively recent agreements, in 2002–03 municipal governments received approximately $165 million or approximately 2.6 percent of net profits (Canadian Partnership for Responsible Gambling, 2004). It is thus apparent that all levels of government in Canada are now reliant to some extent on revenues derived from gambling sources.

With the growth of the volume of dollars involved in legal gambling in Canada, employment in the gambling industry has also risen dramatically. In 1993, 14 000 people were employed in the gambling industry. By 2003, this number had risen to over 50 000 (Marshall & Wynne, 2004).

GAMBLING AND CANADIAN PUBLIC OPINION

Criminologists are interested in various aspects of public opinion regarding law, crime, and criminal justice, mainly because of the possible relationship between such opinion and public policy (Zimmerman et al., 1988). Roberts (1992) claims that public officials' beliefs about public opinion influence criminal justice policy. The public's views concerning gambling may be relevant to an understanding of the development of gambling policy and its potential future directions. However, there is little available in the way of national, systematic, time-series data on Canadians' attitudes toward gambling.

Morton (2003) characterized the attitudes of Canadians toward gambling as ambivalent for most of the 20th century; however, beginning with the 1969 *Criminal Code* amendment, gambling was transformed from a stigmatized minor vice to an acceptable activity regarded as appropriate and perhaps necessary to fund the Canadian welfare state. Morton shows how official condemnation co-existed with unofficial toleration during the first half of the 20th century. She also points to the steady public lobby, beginning in the 1930s, looking for reform and liberalization of gambling law. While the rhetoric of anti-gamblers and the law remained relatively constant from 1919 to 1969, Morton claims there was uneven enforcement of the gambling laws. As well, there were noticeable shifts in public opinion toward more liberal attitudes in both the 1920s and 1950s, at least partly as a function of economic conditions. She summarizes a series of post–Second World War Gallup Polls that showed a gradual increase in support for legalized lotteries and sweepstakes, reaching a 79 percent approval level by 1969. Thus, public attitudes toward this type of gambling shifted over time from viewing gambling as a vice that should be prohibited to an acceptance of its inevitability as a "necessary evil" that could be beneficial to society.

In March of 1984, shortly before the 1985 amendments to the *Criminal Code*, the Gallup Poll asked, "On the whole, are you in favour of or opposed to government-run lotteries?" On a national basis, 76 percent of Canadians were in favour, 16 percent were opposed, and 8 percent were uncertain. So, tolerant attitudes toward one type of gambling persisted after the changes in legislation in 1969 up to a point prior to the 1985 revisions to the *Criminal Code*. However, the 1985 *Criminal Code* amendment finalizing the transfer of authority over legal gambling from federal to provincial jurisdictions and legalizing computer, video, and slot machine–style gambling was legislated without public input and has been an ongoing source of public controversy ever since (Smith & Wynne, 2004). The terms of the amendment were actually negotiated by provincial and federal authorities responsible for culture, fitness, and amateur sport—authorities not typically involved in criminal law revisions. As Osborne and Campbell (1988) have commented, Parliament merely rubber-stamped the amendment in the interests of ending the acrimonious conflict over lotteries and expediting funding for the 1988 Calgary Winter Olympics. They noted the following:

> Following a conspicuous absence of public hearings or discussions, the lotteries bill was given first reading in the House of Commons on 10 October, second and third readings on 6 November, and finally passed after less than three hours of debate; in the Senate it was given first reading 7 November, second reading on 27 November, and third reading and assent on 20 December. It was proclaimed in force on the final day of the year. (Osborne & Campbell, 1988, pp. 24–25)

Although legal gambling has burgeoned over the intervening years, debate continues regarding the appropriate levels and types of gambling that should be allowed in Canadian communities. Recent public opinion on gambling issues has been the subject of only a few polls and surveys. While 6 in 10 Canadians reported partaking in gambling in a 1998 poll, 73 percent felt that problems associated with gambling had increased in their province over the past couple of years (Ipsos News Centre, 1998a). In the same poll, 58 percent indicated that increased revenues do not offset the problems caused by gambling. VLTs and casinos were the formats viewed as most harmful to the community (42 percent and 41 percent, respectively) while charity lotteries were perceived as least harmful (10 percent). Fully 86 percent believed that governments had become addicted to revenue generated from gambling (Ipsos News Center, 1998b).

In the only national random survey of adult Canadian views on gambling, Azmier (2000) reported that 43 percent felt their governments should be doing more to restrict gambling in their province while 47 percent were satisfied with current levels of restriction. However, there was strong support for increased government accountability regarding gambling policy: 84 percent agreed (61 percent strongly) that governments should hold public consultations before introducing new forms of gambling. As well, the survey revealed that

- 60 percent of the sample agreed that gambling problems had increased in their province in the past three years;
- 24 percent perceived the overall impact of gambling to be negative compared to 9 percent who agreed that gambling had an overall positive impact on their community;
- 68 percent disagreed that gambling had improved the quality of life in their province while only 14 percent felt it was beneficial (Azmier, 2000).

There was strong disagreement with current policies allowing VLTs in bars and lounges: 70 percent agreed (49 percent strongly) with restricting VLTs to casinos and racetracks, while 41 percent believed that VLTs should be banned altogether. Overall, respondents saw gambling as a legitimate means for provincial governments to raise revenues, with 67 percent preferring it to raising taxes. However, a strong anti-gambling sentiment is suggested among the 19 percent who preferred to raise revenues through increased taxes.

To the extent it can be gauged from these limited data, Canadian public opinion toward gambling seems ambivalent. On one hand, Canadians generally view gambling as an acceptable community activity, due perhaps to its perceived inevitability and as a source of revenue for governments and charities (Azmier, 2001). On the other hand, many Canadians feel there should be more restrictions on gambling, with the strength of such feelings varying with the type of gambling (e.g., VLTs), the location of venues ("not in my backyard"), and the perceived social costs of gambling. However, as Azmier (2001) has argued, "... gambling policy continues to evolve in Canada with only a minimum of opportunity for public involvement in the decision-making process" (p. 15).

CONTENTIOUS ISSUES IN CANADIAN GAMBLING POLICIES

This section broaches several contentious issues related to how Canadian provincial governments conduct, manage, and regulate legal gambling. In addition, key issues regarding the control and prevention of gambling-related crime and problem gambling are considered.

Ontario Gaming Legislation Review

In 1996 the law firm Morris, Rose & Ledgett was retained by the Ontario Lottery Corporation to provide a legal analysis of Ontario's gaming market. A private-sector proposal seeking the implementation of video lottery terminals (VLTs) based on the Casino Windsor model triggered the review. The analysis, titled the *Ontario Gaming Legislation Review*, ultimately led the provincial government to abandon an intended introduction of VLTs. However, because the analysis challenged the way that existing gambling formats were conducted and managed, the report was not submitted to an all-party provincial justice committee as originally intended, nor was it released to the public.[9]

In reviewing the VLT proposal, the authors found it necessary to analyze the Casino Windsor model on which the VLT proposal was premised, assess charitable gaming, and evaluate the overall legislative framework for gaming in Ontario (Morris, Rose, & Ledgett, 1996). The legal analysis identified the following matters that the authors deemed to be possible contraventions of the gambling provisions of the *Criminal Code*.

a) Broad Interpretation of *Criminal Code* Gambling Provisions

When Ontario implemented casino gambling in Windsor in the early 1990s, the province adopted a hybrid ownership, management, and operation model. Under this model, casinos are owned, controlled, and regulated by the Ontario government but run by private-sector operators. As part of the regulatory structure, two provincial government Crown agencies were initially formed to divide the responsibility for casino gambling oversight (Alfieri, 1994). The Ontario Casino Corporation was made responsible for the business and operating functions of casinos. As well, the Gaming Control Commission was mandated to undertake registration, enforcement, and audit duties. Interested private sector casino operators were invited to respond to a request for proposals, specifying how they would meet various economic, tourism, security, and civic improvement objectives.

The authors of the *Ontario Gaming Legislation Review* argued that this structural arrangement for the management and operation of the Windsor casino was inconsistent with *Criminal Code* provisions on the grounds that it was unclear just who was actually *conducting* and *managing* the gambling operation.

As noted earlier, the *Criminal Code* places the onus for conducting and managing lottery schemes" on provincial governments. The only exemptions are for charitable or religious organizations and fairs or exhibitions licensed by the province. Given that the Ontario casino model is not charity-based, and it is arguable whether the Ontario government is in fact conducting and managing the casino games, the Windsor casino model may be in violation of *Criminal Code* gambling provisions. By the same logic, the report authors held that the proposed Ontario VLT implementation plan, based on the Windsor casino operation, was also of questionable legal status. Because the legal principles underpinning the hybrid government ownership/private sector–operated model have never been tested in court, Ontario casinos continue to operate under this arrangement.

b) Delegation of Authority to Conduct and Manage Gaming Events

As noted earlier, while licensed charities or religious groups can be authorized to conduct and manage lottery schemes to raise monies for worthy causes, a potential problem arises over the involvement of private operators hired to run licensed gambling events. Private operators are allowed to help run gambling operations, but the authorized agent (government/charity/exhibition association) must take "an active and direct participation in the supervision of, and day-to-day operations" (Donovan & Welsh, 1998, p. A26). The issue then becomes this: With hands-on involvement in running gaming events by private operators, can licensed organizations truly claim to be conducting and managing the proceedings as required under section 207(1)(b) of the *Criminal Code*? The *Review of Gaming Legislation in Ontario* makes the case that licensed charities are usually too far removed from the gambling activity, thus giving the private operator de facto control over the gaming event. While approved by the Ontario government in its *Policy Manual* and *Terms and Conditions of the Licence* documents, this practice seemingly breaches *Criminal Code* section 207(1)(b), which states that the authority to lawfully conduct and manage lottery schemes must derive from the *Criminal Code*, not from provincial legislation. In other words, the authority to conduct and manage gambling events cannot be delegated to a third party, neither by the provincial government nor by licensed charitable or religious organizations.

Patrick (2000) concurs that provincial governments and charitable and religious organizations have *Criminal Code* exemptions to conduct and manage lottery schemes and that this authority cannot be delegated to another party. In Patrick's view, private sector entrepreneurs who participate in the profits of gambling machines and who provide business plans, management skills, premises, and staff to facilitate machine gambling are indeed conducting and managing an electronic gaming lottery scheme and, in so doing, are violating the *Criminal Code*. However, in a contrary view, Monahan and Goldlist (1999) have argued that with respect to gaming conducted under section 207(1)(a) of the *Criminal Code*, provinces are able to enter into contractual agreements with private-sector interests to assist in the day-to-day operation of a lottery scheme and are, furthermore, not constrained in how they distribute revenues derived from provincial gaming schemes.

c) Use of Proceeds from Charitable Gambling

The *Criminal Code* dictates that the proceeds from a licensed gambling event are to be used for charitable or religious purposes. At issue is the involvement of private-sector interests who are afforded significant portions of gambling proceeds. The *Ontario Gaming Legislation Review* (Morris, Rose, & Ledgett, 1996) claimed that 42.5 percent of the annual gross wager on Ontario bingos in 1995 was diverted to the private sector in the form of expenses and obviously not used for charitable and religious objects or purposes.

In an interpretation of section 207(1)(b), a 1998 ruling in the Supreme Court of British Columbia held that the provincial government could not appropriate revenues generated by charitable or religious organizations (See *Nanaimo Community Bingo Association v. British Columbia [Attorney General]*).

The provincial government in British Columbia sought to introduce electronic gaming machines in order to increase its revenues from gambling. New regulations were introduced in 1997 that would have increased the overall level of gaming revenues for charitable organizations but would also have directed the largest proportion of the revenues to government coffers. Under the province's plan, proceeds from existing licensed charity bingo events were to be pooled with revenues from electronic games. One-third of the revenues were to be directed to charities to a guaranteed minimum of $118 million annually. The province would direct two-thirds to its Consolidated Revenue Fund.

A number of charitable groups in British Columbia challenged the province, successfully arguing that the plan contravened section 207(1)(b), which does not authorize proceeds from charity lottery schemes to be directed to government. The trial judge agreed but also noted that the government's plan for gambling expansion authorized for-profit management companies to receive a proportion of the proceeds of gaming derived from charitable lottery schemes without regard to what constitutes a reasonable charge for their gaming services. The ruling thus determined that the percentage of revenues allocated to private operators granted them an entitlement regardless of the actual value of the services they provide. This, too, breached the intent of section 207(1)(b), which specifies that revenues be directed to charitable or religious purposes.

In short, the Supreme Court of British Columbia decision had significant repercussions for charitable gaming in British Columbia. In response to the ruling, the province, through the British Columbia Lottery Corporation, assumed direct control under 207(1)(a) of casino and bingo operations in order to introduce electronic gaming machines. As well, it was apparent that the private sector companies could no longer assume such a large share of gambling revenue that is legally intended for the benefit of community-based charitable or religious organizations.

In other provinces, such as Alberta and Ontario, private-sector companies also play a role in providing gaming services to charitable organizations under arrangements similar to that which has been held to contravene the *Criminal Code* in British Columbia. Questions therefore arise regarding the consistency and legality of the interpretations of the *Criminal Code* across the country. Furthermore, questions arise regarding who has the ability and authority to challenge the varying interpretations that are evident across the provinces.

In addition to the concerns listed in the *Ontario Gaming Legislation Review*, other concerns have become apparent.

Regulation of Electronic Gambling Machines (EGMs)

The *Criminal Code* stipulates that provincial governments have exclusive jurisdiction over electronic gaming machines (including computers or video devices used for gaming purposes) and that the exemptions for religious and charitable organizations and fairs and exhibitions that hold for other gambling formats do not apply to electronic gaming. In other words, exempt groups cannot be licensed to conduct and manage electronic gambling machines. Nevertheless, in some provinces electronic gambling machines are housed in casinos, racetracks, and liquor-licensed premises, which means that some exempt groups (e.g., exhibition associations) profit from electronic gambling. Similarly, profits can be taken by owners of bars and lounges where machines are located. In Alberta, for example, VLT retailers receive 15 percent of the annual net profits per machine (the remaining 85 percent goes to the government). With an average VLT retailer profit per machine of approximately $20,000, entrepreneurs with multiple EGMs on site can make upward of $400,000 per year with little effort and minimal financial risk (Smith & Wynne, 2004). Again, the intent of the provisions of the *Criminal Code* that grant exclusive jurisdiction over gambling to provincial governments may be compromised since sizable portions of gambling revenues are directed to private sector interests for allowing EGMs on their properties. Monahan and Goldlist (1999), however, take a different perspective and maintain that provinces are unfettered in their contractual agreements with private operators and are not constrained with respect to the terms of compensation to be paid.

A new twist on the division of EGM proceeds stems from what gaming manufacturers call the recurring revenue model. In addition to selling EGMs outright to Canadian provinces, some manufacturers lease the machines in return for a proportion of the profits (a percentage of the profits as opposed to a flat daily rate). This joint partnership arrangement raises several fundamental questions: (1) Is the "conduct and manage" requirement for provincial governments breached if they do not own the machines? (2) Can the public interest in terms of product safety and gaming machine integrity be protected when provincial governments and private-sector manufacturers share a vested interest in revenue maximization?

Critics have thus questioned whether or not the terms of the *Criminal Code* are strictly applied to gaming machines. As further illustration, Roger Horbay (2004), a software developer, has doubts about who really conducts and manages electronic gaming. In Horbay's view, conducting and managing EGMs entails complete control over the gaming software. Since gaming-machine manufacturers retain proprietary rights to their software, questions arise as to who the controlling mind really is.

A further concern over the operation of Canadian electronic gambling machines pertains to the use of unbalanced reel games. An unbalanced reel game is one where there is a shortage of winning symbols on some reels. Players of these machines see combinations of winning symbols above or below the centre line and gain the mistaken impression that they just missed a large payout or that the machine is easier to beat than it really is (Falkiner & Horbay, 2006). Unbalanced reel games are widespread in Canada and are seen as problematic for consumers because they are intentionally deceptive and there is no way for players to know how the machines actually work. Falkiner and Horbay maintain that unbalanced reel games are fraudulent because they do not meet the standard of a fair game and because the unbalanced reel design takes advantage of those who are susceptible to becoming problem gamblers.

Other questions pertaining to the operation of electronic gambling machines include the following: How are odds and payout rates determined? Who regulates the regulators? Since law-enforcement agencies generally do not have the technical expertise to investigate complaints regarding the integrity of EGMs, they invariably depend on technical advice from provincial gaming regulators—the very authorities that sanctioned the machines. This state of affairs raises questions about the adequacy and independence of checks and balances in the overall gambling regulatory process.

Recently, a Canadian group called Gambling Watch Network, frustrated by provincial government indifference to their concerns, has formally registered a complaint with the Canadian Competition Bureau, alleging that EGMs are cheating the public.

Internet Gambling

Section 207(4)(c) of the *Criminal Code* clearly specifies that only provinces in Canada can operate computer-based lottery schemes. Thus the Code as presently crafted does not allow for charitable organizations or for private-sector operators to operate online gambling within Canada. Moreover, an Internet-based gambling operation conducted and managed by a provincial government cannot take bets from residents of other provinces without the consent of the other provincial governments. Recently, however, the governments of Nova Scotia and British Columbia, through their lottery Crown corporations, have initiated online lottery schemes restricted to residents of their respective provinces and thus in compliance with existing law.

What critics find troublesome in Internet betting schemes is the relative openness of access. Internet gambling games are offered free of charge to anyone who has a computer and Internet access. To wager for money, however, players must register and establish an account, typically using a deposit drawn on a credit card. Given the private and solitary nature of computer betting on the Internet in tandem with the universality of access to the Internet, online gambling is extremely difficult to police. While the *Criminal Code* may prohibit Canadians from participating in gambling on a website located in another country, there is no mechanism to effectively enforce the prohibition (Kelly, Todosichuk, & Azmier, 2001).

According to a report prepared by the Canada West Foundation on Internet gambling, it is a breach of the *Criminal Code* for a private, commercial, Canadian-based gambling site to accept bets from Canadian citizens. The *Starnet Communications International* case set a precedent that enables police and prosecutors to proceed against commercial Internet gambling sites that operate in Canada, but the fact remains that Canadians have the ability to gamble at offshore Internet sites with relative impunity (for greater information on the *Starnet Communications International* case, see Lipton, 2003).

It is also to be noted that the Quebec-based Kahnawá:ke Mohawk First Nation have operated extensive online gambling sites since the late 1990s. Located on the outskirts of Montreal, the Kahnawá:ke Mohawks assert that they are a sovereign nation and entitled to grant gaming licences for lottery schemes. The Kahnawá:ke Mohawks themselves do not operate Internet sites but have established the Kahnawá:ke Gaming Commission (KGC) to license and regulate some 30 gambling websites operated through Internet servers physically located on their tribal lands (Lipton, 2003; Kelly, Todosichuk, & Azmier, 2001).

While the Kahnawá:ke Mohawks are allegedly violating the *Criminal Code*, and while the Quebec and federal governments, together with the provincial police, have investigated their Internet gambling activities, no action has been taken to halt the operations. Even though Internet gambling is not a hugely popular activity for Canadians (less that 0.5 percent of the adult population report having gambled on Internet sites), there are, nevertheless, policy and law-enforcement dilemmas for Canadian authorities (Kelly, Todosichuk, & Azmier, 2001). Of course, as provincial governments continue to expand their repertoire of gaming products through online media, it is likely that Canadian provinces will assert their legal monopoly in this domain as well.

Internet Horse Race Wagering

Critics of the Woodbine Entertainment Group website, which facilitates online betting on horse races in Ontario, formally sought to have federal and provincial authorities explain how and why the online betting operation received approval, alleging that it violates sections 206 and 207 of the *Criminal Code*.

Permission had been granted to the website operators based on the Minister of Agriculture's interpretation that the 1985 amendment to the *Criminal Code* allowing betting on horse racing via telephone also extended to betting via the Internet (another telecommunications device). The federal minister of justice and the Ontario Provincial Police illegal gambling unit ignored queries from a Montreal-based problem gambling counselling firm, Viva Consulting, regarding the legal status of the online betting site.

According to Viva Consulting, given the concerns surrounding Woodbine's entry into Internet wagering, pertinent *Criminal Code* and regulatory questions include the following: (1) Does the minister of agriculture's ruling on Internet betting contravene provisions of the *Criminal Code*? (2) How can non-governmental interests be permitted to conduct online betting schemes? (3) Are regulatory and law-enforcement agencies capable of acting impartially and independently on complaints against government approved gambling operations?[10]

Quebec VLT Class Action Lawsuit

In 2001, Quebec City lawyer Jean Brochu brought a class action lawsuit against Loto-Québec, claiming that it failed to warn players about the potential dangers of the 15 000 video lottery terminals housed in over 4000 bars in the province. The genesis of the legal action stemmed from Brochu's own battle with gambling addiction. As a result of his out-of-control VLT play, Brochu lost his car and home and was disbarred from practising law because he had stolen $50 000 to cover his gambling debts.[11]

At the time of writing, this lawsuit is ongoing. Brochu is suing on behalf of 119 000 Quebecers (a figure derived from a Quebec problem gambling prevalence survey) and asking for $700 million in damages and an admission of liability from Loto-Québec and the EGM manufacturers who provided the machines. At present, five defence law firms are involved (Loto-Québec's and four representing machine manufacturers). Whatever the outcome, this will be a watershed case. A decision that favours the plaintiffs likely will lead to a spate of similar lawsuits. However, a decision in favour of the gaming operators may lead to government's willingness to increase the number and availability of EGMs.

Bill S-11

A private member's bill sponsored by Senator Jean Lapointe was introduced in the Canadian Senate seeking to amend the *Criminal Code*'s provisions that empower provincial and territorial decision making in regard to video lottery terminals (VLTs). In essence, Senator Lapointe sought to have VLTs removed from convenience locations, such as bars, lounges, and restaurants, and restricted to designated gambling venues, such as casinos and racetracks.

The impetus for Bill S-11 was Senator Lapointe's belief that readily accessible VLTs are a major contributor to problem gambling and hence create negative social impacts. Debate on Bill S-11 has included expert testimony from Hal Pruden, counsel, Criminal Law Policy Section, Justice Canada; Jason Azmier, senior policy analyst, Canada West Foundation; and Drs. Jeff Derevensky and Rina Gupta, International Centre for Youth Gambling Problems and High-Risk Behaviors. Discussion on this bill focused on two main issues: (1) How dangerous are VLTs? (2) What repercussions would there be for the federal government, provincial governments, and private business owners if this bill were enacted?

Compelling evidence was presented to the Senate hearings on these issues suggesting that (1) 70 percent of Canadians agree that VLTs should be restricted to gambling venues only; (2) there is no positive economic outcome associated with VLT play, in that VLT revenues exit communities into provincial coffers, while the community is left to deal with the social damages created by problem gamblers; and (3) VLTs are responsible for almost three-quarters of the negative costs of gambling (Canada, 2004, Proceedings of the Standing Senate Committee on Legal and Constitutional Affairs, Dec. 2).

While committee members generally agree that VLTs are hazardous, they have been presented with the following scenarios that would likely occur if this legislation came to pass: (1) the prospect of provincial litigation against the federal government on the grounds that the 1985 agreement, which gave provinces the exclusive authority to manage and conduct lottery schemes, contains a clause stating "this agreement may only be amended or terminated by the unanimous consent of the provinces and the Government of Canada" (Canada, 2004, Proceedings of the Standing Committee on Legal and Constitutional Affairs, Dec. 1); (2) ambiguous terminology in the *Criminal Code* dealing with "slot machines," "video devices," "computers" and "dice games" would need clarifying; and (3) the provinces may hold back their annual gambling revenue payments (which, when adjusted to the Consumer Price Index dollars, amounted to $60 million in 2003) to the federal government as part of the previously noted 1985 agreement.

Bill S-11 presented an interesting dilemma for legislators: Are the social problems created by convenience-location electronic gambling machines worth provoking federal–provincial acrimony? The answers perhaps became apparent when, after passing third reading, Bill S-11 was allowed to die on the Order Paper when Parliament was dissolved on November 29, 2005.

CROSS-NATIONAL LESSONS FOR CANADA

The comparative analysis presented in this section begins with a brief review of the nature and scope of gambling in three countries (Australia, Great Britain, and the United States), followed by a synopsis of each country's national gambling study and the identification of key regulatory issues. The section concludes with suggestions for improvement to Canada's regulatory structures based on policies and practices in the countries we observed. The countries were selected for comparison for particular reasons. All three are English-speaking nations and have similar legal systems and traditions. In addition, they are industrialized countries with free-market economies, and they broadly espouse similar cultural values. They also evidence a variety of legal gambling formats, considerable annual wagering totals, and high per capita gambling expenditures.

Notwithstanding these parallels, there are significant differences among the countries in terms of their gambling operations and regulatory frameworks. These differences derive largely from the fact that Australia and the United States, like Canada, have federal systems of government while Great Britain, on the other hand, has a unitary system. In other words, the division of legislative powers between central and state or provincial governments in Australia, the United States, and Canada has generally resulted in less federal government control over gambling and its regulation.

Nature and Scope of Gambling in Comparative Countries

Table 1.2 highlights similarities and differences in the way in which gambling is managed and conducted in Canada and the comparative countries.

Lessons for Canada

Each of the three countries' gambling regulatory models has strengths and weaknesses. Gleaning from what works and does not work in the countries we examined, the following observations on bolstering Canadian gambling policies and regulatory regimes are tendered.

Canadian Gambling Study

A Canadian national gambling inquiry is long overdue. Indeed, a recommendation for a national review of gambling activity in Canada was made in 2001 by the Canada West Foundation in its report, *Gambling in Canada: Final Report and Recommendations* (Azmier, 2001).

As is the case with other controversial policy issues, gambling policy is entangled in myriad political, moral, social, and economic concerns that polarize positions. Given that legal gambling is now a $13 billion a year industry in Canada (Azmier, 2005), it behooves us to know the extent of this enterprise: who gains and who loses from the activity, whether net community benefits are being maximized, how gambling policy is rationalized and implemented, how gambling is regulated, whether gambling consumers are protected adequately, and whether the social harms resulting from excessive gambling are being properly addressed.

Our observation regarding the need for a national gambling inquiry is tendered not just because the other countries have followed this path. Rather, a Canadian review is warranted because of perceived deficiencies in current Canadian gambling regulatory policies and practices. The need to assess and to provide guidelines on gambling policy for future generations is paramount. Supporting this view, Beare (1989) contended that the expansion of legal gambling in Canada has created a sense of ambiguity that has "resulted in inconsistent policy, limited research and evaluation, inadequate funding for gaming regulation and enforcement, and little concern for the potential social consequences of gambling" (p. 177). Though now over two decades old, Beare's comments remain valid today.

Clarifying Governments' Roles and Obligations

Why are Canadian governments involved in providing gambling opportunities? Given the perceived inevitability of gambling, Canadian legislators have often claimed that it is appropriate for governments to conduct, manage, license, and regulate legal gambling as a way of constraining such negative impacts as organized crime involvement, corruption of public officials,

Table 1.2   Cross-national Comparisons: Management of Gambling in Australia, Great Britain, the United States, and Canada

Variable:	Australia	Great Britain	United States	Canada
1. Legislative Authority	Individual states and territories determine which gambling formats are allowed. In 2000 the federal government implemented a goods and services tax (GST) designed to lessen state reliance on gambling revenue. States were to reduce their gambling taxes in accordance with GST payments received from the federal government.	Gambling is governed by the federal *Gaming Act* passed in 1968. A process for reforming this act has been in place since 2000 and has included a review (the Budd Report), government responses to the review, and draft legislation. Pending legislation is aimed at implementing many of the recommendations from these sources.	Individual states determine the legal gambling formats offered within their borders; the federal government is involved only if the gambling issue is related to a power granted it by the U.S. Constitution, e.g., regulating interstate commerce, Indian affairs, federal taxation, the U.S. Treasury, or use of the U.S. mail.	The federal *Criminal Code of Canada* dictates which gambling formats are legal; provinces are delegated authority to manage, conduct, or license permitted formats.
2. Legal Gambling Formats*	Poker machines (over 200 000); casinos (14); thoroughbred, harness and dog racing through on-course pari-mutuel wagering and bookmakers and off-course betting shops; sports betting; lotto and scratch tickets; keno; bingo; and Internet gambling. Australia is reputed to have "probably the widest and most accessible variety of legal gambling opportunities in the world"(Costello & Millar, 2000, p. 8).	National lottery; betting shops (private bookmakers who take wagers on sports events, horse races, election results, etc.); casinos (133); horse racing; bingo; slot machines that offer both small and large prizes (no minimum age is required to play the small prize machines). Collins (2003, p. 180) describes the UK as having "one of the most peculiar gambling industries in the world."	Lotto and scratch tickets; slot machines and video lottery terminals; horse and dog racing; casinos (914**); bingo; sports betting and off-track horse wagering in a few states.	Lottery products such as lotto, scratch tickets, and sports betting; pull-tabs; bingo; raffles; casinos (62); slot machines and video lottery terminals; and thoroughbred and harness racing.

(Continued)

Table 1.2 (*Continued*)

Variable:	Australia	Great Britain	United States	Canada
3. Gambling on First Nation Lands	No concessions have been made to allow gambling on Aboriginal lands.	No recognized First Nation groups.	Indian tribes are considered to be sovereign entities with powers that are at least as great and sometimes greater than the states where they reside. Under the terms of the federal statute, the *Indian Gaming Regulatory Act*, commercial gambling already authorized by a state can be offered on tribal lands. At present, over one-third of American tribes provide casino gambling and two-thirds of them offer bingo.	First Nations require provincial approval to offer commercial gambling on their reserves. Currently, three provinces (Ontario, Saskatchewan, and British Columbia) offer casinos; proposals for the creation of First Nation casinos have been approved in Manitoba and Alberta; and in Nova Scotia, 50 percent of revenues from the Sydney Casino are split among First Nations who have signed gaming agreements with the province.
4. Problem Gambling Prevalence Rates	In a national study using a variant of the South Oaks Gambling Screen, the Productivity Commission (1999) reported that 2.1 percent of Australian adults had "significant or severe problems" as a result of their gambling behaviour. A further 2.8 percent of the sample was considered to be "at risk."	A British gambling study conducted by GamCare showed between 0.6 percent and 0.8 percent of those aged 16 and over to be problem gamblers.	A survey conducted for the U.S. National Gambling Impact Study Commission (1999) using the NODS (a DSM-IV-based measure of problem gambling) showed that a combined 4.2 percent of adult Americans scored as "at-risk," "problem" or "probable pathological" gamblers.	A national survey using the Canadian Problem Gambling Index indicated that 5 percent of adult Canadians qualified as "at-risk" or "problem gamblers" (Marshall & Wynne, 2004).

Variable:	Australia	Great Britain	United States	Canada
5. Problem Gambling Support Services Funding	The primary responsibility for providing problem gambling treatment services rests with state and territorial governments. The funds to pay for these services come from levies on the gambling industry. Counselling and group support agencies, clinics, and hospitals are the main providers of these services. The total funding for problem gambling support services for all of Australia in 1999 was $15 million (Productivity Commission, 1999).	A "Responsibility in Gambling Trust" of 3 million pounds per year is contributed by the gambling industry to pay for problem gambling services. GamCare, a national counselling agency, is the primary provider for these services.	Most individual states that have an established gambling industry provide some funds for problem gambling services. These funds come from gambling licence fees, taxes, or operations. Generally, state contributions to problem gambling services have been modest and well below that given to other human service programs. For example, the state most dependent on gambling revenues, Nevada, allocates $0 for problem gambling services.	All provincial governments subsidize problem gambling prevention, treatment, and research programs; however, the funding varies considerably from province to province (e.g., Quebec allots $18 million compared to PEI's $15 000) (Campbell & Smith, 2003). Typically, the responsibility for providing problem gambling services resides with the government agency that delivers substance-abuse programs.
6. National Gambling Study	Productivity Commission Report (1999).	Gambling Review (Budd) Report (2001).	National Gambling Impact Study Commission (1999).	None.

*The legal gambling offerings noted may not be available in all areas of the country.
**U.S. casinos range widely in terms of size, elegance, and density per state. (For example, some states do not allow casinos, while Nevada, with 366 casinos, has 40 percent of the nation's total.)

and unfair gambling practices. But, can it be assumed that Canadian provincial governments oversee gambling mainly to protect the public's welfare, or are governments motivated more by revenue generation in spite of the harms that may result? Both positions are relevant given the official rhetoric used to justify Canadian governments' authority to operate and regulate gambling. However, there is an inherent conflict between revenue maximization and social responsibility objectives. Canadian jurisdictions currently perform multiple roles in the provision of gambling goods and services, including licensing, managing, conducting, marketing, promoting, operating, and regulating the activity, as well as garnering most of the profits.

Government self-regulation in regard to gambling is questionable public policy for several reasons. For example, an inherent tension arises between the dichotomous roles (generating revenue vs. protecting citizen welfare) played by government; to wit, certain gambling formats (EGMs) can be quite addictive but, at the same time, stand as a highly lucrative revenue source. Canadian provincial governments have shown repeatedly that addicting some of their citizens is an acceptable business trade-off for generating provincial government revenue. As well, self-regulation has tended to blunt transparency and accountability; has led to special treatment for private-sector industry partners (such as granting regional monopolies); has created inconsistency between jurisdictions in terms of how gambling is regulated and how *Criminal Code* provisions are interpreted; and has contributed to a systemic unwillingness to address the long-term impact on public welfare of such consequences as problem gambling.

Recognizing and correcting these policy dilemmas would mean that governments could not conduct, manage, regulate, and profit from gambling at the same time. Except for the provision of lottery products, this conflict of interest is avoided in Australia, Great Britain, and the United States by licensing private corporations and/or Indian tribes to conduct and manage gambling enterprises. Without the imperative to maximize gambling revenues, individual jurisdictions can regulate gambling rigorously and impartially. In this scenario, state gambling revenues are indirect, coming from licensing fees, from taxes on corporations that operate gambling, and from income taxes paid by gambling industry employees. Overall, less state revenue is generated, but the profit maximizing and regulatory roles of the state are separated.

An alternative possible solution, although not currently in use in the other countries examined, is to allow states to manage, conduct, and profit from gambling but be regulated by a completely independent body with oversight powers akin to those of auditor generals or ethics commissioners.

Of the four countries examined, Great Britain is the only one with a national gambling policy and the only one where gambling is regulated by the national government. In Australia, where gambling regulation is decentralized, scholars have called for a greater federal government presence in gambling policy and regulation on the grounds that the federal government is more likely to be guided by principles of public and national interest and thus be in a better position to mitigate inter-state competition. As some commentators have suggested, the federal government would be less likely to make hasty decisions based on short-term economic pressures and less likely to be influenced by the gambling industry (Costello & Millar, 2000).

Responsible Gambling and Harm Minimization

Lately, the terms *responsible gambling* and *harm minimization* have been used by governments to indicate a concern for mitigating the individual and social damages associated with widespread legal gambling. While responsibility in this regard is a progressive step, it is to be noted that efforts in this area have been tentative and inconsistent (hiring social responsibility directors and incorporating modest responsible gaming features [RGFs] in the design of new gambling machines). Ostensibly, the reason for moving slowly on the issue is that effective responsible gambling policies and practices may result in declining gambling revenues. Despite overwhelming and incontrovertible evidence that electronic gaming machines are the game of choice for problem gamblers, provincial regulators have done little to mitigate the harms associated with machine gambling.

Lottery products are the most popular gambling format with about 60 percent of adult Canadians participating at least once a year. Despite being the most lucrative gambling format, electronic gambling machines are played by only 15 to 20 percent of adults annually—revenues are high because those who do use the machines, do so frequently and intensely (Williams & Wood, 2004).

It is estimated that about 1 in 15 adult Canadians (6.3 percent) are at risk of developing gambling problems. Demographic factors that increase this risk include gender (men are somewhat more likely to become problem gamblers than are females); education (those with less than a postsecondary education are at greater risk for developing gambling problems); and ethnicity (those from an Aboriginal background are three times more likely than those in the general population to be at risk for problem gambling). Finally, the gambling format that places players at most risk for problem gambling are electronic gambling machines (The Wager, 2004).

It is a truism in the administration of legal gambling in Canada that when revenue-generation priorities and social responsibility clash, economic exigency wins. For example, the Ontario government recently reassessed its gambling policies in light of a study that found that 35 percent of the province's gambling revenues come from the 5 percent of the population that are problem gamblers (Williams & Wood, 2004). The "New Gaming Strategy to Focus on a Sustainable Responsible Industry" is, in the words of then Economic Development Trade Minister Joseph Cordiano, supposed to "put social responsibility front and centre in the delivery of gaming in Ontario" ("New Ontario Gaming Strategy," 2005). A critic of the publicized Ontario policy shift maintains that it gives the appearance that social responsibility objectives have a high priority, but in reality, attention is diverted from the social and economic damages caused by "years of uncontrolled gambling expansion" (Horbay, 2005).

A key point raised about gambling regulation in the *Australian Productivity Commission Report* (1999) is that "governments' failure to follow good regulatory process and design principles, compounded by and combined with revenue raising imperatives, may well have led to perverse regulatory outcomes in gambling" (ch. 12, p. 16). Consequently, the Productivity Commission recommended that the overriding goal of all gambling public policy should be to maximize net community benefits. This has resulted in a concerted effort by Australian state governments and territories to implement stringent harm minimization strategies.

Making social responsibility the focal point of gambling policy requires a more forceful and pre-emptive approach than has been the case so far in Canada. A comprehensive responsible gambling policy implies a commitment to probity and to addressing duty-of-care obligations, even if it means reduced gambling revenues. A recent report issued by the Independent Pricing and Regulatory Tribunal of New South Wales (2004), entitled *Gambling: Promoting a Culture of Responsibility*, provides a state-of-the-art approach to responsible gambling policy. According to the New South Wales report, an exemplary responsible gambling strategy has three main elements:

- Informed choice—being able to make decisions about a gambling format on the basis of adequate information about the nature and foreseeable consequences of the activity, and without controlling influences
- Consumer protection—implementing measures to discourage risky behaviours and to minimize the incidence, prevalence, and negative consequences of problem gambling
- Counselling measures—various programs to assist those who are developing or have developed gambling problems to stop or control their intemperate behaviour and to blunt the negative impacts of these behaviours on the gamblers themselves, their families and friends, their employers, and the wider community

Along with these responsible gambling building blocks, the report calls for government transparency, active monitoring and enforcement of responsible gambling regulations, and the need for evidence-based research to inform decision makers. In general, Canadian provincial governments do a satisfactory job of providing problem gambling counselling and prevention programs, but are deficient in the areas of informed choice and consumer protection. For example, Canadian gamblers are not well-informed about the probabilities of winning or about gambling machine payout ratios, nor are they given instruction about how electronic gambling machines work.

Based on the New South Wales study's standards, Canadian jurisdictions have been lax in implementing certain consumer protection measures. For example, casinos in some provinces extend credit and offer cheque-cashing services; self-exclusion programs generally exist only for casino patrons and are relatively easy to circumvent. Furthermore, research has shown that bill acceptors on gambling machines and gambling location ATMs exacerbate problem gambling behaviour, yet they remain in Canadian gambling venues. As well, while the maximum bet on a New South Wales gambling machine is $10, some Canadian provinces offer machines that take $100 bets.

Canadian provincial governments also tend to lack transparency on gambling issues, are seldom open to public input about their gambling policies, and are often averse to having research evidence guide policy decisions. Presumably, challenging questions and contrary research findings threaten gambling revenues. However, by adopting defensive stances with regard to their gambling policies and operations, governments violate their covenant to promote the public interest.

In this section we have sought to explore gambling policies and regulatory frameworks in three countries for the purpose of informing legal gambling policies and regulations in Canada. In our view, existing Canadian legal gambling regimes fall short of the laudable goal of maximizing net community benefits. Achieving this goal requires that gambling be regulated in an uncompromising and impartial fashion and that social responsibility becomes the paramount objective of all gambling policy.

FINAL OBSERVATIONS

This chapter has shown that there are contentious legal, behavioural, and public-policy issues raised by the legalization and expansion of many forms of gambling. For example, we have seen how questions have been raised concerning the legality of the interpretations by some provinces of certain of the *Criminal Code* amendments pertaining to gambling. There is an absence of consistency in the ways in which these gambling amendments have been applied by different provincial governments. We have also observed that the *Criminal Code* amendments and their interpretation raise questions regarding the division of powers between the federal and provincial governments. How can a proper balance be maintained between local provision and regulation of gambling formats and national consistency in the interpretation and implementation of the *Criminal Code*?

Despite the legalization of many forms of gambling, a number of unwanted and harmful behaviours associated with gambling have persisted and, in some cases, increased. In particular, criminal behaviour and gambling remain linked in a number of ways and new social problems such as excessive or problem gambling have arisen, the latter associated with the availability of electronic gambling machines. A range of provincially funded educational and therapeutic programs directed at preventing and ameliorating problems associated with these new forms of deviance have emerged. Finally, we have highlighted a number of public-policy questions raised by the legalization and expansion of gambling. Most generally, how can the benefits and costs of legal gambling be balanced and the unintended but negative consequences of legalization be mitigated? How should public opinion and values enter into the policy process with respect to the regulation of gambling? Perhaps the most crucial policy issue concerns the potential conflicts of interest that arise for provincial governments when they both regulate and promote gambling. Provincial governments have become increasingly dependent upon the enhanced revenue generated by the expansion of legal gambling; therefore, they have a vested interest in the promotion and expansion of gambling. At the same time, these governments now have almost exclusive power to regulate and control gambling activity. The potential for conflicts inherent in this situation is of pressing concern from the perspective both of public welfare and the integrity of governmental institutions.

Social theory can help place these specific issues regarding the legalization and expansion of gambling within a broader context; explicate the underlying social, economic, and political forces contributing to changes in the social control of gambling; and result in a clarification and generalization of the questions involved. Each of four theoretical perspectives provides some insight into the sources and effects of the changes observed in the social control of gambling in Canada.

One perspective on the criminal law regards it as an expression of a fundamental consensus in society with regard to certain values and norms. This functionalist view of law and punishment emphasizes the expressive and symbolic functions of the criminal law and its enforcement (Durkheim, 1960, p. 1984). From this perspective, then, change in consensus regarding fundamental values should result in legal change, with behaviours once regarded as crimes being decriminalized or legalized. Applied to the topic of gambling, this perspective would argue that the legalization of many forms of gambling in Canada reflects a declining consensus around gambling as a moral evil or vice.

While it seems clear that public opinion did not play a major role in producing the 1969 and 1985 *Criminal Code* amendments, it is also evident that public attitudes toward gambling did shift over time toward greater toleration and acceptance of legalized gambling. Thus, there appears to be evidence of some consensus for aspects of legalized gambling. However, it remains unclear to what extent such consensus facilitated the *Criminal Code* amendments or, rather, was the result of these legislative changes. Furthermore, Canadian public opinion remains generally ambivalent toward gambling, particularly with respect to certain types and locations, as well as the appropriate balance to be struck between benefits and costs. Thus, public policy concerning some aspects of gambling lacks a strong consensus and could result in a backlash against some government regulations. Consensus or functional theory suggests, then, that there are limits on the extent to which legislation/regulation can diverge from the widely held views of the public.

A second theoretical perspective recognizes a major limitation of Durkheim's functional approach, namely a failure to consider the role of power and interest-group activity in legal change. Rather than a consensus on fundamental values, this perspective conceptualizes society as constituted by a variety of interest groups in competition and conflict over scarce resources (Quinney, 1970; Akers, 1994; Akers & Hawkins, 1975). Interest groups with greater power are better situated to influence the legislative process to protect their interests and/or values. While there are a variety of interest group/conflict theories, they all emphasize that law, including criminal law, represents, expresses, and protects the specific interests and/or values of particular groups or segments within society. Applied to gambling legislation, this perspective looks for indications of the influence of business groups, such as the leisure industry, trade associations, charitable groups, and entrepreneurial individuals, in lobbying for the decriminalization of gambling.

Morton's (2003) discussion of the appearance in the early 20th century of both legislative reform groups and an anti-gambling lobby may represent an example of the interest group/conflict perspective. However, there is a lack of evidence of any significant public or interest-group involvement in the 1969 and 1985 amendments. But as a result of these amendments and the subsequent expansion of legalized gambling, a number of special interest groups have arisen—primarily consisting of non-profit, community-based charitable organizations, such as social, cultural, and amateur sporting groups—interested in exerting influence on public policy regarding the social control of gambling. This perspective also focuses attention upon provincial governments as the major interested actors in the evolution of the social control of gambling in Canada. This is certainly evident in our discussion of the federal–provincial struggle over gambling in the 1970s and 1980s and the 1985 Code amendments. But it is perhaps even more apparent as provincial governments have taken on the dual role of major promoter and financial beneficiary of legalized gambling. This perspective suggests, then, that it is unlikely that provincial governments will cede any significant regulatory power over gambling back to the federal government or, indeed, to any other agency.

Another, less comprehensive, perspective has been developed to draw upon the historical and cultural realities of Canada's political economy to interpret strategies used by the federal government for governing in a neo-conservative environment (Hatt et al., 1990; 1992). Termed *managing consent*, "this strategy emphasizes the generation of public support while avoiding direct, open, and hostile confrontation.... An effort is made to institutionalize conflict and turn political problems into technical and administrative ones" (Hatt et al.,1992, p. 246). These authors suggest that a number of external and domestic factors act to constrain federal public policy development; most important for our purposes are federal versus provincial powers. The practice of devolving federal responsibilities to lower levels of government has allowed the federal government "to insulate itself from criticism by shifting frustrations and concerns from its own terrain onto that of the provinces" (Hatt et al., 1992, p. 247).

The *Criminal Code* amendments of 1969 and 1985 with respect to gambling seem to exemplify the strategy of managing consent on the part of the federal government. Maintaining the criminal prohibitions on certain forms of gambling (e.g., keeping a common gaming house; unlicensed gambling formats) while decriminalizing a variety of widely acceptable gambling activities by placing them under provincial authority is one way of managing the competing federal and provincial powers. But this may also have represented a way in which the federal government could "insulate itself from criticism" (Hatt et al., 1992, p. 247) from segments of the population opposed to gambling expansion and from concerns regarding possible increased social costs of such action. While ceding social control to the provinces, as well as much of the revenue-generating potential of legalized gambling, the federal government also effectively withdrew itself from responsibility for dealing with the various problems associated with gambling expansion. In this way the federal government can be seen as simultaneously decriminalizing a variety of now widely acceptable activities while upholding the public condemnation of some remaining public vices.

A recent theme in the literature of social control is the mutation of welfare capitalism with the primacy of the social activist state into neoliberalism, with its emphasis on individualism and minimal state structure and its preoccupation with the containment of risk (Garland, 1996, 2001; Hudson, 2003; O'Malley, 1999). Neoliberalism allows the state only a minimum of functions; punishment and control of the dangerous and predatory are the functions of states in relation to crime (Hudson, 2003). Among the cultural characteristics of late modernity noted by Garland (2000) are hyperindividualism (with less emphasis on collective interests or the community), distrust of the state, and the dominance of economic rather than social reasoning. Garland (1996; 2001) argued that the problem of crime control in late modernity demonstrates the limits of sovereign states: they can no longer govern by means of sovereign commands to obedient subjects and therefore "see the need to withdraw or at least qualify their claim to be the primary and effective provider of security and crime control..." (Garland, 1996, p. 449).

Garland (1996) discusses several strategies devised by the administrative machine of the state to adapt to its limitations with respect to crime control. One of these is to "define deviance down" (p. 248) either by filtering it out of the system altogether or by lowering the degree to which certain behaviours are criminalized and penalized. (See also Moynihan, 1992.) Thus, behaviours that were once routinely prosecuted may be decriminalized; or the police may decide that they will no longer use scarce investigative resources on certain offences having a low likelihood of detection and/or a low priority for the public.

Several aspects of the neo-liberal/minimal state perspective apply to key features of the changes observed in the social control of gambling. For example, economic reasoning has become an important feature of discussion regarding the regulation of gambling, particularly in view of the huge profits generated. But even at the outset of federal–provincial negotiation around amendments to the *Criminal Code*, economic more so than social considerations predominated. We have also observed, beginning with the amendments to the *Criminal Code*, several instances of the "minimal state" working to "define deviance down." The federal government has shifted much of the regulatory control to the provinces, who, in turn, have used various means for downloading control of licensed gambling to Crown corporations and private-sector gambling interests. These agencies thus acquire much of the responsibility for the prevention of gambling-related crime on their premises, as well as some law enforcement in view of the low priority assigned to such crime by the public police (Smith et al., 2003; Smith & Wynne, 1999). This fits Garland's (1996, p. 452) responsibilization strategy—whereby central government seeks to act upon crime indirectly by seeking to activate action on the part of non-state agencies and organizations rather than directly through state agencies. Perhaps paradoxically, this may result in an extension of social control as these gambling enterprises employ a variety of surveillance techniques over all customers in efforts at situational crime control. With this privatization of the social control of licensed gambling, along with the increased tolerance of gambling by the public, there is some evidence that the criminal justice system is assigning enforcement a lower priority.

Other recent works have endeavoured to explicate the cultural meaning of modern gambling and have linked its current global popularity and legitimation to the aggressive involvement of the state and to changes in social and economic morality (Cosgrave & Klassen, 2001; Reith, 2007).

Along with the emergence of neo-liberal states, an emphasis was placed on consumer-driven, service-based free market economies, and on a general downsizing and outsourcing of functions of the welfare state. Politicians began to recognize that legal gambling could undercut some criminal elements, bolster state budgets, and generate funds for charitable and non-profit organizations—all while restraining tax increases. In short, a utilitarian worldview took root, based on the premise that if gambling could not be suppressed, then at least some public good should come from it. In turn, greater public acceptance of legal gambling allowed criminal justice authorities to relax their formal surveillance of illegal gambling, believing that resources could be better spent monitoring more serious crime (Smith & Wynne,1999).

In a similar vein, Kingma (2004) has argued that the liberalization and expansion of gambling was part of an international phenomenon that saw state gambling public policy shift from alibi model to risk-model principles. Although discussing gambling in the Netherlands, Kingma's analysis applies to the gambling policies of other industrialized nations, including Canada. According to Kingma, an alibi model was in vogue prior to gambling's expansion and was typified by tightly regulated gambling under the following conditions: (a) legalization that was intended to avoid illegal markets, (b) the discouragement of private profiteering, and (c) gambling proceeds that were directed to social programs, such as welfare, sports, and other "worthy causes" (Kingma, 2004, p. 49). A risk model subsequently emerged along with, and as a result of, global gambling expansion in the 1980s and is exemplified by (a) gambling's being viewed as a legitimate form of commercial entertainment, (b) a belief that gambling revenues should augment government coffers and spur the economy, and (c) gambling "markets" require state control to minimize the risks of addiction and crime (Kingma, 2004; see also Smith & Campbell, 2007).

Using Habermas's (1975) legitimation crisis as an explanatory tool, Kingma (2004) postulated that the paradigm shift occurred during the 1970s and 1980s, when legislation lagged behind aggressive gambling practices, ultimately creating a situation where "politics gave in to market demands without convincing and conclusive (legal) justification (p. 55). The upshot of this policy inversion was gambling proceeds being largely redirected from decentralized welfare initiatives toward government coffers and the introduction of new gambling formats designed not as intrinsically pleasing, recreational amusements but for profit maximization (Smith & Campbell, 2007).

Cosgrave (2006, p. 5) has characterized this redirection as a shift from local to global markets and a colonization of gambling by both the gambling industry and the state working collaboratively in what Reith regards as a "symbiotic relationship" (Reith 2007, p. 36). No longer a threat to the rationality essential to the work/production ethic of modernist capitalism, gambling has been thus commodified as a legitimate leisure activity and constituted as a fundamental aspect of the consumption ethic prevalent now in late modernity (Reith, 2007; Cosgrave, 2006).

The containment of risk is another theme from this perspective that seems applicable to the social control of gambling. When the social costs involved in gambling expansion are considered, the relatively small percentage of problem gamblers often dominate discussion in lieu of a broader debate focused upon public welfare. In conjunction with this attention to risk assessment and harm minimization for problem gamblers, the degree of social control over gambling may actually be extended, at least for segments of the population through monitoring and/or restricting their gambling behaviour and instituting various treatment regimes.

As Reith (2007) has pointed out, the emergence of problem gambling as an unintended consequence of liberalized, commercialized gambling illuminates "…some of the contradictions of modern consumer societies, namely, the increasing emphasis on individual self-control through freely willed practices of consumption that accompanies the reduction in external forms of regulation in economic and social life" (p. 50). The emphasis on individual self-control is evident in the development of responsible gambling strategies, wherein state and commercial interests actively promote the notion that individuals are responsible for holding their inappropriate gambling consumption to acceptable levels and by providing an array of experts in the form of psychologists, counsellors, and other treatment specialists who actively work both to constitute and cure the problem gambler. In this sense, the self-imposition of norms and values conducive to appropriate gambling consumption is achieved and therapy itself becomes a form of regulation (Reith, 2007, pp. 45, 50).

Ultimately, the delegation of authority over gambling from the federal government to the provinces, at the very least is a tacit admission that gambling no longer stands as a matter warranting criminal prohibition. As the preceding discussion has suggested, it is obvious that the delegation of authority over gambling to the provinces has not resulted in increased measures to prevent or to otherwise restrict gambling. Indeed, as much of the discussion confirms, Canadian criminal law has been used principally to consolidate provincial authority over gambling as a revenue-raising instrument and to expand its availability rather than restrict it in any meaningful sense. Brodeur and Ouellet (2004, p. 27) have considered the use of the criminal law for the purpose of creating a limiting monopoly wherein government control of particular activities is justified on the basis of protecting the public. Such an example resides in the *Controlled Drugs and Substances Act*, wherein the intent is to restrict both the availability and use of substances deemed to be potentially harmful if used improperly. Instead, Canadian criminal law in regard to gambling has been used principally to consolidate and legitimize a provincial government "expansionist monopoly" (Brodeur & Ouellett, 2004, p. 27). This, of course, raises the fundamental question of whether or not this is an appropriate function for the criminal law in a democratic society.

QUESTIONS TO CONSIDER

1. Colin Campbell et al. trace a shift in government responses to gambling such that what was often seen as a vice that was liable to criminal prosecution is now tolerated and even encouraged by governments as a source of revenue. In your opinion, how *should* governments respond to gambling behaviours? What gambling practices, if any, should be banned or strictly regulated? Use specific examples in supporting your argument.

2. Review the ongoing conflict over Internet gambling, using this chapter as well as the work of Justin and Jackson (see below, under "Suggestions for Further Reading") and other materials. How should governments act in developing policy concerning Internet gambling, particularly with respect to First Nations stakeholders such as the Kahnawá:ke Mohawk First Nation?

3. What are the major risks associated with gambling activities? To what extent can gambling be seen as a pathological activity? How should legislation and law enforcement be designed to address gambling-linked risks? Use specific examples drawn from this chapter and outside sources.

SUGGESTIONS FOR FURTHER READING

Gardner, D. (2008). *Risk: The science and politics of fear*. Toronto: McClelland and Stewart.

Justin, R., & Jackson, D. J. (2008). The options for internet gambling in Canada. *The American Review of Canadian Studies, 38*(2), 222–223.

Newman, S., & Thompson, A. (2007). The association between pathological gambling and attempted suicide: Findings from a national survey in Canada. *Canadian Journal of Psychiatry, 52*(9), 605–612.

Partington, A. (Ed.). (1997). *The concise Oxford dictionary of quotations* (3rd ed., rev.). New York: Oxford University Press.

NOTES

1. The authors would like to acknowledge the research assistance of three undergraduate students: Lora Lee, Ayren Messmer, and Jessica Sherman. Gary McCaskill provided much appreciated word-formatting support. We also acknowledge the contribution provided by our interview subjects in the United States, the United Kingdom, Australia, and Canada. We are grateful for the support given to this project by Rob Simpson and the Ontario Problem Gambling Research Centre; and by Vickii Williams and the Alberta Gaming Research Institute. Dr. Harold Wynne provided important and helpful comments on an earlier draft of *The Legalization of Gambling in Canada*. We are also especially thankful for the Law Commission of Canada's support and for the opportunity to participate in its "*What Is a Crime?*" project. The Law Commission's senior research officer, Steve Bittle, oversaw the project. His sage advice contributed in immeasurable ways to the original report. This work was developed as part of an anthology coordinated by Professors Joan Brockman of Simon Fraser University and Janet Mosher of York University.

2. We rely upon Devereux's definition of *gambling*: "… an activity in which the parties involved … voluntarily engage to make the transfer of money or something else of value among themselves contingent upon the outcome of some future and uncertain event" (Devereux, 1968, p. 53).

3. See subsequent discussion of public opinion data.

4. "clever but misleading talk… deception" (Bissett, 2002, p. 159).

5. Since its inclusion in the *Criminal Code* in 1906, the term lottery scheme has been liberally interpreted by authorities to encompass a wide variety of gambling formats, such as wheels of fortune and bingo as well as casino games like blackjack and roulette. The expression appears to be distinct to Canadian law.

6. Readers interested in the details of this conflict and the terms of its settlement are referred to Labrosse (1985), Osborne & Campbell (1988), Osborne (1989), Campbell (1994), and Campbell, Hartnagel, & Smith (2005).

7. In a pari-mutuel system, bettors technically wager among themselves rather than with a bookmaker. Payouts to winners are a function of the total amount bet (or handle), divided by the number of winning selections; thus bettors themselves determine the odds. In practice, operators of the pari-mutuel pools deduct a percentage (or takeout) from the handle as a profit for themselves and to pay the owners of the winning horses (Abt, Smith, & Christiansen, 1985, p. 83).

8. Gross profit includes government share of gambling revenues plus the expenses associated with its delivery. Net profit represents the amount of gambling revenue that accrues to government after expenses have been deducted (see Azmier, 2005, p. 2). Some gambling observers refer to gross profit as the win or the amount equal to that lost by gamblers.

9. The report was never released officially to the public, but a leaked copy became available (Donovan & Welsh, 1998). It is available online at http://www.citizenvoice.ca/members/Portals/0/Ontario_Gaming_Legislation_Review.pdf (Retrieved February 7, 2009).

10. See Bailey, S. (2004). *Woodbine Internet betting site under fire as Justice investigates.* Retrieved February 7, 2009, from http://www.vivaconsulting.com/advocacy/woodbine.html

11. See Thorne, D. (2002, April 19). Quebec lawsuit a warning to Alta [Alberta] researcher. Newscan, 4(16). Retrieved February 7, 2009, from http://www.responsiblegambling.org/articles/041902_16.pdf

REFERENCES

Abt, V., Smith, J. F., & Christiansen, E. M. (1985). *The Business of risk: Commercial gambling in mainstream America.* Lawrence, KA: University of Kansas Press.

Akers, R. (1994). *Criminological theories.* Los Angeles: Roxbury.

Akers, R., & Hawkins, R. (1975). *Law & control in society.* Englewood Cliffs, N.J: Prentice Hall.

Alfieri, D. (1994). The Ontario casino project: a case study. In C. Campbell (Ed.). *Gambling in Canada: The bottom line* (pp. 85–91). Burnaby, BC: Criminology Research Centre, Simon Fraser University.

Azmier, J. J. (2000). *Canadian gambling behaviour and attitudes: Summary report.* Calgary, AB: Canada West Foundation.

Azmier, J. J. (2001). *Gambling in Canada: An overview.* Calgary, AB: Canada West Foundation.

Azmier, J. J. (2005). *Gambling in Canada 2005: Statistics and context.* Calgary, AB: Canada West Foundation.

Azmier, J., & Roach, R. (2000). *The ethics of charitable gambling: A survey.* Calgary, AB: Canada West Foundation.

Bailey, S. (2004). *Woodbine Internet betting site under fire as Justice investigates.* Retrieved February 8, 2005, from http://www.vivaconsulting.com/advocacy/woodbine.html

Beare, M. (1989). Current law enforcement issues in Canadian gambling. In C. Campbell, & J. Lowman (Eds.), *Gambling in Canada: Golden goose or Trojan horse?* (pp. 177–194). Burnaby BC: Proceedings of the First National Symposium on Lotteries & Gambling, Simon Fraser University.

Bisset, A. (Ed.). (2002). *The Canadian Oxford compact dictionary.* Don Mills, ON: Oxford University Press.

Bowal, P., & Carrasco, C. (1997). Taking a chance on it: The legal regulation of gambling. *Law Now,* 22(2), 28–30.

Brodeur, J., & Ouellet, G. (2004). What is a crime? A secular answer. In N. DesRosiers and S. Bittle (Eds.), *What is a crime? Defining criminal conduct in contemporary society* (pp. 1–33). Vancouver, BC: UBC Press.

Campbell, C. (1994). *Canadian gambling legislation: The social origins of legalization.* Unpublished doctoral dissertation, Simon Fraser University, Burnaby, BC.

Campbell, C., Hartnagel, T., & Smith, G. (2005). *The legalization of gambling in Canada,* Ottawa, ON: Law Commission of Canada.

Campbell, C., & Smith, G. (1998). Canadian gambling: Trends and public policy issues. *Annals of the American Academy of Political & Social Science,* 556, 22–35.

Campbell, C. & Smith G. (2003). Gambling in Canada—From vice to disease to responsibility: A negotiated history. *Canadian Bulletin of Medical History,* 20(1), 121–149.

Canada. (1956). *Report of the Joint Committee on the Senate and the House of Commons on capital punishment, corporal punishment and lotteries.* Ottawa, ON: Queen's Printer.

Canadian Partnership for Responsible Gambling. (2004). *Canadian Gambling Digest.* Retrieved February 8, 2005, from http://www.cprg.ca/articles/canadian_gambling_digest_2004.pdf

Costello, T., & Millar, R. (2000). *Wanna bet?* St. Leonards, AU: Allen & Unwin.

Cosgrave, J. F. (Ed.). (2006). *The sociology of risk and gambling reader.* New York: Routledge.

Cosgrave J., & Klassen, T. (2001). Gambling against the state: The state and the legitimation of gambling. *Current Sociology,* 49(5), 1–15.

The Budd Report (Gambling Review Report). (2001). London, UK: Department for Culture, Media and Sport.

Devereux, E. C., Jr. (1968). Gambling in psychological and sociological perspective. In *International encyclopedia of social sciences*, (Vol. 6, pp. 53–62). New York: Macmillan.

Dixon, D. (1991). *From prohibition to regulation: Anti-gambling and the law*. Oxford, UK: Claredon.

Donovan, K., & Welsh, M. (1998, October 31). Ontario's casinos illegal, secret report says. The Toronto Star, p. A1.

DSM-IV. (1994). Washington, DC: American Psychiatric Association.

Durkheim, E. (1960). *The division of labour in society*. Glencoe, IL: Free Press.

Durkheim, E. (1984). Two laws of penal evolution. In S. Lukes & A. Scull (Eds.), *Durkheim and the law*. Oxford, UK: Basil Blackwell.

Falkiner, T., & Horbay, R. (2006). Unbalanced reel gaming machines. Paper presented at the 2006 International Pokies Impact Conference, Melbourne, AU. [Editors' note: *Pokies* is a slang term for gambling machines/poker machines.]

Garland, D. (1996) The limits of the sovereign state. *British Journal of Criminology*, 36(4), 445–470.

Garland, D. (2000). The culture of high crime societies. *British Journal of Criminology*, 40(3), 347–375.

Garland, D. (2001). *The culture of control*. Oxford, UK: Oxford University Press.

Habermas, J. (1975). *Legitimation crisis* (T. McCarthy, Trans.). Boston: Beacon.

Hatt, K., Caputo, T. C., & Perry, B. (1990). Managing consent: Canada's experience with neo-conservatism. *Social Justice*, 17, 30–48.

Hatt, K., Caputo, T.C., & Perry, B. (1992) Criminal justice policy under Mulroney, 1984–1990. *Canadian Public Policy*, 18(3), 245–260.

Horbay, R. (2004). EGM Transparency: An essential element of product safety & consumer protection. Presentation at *Myths, Reality and Ethical Public Policy*. International Problem Gambling Conference, October 4–6, Halifax, Nova Scotia.

Horbay, R. (2005, January 24). Guest editorial in Canada's *Gambling Watch Network Weekly Newsletter*, 6(15).

Hudson, B. A. (2003). Understanding justice. Buckingham, UK: Open University Press.

Independent Pricing & Regulatory Tribunal. (2004). Gambling: Promoting a Culture of Responsibility. Sydney, NSW.

Ipsos News Center. (1998a, March 10). Press release, CTV/Angus Reid Group Poll. Ipsos News Center. (1998b, March 9). Press Release, CTV/Angus Reid Group Poll.

Kelly, R., Todosichuk, P., & Azmier, J. J. (2001, October). *Gambling@Home: Internet gambling in Canada*. Calgary: Canada West Foundation.

Kingma, S. (2004). Gambling and the risk society: The liberalization and legitimation crisis of gambling in the Netherlands. In *International Gambling Studies*, 4(1), 47–67.

Labrosse, M. (1985). *The lottery . . . from Jacques Cartier's day to modern times*. Montreal: Stanke.

Lipton, M. (2003). Internet gaming in Canada. Paper presented at the Global Gaming Exposition, September 17, Las Vegas. Available online at http://www.eljlaw.com/Internet.html (Retrieved February 8, 2005).

Marshall, K., & Wynne, H. (July 2004). Against the odds: A profile of at-risk and problem gamblers. *Canadian Social Trends*, 73(Summer).

Martin's Annual *Criminal Code*. (2005). Aurora, ON: Canada Law Books.

Monahan, P., & Goldlist, G. (1999). Roll again: New developments concerning gaming. *The Criminal Law Quarterly*, 42(2), 182–226.

Morris, R., & Ledgett Law Firm. (1996). *Review of gaming legislation in Ontario*. A report prepared for the Ontario Government, Toronto, ON. Retrieved July 1, 2005, from http://www.citizenvoice.ca/members/Portals/0/Ontario_Gaming_Legislation_Review.pdf

Morton, S. (2003). *At odds: Gambling & Canadians 1919–1969*. Toronto, ON: University of Toronto Press.

Moynihan, D. P. (1992, Autumn). Defining deviance down. *The American Scholar*.

Nanaimo Community Bingo Association v. British Columbia (Attorney General), [1999] 2 W.W.R. 428 (B.C.S.C.).

National Gambling Impact Study Commission. (1999). *Final Report*. Washington, DC: Government Printing Office.

O'Malley, P. (1999). Volatile and contradictory punishments. *Theoretical Criminology* 1(3), 175–196.

Ontario. "New Ontario Gaming Strategy to Focus on a Sustainable Responsible Industry." (2005, January 20). Retrieved from http://www.ontario-canada.com/ontcan/page.do?page=5899

Osborne, J. A. (1989). The legal status of lottery schemes in Canada: Changing the rules of the game. Unpublished LL.M. thesis, Faculty of Law, University of British Columbia, Vancouver, BC.

Osborne, J. A., & Campbell, C. S. (1988, Spring). Recent amendments to Canadian lottery & gaming laws: The transfer of power between federal and provincial governments, *Osgoode Hall Law Journal*, 26(1), 19–43.

Patrick, T. (2000). No dice: Violations of the *Criminal Code*'s gaming exemptions by provincial governments. *The Criminal Law Quarterly*, 44(1), 108–126.

Productivity Commission. (1999). *Australia's gambling industries (Vols. 1–2)*. Canberra, AU: ACT.

Quinney, R. (1970). *The social reality of crime*. Boston, MA: Little, Brown & Co.

Reith, G. (2007, September). Gambling and the contradictions of consumption. In *American Behavioral Scientist*, 51(1), 33–55.

Roberts, J. V. (1992). Public opinion, crime, and criminal justice. In M. Tonry (Ed.), *Crime and justice: A review of research*. Chicago: University of Chicago Press.

Smith, G. J., & Campbell, C. S. (2007, September). Tensions and contentions: An examination of electronic gaming issues in Canada. *American Behavioral Scientist*, 51(1), 86–101.

Smith, G., & Wynne, H. (1999). *Gambling and crime in Western Canada: Exploring myth and reality*. Calgary, AB: Canada West Foundation.

Smith, G., & Wynne, H. (2004). *VLT gambling in Alberta*. Edmonton, AB: Alberta Gaming Research Institute.

The wager. (2004). *Gambling in Canada*, 9(28). Retrieved January 26, 2008, from http://www.basisonline.org/2004/07/the-wager-vol-1.html

Thorne, D. (2002, April 19). Quebec lawsuit a warning to Alta [Alberta] researcher. *Newscan*, 4(16). Retrieved February 8, 2005, from http://www.responsiblegambling.org/articles/041902_16.pdf

Williams, R., & Wood, R. (2004). *The demographic sources of Ontario gaming revenue*. A report prepared for the Ontario Problem Gambling Research Centre. Guelph, ON.

Zimmerman, S. E., Van Alstyne, D. J., & Dunn, C. S. (1988). The national punishment survey and public policy consequences. *Journal of Research in Crime and Delinquency*, 25(2), 120–149.

Chapter Two

Just Say No to the War on Drugs

*Barney Sneiderman**

Editors' Note: The next chapter is Barney Sneiderman's discussion of drug enforcement policies. This chapter has been very well received by our students, and we wanted to retain his work for this latest edition of the book. Sneiderman's critical and creative take on government policies toward illicit drugs generates much debate. In "Just Say No to the War on Drugs," he analyzes the failure of the current drug-prohibitionist policies employed in Canada and the United States. He begins by outlining the origins of the war on drugs in the aftermath of the Vietnam War and traces the development of that policy into a volatile political issue that has seen the United States imprison a greater proportion of its citizens than South Africa did during the apartheid era.

Using a satirical style that takes the form of conversations between a visiting alien and various Canadian drug experts, Sneiderman critically discusses many of the myths and misconceptions that motivate present-day drug-enforcement policies in Canada and the United States. Besides questioning the link between drugs and crime, he also criticizes the hypocrisy implicit in the contradiction between the legality of alcohol and tobacco and the criminal status of marijuana. He argues that during the 1920s, prohibition of alcohol in the United States was unsuccessful, and that our current prohibitionist approach to marijuana and other drugs is also doomed to fail. He concludes by arguing for the decriminalization of marijuana, combined with the adoption of a non-punitive health model to deal with other forms of drug abuse.

INTRODUCTION

I would like to begin by dedicating this presentation to George Orwell (1903–1950), the renowned English novelist, essayist, and social critic, and that is because of his brilliant and incisive commentary about the perversion of language to serve political goals. Accordingly, I am going to talk about the Orwellian distortion of language under the following headings: *The War on Drugs*; *Drugs*; *Use versus Abuse*; and *Addiction versus Habit*. I also dedicate this presentation to Lady Godiva (who, according to legend, rode naked through the streets of Coventry in the 11th century); to E.T. (that adorable extraterrestrial); and to that noble bird that, alas, cannot fly: the ostrich. Last but not least, an acknowledgment (dedication seeming inappropriate here) to Dr. Joseph Goebbels, Minister of Popular Enlightenment and Propaganda, Nazi Germany, 1933–1945.

THE WAR ON DRUGS

As the United States was winding down its military commitment in Vietnam, President Richard Nixon replaced one conflict with another by declaring "all out global war on the drug menace."[1] In 1986, President Ronald Reagan and the First Lady redeclared the War on Drugs in a joint

Source: Barney Sneiderman, "Just Say No to the War on Drugs," *The Manitoba Law Journal*, 24, No. 2, 1996–97, pp. 497–531. Reprinted by permission of *The Manitoba Law Journal*.
*Professor Sneiderman passed away in 2006. For a brief biography, see http://www.passagesmb.com/obituary_details.cfm?ObitID=109273

television address to the American people, during which Nancy spoke that memorable war cry, "Just say no to drugs." Actually, the word *war* was only spoken once, although in the press secretary's announcement of the address ten days earlier, it appeared six times: e.g., "The President and Mrs. Reagan will address the Nation from their living quarters in the White House on what we, the American family, can do to win the war on illegal drugs."[2] The following are excerpts from the President's opening remarks:

> Drugs are menacing our society. They're threatening our values and undercutting our institutions. They're killing our children.... Drug trafficking is a threat to our national security.... Let us not forget who we are. Drug abuse is a repudiation of everything America is. The destructiveness and human wreckage mock our heritage. Think for a moment how special it is to be an American. Can we doubt that only a divine providence placed this land, this island of freedom, here as a refuge for all those people in the world who yearn to breathe free.[3]

After a few comments along the same line by the First Lady, the President responded that "Nancy's personal crusade [against drugs] ... should become our national crusade." He then went on to use the word *crusade* four more times, while also referring to the "*battle* against this cancer of drugs."[4] In his continuing rhetorical flourish, he proceeded to draw a linkage between World War II and the War on Drugs and then concluded with a stirring appeal to patriotism:

> My generation will remember how America swung into action when we were attacked in World War II. The war was not just fought by the fellows flying the planes or driving the tanks. It was fought at home by a mobilized nation, men and women alike, building planes and ships, clothing sailors and soldiers, feeding marines and airmen; and it was fought by children planting victory gardens and collecting cans. Well, now we're in another war for our freedom, and it's time for all of us to pull together again.... It's time, as Nancy said, for Americans to "just say no" to drugs. When we all come together, united, striving for this cause, then those who are killing America and terrorizing it with slow but sure chemical destruction will see that they are up against the mightiest force for good that we know. Then they will have no dark alleyways to hide in.... We Americans have never been morally neutral against any form of tyranny. Tonight we're asking no more than that we honor what we have been and what we are by standing together.[5]

The First Lady then chimed in with the last word: "Now we go on to the next stop: making a final commitment not to tolerate drugs by anyone, any time, any place. So won't you join in this great, new national crusade."[6]

All in all, it was a brilliant performance, orchestrated by a media star turned president who years earlier had tellingly extolled television's power to shape public perceptions: "Television has the power to shape thoughts, stir emotions, and inspire actions. It teaches, it sells, it entertains, it informs, and it has the capacity to influence powerfully."[7]

He certainly knew whereof he spoke. His "Declaration of War Against Drugs" was promptly embraced by the "liberal" media that right-wingers love to excoriate, and I vividly recall how television responded to the Ron and Nancy Show with a flood of stories about the cocaine menace. Nancy's war cry, "Just say no to drugs," calls to mind another memorable phrase calling the nation to arms—"a date which will live in infamy"—which is how President Franklin D. Roosevelt described the 7 December 1941 attack on Pearl Harbor when he asked Congress on the following day for a declaration of war against Japan. Admittedly, although "just say no" doesn't have the ring to it that "day of infamy" does, Nancy set the tone for a relentless national policy on illicit drugs that continues to the present day.

When his turn came, President George Bush I chose "the drug problem" as the theme of his first Address to the Nation. Seven years later, that war continues in full force, and it is perhaps appropriate that President Clinton appointed a retired four-star general as his drug czar. After all, if one is fighting a war, then who else but a general should be waging the campaign dictated by the Commander-in-Chief? Although my purpose is not to catalogue the horrific social costs that have been engendered by the so-called War on Drugs, I must at least give them their due. We tend to associate the War on Drugs with the United States because it is the major player; and it is the very nature of that war that the more vigorously a nation wages it, the more catastrophic are the social consequences inflicted upon itself. We in Canada have suffered less only because we have not pursued the war with the ardor and single-minded determination of the Americans. A capsule summary of the war's impact upon the United States is noted by Nova University law professor Steven Wisotsky in his book, *Beyond the War on Drugs*, where he tells us that it " ... has spun a spider's web of Black Market Pathologies, including roughly 25% of all urban homicides, widespread corruption of police and other public officials, street crime by addicts, and subversive narco-terrorist alliances between Latin American guerrillas and drug traffickers as well as wholesale corruption of governments in Latin America and the Caribbean. These pathologies were foreseeable because they are a function of money."[8]

Yet there is even more—in truth, far more—to the debit side of the War on Drugs. The U.S. has long since passed South Africa as the country with the world's highest prison population per capita, and that is thanks to the War on Drugs. It is a war that is flooding the penal system with so many drug offenders that it is necessary to keep building more and more institutions to house these prisoners of war. Moreover, although illicit drug use cuts across racial lines, what is striking is that it is primarily young black males who are being swept off the streets of their ghettos into the correctional system. (In 1989, the newspaper *USA Today* reported that although only 12 percent of those using illicit drugs were black, 38 percent of those arrested for drug violations were black males.[9]) In the federal prison system alone, 62 percent of inmates—47 000 men and women—are drug offenders. Altogether, more than a third of a million Americans are doing time for violating drug laws, and roughly another million are on probation or parole.[10] Prisons are also the fastest-growing part of many state budgets. The war ties up the courts and diverts the police from dealing with criminals who commit the traditional-type crimes that form the basis of the FBI's annual crime index (crimes against the person and property). In the U.S. the concept of civil liberties has been subverted by the practice of mandatory drug testing, the judicial removal of safeguards for obtaining search warrants in drug cases, and the random search for drugs in high-school students' lockers.

And there are the horrendous civil forfeiture statutes that buttress the so-called "zero tolerance" policy. If, for example, a family member or house guest is found in possession of marijuana in your home, you the home-owner can lose your property to the U.S. government unless you can prove—that's right, you have the burden of proof—that not only were you ignorant of the drug's presence, but also that your ignorance was not the result of negligence. In fact, not even that limited defence was allowed until the *Anti-Drug Abuse Act* (1988) was accordingly amended; before then the mere presence of the drug was sufficient in itself to trigger forfeiture.[11] Last but not least, there is the DEA (the U.S. Drug Enforcement Agency), those noble drug warriors who, in their zeal, have been known to break into homes, terrorizing the occupants, and occasionally killing law-abiding residents who get caught in the confusion. But, then, all wars produce their "friendly fire" casualties.

Not a pretty picture, but then war never is. Furthermore, when one fights a war, one must vilify the enemy because how otherwise can the troops be motivated to fight? After all, if our adversaries are really no different from us, then why should we be warring against them? It has thus happened that those who wage the War on Drugs brand the enemy as diabolical creatures who threaten the lives and well-being of those who do not follow in their wicked ways.

As defined in *Webster's Dictionary*, *dope* is a slang expression for "any drug or narcotic." Actually, it is a slang expression for illicit drugs; no one refers to alcohol or tobacco as dope but only drugs such as heroin, cocaine, LSD, and marijuana—all of which tend to get lumped together under that pejorative heading. And who are the consumers and purveyors of such drugs—dope addicts, dope fiends, dope peddlers (invariably lurking in school grounds), or simply dopers. If one is using dope, then one is beyond the pale. The very word conjures up images of people who are out of control and behaving like crazed animals who would be pitied except that they have wilfully brought about their own degradation.

Of course, when one is waging a Manichean struggle between the forces of good and evil, one cannot be expected to wage war in accordance with the Marquis of Queensbury's rules of gentlemanly conduct. It is thus that the Reagan/Bush Drug Czar William Bennett has publicly advocated that drug traffickers be beheaded in public squares. He presumably includes those dealing in marijuana, because I heard him proclaim on the *NBC Nightly News* that "marijuana is the most dangerous drug of them all." (Bennett, America's self-anointed moral philosopher king and author of *The Book of Virtues*, a best-selling anthology of moral tales, is a close political ally of North Carolina Senator Jesse Helms, who aggressively represents the interests of the tobacco industry whenever it comes under threat. Commanding $40 000 per speech on the lecture circuit, Bennett is living proof that virtue is its own reward.) Then there is Newt Gingrich, the Speaker of the U.S. House of Representatives, who has recently called for the mandatory execution of convicted drug smugglers. In introducing a bill to that effect, he said that if we kill enough of them: "it will have a very chilling effect on people bringing drugs into the U.S."[12] On the other hand, Daryl Gates, former chief of the Los Angeles Police Department, would not stop at traffickers. As he testified before the U.S. Senate, casual drug users should be taken out and shot. He explained, "we're in a war!"[13]

Although William Bennett comes across as a bleeding heart compared to Chief Gates, he too is no less adamant in sounding the alarm of a nation imperiled by (illicit) drugs. According to the first National Drug Defense Control Strategy, prepared by the Office of National Drug Control Policy under his direction: "Illicit drug use degrades human character, and a purposeful, self-governing society ignores its people's character at great peril. Drug users make inattentive parents, bad neighbors, poor students, and unreliable employees…. [Using drugs is] a hollow, degrading, and deceptive pleasure … and pursuing it is an appallingly self-destructive impulse."[14]

In a sense, then, drug use is an atrocious crime, perhaps exceeded only by murder—although in the opinion of Nancy Reagan, "if you're a casual drug user, you are an accomplice to murder."[15] So drugs, after all, ranks with the most serious crime that one can commit. (Though tell me, Nancy, if as your drug czar has said, drug use is an "appalling self-destructive impulse," wouldn't it be better labelled as suicide instead of murder?) In any event, it is no wonder that the propaganda arm of the War on Drugs is waging a relentless campaign to discourage that "self-destructive impulse." At the forefront of the propaganda war stands the Partnership for a Drug-Free America, whose self-avowed mission is to "reduce demand for illegal drugs by using media communications to help bring about public intolerance of illegal drugs, their use, and users."

Hence, for example, the Frying Pan commercial. As butter sizzles in an iron skillet, the announcer intones, "This is drugs." After a sunny-side-up egg appears and sizzles in the pan, he informs the viewer, "This is your brain on drugs. Any questions?" Or the Russian roulette print spot, depicting two fingers loading a hand-rolled marijuana cigarette into the chamber of a revolver. As the caption reads: "The odds are that marijuana won't ruin your life. And that Russian roulette won't kill you."[16] And then there is the video in which a terrified patient cowers in his bed as his hysterically giggling surgeon, puffing away at a marijuana cigarette, asks him, "What's wrong with you—tonsillitis?" He replies, "No, appendicitis," and then—as the anaesthetist (presumably also stoned) installs the face mask—he utters a pitiful "Oh, no." At which point the voice-over asks, "Would you still say marijuana is harmless?"[17]

It is of course the nature of propaganda that it distorts the truth; all that counts is whether the message gets across. It was the Nazi Propaganda Minister, Joseph Goebbels, who expressed the cynical view that if the state incessantly repeats a Big Lie, then people will come to believe it. The Big Lie propounded by the Partnership for a Drug-Free America is that society is divided into two camps: the good people who don't use illicit drugs and the evil others who do, and that the latter must be eliminated by measures, however drastic, just as one resorts to the drastic remedy of chemotherapy to root out cancer. In short, the end justifies the means.

Goebbels also believed that propaganda for the masses had to be simple, aimed at the lowest level of intelligence, and reduced to easily learned slogans repeated over and over. The Frying Pan, Russian Roulette, and Stoned Surgeon scenarios would have been right up his alley. As the old saying goes, truth is the first casualty in war.

By the way, it is not only the Partnership for a Drug-Free America that distorts the truth. Consider, for example, a story on marijuana by reporter Roger O'Neil which appeared on 12 September 1995 on the *NBC Nightly News*. The gist of the story was as follows. Marijuana is a dangerous drug threatening the youth of America. A new study suggests that it is addictive. It impairs learning. Once you use marijuana you then go on to cocaine, from cocaine to heroin, and from heroin to the gutter. When O'Neil delivered that final grim message, he stood next to a bum lying in the gutter of some American ghetto. The implicit message, of course, was that the bum had started down the inevitable road to degradation when he smoked his first joint. As the story faded out, the camera panned to anchorman Tom Brokaw, who had the look of concern and anguish that one would expect after hearing such a terrifying account of the ravages wrought by reefer madness.

It is not only in the realm of propaganda that Joseph Goebbels offers a parallel to the War on Drugs. At the beginning of World War II, Germans were forbidden to listen to the BBC under threat of death or imprisonment; and it was Goebbels who urged members of the Hitler Youth to inform upon their parents and anyone else that they caught listening. In that regard, consider this recent parallel that proves that, as in any war, just about anything goes in the War on Drugs. On November 6, 1991, a story appeared in the *Winnipeg Free Press* under the headline: "Turning in dope dealer pays double in November." As the article opens: "Crime pays—now more than ever. Winnipeg police are counting on the lure of big bucks to get people to turn in their neighbours, friends, or even family for cultivating marijuana.... According to the Winnipeg Police Crime Stoppers co-ordinator, 'If it takes a drug problem off the street, we don't care who makes the phone call.'"[18] So for the month of November, anyone informing on someone growing marijuana, even for his own use, was promised double the normal cash reward. This, by the way, was not the first or the last time that such a policy has been promoted by the Winnipeg Police Department.

In that same article, Winnipeg Police Vice Inspector Ray Johns was quoted as stating that: "[i]t's our belief that young people get their introduction into narcotics through marijuana." (At least, the learned Vice Inspector recognizes that marijuana is not a narcotic, which is more than one can say for our Parliamentarians, who include marijuana as a prohibited drug under the *Narcotic Control Act*.) What Johns is referring to is the so-called "stepping-stone" or "gateway" theory, which is a matter of holy writ for the police in their waging of war against marijuana. The implicit admission behind the theory is that marijuana is not the killer drug it is often made out to be. But it must be vigorously suppressed nonetheless because there is something about the drug—what that is, is never explained—that somehow compels its user to go on to cocaine and heroin, the so-called "hard" drugs. (Recall that this was the theme of that NBC newscast that I earlier referred to.)

With all due respect for the Vice Inspector, the disreputable gateway theory presents a notion of cause and effect that is simply another example of the Big Lie. Firstly, since there are multiples of marijuana consumers for every heroin and cocaine consumer, how can one say that the marijuana user of today is the heroin/cocaine user of tomorrow? It is estimated that as many as 70 million Americans have smoked marijuana at one time or another.[19] Thus, if the gateway theory had any validity, then the total population of Canada would be outnumbered by Americans snorting cocaine and/or shooting heroin! I would think that most consumers of these two drugs have either used or continue to use marijuana. However, it is also true that heroin/cocaine users have also indulged in alcohol, tobacco, and a variety of prescription and over-the-counter drugs.

The fact that a cocaine user has used marijuana no more proves a cause and effect relationship than the fact that before cocaine he experienced tobacco, coffee, or mother's milk. The gateway theory illustrates the logical fallacy called by the Latin phrase, *post hoc, ergo propter hoc* ("after the fact, therefore before the fact"). In other words, the fact that event A occurs before event B does not in itself prove that the former caused the latter. One is thus tempted to conclude that all that is proved by the gateway theory is the muddledness of its proponent. But not quite. What I mean is illustrated by the Dutch policy on marijuana, whereby the government allows its sale in specially licensed and strictly regulated coffee shops. Cultivation for personal use is also tolerated, and consequently there are hydroponic stores that furnish the means for doing so. By adopting this approach, the Dutch government is promoting a principle that it calls the "separation of markets."[20] In other words, if the marijuana consumer does not have to seek out an underworld connection for his drug of choice, he is less likely to be exposed to the so-called hard drugs like heroin and cocaine. In a sense, then, separation of markets acts as a *gateway* against exposure to heroin and cocaine. (By the way, the per capita use of marijuana in The Netherlands is about half what it is in Canada and the United States.)

I'll be returning to the Dutch policy on drugs in my concluding remarks, but suffice it to note that American and Canadian drug warriors treat the Dutch approach with contempt. They remind me of the hawks during the Vietnam War, who kept insisting that the only way to victory was to commit ever more resources to a cause that its critics rightly branded as unwinnable. But the War on Drugs is not being won, and more of the same isn't going to do it either. We can distort language to paint a disastrous social policy as a war that must be fought against the menace of dope, but that does not alter the reality that the war is a losing proposition that makes the social disruption caused by Prohibition—the American war against alcohol that marked the turbulent decade called the Roaring Twenties—pale in comparison.

And now, begging your indulgence, a play in three acts, respectively titled: *Drugs, Use versus Abuse,* and *Addiction versus Habit.* The cast (in order of appearance): E.T., the Police Inspector of Vice (hereinafter called the Vice-Inspector), the Pharmacologist, and the Criminologist.

THE PLAY, ACT I: DRUGS

As in the War on Drugs, The Coalition for a Drug-Free America, Just Say No to Drugs.

An inhabited planet in our galaxy has dispatched an emissary by spaceship to Canada to learn about the War on Drugs. They select someone who has been studying our planet from afar but who admits that he finds our species hard to understand. And so arrives one E.T. whose first appointment is with the Vice-Inspector of the local police force.

E.T.: On my way to your office, we passed a number of Drug Stores and I am wondering what they have to do with the War on Drugs.

Vice-Inspector: Actually, Drug Stores is not what the war is all about. That is because Drug Stores are legitimate businesses selling drugs for medicinal purposes, whereas the War on Drugs is directed against the non-medicinal or recreational use of drugs. I am referring here to such drugs as heroin, cocaine, LSD, and marijuana. In fact, it is because these drugs are so harmful that it is not enough simply to outlaw manufacture and distribution. It is also necessary to target the consumer by banning possession for personal use.[21]

Well, so much then for Drug Stores and their drugs. Let us assume at this point that, being a clever fellow, E.T. knows that a police officer is not an expert on the properties of drugs. So he asks to meet with someone who has scientific credentials in the field and can brief him about those dangerous recreational drugs. He is accordingly directed to a professor of pharmacology at a prestigious medical school, who graciously agrees to help him with his inquiries.

E.T.: Since the War on Drugs is a war against recreational drugs, I am wondering what are the recreational drugs that cause the most harm to consumers?

The Pharmacologist: That's easy to answer—tobacco and alcohol. And unfortunately, because these are two of the most widely used recreational drugs, the harm they cause is therefore quite substantial.

E.T.: I'm frankly surprised because I have studied the video and print materials produced by the Partnership for a Drug-Free America—and nowhere did I come across any reference to those two drugs.

The Pharmacologist: Well, that is because the Partnership is only concerned with illegal drugs, and alcohol and tobacco are perfectly legal. So what it means by "Drug-Free" is an America free of the use of illicit drugs.

E.T.: I find this puzzling, because I would think that if your society is going to ban certain drugs—a concept unknown in our world—you would ban the drugs that have the most potential to harm consumers.

The Pharmacologist: That's not how it works here. In any event, perhaps a good place to begin your education is by highlighting the harm caused by alcohol and tobacco. To begin with, there is the carnage wrought on the highways by drunk drivers and the drug's association with crimes of violence such as spousal abuse. Take a look at this brochure, *Alcohol the Drug*, produced by the Addictions Foundation of Manitoba. As it explains,

> Alcohol like any other drug can be misused. It can be addicting. Statistics cite alcohol as a factor in:
>
> 64% of all homicides
> 31% of all suicides
> 40% of all hospital admissions
> 50% of all highway deaths
> 34% of all rapes
> 40% of all family court appearances.

Overindulgence can also wreak havoc upon the consumer's physical and mental well-being. And beyond that is the fact that the most preventable cause of mental retardation is the drinking of alcohol during pregnancy. In fact, Fetal Alcohol Syndrome (FAS) is the single leading cause of mental handicap in North America. There are children and adults in our midst with literally holes in their brains because when they were in the womb they were being bathed in alcohol. To add insult to injury, the Canadian liquor industry does nothing to fund programs for these drug victims and it steadfastly opposes labels on their products warning against drinking while pregnant. You will recall that, according to the Partnership for a Drug-Free America, if you use any drug (i.e., any illicit drug), then the drug fries your brain like a pan fries an egg. Yet, that is precisely what alcohol can do to the fetal brain.

By the way, tobacco also takes a fearful toll upon fetal development. According to a 1995 article in the *Journal of Medical Practice*, smoking mothers in the United States annually cause the deaths of about 5000 infants (about 2000 from Sudden Infant Death Syndrome), suffer about 115 000 miscarriages, and give birth to about 50 000 low weight infants (40 percent of whom require neonatal intensive care).[22]

The public generally doesn't think of alcohol and tobacco as drugs; but there is another drug—cocaine—that is illegal, and the cocaine/pregnancy connection is being addressed. In fact, a number of American states prosecute mothers for using cocaine during pregnancy (charging them under drug laws), aided and abetted by physicians informing on their patients. Some have even gone so far as to charge mothers delivering cocaine-affected infants with ""trafficking in a controlled substance to a minor." The prosecutions have rested on the dubious theory that cocaine must have passed into the newborn's blood system before the umbilical cord was severed.

No matter that—as a number of American medical and public health organizations have stressed—such practices are likely to drive pregnant women using drugs away from pre-natal care. During his tenure as Drug Czar, William Bennett suggested that pregnant women using cocaine be forced into treatment to avoid the "real catastrophe" of a generation of children with potentially severe learning disabilities. As he explained, "If we stopped the drug problem tomorrow dead in its tracks, we would have this generation of children."[23] Not surprisingly, there is no public record of his expressing concern for the generation of children harmed in utero by alcohol and tobacco.

The Drug Czar's moral blind spot is frankly no surprise. Unfortunately, we can expect no better from the media, even from the best that the media has to offer. When *60 Minutes*, the much heralded CBS TV news program, did a recent segment on what it labelled as a major drug problem—cocaine use during pregnancy—the A and T words (alcohol and tobacco) were never even mentioned. No, all we heard from *60 Minutes* is that the drug-during-pregnancy problem is cocaine. But then of course alcohol and tobacco really aren't drugs, right, whereas cocaine is a drug and there are the drug laws in place to use against women ingesting that drug in pregnancy. But rest assured that, as with alcohol, the *60 Minutes* segment never touched upon the havoc wrought by tobacco consumption in pregnancy. Ironically, *60 Minutes* is no friend to the tobacco industry as it has done a number of highly critical segments about its practices. But still, it just never made the alcohol/tobacco connection to the hazards of mixing drugs and pregnancy.

E.T.: Given what you have told me about the effects of tobacco on fetal development, I wonder what it does to those who smoke this drug.

The Pharmacologist: I can't help but smile when you call tobacco a drug. That it certainly is, although like alcohol the public doesn't think of it as a drug. To put it bluntly, the more we learn about tobacco, the more lethal it looks, the protestations of the tobacco companies to the contrary. In fact, the most preventable cause of death is smoking; if everyone stopped smoking, our mortality and morbidity rates would plummet. But there is Joe Camel, that lovable advertising figure who has captured an impressive share of teenage smokers for his parent company; there are also cigarette ads in American fashion magazines that show anorexic models and convey the message that smoking is the way to stay slim. In fact, there is a brand of American cigarettes called Virginia Slims that is marketed particularly for women and whose slogan is, "You've come a long way, baby." Women have indeed come a long way. More are being killed by lung cancer than by breast cancer,[24] and teenaged girls are taking up smoking to a significantly greater extent than their male peers.

Twenty-five years ago, journalist Thomas Whiteside published a book called *Selling Death*,[25] subtitled *Cigarette Advertising and Public Health*. Nothing has really changed since then except that we know now that cigarettes are even more lethal than we assumed a quarter century ago. That title—*Selling Death*—is certainly an apt description of what the tobacco industry is all about. To that industry the cigarette is conceived as a nicotine delivery system. As the public is well aware from extensive media coverage, there have been recent revelations that cigarette companies have been manipulating nicotine levels in order to fine-tune the drug's impact on smokers.

By the way, cigarettes kill about 400 000 Americans and 40 000 Canadians per annum—which is roughly the number of Americans and Canadians killed during all of World War II—and all the deaths from all illicit drugs amount to only a tiny fraction of the cigarette mortality toll.[26] In 1995 the World Health Organization went out of its way to castigate tobacco companies for ignoring death and suffering in their pursuit of profits. According to the UN agency: "Every year, tobacco is responsible for the deaths of three million people around the world, one death in every 10 seconds." It also noted that one-third of tobacco-related deaths occur in developing economies where teens and women are special targets of cigarette advertising. And these dismal figures are steadily going up, not down.[27]

Here in Winnipeg as elsewhere, there are liquor stores and cigarette vending machines that make these drugs readily available to consumers. The drugs are heavily taxed, which means that the government has a vested interest in their sale. In fact, in Manitoba, it is the government that directly runs the trade in alcohol; in other words, the same government that wages the War on Drugs is the province's major drug trafficker.

As E.T. raises his four eyebrows in surprise, the Pharmacologist smiles and continues.

Well, the thinking goes like this. For one thing, about 90 percent of those who drink are so-called social drinkers who don't harm themselves or others, so why punish them because of the 10 percent who do cause harm because of excessive drinking. Besides, just about everyone drinks. The drug is so deeply ingrained in our culture that it would be impossible to enforce even a marginally effective ban against it.

From 1920 to 1933—a time frame called the Prohibition Era—the United States engaged in such an act of folly. If you were to advocate Prohibition as a response to the ravages wrought by that drug, a liquor industry spokesperson would doubtless refer to that era of lawlessness and social chaos as an historical precedent against criminalization. I would agree, although one would be curious to know if he would make the same connection to cocaine. As is the case with alcohol, most consumers of cocaine are not harmed by its use (roughly the same percentage of consumers abuse cocaine as abuse alcohol). Still, the cocaine front is the major battleground of the War on Drugs, and cocaine is to the Drug Warriors as the Eastern Front was to the German Army in World War II—an unmitigated disaster.

There is, by the way, a derivative of cocaine called crack cocaine, which certainly has a high harm potential. The irony is that crack cocaine is a stepchild of the War on Drugs. Because of the grossly inflated black market price of cocaine, crack was developed as a cheap alternative. But that's another story.

Regarding cigarettes, an interesting point is that—unlike any of the illicit drugs, or alcohol for that matter—there is little casual use. In other words, once you begin to smoke, the odds are quite high that not only will you smoke every day, but also that you will smoke multiple cigarettes every day. You will smoke year in and year out, and unless you muster the awesome amount of willpower required to quit the drug, you run the risk of dying of cancer or heart disease. But if we ban cigarettes we would create a black market of nightmarish proportions (which is bad enough as it is with cheaper cigarettes flowing across the American border). Besides, does it really make any sense to treat someone as a criminal just because he or she is a cigarette smoker? Better to try to educate the consumer about the health consequences of smoking; and in Canada we have been getting the message across and consumption has been dropping, except unfortunately among our teenaged population (especially girls).

E.T.: True enough, but if your society had banned alcohol and tobacco way back when, isn't it fair to say that you wouldn't now be experiencing the widespread harm caused by those two drugs?

The Pharmacologist: Not likely. That is because of what Nova University law professor Steven Wisotsky so aptly calls *black market pathologies*, which are an ineradicable byproduct of the War on Drugs.

After explaining Wisotsky's phrase—see Part I of this chapter—she continues.

Can you imagine the nightmare that would be created by the criminalization of these two recreational drugs? Given the enormous demand for alcohol and tobacco, the law that would ban them would not cause the demand to vanish. Simply put, the criminal law is not a magic wand; it cannot work miracles. Instead, what would happen is the emergence of a black market to satisfy the demand. That is the way it is with the currently illegal drugs, and that is the way it would be with the outlawing of alcohol and tobacco.

Still, we are making a dent on tobacco and that is by educating consumers with the straight goods. If you keep stressing the high harm potential of the drug, then many consumers will get the message and either quit smoking—no mean achievement given the addictive properties of the drug—or never start. Regarding alcohol, it is true that most who indulge are responsible consumers; but a problem with that drug is our culture, a culture that out of one side of its mouth preaches moderation but from the other side glamorizes the drug and fails to instill inhibitions against its destructive effects. We are, after all, a booze culture, and how do you deal with that?

E.T.: Although I am endowed with a superintelligence that has no equal on your poor planet, I admit that I am still befuddled. What, then, is the War on Drugs all about? What determines which drugs are legal and which are not?

The Pharmacologist: If you'll excuse me for a minute, I can help you to a quick understanding of the War on Drugs after I make a quick trip to the Roman Catholic Church next door.

E.T. scratches his pointed green head with wonderment but waits patiently until she returns with two bowls of water.

One of these bowls is filled with ordinary tap water and the other with holy water, which means that it is sanctified by the Church. How can you determine which is which?

E.T.: I would think that chemical testing would answer that.

The Pharmacologist: That certainly is an intelligent answer, but it is not the right answer. The truth is that both would test chemically as ordinary tap water; the difference between them is ceremonial.[28] And that, my extraterrestrial friend, is what you have to know to begin to understand the War on Drugs—that it is not the inherent properties of a drug that determine whether it is legal or illegal, that to try to understand the War on Drugs by studying the effects of the drugs themselves would make as much sense as trying to understand the difference between tap water and holy water by comparing samples of each under a microscope. The War on Drugs is really an exercise in ceremonial chemistry.

To illustrate the point, take a look at this book. It is titled Licit and Illicit Drugs, and its subtitle is: The Consumers Union Report on Narcotics, Stimulants, Depressants, Inhalants, and

Marijuana—including Caffeine, Nicotine, and Alcohol.[29] Published in 1972 by the consumer watchdog organization the Consumers Union, it remains a valuable, comprehensive, and objective study of its subject matter.

Given his superbrain power, E.T. is able to digest the 600-page book in 30 minutes. She then continues.

Do you now understand why I said that the holy/tap water demonstration would help explain what the War on Drugs is all about?

E.T.: Yes, I do, because as the book makes clear, there is no correlation between the harm potential of a drug and its legal classification. I was also struck by the comment that "no drug is safe or harmless at all dosage levels or under all conditions of use."[30] In that regard, the authors note that "caffeine can be a dangerous drug," which I suppose would surprise most people who wouldn't even think of their morning cups of coffee as a drug. They also have this to say about coffee, which I imagine is equally applicable to tobacco and alcohol: "By keeping coffee legal, society has avoided extortionate black-market prices that might otherwise bankrupt coffee drinkers and lead them into lives of crime. And coffee drinkers are not stigmatized as criminals, driven into a deviant subculture with all that criminalization entails."[31]

The Pharmacologist: You certainly catch on fast. There is, by the way, a voluminous body of literature that echoes the findings reported in 1972 by the Consumers Union. I won't belabour the point, but consider this statement by the U.S. National Commission on Marijuana and Drug Abuse. It dates from 1973 but is as true today as it was then:

> The imprecision of the term "drug" has had serious social consequences. Because alcohol is excluded, the public is conditioned to regard a martini as something fundamentally different from a marijuana cigarette, a barbiturate capsule or a bag of heroin. Similarly, because the referents of the word "drug" differ so widely in the therapeutic and social contexts, the public is conditioned to believe that "street" drugs act according to entirely different principles than "medical" drugs. The result is that the risks of the former are exaggerated and the risks of the latter are overlooked.[32]

E.T.: I still don't get what the War on Drugs is all about. But I'm beginning to think that what may explain it is that you earthlings are even stranger than I thought.

The Pharmacologist: I can't comment on that, but I can help you understand why the War on Drugs is not about the drugs that have the most harm potential. Rather, what determines whether a particular drug is criminalized is not its inherent properties and/or potential for social harm but rather the kinds of people associated with its use. Since this takes us outside my field of expertise, I have taken the liberty to ask a colleague in the Department of Criminology to join us. He specializes in the area of Drug Control, and here he is now.

After the introductions, the Criminologist tells E.T. that he can understand his confusion and that he will do his best to clear it up. He continues.

The Criminologist: What we have learned is that the behaviour in which people indulge is often less important than the social category assigned to them. Why do certain drugs get labelled as deviant whereas others do not? Well, it is necessary to understand that the drugs of choice of the so-called "moral centre"—the so-called solid citizens, the professional and business classes, the police, politicians, etc.—don't get criminalized. It is only the drugs whose primary indulgers are the so-called "morally susceptible" that are placed beyond the pale. Of course, these so-called deviants also use alcohol and tobacco, but the fact that these are also the drugs of choice of the moral centre ensures that they remain legal.[33]

E.T.: Excuse me for interrupting, but isn't this concept of the "moral centre" contradicted by the notorious American experience with Prohibition?

The Criminologist: Good point, but not really. The so-called Prohibition Era—the banning of alcohol in the United States from 1920 to 1933—is simply the exception that proves the rule. Prohibition was a product of the moral fervour engendered by World War I—that a nation couldn't fight the Germans if its soldiers and armaments workers were soused with booze. Although, admittedly, also at play were the so-called Temperance Societies, which had been lobbying for the banning of alcohol for years because of its horrific social costs. But still, it was the entry of the United States into the war that made Prohibition a politically viable measure. Compared to the long drawn out War on Drugs, Prohibition was a short run experiment. The reason that it was repealed was that the "moral centre" could not abide the continued criminalization of its preferred recreational drug.

It is particularly instructive to study the history of drug criminalization in the United States and Canada—the reasons why particular drugs were banned. Indeed, as I've said, what one finds is that the currently illegal drugs were criminalized because of the people associated with their use.[34] In fact, it was the Canadian Parliament that set the precedent for the Americans, banning trafficking in opium for nonmedicinal purposes in the *Opium Act* (1908), followed by a ban on possession in the *Opium and Narcotic Drug Act* (1911). The legislation reflected the anti-Oriental sentiment of the day and was directed at the "heathen" Chinese consumers of the drug, even though there was no evidence that their recreational opium use was a social problem.[35] (Incidentally, the Americans did not adopt a criminal law model of drug control until 1914, when Congress passed the *Harrison Narcotic Act*.) In 1923, marijuana was added to the schedule of prohibited drugs in the *Opium and Narcotic Drug Act* and was approved by Parliament with no discussion whatsoever.[36] (Once again, Parliament was one step ahead of Congress, which did not outlaw marijuana until the 1937 enactment of the *Marijuana Tax Act*; it is pertinent to note that at that time the drug's consumers in the United States were primarily Mexicans, blacks, and jazz musicians.) The 1923 amendment had been prompted by a series of sensationalist articles that were published in *Maclean's Magazine* in 1920 and whose stated purpose was to pressure the government to enact stricter drug laws.

Written by Emily Murphy, a champion and spokesperson for various social causes (including women's suffrage), the articles were published in book form in 1922 under the title *The Black Candle*.[37] Her writings on the subject of drugs reek of "popular racial bias, fables, and sensationalism."[38] But her views were widely publicized and endorsed in newspaper editorials across the country. Her chapter titled "Marijuana—A New Menace" is replete with "documented" cases reported by police officials of the most horrific crimes committed by crazed marijuana addicts. Most of the horror stories involved Mexicans, although none was said to have happened in Canada. Still, *The Black Candle* was of sufficient influence to lead to the banning of the drug in Canada.

Regarding marijuana, the drug was not that popular until the 1960s, and it is clear that the current war on marijuana, which is conducted with even greater intensity in the United States than here, is a war against the 1960s! The war against marijuana is a war against the 1960s because no drug is more associated with that era of political dissent, hippies, and alternative life-styles. What other explanation is there for the continued criminalization of a drug whose ill effects pale in comparison to those of alcohol and tobacco? Why else would William Bennett call it the most dangerous drug of them all? The answer is simple—holy versus tap water. It is true, of course, that there are marijuana smokers who harm themselves by overindulgence in the drug. But, as you know, one can say that about virtually any drug—whether licit or illicit. Aspirin, for example, is truly a wonder drug, but it can do you serious, even life-threatening, harm. As the Consumers Union Report explains, there is virtually no drug—legal, illegal, prescription, over-the-counter—that is harm free. Two years after the publication of *Licit and Illicit Drugs*, that point was underscored when the distinguished medical authors of a book called *Pills, Profits, and Politics* reported that an estimated 130 000 deaths occurred annually in the United States from adverse reactions to prescription drugs![39] The figures are even higher now but are never connected to the so-called drug problem, and William Bennett would no doubt respond that these are medicinal drugs and that somehow this makes the difference.

So, now you have a clear understanding of the term "ceremonial chemistry," which might also be called "political pharmacology" or "Calvinist pharmacology." In short, it is not the inherent pharmacological properties of drugs that determine their legal status. It is rather at the political level that these decisions are made.

The Pharmacologist: There is an important point that I should reiterate. Over time the public has been so brainwashed that most people do not even think of alcohol and tobacco as drugs, a mindset illustrated by that oftspoken phrase, "alcohol and drugs"—as in, "Such-and-such a community is having problems with alcohol and drugs." Its explicit meaning is that although alcohol may be a problem, it is not a drug problem. In the early 1970s, a "substances regarded as drugs" survey was conducted in the United States. When asked which substances on a list were drugs, regarding alcohol only 39 percent of adults and 34 percent of minors said Yes, and regarding tobacco only 27 percent of adults and 16 percent of minors said Yes.[40] Is there reason to think that the brainwashed public is any less misinformed today than two decades ago? I think not.

Although alcohol is far and away the major drug problem affecting our youth, one hears time and time again that young people do not regard alcohol as a problem because, after all, it is not a drug! I recently watched a Detroit television news programme, in which some teenagers were deploring the effects of alcohol on many of their peers and were saying, "Just because it's not a drug doesn't mean that it can't harm you."

What could be more absurd than to watch a baseball or football game on TV where an anti-drug commercial is followed by a beer commercial, the latter extolling the connection between beer and being a real man. In a 50-page booklet titled *Myth, Men and Beer*, even as respectable an organization as the AAA (Automobile Association of America) has called for the banning of beer commercials. As the booklet (published in 1988) states: "Beer is represented as an essential element in masculinity, so that one cannot be attained without the other. In our view, this is a distorted and dangerous message to broadcast to young people."

The Criminologist: The only thing I'd like to add is that all those Drug Warriors—the Reagans, George Bush I and II, William Bennett, Newt Gingrich, Daryl Gates, and their Canadian allies—are quick to bemoan government intrusion into the private lives of the citizenry. Get government off the backs of the people, they have all said. But, hey, drugs are different, right?

E.T.: Thank you both for enlightening me, but I still find this somewhat confusing. I suppose that if I were not a stranger to your planet and in particular to your species, I would have a better understanding of what you call the War on Drugs. But as it is I still find it difficult to grasp why you earthlings would pursue such a mindless policy.

The Pharmacologist: I have the same trouble. All I can say is that it might help you get a handle on the War on Drugs by reading this book. It is called *Alice in Wonderland*.

THE PLAY, ACT II: DRUG USE VERSUS DRUG ABUSE

The Pharmacologist: In any event, continuing with your education, let me tell you about the "use" and the "abuse" of drugs. When I use the term "drug abuse," I mean that the consumer is being harmed by the drug (either in the physical and/or psychological sense or in his relationships with others—family, friends, workmates, even strangers). In other words, what abuse means is that for the user the burdens stemming from consumption have exceeded its benefits. For example, as used nonmedically in our society, alcohol is taken occasionally and in moderation with few undesirable side effects by the great majority of users. But then there is abuse, and I am here referring to those who get into trouble with the drug: impairing judgment and coordination sufficient to cause an auto accident, increasing aggressiveness that results in crimes of violence (more often than not against one's spouse), or causing irreversible damage to the brain, liver, and other body parts. So much, then, for the distinction between drug use and drug abuse.

However, when a drug is criminalized, there is no use but only abuse. If you smoke a joint on the weekend as part of a social evening with your friends—if the drug is one aspect of a good time had by all—then you are a drug abuser simply because there is no legally recognized use of illicit drugs. Even if you are smoking marijuana for its medicinal properties—for example, to combat the nausea of chemotherapy—you are still considered a drug abuser! In any case, I know that my colleague would like to pick up this theme of use versus abuse.

The Criminologist: Students of criminal law are familiar with two Latin terms: *malum in se* and *malum prohibitum* (wrong in itself and wrong by the force of law). On the one hand, there are such traditional crimes as murder, robbery, kidnapping, and assault, which regardless of any particular penal code would be universally regarded as wrong in themselves: i.e., *malum in se*. Consider, on the other hand, offences such as carrying open liquor in your vehicle, an act which is not wrongful in itself (e.g., an unsealed bottle of whiskey on the back seat that is just sitting there). It is wrongful because the act is so defined by law: it is *malum prohibitum*.

In summary, then, one must understand that when a drug is criminalized, whether the drug harms the user is beside the point. By definition, then, one cannot use an illicit drug. One can only abuse, and surely abuse is wrong in itself. In other words, the public at large has been conditioned to accept illicit drug use as *malum in se*.

THE PLAY, ACT III: DRUG ADDICTION VERSUS DRUG HABIT

The Pharmacologist: Finally, a word about drug addiction and the tobacco habit. In the War on Drugs, addiction is a term that is used all too lightly. If you use heroin or cocaine, then you are an addict. But the evidence is that the majority of those who use heroin and cocaine do not do so on a day in, day out basis. I am certainly not saying that these drugs cannot be addictive, but since most users are not addicted, it is the properties of the drug combined with the psycho-social makeup of the user that determine whether a person becomes hooked.[41] But, still, we do know that there is one drug for which casual use is a rarity—that most of those who start using it will wind up consuming it compulsively over time. And quitting it is harder than quitting heroin, and that drug is nicotine! Consider the following excerpt from a chapter in the Consumers Union Report, titled "Nicotine as an Addictive Drug":

One hallmark of an addicting substance is the fact that users seek it *continuously* day after day. If they can take it or leave it—take it on some days and not be bothered by lack of it on other days—they are not in fact addicted. Judged by this standard, nicotine is clearly addicting; the number of smokers who do not smoke every day ... is very small. The typical pattern of nicotine use, moreover, is not only daily but hourly. Nearly four male smokers out of five and more than three female smokers out of five consume 15 or more cigarettes a day—roughly one or more per waking hour.... No other substance known to man is used with such remarkable frequency. Even caffeine ranks a poor second.[42]

By the way, tobacco shows stunning parallels with heroin in terms of its addictive power. But the point is that we talk only about the tobacco habit. If we were to call it what it is—an addiction—then we might have to admit that it is, after all, a drug. On the other hand, if you are an infrequent user of heroin or cocaine—in other words, if you can take it or leave it—you are still at risk to be labelled a drug addict.

Be that as it may, the tobacco industry not only continues to assert that there is no scientific proof that their product is harmful but also heatedly denies that it is addictive. The industry has transformed its stance of wallowing in righteous indignation into an art form, as illustrated by an Associated Press release on 4 April 1988. When the then U.S. Surgeon-General C. Everett Koop stated that nicotine was addictive, the vice-president of the U.S. Tobacco Institute responded that: "It is apparent that anti-tobacco zeal has overtaken common sense and good judgment." In a comment that can be described only as pure unadulterated *chutzpah*, he added: "To imply that the 55 million American tobacco-smokers are drug-abusers is to subvert and divert attention from the nation's war on illicit drugs. It is a trivialization of the country's urgent concerns with hard drugs and verges on irresponsibility."

So endeth the extraterrestrial's lesson on the subversion of language to serve a political agenda. As he prepares to leave our planet, E.T. telepathically dispatches the following message to home:

"I have encountered earthlings. They have a bizarre and nonsensical custom. They proudly call it the War on Drugs. I regret to report that my mission has failed—we have yet to discover intelligent life elsewhere in the universe."

THE OSTRICH AND THE NAKED EQUESTRIENNE

In December 1993, Jocelyn Elders, the then U.S. Surgeon-General, publicly stated that it was time to consider whether legalizing drugs might help fight crime. I heard former Drug Czar William Bennett's response on CNN: "She's morally obtuse, nutty, just plain nutty." And President Clinton reacted quickly to disassociate his administration from her comment, authorizing the White House communications director to inform the media that "it's nothing we would ever entertain." Clinton himself announced that he had no intention of reviewing the War on Drugs agenda of Ronald Reagan and George Bush. Like them, he is content to bury his head in the sand whilst the war continues to wreak its havoc upon a beleaguered public. Still, the ostrich cannot fly and neither can the War on Drugs. The difference is that the ostrich accepts nature's will whereas the Drug Warriors remain unshaken in the mad belief that a war that by its very nature is unwinnable is actually winnable. John Cleese of Monty Python fame could capture the essence of the War on Drugs in a two-minute routine. His gangly body covered with feathers, he jumps out a window, furiously flapping his arms and chanting a "Just Say No to Drugs" mantra. Not surprisingly, he plummets to the ground, landing on John Q. Public and crushing him like a bug. Cleese gets up, brushes himself off, and says, "I'll get it right next time"—and with a look of grim determination, he leaps up the stairs on his way back to the same window. Repeat the scene *ad nauseam* and one has a capsule history of the War on Drugs.

It may well be that President Clinton is not a true believer in the holy drug crusade. But he is a shrewd politician, who no doubt fears that questioning the legitimacy of the War on Drugs is politically the kiss of death. During the Cold War, there were politicians who profited by accusations of "soft on Communism" levelled against their political opponents, and Clinton knows that the accusation of being "soft on drugs" would provoke the same kind of backlash. In welcome contrast, there are a number of public figures with solid conservative credentials who have expressed the same view as Dr. Elders, including free market economist Milton Freedman, Reagan's Secretary of State George Schultz, and William F. Buckley, conservative media pundit and editor of the magazine *National Review*.[43]

What they have come to recognize is that the criminalization of drugs carries in its wake social costs that typify efforts to stamp out so-called consensual crimes; and that the greater the zeal invested in the process—as in the War on Drugs—the more the havoc that is wreaked. To know what the War on Drugs is really all about is to know the nature of the society that pursues it with such grim determination. Of course, I am referring to the United States. I suggest to you that the War on Drugs is really about scapegoating, about the need to conjure up enemies with whom to wage battle. It is about a characteristic of American society that dates back to the Salem witch trials of 1692 and that carries an unbroken thread through the Red Scare of the early 1920s, the McCarthy Era of the 1950s (the so-called Communist witchhunts), the War on Drugs, and the recent spate of cases involving unfounded allegations of ritual sexual abuse of children (particularly notorious are the cases involving day care centres). In short, the War on Drugs is as American as apple pie.

It is a war waged by a country whose tobacco industry has found prosperous new markets in third world countries, and whose tobacco farmers benefit from generous government subsidies to promote their lethal product overseas. By the way, keep in mind that the reason for one of Canada's drug smuggling problems—tobacco—is that the Americans won't use the taxing power to discourage consumption as we do. What I'm talking about is hypocrisy, about a war that wallows in it up to its red-white-and-blue eyeballs.

I'm talking about an America whose black ghettoes are awash with crack cocaine; and instead of confronting the socioeconomic breeding grounds for crack, it mounts what is in effect a race war against the drug's consumers. About a country that invades Panama to get rid of one drug trafficker (formerly on their payroll)—killing hundreds of innocent people in the process—and then quickly pulls out its troops, in effect guaranteeing that the illicit drug business would continue as usual. Panama was President Bush's doing; he called it Operation Just Cause. Good old George, as a Drug Warrior he stood as tall in the saddle as his mentor, Ronald Reagan.

I am here reminded of that 19th century Mexican general who lamented, "Poor Mexico, so far from God, so near the United States." I won't comment on the theological aspect of his remark, but regarding the geographical, all I'll say is, poor Canada. It is true that we have not embraced the war with the singleminded fanaticism of the Americans, but being neighbours, we cannot escape the taint of their unrelenting Drug War rhetoric. Yet it is equally true that Canada, no less than the United States, embraced the Police Model of drug control early in this century; and that, albeit we do not enforce the law with the same rabid intensity of the Americans, we are still committed to the pursuit of a bankrupt and shameful policy that has caused far more harm than any good that it has sought to accomplish.

Of course, the War has been good—good for the politicians who garner votes by showing that they are not soft on drugs, good for those in the business of building and running prisons, good for bloated bureaucracies like the DEA, good for people in the burglar alarm business because of all the break-ins committed by those who steal to get the money to pay the inflated black market price for their drugs of choice, and finally, last but not least, good—hey, wonderful—for organized crime.

Is there another way? Is there anything to learn from elsewhere? I have referred to the principle of *separation of markets* that informs Dutch drug policy. It operates in tandem with another principle: what the Dutch call *harm reduction*.[44] Although Dutch law prohibits the possession and sale of cocaine and narcotic drugs such as heroin, the provisions against possession are in effect not enforced. The rationale is as follows. If the person's use of an illicit drug is not dysfunctional, then there is no reason for state intervention. However, if the drug use is dysfunctional, then the arm of the state that should be involved is not law enforcement but rather public health. And why not? If someone is having a drug problem, what do we accomplish by labelling him a criminal? In any event, we would much sooner get him into treatment if the state treats him as a patient—as one with a health problem—rather than as a criminal. In short, if drug use, then it is not the state's business; if drug abuse, then it is the business of public health, not criminal justice.

What we have to recognize is that the pursuit of pleasure through recreational drugs— whether licit or illicit—is part and parcel of the human condition. In his insightful book, *Intoxication: Life in Pursuit of Artificial Paradise*, Dr. Ronald Siegel, a renowned professor of psychopharmacology at UCLA, refers to recreational drug use as the "fourth drive."[45] Exhibited by both animals (e.g., cats and catnip) and humans, the pursuit of intoxication, according to Dr. Siegel, is as natural and powerful a drive as sex, hunger, and thirst. His thesis probably explains why anthropologists have yet to discover a society that has not featured the nonmedical use of drugs. In other words, it is human nature that we are talking about, and the notion of a society rid of recreational drug use is an impossible dream. The War on Drugs is a war on the biological and social nature of our species; it is a civil war, a war on our own people, those who do not use the right drugs. As Pogo says, the enemy is us.

The era of the compact disk is no place for that old fashioned and terribly outdated record player that keeps grinding out the message that a drug is either legal or illegal, and if it is illegal, then that means War. A century ago, Queen Victoria referred to the women's suffrage movement (women seeking the right to vote) as a "mad wicked folly." That it surely wasn't, but if ever there was a social policy that deserved that label—a "mad wicked folly"—it is the War on Drugs.

So, where do we go from here? Are there feasible alternatives to a social policy that wallows in hypocrisy and moral bankruptcy? The Drug Warriors and their allies have buried their heads in the sand because they cannot abide a different way; but the point is that we'll never know of alternatives until we come up for air and start looking. For those who are prepared to extricate their heads (and brains) from the sand, I suggest the following points to ponder.

There is a need to guide the public policy of drug control according to the harm principle. Each drug, regardless of its label as licit or illicit, must be considered on its own merits. What is the particular drug's relative potential for both personal and social harm? And what can we do to minimize the harm? In other words, we need a policy that is tailor-made for each particular drug. For example, in Canada we have done a fairly good job along that line with regard to tobacco, as a combination of public education and high taxes has served to decrease consumption. But we must keep in mind not only that every drug has the potential to cause harm but also that what determines any drug's impact upon the consumer and society is not simply the chemistry of the drug. It is rather the interaction between the drug and the consumer. As the authors of the Consumers Union Report explain in their introduction: "Readers who traditionally think in terms of the effect of a drug will learn here that even the simplest (psychoactive) drugs have a wide range of effects—depending not only on their chemistry but on the ways in which they are used, the laws that govern their use, the user's attitudes and expectations, and countless other factors."[46]

Marijuana is a case in point. Recall my reference to the reefer madness NBC news item and the statement that the drug impairs learning. What I object to is its presentation as a categorical statement: marijuana impairs learning. Actually, the reference was to a study suggesting that even if they have not smoked marijuana for a day, some heavy smokers may have trouble performing simple tasks that involve sustaining and shifting attention. Still, that is a far cry from saying that the drug inevitably produces that result. Furthermore, to say that a drug "'impairs' learning" is more ominous than to say that it affects attention. But I'll say once again that there are no totally harmless drugs. After all, even that wonder drug aspirin can cause gastric bleeding, mental confusion, blood clotting, and a host of other unpleasant and sometimes life-threatening side effects.[47] The solution is not to criminalize those who have a drug problem but rather to formulate nonpunitive strategies to deal with their dysfunctioning. It makes no sense to treat alcohol and tobacco abusers as criminals, just as it makes no sense to treat marijuana, cocaine, and heroin abusers as criminals.

Drug law reformers have publicly called for the decriminalization of possession of small amounts of marijuana and hashish.[48] I applaud their sentiment, albeit I would go further as I believe it unconscionable to criminalize the possession of any drug for personal use. I simply cannot accept the concept that a person becomes a criminal because of what she ingests into her own body, whether it be marijuana, tobacco, cocaine, alcohol, or a steady diet of cream puffs, cheese blintzes awash in sour cream, and Big Macs. To my mind, the very notion of the crime of possession of drugs for personal use invokes the spectre of the state as Orwellian Big Brother. If the substance leads the consumer to batter his spouse or cause an auto accident, then prosecute him for the substantive offence. But otherwise leave him alone, although offer him help if his drug consumption proves dysfunctional. But that is of course a far cry from branding him as a criminal. I am here reminded of what Dr. Helen Nowlis, a renowned drug researcher, has aptly called "the drug problem problem"—the harm caused by the manner in which society has approached the question of drug control.[49]

By the way, the possession of alcoholic beverages for personal use was not criminalized during the Prohibition Era. Rather the law was directed against manufacture, sale, and importation. So at least the tragic social costs of Prohibition were not compounded by grinding ordinary consumers into the jaws of the criminal justice system.

Way back when, I read a marvelous book, a true classic, called *The Limits of the Criminal Sanction*, by Stanford law professor Herbert Packer.[50] Packer outlines six criteria as "a benchmark for the optimal use of the criminal sanction."[51] The final one—which he suggests is the most important—is that, with regard to the conduct in question: "There are no reasonable alternatives to the criminal sanction for dealing with it."[52] I would suggest that this ground alone furnishes sufficient reason to decriminalize possession for personal use. Surely, a Health Model that truly distinguishes between use and abuse and seeks to help, not criminalize, abusers is a far preferable mechanism of social control than the Police Model. Another criterion that Packer weighs heavily is that "the conduct ... is not condoned by any significant segment of society."[53] Aside from those who do not use marijuana but who don't mind that others do, there are an estimated 2 000 000 marijuana smokers in Canada, who in one fell swoop are branded as criminals. I personally deplore a system of criminal law that brands such sizeable numbers of its subjects as outlaws not because they commit crimes against persons or property but because they choose to ingest a particular drug. In Victorian England over a hundred years ago, the renowned philosopher John Stuart Mill published his memorable book-length essay, *On Liberty*, in which he had this to say about the limits of criminal sanctions: "The principle is, that the sole end for which mankind are warranted ... in interfering with the liberty of action of any of their members is self-protection. That the only purpose for which power can be rightfully exercised over any member of a civilized community against his will is to prevent harm to others. His own good, either physical or moral, is not a sufficient warrant."[54]

Those were wise words then and they are wise words today. Would that those who rant and rave about "getting government off the backs of the people" come to make that connection to the War on Drugs! Of course, it is true that there are consumers of illicit drugs whose drug use directly leads to crimes committed against persons and property. But that is a byproduct of the war itself—the artificially inflated black market cost of drugs that are criminalized is bound to drive abusers to commit crimes for the money, to afford that cost. That aspect of the War on Drugs is, I suggest, as bizarre and nonsensical as anything that Alice ever stumbled upon in Wonderland.

In any event, I can well imagine a loud chorus of angry voices protesting that decriminalizing possession for personal use sends the wrong message—that it would encourage the use of illicit drugs. I doubt that. It is fanciful to believe that there are hordes of solid citizens who have thus far shied away from illicit drugs but who would somehow be prompted to indulge if possession were decriminalized. (Bear in mind that when a number of American states drastically reduced penalties for marijuana possession in the 1970s, there was no discernible increase in consumers.) I rather think that my proposal would be sending the right message—that the time has come to seek a new way and that, in the meantime, the least we can do is to proclaim an armistice in the war against those who possess illicit drugs for personal use. That is the first step, but who can say at this juncture where we will end up? But at least that would be a good beginning.

But beyond that one small but needed step, we must seek to devise a model of drug control that is markedly different from the Police Model framework of the War on Drugs. In the quest for a new way, I suggest that we see what there is to learn from the Dutch drug control policy, what one could call an integrated Health/Police Model. Its two overriding principles—separation of markets and harm reduction—are health-oriented, albeit the Health Model rebounds to the benefit of the Police Model because the latter is ill-equipped to suppress consumer demand for drugs. As Professor Ethan Nadelman, the director of the Lindesmith Center, a drug policy research institute in New York City, sums up the Dutch experience:

American drug warriors like to denigrate the Dutch, but the fact remains that Dutch drug policy has been dramatically more successful than U.S. drug policy. The average age of heroin addicts in the Netherlands has been increasing for almost a decade; HIV rates among addicts are dramatically lower than in the United States; police don't waste resources on non-disruptive drug users but, rather, focus on major dealers or petty dealers who create public nuisances. The decriminalized cannabis (marijuana) markets are regulated in a quasi-legal fashion far more effective and inexpensive than the U.S. equivalent.[55]

Dutch drug policy reflects two aspects of the Dutch national character: a tolerance for diversity coupled with pragmatism (if one cannot suppress an activity—e.g., drugs or prostitution—then bring it out into the open and regulate it). There is much to be said for that philosophy. Our way has been different, ever since Canada embraced the Police Model in 1908 and the United States did likewise in 1914. But it is incumbent upon us to seek a new way, one that inevitably will proceed by bumps and starts, requiring fine tuning as we learn from our mistakes along the road to developing a social policy that minimizes the harm caused by dysfunctional drug use (i.e., drug abuse). That hope was expressed two years ago by Barbara Ehrenreich in a thoughtful essay, "Kicking the Big One," in which she indicted drug prohibition as "an evil [that] grips America, a life-slapping, drug-related habit" and proposed that, "It's not necessary to quit cold turkey. Consider starting with marijuana, then easing up on cocaine and heroin possession, concentrating law enforcement on the big-time pushers. Take it slowly, see how it feels. One day at a time."[56]

I agree with Ehrenreich that the place to begin is with marijuana but that drug law reform cannot end there. It is thus my fervent hope that, if Senators are prepared to question the criminalizing of small amounts of marijuana, they will go on to question the very legitimacy of the war itself.[57] There is a voluminous body of literature—both American and Canadian—presenting alternatives to the Police Model of drug control, and all that it takes to seek new paradigms is the moral courage to just Say No to the War on Drugs. A good place to start the quest for a new way is by reading the cover story in the 12 February 1996 issue of William Buckley's magazine, *National Review*. Titled "The War on Drugs Is Lost," it contains seven articles (the first by Buckley himself) that prove the point. The final article is by Yale Law Professor Steven Duke, co-author of *America's Longest War: Rethinking Our Tragic Crusade Against Drugs*. I'll leave you with Duke's final paragraph—the cover story's last word: "The only benefit to America in maintaining prohibition is the psychic comfort we derive from having a permanent scapegoat. But why did we have to pick an enemy the warring against which is so self-destructive? We would be better off blaming our ills on celestial invaders flying about in saucers."[58]

Unfortunately, that "psychic comfort" is very much in evidence in the 1996 U.S. presidential campaign, as the incumbent and his opponent strive to outdo one another in their commitment to the War on Drugs. The President stood as a true Drug Warrior when he proclaimed "I hate drugs" during his renomination speech before his party's national convention. He reiterated that war cry in the first televised debate with Senator Dole. But he is not to be outdone by the Senator, who by the way is a staunch defender of the tobacco industry and who has informed the American public that cigarettes really aren't addictive (although he has recently backtracked from that position, saying that since he is not a doctor, he cannot say for certain). The Senator has called for more police and more prisons to combat the menace of drugs. When asked if he would implement a "zero tolerance" policy, he replied that it would be "zero, zero, zero, zero tolerance." And he has managed to blame the President for the recent upsurge in illicit drug use by teenagers.

Yet, the inescapable truth bears repeating: that more of the same—more police, harsher penalties, and more prisons—is not going to win a war that by its very nature is unwinnable. That is because of the Black Market Pathologies referred to earlier; there are such enormous amounts of money to be made that the market in illicit drugs is virtually unstoppable. As the author of a recent magazine article titled "The Phony Drug War" expressed it: "Putting a murderer in jail means one less murderer on the street. Putting a dealer in jail creates a job opening."[59] Simply put, law enforcement efforts to suppress the importation and cultivation of illicit drugs have a *push down, pop up* effect. If one hydroponic marijuana operation is uncovered, then another simply pops up in its place. If cocaine production were to vanish overnight in Colombia, it would soon flourish elsewhere in South America. And if it stopped throughout South America, it would thrive in Asia. And if not Asia, then Africa. Alas, one can also say the same about heroin. It is the same push down, pop up effect that bedevilled the American military in Vietnam with its body count obsession. It did not matter how many North Vietnamese and Viet Cong were killed, because there were always others to take their place.

In a telegram to Prime Minister Chrétien, an organization of concerned parents—who describe themselves as "volunteers working to stop substance abuse by children"—expressed its impassioned opposition to the relaxation of criminal penalties for marijuana. As it asked the

Prime Minister, "What do you want for Canada, a drug-free society or a drug-filled society?"[60] But the truth is that we will never have a "drug-free" society. Recreational drugs are here to stay; as I have been told by more than one high school and junior high school teacher, marijuana is available to virtually any student who wants it.

I too as a parent share the concern of those parents who worry about children abusing drugs. But what reason is there to believe that we have no choice but to persevere in a rigid commitment to a policy that has done such a dismal job of keeping children (and adults) away from drugs? If a business conducted an enterprise with the dismal track record of the War on Drugs, its board of directors would long since have been turfed by outraged shareholders. Is there a better way? The point is that we'll never know until we begin to look, to expand our horizons beyond the limited vision of the Drug Warriors. I have suggested that at the very least we consider the *decriminalization* of illicit drug use: that whatever the drug, possession for personal use fall outside the ambit of the criminal law. As the distinguished American criminologist Elliott Currie has commented: "decriminalization is not a panacea; it will not end the drug crisis, but it could substantially decrease the irrationality and inhumanity of our present punitive war on drugs."[61]

Since decriminalization is only a halfway measure, should we go all the way to *legalization*: a free market in which illicit drugs are made as legally available as tobacco and alcohol? Professor Currie says no, at least as regards heroin and cocaine, and as he explains, his view is coloured by the nature of American society:

> Evidence ... confirms that much (though, of course, not all) of the harm caused by endemic drug abuse is intrinsic to the impact of hard drugs themselves (and the street culture in which drug abuse is embedded) within the context of a glaringly unequal, depriving, and deteriorating society. And it affirms that we will not substantially reduce that harm without attacking the social roots of the extraordinary demand for hard drugs in the United States. Just as we cannot punish our way out of the drug crisis, neither will we escape its grim toll by deregulating the drug market.[62]

On the other hand, he also acknowledges that "there is a strong argument for treating marijuana differently from the harder drugs."[63] Professor Currie is but one of many thoughtful critics who have argued against the call for escalation of the War on Drugs on the grounds that "more of the same [won't] do the job."[64] But if we don't simply want more of the same, then we must do what we are supposed to do in a democracy on contested issues of public policy: proceed in a calm and measured fashion to talk and listen and debate the merits of conflicting views.

I am pleased to report that this kind of debate has already happened on Parliament Hill. The House of Commons Health Committee has held hearings on Canada's drug policy, as a follow-up to the recent enactment of *The Controlled Drugs and Substances Act*. The new *Act*, which replaced the *Narcotic Control Act* and sections of the *Food and Drug Act*, embodies the Police Model and, if anything, is even more punitive than the old law. When the *Act*, originally called Bill C-7 and then Bill C-8, was before the Senate Legal and Constitutional Affairs Committee, it drew the ire of the Canadian Bar Association. In expressing its strong opposition to Bill C-7, the CBA's National Criminal Justice Section rightly noted that, "[T]he criminalization approach to drug control has proven ineffective for decreasing drug use, reducing crime, or improving health status in the general population."[65] The brief then went on to make the startling admission that: "To recommend diminishing the prohibitionist approach ... is in direct contradiction to the self-interests of lawyers, in that any decriminalization would ultimately mean less work for lawyers.... However, the National Criminal Justice Section takes the position against continued prohibition, contrary to the economic self-interests of lawyers, because we firmly view that position to be in keeping with our professional responsibility to advance the public interest."[66] In its later submission to the Senate against Bill C-8, the CBA reaffirmed its stand: "We submit that it is in the public interest to take the harm-reduction approach rather than the criminalization approach. It will mean, of course, less work for lawyers."[67]

Wonder of wonders—that an organization of lawyers has advocated against the profession's own economic interests! The CBA's principled stand is a clarion call that I hope will inspire the House's Health Committee to take a critical look at what we have wrought by our single-minded devotion to the War on Drugs. In any event, the Canadian Ministry of Justice has introduced a bill to decriminalize possession of 15 grams or less of marijuana. Possession would be subject to a fine but it would not be treated as a criminal offence. Although about nine American states have enacted comparable legislation, the administration of George Bush II has ranted and raved at the proposal and vowed to tie up border traffic if enacted.

Finally, a word to Nancy and Ronald Reagan, George Bush I and II, Bill Bennett, Newt Gingrich, Daryl Gates, their newest ally, Bill Clinton, and all the other Drug Warriors, American and Canadian, who keep telling us that what we require is more of the same: more drug police, harsher punishments, more prisons and more education on the evils of illicit drugs. You remind me of the story of the emperor strutting around in what he believed was a splendid new cloak, and all save a small boy were too embarrassed to tell him the truth: that he was wearing nothing but the suit he was born with. So to all of you cloaked in the mantle of the War on Drugs—surprise, it's made of see-through glass, and if you glance in the mirror, you'll discover that you too have the look of Lady Godiva on that memorable day in Coventry so long ago. But at least she could hold her head proudly. Yours should be bowed down with shame.

QUESTIONS TO CONSIDER

1. Summarize several important points Sneiderman makes about the impact of the War on Drugs. Do you agree or disagree with his arguments?

2. Outline the reasons why drugs such as opium, marijuana, and cocaine were criminalized in Canada and the United States. Does this discussion support or refute the argument that drugs are criminalized because they are dangerous?

3. Is the War on Drugs "winnable"? Discuss the steps that would be necessary for Canada to eliminate illegal drug use. Also discuss whether these steps would be acceptable in Canadian society.

SUGGESTIONS FOR FURTHER READING

Carrier, N. (2007). The autonomy and permeability of law: The case of the Canadian prohibition of cannabis. *Canadian Journal of Law and Society, 22*(1), 123–138.

Jensen, E., Gerber, J., & Mosher, C. (2004). Social consequences of the war on drugs: The legacy of failed policy. *Criminal Justice Policy Review 15,* 100–121.

O'Mahony, P. (2008). *The Irish war on drugs: The seductive folly of prohibition.* New York: Palgrave.

Walby, K. (2008). Hunting for harm: Risk-knowledge networks, local governance, and the Ottawa needle hunter program. *Canadian Journal of Law and Society, 23*(1), 161–178.

NOTES

1. S. Duke, "The War on Drugs Is Lost" *National Review* (12 February 1996) at 47.

2. Administration of Ronald Reagan (4 September 1986). National campaign against drug abuse: Statement by the principal press secretary to the president announcing an Address to the Nation by the President and Mrs. Reagan. *Weekly Compilation of Presidential Documents*, 22 (38) at 1138–39. Cited in W.N. Elwood, *Rhetoric in the War on Drugs: The Triumphs and Tragedies of Public Relations* (Westport: Praeger, 1994) at 28.

3. Ronald Reagan (14 September 1986). National campaign against drug abuse: Address to the Nation. *Weekly Compilation of Presidential Documents*, 22 (38) at 1183–87. Cited in Elwood, *supra* note 2 at 28–29.

4. *Ibid.* at 1187. Cited in Elwood, *supra* note 2 at 30.

5. *Ibid.* at 1186–87. Cited in Elwood, *supra* note 2 at 31.

6. *Ibid.* at 1187. Cited in Elwood, *supra* note 2 at 32.

7. *Ibid.* at 1183–87. Cited in Elwood, *supra* note 2 at 28–29.

8. S. Wisotsky, *Beyond the War on Drugs* (Buffalo: Prometheus Books, 1990) at xx.

9. Elwood, *supra* note 2 at 99.

10. R. Reynolds. "Hooked on the Drug War" *The Hartford Advocate* (26 January 1995) 14.

11. S. Duke & A.C. Gross, *America's Longest War* (New York: Putnam's Sons, 1993) at 135–45.

12. "Gingrich Urges Death Penalty for Illegal Drug Smugglers" *Washington Post* (27 August 1995) 3.

13. J.D. McNamara, "The War on Drugs Is Lost" *National Review* (12 February 1996) 42.

14. Office of National Drug Control Policy, Executive Office of the President, National Drug Control Strategy (1989) at 7 and 9.

15. Duke Gross, *supra* note 11 at 106.

16. *Supra* note 2 at 84–85. Chapter 4 (81–101) presents a fascinating account of the Partnership for a Drug-Free America.

17. The Stoned Surgeon video appears in a PBS documentary, *Altered States*, that was broadcast in April 1995.

18. *Winnipeg Free Press* (6 November 1991) A17.

19. E.A. Nadelman, "The War on Drugs Is Lost" *National Review* (12 February 1996) 38.

20. J.H. VanVliet, "Separation of Drug Markets and the Normalization of Drug Problems in the Netherlands: An Example for Other Nations?" (1990) 20 *Journal of Drug Issues* 463.

21. As an aside, if E.T. pursued his inquiry elsewhere, he would learn about the role of pharmaceutical companies in promoting the use of drugs that are a mixed blessing: drugs that harm as well as benefit consumers; drugs that are grossly overused because of aggressive market promotion and over-prescribing by physicians. That, by the way, is the theme of a study by J. Lexchin, M.D., *The Real Pushers: A Critical Analysis of the Canadian Drug Industry* (Vancouver: New Star Books, 1984).

22. J.R. DiFranza & R.A. Lew, "Effect of Maternal Cigarette Smoking on Pregnancy Complications and Sudden Infant Death Syndrome" (1995) 40 *Journal of Medical Practice* 385.

23. "Bennett Suggests Forced Treatment" *Winnipeg Free Press* (18 June 1989) A21.

24. "Women's Lung Cancer Deaths Up" *Winnipeg Free Press* (2 September 1992) A8.

25. T. Whiteside, *Selling Death* (New York: Liveright, 1970).

26. "Smoking Accounts for 20% of Deaths, Study Suggests" *Winnipeg Free Press* (11 October 1991) A5. See also J. Urschel, "Want a War on Drugs? Let's Take 'Em All On" *USA Today* (14 December 1993) A7.

27. "WHO Hits Tobacco Firms Over Death Rate" *Winnipeg Free Press* (31 May 1995) A7.

28. Alas, the very clever holy/tap water metaphor is not mine but that of the renowned psychiatrist and social critic, Dr. Thomas Szasz. See T. Szasz, *Ceremonial Chemistry* (New York: Anchor Press/Doubleday, 1974).

29. E.M. Brecher *et al.*, *Licit and Illicit Drugs* (Toronto: Little, Brown Co., 1972).

30. *Ibid.* at 536.

31. *Ibid.* at 206.

32. National Commission on Marijuana and Drug Abuse, *Drug Abuse in America: Problem in Perspective*, 2d report (1973) at 11.

33. T. Duster, *The Legislation of Morality* (New York: The Free Press, 1970) at 247–48.

34. J. Helmer, *Drugs and Minority Oppression* (New York: Seabury Press, 1975); M. Green. "A History of Canadian Narcotics Control" (1979) 37 *U.T. Fac. L. Rev.* 42.

35. S. Small, "Canadian Narcotics Legislation, 1908–23: A Conflict Model Interpretation" in W. Greenaway & S. Brickey, eds., *Law and Social Control in Canada* (Scarborough: Prentice-Hall, 1978) 28.

36. At the present time, marijuana is a prohibited drug under the *Narcotic Control Act*. Parliament has chosen to classify marijuana as a narcotic, although botanically it is not. In section 2, the *Act* broadly defines "trafficking" as including "to manufacture, sell, give, administer, transport, send, deliver, or distribute...." Thus, if you *give* a joint to a friend, then—*in the eyes of the law*—you are a narcotics trafficker!

37. E. Murphy, *The Black Candle* (Toronto: Thomas Allen, 1922).

38. B. Anthony & R. Silverman. "Introduction" in E. Murphy, *The Black Candle* (Toronto: Coles Publishing Company, 1973) [reprint] at 3.

39. M. Silverman & P.R. Lee, *Pills, Profits, and Politics* (Berkeley: University of California Press, 1974) at 264.

40. *Supra* note 24 at A10.

41. Note that genetic predisposition may also be involved; it is certainly a contributing factor in some cases of alcoholism.

42. *Supra* note 29 at 223.

43. *Supra* note 11 at xviii.

44. *Supra* note 20. As indicated by his article's title, Van Vliet also uses the phrase "normalization of drug problems" as another description of "harm reduction."

45. R. Siegel, *Intoxication: Life in Pursuit of Artificial Paradise* (New York: E.P. Dutton, 1989).

46. *Supra* note 29 at xi.

47. M.J. Rodman & D.W. Smith, *Pharmacology and Drug Therapy in Nursing* (Toronto: J.B. Lippincott Company, 1968) at 163.

48. "Senators High on Legalizing Marijuana" *The Toronto Star* (17 May 1996) 3.

49. *Supra* note 29 at 521.

50. H. Packer, *The Limits of the Criminal Sanction* (Stanford: Stanford University Press, 1968).

51. *Ibid.* at 296.

52. *Ibid.*

53. *Ibid.*

54. Quoted in N. Morris & G. Hawkins, *The Honest Politician's Guide to Crime Control* (Chicago: University of Chicago Press, 1969) at 4.

55. *Supra* note 19 at 39.

56. B. Ehrenreich. "Kicking the Big One" *Time* (28 February 1994) 60.

57. I would also couple the decriminalization of possession for personal use with the legal availability of marijuana for medicinal purposes: e.g., for cancer (reducing the nausea caused by chemotherapy), for multiple sclerosis (easing pain), for glaucoma (reducing pressure on the eyeballs), and for AIDS (stimulating appetite). There is no more cruel aspect of the War on Drugs than the denial of the drug to those who can benefit from its medicinal properties and for whom there are no adequate legal substitutes.

58. *Supra* note 1 at 48.

59. J.W. Shenk, "The Phony Drug War" *The Nation* (23 September 1996) 11.

60. Lambton Families in Action for Drug Education, Inc. telegram to the Right Honourable Jean Chrétien, 7 June 1994.

61. E. Currie, "Towards a Policy on Drugs" in H.T. Wilson, ed. *Drugs, Society, and Behavior* (Guilford, CT: Dushkin Publishing, 1996) at 216.

62. *Ibid.*

63. *Ibid.*

64. *Ibid.* at 214.

65. National Criminal Justice Section of the Canadian Bar Association, *Submission on Bill C-7* (May 1994) at 1.

66. *Ibid.* at 19.

67. (28 March 1996) 3 Proceedings of the Standing Senate Committee on Legal and Constitutional Affairs at 3.5.

Chapter Three

Euthanasia and Assisted Suicide in the Post-*Rodriguez* Era: Lessons from Foreign Jurisdictions

*Michael Cormack**

Editors' Note: Michael Cormack deals with a controversial issue that has become increasingly important in Canada over the past two decades. In "Euthanasia and Assisted Suicide in the Post-Rodriguez Era," Cormack compares the approaches to euthanasia and assisted suicide taken by Australia, Canada, the Netherlands, and the United States. He notes that euthanasia and assisted suicide, as well as "counselling a suicide," are illegal in Canada and carry maximum sentences ranging from 14 years to life imprisonment. Cormack discusses the Rodriguez case, in which the British Columbia Supreme Court, the British Columbia Appeals Court, and the Supreme Court of Canada all refused to grant a 42-year-old ALS sufferer the right to assistance in committing suicide. He notes that this decision is consistent with the official position of the Canadian Medical Association, although many Canadian physicians support some law reform on euthanasia and assisted suicide.

Cormack cites opinion polls that indicate that most Canadians favour assisted suicide for people suffering from an incurable disease. Despite this public support and the ambivalence within the medical profession, numerous attempts to codify Canadian jurisprudence on end-of-life decision making have failed. Cormack compares this to Australia, where some states experimented with assisted suicide and voluntary euthanasia before the federal government outlawed the practice, and the United States, where assisted suicide is illegal in all states except Oregon. (Editors' note: Oregon passed the Death with Dignity Act in 1997, and Washington State became the second state to adopt similar legislation in 2008.) Cormack outlines the approach taken in the Netherlands, where euthanasia and assisted suicide are illegal but not prosecuted as long as certain safeguards are followed. (This practice has changed since the article was written. The Dutch Penal Code was amended in 2001 to remove voluntary euthanasia and assisted suicide from its purview.)

Cormack turns his attention to several philosophical issues that have had an impact on the debate over euthanasia and assisted suicide in Canada. The most important of these include "killing versus letting die," "autonomy and the right to die," "the sanctity of life," and the "slippery slope" argument. He argues there is much less difference between letting patients die and taking proactive steps to end life than is frequently believed because both involve a conscious decision to take action (e.g., withdraw treatment in the case of the former) that will hasten death. Insofar as autonomy and the right to die is concerned, Cormack notes that Canadians already have the right to commit suicide without fear of repercussions and that such autonomy also gives people the right to refuse life-sustaining treatment. The key question is whether the notion of autonomy can be extended to include the right to assisted suicide and voluntary euthanasia. After all, true autonomy should include both the right to live one's life as one chooses and the right to end it if one chooses.

These arguments lead directly into two further philosophical conundrums, namely the sanctity of life and slippery-slope issues. In dealing with the sanctity-of-life issue, Cormack discusses the argument that euthanasia and assisted suicide tend to devalue the importance of life generally and especially as it

Source: *Osgoode Hall Law Journal*, Vol. 38, No.4, pp. 591–641. Reprinted by permission of the author.

*B.A., Simon Fraser University (School of Criminology), LL.B. Candidate, University British Columbia. Special thanks to Professor Neil Boyd at Simon Fraser University: Your insight was invaluable. I also wish to thank the anonymous reviewers for their thoughtful critiques.

relates to handicapped people. Although he accepts the validity of these arguments, he also notes that the sanctity of life is far from absolute and may be overridden by autonomy concerns. As for the slippery-slope argument, Cormack accepts the contention that allowing assisted suicide and voluntary euthanasia may lead to abuses. In this respect, he reviews some of the criticisms levelled at the Dutch experience, and concedes that there is considerable evidence to suggest that the Dutch process is rife with abuse. However, he argues that there is little evidence of abuse in Oregon, where stringent safeguards are in place. In any event, Cormack argues that assisted suicide and euthanasia have always existed in Canada and that a political response to the issue is desirable. He argues that the experiences of Oregon, Australia, and the Netherlands must be considered in any attempt to legalize assisted suicide or voluntary euthanasia in Canada. Cormack concludes by outlining a proposal for how legalized assisted suicide and euthanasia should be operationalized in Canada, complete with mandatory safeguards.

I. INTRODUCTION

Terry Graham, a resident of Brampton, Ontario, suffers from a rare degenerative muscle disease known as mitochondrial myopathy. With little muscle to protect his nerves, he experiences overwhelming pain that cannot be entirely alleviated by morphine. He has been lobbying federal officials for the right to have a physician-assisted death, but his efforts have gone unrewarded.[1] The Graham case is only the tip of the iceberg. Euthanasia and assisted suicide are highly controversial subjects that have drawn much attention in Canada over the last two decades. The issues surrounding the prohibition of both practices are extremely complicated and demand an equally complex examination. The discussion below will outline how the Netherlands, the United States, Australia, and Canada have approached euthanasia and assisted suicide. Jurisprudence, public opinion polls, legislative developments, and the position of medical organizations and their members will be included in the analysis. A number of arguments for and against the continued prohibition of the practices in Canada will be evaluated. As well, information regarding the extent to which euthanasia and assisted suicide are performed in these countries will be assessed. It will be shown that Canadians currently enjoy much control over decisions concerning the end of life. The principles of autonomy and beneficence provide the foundation necessary to justify lifting the prohibition of voluntary euthanasia and assisted suicide in Canada. With regard to the development of safeguards in order to prevent abuse, the way in which foreign jurisdictions have dealt with both practices is highly instructive. Legislative reform is in order; the matter should not be left to the courts. Workable legislation can be drafted and a proposal of just what that should entail will also be presented.

II. DEFINING EUTHANASIA AND ASSISTED SUICIDE

Euthanasia can be classified as voluntary, non-voluntary, or involuntary.[2] Voluntary euthanasia does not involve a request for assistance, because the person involved has never had the capacity or has lost the capacity to make a request. Involuntary euthanasia occurs when the person killed is capable of making a request but refuses or is not consulted in the matter. Unbearable suffering underscores the motive for killing in such an instance. However, legitimate cases of involuntary euthanasia are hard to conceive of and closely parallel homicide.[3]

Euthanasia can also be characterized as active or passive.[4] This distinction is similar to the acts and omissions legal doctrine and rests on the manner in which a person dies. While the distinction is sometimes important, for reasons that will become evident, passive euthanasia will not generally be referred to as euthanasia. Instead, passive euthanasia will be classified as both: withholding life-sustaining treatment—foregoing treatment that is potentially life-sustaining; and, withdrawing life-sustaining treatment—ceasing previously initiated life-sustaining treatment.[5]

As a result, voluntary euthanasia will be defined as a deliberate act by one party with the intention of ending the life of another, at the request of the latter, where the act causes death.[6] Non-voluntary euthanasia and involuntary euthanasia differ from voluntary euthanasia with regard to the lack of a request or a refusal of death and the competence of the person killed. Euthanasia, when referred to, will encompass all three variants. Assisted suicide is less complex conceptually and will be defined as: a deliberate act by one party with the intention of assisting another to take his/her own life, by providing the knowledge and/or means to do so, at the request of the latter.[7] The most important distinction between the above definitions of euthanasia and assisted suicide concerns the person performing the act that terminates life. In the case of euthanasia, another party performs the act as opposed to assisted suicide where the person dying does so. In the medical context, this difference implies that a physician administers a death-causing substance in the case of voluntary euthanasia. With regard to assisted suicide, the physician supplies the substance to the patient for self-administration.[8] At this point, an examination of the legality of the above end-of-life practices in selected countries is in order.

III. THE LEGAL STATUS OF EUTHANASIA AND ASSISTED SUICIDE IN CANADA

Attempted suicide was prohibited in Canada's first *Criminal Code*.[9] The ban was lifted in 1972.[10] Assisted suicide was also prohibited under the *Code, 1892*[11] and, today, it remains a separate offence.[12] Section 241 of the *Code, 1985* prohibits counselling or aiding suicide, whether suicide ensues or not, and provides for a punishment of imprisonment for a maximum term of fourteen years.[13] Acts of euthanasia fall under the provisions relating to homicide.[14] Life imprisonment is the mandatory punishment for both first and second degree murder, and a person is eligible for parole after serving a minimum of twenty-five years or ten years of his or her sentence, respectively.[15] Manslaughter carries a maximum penalty of life imprisonment but no mandatory minimum sentence, except when a firearm is used (four years).[16] There are a number of other sections of the *Code, 1985* that are also relevant to euthanasia, assisted suicide, and end-of-life decisions.[17] Furthermore, Canadians cannot legally consent to have death inflicted upon them.[18]

With regard to medical treatment, the *Code, 1985* does not require that patients accept unwanted treatment nor does it require the administration of futile treatment (completely ineffective treatment). Necessary palliative care (care aimed at relieving, as opposed to curing, a person's physical, psychological, emotional, or spiritual suffering) that results in the patient's death is not prohibited by the *Code, 1985* as long as it conforms to medically accepted practice. The practice of total sedation (rendering an individual totally unconscious via the administration of drugs with no potential shortening of life) is legal if the patient, or the patient's surrogate, consents.[19] As for surrogate and proxy decisionmaking, advance directive legislation (legislation that enables competent individuals to execute documents regarding health care decisions to be made if the person becomes incapable of making such decisions) has been enacted in nine provinces and one territory.[20]

At common law, medical treatment decisionmaking rests largely with the patient. Except in emergency situations, physicians are required to obtain informed consent from the patient before treatment is administered and an action in battery lies against the physician if there is treatment without consent.[21] Consent that is inadequately informed serves as the basis for an action in negligence against a physician.[22] A physician must adhere to a patient's refusal of life-sustaining treatment.[23] Patients also have the right to have life-sustaining treatment withdrawn.[24] Respect for patients' decisions concerning their own bodies, even though such decisions may result in death, are rooted in the motions of autonomy and self-determination.[25] However, the Supreme Court of Canada decided that these principles do not justify ending the prohibition of euthanasia or assisted suicide.[26]

The leading case in Canada concerning euthanasia and assisted suicide is the *Rodriguez*[27] decision. Sue Rodriguez was forty-two years old and suffered from amyotrophic lateral sclerosis (ALS). Her condition was deteriorating rapidly and she would have lost the capacity to speak, swallow, move, and breathe without assistance. She sought an order entitling her to assistance in committing suicide when the condition became intolerable. She wanted a physician to establish the technological means by which she could end her life by her own hand. Thus, she sought to have section 241 of the *Code, 1985* declared invalid and to be of no force and effect pursuant to section 52 of the *Constitution Act, 1982*,[28] to the extent that it prevented a terminally ill individual from committing physician-assisted suicide. Rodriguez claimed that section 241 violated her rights under sections 7, 12, and 15(1) of the *Charter of Rights and Freedoms*.[29] The British Columbia Supreme Court dismissed the application. The majority of the British Columbia Court of Appeal affirmed the decision and a majority (5–4) of the Supreme Court of Canada dismissed the appeal.[30] The justices in *Rodriguez* clearly advocated different approaches to euthanasia and assisted suicide. The majority upheld the prohibition of both practices. Chief Justice Lamer, and Justice Cory, dissenting, advocated the decriminalization of assisted suicide only,[31] while Justices McLachlin and L'Heureux-Dubé, dissenting, indicated that euthanasia would also be permissible.[32]

The Supreme Court of Canada is not the only body to consider legal reform in this area. The Law Reform Commission of Canada released its working paper in 1982 and its report in 1983 on euthanasia, assisted suicide, and the cessation of treatment.[33] The Commission recommended against decriminalizing or legalizing voluntary euthanasia and assisted suicide. It suggested that the *Code, 1985* be amended to make it clear that physicians do not attract criminal liability for administering appropriate palliative care that has the effect of shortening a patient's life expectancy. Additionally, the Commission recommended that the *Code, 1985* be amended so that physicians would not be held criminally responsible for not initiating or discontinuing treatment for incompetent patients, when treatment was therapeutically useless and not in the patient's best interest.[34] In 1987, it reiterated its recommendation regarding palliative care that shortens life. As well, it proposed that mercy killing be treated as second-, not first-degree murder, and that no fixed sentence be attached to second-degree murder.[35]

In 1991, Private Member's Bill C-261 was introduced in the House of Commons. Among other things, it proposed legalizing euthanasia and would have protected physicians who administered pain-killing treatment that simultaneously hastened death.[36] The Bill was dropped from the Order Paper after second reading.[37] Also in 1991, the British Columbia Royal Commission on Health Care and Costs recommended that the *Code, 1985* be amended to exempt health care workers from liability when assisting terminally ill patients in suicide. However, a consensus on voluntary euthanasia could not be reached and no recommendations were made on the issue.[38] In 1994, Bill C-215 was introduced, proposing to decriminalize physician-assisted suicide for terminally ill patients, but died in the same manner as Bill C-261.[39]

In 1995, the Special Senate Committee on Euthanasia and Assisted Suicide released its report. The majority of the Committee recommended that no changes be made to section 241 of the *Code, 1985*. Concerns expressed included: the apprehension that legalizing assisted suicide would undermine the social value of respect for life; the fear that changes could lead to abuses; and the worry of the slippery slope—permitting assisted suicide in cases where persons were competent would inevitably lead to changes that would allow the procedure for incompetent persons.[40] The majority of the Committee recommended that non-voluntary, involuntary, and voluntary euthanasia remain criminal offences. However, the Commission suggested that the *Code, 1985* be amended so as to provide for less severe penalties in cases of voluntary euthanasia that involve mercy or compassion. The majority opposed euthanasia for essentially the same reasons it opposed assisted suicide.[41]

In 1996, the Ontario Law Reform Commission released a study paper that advocated an amendment to section 241 of the *Code, 1985* that would have exempted health care professionals from liability when assisting in another's suicide. However, the Commission recommended that euthanasia remain a criminal offence.[42] Bill C-304, which would have decriminalized assisted suicide for the terminally ill, was introduced in 1997, but was dropped from the Order Paper after second reading.[43] Bill S-2 was first read on 13 October 1999 and recommended codifying the common law practices relating to withdrawing and withholding life-sustaining treatment. It also clarified that health care providers were not liable to criminal sanction when medication that might shorten life was administered for pain relief purposes. It died on the Order paper in October of 2000.[44]

End-of-life decisions have been continuously addressed in Canada over the past two decades. The attempts to codify Canadian jurisprudence have not borne fruit. The Canadian Medical Association's (CMA) position is that "[t]he withholding or withdrawal of inappropriate, futile or unwanted medical treatment and the provision of compassionate palliative care, even when that shortens life, is considered good and ethical medical practice."[45] However, in other respects, CMA policy is reflected in the law; changes to the law regarding voluntary euthanasia and assisted suicide have outright failed. This complements official CMA policy, which condemns physician participation in both situations.[46] However, the CMA's policy does not mirror physician opinion. A 1993 survey revealed that of the 923 respondent physicians, 60.5 per cent supported some type of legal change regarding voluntary euthanasia and physician-assisted suicide, while 28.9 per cent opposed such measures.[47] In 1994, 866 Alberta physicians were asked whether it is sometimes right to practice active euthanasia: 42 per cent replied yes, 47 per cent no, and 11 per cent were uncertain. In response to whether the law should be changed to permit active euthanasia, the answers were 37 per cent yes, 47 per cent no, and 16 per cent uncertain.[48] In 1999, the findings of a survey administered in 1995 were published. Of the 1,855 Canadian physicians polled, 49 per cent supported changing the law to permit physician-assisted suicide; however, only 20 per cent would be willing to practice it if it were legal; 57 per cent would not, and 23 per cent were uncertain.[49] The above results indicate that the medical community is extremely divided with regard to these practices.

Given the highly political nature of the debate, public sentiment must also be considered. Since 1968, Gallup Polls have been conducted in Canada using the following question: "When a person has an incurable disease that causes great suffering, do you, or do you not think that competent doctors should be allowed by law, to end the patient's life through mercy killing, if the patient has made a formal request in writing?"[50] The results indicate that support increased dramatically between 1968 (45 per cent yes, 43 per cent no, 12 per cent undecided) and 1989 (77 per cent, 17 per cent, 6 per cent, respectively). Since then, public support has been relatively constant.[51] The polling question appears to encompass only voluntary euthanasia, in the medical context, for those suffering from an incurable illness; although, it should be expected that physician-assisted suicide in the same circumstances would evoke similar support. In 1997, the Angus Reid Group conducted a national poll on "Canadians' Views on Euthanasia."[52] While the question appeared to refer only to suicide and assisted suicide for the terminally ill, the results echoed the findings of a 1993 Angus Reid survey: 76 per cent supported the right to die, 17 per cent opposed, and 7 per cent were unsure.[53] Overall, there is substantial public support in Canada for permitting the practices of assisted suicide and voluntary euthanasia in certain circumstances.

IV. THE LEGAL STATUS OF EUTHANASIA AND ASSISTED SUICIDE IN OTHER LEGAL REGIMES

A. Australia

Like Canadians, Australians have the right to refuse life-sustaining treatment and have it withdrawn.[54] Currently, euthanasia and assisted suicide are illegal in all states and territories.[55] Various bills aimed at legalizing voluntary euthanasia had been introduced in Australia during the 1990s.[56] In 1995, after a mere three-month period, legislation legalizing voluntary euthanasia and assisted suicide was passed in a "conscience vote" in the Northern Territory Legislative Assembly.[57] After the supreme court upheld the validity of the legislation,[58] the *Rights of the Terminally Ill Act, 1995*[59] came into force in July of 1996, and the Northern Territory became the first district in the world to legalize the procedures.[60] However, the legislation's life was short. In March of 1997, *ROTTI* was effectively repealed by federal legislation, the *Euthanasia Laws Act, 1997*,[61] which prohibited the territories from legalizing voluntary euthanasia. The primary reason for the repeal of *ROTTI* was the fear that the legislation would lead to abuse.[62] Only four persons ended their lives under *ROTTI*.[63]

ROTTI provided that a patient, at least eighteen years of age, could request that a health care practitioner assist her or him in dying. The practitioner or the patient could have administered the lethal substance. The administering practitioner did not have to be a physician. The patient had to be [afflicted] with an illness causing severe pain or suffering that would have resulted in death. The practitioner must have been satisfied that there was no reasonable medical treatment acceptable to the patient that might have reasonably been undertaken in hope of realizing a cure. Such reasonable treatment was confined to the relief of suffering, pain, and/or distress, with the purpose of allowing the patient to die comfortably. The patient could not have been diagnosed with treatable clinical depression. The practitioner had to inform the patient of the nature of the condition and all forms of treatment. A practitioner, with special qualifications in the area, must have advised the patient of his or her palliative care options and was required to refuse to assist if there were alternatives reasonably available that would have alleviated the patient's suffering to a degree acceptable to the patient. A psychiatrist and another practitioner with prescribed experience in the treatment of the particular illness afflicting the patient must have confirmed the first provider's diagnosis and prognosis. The patient had to be of sound mind and had to have considered the effect that the decision would have had on his or her family. The practitioner must have been reasonably satisfied that the decision was made voluntarily, freely, and after due deliberation. The patient was required to have signed a request certificate no sooner than seven days after the initial request. If the patient was unable to sign, he or she could request that a disinterested party sign on his or her behalf. The medical practitioner must have witnessed the signature. A second practitioner must have signed the certificate in the presence of the patient and the first doctor. The practitioners could not have stood to gain financially from the patient's death. At least forty-eight hours must have elapsed between the time the certificate was signed and the procedure was performed. The patient had the ongoing right to rescind the request in any manner and at any time. The practitioner must have assisted the patient and/or remained present until the patient died. After the patient's death, the assisting practitioner had to submit a report to the coroner. Fines and terms of imprisonment for violations relating to objectionable or improper conduct on behalf of the practitioner or another party, and inaccurate record keeping, were also provided for in *ROTTI*. A practitioner was entitled to refuse to grant a patient's request at any time, for any reason.[64] It should be noted that the patient need not have been competent at the time of administration; rather, it was adequate that the patient had not indicated to the doctor a contrary intention to go through with the procedure.[65] Parliamentary debates indicate that this provision was intended to accommodate persons who had requested assistance but had subsequently lost decisionmaking capacity.[66]

Although the Australian Medical Association has always opposed voluntary euthanasia,[67] medical practitioners endorse law reform. Pooled data from Australia health practitioner surveys indicate that 57 per cent of doctors and 71 per cent of nurses support legal change to permit voluntary euthanasia.[68] Moreover, public opinion advocates the legalization of voluntary euthanasia and assisted suicide. Since 1962, a majority of those polled have been in favour of some form of assistance in dying. In 1995, a Morgan Gallup Poll indicated that 78 per cent of respondents were in favour of permitting the administration of a lethal dose by a doctor to a hopelessly ill and suffering patient, 14 per cent against, and 8 per cent undecided.[69] Of the ten separate polls conducted since 1983 using the same question, the lowest level of support occurred in 1986; 66 per cent for, 21 per cent against.[70] The results suggest that the public supports changes in the law to allow for voluntary euthanasia.

B. The United States

Americans also have the right to refuse life-sustaining treatment or have it withdrawn.[71] The United States Supreme Court has ruled that this right, for competent individuals, is constitutionally protected and is underscored by liberty interests.[72] Despite two federal appeal court decisions to the contrary,[73] the Supreme Court in *Glucksberg* held that withdrawing and withholding treatment can be distinguished from assisted suicide and as a result of the court's unanimous decision, Americans do not have a constitutional right to assisted suicide.[74] Forty-one states have criminalized assisted suicide via statute. In six states and the District of Columbia, it is a common law crime.[75] In states that do not have specific legislation, assisted suicide can be dealt with under general criminal law statutes and can be treated as murder or manslaughter. All acts of euthanasia are illegal in every state and are classified as murder.[76]

In 1994, Oregon's *Death and Dignity Act*[77] was passed by a citizens' initiative.[78] Implementation of the *DDA* was delayed by a court injunction until 27 October 1997. Oregonians voted on Measure 51, aimed at repealing the *DDA*, in November of that year. Sixty per cent of voters opted to retain the *DDA*, as opposed to 40 per cent who voted against it.[79] Still in force, the Act legalizes assisted suicide under certain conditions. Patients, at least eighteen years old, can request lethal medical prescriptions from their physicians. The patient must be a resident of Oregon and be suffering from a terminal disease (an irreversible and incurable disease that will result in death within six months). The physician must inform the patient of his/her diagnosis, prognosis, the probable risks and results of the prescribed medication, and the feasible alternatives. The physician must also refer the patient to another physician for confirmation of the diagnosis, the patient's capability, and the voluntariness of the request. The physician must refer the patient to counselling where appropriate and recommend that his/her family be informed of the decision. The patient is required to make a total of three requests (two oral and one written). The patient must be able to make and communicate health care decisions and the request must be voluntary and signed without coercion. At least two persons, other than the attending physician, must witness the signing. Additionally, one witness cannot be related to the patient, stand to gain financially from the death, nor be associated with the health care facility. The second oral request must be made no sooner than fifteen days after the initial one, at which time the physician must give the patient the chance to rescind the request. No less than forty-eight hours must pass between the writing of the prescription and the patient's written request. Thus, patients must wait for at least fifteen days for their lethal prescription to be written. The patient has the right to rescind the request in any manner, at any time. Physicians are required to report all lethal prescriptions written to the Oregon Health Division. No physician is under a duty to provide assistance. If a physician refuses or is unable to fulfil the patient's request and the patient changes providers, then the physician must deliver a copy of the patient's medical records to the new provider. Additionally, the *DDA* explicitly states that it does not authorize active euthanasia or mercy killing.[80] In 1998, sixteen people and in 1999, twenty-seven people, ended their lives pursuant to the *DDA*.[81]

The American Medical Association (AMA) has approved of the withholding and withdrawing of treatment in certain circumstances.[82] Furthermore, the AMA has unequivocally endorsed the practice of administering pain-medication to the terminally ill despite its life-shortening effect.[83] Nonetheless, the AMA has consistently opposed active euthanasia.[84] With regard to physician-assisted suicide, the AMA stated that it "is fundamentally incompatible with the physician's role as healer."[85] However, a national survey of physicians conducted in 1996 revealed that, of 1902 respondents, 11 per cent indicated "that under current legal constraints, there are circumstances in which they would prescribe a medication for a competent patient to use with the primary intention of ending his or her life: 36 per cent ... said they would prescribe a medication if it were legal to do so."[86] Similarly, under present legal constraints, 7 per cent stated that they could envision circumstances involving a competent patient in which they would be willing to administer a lethal injection; 24 per cent would be willing to do so if it were legal.[87] The findings of a study conducted in Oregon in 1999 showed that, of the 144 respondents who received requests for lethal prescriptions, 51 per cent were willing to prescribe the medication, 37 per cent were not, and 12 per cent were uncertain.[88] With regard to public opinion, Gallup Poll results reveal that support for the legalization of voluntary euthanasia has grown from 37 per cent in 1947[89] to 75 per cent in 1996.[90] In 1994, a Harris Poll disclosed that 73 per cent of those polled approved of physician-assisted suicide.[91] Once again, the medical community's official stance on both procedures does not mesh well with physician and public opinion.

C. The Netherlands

Euthanasia and assisted suicide are prohibited under the Dutch *Penal Code*[92] pursuant to the articles relating to murder, manslaughter, and inciting or assisting suicide. In contrast to Canadian law, the *Penal Code* does not provide for mandatory minimum penalties,[93] the consent of the person killed mitigates the crime,[94] and assisting suicide is only punishable when a suicide actually ensues.[95] Furthermore, a person avoids criminal liability when the offence was committed as a result of a *force majeure* (*overmacht*). [96] Notwithstanding the official illegality of voluntary euthanasia and assisted suicide, both practices are legally permitted. The Dutch courts, in conjunction with the medical establishment, have developed the policy relating to voluntary euthanasia and assisted suicide.[97] The legitimacy of both practices is grounded in the principles of autonomy and beneficence.[98]

In 1993, the law governing the disposal of corpses was amended. New forms regarding the death of patients were introduced. The form relating to voluntary euthanasia and assisted suicide outlined various points requiring attention by the reporting physician. In essence, the elements corresponded to the requirements of "careful practice" (outlined below) delineated in the case law. The amendment did not affect the legality of either practice.[99] Today, both practices are permitted if certain conditions are met. The substantive requirements dictate that a patient make an explicit request that is voluntary, well considered, and enduring. The patient must be suffering unbearably and hopelessly. The suffering need not have a somatic basis and in such a case there must be no realistic prospect of treatment. If the suffering is somatically based, then other possibilities for relieving the distress or treating the condition must have been exhausted or refused by the patient. Only physicians can legally perform euthanasia. With regard to the procedural requirements (requirements of careful practice), a doctor must formally confer with at least one other physician as to the patient's condition, prognosis, and the alternatives available. A written record of the matter should be kept and the procedure should be performed in a professionally responsible manner. The physician should remain with the patient or be readily available until death. Instances of euthanasia cannot be reported as natural deaths.[100] Physicians are obligated to notify the authorities, but prosecutions do not result if the guidelines are adhered to. The physician's actions are evaluated by a regional review committee whose final opinion is submitted to the Public Prosecutions Service and has much bearing on whether a prosecution will proceed.[101]

The current situation in the Netherlands seems to sit well with the Dutch population. A 1991 survey conducted by the Social and Cultural Planning office revealed that 57 per cent of respondents were in favour of a doctor administering a lethal injection in order to relieve the suffering of a patient at her/his explicit request, 32 per cent said it depends, 3 per cent were unsure, and 9 per cent were opposed.[102] A more recent university study claims that 92 per cent of the population supports euthanasia.[103] Similar support can be found in the political realm. In 1993, the positive responses of all three major political parties (the Liberals, the Social-Democrats, and the Christian-Democrats) to the following question were overwhelming: "Do you feel that someone who is, for him- or herself, in an unacceptable and hopeless situation, always has the right to request a termination of his/her own life?"[104]

Over the years, a number of legislative proposals have been made in an attempt to codify voluntary euthanasia and assisted suicide policy. They failed, not because there was a lack of majority support, but because of the needs of placating the Christian-Democrats to ensure the survival of coalition governments.[105] Since 1951, nearly all coalitions have included the Christian-Democrats.[106] However, in 2000, that changed; the Christian-Democrats were not part of the government.[107] On 28 November 2000, the Lower House of the Dutch Parliament approved a bill that will remove voluntary euthanasia and assisted suicide from the sphere of the criminal law.[108] Provisions will be added to articles 293 and 294 of the *Penal Code* that absolve physicians of liability.[109] Sixty-six per cent of the 362 Dutch physicians surveyed in 1991 favoured similar amendments.[110] The physician must fulfil the requirements of due care provided for in a new act: the *Termination of Life on Request and Assistance with Suicide (Review) Act*.[111] Physicians must also report their actions to the municipal coroner. The new legislation will not substantively change the present due care requirements. It recognizes the validity of euthanasia declarations (advance directives). Physicians can act on the directive unless they have good reason not to. Persons as young as sixteen years old can request voluntary euthanasia and assisted suicide as long as their parents participate in the decision making process. Children between the ages of twelve and sixteen can also request the procedures, but the consent of their parents or guardians is required. Review committees will continue to conduct investigations, but only have to refer cases to the prosecutor when they deem it necessary to do so.[112] The legislation received the support of the Social-Democratic, Liberal-Democratic, and Liberal coalition government, but was opposed by three small right-wing religious parties and the Christian-Democratic Party.[113] On 10 April 2001, the Dutch Senate passed the bill and it is anticipated that it will go into force in autumn 2001.[114]

V. NORMATIVE JUSTIFICATION OF VOLUNTARY EUTHANASIA AND ASSISTED SUICIDE IN CANADA

A number of positions have been advanced in favour of, and in opposition to, the legalization of voluntary euthanasia and assisted suicide. Some of the more compelling arguments will be examined in detail below, with particular attention being paid to the Canadian situation.

A. The *Rodriguez* "Consensus"

The majority in *Rodriguez*[115] interpreted such things as the prohibition of voluntary euthanasia and assisted suicide in foreign jurisdictions and the official positions of medical associations as evidence that there is a consensus that the practices should not be permitted.[116] This approach is problematic for various reasons. The weight to be given to an alleged consensus when formulating or amending public policy and the law should be cautiously assessed.[117] As well, the courts should not use the purported consensus in foreign jurisdictions to define the extent to which the rights of Canadians are protected by the *Charter*.[118] Instead, if consensus is to be utilized, then it should be informed by the Canadian experience.[119] If one examines the results of the public and physician opinion polls listed above, then the consensus arrived at in *Rodriguez* is anything but accurate. Rather, sentiment appears to significantly favour law reform. Moreover, the recent legislative development in Oregon throws the entire "prohibition-therefore-consensus" argument into question. However, a consensus alone does not necessarily justify permitting voluntary euthanasia and assisted suicide. The *Charter* protects the rights and freedoms of all Canadians (minorities included)[120] and a consensus is merely one factor that needs to be taken into account.

B. Killing Versus Letting Die

There has been much controversy surrounding the distinction between "killing" and "letting die." Roughly, the argument for maintaining the distinction is as follows: withdrawing or withholding life-sustaining treatment constitutes an omission, not a positive act; death is caused by the underlying disease, not by the omission nor by the administration of a lethal substance; thus, the doctor does not kill, but lets the patient die.[121] As a result, culpability differs. Each claim will be dealt with in turn.

Withholding treatment is obviously an omission and Lord Browne-Wilkinson in *Airedale*[122] articulated why withdrawing treatment can also be classified as such:

> The positive act of removing the nasogastric tube presents more difficulty. It is undoubtedly a positive act, similar to switching off a ventilator in the case of a patient whose life is being sustained by artificial ventilation. But in my judgment in neither case should the act be classified as positive, since to do so would be to introduce intolerably fine distinctions. If, instead of removing the nasogastric tube, it was left in place but no further nutrients were provided for the tube to convey to the patient's stomach, that would not be an act of commission. Again, as has been pointed out ... if the switching off of a ventilator were to be classified as a positive act, exactly the same result can be achieved by installing a time-clock which requires to be reset every 12 hours: the failure to reset the machine could not be classified as a positive act.

This line of reasoning reflects the difficulties in reconciling the acts/omissions doctrine with acceptable medical practice. Yet, if one concedes that, in some circumstances, withdrawing treatment should be classified as an omission, then the procedure can be distinguished from voluntary euthanasia and assisted suicide, since these practices involve positive acts.

It has been asserted that the cause of death when treatment is withheld or withdrawn is the underlying disease; nature simply takes its course.[123] It is hard to envision though, that withdrawing life-sustaining treatment does not fall within the ambit of legal causation, especially when the withdrawal is contrary to the patient's wishes.[124] Legal causality in this area is based on policy considerations: whether consent has been given, whether treatment is futile,[125] and who is withdrawing the treatment. Nonetheless, voluntary euthanasia and assisted suicide do involve the administration of substances that undoubtedly cause death. Additionally, it can be argued that the act of giving a lethal substance to a patient invokes different feelings on behalf of the facilitator.[126]

Intent can also serve to differentiate other end-of-life decisions from voluntary euthanasia and assisted suicide; that is, with regard to the latter procedures, the primary intent of the facilitator is to kill.[127] In *Rodriguez*, Justice Sopinka reiterated that such distinctions form the basis of Canadian criminal law.[128] However, other end-of-life decisions also involve subjective foresight of death, and a person should not simply avoid responsibility by turning one's attention to one effect as opposed to another.[129]

Do the above distinctions serve to isolate voluntary euthanasia and assisted suicide from other end-of-life decisions and as a result, justify prohibition? The matter is further obscured when one considers common medical practice regarding the withdrawal of life-sustaining treatment in Canada. In a case involving the withdrawal of a respirator, the Quebec Superior Court permitted the physician to ask the hospital for any "necessary assistance" in such circumstances "so that everything can take place in a manner respecting the dignity of the plaintiff."[130] In a medical disciplinary hearing in Ontario in 1995, the committee heard testimony from three expert witnesses:

> They testified that, once the decision is made to withdraw life-support by removing the intratracheal tube, it is the attending physician's duty to do everything necessary to keep the patient comfortable and prevent suffering. Morphine is the drug of choice and should be given in doses to relieve feelings of suffocation and anxiety that would otherwise occur … the physician should err on the side of giving too much rather than not enough, to ensure that this goal is reached … whether morphine administration hastens death while relieving suffering, in a situation where death is imminent and inevitable, is immaterial.[131]

The contrast between killing and letting die is far from being crystal clear. All of the aforementioned end-of-life decisions involve the inevitable death of the patient and the facilitator's subjective foresight of that outcome. Moreover, many of the distinctions are circumstantially dependent. For example, withdrawing treatment would certainly be classified as a positive act if it were not consensual and involved a malefactor. Additionally, legal causation in the context of withdrawing treatment is contingent upon consent. If a dying patient had the potential to live for quite some time, desired to do so, and a physician withdrew life-sustaining treatment despite the patient's wishes, then surely the underlying disease could not be held out to be the legal cause of death. As well, the feelings invoked on behalf of the facilitator that administers a lethal substance need not be interpreted in a negative manner; facilitators should perceive their actions as providing appropriate care for their patients.

Although it is possible to maintain certain distinctions between voluntary euthanasia or assisted suicide and other end-of-life decisions in some situations, the above discussion supports the contention that the procedures differ in degree and not in kind. Furthermore, such differences are not determinative of whether prohibition is warranted. Justice McLachlin (as she was then), dissenting, in *Rodriguez*, held that if a justification is established, it does not matter whether the assistance to end life is passive (withdrawing treatment) or active (providing the necessary means).[132] It is necessary to look elsewhere in order to decide whether the prohibition of voluntary euthanasia and assisted suicide can be justified.

C. The Sanctity of Life

It is commonly argued that human life is sacred and inalienable.[133] The majority of *Rodriguez* accepted this proposition.[134] Human life is well protected under Canadian law and there is little doubt that its value should be enthusiastically revered. However, the strength of the argument needs to be evaluated. As previously indicated, Canadians are free to terminate their own lives if they so wish. With regard to the killing of others, Justice Sopinka, in *Rodriguez*, asserted that participating in the death of another is inherently "morally and legally wrong."[135] However, Justice McLachlin stated that people are not necessarily criminally sanctioned when their omissions result in another's death. Those under a legal obligation to provide the necessaries of life are not criminally liable when a lawful excuse is established, such as the incapacity to provide or the consent of the person who dies. A person who kills in self-defence is not culpable either. Thus, the legal rule that killing is wrong is not absolute. Culpability is dependent upon the circumstances and whether a valid justification can be made out.[136] As far as morality is concerned, it can be argued that causing a person's death is morally wrong when it is unauthorized, unjustified, and deprives a person of benefits that would otherwise have been afforded. No moral wrong exists when these elements are absent.[137] As a result, the contention that killing is inherently wrong is highly debatable.

The "sanctity of life" argument is further called into question when one considers that Canadians can refuse life-sustaining treatment and have it withdrawn. Doctors can also withhold futile treatment and the administration of palliative care that has the effect of shortening life is medically accepted practice in Canada. Moreover, the argument cannot be viewed in the abstract. Life must be valuable to someone or for something: "[t]he sanctity of life is acknowledged to be of overwhelming value to society when chosen, but its value in the particular case is not so clearly seen when it offers only suffering."[138] The "sanctity of life" argument is by no means devoid of merit, but it does not serve as an adequate justification for the continued prohibition of voluntary euthanasia and assisted suicide.

D. The Right to Die?

There may or may not be a "right" to die in Canada. As it stands, a person can, without fear of criminal punishment, express one's autonomy and end her or his life. There has not been a push for the re-criminalization of suicide in Canada. People also have much control over other end-of-life decisions. Thus, Canadians apparently accept that the notion of autonomy or personal choice extends to self-destructive behaviour.[139] Whether a general "right to die" exists and just what that entails (a positive or negative right) is open to debate. Regardless, it is not necessary to find such a right in order to justify voluntary euthanasia and assisted suicide.

E. The Integrity of the Medical Profession

As mentioned above, the American Medical Association considers assisted suicide to be at odds with the traditional role of the physician as "healer" and the state has an interest in protecting the honour of the medical profession.[140] Additionally, it is argued that allowing physician-assisted suicide "would desensitize doctors to killing, destroy physicians' moral credibility, subvert society's faith in physicians and generally make life more difficult for physicians whether they agree or refuse to assist."[141] However, Justice Stevens, in *Glucksberg*, acknowledged that a physician's refusal to administer medication that renders death dignified and tolerable could contradict the physician's role as healer.[142] The dying patient may view a physician's refusal to hasten death as a rejection, abandonment, or a declaration of inappropriate paternalistic authority. Complying with a patient's request for physician-assisted suicide would not harm the doctor-patient relationship. Moreover, there is already tension between the traditional role of physicians and contemporary reality; doctors engage in practices that shorten life, such as withdrawing or withholding life-sustaining treatment and terminal sedation.[143] The "medical integrity" objection and the concerns above should also apply to these practices.[144] Yet, as previously mentioned, these practices have been accepted in Canada to the extent that there has been a push to recognize the legality of these common medical procedures through legislation.[145] Furthermore, palliative care in Canada has recently been at the forefront of political discussion. The Standing Senate Committee on Social Affairs, Science and Technology, following up on the 1995 Senate report on euthanasia and assisted suicide, concluded, among other things, that: "Each person is entitled to die in relative comfort, as free as possible from physical, emotional, psychosocial, and spiritual distress. Each Canadian is entitled to access skilled, compassionate, and respectful care at the end of life."[146] Consistent with this view, there comes a time in the doctor-patient relationship when the physician's role is no longer curative, but transforms into one that involves comforting.[147] Death is an inevitable part of life and medical care should address the event appropriately. The basic ethical principles espoused by the Canadian Medical Association (CMA) provide for compassionate end-of-life care. The CMA's Code of Ethics does not explicitly mention euthanasia or assisted suicide, but "has traditionally been *interpreted* as opposing these practices."[148] The continued prohibition of voluntary euthanasia and physician-assisted suicide on the grounds that there is a need to protect the medical profession's integrity is not persuasive.

F. Quality Palliative Care Is Not the Solution

It can be argued that adequate palliative care can reduce or eliminate requests for euthanasia and assisted suicide. According to some, the lack of palliative care services underscores the push for assisted suicide in Canada.[149] In some cases, palliative care may inhibit or end one's desire to die. However, this is not true in all cases. For example, Justice Stevens, in *Glucksberg*, referred to sources that assert that such care is not always effective because pain becomes more difficult to treat as death draws near.[150] Additionally, inadequate pain management is not necessarily the prime concern of dying patients. A study of the characteristics of those that died under Oregon's *DDA* in 1998 and 1999 revealed that patients were very much concerned about end-of-life issues unrelated to pain.[151] Furthermore, a Canadian study of 126 patients indicated that they were most anxious about the following: avoiding inappropriate prolongation of dying (61.1 per cent), strengthening relationships with loved ones (38.9 per cent), achieving a sense of control (38.1 per cent), relieving burden (38.1 per cent), receiving adequate symptom and pain management (22.2 per cent).[152]

There is often more behind a request for death than the alleviation of pain. Admittedly, palliative care encompasses more than just pain control and can be of assistance in other areas that might influence an end-of-life decision. But this does not directly challenge the permissibility of voluntary euthanasia or assisted suicide; these practices are independently justifiable. Palliative care, and voluntary euthanasia and assisted suicide, can be conceptualized as legitimate alternatives on the health care continuum, not as dichotomies.[153] Comprehensive care for the dying should be adopted in Canada.

G. Autonomy and Beneficence

The right to refuse life-sustaining treatment or have it withdrawn in Canada is premised on the notion of autonomy. The Standing Senate Committee on Social Affairs, Science and Technology stated that, in general, the principles of autonomy, beneficence, and justice guide ethical discussions concerning end-of-life care:

> Autonomy generally encompasses self-determination, personal liberty and freedom of choice. Justice refers to the overall question of fairness, of equitable distribution of scarce resources. Beneficence seeks to ensure that any intervention is for the benefit of the patient and not for experimental, economic, or other reasons. The trend is away from an ethic of prolonging life at all costs and toward an ethic that emphasizes the quality of life and of dying.[154]

The principles of autonomy (explicitly mentioned) and beneficence (implicit in the discussions involving suffering) were extensively examined in the *Rodriguez* decision and, according to the dissent, justified assistance in dying.[155] Additionally, beneficence and autonomy underscore the CMA's code of ethics.[156] These principles are the driving force behind the push for palliative care in Canada and, when taken together, can justify voluntary euthanasia and assisted suicide as well. When people make voluntary and informed decisions that continuing life is not to their benefit, they should be free (with qualification) to seek assistance so that they can end their lives in a compassionate and acceptable manner. However, there are some objections to this assertion.

There is some concern that permitting "death with dignity" will spread the message that disabled life is not worth living.[157] But the same criticism can be levelled against the practice of withdrawing and withholding of life-sustaining treatment, yet the total devaluation of disabled lives has not resulted. Most severely disabled persons do not consider themselves as being "better off dead." However, commitment to autonomy demands that such persons' wishes be respected whether they decide to live or reject treatment.[158] If a disabled person desires death, is not receiving life-sustaining treatment, and is unable to take his/her own life, then the principles of autonomy and beneficence support permitting voluntary euthanasia or assisted suicide in such a case. A fear of what might occur in the future should not override individual choices to end suffering in the present.

Various attempts have also been made to undermine the notion that autonomous decision-making is possible in the "terminally ill" context. First, there is concern that treatable depression is related to the desire to die in terminally ill patients and that proper treatment can reverse such feelings.[159] Recognizing and treating endogenous depression is an ongoing problem for medical practitioners.[160] Although depression is not uniformly present in dying patients, it has been argued that severe depression casts serious doubt on whether an individual's request is well-reasoned, because depression "is an intrinsic part of the disease."[161] However, not all depressive conditions affect the decision-making process.[162] As a result, autonomy is not necessarily undermined.

Second, it has been contended that some psychologists are not qualified to conduct mental competency assessments, that the degree of confidence based on single evaluations is very low, and that these limitations may adversely affect free choice.[163] Nonetheless, such assessments are made daily, in a variety of important contexts, and their validity is not seriously questioned. Furthermore, this objection, as well as the first, does not directly challenge the notion of autonomous decisionmaking. Rather, it highlights the need for legislative safeguarding to reasonably ensure that autonomous decisionmaking will be realized.[164]

Third, it has been argued that autonomous decisionmaking that is "fully informed, non-coerced ... in rational furtherance of one's own goals, is an ideal which is never fully realized."[165] For this reason, even voluntary euthanasia should not be permitted. The stylized argument for this conclusion is as follows: decisions are always subject to external influences. Due to the extreme circumstances, the autonomy of an incurably or terminally ill patient is seriously compromised. In such cases, the person desiring death may be making a terrible mistake. There are no satisfactory means of identifying these cases. Therefore, an absolute prohibition on assisted suicide is justified in order to prevent disregarding a person's "authentic autonomy."[166] Implicit in the argument is the premise that terminally ill individuals who exercise a reasonable degree of autonomy do not generally request death. Thus, a request is evidence of a lack of autonomy and assistance should not be given. The argument also requires one to accept that totally autonomous decisions cannot be made, especially by the terminally ill. As a result, any argument from autonomy that advocates voluntary euthanasia or assisted suicide for the terminally ill automatically fails. However, decisions are always made within a context and the fact that they are made in difficult circumstances does not render them non-autonomous. The dismissal of terminally ill patients' autonomous decisionmaking ability in the above manner is paternalistic. Moreover, autonomous capacity is not generally an issue in the context of refusing or withdrawing life-sustaining treatment and it should not be questioned simply because a person is asking for assistance in dying. Furthermore and again, this argument emphasizes the need for caution in drafting legislation that protects against abuse and does little to undermine the notion of autonomy. With the above discussion in mind, the combined principles of autonomy and beneficence provide the foundation necessary to support the permissibility of voluntary euthanasia and assisted suicide in Canada.

H. Slippery Slopes

By far, the most common argument used to oppose voluntary euthanasia and assisted suicide takes the form of the slippery slope. Slippery slope arguments usually entail that an alleged action, although acceptable in the circumstances, would set off a disastrous set of subsequent events. Thus, the initial step should not be taken.[167] These types of arguments present analytical difficulties in the voluntary euthanasia and assisted suicide context because: "[t]hey involve essentially factual claims being made about … probable or possible consequences … [b]oth the prediction and its denial are speculative—not satisfactorily provable or refutable."[168] Nevertheless, the arguments cannot be taken lightly due to the seriousness of the allegations.

It has been argued that permitting voluntary euthanasia and assisted suicide could lead to an increase in the prevalence of the practices.[169] This may or may not be the case. After all, most people cherish life and fight to survive. Increased medical technology and better end-of-life care should also help prevent the practices from reaching epidemic proportions. But even if the incidents of voluntary euthanasia and assisted suicide were to increase, that would not necessarily be an unfavourable outcome. The practice of voluntary euthanasia may be more humane than other permissible end-of-life procedures as it can lead to less suffering.[170]

Permitting voluntary euthanasia and assisted suicide could also lead to abuses.[171] For example, the vulnerable could be coerced into asking for the procedures. The Ontario Law Reform Commission employed this reasoning to justify assisted suicide but not voluntary euthanasia. The Commission stated that active participation negates much of the potential for abuse that could occur when someone else administers a lethal substance.[172] This argument is unconvincing. It is not difficult to imagine a situation where a person has been persuaded to ask for assisted suicide. More importantly, the same criticism can be levelled against the practices of withholding, withdrawing, and refusing life-sustaining treatment.[173] It can be argued that these practices are even more susceptible to abuse in light of advance directive legislation and proxy decisionmaking ability, yet, there has not been a push to prohibit these practices. The assertion that abuses, such as the coercion of the vulnerable, might occur if voluntary euthanasia and assisted suicide are permitted stresses the need for enacting stringent legislative safeguards, not maintaining a blanket prohibition.

It has additionally been alleged that permitting the practices could lead to non-voluntary and involuntary euthanasia.[174] These latter forms of euthanasia categorically differ from voluntary euthanasia in that they do not involve voluntariness and explicit requests. Thus, in the logical sense, the argument fails. Nonetheless, the argument is continually made and those opposed to voluntary euthanasia and assisted suicide point to the situation in the Netherlands for evidence that this slide and other abuses have occurred in reality.[175] This claim greatly fortifies the position of those opposed to lifting the prohibition and is arguably the most significant obstacle that proponents of change have to face.

I. Summary and Conclusion

The previous discussion lends support to the following propositions. First, there is a general sentiment that the laws prohibiting voluntary euthanasia and assisted suicide in Canada are in need of change. Second, while it is possible to maintain some distinctions between voluntary euthanasia or assisted suicide and other end-of-life practices, the procedures differ in degree and not in kind. Third, the "sanctity of life" is not an absolute value. Patients and physicians currently have much control over end-of-life matters in Canada. As a result, the argument that human life is inviolable and inalienable fails to justify the continued prohibition of voluntary euthanasia and assisted suicide. Fourth, the practices do not pose a threat to the medical profession's integrity. Fifth, comprehensive care for the dying should include not only palliative care, but also voluntary euthanasia and assisted suicide. Sixth, the twin principles of autonomy and beneficence provide the foundation for permitting the procedures in Canada. Finally, although slippery slope arguments can generally be dismissed, they do raise some legitimate concerns. If allowing voluntary euthanasia and assisted suicide inevitably leads to non-voluntary or involuntary euthanasia and/or widespread abuse, then continued prohibition is warranted; the evidence must be examined.

VI. THE NORMATIVE QUESTION MARK: THE SLIPPERY SLOPE

Allegations that voluntary euthanasia and assisted suicide lead to non-voluntary and involuntary euthanasia as well as other abuses abound. The goings-on in the Netherlands are used to substantiate such claims. The validity of these claims will be examined below. The extent to which voluntary euthanasia and assisted suicide are being practiced, and whether similar criticisms can be levelled against the state of affairs in other countries will also be discussed.

A. The Netherlands

Dutch jurisprudence suggests that the situation in the Netherlands is far from being trouble-free.[176] However, the empirical evidence must be examined in order to provide an accurate account of the overall situation. Unfortunately, reliable and valid research in the Netherlands did not exist before 1990.[177] In 1991, the state-authorized Remmelink Commission delivered its national report on euthanasia and other end-of-life decisions.[178] The Commission conducted three separate studies and ensured confidentiality. The "physician interview" (PI) study entailed in-depth interviews with 405 physicians. The "death certificate" (DC) study was based on a stratified sample of 7,000 deaths. The physicians that participated in the PI study answered questionnaires concerning their actions in the subsequent six months; this was referred to as the "prospective" study.[179] A number of medical decisions concerning the end-of-life were examined. With regard to euthanasia, the Commission adopted the definition accepted in the Netherlands: "the purposeful acting to terminate life by a person other than the person concerned upon request of the latter."[180] Thus, only voluntary euthanasia is classified as euthanasia in the Netherlands. Assisted suicide was defined as "the purposeful assisting of the person concerned to terminate life upon request of the latter."[181] Life-terminating acts without the patient's explicit request (LAWER) entailed "acts" such as the administration of drugs (withdrawing treatment not included) and a non-explicit request (no request at all or vague remarks).[182] LAWER includes non-voluntary and involuntary euthanasia as defined in this paper. The results of the PI study were weighted so as to enable extrapolation.[183] In 1995, the PI and DC studies were duplicated.[184] The table on the following page offers a detailed comparison of the studies' findings.[185]

Although a great number of requests for voluntary euthanasia and assisted suicide are made, relatively few are granted. It is generally agreed upon that the best estimates for voluntary euthanasia equalled 1.8 per cent (2,300) and 2.4 per cent (3,200) in 1990 and 1995, respectively. For both years, the agreed upon total for assisted suicide is 0.3 per cent (400). With regard to LAWER, the figure for 1990 is 0.8 per cent (1,000) and 0.7 per cent (900) for 1995.[186] However, commentators[187] rightly point out that opioids given with the intention to end life (not included in the above analysis) should be added to the number of deaths that occurred without an explicit request: 1 per cent (1,300) in 1990; 1.4 per cent (1,900) in 1995. Thus, estimated deaths caused by active physician intervention total 5,000 (3.9 per cent) in 1990 and 6,400 (4.7 per cent) in 1995.

In the 1990 study, 54 per cent of physicians indicated that they had performed voluntary euthanasia or assisted suicide at some time and 34 per cent had not but could conceive of doing so.[188] In 1995, the corresponding figures were 53 per cent and 35 per cent, respectively.[189] In 1990, 54 per cent of the physicians surveyed stated that circumstances exist where a doctor should raise voluntary euthanasia as a possibility with the patient. [190] There is a concern that the voluntariness of a request can be compromised by such a suggestion. [191] In all cases of voluntary euthanasia, assisted suicide, and LAWER in 1990, the doctor initiated the discussion 21 per cent of the time. In voluntary euthanasia and assisted suicide cases only, the doctor initiated the discussion 12 per cent and 15 per cent of the time for 1990 and 1995, respectively.[192] While such instances are infrequent, they occur nonetheless and voluntariness must be questioned in at least some cases.

Reported cases of physician-assisted death increased from 486 in 1990 to 1,466 in 1995. In light of the estimates of voluntary euthanasia and assisted suicide, the notification rate increased from approximately 18 per cent to 41 per cent. Only two cases of physician-assisted death without the explicit request of the patient in 1990 and three cases in 1995 were reported.[193] Thus, while the situation is improving, reporting rates are low and this is extremely troubling.

Table 1 The incidence of euthanasia and assisted suicide in the Netherlands*

Variable		Phys. Interview (PI) Study				Death Cert. (DC) Study			
		1990		1995		1990		1995	
Explicit requests for VE**or AS***		8,900		9,700		no data		no data	
VE:	% of deaths (number)	1.8	(2,300)	2.4	(3,200)	1.7	(2,200)	2.4	(3,200)
PAS****:	% of deaths (number)	0.3	(400)	0.4	(500)	0.2	(300)	0.2	(300)
LAWER:	% of deaths		no data	0.7	(900)	0.8	(1,000)	0.7	(900)

*Percentages are based on total number of deaths in the Netherlands: 128,786 (1990); 135,546 (1995), numbers have been rounded; **VE—voluntary euthanasia; ***AS—assisted suicide; ****PAS—physician-assisted suicide.

According to the PI study in 1990, the patients had good insight into the disease and prognosis in all of the voluntary euthanasia and assisted suicide cases. There were no alternatives 79 per cent of the time. In 17 per cent of the cases, alternatives were available but the patient no longer wanted them. Four per cent of the voluntary euthanasia and assisted suicide cases did not involve an explicit request. Similarly, 6 per cent of the cases did not involve a repeated request. Eighty-four per cent of the physicians consulted with colleagues and only 60 per cent kept written records.[194] The DS study in 1995 revealed that 100 per cent of voluntary euthanasia and assisted suicide cases involved an explicit request; however, 3 per cent of the patients were not competent. Of all voluntary euthanasia and assisted suicide cases, 4 per cent were discussed with no one.[195] A comparison between the most recent reported and unreported cases in 1990 and 1995 indicated that, as far as the satisfaction of the substantive requirements was concerned, no differences existed. However, procedural requirements showed a decrease in cases not discussed with colleagues in 1995 (11 per cent) compared to 1990 (16 per cent). Written reports were also more available in 1995: 81 per cent of the cases as opposed to 60 per cent of the cases in 1990.[196] Another report on the 1990/1995 data indicated that a physician administered some or all of the medication in 91 per cent of the voluntary euthanasia cases, and a nurse or person other than the physician or nurse did so 5 per cent of the time. While 72 per cent of the doctors interviewed remained present until death, a physician was not present at all in 2 per cent of the cases. With regard to assisted suicide, only 52 per cent of the cases involved the continuous presence of a physician and the absentee rate was 10 per cent.[197]

With regard to LAWER, the PI study in 1990 indicated that 27 per cent of the respondents had performed such an act at some time and 32 per cent had never done so but could conceive of doing so.[198] The corresponding figures for 1995 were 23 per cent and 32 per cent, respectively.[199] Of the most recent cases in 1990, patients were totally able to make a decision 14 per cent of the time and there were alternatives in 8 per cent of the cases.[200] In 1995, there was no explicit request but the issue was discussed or a wish was stated in 52 per cent of the cases. In the remaining 48 per cent of the cases, the decision was not discussed and there was no previous wish. Of all cases in 1995, 21 per cent involved competent patients and 5 per cent were discussed with no one.[201] LAWER is of great concern as such cases can be treated as non-voluntary or involuntary euthanasia.[202]

The information above indicates that there are problems in the Netherlands. Many of the substantive and procedural requirements listed in Part IV are not being adhered to. The majority of the cases are not being reported. Additionally, Dutch physicians are participating in non-voluntary and quite possibly, involuntary euthanasia. Given the abundance of data, it is not difficult to understand why the situation in the Netherlands draws so much attention. Since there was no reliable research before 1990, however, it is unclear whether the voluntary euthanasia and assisted suicide rates have substantially increased. Thus, there is no evidence of the presence of a slippery slope.[203] Furthermore, while some abuses are occurring, it is far from certain that the situation is out of control or that the cause of any problems is related to the permissibility of voluntary euthanasia and assisted suicide. Before commentators point their fingers at the Dutch sliding down the slippery slope, these critics might do well to look at the goings-on in their own countries.

B. Australia

Research on end-of-life decisions in Australia is rather plentiful and quite enlightening. In a study of 943 Australian nurses reported in 1993, 218 stated that they had been asked by a doctor to participate in euthanasia, and 85 per cent complied with the request. Additionally, sixteen nurses, without having been approached by a doctor, granted a patient's request for euthanasia. In a survey published in 1994, 52 per cent of the 278 Australian nurses sampled took active measures in order to bring about a patient's death, frequently without a request to do so from the patient or his/her family.[204] Another 1994 report indicated that 47 per cent of the Southern Australian physicians sampled received a request for assisted death or euthanasia at some time and that 19 per cent had participated in the practices.[205] In a 1995 paper delivered at an Australian HIV conference, 18 per cent (forty-one) of the doctors surveyed had participated in assisted suicide. These physicians had received 438 requests. Surprisingly, four people who received assistance were healthy.[206] Evidently, Australian doctors and nurses are participating in acts of euthanasia and assisted suicide, sometimes in extremely dubious circumstances.

In 1996, a study was conducted that largely duplicated the "prospective study" in the Netherlands.[207] Of the 800 physicians that made medical decisions concerning the end of life (MDEL), 3.2 per cent (twenty-six) reported engaging in euthanasia or assisted suicide. Of these, 100 per cent involved an explicit request but 4 per cent did not involve a competent patient. In 12 per cent of the cases, the decision was discussed with no one. With regard to life-terminating acts without the patient's explicit request (LAWER), 6.4 per cent (fifty-one) of physicians reported having done so. Of these, 31 per cent reported that there was no explicit request, no wish expressed, and no discussion of the action with the patient. Moreover, 6 per cent of the physicians engaging in LAWER indicated that the action was neither requested nor discussed with the patient and the patient was competent. Sixteen per cent of the physicians discussed the decision with absolutely no one.[208] The study also estimated the percentage of total deaths due to MDEL in Australia. The results were compared to those of the Netherlands in 1995. The rates of death in Australia during 1995 resulting from acts of euthanasia (1.8 per cent) and physician-assisted suicide (0.1 per cent) were slightly lower than those in the Netherlands (2.4 per cent and 0.2 per cent, respectively). However, the LAWER rate was substantially higher: 3.5 per cent in Australia as compared to 0.7 per cent in the Netherlands.[209] This information indicates that incidents of assisted suicide and voluntary, non-voluntary, and involuntary euthanasia are occurring in Australia. The situation definitely invites "Dutch-like" criticism, especially with regard to LAWER.

C. The United States

Assisted suicide and euthanasia (save perhaps for involuntary euthanasia) are practiced in the United States. Retired pathologist Dr. Jack Kevorkian had no qualms about openly performing dozens of so called "medicides."[210] But much also goes on behind closed doors. In 1995, 53 per cent of 117 doctors working with HIV patients in the San Francisco Bay Area admitted to granting an assisted-suicide request on at least one occasion to a patient suffering from AIDS.[211] The results of a 1996 survey involving 852 critical care nurses showed that 16 per cent had participated in an act of euthanasia or assisted suicide at least once during their careers, 65 per cent doing so three times or less, and 5 per cent doing so twenty or more times.[212] In that same year, over 1,900 American physicians completed surveys on euthanasia and assisted suicide.[213] The results indicated that 18.3 per cent and 11.1 per cent received a request for assisted suicide or a lethal injection, respectively. Of the entire sample, 3.3 per cent had written a prescription conducive to suicide and 4.7 per cent had administered a lethal injection. The patient characteristics of the most recent cases of euthanasia or assisted suicide (eighty-one) showed that assisted suicide cases involved: a patient request (95 per cent), an explicit request (75 per cent), a repeated request (51 per cent), twelve or more years of education (93 per cent), a second opinion (less than 1 per cent), and cancer (70 per cent). Cases of euthanasia involved: a patient request (39 per cent), an explicit request (21 per cent), a repeated request (53 per cent), twelve or more years of education (83 per cent), a second opinion (32 per cent), and cancer (23 per cent).[214]

A study published in 1998 was conducted in order to determine whether American physicians were adhering to the proposed safeguards for euthanasia and physician-assisted suicide.[215] Of the 355 oncologist respondents, 15.8 per cent (fifty-six) admitted to participating in one of the practices. The results of in-depth interviews with thirty-eight of the fifty-six oncologists revealed that 5.3 per cent reported administering lethal injections, 73.7 per cent prescribed medication knowing the patient would commit suicide, and 21.1 per cent engaged in both procedures. Cancers were the most common underlying conditions.[216] In 78.9 per cent of the cases, the patient initiated the request and 63.2 per cent of the time it was repeated. Cases were only discussed with other doctors 39.5 per cent of the time.[217]

A study released in the year 2000 revealed that of the 152 United States oncologists sampled, 48 per cent received requests for euthanasia or assisted suicide. None performed euthanasia, 7 per cent (eleven) engaged in assisted suicide, and 2 per cent (three) ended life without a request. The most frequent diagnosis was cancer, and cases were only discussed with other physicians 8 per cent of the time.[218] The results of a comparative study of those that died under Oregon's *DDA* in 1998 (sixteen) and 1999 (twenty-seven) was also published in 2000.[219] The median age of those assisted was seventy and seventy-one in 1998 and 1999, respectively. High school and college graduates comprised 81 per cent of those aided in 1998 and 92 per cent in 1999. The most common underlying illness was cancer in both years. At the time of request in 1998, 67 per cent were enrolled in a hospice program; the corresponding figure for 1999 was 44 per cent. Immediately before death, 73 per cent (1998) and 78 per cent (1999) of those receiving assistance were enrolled in such programs. All of the persons in 1999 were insured and 6 per cent (one) in 1998 were not.[220]

A number of propositions may be drawn from this information. The notion that vulnerable persons/groups, such as the uneducated, the uninsured, and the disabled (the most common underlying condition being cancer) will end up requesting assisted suicide (in light of the *DDA* research) or euthanasia, is highly questionable. Hospice and palliative care do not necessarily eliminate a person's desire to die. Moreover, assisted suicide, voluntary and non-voluntary euthanasia, and quite probably involuntary euthanasia, are being practiced in America, both within and outside the medical context. Violations of proposed guidelines are also occurring. American critics of the Dutch experience should consider being a little more attentive to their own situation.

D. Canada

Research on voluntary euthanasia and assisted suicide in Canada is quite scarce, but what little does exist is illuminating. A small study in 1992–1993 indicated that respondents from various professional backgrounds participated in the deaths of thirty-four persons with AIDS and one afflicted with cancer.[221] The results of an Alberta survey published in 1993 revealed that, of the 1391 physician respondents, 19 per cent had received at least one request for euthanasia.[222] Of all respondents, 33 per cent stated that they would not report a colleague who had engaged in euthanasia to anyone.[223] Unfortunately, the survey did not ascertain whether doctors had actually participated in the practice. A minor study reported in 1996 revealed that at least eleven persons assisted in twenty-five AIDS-related deaths.[224] Another small study involving Canadian nurses in AIDS care was published in 1998 and indicated that 22.2 per cent (ten) of forty-four respondents received patient requests for voluntary euthanasia. The corresponding figure for assisted suicide was 11.1 per cent (five) of forty-two respondents. Of the total nurses responding (forty-five), 57.8 per cent (twenty-six) stated that physicians perform voluntary euthanasia and assisted suicide and 28.9 per cent (thirteen) stated that nurses do likewise.[225]

Further insight as to the occurrences of euthanasia and assisted suicide in Canada can be attained through an examination of criminal trials and non-criminal hearings. In 1941, an Alberta couple was acquitted of killing their two-year-old son who suffered from cancer; he was asphyxiated with carbon monoxide.[226] In 1991, a physician administered a lethal dose of morphine to two elderly patients and was not criminally charged. In that same year, a nurse gave a lethal injection to a seventy-eight-year-old patient. He was convicted of administering a noxious substance, received three years' probation, a suspended sentence, and was prohibited from ever practicing nursing.[227] In 1992, it was reported that a Montréal doctor administered a lethal injection to an AIDS patient. The matter was not pursued, as the Québec College of Physicians advised against prosecution.[228] In 1993, a doctor was convicted of administering a noxious substance (potassium chloride) to a cancer patient that had been removed from a ventilator. He received a suspended sentence and three years probation.[229] In 1994, Sue Rodriguez apparently died with the help of a physician and to this day, the doctor remains anonymous.[230] In 1993, Robert Latimer was charged with second-degree murder for asphyxiating his daughter with carbon monoxide; she had severe cerebral palsy. Several years later, after a prolonged court battle, Latimer's conviction and sentence were upheld by the Supreme Court of Canada.[231] In 1995, an eighty-one-year-old woman helped her ill husband commit suicide and attempted to take her own life. She pleaded guilty to manslaughter and received eighteen months probation.[232] In 1996, Dr. Nancy Morrison administered potassium chloride to a patient after he had been removed from a respirator. The judge at the preliminary inquiry held that there was insufficient evidence to commit Dr. Morrison to stand trial for first-degree murder. The Crown application to quash the decision was dismissed in 1998.[233] In 1999, the Court of Appeal of Ontario dismissed the appeal of a doctor who pled guilty to two counts of aiding suicide after he prescribed lethal doses of Seconal to two HIV patients who were not suffering from AIDS. The trial judge imposed sentences of incarceration for two years less a day and three years probation to be served concurrently.[234] In July of 2000, the Manitoba Crown stayed charges against Bert Doerkson, eighty-one, for assisting in his cancer-stricken wife's suicide.[235]

The information suggests several things. The courts have dealt with many cases leniently. Little is known about the frequency of voluntary euthanasia and assisted suicide in the medical context and more research is necessary. But the material does verify that incidents of voluntary and non-voluntary euthanasia, and assisted suicide, are occurring in Canada. In light of the more extensive research from other countries, it might well be surmised that involuntary euthanasia within the medical context is being practiced here also.

E. Summary and Conclusion

The situation in the Netherlands is far from perfect. Assisted suicide, voluntary and non-voluntary euthanasia, and quite possibly, involuntary euthanasia are practiced, often in questionable circumstances. Many of the substantive and procedural requirements are also violated. By acknowledging the existence of such practices, the Dutch have invited criticism. Although euthanasia and assisted suicide are prohibited elsewhere, they are practiced nevertheless. Whatever one might think of the Dutch approach, it is speculation to conclude that a slippery slope exists or that the slide is already complete in the Netherlands. Since there is no reliable research in the Netherlands before 1990, the claim that "permissibility" necessarily entails "slippery slopes" cannot be established. The research emerging from Oregon casts further doubt on such a claim. This is not to say that permitting the practices will not lead to problems; the potential is real. It does not follow, however, that adequate safeguards cannot be developed elsewhere because the situation in the Netherlands is problematic. A different approach is necessary.

VII. PRACTICAL MEASURES

Arguably, too much medical and judicial discretion, a *post hoc* reporting procedure, and a lack of legislative input, has given rise to the current state of affairs in the Netherlands. In Canada, Parliament has declined and still refuses to deal with the continued prohibition of voluntary euthanasia and assisted suicide, preferring instead that the courts consider the issue.[236] Canadian and American case law suggests that the topic warrants a political response.[237] Justice Souter, in *Glucksberg*, explained why the matter is best left for legislators: "[n]ot only do they have more flexible mechanisms for factfinding than the Judiciary, but their mechanisms include the power to experiment, moving forward and pulling back as facts emerge within their own jurisdictions."[238] Although the drafting of adequate legislation may be a cumbersome task, it is possible. Foreign schemes, such as the *DDA*,[239] *ROTTI*,[240] and the Dutch requirements are highly instructive. What follows is a proposal of what voluntary euthanasia and assisted suicide legislation in Canada should include.

A. Proposed Legislation

First of all, the title of an Act should attempt to convey what lies at the foundation of the legislation. For example, the "Voluntary and Compassionate Death Act" might appropriately characterize Canadian legislation. The Act would include a preamble to the following effect: Nothing in this Act should be construed so as to permit the practices of non-voluntary or involuntary euthanasia. It would also include a suitable definition section and a residency provision. The Act would permit the practice of both voluntary euthanasia and assisted suicide in the medical context. It can be argued, however, that assisted suicide is preferable for a number of reasons. First, it minimizes the involvement of third parties. Second, persons should not ask others to do what they can do for themselves. Third, assisted suicide decreases the risk of traumatizing another party.[241] Additionally, it increases the patient's involvement and stresses the voluntariness and genuineness of the request. Finally, it might also ease the consciences of those that assist.[242] Nonetheless, given the similarity between voluntary euthanasia and assisted suicide, and the justifiability of each, voluntary euthanasia must also be permitted. Forcing life on those physically unable to complete the act would be cruel since they have, potentially, years of agony to experience as compared to one who is "knocking on death's door."[243] As well, such policy does not adequately respect the principles of autonomy and beneficence. Moreover, if problems are experienced during an assisted suicide, then medical staff might need to intervene.[244] Permitting voluntary euthanasia would also help to insulate the legislation from a constitutional challenge pursuant to section 15 of the *Charter*.[245]

As opposed to the *post hoc* reporting procedures in all of the jurisdictions mentioned above, a system of pre-authorization should be in place.[246] Such a procedure would ensure predictability in the law. Applications would be submitted to a provincial panel for approval.[247] The panel could include permanent and rotating positions for: a medical ethicist; a palliative care specialist; a psychologist; a lawyer; a social worker; a coroner's representative; a specialist with experience relevant to the specific case;[248] a criminologist, sociologist, or other academic with a background in the humanities; a nurse; a patient advocate. Such a panel would be in a better position than a court to evaluate the legitimacy of individual cases.[249] Although the application process would detract from patient autonomy,[250] the procedure strikes an appropriate balance between absolute prohibition and unqualified respect for autonomy.[251] The number of members on a given panel should be no less than five, in order to ensure a balanced appraisal. Majority opinion would be decisive. A national committee could monitor provincial decisions, direct research (integral to such a legislative scheme) and report its findings, and suggest whether adjustments are in order.

A written application for assistance in dying would have to be filed by the patient. Where a patient is physically unable to sign an application, a proxy signor would be allowed to do so. Given the gravity/finality of the practices, restricting eligibility to those eighteen years of age and older would be acceptable.[252] The patient would have to be competent and all applicants would be required to submit to mental status assessments. Since the Act would not permit non-voluntary or involuntary euthanasia, patients would have to be competent immediately before the procedure is initiated. As a consequence, requests cannot be premised on advance directives or on decisions made by proxies. The patient would have to be informed of all the relevant medical facts. The request must be repeated in order to account for any variability involved in the desire to die.[253] There would also be a mandatory waiting period between the making of requests and the performance of the procedures. The patient would have the right to rescind the request at any time, in any manner.

The practices of voluntary euthanasia and assisted suicide would be limited to instances where pain and suffering is reasonably unacceptable to the individual. Reasonable alternatives would also need to be explored. Thus, assessments of suffering and health care alternatives would be based on a mixed subjective/objective model: a balanced approach. With regard to alternative care, the more intrusive the procedure, the more reasonable it would be to refuse it. Ample weight should be given to the principles of autonomy and beneficence at all times. Suffering would need to stem from an irreversible physiologically based condition.[254] A "Schedule of Medical Conditions" would outline the eligible medical conditions and corresponding time limitations within which the procedures could be performed. For example, amyotrophic lateral sclerosis (ALS), AIDS, various types of cancer, and total physical incapacity could have tailored time limitations of six months, one year, or none at all. The medical profession (including nurses), in conjunction with the legal community, would determine these time limits in order to account for all of the medical issues and legal ramifications. Such a schedule would eliminate ambiguities, and provide for flexibility, and ensure that amendments are debatable and occur in the open. In cases of total physical incapacity when death is not imminent, patients would have to consult with a patient advocate. Given the length of life shortening involved, this further requirement would be justified.

An applicant would have to be examined by two physicians that verify the above requirements have been met. The physicians and the psychologist would have to submit independent reports, not simply sign another's assessment. This would guard against abuse and promote accountability. Someone with palliative care experience would have to consult with the patient. A physician would be entitled to introduce the options of voluntary euthanasia and assisted suicide; they would be legitimate alternatives and should be openly discussed. Second opinions and mental assessments would ensure that such suggestions do not unduly affect the decision-making process.

The medical profession would determine the appropriate drugs to be utilized and establish a procedure of acceptable administration. Persons eligible to give assistance would not be limited to physicians. A qualified nurse, in the presence of a physician, could carry out the procedure as long as the established standards of practice are adhered to. This would allow for the maximization of medical personnel autonomy and ensure adequate procedural availability. A physician would be required to remain present until the individual died. The procedure would be performed in front of witnesses in order to provide a check on abuse and error.[255] One of the witnesses would have to be unrelated to the patient and could not stand to gain from the death. The practices would not have to be performed in a medical setting; rather, they could be carried out at the homes of people choosing to die in more comfortable surroundings. No medical professional would be required to perform either procedure. There would be no need to impose new criminal penalties, as the *Code, 1985*[256] provisions would remain in force. However, since the courts tend to treat physicians leniently, minimum three to six month suspensions of medical licences might accompany violations.[257] The Act would also delineate its effect on the construction of contracts, wills, statutes, and annuity and insurance policies.[258]

VIII. CONCLUSION

Autonomy underscores the right of Canadians to have life-sustaining treatment withheld or withdrawn. Together, the principles of autonomy and beneficence propel Canadian palliative care policy, the CMS's Code of Ethics, and informed the *Rodriquez* decision. These principles provide the foundation for justifying voluntary euthanasia and assisted suicide. When people make voluntary and informed decisions that the continuation of life is not to their benefit, they should be free, with qualification, to seek assistance in order to end their lives in a compassionate and acceptable manner. Withdrawing and withholding life-sustaining treatment and administering palliative care that has the effect of shortening life, differ from voluntary euthanasia and assisted suicide only in degree, not in kind. All of these practices can be viewed as legitimate exceptions to the principle of the "sanctity of life."

While slippery slope arguments raise some serious concerns, they can ultimately be dismissed. Admittedly, there are risks with the Dutch model due to the possibility of a slippery slope. However, the other countries discussed have not adequately explored what is transpiring in their own back yards. They are open to many of the same criticisms given that euthanasia and assisted suicide are being practiced in these countries. There is evidence of cause for concern in the Netherlands, but the evidence is insufficient to warrant a blanket prohibition in Canada. Too much medical and judicial discretion, a *post hoc* reporting procedure, and a lack of legislative input have given rise to the Dutch status quo. A different approach, such as the one delineated above, would prevent abuses from occurring and maintain the prohibition of non-voluntary and involuntary euthanasia. The experience in Oregon supports the assertion that similar legislation is feasible. Public opinion strongly supports legislative reform, as does much of the Canadian medical community. Consequently, since legislators are in the best position to deal with these issues, change in the existing law should be accomplished by the government, not the judiciary.

QUESTIONS TO CONSIDER

1. In his article on euthanasia and assisted suicide, Michael Cormack outlines several philosophical positions regarding legalizing euthanasia and assisted suicide, including the "slippery slope" argument. Do you think the model legislation that he proposes contains enough safeguards to ensure that a "slippery slope" would not develop if euthanasia and assisted suicide were legalized in Canada? Why? Why not?

2. Cormack reviews information regarding the Dutch experience, which suggests that there is a significant danger of abuse inherent in legalizing euthanasia. However, he also notes that the Oregon case has not given rise to similar abuse. How would you rate the possibility of abuse? Which experience, i.e., Oregon or the Netherlands, do you think would be replicated in Canada if we were to legalize euthanasia? Why?

3. Do you feel that euthanasia and/or assisted suicide should be legalized in Canada? If no, why do you feel this way? If yes, what safeguards do you feel should be incorporated into the law?

SUGGESTIONS FOR FURTHER READING

Griffiths, J., Weyers, H., & Adams, M. (2008). *Euthanasia and law in Europe*. Portland, OR: Hart.

Patterson, C. (2008). *Assisted suicide and euthanasia: A natural law ethics approach*. Aldershot: Ashgate.

Tiedemann, M., & Valiquet, D. (2008). *Euthanasia and assisted suicide: International experiences*. Parliamentary Information and Research Service, Law and Government Division, revised July 17, 2008. Retrieved February 12, 2009, from http://site.ebrary.com/lib/sfu/docDetail .action?docID=10248688

Young, M. G. (2006). *U.K. social workers' attitudes toward assisted death, policies guiding practice, and transformational collaboration: Holding fast to medio-ethical principles of beneficence, non-malfeasance and social justice*. Unpublished Ph.D. thesis, Special Arrangements, Simon Fraser University, Burnaby, B.C.

NOTES

1. M. Mandel, "Fighting for a Chance to End his Life of Misery Terry Graham Dreams of Death with Dignity, but his Life is the Real Nightmare" *Toronto Sun* (2 April 2000) 5 [hereinafter "Death with Dignity in Toronto"].
2. P. Singer, *Practical Ethics*, 2d ed. (Cambridge: Cambridge University Press, 1993) at 176–81.
3. *Ibid.* at 179.
4. *Ibid.* at 202–13.
5. Special Senate Committee on Euthanasia and Assisted Suicide, *Of Life and Death—Final Report* (Ottawa: Senate of Canada, 1995) at c. 2, online: Government of Canada < http://www.parl.gc.ca/ english/senate/com-e/ euth-e/rep-e;lad-e-htm#ii> (date accessed: 11 May 2001) [hereinafter *Of Life and Death*].
6. This definition is a composite (some elements omitted) of those outlined in: *Ibid.* P.J. van der Maas, J.J.M. van Delden, L. Pijnenborg, "Health Policy Special Issue: Euthanasia and Other Medical Decisions Concerning the End of Life" (1992) 22 Health Pol'y at 23 [hereinafter "Special Issue"].
7. See "Special Issue," *ibid.*
8. *Ibid.*
9. *Criminal Code*, S.C. 1892, c. 29, s. 238 [hereinafter *Code, 1892*].
10. *Criminal Law Amendment Act*, 1972, S.C. 1972, c.13, s. 16.
11. *Supra* note 9, s. 237.
12. *Criminal Code*, R.S.C.1985, c. C-46, s. 241 [hereinafter *Code, 1985*].
13. *Ibid.*
14. *Ibid.* ss. 222, 229, 231, 234–36.
15. Ibid., ss. 231, 235. Ibid. s. 742, as am. by An Act to amend the Criminal Code (sentencing) and other Acts in consequence thereof, S.C.1995, c. 22, s. 6.
16. Ibid., ss. 234, 236.
17. See, for example, ibid., ss. 45 (surgical operations), 215 (duty of persons to provide necessaries), 216 (duty of persons undertaking acts dangerous to life), 217 (duty of persons undertaking acts), 220 (causing death by criminal negli-gence), 221 (causing harm by criminal negligence), 245 (administering noxious thing), 265 (assault), 266 (assault), 267 (assault with a weapon or creating bodily harm), 268 (aggravated assault), 269 (unlawfully causing bodily harm).
18. Ibid., s. 14.
19. Of Life and Death, supra note 5 at c. 4.
20. Personal Directives Act, S.A. 1996, c. P-4.03, Representation Agreement Act, R.S.B.C. 1996, c. 405; Health Care Directives and Consequential Amendments Act, S.M. 1992, c. 33; Advance Health Care Directives Act, S.N. 1995, c. A-4.1; Medical Consent Act, R.S.N.S. 1989, c. 279; Substitute Decisions Act, 1992, S.O. 1992, c. 30; Consent to Treatment and Health Care Directives Act, S.P.E.I. 1996, c. 10; Public Curator Act, S.Q. 1989, c. 54; Civil Code of Quebec, S.Q. 1991, c. 64, ss. 10–34; Health Care Directives and Substitute Health Care Decision Makers Act, S.S. 1997, c. H-0.001; Health Act, S.Y. 1990, c. 36, s. 45, am. by Enduring Powers of Attorney Act, S.Y. 1995, c. 8, ss. 19–20.

21. Mulloy v. Sang, [1935] I.W.W.R. 714 (Alta. C.A.); and Malette v. Shulman (1990), 67 D.L.R. (4th) 321 (Ont. C.A.) [hereinafter Malette].

22. Reibl v. Hughes, [1980] 2 S.C.R. 880; Arndt v. Smith, [1997] 2 S.C.R. 539; Hopp v. Lepp, [1980] 2 S.C.R. 192; and Ciarlariello v. Schacter, [1993] 2 S.C.R. 119 [hereinafter Ciarlariello].

23. Malette, supra note21.

24. Nancy R. v. Hôtel-Dieu de Québec (1992), 86 D.L.R. (4th) 385 (Que. Sup. Ct.) [hereinafter Nancy B.].

25. Ibid.; and Ciarlariello, supra note 22.

26. Rodriguez v. British Columbia (A.G.), [1993] 3 S.C.R. 519 [hereinafter Rodriguez].

27. Ibid.

28. Constitution Act, 1982, being Schedule B to the Canada Act 1982 (U.K.), 1982, c. 11, s. 52 [thereinafter Constitution Act, 1982].

29. Canadian Charter of Rights and Freedoms, Part 1 of Constitution Act, 1982, supra note 28, ss. 7, 12, 15(1) [hereinafter Charter].

30. Rodriguez, supra note 26.

31. Ibid. at 578–79, Lamer C.J.C., 630–31, Cory J.

32. Ibid. at 624.

33. Law Reform Commission of Canada, *Euthanasia, Aiding Suicide and Cessation of Treatment* (Working Paper 28) (Ottawa: Law Reform Commission of Canada, 1982); and Law Reform Commission of Canada, *Report on Euthanasia, Aiding Suicide and Cessation of Treatment* (Report 20) (Ottawa: Law Reform Commission of Canada, 1983) [hereinafter *Euthanasia, 1983*].

34. *Euthanasia, 1983, ibid.* at 27–28.

35. Law Reform Commission of Canada, *Report on Recodifying Criminal Law* (Report 31, Revised and Enlarged Edition of Report 30) (Ottawa: Law Reform Commission of Canada, 1987) at 58–61.

36. Bill C-261, *An Act to Legalize the Administration of Euthanasia Under Certain Conditions to Persons Who Request It and Who Are Suffering from an Irremediable Condition and Respecting the Withholding and Cessation of Treatment and to Amend the Criminal Code*, 3rd Sess., 34th Parl., 1991, (1st reading 19 June 1991).

37. *Of Life and Death, supra* note 5 at "Appendix D: Chronology of Major Canadian Developments and Events," online: Government of Canada http://www.parl.gc.ca/35/2/parlbus/chambus/senate/com-e/euth-e/rep-e/lad-a2-e.htm#d> (date accessed: 14 May 2001).

38. M. Otlowski, *Voluntary Euthanasia and the Common Law* (Toronto: Clarendon Press, 1997) at 380–81.

39. Bill C-215, *An Act to Amend the Criminal Code*, 1st Sess., 35th Parl., 1994, (1st reading 16 February 1994); and *Of Life and Death, supra* note 5 at "Appendix E: Legislative Proposals Previously Introduced in Parliament," online: 'Government of Canada < http://www.parl.gc.ca/35/2/parlbus/chambus/senate/com-e/euth-e/rep-e/lad-a2-e.htm#e> (date accessed: 14 May 2001).

40. *Of Life and Death, ibid.* at c. 7

41. *Ibid.* at c. 8.

42. J.M. Gilmour et al., Ontario Law Reform Commission, *Study Paper on Assisted Suicide, Euthanasia and Foregoing Treatment* (Toronto: Ontario Law Reform Commission, 1997) at 261.

43. Bill C-304, *Act to Amend the Criminal Code (Aiding Suicide)*, Sess., 35th Parl., 1996, (1st reading on 12 June 1996 and debated at second reading and dropped from the Order Paper on 6 March 1997).

44. Bill S-2, *Act to Facilitate the Making of Legitimate Medical Decisions Regarding Life-sustaining Treatments and the Controlling of Pain*, 2d Sess., 36th Parl., 1999 (1st reading on 13 October 1999, referred to the Standing Committee on Legal and Constitutional Affairs on 23 February 2000 and died on the Order Paper on 22 October 2000) [hereinafter Bill S-2].

45. British Columbia Ministry of Attorney General, "British Columbia Guidelines on Active Euthanasia and Assisted Suicide" *Press Release* (4 November 1993), online: QL (LNHE).

46. Canadian Medical Association, "Euthanasia and Assisted Suicide (Update 1998)" (Canada: Canadian Medical Association, 1998), online: Canadian Medical Association < http://www.cma.ca/inside/policybase/1998/06-19f.htm> (date accessed: 11 May 2001).

47. Otlowski, *supra* note 38 at 315.

48. M.J. Verhoef & T.D. Kinsella, "Alberta Euthanasia Survey: 3-Year Follow-up" (1996) 155 Can. Med. Ass'n. J. 885 at 888.

49. T.D. Kinsella & M.J. Verhoef, "Determinants of Canadian Physicians' Opinions About Legalized Physician-Assisted Suicide: A National Survey" (1999) 32 Annals, Royal College of Physicians and Surgeons of Canada 211 at 213–14.

50. Otlowski, *supra* note 38 at 261–62.

51. *Ibid.* at 262. In response to the same question, 75 per cent answered yes, 17 per cent no, and 8 per cent undecided in 1995.

52. Angus Reid Group, "Canadians' Views on Euthanasia" (Ipsos-Reid, 1997), online: Angus Reid Group < http://www.angusreid.com/media/content/displaypr.cfm?id_to_view=878 > (date accessed: 11 May 2001).

53. *Ibid.*

54. P.S. Florencio & R. H. Keller, "End-of-Life Decision Making Rethinking the Principles of Fundamental Justice in the Context of Emerging Empirical Data" (1999) 7 Health L.J. 233 at 239 [hereinafter "Fundamental Justice"]; J.I. Fleming, "Death, Dying and Euthanasia: Australia Versus The Northern Territory" (2000) 15 Issues in Law and Medicine 291 [hereinafter Fleming]; B. Kitchener & A.F. Jorm, "Conditions Required for a Law on Active Voluntary Euthanasia: A Survey of Nurses' Opinions in the Australian Capital Territory" (1999) at 25 Journal of Medical Ethics 25 [hereinafter "Conditions Required"].

55. See, for instance, "Fundamental Justice," *ibid.*; and Fleming, *ibid.*

56. See, for instance, Fleming, *ibid.*; and "Conditions Required," *supra* note 54.

57. R. S. Magnusson, "The Sanctity of Life and the Right to Die: Social and Jurisprudential Aspects of the Euthanasia Debate in Australia and the United States" (1997) 6 Pac. Rim L & Pol'y J. 1 at 59, online: WL (PACRLPJ); "Conditions Required," *ibid.*

58. *Wake v. Northern Territory of Australia* (1996), 109 N.T.R. 1 (S.C.).

59. *Rights of the Terminally Ill Act 1995* (N.T.) [hereinafter *ROTTI*].

60. "Fundamental Justice," *supra* note 54 at 240.

61. *Euthanasia Laws Act, 1997* No. 17 of 1997, online: Australian Legal Information Institute < http://www.austlii. edu.au/cgi-bin/disp.pl/au/legis/cth/consol%5fact/ela1997161/sch1.html?query=%7e+euthanasia+law+ act+ 1997> (date accessed: 11 May 2001).

62. "Fundamental Justice," *supra* note 54 at 251; and S.I. Fraser & J.W. Walters, "Death—Whose Decision? Euthanasia and the Terminally Ill" (2000) 26 Journal of Medical Ethics 121 at 122 [hereinafter "Whose Decision"].

63. "Whose Decision," *ibid.*

64. *ROTTI, supra* note 59 at ss. 3–12, 14.

65. *Ibid.*, s. 7(1)(o).

66. Otlowski, *supra* note 38 at 483–84.

67. *Ibid.* at 318.

68. "Conditions Required," *supra* note 54 at 26.

69. The question asked was: "If a hopelessly ill patient, in great pain with absolutely no chance of recovering, asks for a lethal dose, so as not to wake again, should a doctor be allowed to give a lethal dose, or not?": Otlowski, *supra* note 38 at 263, n. 10.

70. Ibid.

71. Cruzan v. Director, Missouri Department of Health, 497 U.S. 261 (1990).

72. Ibid.; and Washington v. Glucksberg, 521 U.S. 702 (1997) [hereinafter Glucksberg].

73. Compassion in Dying v. State of Washington, 79 F. 3d 790 (9th Cir. 1996) (en banc); and Quill Vacco, 80 F. 3d 716 (2d Cir. 1996).

74. Glucksberg, supra note 72.

75. A. Meisel & K.L. Cerminara, The Right to Die, 2001 Cumulative Supplement to the 2d ed. (Toronto: Aspen Law & Business, 2001) at 434; and Md. Ann. Code art. 27, §416 (2001). Assisted suicide is both prohibited via statute and is considered a common law crime in the states of Maryland, Nevada, and South Carolina.

76. Of Life and Death, supra note 5 at "Appendix P: Assisted Suicide and Euthanasia in Foreign Jurisdictions," online: http://www.parl.gc.ca/35/2/parlbus/chambus/senate/com-e/euth-e/rep-e/lad-a3-e.htm#p (date accessed: 14 May 2001); "Fundamental Justice," supra note 54 at 239.

77. Death with Dignity Act, Ore. Stat. §127.800–127.897 (1994), online: Oregon Health Division <http://www.ohd.hr.state.or.us/chs/pas/ors.htm> (date accessed: 16 May 2001) [hereinafter DDA].

78. Oregon Health Division, "Oregon's Death with Dignity Act" (1994), online: Oregon Health Division <http://www.ohd.hr.state.or.us/chs/pas/pas.htm> (date accessed: 16 May 2001).

79. Ibid.

80. DDA, supra note 77, §127.880, s. 3.14.

81. A.D. Sullivan, K. Hedberg & D.W. Fleming, "Legalized Physician-Assisted Suicide in Oregon—The Second Year" (2000) 342 New Eng. J. Med. 598 at 598 [hereinafter "Suicide in Oregon"].

82. Otlowski, *supra* note 38 at 305.

83. *Glucksberg, supra* note 72 at 750–51.

84. Otlowski, *supra* note 38 at 305.
85. *Glucksberg, supra* note 72 at 731.
86. D.E. Meier *et al.*, "A National Survey of Physician-Assisted Suicide and Euthanasia in the United States" (1998) 338 New Eng. J. Med 1193 at 1195.
87. *Ibid.*
88. L. Ganzini *et al.*, "Physicians' Experiences with the Oregon Death with Dignity Act" (2000) 342 New Eng. J. Med. 557 at 559.
89. Voluntary Euthanasia Society, "USA," online: Voluntary Euthanasia Society <http://www.ves.org.uk/D/ FS_USA.html> (date accessed: 11 May 2001).
90. Voluntary Euthanasia Society, "Public Opinion," online: Voluntary Euthanasia Society <www.dignityindying.org.uk> (date accessed: 11 May 2001).
91. "Whose Decision," *supra* note 62 at 122.
92. *The American Series of Foreign Penal Codes: the Dutch Penal Code,* trans. L. Rayar & S. Wadsworth, intro. G. van den Heuvel & H. Lensing (Littleton, Colo.: Rothman, 1997), Art. 289, 287, 294 [hereinafter *Penal Code*].
93. *Ibid.* Art. 287, 289, 293, 294.
94. *Ibid.* Art. 293.
95. *Ibid.* Art. 294. For a more detailed comparison of the law in Canada and the Netherlands, see: B. Sneiderman & Marja Verhoef, "Patent Autonomy and the Defence of Medical Necessity: Five Dutch Euthanasia Cases" (1996) 34 Alta. L. Rev. 374 [hereinafter "Patient Autonomy"].
96. *Penal Code, ibid.*, Art. 40.
97. For an in-depth look into the development of euthanasia and assisted suicide policy in the Netherlands via jurisprudence and the recommendations of the Committee of the Royal Dutch Medical Association, see "Patient Autonomy," *supra* note 95 at 385–407; J. Griffiths, A. Bood & H. Weyers, *Euthanasia and Law in the Netherlands* (Amsterdam: Amsterdam University Press, 1998) at 83–4, 118–27, 341–51 [hereinafter *Euthanasia and Law*].
98. *Euthanasia and Law, ibid.* at 97, 172–74; and "Patient Autonomy," *ibid.* at 393–96, 407–14.
99. *Euthanasia and Law, ibid.* at 79–80.
100. *Ibid.* at 100–106.
101. Minister of Justice of The Netherlands, "Bill for 'Review of Cases of Termination of Life on Request and Assistance with Suicide' Sent to the Lower House of Parliament" (1999), online: Department of Justice < http://www.minjust.nl:8080/a_BELEID/fact/euthanasia.htm > (date accessed: 15 May 2001) [hereinafter "Review of Cases"].
102. P.J. van der Maas, L. Pijnenborg & J.J.M. van Delden, "Changes in Dutch Opinions on Active Euthanasia, 1966 Through 1991" (1995) 273 J. Am. Med. Ass'n 1411 at 1413 [hereinafter "Changes in Dutch Opinions"]. It is assumed that the totals in 1991 are rounded since the total exceeds 100 per cent.
103. R. Janssen, "Government Supports Euthanasia Law" (1999) 390 Europe 41.
104. D.J. Hessing, J.R. Blad & R. Pieterman, "Practical Reasons and Reasonable Practice: The Case of Euthanasia in The Netherlands" (1996) J. Soc. Issues 149 at 163–064 [hereinafter "Practical Reasons"]. The Liberals replied 95.4 per cent yes, 3.8 per cent don't know, and 0.8 per cent no. The corresponding data for the Social-Democrats was 86 per cent, 10.3 per cent and 3.7 per cent. The Christian-Democrat response was 66.3 per cent, 16.7 per cent and 17.1 percent, respectively.
105. *Euthanasia and Law, supra* note 97 at 85.
106. "Practical Reasons," *supra* note 104 at 162.
107. "Review of Cases," *supra* note 101.
108. The vote was 104–40. "Legalizing Euthanasia in the Netherlands" *Maclean's* (11 December 2000), online: LEXIS-NEXIS (news, 90 DAYS); and Minister of Justice of The Netherlands, "Review of Cases of Termination of Life On Request and Assistance with Suicide: Bill Passed in Parliament" (2000), online: Department of Justice <http://www.minjust.nl:8080/c_actual/persber/pb0668.htm> (date accessed: 28 May 2001) [hereinafter "Bill Passed"].
109. *Ibid;* and "Review of Cases," *supra* note 101.
110. "Special Issue," *supra* note 6 at 103. An additional 20 per cent thought voluntary euthanasia should remain punishable in principle but not when the rules of due care were adhered to. Seven per cent opined that voluntary euthanasia was never punishable. One per cent thought it should always be punished.
111. "Review of Cases," *supra* note 101; and "Bill Passed," *supra* note 108.
112. "Review of Cases," *ibid.*
113. Janssen, *supra* note 103.

114. The vote was 46–28: Minister of Justice of The Netherlands, "Bill for Testing Requests for Euthanasia and Help with Suicide Passed by Dutch Parliament" (2001), online: Department of Justice <http://www.mini-just.nl:8080/c_actual/persber/pb0715.htm> (date accessed: 28 May 2001).

115. *Rodriguez, supra* note 26.

116. *Ibid.* at 601–608, 612–15.

117. E.W. Keyserlingk, "Assisted Suicide, Causality and the Supreme Court of Canada (Case Comment)" (1994) 39 McGill L.J. 708 at 715.

118. "Fundamental Justice," *supra* note 54 at 250–51.

119. *Ibid.*

120. See, for example, the provisions pertaining to fundamental freedoms, equality rights, and minority language educational rights in *Charter, supra* note 29, ss. 2, 15, 23.

121. B. Sneiderman, "The Case of Nancy B: A Criminal Law and Social Policy Perspective" (1993) 1 Health L.J. 25 at 28–29 [hereinafter "The Case of Nancy B"].

122. *Airdale N.H.S. Trust v. Bland*, [1993] A.C. 789 at 881–82 [hereinafter *Bland*]. Another case considered and distinguished *Bland* on the grounds that an invasive surgical procedure to separate conjoined twins could not accurately be classified as an omission: *Re A (children) (conjoined twins: surgical separation)*, [2000] 4 All E.R. 961 (C.A.)

123. See, for example, *Nancy B, supra* note 24; and N. Cantor & G.C. Thomas III, "The Legal Bounds of Physician Conduct Hastening Death" (2000) 48 Buff. L. Rev. 83 at 153 [hereinafter "Legal Bounds"].

124. A. Fish & P.A. Singer, "Nancy B: The Criminal Code and Decisions to Forgo Life-Sustaining Treatment" (1992) 147 Can. Med. Ass'n. J. 637 at 639.

125. Keyserlingk, *supra* note 117 at 712.

126. M.A. Somerville, "'Death Talk' in Canada: The *Rodriguez* Case (Case Comment)" (1994) 39 McGill L.J. 602 at 612–13.

127. *Ibid.*

128. *Rodriguez, supra* note 26 at 607.

129. Singer, *supra* note 2 at 209–10.

130. *Nancy B., supra* note 24 at 395.

131. *Re de la Rocha*, [1995] O.C.P.S.D. No. 6 at para. 29, online: QL (OCPS) [hereinafter *de la Roche*].

132. *Rodriguez, supra* note 26 at 624.

133. Otlowski, *supra* note 38 at 21.

134. *Rodriguez, supra* note 26 at 595–96.

135. *Ibid.* at 601.

136. *Ibid.* at 623–24.

137. T.L. Beauchamp, "The Medical Ethics of Physician-Assisted Suicide" (1999) 25 J. Med. Ethics 437 at 438.

138. G. Du Val, "Assisted Suicide and the Notion of Autonomy" (1995) 27 Ottawa L. Rev. 1 at 13.

139. *Ibid.* at 12.

140. *Glucksberg, supra* note 72 at 731, 748–94.

141. *Du Val, supra* note 138 at 16.

142. *Glucksberg, supra* note 72 at 748–49.

143. *Ibid.*

144. *Du Val, supra* note 138 at 16.

145. Bill S-2, *supra* note 44.

146. Standing Senate Committee on Social Affairs, Science and Technology, *Quality End-of-Life Care: The Right of Every Canadian* (2000) at "The Subcommittee's Conclusions," online: Government of Canada <http://www.parl.gc.ca/36/2/parlbus/commbus/senate/com-e/upda-e/rep-e/repfinjun00-e.htm> (date accessed: 16 May 2001) [hereinafter *End-of-Life Care*].

147. N. Testa, "Sentenced to Life? An Analysis of the United States Supreme Court's Decision in *Washington v. Glucksberg*" (1998) 22 Nova L. Rev. 821 at 850.

148. Canadian Medical Association, "Euthanasia and Assisted Suicide (update 1998)" (1998), online: Canadian Medical Association <http://www.cma.ca/inside/policybase/1998/06-19f.htm> (date accessed: 16 May 2001) [hereinafter "Euthanasia and Assisted Suicide"] [emphasis added].

149. CBC Staff, "Senate Releases Report on Quality of Care for Dying" CBC News (7 June 2000), online: CBC News <http://www.cbc.ca/cgi-bin/templates/view.cgi?/news/2000/06/05/palliative00605> (date accessed: 16 May 2001).

150. *Glucksberg, supra* note 72 at 747–48.

151. "Suicide in Oregon," *supra* note 81 at 603: While the families of nineteen patients indicated that physical suf-fering was quite a concern to those dying (53 per cent), the physicians of all forty-three patients identified the following concerns: burden on family, friends, or other care-givers (21 per cent); loss of autonomy (79 per cent); inability to participate in enjoyable activities (77 per cent); losing control over bodily functions (58 per cent); inadequate pain control (21 per cent).

152. P.A. Singer, D.K. Martin & M. Kelner, "Quality End-of-Life Care: Patients' Perspectives" (1999) 281 J. Amer. Med. Ass'n 163 at 165.

153. M.G. Young & R.D. Ogden, "The Role of Nurses in AIDS Care Regarding Voluntary Euthanasia and Assisted Suicide: A Call for Further Dialogue" (2000) 31 J. Advanced Nursing 513 at 517.

154. *End-of-Life Care, supra* note 146 at Part I.

155. *Rodriguez, supra* note 26.

156. "Euthanasia and Assisted Suicide," *supra* note 148.

157. C. Mwaria, "Physician-Assisted Suicide: An Anthropological Perspective" (1997) 24 Fordham Urb. L.J. 859 at 864–85, online: WL (FDMULJ).

158. "The Case of Nancy B," *supra* note 121 at 37–38.

159. J. Belian, "Deference to Doctors in Dutch Euthanasia Law" (1996) 10 Emory Int'l L. Rev. 255 at 285, online: WL (EMORYILR); and H. Hendin, "Seduced by Death: Doctors, Patients, and the Dutch Cure" (1994) 10 Issues L. Med. 123 at 164, online: WL (ISSULM) [hereinafter "Seduced by Death"].

160. P. Baume, "Voluntary Euthanasia: Responses of Medical Practitioners in NSW and the Act to Six Open-Ended Questions" (1998) 22 Austl. N.Z. J. Pub. Health 269, online: Geerstein Science Information Centre at the University of Toronto, e-journals (date accessed: 24 May 2001).

161. D.K. Gittelman, "Euthanasia and Physician-Assisted Suicide" (1999) 92 S. Med. J. 369 at 371.

162. M.A. Drickamer, M.A. Lee & L. Ganzini, "Practical Issues in Physician-Assisted Suicide" (1997) 126 Annals of Internal Medicine 146 at 147.

163. M. Larkin, "Psychologists Grapple with Patient Requests to Hasten Death" (1999) 353 *Lancet* 2133.

164. Singer, *supra* note 2 at 196–97.

165. Du Val, *supra* note 138 at 20.

166. *Ibid.* at 20–22, 29, 30–31.

167. See, for example, T. Govier, *A Practical Study of Argument*, 2nd ed. (Belmont, Calif.: Wadsworth, 1988) at 388.

168. Du Val, supra note 138 at 15.

169. *Rodriguez, supra* note 26 at 581–601; "Fundamental Justice," *supra* note 54 at 251–52.

170. J. Rachels, "Active and Passive Euthanasia" in M. Velasquez & C. Rostankowski, eds., *Ethics: Theory and Practice* (Englewood Cliffs, N.J.: Prentice-Hall, 1985) 285 at 286.

171. *Rodriguez, supra* note 26 at 581–601; "Fundamental Justice," *supra* note 54 at 251–52.

172. Gilmour, *supra* note 42 at 258.

173. D. Gorman, "Active and Passive Euthanasia: The Cases of Drs. Claudio Alberto de la Rocha and Nancy Morrison" (1999) 160 Can. Med. Ass'n J. 857 at 860.

174. J. Keown, "Euthanasia in The Netherlands: Sliding Down the Slippery Slope?" (1995) 9 Notre Dame J.L. Ethics & Pub. Pol'y 407, online: WL (NTDJLEPP): "Euthanasia and Assisted Suicide," *supra* note 148; and *Rodriguez, supra* note 26 at 581–601.

175. See, for example, Keown, *ibid.* at 407–48; *Rodriguez, supra* note 26 at 603–604; *Glucksberg, supra* note 72 at 734–35; and T. Lemmens, "Legalizing Euthanasia" (1995) 2 Can. HIV/AIDS Pol'y Newsl. 7 at 8–9.

176. Assistance was given in questionable circumstances and/or in breach of the established guidelines in the *Kors, Duintjer,* and *Chabot* cases. For a detailed case analysis see: "Patient Autonomy," *supra* note 95 at 393–405. It has been argued that accepting a suicide plea from a patient with psychiatric problems is simply poor psychiatry: "Seduced by Death," *supra* note 159 at 164. Technically, the Dutch have also condoned the practice of non-voluntary euthanasia as the *Prins* and *Kadijk* cases did not involve the request of the infants involved. For more details see: *Euthanasia and the Law, supra* note 97 at 830–48, 341–51; Approximately fifteen severely disabled infants are euthanized every year in the Netherlands: *Euthanasia and the Law, supra* note 97 at 230.

177. *Euthanasia and the Law, ibid.* at 202; "Changes in Dutch Opinions," *supra* note 102.

178. *Euthanasia and the Law, ibid.* at 77–79.

179. "Special Issue," *supra* note 6 at 13; P.J. van der Maas *et al.*, "Euthanasia and Other Medical Decisions Concerning the End of Life" (1991) 338 *Lancet* 669 at 669–70 [hereinafter "Other Medical Decisions"].

180. "Special Issue," *ibid.* at 23.

181. Ibid.

182. L. Pijnenborg et al., "Life-Terminating Acts Without Explicit Request of Patient" (1993) 341 Lancet 1196 at 1197.
183. "Other Medical Decisions," supra note 179 at 670.
184. P.J. van der Maas et al., "Euthanasia, Physician-Assisted Suicide, and Other Medical Practices Involving the End of Life in The Netherlands, 1990–1995" (1996) 335 New Eng. J. Med. 1699 [hereinafter "End of Life in The Netherlands"].
185. Ibid. Based on the figures contained in Table 1.
186. H. Jochemsen J. Keown, "Voluntary Euthanasia Under Control? Further Empirical Evidence from the Netherlands" (1999) 25 J. Med. Ethics 16 at 17 [hereinafter "Under Control"]. See also, Ministerie van Buitenlandse Zaken, "Assistance in Discussing End of Life Issues and Care at the End of Life in the Netherlands" (2001), online: Ministerie van Buitenlandse Zaken <http://www.minbuz.a.nl/english/Content.asp?key=409696&pad=257570,257588,257609,411276> [hereinafter "Euthanasia and Other Decisions"].
187. H. Hendin et al., "Physician-Assisted Suicide and Euthanasia in the Netherlands: Lessons From the Dutch" (1997) 277 J. Am. Med. Ass'n 1720 at 1710. The reader should note that five of the twelve Hendin et al. calculations of the "actual figures" are incorrect. The miscalculations are as follows: in the 1990 questionnaire, 244 for PAS should be 257; in the 1990 interview study, 2445 for euthanasia should be 2446, 380 for PAS should be 386 and 1350 for opioids given with explicit intention should be 1287; in the 1995 interview, 1896 for opioids given with explicit intention should be 1897. In addition, Hendin et al, based their "actual figure" calculations on percentage estimates, which suggests that rounding is appropriate. This is consistent with the approach of other authors. See, for example, "Under Control," supra note 186; and "Euthanasia and Other Decisions" supra note 186.
188. "Special Issue," *supra* note 6 at 40: 8 per cent would never perform the practices but would refer a patient to another physician, and 4 per cent would never participate and would not refer.
189. "End of Life in The Netherlands," *supra* note 184 at 1702: 9 per cent would never perform the practices but would refer a patient to another physician and 3 per cent would never participate and would not refer.
190. "Special Issue," *supra* note 6 at 102.
191. H. Hendin, "Correspondence: Euthanasia and Physician-Assisted Suicide in the Netherlands" (1997) 336 New Eng. J. Med. 1385 at 1385 [hereinafter "Euthanasia"].
192. P.J. van der Maas & G. van der Wal, "Correspondence: Euthanasia and Physician-Assisted Suicide in the Netherlands" (1997) 336 New Eng. J. Med. 1385.
193. G. van der Wal *et al.*, "Evaluation of the Notification Procedure for Physician-Assisted Death in the Netherlands" (1996) 335 New Eng. J. Med. 1706 at 1707.
194. "Special Issue," *supra* note 6 at 50.
195. "End of Life in the Netherlands," *supra* note 184 at 1704: 83 per cent were discussed with a colleague, 33 per cent with a nurse, and 70 per cent with relatives or others (more than one answer was possible).
196. van der Wal, *supra* note 193 at 1708.
197. J. Groenewoud *et al.*, "Clinical Problems with the Performance of Euthanasia and Physician-Assisted Suicide in the Netherlands" (2000) 342 New Eng. J. Med. 551 at 553.
198. "Special Issue," *supra* note 6 at 58: 41 per cent would never do so.
199. "End of Life in the Netherlands," *supra* note 184 at 1701:45 per cent would never do so.
200. "Special Issue," *supra* note 6 at 61–62. Patients were not totally able to make a decision in 11 per cent of the cases and totally unable 75 per cent of the time.
201. "End of Life in The Netherlands," *supra* note 184 at 1704.
202. "Euthanasia," *supra* note 191.
203. R. Gillon, "Euthanasia in the Netherlands—Down the Slippery Slope" (1999) 25 J. Med. Ethics 3 at 4.
204. D.A. Asch, "The Role of Critical Care Nurses in Euthanasia and Assisted Suicide" (1996) 334 New Eng. J. Med. 1374 at 1374 [hereinafter "Critical Care Nurses"].
205. C.A. Stevens & R. Hassan, "Management of Death, Dying and Euthanasia: Attitudes and Practices of Medical Practitioners in South Australia" (1994) 20 J. Med. Ethics 41 at 41.
206. D. Buchanan, "Australia—Lenient Sentence in Euthanasia Case" (1996) 2 Can. HIV/AIDS Pol'y Newsl. 25 at 25–26.
207. H. Kuhse, "End-of-Life Decisions in Australian Medical Practice" (1997) 166 Med. J. Australia 191 at 196.
208. *Ibid.* at 193–94.
209. *Ibid.* at 196: based on total number of deaths in Australia July 1994–June 1995 (125,771).
210. D.A. Pratt & B. Steinbock, "Death with Dignity or Unlawful Killing: The Ethical and Legal Debate Over Physician-Assisted Death" (1997) 33 Crim. L. Bull. 226 at 229.

211. L.R. Slome *et al.*, "Physician-Assisted Suicide and Patients with Human Immunodeficiency Virus Disease" (1997) 336 New Eng. J. Med. 417 at 419.

212. "Critical Care Nurses," *supra* note 204 at 1375. Not all of the reported cases of euthanasia were performed pursuant to requests or with the knowledge of family members, surrogates, or the patients themselves.

213. Meier, *supra* note 86 at 1194.

214. *Ibid.* at 1197.

215. E.J. Emanuel *et al.*, "The Practice of Euthanasia and Physician-Assisted Suicide in the United States: Adherence to Proposed Safeguards and Effects on Physicians" (1998) 280(6) J. Am. Med. Ass'n 507 at 508.

216. *Ibid.* at 509.

217. *Ibid.* at 510.

218. D.L. Willems *et al.*, "Attitudes and Practices Concerning the End of Life: A Comparison Between Physicians From the United States and the Netherlands" (2000) 160 Arch. Intern. Med. 63 at 66.

219. "Suicide in Oregon," *supra* note 81.

220. *Ibid.* at 600.

221. R. D. Ogden, *Euthanasia and Assisted Suicide in Persons with Acquired Immunodeficiency Syndrome (AIDS) or Human Immunodeficiency Virus (HIV)* (Pitts Meadows, B.C.: Perreault Goedman, 1994) at 67.

222. T.D. Kinsella & M.J. Verhoef, "Alberta Euthanasia Survey: 1. Physicians' Opinions About the Morality and Legalization of Active Euthanasia" (1993) 148 Can. Med. Ass'n J. 1921 at 1921.

223. T.D. Kinsella & M.J. Verhoef, "Alberta Euthanasia Survey: 2. Physicians' Opinions About the Acceptance of Active Euthanasia as a Medical Act and the Reporting of Such Practice" (1993) 148 Can. Med. Ass'n J. 1929 at 1929.

224. L. Shap, "Canadian Study on Euthanasia, Assisted Suicide and HIV/AIDS" (1997) 3 Can. HIV/AIDS Pol'y Newsl. 24.

225. M.G. Young & R.D. Ogden, "End-of-Life Issues: A Survey of English-Speaking Canadian Nurses in AIDS Care" (1998) 9:2 J. Ass'n Nurses in AIDS Care 18 at 22–23.

226. B. Sneiderman, "Latimer, Davis, and Doerksen: Mercy Killing and Assisted Suicide on the Op. Ed. Page" (1998) 25 Man. L.J. 449 at 455.

227. The cases of Dr. Peter Graff and Scott Mataya cited in Ogden, *supra* note 221 at 20–24.

228. B. Sneiderman, "The Rodriguez Case; Where do We Go From Here—A Multi-Dimensional (6-Layered) Approach" (1994) 2 Health L. J. 1 at 9.

229. *de la Rocha, supra* note 131.

230. "Death with Dignity in Toronto," *supra* note 1.

231. Latimer was initially convicted of second-degree murder in 1994. Latimer appealed the decision to the Saskatchewan Court of Appeal, but his appeal was dismissed *R. v. Latimer*, [1995] 8 W.W.R. 609. However, Latimer's conviction was quashed and a new trial was ordered by the Supreme Court of Canada when it was ascertained that the prosecutor interviewed potential jurors regarding their views on subjects of significance in the case: *R. v. Latimer*, [1997] S.C.R. 217. At his second trial, Latimer was once again convicted for second-degree murder; however, Justice Noble, the trial judge, granted Latimer a constitutional exemption from the mandatory minimum sentence and instead sentenced Latimer to one year of imprisonment and one year on probation. The Crown appealed the decision to grant a constitutional exemption and Latimer appealed his conviction to the Saskatchewan Court of Appeal. The court dismissed Latimer's appeal and allowed the Crown's appeal from the decision to grant a constitutional exemption: *R. v. Latimer* (1998), [1999] 6 W.W.R. 118 (1997). Latimer appealed his conviction and sentence to the Supreme Court of Canada. The Court dismissed Latimer's appeal and upheld Latimer's conviction for second-degree murder and the accompanying mandatory minimum sentence of ten years: *R. v. Latimer*, [2001] S.C.J. No. 1, online: QL (SCJ).

232. *R. v. Brush*, [1995] O.J. No. 656 (Prov. Div.), online: QL (OJ) [hereinafter *Brush*].

233. *R. v. Morrison* (1998), 174 N.S.R. (2d) 201 (S.C.).

234. *R. v. Genereux* (1999), 44 O.R. (3d) 339. Both the Crown and the accused appealed sentence. Leave was granted to both parties, but the court of appeal dismissed both appeals.

235. Vancouver Province, "Winnipeg (CP) - The Manitoba Crown … "(28 July 2000), online: Vancouver Province <http://www.vancouverprovince.com/cgi-bin/newsite.pl?adcode=p-nw&modul.../n072825.htm> (date accessed: 28 July 2000).

236. Hon. B. McLachlin, "Charter Myths" (1999) 33 U.B.C.L. Rev. 23 at 32.

237. *Rodriguez, supra* note 26; *Brush, supra* note 232; and *Glucksberg, supra* note 72 at 788.

238. *Glucksberg, ibid.*

239. *DDA, supra* note 77.

240. *ROTTI, supra* note 59.

241. Otlowski, *supra* note 38 at 465–66.

242. "Legal Bounds," *supra* note 123 at 166–67.

243. *Ibid.*

244. Otlowski, *supra* note 38 at 466.

245. See, for example, *Rodriguez, supra* note 26.

246. A system of pre-authorization was also suggested by Gilmour, *supra* note 42 at 257–58; and T.O. Nielsen, "Guidelines for Legalized Euthanasia in Canada: A Proposal" (1998) 31:7 Annals, Royal College of Physicians and Surgeons of Canada 314 at 317 [hereinafter "Guidelines for Canada"].

247. Regional ethics committees were suggested by "Guidelines for Canada," *ibid.*

248. *Ibid.*

249. *Ibid.*

250. M.A. Somerville, "Guidelines for Legalized Euthanasia in Canada: A Rejection of a Proposal" (1999) 32 Annals, Royal College of Physicians and Surgeons of Canada 8 at 8–9.

251. T.O. Nielsen, "Response" (1999) 32:1 Annals, Royal College of Physicians and Surgeons of Canada 9 at 10.

252. Otlowski, *supra* note 38 at 479.

253. H.M. Chochinov *et al.*, "Will to Live in the Terminally Ill" (2000) 125 Issues L. & Med. 334 at 335.

254. It should be remembered that unassisted suicide is an option for a person suffering from a non-somatically based condition where there is a wish to die.

255. Otlowski, *supra* note 38 at 491.

256. Code, 1985, supra note 12.

257. "Guidelines for Canada," supra note 246 at 317.

258. See, for example, DDA, supra note 77 at §127.870, s. 3.12, §127.875, s. 3.13, §127.880, s. 3.14; and ROTTI, supra note 59, ss. 16, 18, 19, 20.

Chapter Four

Lost Lives at Westray: Official Discourse, Public Truth and Controversial Death

John McMullan*

Editors' Note: The final chapter in this section on law and morality highlights the bitter aftermath of a mining explosion at Westray mine in Nova Scotia on May 19, 1992. Twenty-six miners were killed in the explosion. A formal report on the tragedy was completed and both criminal and non-criminal charges were laid in the aftermath of this tragedy.

In "Lost Lives at Westray," Professor John McMullan provides important background on this event and a detailed, critical account of how various stakeholders—families of the victims, Curragh Resources (owner of the Westray Mine), medical professionals, lawyers, and reporters, to name a few—took part in an embedded conflict over what happened, who should be liable, and how such deaths might be prevented. McMullan offers an original look at the Westray controversy, building on medical reports, miners' testimony to the public inquiry on Westray, and critical theory on truth seeking, knowledge, and power.

This critical approach relies on ways in which truth, fact, accountability are contested, sometimes with the result that governments are toppled or corporate bodies are held liable, but more often than not, there is a very different result where these same stakeholders are not punished or otherwise subject to substantial penalties. McMullan makes the case for a nexus of two powerful disciplines—medicine and law— whereby some considerations became more prominent than others, and some discourses became taken for granted while others were not "sayable." In Professor McMullan's own words, "… medicine and law [often] work together in constructing public truth. Medicine maps the physical body, law arranges the social body and together these disciplines constitute a formidable alliance of truth discovery and truth delivery."

THE WESTRAY DISASTER AND AFTER

At 5:20 a.m. on May 9, 1992, an explosion ripped through an underground mine in Pictou County, Nova Scotia claiming the lives of 26 miners. According to the *Report of the Westray Mine Public Inquiry*, sparks caused by the cutting head of a continuous miner machine ignited methane gas. The methane fire intensified into a methane explosion. The shock wave from the explosion then caused dust particles to become airborne and this created a full-blown coal-dust explosion underground. The explosions were so strong that they blew the top off the mine entrance, more than a mile above the blast center.[1] In the early hours after the explosion, numerous groups positioned themselves to prepare for, respond to and understand the disaster. The families of the trapped miners and their friends gathered to provide support and await information. Curragh Resources, the owners of the Westray Mine, took control of the site, managed the incident and kept reporters and family members at a distance from company premises.

Source: John McMullan, "Lost Lives at Westray: Official Discourse, Public Truth and Controversial Death," *Canadian Journal of Law and Society*, (22:1) 2007, pp. 21–42. © University of Toronto Press Incorporated. Reprinted by permission of *Canadian Journal of Law and Society/Revue Canadienne Droit et Societe* and UTP Journals, www.utpjournals.com.
*Research for this article was aided by a grant from the Social Sciences and Humanities Research Council of Canada. The author thanks Melissa McClung and Jan Cavicchi for assistance in coding the data, and two anonymous reviewers for the critical comments on an earlier draft.

Draegermen,[**] miners trained in rescue operations, quickly went into action picking their way through the debris looking for survivors. The R.C.M.P. managed the flow of traffic and isolated the families from the 200 reporters who converged on the small town of Plymouth. The entire site had the feel of a siege; information was strategically gathered, calibrated, and released.[2]

The social impacts of the tragedy immediately extended beyond those directly involved. The Premier promised a public inquiry and on May 15th, he appointed Justice Richard to investigate the disaster. The Department of Labor, who had oversight responsibilities for the Westray mine, launched an internal review and the police (R.C.M.P.) initiated their own belated criminal investigation. On April 20, 1993, almost a year after the explosion, they laid charges of manslaughter and criminal negligence causing death against the company, Curragh Resources and two mine managers, alleging that they were operating an unsafe mine by failing to keep coal dust in check and by failing to control methane levels in the mine.[3] For five years afterwards, however, state officials, mining experts, police investigators, judges, and criminal lawyers could not decide who was responsible for the loss of lives. Regulatory agencies filed 54 retroactive violations of the *Occupational Health and Safety Act* against Curragh Resources, and then dropped them in favour of a criminal prosecution.[4] The criminal trial [1995], which cost an estimated $4.5 million, ended in a mistrial and a staying of all charges against the Westray accused.[5] The public inquiry [1995-1997], which cost a further $4.8 million, allocated some responsibility: "management failed, the inspectorate failed, and the mine blew up."[6] Yet no criminal charges followed. Nor have civil actions fared any better. The Supreme Court of Canada concluded that the Nova Scotia government can not be held legally accountable for the Westray deaths even if it was negligent in licensing and administering an unsafe mine.

This paper examines the role of official inquiry and the production of truth: mundane forms of governance such as medical investigations that are signed off as a record of an agency's performance and ceremonial forms of governance such as full-blown public inquiries that examine broader issues.[7] I start from the premise that the constitution of death in tragedies such as Westray rests in large measure on how medical procedures and classification come together to form fields of enunciation about death, which are then communicated to waiting publics. I am concerned here with the determination of what counts as truth in a discourse and how it is produced over time. To that end, I study the texts of medical discourse and the context of their narrative production in registering and re-registering official truth messages. I draw upon death certificates, doctor's reports, the final report of the chief medical examiner, and legal testimony of medical experts at the criminal trial (1167 pages of text) as my primary source materials. But I also recognize that truth may be an unsettled account, an effect or not, of the resolution of disputes over time. Truth in this sense results from experience rather than inquiry. It is realized in challenging experiences where individuals are forced to question their values, beliefs, and perceptions that they had once accepted without hesitation.[8] Thus I also examine 30 miners' accounts presented before the public inquiry from 1995 to 1997, [4202 pages of transcript] to determine the existence and elements of a subaltern discourse and its relationship to the exercise of power. I coded the content of these documents to measure the following general themes and questions: power, knowledge and the body—what practices, procedures, and rules were considered credible in constituting understandings of the body in the determination of controversial death; regimes of truth—what "truth statements" were formulated and circulated about the cause and manner of death at Westray, by whom, and with what effects; truth, justice, and reconciliation—what was the play of governance surrounding the criminal trial and the public inquiry and how did it affect the relations between truth, justice and the body at Westray and after; and official discourse, resistance and the state— how did "knowing" about Westray transform the politics of truth and official discourse?

[**]Dictionary.com notes that a draegerman is "a miner, usually a member of a special crew, trained in underground rescue work and other emergency procedures" (http://dictionary.reference.com/browse/draegerman?qrsc=2446)

The paper is organized as follows: first, I discuss the relationship between power, medical discourse, and the production of truth; second, I explore how medical science and law contributed to the social production of an official knowledge about the Westray dead; third, I explain the significance of this public truth-telling on the constitution and registration of alternate truth accounts or counter-memories; finally, I discuss the role of the public inquiry and the subsequent transformation of truth about death at Westray. I argue that subaltern truth accounts circulated by miners and relatives of the deceased were simultaneously acknowledged and denied within the official inquiry and that official discourse was transformed in the aftermath of the Westray disaster, but with different effects from those intended by oppositional voices.

POWER, DISCOURSE AND TRUTH

Truth is a difficult concept that is almost always implicated in political and communicative processes involving perception, representation, and interpretation.[9] Yet inquests, public courts, inquiries, and truth commissions all claim to offer mechanisms and procedures by which "truth" can be aggregated, confirmed or denied, and fairness and justice allocated.[10]

Medicine is an especially important site in the "systematisation of modes of argument that proclaim the state's legal and administrative rationality."[11] Sudden disasters such as Westray are often followed by official investigations whose purposes are to discover the facts, investigate improprieties, review policies and programs, provide solutions, and maintain public confidence.[12] Coroners, nurses, laboratory technicians and forensic experts are typically empowered to create representations—what can and cannot be said—and to pronounce authoritatively on the causes of death. Of course, their discourses can be invalidated by law or challenged by lay or expert alternate accounts. But more often medicine and law work together in constructing public truth. Medicine maps the physical body, law arranges the social body and together these disciplines constitute a formidable alliance of truth discovery and truth delivery.[13]

So truth in this perspective is not outside power or lacking in it. There is no power relation without the constitution of a field of truth, nor any truth that does not presuppose and at the same time constitute a power relation. As Foucault notes, "power never ceases its interrogation, its inquisition, its registration of truth; it institutionalizes, professionalizes and rewards its pursuit."[14] What medicine typically produces is an official "regime of truth" that is marked by rules and procedures that limit the sayable, condition discursive relations and performance, and situate medical discourses among other discourses and non-discursive institutions.[15] Medical and social categories are routinely deployed as resources in constructing the normal and the pathological. Laboratory techniques, autopsy reports, and the compilation of case records, all work to separate, analyze and classify bodies, so that they become both the object and the subject of the exercise of power in the determination of official knowledge.[16] Procedural codes govern the doing of things; verification codes provide principles and justifications for the ways of doing things. These codes act as grids for organizing things—diseases, anatomical functions, and nosologies—and for announcing public truths. They establish the appropriate enunciations that are deemed acceptable or not, the technologies used to judge true and false statements, and the valorization of specific sources as truth-sayers.[17]

Medical science produces texts that are considered "true" because they follow scientific rules that allow for proofs and refutations. But these texts are not the final reflections of an external reality; instead they are more properly representations of what is assumed to exist. Studies of the International Classification of Diseases causing death (ICD) and the American Psychiatric Association's diagnostic and statistical manual (DSM) indicate that these classifications are constantly revised.[18] Their "archaeologies" reveal a myriad of twists and turns about the truth of biological subsystems, the symptoms of mental illnesses, the character of diseases, and the causes of death. Like star atlases or ornithological guides that tell us how to "read" the night sky or "observe" bird life, these official templates advise us how to see and understand loss of life.[19] As Prior observes: " ... in most cases of violent death, all that is discovered is a corpse. The cause of death for that corpse always remains a matter to be negotiated—usually and principally—through the procedures of coroners and other legal officials."[20]

Suicide verdicts, for example, are manufactured [or not] from a complex of situated contexts, organizational factors, and background expectancies. They are arrived at via a process of practical reasoning or "digging" based on what suicides are thought to "look like."[21] Homicide verdicts are also social constructs. Pathological findings, for example, may suggest one cause of death [natural] but be unable to determine the process that led up to it actually occurring because the means of death left no evidence such as suffocation with a pillow [homicide.][22] In workplace disasters, where serious crime is not suspected, the diagnostic "digging" can be perfunctory if the suspicion is that a mortality is not expected to be a homicide[23] or if deaths are not typically recorded as workplace related because they happen in circumstances that are not usually identified with occupational harm, such as highway fatalities involving truckers, bus drivers, retail estate agents and the like who work on the road.[24]

Truth is thus a consequence of the way that different claims are given credibility. Death is made true by events over time. And it is here in the spaces where institutional sites and professional discourses intersect that views from above become organized and rationalized, while other views become ignored, debated or disqualified. As Latour puts it, "truth is an effect of the settling of disputes."[25] But establishing truth is by no means easy when power is at stake and official institutions stand accused. Deceit is often built into the fabric of state and corporate truth-telling.[26] In Becker's words, "officials develop ways of denying the failure of the institution to perform as it should and explaining those failures that cannot be hidden."[27] Arendt and Cohen identify two forms of reaction that are critical to the production of official discourses: (a) literal denial "nothing is happening" and (b) interpretive denial—"what is happening is really something else."[28] Literal denial amounts to corporate and government rearrangements of information into benign narratives by exempting or denying the credibility of alternate accounts. Interpretive denial admits the raw facts "but denies the interpretive framework placed on the events." It entails claims and counter-claims and is embedded in a legal language that emphasizes euphemism or uses technical rules to minimize harm, avoid causality and evade responsibility.[29] So little is true in discourse that is not a product of power and the uses of truth are both constitutive and criterial and are therefore concerned with what counts as truth and how it is produced in discourse. Thus official discourses are frequently conceptual efforts to organize noumenal realities, or equally they are efforts to understand unexpected events and explain them retrospectively. This is what Foucault calls truth resulting from inquiry where it is acquired by deliberation or study.

Official discourses and their truth claims, however, are not always legitimation exercises for the powerful. Public inquiries, truth commissions, and judicial investigations can expose wrongdoings, cover-ups, and official negligence.[30] The Marchioness action group eventually won a public inquiry that led to inquest verdicts of unlawful killing in a boat sinking tragedy off the coast of Britain. A decade of investigation into the Hillsborough Soccer disaster eventually exposed the police, the coroner and the home office as parties involved in withholding and doctoring information and obfuscating the truth of death as so many acts of hooliganism when it was in fact caused by poor police practices.[31] Official inquiries have provided opportunities for a variety of interest groups to make submissions and foster broad-ranging investigations that invalidated preferred official claims to truth. For example, the Stevens Inquiry into the security forces and the loyalist paramilitaries in Northern Ireland deeply damaged the reputation of the British army and the credibility of the labour government.[32] Justice Hickman's Inquiry into the wrongful conviction of Donald Marshall, Jr., a Mi'kmaq Aboriginal, was profoundly prejudicial to the Nova Scotia government's entire criminal justice system[33] and Justice Gomery's inquiry into sponsorship scandals in Canada helped defeat the very government that called it into existence. "Breathing spaces" can be transformed into "garrulous spaces" and the play of governance can be ironic and emote random unexpected outcomes. Different uses of truth can qualify and limit one another.

Indeed truth may also form from difficult events when cognitive elements are reassembled to visualize something differently because of sudden and shocking experiences. According to Foucault, "limit experiences" are achieved through mental reflections that crises force on people. This "experiential" form of truth is about changes of mind due to emotional rather than rational factors where individuals reconceive who and what they are and value because they experience religious loss, political conversion, personal betrayal, or under unexpected trauma. These are circumstances where epistemic ruptures occur, and where truths are gained or established because of how things come together during personal turmoil rather than from conclusions reached on the basis of intense investigation. Previously accepted values, attitudes or ideas are questioned as are the evidential criteria previously used to think normatively and resolve everyday problems. Truth found in limit experiences is based on an "appropriation" by individuals rather than a "production" by power. This use of truth leads to the adoption of new perceptions, new-self images and new correctness claims about the world and how and why it operates the way it does. Truths embedded in such challenging experiences often resist or oppose power-produced truth and offer a counter memory to the ever-tightening grip of official institutions and their claims-making. Truth forged in limit experiences not only sets restraints on the play of power, it explains why the production of official truth is not monolithic or wholly determining of what people believe or of how they are governed as subjects.[34]

So how did medical knowledge represent the official truth about lives lost at Westray? Was there a contested space about Westray as truth? Did the limit experience of the disaster and its aftermath lead to the wrestling of new truths from the circumstances of trauma and tragedy? What was the politics of truth of the official public inquiry?

MEDICO-LEGAL EXAMINATIONS AND THE PUBLIC TRUTH OR DEATH

Soon after the search and rescue mission commenced, dragaermen indicated that the damage inside the mine was more extensive than anticipated. The rescuers first worked at establishing a fresh air base underground from which they could launch their search. Then they cleared the debris so that travel would be quicker and less hazardous inside the mine. Eventually they discovered six dead victims. Their bodies were clustered together and showed little evidence of burning. Then they came upon the bodies of another five miners, all showed signs of burning and most showed signs of pink lividity, the effects of methane poisoning. On Wednesday, May 13, draegermen located four more badly burned bodies. But this was the last attempt at rescue: the sad conclusion was that no one could have survived the fire and explosion and eleven bodies remain buried underground to this day.[35]

Disasters are routinely caused by predictable situations coming together dramatically and unexpectedly. Essential to disaster management are agreed upon procedures to bring order from chaos: where to hold the deceased, how to accommodate survivors, relatives and friends, when and how to identify bodies, when to secure sites for investigation, how to collect evidence when wrongdoing is suspected, and how to provide accurate information to anxious publics. An array of emergency personnel—a medical team, firefighters, the R.C.M.P., and community volunteers—quickly set up as self-supporting units to aid the rescue operation at the mine. Police immediately contacted the medical examiner's office, and three doctors and several nurses from the local hospital came to assist in the identification of the dead. They constructed a temporary mortuary at a local sports arena and planned for an anticipated "worst case" scenario.

The R.C.M.P. guarded the perimeter of the disaster site to keep the public out and to regulate and monitor communication between the media, medical examiners, rescue teams and the bereaved. The medical examiners policed the boundaries between the lost and the living by controlling the processing of the dead, and deciding when, where, and to whom information would be released. As the medical examiner noted at the trial:

> Q: What types of facilities were set up....?
> A: Ultimately, on May 10th, '92, 11 bodies were recovered and they arrived at the New Glasgow stadium.... In any event, before that what I had done was had a number of body numbers made up which also included syringes, needles, tubes and screw-top jars for the collection of blood and, if any urine was present, to collect urine.[36]

The objective of a medico-legal examination is to determine a preferred "cause of death and gain expert forensic evidence for adjudication."[37] In these examinations, the procedures are typically inquisitorial with no prosecution and no accused: an unspeaking body is mapped and put into discourse. Medical examiners instruct the bereaved that it is "their" role, and "their" responsibility, carefully conducted and communicated, to determine who died, when, where, and how.[38] In disasters like Westray, families usually are aware of the first three; their principal concern is how they died. The medical examinations of the miners probed the exterior surface of the bodies (clothing, personal items, skin, hair, face) and their internal physiological elements (tissues, organs, blood and urine). Truth discovery was predicated on the body as the *sine qua non* of human mortality.

> A: I [chief medical examiner] stated at that time that since this appeared to be an accident and nothing—I shouldn't say nothing further would come of it, of course, at the very least there would either be an inquiry, but I said that what I could do is, after giving the specimens to him [RCMP officer] ... that I would later ... get the specimens at the RCMP headquarters in Stellarton.
> Q: Now as a result of receiving those analyses back and combining those, I take it, with observations and the examinations you conducted at the New Glasgow arena, what conclusions, if any, did you come to with respect to the other 10 bodies which we have noted, here ...
> A: They all died of carbon monoxide poisoning from smoke inhalation, and given the nature of the event, death probably occurred very rapidly, probably within one to three minutes, in that general time.[39]

Examinations did not initially require doctors to dismember bodies. Official autopsies were performed on four of the bodies; only those discovered after the first eleven were examined in much detail. Loss of life was sited within organs, tissues, and cells. The chief medical examiner recollects his verdicts:

> A: So in all—in this incident, identification was easy; the cause of death was easy. There was no real damage to the bodies that made identification a real problem. The next four that we're going to talk about were more of a problem, but even there, there was really no real problem.
> Q: Was there then, any necessity, in your opinion, to conduct internal examinations of these bodies in order to confirm further? Or did you have any other suspicions that the cause of death might be anything other than carbon monoxide poisoning ...
> A: No, I had no ... I had no problem.[40]

One miner's body, at the request of his family, was re-examined by an independent forensic pathologist whose results opened up a consideration of a wider context of death.

> A: The only other change which I saw … on microscopic examination … was the rupture of some of the minor … spaces in the lungs … consistent with blast injury.
> Q: Could you just go into that in a little bit more detail?
> A: What happens … is that areas like the lung are … most susceptible to injury, presumably because they have a more wide range of movement and can be injured due to the motion of the blast. And what that does is it causes the small air spaces to rupture and it leads to hemorrhage within these air spaces.
> Q: I see. And the blast as you described it, could it affect any other part of the body?
> A: Interestingly enough, the solid areas of the body tend not to be affected. See, what happens is that the blast may have injured the lung and may have led to his death … which is the accumulation of fluid in itself, but in this case, he did not have the opportunity to develop those symptoms and he died because of the carbon monoxide ingestion and the absence of oxygen presumably.[41]

While this autopsy yielded new findings implicating conditions in the mine, it was quickly decontexualized. The politics of medical truth-telling incorporated blast evidence into its official "accident" narrative, but it disqualified controversial causes or circumstances such as workplace conditions, mine mismanagement, or regulatory improprieties. A framework that viewed events as the result of unmotivated and purely physical processes predominated. Medical investigation masked the presence of social structure and social action in death by quickly adopting a natural anatomical framework and the catch-all of the accidental verdict. Speaking the truth of death at Westray entailed making very specific moves in a discourse where what was right was dictated by the truth regime's bio-medical correctness criteria.

This somatic discourse was further bolstered by a categorization system that emphasized two interrelated procedures that effectively constituted the structure and limits of the sayable, enabling the calibration of true and false statements: the direct "causes of death" that established the immediate loss of life and the "manner of death" that indicated the antecedent factors that brought about the cause of death in the first place. Normally manner of death is classified by medical examiners as either "natural" or unnatural." The element of unnaturalness," however, were not determined by the eccentricities of individual examiners but by the system of discourse operated by medical investigators that set the specific content of a directive, assertive, and declarative discourse. When deaths occur by "unnatural" causes, they are filtered into five mutually exclusive categories: accident, suicide, homicide, undetermined, and unclassified.[42] The rules governing the classification of carbon monoxide poisoning, heat spasm, and blunt trauma injuries interpellated a specific vision of death. As the chief medical examiner stated under cross examination:

> Q: And all 15 were determined to be, in terms of the manner of death, accidental?
> A: Yes.[43]

This "table of death" based on physico-anatomical data and routine pathological procedures permitted medical "causes of death" to stand proxy for the "manner of death."

Q: And you [medical examiner], under that statutory duty, you actually filled in the certificate of death as saying accident/mine explosion?

A: Yes. That's a generic determination. Any legal follow-ups from that have nothing to do with the medical examiner. For example, somebody can be drinking and driving and run into somebody. And unless they are clearly aiming to hit the person, the death is classified as an accident. Of course, legally, they then can be charged with whatever crime they—the Crown— ... I'm saying it's the same thing as murder. "Murder" is a legal term. "Homicide" is a medical term.[44]

The rationale for this distinction, of course, was to not pre-empt decisions which are constitutionally the province of criminal and civil courts. But "homicide" is a proper medical verdict and to establish it when mass deaths have occurred requires a larger view of what constitutes the manner of such an incident. Antecedent causes at Westray were determined without reference to situated knowledge that typically informs suicide verdicts, for example. As Atkinson notes, coroners used "operational decisions" to determine suicides. They combined "positive evidence of intent" (suicide notes) with "cues," "signs" or "warnings" (drugs on the person, personal histories, facts out of place, etc.) to arrive at the social meaning of suicide. They pursued conflicting and complex agendas in their process of interpretative reasoning.[45] Diagnostic judgements, however, did not situate the Westray deaths in time or space. Although the concept "manner of death" empowered medical experts to relate their causal findings to wider work contexts, their discursive system of classification did not do so. Medical truth was discourse-relative, a set of practices and rules that dictated limited moves of "correctness" concerning death as codified by the disciplinary principles of coroners and expert examiners. The category "unclassifiable," for example, is used for deaths where the absence of bodily injuries makes classification difficult. This category includes deaths that otherwise would be classified as accidents or suicides when the manner of death can not be established because the "intent" of the victim is unknown. A similar logic arises with deaths that are caused by unintentional acts of omission. While such acts are defined as actionable in murder and manslaughter cases in the legal realm, the category of 'homicide' is used only in deaths where active intent to kill is established. In the apparent absence of this will to kill, the Westray deaths were framed as analogous to other types of mishaps—house fires, automobile crashes, boating tragedies—all of which are coded as unpredictable and unintentional. Nor were the Westray deaths even classified as "undetermined"; an apparent lack of information made this impossible. Yet there was enough medical data to consider the explosion not suspicious and to classify the deaths as accidental! Slapper's observation that medical officials view deaths in workplaces "through drinking straws" was confirmed in the Westray case.[46] Indeed the medical verdict reinforced the company's claim that the dead were "courageous workers," the victims of "mother nature who cannot always be predicted" and where there had been "no warnings of any kind."[47] This rather strict medical interpretation of the word "how," as applied to manner of death, seemed to assume that companies cannot really kill people. Medical knowledge was foremost "a discourse of confidence,"[48] to borrow Burton and Carlen's term, that reaffirmed the competence of state practices and valorized corporate accounts and the formal systems they operated in the mine.

The medical examination of the Westray deaths also involved a specialist network of writing: aggregating, recording, revising and registering for political purposes. The network was organized hierarchically: nurses and laboratory analysts were at the bottom; above them were the medical doctors who identified and examined the bodies in the immediate aftermath of the explosion, and at the top, was the chief medical examiner's office with extensive powers to interpret and reinterpret the findings and to speak the official truth with credibility to government and the public. Dr. Barclay's [a doctor in the medical examiners office] testimony at the criminal trial is instructive: "Yes … notes were dictated to a nurse…. I did prepare a report from the notes but it was not an official medical report. All the official reports were done by Mr. Perry [chief examiner] on all the deceased."[49] Defense lawyers for the Westray accused bolstered this hierarchy of credibility. They downplayed the accounts of other medical experts and at the trial endorsed only the chief medical examiner's texts as truthful. Consider the objections by the defense to three written reports by other doctors submitted as part of the prosecution's case.

> The three—or the typed version of these reports which we have difficulty with, number one is where it says "Doctor," it says "Dr. Perry, Chief Medical Examiner." All three, Dr. Perry has not signed. So it does not list this witness as the doctor. It lists Dr. Perry as the doctor and Dr. Perry hasn't signed it. Also, the date—although they are undated, there is a handwritten date on those documents which is November 3, 1994. So it appears that, in fact, Dr. Sebastian did comply with Staff Sergeant MacDonald's request and provide some type of document back. We assume that this is the document but it lists Dr. Perry, it doesn't list Dr. Sebastian as being the doctor, so first off, Dr. Perry is not signing. Number two is it appears that they are clearly based upon recollection…. The documents which we have which are the notations at the time the autopsies were performed, we have no difficulty with; it's the November documents which were prepared apparently on the basis of recollection, which it says on the face of the document, and particularly where it has Dr. Perry as being the doctor involved and they're unsigned by Dr. Perry. We have Dr. Perry's report. That's the objection to those three pieces.[50]

The registration of death was profoundly paradoxical. On the one hand it was akin to an operational closure that initially affirmed explanations preferred by official power-holders. As the chief medical examiner put it, "[i]t is not up to the medical examiner to ascertain blame. That's in the field of law enforcement and then, I'd presume prosecution."[51] On the other hand, medical knowledge was not separate from the field of prosecution. Reports, memoranda and letters were collected and tagged as forensic evidence for the prosecution. At the criminal trial, some medical experts suggested that a wider wrongdoing may have caused the explosion and the deaths. They now spoke of "large quantities of coal dust," and "high methane levels" as causal factors and presented non-medical evidence that was discovered as part of their investigation: "He [a dead miner] had a battery back and a breathing pack and he also had a methane gas meter. The meter reading by the way was zero."[52] Some even questioned their previous reports suggesting a different interpretation of death other than accident. But this discursive re-registering was shut down in cross-examination:

> Q. Dr. Perry, perhaps, for clarification, you used what we might, in this trial, call mining terms. You talked about dust, explosion, fires, smoke inhalation, when you were talking about your medical findings…. But your examination—didn't tell you that, that your medical examination told you that he had a fused larynx and wasn't able to breathe because of that, isn't that correct?
> A. Yes, but the cause of death is also related to the history. It's not only examining the body.[53]

The "plasticity of law,"[54] to borrow Cohen's phrase, enabled defense lawyers to resist a discourse of wider causes and to normalize the disaster as an event with a non-culpable legal subject. Causes related to the history of the explosion were ruled out in medicine and in law. Soot covered clothing, burnt body parts, scorched skin, multiple lacerations, soot in the trachea and bronchi, blunt trauma injuries, and carbon dioxide poisoning were all registered without much of a hint of suspicious circumstance or possible negligence. No one would think of describing a sudden death in a hospital as a "homicide" until such a cause had been convincingly established, but it seemed normal to refer to work deaths at Westray as "accidents" without questions being asked or answered and to place the deceased in a default category that came to terms with human agency by means of erasure and denial. As Scraton observes, medico-legal inquiries, "are places of illusion that have to bear the full weight of responsibility for resolving and revealing the circumstances of death, while giving not so much as a nod towards individual or corporate liability."[55]

Indeed it is difficult to see how "homicide" can ever be returnable in respect to deaths at work like Westray. There are predispositions to downplay a "homicide" verdict: it is labour intensive, costly, uses up a lot of resources, causes a lot of upset in other parts of the legal system, and cuts across the supposed consensual, contractually governed settings where much work occurs.[56] None of the 35 medical officers in one recent study could even remember suggesting an "unlawful killing" related to a death at work.[57] In Bourdieu's words, medical knowledge constituted an underlying "thought element" for death determination at Westray, a system of presuppositions and categories that were largely accepted without much questioning, and an "unthought element" that imagined corporate and state involvement to the margins and out of discursive play.[58] Taken together, medical and legal procedures were "techniques of discursive affirmation" that promoted explanations acceptable to official discourse and saw to it that they predominated in the public mind, at least in the early years after the explosion and during the criminal trial.[59]

THE LIMIT EXPERIENCES OF WESTRAY, COUNTER-MEMORY AND THE PARADOXES OF OFFICIAL INQUIRY

The deletion of human agency naturalized deaths at Westray and the deletion of intent relegated them to a status in which the proximate causes were agreed upon, but the social context was left to happenstance. An accidental death in this logic would be transformed into the equivalent of a manslaughter or a murder, if and only if, criminal procedures could reveal the precise circumstances of the deaths to be other than what medical knowledge had already proclaimed them to be. A defiant logic that forced the families of the bereaved to live with the determinant weight of "accident theory" that added to their grief and trauma. But how can medical thinking decide that there was no homicide without fully examining the broader context of the deaths to see whether mistakes, recklessness, or incompetence in the workplace were at fault? How can the bereaved ascertain that it was a homicide that killed their relatives, not simply an unforseen danger in the dark?

These questions inform surviving miners' and bereaved family members' discourse on death at Westray. This discourse, it must be said, was wrenched from a painful experience in which cognitive changes "happened" as the shock wore off and the re-examination of events commenced. From the perspective of those who experienced the trauma of the tragedy maintaining the official medical version of the public truth evinced an unwillingness to confront disturbing information. For them, the Westray story contained abundant *earlier* evidence of illegal mining practices, including unauthorized tunneling in the dangerous gaseous coal seam in Pictou County, a culture of *laissez-faire* coal production where the existing inspectorate did not enforce occupational health and safety laws at the mine site, and a system of government collusion with the mine owner involving widespread political favouritism, guaranteed public loans, subsidies, tax incentives and infrastructure grants, and a protected coal market at three times the market value to broker the mine into existence.[60] For the miners and their families this created a climate of high risk extraction and low duty of care. As one miner put it, "management ... was notorious for doing things in a half-arsed way and then not fixing them until something happened."[61]

Furthermore this experiential-based discourse linked the human catastrophe to a subsequent series of state failures in the legal domain: a botched police investigation that resulted in incomplete, inaccurate and poorly presented evidence for purposes of prosecution, a state prosecution that was deliberately denied the financial resources, the administrative organization and the appropriate legal expertise to make a credible criminal case, a biased judge who inappropriately interfered in the judicial proceedings and instigated an unwarranted mistrial, a hesitant public prosecutor who decided to stay all charges even though he was given leave by the Appeal Court to retry the case, and a government who rejected responsibility for the disaster, tried to scapegoat the miners as the architects of their own misfortune, and refused to acknowledge the victimization of the dead and their families or offer compensation for their losses.[62] One woman remembers how a company executive responded to family requests for the retrieval of the eleven bodies not recovered from the mine: "We're here to make money not spend money, and if you want to get the bodies back, go see your politicians."[63] Two other family members recall how they were made to wait before being able to claim a miner's body.

> Father-in-law: … our [son-in-law's] body was one of the first recovered … we decided almost immediately that we wanted a complete autopsy.…
> Mother-in-law: … we were told that we would be able to see his body at seven o'clock in the evening. We left the fire hall at about two in the afternoon. We got word … to be at the basement of the church at seven [pm] but we didn't see his body until, what six in the morning?… it bothered me that officials, if you will, were taking this long to prepare a body before we would see it.…"[64]

Not surprisingly, eighty per cent of fifty-two family members recently interviewed said that responsibility for the loss of lives had not been adequately determined by the government and two out of three insisted that justice had not been delivered.[65]

While the medical establishment paid no attention to the workplace-related situated contexts, cues, facts out of place, and background warnings in their interpretation of death, the experiential view from below contested medico-legal power and its discourse of the public truth. As one spouse noted, "basically what I had to do was pick up what was left of my life and try to put it in some perspective that would make me and the kid survive."[66] Death at Westray, miners and family members insisted, was also a sentimental order involving trial, loss and melancholia, the expression and normalization of grief, and the process of memorialization. The body was first and foremost a site of personhood; a discursive point at which persona, social relations, and the political interconnected and interacted. It was therefore a language site over which people expressed feelings of loss and love, over which they prayed and eulogized, and over which they expressed concern and anger about larger social, economic, and political interests that affected the loss of lives close to them. The body was interpreted as a cultural entity where the social conditions of mining were literally written into and onto it, and where understanding death included the contingent play of economic and political power and social inequality.[67] For the miners and the bereaved families, Westray was a provocative trial-like event that required a wider contextual truth.

This meant learning from the event and its aftermath and coming to see things in a different light. It meant standing back and trying to understand why institutions they valued let them down. It meant questioning the evidential criteria of medicine, law, and justice and fashioning and applying new criteria to cope with the pressing perplexities of continuous trauma and prolonged loss. It meant acquiring a truth from a limit experience and cognitively rearranging emotional feelings and epistemological thinking to tell a different truth about dying in the mine. The comments of four family members are exemplary:

> Those bastards did this and they are walking away from this…. so I'm trying to see where this friggin' justice system fits in. It doesn't fit nowhere…. I just can't let it go that these people were able to kill twenty-six people and just walk away.[68]
>
> I might have been able to accept it if he had a car accident, or if he had cancer, or something, and dealt with it, but I'm not happy with it, no, and I probably never will be, because maybe there'll never be justice. I don't have any faith in it anymore….
>
> I guess I never thought that anything like this could ever happen. I never thought that we could be made a mockery in public, and I never thought anybody could kill somebody and get away with it, so publicly.
>
> I've learned that you can't trust anyone in government…. I've learned that, yes, you can still kill people and get away with it if you have a little money in the bank.[69]

It meant expressing memories of their own culpability underground: smoking in the mine, permitting tampered equipment to operate without challenge, allowing family and friends to go underground in unsafe conditions, and exposing the deadly practices of mine owners and managers to release the dead from their silence. Most of all it meant standing up and affirming to the public inquiry [referred to hereafter as the Westray Public Inquiry Transcripts] that the Westray dead were not responsible for their demise:

> The coal dust in this area [North Main on May 1 and 2] ranged from ankle deep to mid calf;[70]
>
> The scoop quit between A Road and A-1 Road on 4 Crosscut because methane levels in the mine were very high at that time between 5 and 6.9% methane;[71]
>
> As a general rule stone-dusting was not done;[72]
>
> There were no stone dust barriers at the mine…. No, I never saw them at Westray … doing dust examples;[73]
>
> The stoppings … were plywood … all kind of bent up on and, you know, I mean, there's obviously holes…. they should have been filled as gas was leaking in the mine before the explosion;[74]
>
> When they started plugging vent tubes and … disconnecting the methanometer on the scoop … I was pretty upset. Because … they were taking chances with everybody's lives;[75]
>
> But then we were talking up in the section later on, and John was saying if they have a roof fall in the old gob and that stopping ever lets go, he said, we're all dead in this section;[76]
>
> There was no ventilation plan, there was no mine plan … maybe it was behind closed doors, but I didn't see it;[77]
>
> The compressor at No. 10 Crosscut leaked oil for at least three weeks anyway…. it shouldn't have been in [the mine] but somehow they got an exemption for the thing;[78]
>
> There didn't seem to be too much point to it [outlining the state of the problems] because I b[r]ought up maybe three or four different safety infractions that I thought should be repaired, and after maybe seven or eight times putting it down on the sheets … you just gave up;[79]
>
> And it was a shock to me…. so nobody on that property [Westray mine] was a certified mine manager from what I would call an accreditable authority…;[80]
>
> In my opinion, Westray Coal was operating and operated in the most dangerous manner of any mine I have ever worked in throughout the world….[81]

These testimonials and hundreds more like them, opened up a wider discourse on the body, truth, and social justice that was evinced in the 120 interviews conducted by inquiry lawyers with miners and draegermen and at the official hearings where 30 of them gave oral testimony. A multiplicity of subjugated narratives were recorded and then circulated widely by the media to the public. The limits and forms of the sayable were expanded to include neglect, prior knowledge, cover-up—and prevention. The body was re-coded first and foremost in a discourse of structural violence and thoroughly physical forms of explanation about death were contested. The depoliticalization of death produced by medical and legal power was challenged by a coun-ter-memory that attacked the credibility of medical inquiry to determine death, of government to govern and of the coal industry to mine effectively. The experiential truth-telling of the miners—their particular spoken histories, workplace narratives, stories of complaint and cama-raderie and rituals of remembrance—evoked new visions of Westray and after. Westray was put into discourse as a calamity of cave-ins, underground fires, excessive methane levels, unchecked coal dust residue, faulty equipment, broken promises, careless management, political manipula-tion and corporate indifference. Broadly speaking, the truth-telling that resulted from surviving the ordeal of Westray pieced together a discourse of workplace violence. Dying underground was gradually reconceived and widely proclaimed to be a crisis that need not have happened and both the miners and the bereaved reconsidered who and what they were and valued and how things were with them after their personal trials. As Davis, Wohl and Verberg rightly note "'Westray' was no so much an event as it was the starting point for a series of events and experi-ences that undermined the fundamental beliefs of many—if not most—of the families."[82]

The public inquiry findings acknowledged the experiential truth claims of those who lived the tragedy and the trauma. It offered judgments contrary to the preferred position of the government that appointed it and provided findings at odds with the medical regime that had defined the public truth of official death as accidental. It used experiential truth as a balance to official accounts of non-culpability. The Report of the Westray Inquiry asserted:

> The Westray story ... is a story of incompetence, of mismanagement, of bureaucratic bungling, of deceit, of ruthlessness, of cover-up, of apathy, of expediency, and of cynical indifference....[83]

The pain of death was certainly registered: miners' names, ages and dates of death were listed and their memories were honoured in a dedication at the beginning of the report. As Dodd notes, "this was the first of the Nova Scotia accident reports that ... listed the deceased before the findings of the inquiry," in effect re-rendering the medical discourse as suspicious and prioritizing the presence of the miners in the truth-telling process.[84] The public inquiry not only exonerated the miners of blame, it also criticized the leaders of government and industry: "those serenely uninformed, the willfully blind, or the cynically self-serving." Had there been "adequate ventilation, had there been adequate treatment of coal dust, and had there been ade-quate training and an appreciation by management for a safety ethic," Justice Richard opined, then "sparks would have faded harmlessly." The public inquiry acknowledged that there was a "killing of all 26 miners," and that this loss of life was caused by expedience and greed.[85]

On the one hand, the inquiry was an information hunter that tried to generate account-ability where police investigations and prosecutory processes had previously failed. It offered an opportunity, however delayed, to ensure that political and management failings were exposed to public scrutiny. The reclamation of death and the inscription of a discourse of work violence was an instance of official discourse being worked on by other interests rooted in the experien-tial use of truth and an example of the formation of a contestable space between one official version of state veracity and another.[86] On the other hand, this subversive element in official discourse was plumbed into a wider representational order. The public inquiry was also a technique of governance, a routine political tactic directed at legitimacy building. The tragedy was constituted as a "black mark" against all coal mining that had to be recognized and corrected to prevent future similar events from occurring. But those known to be most responsible for this censorious behaviour did not appear at the hearings, did not explain their actions and have not been held accountable for them. Corporate capital, at the highest level, signaled the absence of a problem as a form of denial to protect their own interests. Indeed correction, as defined by official inquiry, stopped short of identifying culpability and indicating liability. Even the symbolism of law marking out socially unacceptable conduct was absent in the report findings. "Anyone who expects that this Report will single out one or two persons and assess total blame for the tragedy will be similarly disappointed."[87] Prime suspects were left nameless and their acts of omission and commission were not causally related to any deaths. Deaths were the result of a disaster by design that distributed fault to the many without consequence. The loss of 26 lives was not the result of any definable misstep, and incompetence and ignorance were not the cold calculations of coal production at any cost.

The battle for the truth was also a device for social ordering through which the state's and the industry's fractured and damaged images of administrative rationality and democratic legality were rebuilt. Notwithstanding the clarity and credibility of the discourse of workplace violence, experts and their evidence were framed to create a renewed faith in state institutions and the mining industry, their policies, practices and personnel. The oppositional voices of the miners were re-orchestrated into smoothing exercises whose primary goals were to restore respect to the industry and recover credibility for government institutions. Both were anxious to move the tragedy forward to where they could consider recommendations. This "pedagogic task of discursive incorporation," to use Burton and Carlen's apt phrase, acknowledged the voices from below and their experiential use of truth, but incorporated them into a transformative project with entirely different effects.[88] The end result was an odd balance that admitted that the medico-legal regime of truth was a mixture of half-truths, evasions, and legal sophistries, but that sacrificed "justice" for "truth" by granting amnesty to the perpetrators. The final report allowed the bereaved and surviving miners to come to terms with the pain of these losses by registering the legitimacy of their counter-memory, all the while forbidding them a process of recognizable due process to redress their losses. The play of governance permitted a subaltern alterity to exist as a "garrulous space" that both acknowledged and discounted its own truth-telling. It tried to constitute a world that could speak for itself with the agreement of the many but it created a world in which injustice and trauma for the bereaved miners still co-exist in an unending yesterday. Reconciliation trumped justice in the official discourse of controversial death at Westray. Establishing "what happened" without determining "who was responsible" provided some closure for the victims and their families, but this outcome continues to invoke the persistent question, what next in the aftermath of organized truth-telling at Westray and continues to fan the desire for justice, compensation and just laws. At Westray the oppositional discourse's alterity, like the official discourse's hegemony were, in their turns, simultaneously recognized and denied.

QUESTIONS TO CONSIDER

1. In the wake of the deaths at Westray, critically assess the argument that provincial legislatures, courts, and commissions of inquiry are impartial bodies that objectively review facts and reach fair decisions for wronged parties. Consider the counterargument that such bodies are hindered in their search for answers and in the compensation they may recommend.

2. Do you agree with Professor McMullan's thesis that medical professionals and legal professionals may form an alliance that in many ways obscures truth telling and serves to "depoliticize" the events at Westray? Use specific examples drawn from his narrative. Can you think of counterexamples where lawyers or medical professionals are far more critical of state failures?

3. There has been a longstanding concern by victims' advocates that harms are not taken seriously enough by official bodies and that findings are often delayed. What other parallels could be drawn from the Westray deaths and subsequent hearings and inquiries? Use examples such as the Air India Flight 182 bombing in June 1985, with 329 people killed, or the death of Polish national Robert Dziekanski at Vancouver International Airport in October 2007. (The Air India bombing led to the Commission of Inquiry into the Investigation of the Bombing of Air India Flight 182, whereas the death of Robert Dziekanski was the focus of the Braidwood Commission.)

SUGGESTIONS FOR FURTHER READING

Gomery, J. H. (2006). The pros and cons of commissions of inquiry. *McGill Law Journal, 51*(4), 783–798.

McMullan, J. (2006). News, truth, and the recognition of corporate crime. *Canadian Journal of Criminology and Criminal Justice, 48*(6), 905–939.

Michalowski, R. J., & Kramer, R. C. (Eds.). (2006). *State-corporate crime: Wrongdoing at the intersection of business and government.* New Brunswick, NJ: Rutgers University Press.

Mullins, C., & Rothe, D. (2008). Gold, diamonds and blood: International state-corporate crime in the Democratic Republic of the Congo. *Contemporary Justice Review, 11*(2), 81–99.

Roach, K. (2006). Must we trade rights for security? The choice between smart, harsh or proportionate security strategies in Canada and Britain. *Cardozo Law Review, 27*(5), 2157–2221. (Reprinted in David Dyzenhaus (Ed.), *Civil Rights and Security*, Aldershot, Ashgate, 2008, chapter 8).

NOTES

1. Province of Nova Scotia. The Westray Story: A Predictable Path to Disaster, Report of the Westray Mine Public Inquiry (Halifax: Government Printer, 1997) Justice K. Peter Richard, Commissioner [The Westray Story].
2. C. McCormick, "The Westray Mine Explosion: Covering a Disaster and a Failed Inquiry" in C. McCormick, ed., Constructing Danger: The Mis/Representation of Crime in the in the News (Halifax: Fernwood Publishing, 1995) 1 at 197 ["Westray Mine Explosion"]; J. McMullan & S. Hinze, "The Press, Ideology, and Corporate Crime" in C. McCormick, ed., The Westray Chronicles: A Case Study in Corporate Crime (Halifax, Fernwood Publishing, 1999) 183 [Westray Chronicles]; T. Richards, "Public Relations and the Westray Mine Explosion" in Westray Chronicles, ibid. 136.
3. D. Jobb, Calculated Risk: Greed, Politics and the Westray Tragedy (Halifax: Fernwood Publishing, 1994).
4. Ibid.; D. Jobb, "Legal Disaster: Westray and the Justice System" in Westray Chronicles, supra note 2, 163.
5. D.R. Beveridge & P.I. Duncan, Review of the Nova Scotia Public Prosecution Service (Halifax: Nova Scotia Department of Justice, 2000).
6. The Westray Story, supra note 1 at VII.
7. G. Gilligan, "Official Inquiry, Truth and Criminal Justice" in G. Gilligan & J. Pratt, eds., Crime, Truth and Justice: Official Inquiry, Discourse, Knowledge (Cullompton: Willan, 2004) 21 [Crime, Truth and Justice].
8. M. Fourcault, "Politics and the Study of Discourse" in G. Burchell, C. Gordon & P. Miller, eds., The Foucault Effect: Studies in Governmentality (Chicago: University of Chicago Press, 1991a) 53; M. Foucault, "Questions of Method" in Burchell, Gordon & Miller, ibid. 73.

9. H. Arendt, Between Past and Future: Eight Exercises in Political Thought (New York: Viking Press, 1971) [Eight Exercises]; H. Arendt, The Crises of the Republic (New York: Harcourt, Brace Jovanovich, 1972) [Crises of the Republic]; B. Williams, Truth and Truthfulness: An Essay in Genealogy (Princeton, N.J.: Princeton University Press, 2002).

10. G. Gilligan & J. Pratt, "Introduction: Crime, Truth and Justice—Official Inquiry and the Production of Knowledge" in Crime, Truth and Justice, supra note 7, 1; R.I. Rothberg & D. Thompson, eds., Truth vs. Justice: The Morality of Truth Commissions (New Jersey: Princeton University Press, 2000).

11. F. Burton & P. Carlen, Official Discourse: On Discourse Analysis, Government Publications, Ideology and The State (London: Routledge and Kegan Paul, 1997) at 48.

12. P. Scraton, Hillsborough: The Truth (Edinburgh, Mainstream Publishing, 1999) at 83.

13. P. Scraton, "Lost Lives, Hidden Voices: 'Truth' and Controversial Deaths" (2002) 1 Race and Class 107.

14. M. Foucault, "The Eye of Power" in C. Gordon, ed., Power/Knowledge: Selected Interviews and Other Writings (1972–1977) (New York: Pantheon Books, 1980d) 93 [Power/Knowledge].

15. M. Foucault, "Politics and the Study of Discourse" in G. Burchell, Gordon & Miller, supra note 8, 53; M. Foucault, "Questions of Method," ibid. 73.

16. D. Findlay, "The Good, the Normal and the Healthy: The Social Construction of Medical Knowledge about Women" (1993) 18:2 Canadian Journal of Sociology 115.

17. M. Foucault, "Power and Strategies" in Power/Knowledge, supra note 14, 134.; M. Foucault, Fearless Speech (Los Angeles: Semiotexte, 2001).

18. L. Prior, The Social Organization of Death: Social Practices and Medical Discourse in Belfast (Basingstoke: MacMillan, 1989).

19. B. Latour, Science in Action: How to follow Scientists and Engineers through Society (Cambridge, Mass: Harvard university Press, 1987).

20. Supra note 18 at 325.

21. J.M. Atkinson, Discovering Suicide: Studies in the Social Organization of Death (London: MacMillan, 1978); J.D. Douglas, The Social Meaning of Suicide (Princeton: Princeton University Press, 1967).

22. A. Leadbetter, "Confessions of Ignorance of Causation in Coroners' Necropsies" (1996) 49:6 Journal of Clinical Pathology 439 at 442.

23. K. Figlo, "What is an Accident?" in P. Weindling, ed., The Social History of Occupational Health (London: Croom-Helm, 1985); R. Smith, "Forensic Pathology, Scientific Expertise, and the Criminal Law" in R. Smith & B. Wynne, eds., Expert Evidence: Interpreting Science in the Law (London: Routledge, 1989) 56; S. Tombs, "Workplace Injury and Death: Social Harm and the Illusions of Law" in P. Hillyard, C. Pantazis, S. Tombs & D. Gordon, eds., Beyond Criminology, Taking Harm Seriously (London: Pluto Press, 1984) 156.

24. G. Slapper, Blood in the Bank: Social and Legal Aspects of Death at Work (Aldershot: Ashgate, 1999) at 134.

25. Supra note 19 at 100.

26. J. Bakan, The Corporation, The Pathological Pursuit of Profit and Power (Toronto: Penguin Books, 2004); H. Glasbeek, Wealth By Stealth: Corporate Crime, Corporate Law and the Perversion of Democracy (Toronto: Between the Lines, 2002).

27. H. Becker, "Whose Side We On?" (1967) Social Problems 1 at 243.

28. Supra note 9, Eight Exercises and Crises of the Republic; S. Cohen, States of Denial: Knowing About Human Atrocities and Suffering (Cambridge: Polity Press, 2001).

29. Cohen, ibid. at 105–106.

30. G. Gilligan & J. Pratt, "Introduction: Crime, Truth and Justice—Official Inquiry and the Production of Knowledge" in Crime, Truth and Justice, supra note 7, 1; R.I. Rothberg, & D. Thompson, eds., Truth vs. Justice: The Morality of Truth Commissions (New Jersey: Princeton University Press, 2000); E. Tucker, "The Westray Disaster and Its Aftermath: The Politics of Causation" (1995) 10:1 C.J.L.S. 92.

31. P. Scraton, "From Deceit to Disclosure: The Politics of Official Inquiries in the United Kingdom" in G. Gilligan & J. Pratt, supra note 7 ["From Deceit to Disclosure"]; P. Scraton, "Lost Lives, Hidden Voices: 'Truth' and Controversial Deaths" (2002) 44:1 Race and Class 107; P. Scraton, Hillsborough: The Truth (Edinburgh: Mainstream Publishing 1999).

32. G. Gilligan, "Official Inquiry, Truth and Criminal Justice" in G. Gilligan & J. Pratt, supra note 7, 1.

33. P. Stenning, & C. LaPrairie, "'Politics by Other Means'; the Role of Commissions of Inquiry in establishing the 'Truth' about Aboriginal Justice in Canada" in G. Gilligan & J. Pratt, eds., supra note 7.

34. M. Foucault, Fearless Speech (Los Angeles: Semiotexte, 2001); J. Miller, The Passion of Michel Foucault (New York: Simon and Schuster, 1993) at 270–274; C. G. Prado, Searle and Foucault on Truth (Cambridge: Cambridge University Press) at 93–96; P. Carlen, "Official discourse, comic relief and the play of governance" in G. Gilligan & J. Pratt, supra note 7, 271.

35. *Supra* note 1 at 552.
36. Trial Transcript of *R. v. Curragh Inc.*, [1995] N.S.R. (2d) at Feb. 14, 1995 (paginated by day of trial only) [Trial Transcripts].
37. H. Lundsgaarde, *Crime in Space City: A Cultural Analysis of Houston Homicide Patterns* (New York: Oxford University Press, 1977) at 36.
38. "From Deceit to Disclosure", *supra* note 31.
39. Trial Transcripts, *supra* note 36.
40. *Ibid.*
41. *Ibid.* at Feb. 23, 1995.
42. R.A. Perry, *Death Certificates of Explosion Victims* (Halifax: Office of Chief Medical Examiner, 1992a); R.A. Perry, *Report of the Chief Medical Examiner: Westray Mine Explosion* (Halifax: Office of the Chief Medical Examiner, 1992b).
43. Trial Transcripts, *supra* note 36 at Feb. 23, 1995.
44. *Ibid.*
45. J.M. Atkinson, *Discovering Suicide: Studies in the Social Organization of Death* (London: Macmillan, 1978) at 172–181.
46. *Supra* note 24 at 138.
47. S. Cameron & A. Mitrovica, "Burying Westray" *Saturday Night* (May 1994) 54 at 56.
48. F. Burton & P. Carlen, *supra* note 11 at 51.
49. Trial Transcripts, *supra* note 36, at February 2, 1995.
50. Trial Transcripts, *supra* note 36 at April 10, 1995.
51. *Ibid.*
52. *Ibid.*
53. *Ibid.*
54. Cohen, *supra* note 28.
55. Gilligan & Pratt, *supra* note 30 at 132.
56. *Supra* note 24.
57. *Supra* note 24 at 93.
58. P. Bourdieu, *Outline of a Theory of Practice* (Cambridge: Cambridge University Press, 1977) at 169.
59. F. Burton & P. Carlen, *supra* note 11 at 51.
60. H. Glasbeek & E. Tucker, "Death by Consensus at Westray?" in *Westray Chronicles, supra* note 2, 71; T. Hynes & P. Prasad, "The Normal Violation of Safety Rules," *ibid.*, 117; E. Tucker, "The Westray Disaster and Its Aftermath: The Politics of Causation" (1995) 10:1 C.J.L.S. 92.
61. S. Comish, *The Westray Tragedy: A Miner's Story* (Halifax: Fernwood Publishing, 1993) at 53.
62. D Jobb, "Legal Disaster: Westray and the Justice System" in *Westray Chronicles, supra* note 2, 163.
63. S. Dodd, "Unsettled Accounts after Westray" in *Westray Chronicles, ibid.*, 232.
64. *Ibid.* at 230.
65. C.G. Davis, "Picking up the Pieces: The Personal Legacies of Westray" (Paper presented at the *Congress of the Humanities and Social Sciences*, June 1, 2003, Halifax, Nova Scotia, Canada) [unpublished] ["Picking up the Pieces"]; C.G. Davis, M.J.A. Wolh & N. Verberg, "Profiles of Posttraumatic Growth Following an Unjust Loss" Death Studies [forthcoming in 2007].
66. Davis, Wolh & Verberg, *ibid.*
67. N. Krieger & G. Davey Smith, "Bodies Count, and Body Counts: Social Epidemiology and Embodying Inequality" (2004) 26:1 Epidemiologic Reviews 94; Prior, *supra* note 18 at 63.
68. Dodd, "Unsettled Accounts after Westray" in *Westray Chronicles, supra* note 2 230 at 238–239.
69. "Picking up the Pieces," *supra* note 65 at 6.
70. *Westray Public Inquiry Transcripts* (Halifax: Westray Mine Public Inquiry, 1995–1997) Jan 18, 1996 at 3998.
71. *Ibid.* at 3965.
72. *Ibid.* Jan. 22, 1996, at 3941.
73. *Ibid.* at 4344.
74. *Ibid.* Jan. 18, 1996, at 4149.
75. *Ibid.* Jan 25, 1996, at 5150.
76. *Ibid.* Jan. 18, 1996, at 4151.
77. *Ibid.* Jan. 22, 1996, at 4333.
78. *Ibid.* Jan. 18, 1996, at 4136.
79. *Ibid.* Jan. 18, 1996, at 4115.

80. *Ibid.* Jan. 22, 1996, at 4404.

81. *Ibid.* at 4386.

82. Davis, Wohl & Verberg, *supra* note 65 at 19.

83. *Supra* note 1 at 1X.

84. S. Dodd, "Where the Slaughter is Wholesale: Fatality Reports from Nova Scotia's Coal Miners" (2005) [unpublished, archived at Halifax: King's College, Nova Scotia, Canada] at 26.

85. *Supra* note 1 at 3, 14.

86. *Supra* note 7 at 22.

87. *Supra* note 1 at VIII.

88. *Supra* note 11 at 51.

Part Two

Minorities and the Law

The treatment of minority groups can be considered a test of the overall fairness inherent in any legal system. Contemporary legal systems normally embody principles of legal equality that promote the equal treatment of all citizens, yet legal systems also contain systematic biases that exclude or discriminate against certain groups. Thus, discrimination based on race, gender, class, culture, and sexual orientation are evident in the administration of justice and in society at large. The Canadian legal system is no exception. The chapters in this part deal with instances where minority groups have demanded changes to the Canadian legal system to accommodate their needs.

In Chapter Five, Constance Backhouse presents a historical analysis of how racism affected Canadians of African descent. Chapter Six, by Abigail Baken and Audrey Kobiashi, highlights controversies over efforts to secure equity in employment. Chapter Seven, by Laura Westra, deals with issues involved in the increasing demands by Canada's Aboriginal peoples for greater autonomy over their legal affairs. The final chapter in this section is taken from Douglas Janoff's book, *Pink Blood: Homophobic Violence in Canada.* Janoff draws on documented cases of assaults on GLBT (gay, lesbian, bisexual, transgendered) people and ways in which police, prosecutors, defence lawyers, and judges have responded to such attacks.

Chapter Five

"Bitterly Disappointed" at the Spread of "Colour-Bar Tactics": Viola Desmond's Challenge to Racial Segregation, Nova Scotia, 1946

Constance Backhouse

Editors' Note:* Constance Backhouse's discussion of the Viola Desmond Case of mid-1940s Nova Scotia highlights how a colour bar was established in some areas of Canada and how race-based segregation was challenged in the courts, media, and society at large. The case involved charges brought against Viola Desmond, a biracial businesswoman who was considered "coloured." The incident began with a seeming twist of fate: in November 1946, her car had mechanical troubles in New Glasgow, Nova Scotia. While the car was being repaired, Ms. Desmond decided to see a movie playing at the Roseland Theatre, a local cinema. She sat in the downstairs area, designated for white patrons, and refused to leave her seat or relocate in the upstairs area reserved for "coloured" people. Ms. Desmond was forcibly removed from the theatre by a police officer, suffered injuries to her knee and hip, and jailed overnight.

Backhouse provides a detailed analysis of the 1946 trial of Viola Desmond for an alleged violation of the provincial Theatres, Cinematographs and Amusements Act of 1915, legislation that was meant to penalize people who did not pay an "amusement tax," and that did not specify race as part of such an infraction. Backhouse makes the important point that "most challenges to racial segregation in Canada seem to have come from middle-class individuals ... A certain level of economic security furnished a base which enabled such individuals to consider taking legal action against discriminatory treatment." Along with this social-class analysis, Backhouse has a sharp eye for divisions within professions and within the community. She traces differences of opinion within the legal community, among politicians, and certainly inside the black community—where some expressed dislike for the legal action and criticized Viola Desmond for attempting to pass as white, among other things. Backhouse also chronicles legal precedents and social customs that reinforced discriminatory treatment of black Canadians or that undermined discriminatory practices.

The contentious racial incident began on Friday, 8 November 1946, when Viola Irene Desmond's 1940 Dodge four-door sedan broke down in New Glasgow, Nova Scotia.[1] The thirty-two-year-old, Halifax-born Black woman was *en route* to Sydney on a business trip. Forced to wait overnight for repairs, she decided to take in the seven o'clock movie at the Roseland Theatre. Erected on the northeast corner of Forbes and Provost streets in 1913, the theatre was designed in the manner of grand old theatrical halls, and graced with colourful wall murals featuring paintings of "the land of roses." In its early days, the Roseland introduced New Glasgow audiences to silent pictures, with enthusiastic local musicians providing background sound with piano, cymbals, sirens, and bass drums. One of the most popular proved to be the American blockbuster *Birth of a Nation*. Outfitted with the latest modern equipment for sound in 1929,

Source: Constance Backhouse, "'Bitterly Disappointed' at the Spread of 'Colour-Bar Tactics': Viola Desmond's Challenge to Racial Segregation, Nova Scotia, 1946." Reprinted with permission from the Osgoode Society of Canadian Legal History.

* This synopsis is adapted from B. Burtch, *The Sociology of Law* (Toronto: Nelson Education, 2003), pages 128–130.

the theatre premiered Al Jolson's celebrated blackface performance in *The Jazz Singer* in the first month of "talkies." In time, the Roseland came to be New Glasgow's premier movie theatre.[2]

Handing the Roseland cashier a dollar bill, Viola Desmond requested "one down please." Peggy Melanson, the white ticket-seller on duty that evening, passed her a balcony ticket and seventy cents in change. Entirely unaware of what would ensue from her actions, Viola Desmond proceeded into the theatre and headed towards the main-floor seating area. Then Prima Davis, the white ticket-taker inside the theatre, called out after her: "This is an upstairs ticket, you will have to go upstairs."

Thinking there must have been some mistake, Viola Desmond returned to the wicket and asked the cashier to exchange the ticket for a downstairs one. The ticket-seller refused, and when Viola Desmond asked why, Peggy Melanson replied: "I'm sorry but I'm not permitted to sell downstairs tickets to you people."

Peggy Melanson never mentioned the word "Black," or the other terms, "Negro" or "coloured," which were more commonly used in the 1940s. But Viola Desmond recognized instantly that she was being denied seating on the basis of her race. She made a spontaneous decision to challenge this racial segregation, walked back inside, and took a seat in the partially filled downstairs portion of the theatre. As Prima Davis would later testify, "[When] she came back and passed into the theatre, I called to her. She never let on she heard me. She seated herself below."[3]

Prima Davis followed Viola Desmond to her main-floor row. Confronting the Black woman, who was now sitting quietly in her seat, she insisted, "I told you to go upstairs." When Viola Desmond refused to budge, Prima Davis left to report the matter to the white manager, Harry MacNeil. MacNeil was New Glasgow's most prominent "showman," his family having constructed MacNeil's Hall in the late 1870s to serve as the town's first theatre. The MacNeils brought in a series of concert artists, ventriloquists, astrologists, musicians, bell-ringers, jugglers, and tumblers to entertain theatre-goers. Town historians recall innumerable performances in MacNeil's hall of "Uncle Tom's Cabin," with "boozy has-beens of the classic theatre emoting lines of blackface roles with Shakespearean declamations." When moving pictures killed off live theatre, Harry MacNeil built a series of movie houses in New Glasgow, ultimately settling on the Roseland Theatre as the best location in town.[4]

Harry MacNeil came down immediately and "demanded" that Viola Desmond remove herself to the balcony. She had already "been told to go upstairs," MacNeil pointed out, and a notice on the back of the ticket stipulated that the theatre had "the right to refuse admission to any objectionable person." Viola Desmond replied that she had not been refused admission. The only problem was that her efforts to purchase a downstairs ticket had been unsuccessful. Politely but firmly, she requested the manager to obtain one for her. "I told him that I never sit upstairs because I can't see very well from that distance," she later told the press. "He became angry and said that he could have me thrown out of the theatre. As I was behaving very quietly, I didn't think he could." The agitated Harry MacNeil turned heel and marched off in pursuit of a police officer.

THE ARREST AT THE ROSELAND THEATRE

In short order, Harry MacNeil returned with a white policeman, who advised Viola Desmond that he "had orders" to throw her out of the theatre. "I told him that I was not doing anything and that I did not think he would do that," advised Viola Desmond. "He then took me by the shoulders and dragged me as far as the lobby. I had lost my purse and my shoe became disarranged in the scuffle." The police officer paused momentarily to allow Viola Desmond to adjust her shoe, while a bystander retrieved her purse. Then the forcible ejection resumed. As Viola Desmond recounted:

> The policeman grasped my shoulders and the manager grabbed my legs, injuring my knee and hip. They carried me bodily from the theatre out into the street. The policeman put me into a waiting taxi and I was driven to the police station. Within a few minutes the manager appeared and the Chief of Police [Elmo C. Langille]. They left together and returned in an hour with a warrant for my arrest.

She was taken to the town lock-up, where she was held overnight. Adding further insult, she was jailed in a cell alongside male prisoners. Mustering every ounce of dignity, Viola Desmond deliberately put on her white gloves, and steeled herself to sit bolt upright all night long. She later described her experience in the lock-up as follows: "I was put in a cell which had a bunk and blankets. There were a number of men in the same block and they kept bringing in more during the night. The matron was very nice and she seemed to realize that I shouldn't have been there. I was jailed for twelve hours …"[5]

THE TRIAL

The next morning, 9 November 1946, Viola Desmond was brought before New Glasgow magistrate Roderick Geddes MacKay. Born and bred in near-by St. Mary's in Pictou County, MacKay had graduated in law from Dalhousie University in 1904. He was appointed town solicitor for New Glasgow in 1930, where he managed his law practice while simultaneously holding down a part-time position as stipendiary magistrate. The sixty-nine-year-old white magistrate was the sole legal official in court that day. Viola Desmond had no lawyer; she had not been told of her right to seek bail or to request an adjournment, nor of her right to counsel. Indeed, there was no Crown attorney present either. Harry MacNeil, "the informant," was listed as the prosecutor.[6]

Viola Desmond was arraigned on a charge of violating the provincial Theatres, Cinematographs and Amusements Act. First enacted in 1915, the statute contained no explicit provisions relating to racial segregation. A licensing statute to regulate the operations of theatres and movie houses, the act encompassed such matters as safety inspections and the censorship of public performances. It also stipulated that patrons were to pay an amusement tax on any tickets purchased in provincial theatres. Persons who entered a theatre without paying such tax were subject to summary conviction and a fine of "not less than twenty nor more than two hundred dollars." The statute authorized police officers to arrest violators without warrant, and to use "reasonable diligence" in taking them before a stipendiary magistrate or justice of the peace "to be dealt with according to law."[7]

The statute based the rate of the amusement tax upon the price of the ticket. The Roseland Theatre's ticket prices were forty cents for downstairs seats, and thirty cents for upstairs seats. These prices included a tax of three cents on the downstairs tickets, and two cents on the upstairs. The ticket issued to Viola Desmond cost thirty cents, of which two cents would be forwarded to the public coffers. Since she had insisted on sitting downstairs, she was one cent short on tax.[8]

This was the argument put forth by Harry MacNeil, Peggy Melanson, and Prima Davis, all of whom gave sworn evidence against Viola Desmond that morning. The trial was short. The three white witnesses briefly testified that the accused woman had purchased an upstairs ticket, paying two cents in tax, and then insisted on seating herself downstairs. After each witness concluded, Magistrate MacKay asked the prisoner if she wanted to ask any questions. "I did not gather until almost the end of the case that he meant questions to be asked of the witnesses," Viola Desmond would later explain. "It was never explained to me of whom I was to ask the questions." So there was no cross-examination of the prosecution witnesses whatsoever.[9]

At the close of the Crown's case, Viola Desmond took the stand herself. The minutes of evidence from the trial record contain a succinct report of her testimony: "I am the accused. I offered to pay the difference in the price between the tickets. They would not accept it." Magistrate MacKay convicted the defendant and assessed the minimum fine of $20, with costs of $6 payable to the prosecuting informant, Harry MacNeil. The total amount of $26 was due forthwith, in default of which the accused was ordered to spend one month in jail.[10]

Viola Desmond was quite properly angry that she was offered no opportunity to speak about the real issues underlying the taxation charges. "The Magistrate immediately convicted and sentenced me without asking me if I had any submissions to make to the Court on the evidence adduced and without informing me that I had the right to make such submissions," she later explained. Even a casual observer can see that many arguments might have been raised to preclude a conviction. It was far from clear that Viola Desmond had actually transgressed the statute. According to her testimony, she tendered the difference in the ticket prices (including the extra cent in tax), but the manager and ticket-seller refused to accept her money. It is difficult to find the legally required *actus reus* (criminal act) in Viola Desmond's behaviour here. Indeed, if anyone had violated the statute, it was the theatre owner, who was in dereliction of his statutory duty to collect the tendered taxes and forward them to the designated government board.[11]

Furthermore, the price differential between upstairs and downstairs seats was not prescribed by statute. It was simply a discretionary business policy devised by the management of the theatre. The manager could have decided to collapse the two admission prices and ask one single fee at whim. In this instance, Harry MacNeil chose to charge Viola Desmond a mere thirty cents for her ticket, and on this amount she had paid the full tax owing. She was not charged forty cents, so she did not owe the extra cent in tax. The court might have construed the rules regarding alternate seating arrangements as internal business regulations having nothing whatsoever to do with the revenue provisions in the legislation.

Even more problematic was the prosecution's questionable attempt to utilize provincial legislation to buttress community practices of racial discrimination. The propriety of calling upon a licensing and revenue statute to enforce racial segregation in public theatres was never addressed. Did the legislators who enacted the statute design the taxing sections for this purpose? Were racially disparate ticket-selling practices contemplated when the statutory tax rates were set? Were the penalty sections intended to attach alike to theatre-goers deliberately evading admission charges and Blacks protesting racial segregation? As the press would later attest, Viola Desmond "was being tried for being a negress and not for any felony."[12]

Observers of the trial would have been struck by the absence of any overt discussion of racial issues. In the best tradition of Canadian "racelessness," the prosecution witnesses never explained that Viola Desmond had been denied the more expensive downstairs ticket on the basis of her race. No one admitted that the theatre patrons were assigned seats on the basis of race. In an interview with the Toronto *Daily Star* several weeks later, Harry MacNeil would insist that neither he nor the Odeon Theatres management had ever issued instructions that main floor tickets were not to be sold to Blacks. It was simply a matter of seating preferences: "It is customary for [colored persons] to sit together in the balcony," MacNeil would assert.[13] At the trial, no one even hinted that Viola Desmond was Black, that her accusers and her judge were white. On its face, the proceeding appears to be simply a prosecution for failure to pay provincial tax. In fact, if Viola Desmond had not taken any further action in this matter, the surviving trial records would have left no clue to the real significance of the case.[14]

VIOLA DESMOND: THE WOMAN ACCUSED

The day of her conviction, Viola Desmond paid the full fine, secured her release, and returned to her home on 4 Prince William Street in Halifax. She was deeply affronted by her treatment at the hands of the New Glasgow officials. Her decision to protest the racially segregated seating practices at the Roseland Theatre had initially been a spontaneous gesture, but now she was resolved to embark upon a more premeditated course of action. She was also "well known" throughout the Black community in Nova Scotia, and consequently in a good position to do something about it.[15]

Viola Desmond, whose birth name was Viola Irene Davis, was born in Halifax, on 6 July 1914, into a prominent, middle-class, self-identified "coloured" family. Her paternal grandfather, a Black self-employed barber, had established the Davis Barbershop in Halifax's North End. Barbering was an occupation within which a number of Canadian Blacks managed to carve out a successful living in the nineteenth and early twentieth centuries. Hair-cutting and -styling were rigorously segregated by race in many portions of the country, with white barbers and beauticians reluctant to accept Black customers. Black barbers were quick to seize the business opportunities rejected by racist whites, and set up shop servicing both Black and white clientele.[16]

James Albert Davis, Viola's father, worked in the Davis Barbershop for a time, and then took up employment as a shipwright in the Halifax Shipyards. Eventually, he established a career for himself as a businessman, managing real estate and operating a car dealership. Although it was extremely difficult for Blacks to obtain positions within the civil service, two of Viola's male relatives worked for the federal postal service.[17]

Viola's mother, Gwendolin Irene Davis, was the daughter of a Baptist minister who had come to Halifax from New Haven, Connecticut. Gwendolin Davis's mother, Susan Smith, was born in Connecticut and identified herself as white. Gwendolin's father, Henry Walter Johnson, was "seven-eighths white" and although he is described as being "of mixed race," Gwendolin Davis seems to have been generally regarded as white.[18]

The question of racial designation, inherently a complex matter, becomes even more problematic when individuals with different racial designations form blended families. Some have suggested that a fundamental premise of racial ideology, rooted in the history of slavery, stipulates that if individuals have even "one Black ancestor," regardless of their skin colour they qualify for classification as "Black." However, it is equally clear that some light-skinned individuals are able to "pass" for white if they choose, or can be mistaken for "white," regardless of their own self-identification.[19]

Viola's parents married in 1908, creating what was perceived to be a mixed-race family within a culture that rarely welcomed interracial marriage. It was not the actual fact of racial mixing that provoked such concern, for there was undeniable evidence that interracial reproduction had occurred extensively throughout North American history. It was the formalized recognition of such unions that created such unease within a culture based on white supremacy. The tensions posed within a racist society by an apparently mixed-race family often came home to roost on the children born to James and Gwendolin Davis. Viola's younger sister recalls children taunting them in the schoolyard, jeering: "They may think you're white because they saw your mother at Parents' Day, but they haven't seen your father." Viola self-identified both as "mixed-race" and as "coloured," the latter being a term of preference during the 1930s and 1940s.[20]

Viola Davis was an extremely capable student, whose initial schooling was obtained within a racially mixed student body at Sir Joseph Howe Elementary School and Bloomfield High School. Upon her graduation from high school, Viola took up teaching for a brief period at Preston and Hammonds Plains, racially segregated schools for Black students. She saved all of her teaching wages, since she knew from the outset that she wanted to set up a hairdressing business of her own. Modern fashion trends for women, first heralded by the introduction of the "bobbed" haircut in the 1920s, created an explosion of adventurous career opportunities for "beauticians," who earned their livelihood by advising women on hair care and cosmetics. Beauticians provided much-sought-after services within the all-female world of the new "beauty parlours," which came to serve important functions as neighbourhood social centres. Beauty parlors offered steady and socially respectable opportunities to many entrepreneurial women across Canada and the United States.[21]

Despite severely limited employment opportunities in most fields, some Black women were able to create their own niche in this new market, as beauticians catering to a multi-racial clientele with particular expertise in hair design and skin care for Black women. This was Viola Desmond's entrepreneurial goal, but the first barrier she faced was in her training. All of the facilities available to train beauticians in Halifax restricted Black women from admission. Viola was forced to travel to Montreal, where she was able to enrol in the Field Beauty Culture School in 1936. Her aspirations took her from Montreal to New York, where she enrolled in courses to learn more about wigs and other styling touches. In 1940, she received a diploma from the acclaimed Apex College of Beauty Culture and Hairdressing in Atlantic City, founded by the renowned Black entrepreneur Sarah Spencer Washington.[22]

Shortly before she left for her first training in Montreal, Viola met John Gordon (Jack) Desmond, a man ten years her senior. Their courtship would ultimately lead to her marriage at the age of twenty-two. Jack Desmond was a descendant of generations of Black Loyalists who had settled in Guysborough County in 1783, when several thousand free Blacks took up land grants from the Crown. He was born into a family of eight children in Tracadie, Nova Scotia, on 22 February 1905, and lived for some years in New Glasgow. He moved to Halifax in 1928 and took employment with a construction company, but the loss of his eye to a metal splinter in a work accident in October 1930 cost Jack Desmond his job.[23]

Shifting careers by necessity, in 1932 Jack Desmond opened his own business, Jack's Barbershop on Gottingen Street, a central thoroughfare in the "Uptown Business District" in a racially mixed neighbourhood in the old north end of Halifax. The business attracted a racially mixed clientele, drawn in part from the men who came in on the ships at the naval dockyard. The first Black barber to be formally registered in Nova Scotia, Jack Desmond was popular, with an easy-going personality that would earn him the title "The King of Gottingen Street." Jack became romantically interested in the young Viola Davis, took the train up to Montreal to see her while she was in training, and ultimately proposed marriage there. In 1936, the couple was married before a Baptist minister in Montreal.[24]

When Viola returned to Halifax in 1937, she set up Vi's Studio of Beauty Culture alongside her husband's barbershop on Gottingen Street. She offered her customers a range of services, including shampoos, press and curl, hair-straightening, chignons, and hairpieces and wigs. Former customers recall the weekly Saturday trip to "Vi's" as the social highlight of the week. Viola Desmond amassed a devoted clientele, many of whom still recollect with great fondness her sense of humour, her sympathetic nature, and her cheerful, positive outlook on life. The younger women thought of her as inspirational, someone who "took all of us kids from this area under her wing, and was like a mother to us all."[25]

Ambitious and hard-working, Viola Desmond soon developed plans to expand her business. She branched out into chemistry and learned how to manufacture many specialized Black beauty powders and creams, which she marketed under the label "Vi's Beauty products." She added facials and ultra-violet-ray hair treatments to her line of services. Viola Desmond's clientele encompassed legendary figures such as the Black classical singer Portia White, who came for private appointments on Sundays because her hectic schedule did not permit regular appointments during the week. Gwen Jenkins, the first Black nurse in Nova Scotia, began weekly visits to "Vi's Children's Club" for washing and braiding at the age of ten. Despite the hectic pace of business, Viola continued to take courses in the latest hair styles and make-up, travelling to New York every other year to update her expertise. In 1945, she was awarded a silver trophy for hair styling by the Montreal Orchid School of Beauty Culture. Recognizing that there were additional opportunities outside of Halifax, Viola began to travel around the province, setting up temporary facilities to deliver products and services to other members of the Black communities.[26]

Although Jack was initially supportive of his wife's choice of career, her ambitious business plans began to cause him some distress. He became concerned that all of the travel required was inappropriate for a married woman. Both spouses in Black families frequently held down jobs in the paid labour force, contrary to the pattern in white middle-class households. But middle-class Black women who sought work outside the home often faced bitter tensions within their marriages. Their careers tended to clash with society's prevailing ideals of gender, which required that men be masters in their own homes, ruling over dependent women and children. Even women who remained childless, such as Viola Desmond, found themselves subject to pressure to retire from the paid workforce.[27]

At odds with her husband on this point, Viola Desmond held firm convictions that Black women ought to have greater access to employment opportunities outside their traditionally segregated sphere of domestic service. A few years after she set up her own studio, she opened the Desmond School of Beauty Culture, which drew Black female students from across Nova Scotia, New Brunswick, and Quebec. Viola Desmond's long-range plans were to work with the women who graduated from her school to establish a franchise operation, setting up beauty parlours for people of colour across Canada. Her former students recall that she kept the shop immaculately; that all the beauticians, including Viola, wore uniforms and regulation stockings; and that their appearance was rigorously inspected each day. Viola Desmond personified respectability to her students, who always called her "Mrs. Desmond" and were struck by the "way that she carried herself" and her "strength of character."[28]

The evidence suggests that most legal challenges to racial segregation in Canada seem to have come from middle-class individuals. This appears not to be a coincidental factor, for class issues are intricately related to such matters. A certain level of economic security furnished a base which enabled such individuals to consider taking legal action against discriminatory treatment. Furthermore, given contemporary class biases, middle-class status appears to have underscored the indignity of racist treatment. Viola Desmond's elite position within the province's Black community was well established. She and her husband, Jack, were often held up as examples of prosperous Black entrepreneurs, whose small-business ventures had triumphed over the considerable economic barriers that stood in the way of Black business initiatives. Yet regardless of her visible financial standing in the community, Viola Desmond remained barred from entry into the more expensive seating area of the New Glasgow theatre. For those who believed that economic striving would eventually "uplift" the Black race, the response of the manager of the Roseland Theatre crushed all hope of eventually achieving an egalitarian society.[29]

The matter of gender is also important in understanding the significance of Viola Desmond's ejection from the Roseland Theatre. In making her decision to challenge racial segregation in the courts, Viola Desmond became one of the first Black women in Canada to do so. As the controversy spread, Viola Desmond also came to symbolize the essence of middle-class Black femininity. She was a celebrated Halifax beautician, described as both "elegantly coiffed and fashionable dressed," a "fine-featured woman with an eye for style." Her contemporaries recall that she was always beautifully attired, her nails, make-up, and hair done with great care.

Described as a "petite, quiet-living, demure" woman, who stood four foot eleven inches, and weighed less than one hundred pounds, Viola Desmond was a well-mannered, refined, demonstrably *feminine* woman, physically manhandled by rude and forcibly violent white men. The spectacle would undoubtedly have provoked considerable outcry had the principal actors all been middle-class whites. Customary white gender relations dictated that, at least in public, physically taller and stronger men should exercise caution and delicacy in their physical contact with women. Roughing up a lady violated the very core of the ideology of chivalry.[30]

The extension of traditional white gender assumptions to Black women provoked more pause. Racist practices condoned and nurtured throughout North America during times of slavery denied Black women both the substance and the trappings of white femininity. Slave masters compelled their male and female slaves alike to labour alongside each other, irrespective of gender. Black women found their reproductive capacity commodified for material gain, and frequently experienced rape at the hands of their white owners and overseers. Denied the most fundamental rights to their own bodies and sexuality, Black women were barred by racist whites from any benefits that the idealized cult of "motherhood" and "femininity" might have offered white women. The signs on the segregated washrooms of the Deep South, "white ladies" and "black women," neatly encapsulated the racialized gender assumptions. As Evelyn Brooks Higginbotham has described it, "no black woman, regardless of income, education, refinement, or character, enjoyed the status of lady."[31]

Whites who [subscribed] to attitudes such as these were somewhat unsettled by women such as Viola Desmond. Throughout her frightening and humiliating ordeal, she had remained the embodiment of female respectability. Her challenge to the racially segregated seating policies was carried out politely and decorously. Her dignified response in the face of the volatile theatre manager's threat to throw her out was that she "was behaving very quietly," and so "didn't think he could." Even the white matron from the New Glasgow lock-up recognized the incongruity of exposing a refined woman to the rough-and-tumble assortment of men collected in the cell that night: "She seemed to realize that I shouldn't have been there," emphasized Viola Desmond. By the standards of the dominant culture, Viola Desmond was undeniably feminine in character and deportment. The question remained whether the ideology of chivalry would be extended to encompass a Black woman who was insulted and physically mauled by white men.

THE COMMUNITY RESPONDS TO THE CONVICTION

The first to hear about the incident was Viola Desmond's husband, Jack, who was upset but not surprised. Jack was quite familiar with New Glasgow's Roseland Theatre. In fact, he had watched the Roseland Theatre being built while he worked as a child in the drugstore next door. "[T]here were no coloreds allowed downstairs," he recalled later. "She didn't know that—I knew it because I grew up there." A deeply religious man, Jack Desmond held philosophical views that were rooted in tolerance: "You've got to know how to handle it," he would counsel. "Take it to the Lord with a prayer."[32]

Viola Desmond was considerably less willing to let temporal matters lie, as the interview she gave to the Halifax *Chronicle* shortly afterward indicates:

I can't understand why such measures should have been taken. I have travelled a great deal throughout Canada and parts of the United States and nothing like this ever happened to me before. I was born in Halifax and have lived here most of my life and I've found relations between negroes and whites very pleasant. I didn't realize a thing like this could happen in Nova Scotia— or in any other part of Canada.[33]

The shock that underlies this statement clearly communicates the magnitude of the insult that Viola Desmond experienced in the Roseland arrest. She must have been no stranger to racial segregation. She taught in segregated schools, was denied occupational training on the basis of race, and was keenly aware of segregated facilities in her own business. But unexpectedly to encounter segregated seating in a Nova Scotian theatre seems to have struck Viola Desmond as a startling injustice. The unforeseen discrimination was magnified by the heinous actions of the theatre manager and various officials of the state, who responded to her measured resistance with armed force and criminal prosecution. To see the forces of law so unanimously and spontaneously arrayed against her quiet protest must have struck Viola Desmond as outrageous. Couching her complaint in the most careful of terms, with polite reference to the "very pleasant" relations that normally ensued between the races, she challenged Canadians to respond to this unconscionable treatment, to side with her against the legal authorities who pursued her conviction.

A considerable portion of the Black community in Halifax seems to have shared Viola Desmond's anger and concern over the incident. Pearleen Oliver was one of the first to take up the case. One of the most prominent Black women in Nova Scotia, Pearleen Oliver was born into a family of ten children in Cook's Cove, Guysborough County, in 1917. She "put herself through high school by doing housework," the first Black graduate of New Glasgow High School in 1936. After graduation, she married the young Reverend William Pearly Oliver. The Olivers presided over an almost exclusively Black congregation at Cornwallis Street Baptist Church, where the Rev. Oliver was posted as minister. Viola and Jack Desmond belonged to the Cornwallis Church, and the morning after her arrest Viola Desmond came over to seek advice from the Olivers. Only Pearleen was home, but she recalls vividly that Viola Desmond was shaken and tearful as she related her experience. "I said, 'Oh Dear God, Viola, what did they do to you, what did they do to you?'" Pearleen Oliver was appalled by what had happened, and told Viola that she should seek legal advice. "I figured it was now or never," explained Mrs. Oliver, "Hitler was dead and the Second World War was over. I wanted to take it to court."[34]

Pearleen Oliver had an enviable record as a confirmed proponent of racial equality. In 1944, she spearheaded a campaign of the Halifax Coloured Citizens Improvement League to force the Department of Education to remove racially objectionable material from its public-school texts. The insulting depiction of "Black Sambo" in the Grade 11 text should be stricken from the books, she insisted, and replaced by the "authentic history of the colored people" and accounts of "their contribution to Canadian culture." The leader of the Ladies Auxiliary of the African United Baptist Association, who campaigned extensively to eliminate racial barriers from the nursing profession, Pearleen Oliver, also took matters affecting Black women extremely seriously.[35]

When he learned of Viola's treatment later that weekend, the Rev. William Oliver was equally concerned. An influential member of the African United Baptist Association of Nova Scotia, the Rev. Oliver had achieved public acclaim as the only Black chaplain in the Canadian army during the Second World War. A confirmed proponent of racial equality in education and employment, William Oliver was no stranger to humiliating practices of racial segregation himself. He had been refused service in restaurants, barred from social activities organized by whites, and challenged when he attempted to participate in white athletic events. William Oliver was on record as opposing racial segregation in hotels, restaurants, and other public facilities, stressing that businesses should "cater to the public on the basis of individual behavior, regardless of race."[36]

The Olivers were shocked by the visible bruises on Viola Desmond's body, and they advised her to get immediate medical attention. The Black physician whom Viola consulted on 12 November treated her for injuries to her knee and hip, and also advised his patient to retain a lawyer to appeal the conviction.[37]

Recognizing that they needed to gather assistance from the wider community, Pearleen Oliver sought public support for Viola's case from the Nova Scotia Association for the Advancement of Colored People (NSAACP). The NSAACP, dedicated to eradicating race discrimination in housing, education, and employment, was founded in 1945. Pearleen Oliver found about half of the NSAACP members supportive of Viola Desmond's court challenge, while half expressed initial reluctance. Divisions of opinion about strategies for change seem to be inherent in all social reform movements, and the NSAACP was no exception. Fears of fostering racist backlash, concerns about using the law to confront racial segregation, and questions about whether equal admission to theatres was a pressing issue seem to have motivated the more cautious.[38]

Pearleen Oliver made a convincing case for supporting a legal claim, however, and all of the members of the NSAACP ultimately backed the case. They pledged to call public meetings about Viola Desmond's treatment and to raise funds to defray any legal costs. As Pearleen Oliver would explain to the Halifax *Chronicle*, the NSAACP intended to fight Viola Desmond's case to prevent "a spread of color-bar tactics" across the province.[39]

Some dissent continued to linger within the Black community. One individual wrote to *The Clarion*, a bi-weekly Black newspaper founded in New Glasgow in July 1946:

> About all we have to say about our Country is "Thank God" for it. With all its shortcomings it is still the best place on earth. I would like to start complaining about segregation in theatres and restaurants, but as I look around me and see the food stores filled to overflowing while countless millions are starving I just can't get het up over not eating in certain places. I am EATING and REGULARLY. Later on, maybe, but not now. Canada is still all right with me.[40]

The argument made here seems partially rooted in economic or class-based concerns. The letter focused on issues of basic sustenance, intimating indirectly that those who could afford to eat in restaurants or attend the theatre were not fully representative of the Black community. In contrast, Carrie M. Best, the forty-three-year-old Black editor of *The Clarion*, believed that the question of racial segregation in public facilities was extremely important to the entire Black population. She wrote back defending those who would challenge such discrimination:

> It is sometimes said that those who seek to serve are "looking for trouble." There are some who think it better to follow the line of least resistance, no matter how great the injury. Looking for trouble? How much better off the world would be if men of good will would look for trouble, find it, and while it is merely a cub, drag it out into the open, before it becomes the ferocious lion. Racial and Religious hatred is trouble of the gravest kind. It is a vicious, smouldering and insidious kind of trouble, born of fear and ignorance. It often lays dormant for years until some would[-]be Hitler, Bilbo or Rankin emerges to fan the flame into an uncontrollable catastrophe.
>
> It is heartening to know how many trouble shooters have come to the aid of *The Clarion* since the disgraceful Roseland incident. They are convinced, as we are, that it is infinitely wiser to look for trouble than to have trouble looking for them.[41]

Carrie Best would profile Viola Desmond's treatment on the front pages of *The Clarion*, denouncing it as a "disgraceful incident," and claiming that "New Glasgow stands for Jim-crowism, at its basest, over the entire globe." She also gave prominent placement to a notice from Bernice A. Williams, NSAACP secretary, announcing a public meeting to solicit contributions for the Viola Desmond Court Fund. *The Clarion* urged everyone to attend and give donations: "The NSAACP is the Ladder to Advancement. Step on it! Join today!" Money began to trickle in from across the province, with donations by whites and Blacks alike.[42]

Carrie Best, who was born and educated in New Glasgow, was well acquainted with the egregious forms of white racism practised there. A woman who defined herself as an "activist" against racism, she did not mince words when she claimed there were "just as many racists in New Glasgow as in Alabama."[43] She was thrown out of the Roseland Theatre herself in 1942, for refusing to sit in the balcony, and tried unsuccessfully to sue the theatre management for damages then.[44]

Nor was she a stranger to the heroism of Black resisters. One of her most vivid childhood memories involved a race riot that erupted in New Glasgow at the close of the First World War. An interracial altercation between two youths inspired "bands of roving white men armed with clubs" to station themselves at different intersections in the town, barring Blacks from crossing. At dusk that evening, Carrie Best's mother was delivered home from work by the chauffeur of the family who employed her. There she found that her husband, her younger son, and Carrie had made it home safely. Missing was Carrie's older brother, who had not yet returned from his job at the Norfolk House hotel. Carrie described what ensued in her autobiography, *That Lonesome Road*:

> In all the years she lived and until she passed away at the age of eighty-one my mother was never known to utter an unkind, blasphemous or obscene word, nor did I ever see her get angry. This evening was no exception. She told us to get our meal, stating that she was going into town to get my brother. It was a fifteen minute walk.
>
> At the corner of East River Road and Marsh Street the crowd was waiting and as my mother drew near they hurled insults at her and threateningly ordered her to turn back. She continued to walk toward the hotel about a block away when one of the young men recognized her and asked her where she was going. "I am going to the Norfolk House for my son," she answered calmly. (My mother was six feet tall and as straight as a ramrod.) The young man ordered the crowd back and my mother continued on her way to the hotel. At that time there was a livery stable at the rear entrance to the hotel and it was there my mother found my frightened older brother and brought him safely home.[45]

This was but one incident in an increasingly widespread pattern of white racism, that exploded with particular virulence across Canada during and immediately following the First World War. White mobs terrorized the Blacks living near New Glasgow, physically destroying their property. White soldiers also attacked the Black settlement in Truro, Nova Scotia, stoning houses and shouting obscenities. Throughout the 1920s, Blacks in Ontario and Saskatchewan withstood increasingly concerted intimidation from the hateful Ku Klux Klan. But race discrimination had a much longer history in Canada.[46]

THE HISTORY OF BLACK SEGREGATION IN CANADA

From the middle of the nineteenth century, Blacks and whites in two provinces could be relegated to separate schools by law.[47] Ontario amended its School Act in 1849 to permit municipal councils "to authorize the establishing of any number of schools for the education of the children of colored people that they may judge expedient." The preamble to the statute was quite specific. The legislation was necessary, it admitted, because "the prejudices and ignorance" of certain Ontario residents had "prevented" certain Black children from attending the common schools in their district. The statute was amended in 1850, to direct local public school trustees to establish separate schools upon the application of twelve or more "resident heads of families" in the area. In 1886, the legislature clarified that schools for "coloured people" were to be set up only after an application had been made by at least five Black families in the community.[48]

Although drafted in permissive language, white officials frequently used coercive tactics to force Blacks into applying for segregated schools.[49] Once separate schools were set up, the courts refused Black children admission to any other schools, despite evidence that this forced many to travel long distances to attend schools they would not have chosen otherwise.[50] Separate schools for Blacks continued until 1891 in Chatham, 1893 in Sandwich, 1907 in Harrow, 1917 in Amherstburg, and 1965 in North Colchester and Essex counties.[51] The Ontario statute authorizing racially segregated education would not be repealed until 1964.[52] As white historian Robin Winks has noted:

> The Negro schools lacked competent teachers, and attendance was highly irregular and unenforced. Many schools met for only three months in the year or closed entirely. Most had no library of any kind. In some districts, school taxes were collected from Negro residents to support the [white] common school from which their children were barred ... The education received ... could hardly have been regarded as equal ...[53]

Similar legislation dating from 1865 existed in Nova Scotia, where education authorities were authorized to establish "separate apartments or buildings" for pupils of "different colors."[54] A campaign for racial integration in the schools, organized by leaders of the Black community in 1884, prompted an amendment to the law, stipulating that Black pupils could not be excluded from instruction in the areas in which they lived.[55] The original provisions for segregation within the public school system remained intact until 1950.[56] In 1940, school officials in Lower Sackville, in Halifax County, barred Black children from attending the only public school in the area, and until 1959 school buses would stop only in the white sections of Hammonds Plains. In 1960, there would still be seven formal Black school districts and three additional exclusively Black schools in Nova Scotia.[57]

Beyond the schools, racial segregation riddled the country. The colour bar was less rigidified than in the United States, varying between regions and shifting over time.[58] But Canadian employers commonly selected their workforce by race rather than by merit.[59] Access to land grants and residential housing was frequently restricted by race.[60] Attempts were made to bar Blacks from jury service.[61] The military was rigorously segregated.[62] Blacks were denied equal access to some forms of public transportation.[63] Blacks and whites tended to worship in separate churches, sometimes by choice, other times because white congregations refused membership to Blacks.[64] Orphanages and poor-houses could be segregated by race.[65] Some hospitals refused access to facilities to non-white physicians and service to non-white patients.[66] Blacks were even denied burial rights in segregated cemeteries.[67] While no consistent pattern ever emerged, various hotels, restaurants, theatres, athletic facilities, parks, swimming pools, beaches, dance pavilions, skating rinks, pubs and bars were closed to Blacks across the country.[68]

There were as yet no Canadian statutes expressly prohibiting such behaviour. The first statute to prohibit segregation on the basis of race did not appear until more than a year after Viola Desmond launched her civil suit, when Saskatchewan banned race discrimination in "hotels, victualling houses, theatres or other places to which the public is customarily admitted." The 1947 Saskatchewan Bill of Rights Act, which also barred discrimination in employment, business ventures, housing, and education, constituted Canada's first comprehensive human rights legislation. The act offered victims of race discrimination the opportunity to prosecute offenders upon summary conviction for fines of up to $200. The Court of King's Bench was also empowered to issue injunctions to restrain the offensive behaviour.[69] But none of this would assist Viola Desmond in November 1946.

PREPARING FOR LEGAL BATTLE

Had Viola Desmond wished to retain a Black lawyer to advise her on legal options, this would have presented difficulties. Nine Black men appear to have been admitted to the bar of Nova Scotia prior to 1946, but few were available for hire.[70] The only Black lawyer practising in Halifax in 1946 was Rowland Parkinson Goffe. A native of Jamaica, Goffe practised initially in England, taking his call to the Nova Scotia bar in 1920. Goffe travelled abroad frequently, operating his legal practice in Halifax only intermittently. For reasons that are unclear, Viola Desmond did not retain Goffe. He may have been away from Halifax at the time.[71]

Four days after her arrest, on 12 November, Viola Desmond retained the services of a white lawyer named Frederick William Bissett. Rev. William Oliver knew Bissett, and it was he who made the initial arrangements for Viola to see the lawyer. A forty-four-year-old native of St. John's, Newfoundland, Bissett graduated in 1926 from Dalhousie Law School with a reputation as a "sharp debater." Called to the bar in Nova Scotia that year, he opened his own law office in Halifax, where he practised alone until his elevation to the Supreme Court of Nova Scotia in 1961. A noted trial lawyer, Bissett was acclaimed for his "persistence and resourcefulness," his "keen wit and an infectious sense of humour." Those who knew him emphasized that, above all, Bissett was "gracious and charming," a true "gentleman." This last feature of his character would potentially have been very helpful to Viola Desmond and her supporters. Their case would be considerably aided if the courts could be induced to visualize Viola Desmond as a "lady" wronged by rough and racist men. The affront to customary gender assumptions might have been just the thing to tip the balance in the minds of judges who would otherwise have been reluctant to oppose racial segregation. A "gentleman" such as Bissett would have been the perfect choice to advocate extending the mantle of white chivalry across race lines to cover Black women.[72]

Bissett's first task was to decide how to frame Viola Desmond's claim within the doctrines of law. One option might have been to mount a direct attack on the racially restrictive admissions policy of the theatre. There was an excellent precedent for such a claim in an earlier Quebec Superior Court decision, *Johnson v. Sparrow*. In 1899, the court awarded $50 in damages to a Black couple barred from sitting in the orchestra section of the Montreal Academy of Music. Holding that a "breach of contract" had occurred, a white judge, John Sprott Archibald, reasoned that "any regulation which deprived negroes as a class of privileges which all other members of the community had a right to demand, was not only unreasonable but entirely incompatible with our free democratic institutions." The Quebec Court of Queen's Bench affirmed the ruling on appeal, although it focussed exclusively on the breach of contract and held that the issue of racial equality did not need to be directly addressed at the time.[73]

A similar position was taken in British Columbia in 1914, in the case of *Barnswell v National Amusement Company, Limited*. The Empress Theatre in Victoria promulgated a "rule of the house that coloured people should not be admitted." When the white theatre manager turned away James Barnswell, a Black man who was a long-time resident of Victoria, he sued for breach of contract and assault. The white trial judge, Peter Secord Lampman, found the defendant company liable for breach of contract, and awarded Barnswell $50 in damages for humiliation. The British Columbia Court of Appeal affirmed the result.[74]

A string of other cases had done much to erode these principles. In 1911, a Regina newspaper announced that a local restaurant was planning to charge Black customers double what whites paid for meals, in an effort to exclude them from the local lunch-counter. When William Hawes, a Black man, was billed $1.40 instead of the usual $0.70 for a plate of ham and eggs, he took the white restaurant-keeper, W. H. Waddell, to court one week later. His claim was that Waddell had obtained money "by false pretences." The case was dismissed in Regina's Police Court, with the local white magistrates concluding that Hawes had known of the double fare when he entered the restaurant, and that this barred a charge of false pretences.[75]

Another example of judicial support for racial segregation occurred during the upsurge of racial violence at the close of the First World War. In 1919, the majority of the white judges on the Quebec Court of King's Bench held in *Loew's Montreal Theatres Ltd. v Reynolds* that the theatre management had "the right to assign particular seats to different races and classes of men and women as it sees fit." White theatre proprietors from Quebec east to the Maritimes greeted this ruling with enthusiasm, using it to contrive new and expanded policies of racially segregated seating.[76] In 1924, in *Franklin v. Evans*, a white judge from the Ontario High Court dismissed a claim for damages "for insult and injury" from W. V. Franklin, a Black watch-maker from Kitchener, who was refused lunch service in "The Cave," a London restaurant.[77] In 1940, in *Rogers v Clarence Hotel*, the majority of the white judges on the British Columbia Court of Appeal held that the white female proprietor of a beer parlour, Rose Elizabeth Low, could refuse to serve a Black Vancouver businessman, Edward Tisdale Rogers, because of his race. The doctrine of "complete freedom of commerce" justified the owner's right to deal "as [she] may choose with any individual member of the public."[78]

Fred Christie v The York Corporation, ultimately reaching a similar result, wound its way through the Quebec court system right up to the Supreme Court of Canada in 1939. The litigation began when the white manager of a beer tavern in the Montreal Forum declined to serve a Black customer in July 1936. Fred Christie, a resident of Verdun, Quebec, who was employed as a private chauffeur in Montreal, sued the proprietors for damages. Judge Louis Philippe Demers, a white judge on the Quebec Superior Court, initially awarded Christie $25 in compensation for humiliation, holding that hotels and restaurants providing "public services" had "no right to discriminate between their guests." The majority of the white judges of the Quebec Court of King's Bench reversed this ruling, preferring to champion the principle that "chaque propriétaire est maître chez lui." This philosophy was endorsed by the majority of the white judges on the Supreme Court of Canada, who agreed that it was "not a question of motives or reasons for deciding to deal or not to deal; [any merchant] is free to do either." Conceding that the "freedom of commerce" principle might be restricted where a merchant adopted "a rule contrary to good morals or public order," Judge Thibaudeau Rinfret concluded that the colour bar was neither.[79]

In contrast, a series of judges dissented vigorously throughout these cases. In *Lowe's Montreal Theatres Ltd. v Reynolds*, white judge Henry-George Carroll took pains to disparage the situation in the United States, where law was regularly used to enforce racial segregation. Stressing that social conditions differed in Canada, he insisted: "Tous les citoyens de ce pays, blancs et noirs, sont soumis à la même loi et tenus aux mêmes obligations." Carroll spoke pointedly of the ideology of equality that had suffused French law since the revolution of 1789, and reasoned that Mr. Reynolds, "un homme de bonne éducation," deserved compensation for the humiliation that had occurred.[80]

In *Rogers v Clarence Hotel*, Judge Cornelius Hawkins O'Halloran wrote a lengthy and detailed rebuttal to the majority decision. Noting that the plaintiff was a British subject who had resided in Vancouver for more than two decades, with an established business in shoe-repair, O'Halloran insisted that he should be entitled to obtain damages from any beer parlour that barred Blacks from admission. "Refusal to serve the respondent solely because of his colour and race is contrary to the common law," claimed the white judge. "All British subjects have the same rights and privileges under the common law—it makes no difference whether white or coloured; or of what class, race or religion."[81]

In *Christie v The York Corporation*, the first dissent came from Antonin Galipeault, a white judge of the Quebec Court of King's Bench. Pointing out that the sale of liquor in Quebec taverns was already extensively regulated by law, he concluded that the business was a "monopoly or quasi-monopoly" that ought to be required to service all members of the public. Galipeault noted that if tavern-keepers could bar Blacks, they could also deny entry to Jews, Syrians, the Chinese, and the Japanese. Bringing the matter even closer to home for the majority of Quebecers, he reasoned that "religion" and "language" might constitute the next grounds for exclusion. Galipeault insisted that the colour bar be struck down.[82]

At the level of the Supreme Court of Canada, Henry Hague Davis expressly sided with Galipeault, concluding that racial segregation was "contrary to good morals and the public order." "In the changed and changing social and economic conditions," wrote the white Supreme Court justice, "different principles must necessarily be applied to new conditions." Noting that the legislature had developed an extensive regulatory regime surrounding the sale of beer, Davis concluded that such vendors were not entitled "to pick and choose" their customers.[83]

What is obvious from these various decisions is that the law was unsettled, as Judge Davis frankly admitted: "The question is one of difficulty, as the divergence of judicial opinion in the courts below indicates."[84] Where the judges expressly offered reasons for arriving at such different results, their analysis appears to be strained and the distinctions they drew arbitrary. Some tried to differentiate between a plaintiff who had prior knowledge of the colour bar and one who did not. Some considered the essential point to be whether the plaintiff crossed the threshold of the premises before being ejected. *Ad nauseam* the judges compared the status of theatres, restaurants, taverns, and hotels. They argued over whether public advertisements issued by commercial establishments constituted a legal "offer" or merely "an invitation to buy." They debated whether a stein of beer had sufficient "nutritive qualities" to be regarded as food.

Despite the endless technical arguments, the real issues dividing the judges appear to be relatively straightforward. There were two fundamental principles competing against each other: the doctrine of freedom of commerce and the doctrine of equality within a democratic society. Although the judges seem to have believed that they were merely applying traditional judicial precedents to the case at hand, this was something of a smoke screen. Some judges were choosing to select precedents extolling freedom of commerce, while others chose to affirm egalitarian principles. There was nothing that irretrievably compelled them to opt for one result over the other except their own predilections. A white law professor, Bora Laskin, made this explicit in a legal comment on the *Christie* case, written in 1940: "The principle of freedom of commerce enforced by the Court majority is itself merely the reading of social and economic doctrine into law, and doctrine no longer possessing its nineteenth century validity."[85]

Furthermore, no court had yet ruled on the validity of racial segregation in hotels, theatres, or restaurants in the province of Nova Scotia. A cautious lawyer, one easily cowed by the doctrinal dictates of *stare decisis*, might have concluded that the "freedom of commerce" principle enunciated by the majority of judges in the Supreme Court of Canada would govern. A more adventuresome advocate might have surveyed the range of judicial disagreement and decided to put the legal system to the challenge once more.

The reform-minded lawyer could have gone back to the original decisions in *Johnson v Sparrow* and *Barnswell v National Amusement Co.*, which most of the judges in the later cases had curiously ignored.[86] Quebec Judge John Sprott Archibald, in particular, laid a firm foundation in *Johnson v Sparrow*, eloquently proclaiming the right of Canadians of all races to have equal access to places of public entertainment. Roundly criticizing the policy of racially segregated seating, he explained:

> This position cannot be maintained. It would perhaps be trite to speak of slavery in this connection, and yet the regulation in question is undoubtedly a survival of prejudices created by the system of negro slavery. Slavery never had any wide influence in this country. The practice was gradually extinguished in Upper Canada by an act of the legislature passed on July 9th, 1793, which forbade the further importation of slaves, and ordered that all slave children born after that date should be free on attaining the age of twenty-one years. Although it was only in 1834 that an act of the imperial parliament finally abolishing slavery throughout the British colonies was passed, yet long before that, in 1803, Chief Justice Osgoode had declared slavery illegal in the province of Quebec. Our constitution is and always has been essentially democratic, and does not admit of distinctions of races or classes. All men are equal before the law and each has equal rights as a member of the community.[87]

Judge Archibald's recollection of the legal history of slavery in Canada is something of an understatement. The first Black slave arrived in Quebec in 1628, with slavery officially introduced by the French into New France on 1 May 1689.[88] After the British Conquest in 1763, the white general Jeffery Amherst confirmed that all slaves would remain in the possession of their masters.[89] In 1790, the English Parliament expressly authorized individuals wishing to settle in the provinces of Quebec and Nova Scotia to import "negroes" along with other "household furniture, utensils of husbandry or cloathing" free of duty.[90] In 1762, the Nova Scotia General Assembly gave indirect statutory recognition to slavery when it explicitly adverted to "Negro slaves" in the context of an act intended to control the sale of liquor on credit.[91] In 1781, the legislature of Prince Edward Island (then Île St-Jean) passed an act declaring that the baptism of slaves would not exempt them from bondage.[92]

The 1793 Upper Canada statute, of which Judge Archibald was so proud, countenanced a painfully slow process of manumission. The preamble, noting that it was "highly expedient to abolish slavery in this province, so far as the same may gradually be done without violating private property," said it all. The act freed not a single slave. Although the statute did ensure that no additional "negro" slaves could be brought into the province, it confirmed the existing property rights of all current slave-owners. Furthermore, children born of "negro mother[s]" were to remain in the service of their mothers' owners until the age of twenty-five years (not twenty-one years, as Judge Archibald had noted). The act may actually have discouraged voluntary manumission, by requiring slave-owners to post security bonds for slaves released from service, to cover the cost of any future public financial assistance required.[93] Confronted with litigants who contested the legal endorsement of slavery, white judges in Lower Canada, Nova Scotia, and New Brunswick dispatched inconsistent judgments.[94] Portions of the area that was to become Canada remained slave territory under law until 1833, when a statute passed in England emancipated all slaves in the British Empire.[95] Slavery persisted in British North America well after it was abolished in most of the northern states.[96] Even after abolition, Canadian government officials approved the extradition of fugitive African Americans who escaped from slavery in the United States and sought freedom in Canada.[97]

However, Judge Archibald's ringing declaration that the constitution prohibited racial discrimination was an outstanding affirmation of equality that could potentially have been employed to attack many of the racist practices currently in vogue. Long before the enactment of the Canadian Bill of Rights or the Canadian Charter of Rights and Freedoms, here was a judge who took hold of the largely unwritten, amorphous body of constitutional thought and proclaimed that the essence of a democracy was the legal eradication of "distinctions of races or classes." A thoughtful attorney could have created an opening for argument here, reasoning that the "freedom of commerce" principle should be superseded by equality rights as a matter of constitutional interpretation. These arguments had apparently not been fully made to the Supreme Court of Canada when the *Christie v York Corporation* case was litigated. There should have been room for another try.

In addition, the Supreme Court had expressly admitted that "freedom of commerce" would have to give way where a business rule ran "contrary to good morals or public order." No detailed analysis of the ramifications of racial discrimination was ever presented in these cases. A concerted attempt to lay out the social and economic repercussions of racial segregation might have altered the facile assumptions of some of the judges who could find no fault with colour bars. So much could have been argued. There was the humiliation and assault on dignity experienced by Black men, women, and children whose humanity was denied by racist whites. Counsel could have described the severe curtailment of Black educational and occupational opportunities that placed impenetrable restrictions upon full participation in Canadian society. The distrust bred of racial segregation had triggered many of the instances of interracial mob violence that marred Canadian history. A creative lawyer might have contended that rules that enforced racial divisions undeniably fomented immorality and the disruption of public peace.

Similar arguments had been made before the Ontario Supreme Court in 1945, in the landmark case of *Re Drummond Wren*. The issue there was the legality of a restrictive covenant registered against a parcel of land, enjoining the owner from selling to "Jews or persons of objectionable nationality." Noting that there were no precedents on point, Judge John Keiller Mackay, a white Gentile, quoted a legal rule from *Halsbury* "Any agreement which tends to be injurious to the public or against the public good is void as being contrary to public policy." Holding that the covenant was unlawful because it was "offensive to the public policy of this jurisdiction," Mackay stated:

> In my opinion, nothing could be more calculated to create or deepen divisions between existing religious and ethnic groups in this Province, or in this country, than the sanction of a method of land transfer which would permit the segregation and confinement of particular groups to particular business or residential areas ... It appears to me to be a moral duty, at least, to lend aid to all forces of cohesion, and similarly to repel all fissiparous tendencies which would imperil national unity. The common law courts have, by their actions over the years, obviated the need for rigid constitutional guarantees in our polity by their wise use of the doctrine of public policy as an active agent in the promotion of the public weal. While Courts and eminent Judges have, in view of the powers of our Legislatures, warned against inventing new heads of public policy, I do not conceive that I would be breaking new ground were I to hold the restrictive covenant impugned in this proceeding to be void as against public policy. Rather would I be applying well-recognized principles of public policy to a set of facts requiring their invocation in the interest of the public good.

The common law was not carved in stone. Nor was the judicial understanding of "public policy," which as Judge Mackay stressed, "varies from time to time."[98]

In assessing his strategy in the *Desmond* case, Bissett had to consider many factors: the wishes of his client, the resources available to prepare and argue the case, the social and political climate within which the case would be heard, and the potential receptivity of the bench.

Viola Desmond would have been soundly behind a direct attack on racial segregation. She had come seeking public vindication for the racial discrimination she had suffered. The community support and funding from the NSAACP would have strengthened her claim. The Halifax beautician would have been viewed as a conventionally "good" client, a successful business entrepreneur, a respectable married woman who had proved to be well mannered throughout her travails. The traditional assumptions about race relations were also under some scrutiny. Although white Nova Scotians continued to sponsor racial segregation in their schools, housing, and workforce, the unveiling of the Nazi death camps towards the end of the Second World War riveted public attention upon the appalling excesses of racial and religious discrimination. In October 1945, the Canadian Parliament entertained a motion to enact a formal Bill of Rights, guaranteeing equal treatment before the law, irrespective of race, nationality, or religious or political beliefs. Public sentiment might have been sufficiently malleable to muster support for more racial integration. Viola Desmond's case potentially offered an excellent vehicle with which to test the capacity of Canadian law to further racial equality.[99]

But Frederick William Bissett decided not to attack the racial segregation directly. Perhaps he simply accepted the Supreme Court of Canada ruling in *Christie v York Corporation* as determinative. Perhaps he could not imagine how to push the boundaries of law in new, more socially progressive directions. Perhaps he was intimately acquainted with the white judges who manned the Nova Scotia courts, and knew their predilections well. Whatever the reason, Bissett settled upon a more conventional litigation strategy. That he would fail, even in this more limited effort, may suggest that a more dramatic challenge would have fallen far short of the goal. I prefer to think that the stilted narrowness of the vision dictated an equally narrow response.

REX V DESMOND

Bissett issued a writ on Wednesday, 14 November 1946, naming Viola Desmond as plaintiff in a civil suit against two defendants, Harry L. MacNeil and the Roseland Theatre Co. Ltd. Bissett alleged that Harry MacNeil acted unlawfully in forcibly ejecting his client from the theatre. He based his claim in intentional tort, a legal doctrine that contained little scope for discussion of race discrimination. The writ stipulated that Viola Desmond was entitled to compensatory damages on the following grounds: 1 / assault; 2 / malicious prosecution; and 3 / false arrest and imprisonment. Bissett did not add a fourth and lesser-known tort, "abusing the process of the law," which might have offered more scope for raising the racial issues that concerned his client. The three grounds he did enunciate were all advanced in racially neutral terms.[100]

Whether there would have been an opportunity to address the issue of race discrimination indirectly within the common-law tort actions will never be known. The civil claim apparently never came to trial, and the archival records contain no further details on the file. Why Bissett decided not to pursue the civil actions is unclear. Perhaps he felt that the tort claim would be difficult to win. The common-law principle of "defence of property" might have been invoked to justify the use of force by property owners against trespassers. The defendants would also have been entitled to raise the defence of "legal authority," asserting that they were within their rights in removing someone who had breached the tax provisions of the Theatres Act. The conviction registered against Viola Desmond bolstered this line of argument, confirming that at least one court had upheld the defendants' actions. It also served as a complete defense to the claim for "malicious prosecution." Upon reflection, Bissett may have decided that he needed to overturn the initial conviction before taking any further action upon the civil claim.[101]

On 27 December 1946, Bissett announced that he would make an application for a writ of *certiorari* to ask the Supreme Court of Nova Scotia to quash Viola Desmond's criminal conviction. There was "no evidence to support" the conviction, he contended, and the magistrate lacked the "jurisdiction" to convict her. Bissett filed an affidavit sworn by Viola Desmond, outlining how she had asked for a downstairs ticket and been refused, describing in detail her physical manhandling by the theatre manager and police officer, and documenting the failings in the actual trial process itself. Nothing in the papers filed alluded directly or indirectly to race. Viola Desmond, Reverend W. P. Oliver, and William Allison (a Halifax packer) jointly committed themselves to pay up to two hundred dollars in costs should the action fail.[102]

A writ of *certiorari* allowed a party to transfer a case from an inferior tribunal to a court of superior jurisdiction by way of motion before a judge. In this manner, the records of proceedings before stipendiary magistrates could be taken up to the Supreme Court for reconsideration. The availability of this sort of judicial review was restricted, however. Parties dissatisfied with their conviction could not simply ask the higher court judges to overrule it because the magistrate's decision was wrong. Instead, they had to allege that there had been a more fundamental denial of justice or that there was some excess or lack of jurisdiction.[103]

There is no written record of what Bissett argued when he appeared before Nova Scotia Supreme Court Justice Maynard Brown Archibald on 10 January 1947.[104] But the white judge was clearly unimpressed. A native of Colchester County, Nova Scotia, Judge Archibald had studied law at Dalhousie University and was called to the Nova Scotia bar in 1919. He practiced law in Halifax continuously from 1920 until his appointment to the bench in 1937. Although he was an erudite lecturer in Dalhousie's law school, Archibald did not choose to elaborate upon legal intricacies in his decision in the *Desmond* case. Viola Desmond had no right to use the process of *certiorari*, he announced, and he curtly dismissed her application on 20 January. The cursory ruling of less than two pages contained a mere recitation of conclusion without any apparent rationale. "It is clear from the affidavits and documents presented to me that the Magistrate had jurisdiction to enter upon his inquiry," Archibald noted. "This court will therefore not review on *certiorari* the decision of the Magistrate as to whether or not there was evidence to support the conviction."[105]

The best clue to deciphering the decision is found in the judge's final paragraph:

> It was apparent at the argument that the purpose of this application was to seek by means of *certiorari* proceedings a review of the evidence taken before the convicting Magistrate. It is obvious that the proper procedure to have had such evidence reviewed was by way of an appeal. Now, long after the time for appeal has passed, it is sought to review the Magistrate's decision by means of *certiorari* proceedings. For the reasons that I have already given, this procedure is not available to the applicant.[106]

A part-time stipendiary magistrate for a brief period during his days of law practice, Judge Archibald was concerned that lower court officials be free from unnecessary, burdensome scrutiny by superior court judges. Earlier Nova Scotia decisions had reflected similar fears, suggesting that access to judicial review be restricted to prevent "a sea of uncertainty" in which the decisions of inferior tribunals were subjected to limitless second-guessing. The proper course of action, according to Archibald, would have been to appeal Magistrate MacKay's conviction to County Court under the Nova Scotia Summary Convictions Act.[107]

Why Bissett originally chose to bring a writ of *certiorari* rather than an appeal is not clear. The Summary Convictions Act required litigants to choose one route or the other, not both. An appeal permitted a full inquiry into all of the facts and law surrounding the case, with the right to call witnesses and adduce evidence, and the appeal court entitled to make a completely fresh ruling on the merits. Although an appeal would seem to have offered greater scope to the defence, Bissett may have preferred to make his arguments before the more elevated Nova Scotia Supreme Court, which heard applications for *certiorari*, rather than the County Court, which heard appeals from summary convictions. Or he may simply have missed the time limit for filing an appeal, which was set as ten days from the date of conviction. He issued the civil writ a mere five days after the initial conviction, but the writ of *certiorari* was not filed until almost a full month afterwards. Possibly by the time Bissett turned away from the civil process to canvas his options with respect to the criminal law, it was already too late for an appeal.[108]

Since the limitation period for appeals had already run, Bissett had no other option but to seek to overturn Archibald's ruling before the full bench of the Nova Scotia Supreme Court.[109] The case was set down for argument on 13 March. Jack Desmond refused to accompany his wife to court, since he continued to oppose Viola's actions and blamed her for stirring up trouble. The tensions within the marriage were increasing by the day, and would ultimately result in the couple's permanent marital separation.[110] Carrie Best, who did accompany Viola Desmond to court, acknowledged in *The Clarion* that it was an emotionally tense experience to sit through the hearing, "hoping against hope that justice will not be blind in this case." Carrie Best admitted that she "watched breathlessly as the calm, unhurried soft spoken Bissett argued his appeal." Bissett conceded that the time to lodge the original appeal had "inadvertently slipped by," but that this should not bar the court from reviewing on *certiorari*. "The appellant is entitled to the writ," claimed Bissett, "whether she appealed or not, if there has been a denial of natural justice."[111]

The affidavit Viola Desmond filed to support her case set out in detail the many ways she felt the trial had been procedurally unfair. She had not been told of her right to counsel or her right to seek an adjournment. She did not understand that she was entitled to cross-examine the prosecution witnesses. She was sentenced without any opportunity to make submissions to the court. These several omissions would have more than sufficed to constitute a denial of natural justice, as lawyers understand the meaning of that term in the latter half of the twentieth century. But at the time of the *Desmond* appeal the concept of due process was much less clear. Judge John Doull, who issued his decision on this case on 17 May 1947, even disputed the use of the term "natural justice." A former attorney general of Nova Scotia, Doull wrote:

> A denial of justice apparently means that before the tribunal, the applicant was not given an opportunity of setting up and proving his case. (The words "natural justice" were used in some of the opinions of the judges but I doubt whether that is a good term.) At any rate a denial of the right to be heard is a denial of a right which is so fundamental in our legal practice that a denial of it vitiates a proceeding in which such denial occurs.[112]

The white judge conceded that if a "denial of justice" was established in Viola Desmond's affidavit, the failure to appeal would no longer suffice to bar her claim. But then Judge Doull, a former mayor of New Glasgow, concluded that there had been no such procedural omissions in the present case. None of the other white Supreme Court judges differed from this view.[113]

Bissett's other argument, on the lack of jurisdiction, was vigorously disputed by respondent's counsel, Edward Mortimer Macdonald, Jr, KC. Harry MacNeil's lawyer was a forty-seven-year-old white New Glasgow resident who had received degrees from Dalhousie University, Bishop's College, and McGill. He practised law in Montreal from 1924 to 1930, then returned to practice in his birth province of Nova Scotia, where he served as the town solicitor for New Glasgow. "The magistrate [had] jurisdiction, [and] tried the case on the evidence before him," asserted Macdonald. "The sole objection remaining to the appellant is that the evidence does not support a conviction. The proper remedy therefore is by way of appeal."[114]

Bissett did not argue that it was beyond the jurisdiction of a magistrate to apply the Nova Scotia Theatres, Cinematographs and Amusements Act to enforce racial segregation. He should have. Courts had long held that it was an abuse of process to bring criminal charges as a lever to enforce debt collection. Here the theatre manager was not trying to help the province collect tax, but to bring down the force of law upon protesters of racial segregation. That Bissett might have drawn an analogy to the abuse of process decisions was suggested months later in a *Canadian Bar Review* article written by J. B. Milner, a white professor at Dalhousie Law School. Calling the *Desmond* case "one of the most interesting decisions to come from a Nova Scotia court in many years," Milner asserted that Harry MacNeill was prosecuting Viola Desmond "for improper reasons." MacNeill's "desire to discriminate between negro and white patrons of his theatre" transformed the criminal proceeding into "a vexatious action," Milner argued.[115]

None of this was addressed before the court. Instead, Bissett confined his jurisdictional point to the insufficiency of evidence at trial, leaving himself wide open to procedural critique. Judge Robert Henry Graham emphasized that the evidentiary matters in this case did not relate to jurisdiction: "A justice who convicts without evidence is doing something that he ought not to do, but he is doing it as a Judge and if his jurisdiction to entertain the charge is not open to impeachment, his subsequent error, however grave, is a wrong exercise of a jurisdiction which he has, and not a usurpation of a jurisdiction which he has not." There could be no question "raised as to the jurisdiction of the stipendiary magistrate" in this case, concluded Judge Graham, himself another former white mayor and stipendiary magistrate from New Glasgow. Furthermore, Judge Graham added, "no reason except inadvertence was given to explain why the open remedy of appeal was not taken." William Francis Carroll and William Lorimer Hall, the other two white judges who delivered concurring opinions in the case, agreed that *certiorari* was not procedurally available to overturn the conviction.[116]

Three of the judges, however, felt inclined to make some comment about the sufficiency of evidence at trial. Graham's view was that the charge had been substantiated: "[Viola Desmond] knew that the ticket she purchased was not for downstairs and so that she had not paid the full tax." Carroll disagreed: "the accused did actually pay the tax required by one purchasing such a ticket as she was sold." Hall, the only judge to make even passing reference to the racial issues, was most explicit:

> Had the matter reached the Court by some method other than *certiorari*, there might have been opportunity to right the wrong done this unfortunate woman.
>
> One wonders if the manager of the theatre who laid the complaint was so zealous because of a *bona fide* belief there had been an attempt to defraud the Province of Nova Scotia of the sum of one cent, or was it a surreptitious endeavour to enforce a Jim Crow rule by misuse of a public statute.[117]

Despite their differing opinions, all four judges took the position that Viola Desmond's efforts to overturn Magistrate MacKay's original ruling should be denied. Her conviction would stand.

The decision to apply for *certiorari* rather than to appeal had cost Viola Desmond dearly. Respondent's counsel, E. M. Macdonald, laid the blame squarely at Bissett's feet. "The appellant had full benefit of legal advice before the expiry of the delays for appeal," he insisted at the Supreme Court hearing. More than five days before the expiration of the time for appeal, Bissett was actively on the case, having already launched the civil action for assault, malicious prosecution, and false arrest and imprisonment. His decision to opt for judicial review rather than an appeal of the original conviction proved disastrous. He chose to argue the case in a conservative and traditional manner, relegating the race issues to the sidelines of the legal proceeding. Even within this narrow venue, Bissett failed to deliver.

THE AFTERMATH

What must Viola Desmond have thought of the ruling? Although she left no letters or diaries reflecting her views, her sisters recall something of her feelings at the time. Wanda Robson, Viola's younger sister, explains:

> The day she came back from the court, knowing she had lost the case, she was very disappointed. A person like my sister never liked to lose. A person like my sister, who was such a hard worker, had always been told if you do hard work, you're going to win. If you're Black or Negro or whatever, you're going to work hard, get that scholarship and win. We forgot about our colour and educated ourselves. She felt that she should have won the case, and she was bitterly disappointed.[118]

Viola Desmond must have been appalled, not only by the ruling, but by the way her attempt to seek legal protection from racial discrimination was turned into a purely technical debate over the intricacies of criminal procedure. None of the judges even noted on the record that she was Black. The intersection of "white male chivalry" with "Black womanhood" lay completely unexamined. Nor was there any direct reference to the Roseland theatre's policy of racially segregated seating. Judge Hall was the only one to advert to the "Jim Crow rule," a reference to the practices of racial segregation spawned in the United States after the abolition of slavery. Even Judge Hall's professed concern did not dissuade him from reaching the same conclusion as his brothers on the bench: that the court was powerless to intervene.

Professor Milner took up this very point in his review of the case; "discrimination against colour," he noted, took place "outside the sphere of legal rules." The theatre manager "apparently violated no law of human rights and fundamental freedoms in this free county in refusing admission to part of his theatre to persons of negro extraction." What struck Milner as particularly unfair was that the manager not only removed Viola Desmond, "as our democratic law says he may," but also successfully prosecuted her for violating a quasi-criminal provision in a provincial statute.[119]

The *Clarion's* coverage of the "disappointing" decision, on 15 April 1947, was muted. Politely expressing appreciation for "the objective manner in which the judges handled the case," the editor noted: "It would appear that the decision was the only one possible under the law. While in the moral sense we feel disappointed, we must realize that the law must be interpreted as it is. The Clarion feels that the reason for the decision lies in the manner in which the case was presented to the Court. This was very strongly implied by the Supreme Court. This is a regrettable fact."[120]

Bissett, who is not mentioned by name, is clearly taking the fall here. It was his choice of an application for *certiorari*, rather than appeal, which was singled out as the reason for the legal loss. His conservative strategy of camouflaging race discrimination underneath traditional common-law doctrines, his decision not to attack the legality of racial segregation with a frontal assault, was not discussed.

The *Clarion* did, however, take some solace from Judge Hall's "Jim Crow" remarks, which it quoted in full, adding:

> The Court did not hesitate to place the blame for the whole sordid affair where it belonged. [...] It is gratifying to know that such a shoddy attempt to hide behind the law has been recognized as such by the highest Court in our Province. We feel that owners and managers of places of amusement will now realize that such practices are recognized by those in authority for what they are,—cowardly devices to persecute innocent people because of their outmoded racial biases.[121]

Some Blacks believed the whole incident better left alone. There were accusations that Viola Desmond had caused all the trouble by trying to "pass" for white, that her mother's white heritage caused her to put on airs and sit where she ought never to have sat. Walter A. Johnston, a Black Haligonian employed as a chef with the Immigration department, made a point of criticizing Viola Desmond at an Ottawa national convention of the Liberal party in October 1948. Viola Desmond had been "censured by the Halifax colored group" for her activism, he advised. "We told her she was not helping the New Glasgow colored people by motoring over there to cause trouble." Johnston complained of racial "agitators" who would "increase the racial problem and set back the progress towards good feeling." The policy he counselled: to "shrug ... off the trouble we met" with a "soft-answer-that-turneth-away-wrath."[122]

James Calbert Best, Carrie Best's son and the associate editor of *The Clarion*, had an entirely different perspective. Calling for legislation that would put the right to racial equality above the privileges of those in business, he claimed: "People have come to realize that the merchant, the restaurant operator, the theatre manager all have a duty, and the mere fact that such enterprises are privately owned is not longer an excuse for discrimination on purely racial grounds. [...] Here in Nova Scotia, we see the need for such legislation every day."[123]

Comparing the situation of Blacks in Nova Scotia with those in the American South, Best castigated Canadians for their complacency:

> We do have many of the privileges which are denied our southern brothers, but we often wonder if the kind of segregation we receive here is not more cruel in the very subtlety of its nature. [...]
>
> True, we are not forced into separate parts of public conveyances, nor are we forced to drink from separate faucets or use separate washrooms, but we are often refused meals in restaurants and beds in hotels, with no good reason.
>
> Nowhere do we encounter signs that read "No Colored" or the more diplomatic little paste boards which say "Select Clientele," but at times it might be better. At least much consequent embarrassment might be saved for all concerned.[124]

Bolstered by the apparent inability of the courts to stop racial discrimination, Canadian businesses continued to enforce their colour bars at whim. The famous African-American sculptress Selma Burke was denied service in a Halifax restaurant in September 1947. "We had expected to find conditions in Canada so much better than in the States," explained her white companion, "but I'm sorry to say we were mistaken."[125] Grantley Adams, the Black prime minister of Barbados, was refused a room in a Montreal hotel in 1954 because the hotel had "regulations."[126] The racial intolerance in New Glasgow intensified and spread to other groups. In September 1948, a gang of hooded marauders burned a seven-foot cross on the front lawn of the home of Joe Mong, the Chinese proprietor of a New Glasgow restaurant. Police investigated but pronounced themselves sceptical that the incident had "anything to do with K.K.K. activities." It was simply "a private matter," they concluded.[127] Akin to "freedom of commerce."

After her loss in court, Viola Desmond seems to have withdrawn from public gaze and taken steps to consolidate her business. Her younger sister recalls that Viola sought advice from her father. "She was wondering what she should do, and my father said: 'Viola, I think you've gone as far as you should go. It's time to get on and put this behind you. I won't say that nothing's been gained. Something has, but at what cost? Your business is sliding.' So she set her lips, and got back to her business."[128] But even the business seems to have lost some of its lustre. Angry at the failure of the legal system to erase her conviction, Viola Desmond set aside her plans to establish franchise operations throughout Canada. She began to invest her money in real estate, believing that this represented greater security in a racially torn society. She bought up homes, renovated them, and rented them out to Black families. Eventually she closed up her shop and moved to Montreal, where she enrolled in business classes, hoping to become a consultant in the entertainment industry. She moved down to New York City, where she had just begun to establish her business when she fell ill. On 7 February 1965, at the age of fifty, Viola Desmond died in New York of a gastro-intestinal haemorrhage.[129]

"As a matter of legal precedent, the *Viola Desmond* case was an absolute failure. The lawsuit was framed in such a manner that the real issues of white racism were shrouded in procedural technicalities. The judges turned their backs on Black claims for racial equality, in certain respects openly condoning racial segregation. But the toll that her battle with racial segregation took on Viola Desmond was not entirely for naught. According to Pearleen Oliver, the legal challenge touched a nerve within the Black community, creating a dramatic upsurge in race consciousness. The funds raised for legal fees were diverted to serve as seed money for the fledgling NSAACP, after Frederick William Bissett declined to bill his client, substantially strengthening the ability of the Black organization to lobby against other forms of race discrimination.[130]

While there were undeniably those who thought the struggle better left unwaged, the leaders of Nova Scotia's Black community felt differently. Asked to reflect on Viola Desmond's actions fifteen years later, Dr. William Pearly Oliver tried to explain the enormous symbolic significance of the case. His appreciation for her effort transcends the failures of the legal system, and puts Viola Desmond's contribution in clearer perspective: " ... this meant something to our people. Neither before or since has there been such an aggressive effort to obtain rights. The people arose as one and with one voice. This positive stand enhanced the prestige of the Negro community throughout the Province. It is my conviction that much of the positive action that has since taken place stemmed from this ..."[131]

QUESTIONS TO CONSIDER

1. Discuss ways in which the Desmond case and the Hawes case, discussed in this chapter, corresponded to or violated public sentiments of the day concerning race, dignity, and justice. Use the specific examples of those who supported or opposed Viola Desmond's challenge to colour-bar measures.

2. Trace the tensions between legislators and judges in their interpretation of race-based practices, including legislation. Whose interests were at stake when such legislation was implemented and challenged?

3. In your view, are racial minorities in contemporary Canada no longer discriminated against by race-specific legislation? Are such minorities disadvantaged in economic, social, and political life despite formal equality provisions in law? Use Backhouse's essay and outside readings to support your answer.

SUGGESTIONS FOR FURTHER READING

Cooper, A. (2006). *The hanging of Angelique: Canada, slavery and the burning of Montréal.* Toronto: HarperCollins.

Hill, L. (2007). *The book of Negroes.* Toronto: HarperCollins. This novel was published in Australia, the United States, and New Zealand under the less provocative but rather generic title, *Someone Knows My Name.* Hill discusses his most recent work on a blog: http://www.cbc.ca/national/blog/video/immigrationdiversity/lawrence_hills_book_of_negroes.html (accessed January 16, 2009).

NOTES

1. Details surrounding the arrest are taken from "Affidavit of Viola Irene Desmond," 29 January 1947, *His Majesty the King v Viola Irene Desmond,* Public Archives of Nova Scotia (hereinafter cited as PANS), RG39 "C" Halifax, v-937, Supreme Court of Nova Scotia no. 13347; "Negress Alleges She Was Ejected from Theatre," Halifax *Chronicle,* 30 November 1946, p. 2; "Ban All Jim Crow Rules Is Comment on N.S. Charge," Toronto *Daily Star,* 30 November 1946, p. 3. Material from this chapter was presented at the Seventh Annual Gibson-Armstrong Lecture in Law and History at Osgoode Hall Law School in February 1994, and an earlier version was published as "Racial Segregation in Canadian Legal History: Viola Desmond's Challenge, Nova Scotia 1946," *Dalhousie Law Journal* 17:2 (Fall 1994), 299–362.
2. On the history of the Roseland Theatre and the racist nature of *The Birth of a Nation* (film) and blackface minstrelsy, see*
3. For details concerning a number of Canadian cases that set historical precedents for Viola Desmond's direct-action approach, see*
4. On MacNeil and his theatre, see*
5. "Negress Alleges She Was Ejected from Theatre," Halifax *Chronicle,* 30 November 1946, p. 2; "Affidavit of Viola Irene Desmond," PANS. For the reference to the gloves and posture, see the notes of the researcher who assisted with the compilation of material for this chapter: Tanya Hudson, "Interview with Dr. Pearleen Oliver," Halifax, 28 August 1995.
6. For biographical details on MacKay, see "Former Magistrate Dies at 84 [Obituary]," Halifax *Chronicle-Herald,* 29 September 1961, p. 2.
7. See R.S.N.S. 1923, c. 162, s.8(8), 9, 10, 14. The initial enactment is *Theatres and Cinematographs Act,* S.N.S. 1915, c.9, as amended.
8. For details of the statutory provision and the pricing arrangement at the Roseland, see *
9. "Record," Rod G. MacKay, Stipendiary Magistrate for the Town of New Glasgow, County of Pictou, 9 November 1946 R.- (*Inf. Henry MacNeil*) *v Viola Desmond,* PANS; "Affidavit of Viola Desmond," PANS.
10. "Record," Rod G. MacKay, PANS. The ultimate disposition of the costs is unclear. One handwritten document signed by Magistrate MacKay indicates that the accused was to pay Harry MacNeil, "the Informant herein, the sum of six dollars for his costs in this behalf." Another handwritten document signed by the magistrate indicates that the costs were broken down: $2.50 to be paid to himself as magistrate, and $3.50 to Police Chief Elmo G. Langille.

*Extensive notes with complete details, indicated by an asterisk, can be found [under Catalogues/History/Canadian History/*Colour-Coded: A Legal History of Racism in Canada, 1900–1950* (Toronto: University of Toronto Press © 1999), Chapter 7] at the following website: www.utpress.utoronto.ca/.

11. "Affidavit of Viola Desmond," PANS; R.S.N.S. 1923, c.362, s.8(3), 3(10). *Saturday Night* raises this point in its coverage of the trial, 7 December 1946, p. 5: "[T]he action of the magistrate in fining the lady in question for defrauding the province, when she had most expressly tendered to the box office the proper price, including tax, of the seat in which she later insisted on sitting, is a travesty of justice."

12. "Negress Alleges She Was Ejected from Theatre," Halifax *Chronicle*, 30 November 1946, p. 2. On the historical use of the terms "Negro" and "Negress" and the preference of the Black community for the word "coloured," see*

13. "Ban All Jim Crow Rules Is Comment on N.S. Charge," Toronto *Daily Star*, 30 November 1946, p. 3. MacNeil continued: "We have a large colored patronage at our theatre and we don't permit color discrimination to be a determining factor. It would be poor policy for us to set up a color bar. […] There was no discrimination."

14. This raises the important question of how many other trials lie buried, lost to historical scrutiny, because the real issues relating to racial divisions were (consciously?) unspoken or camouflaged with unrelated legal matters. On the tendency to delete references to race in evidence filed on racial-discrimination matters, see Robin W. Winks, *The Blacks in Canada: A History*, 2d ed. (Montreal: McGill-Queen's University Press, 1997), at 424, discussing the 1920 hearing under the Industrial Disputes Investigation Act into the racially motivated discharges of thirty-six Black porters from the CPR. On a comparative note, see the discussion of the appeal of the conviction of Rosa Parks in the Montgomery bus boycott in Alabama in 1955, which never mentioned the Alabama bus segregation statute or racial segregation. "One reads the opinion in vain trying to understand the issue that her appeal raised," notes Robert Jerome Glennon in "The Role of Law in the Civil Rights Movement: The Montgomery Bus Boycott, 1955–1957," *Law and History Review*, vol. 9 (1991), 59 at 88.

15. Viola Desmond's older sister recalls her sister's actions as unpremeditated: "I think it was a spontaneous action. She was aware of prejudice, but she had not been exposed to that kind of prejudice. In Halifax, you could sit where you liked in the theatre. So I think it came as a shock to her. She was well-known in Halifax, she felt herself to be an entrepreneur, she paid taxes, and she was part of the city. She knew people at different levels, so it was more of a shock for her. She acted spontaneously and I truly believe she never thought she would be physically mishandled. I think she was more shocked than surprised." See Constance Backhouse, "Interview with Mrs S. A. (Emily) Clyke, Viola Desmond's older sister," Montreal, 28 April 1995. For reference to Viola Desmond as "well known throughout the province," see *The Clarion* 1:1 (December 1946), PANS Reel 4340.

16. Constance Backhouse, "Interview with Wanda Robson, Viola's younger sister," North Sydney, 22 March 1995; Backhouse, "Interview with Mrs S. A. (Emily) Clyke." Judith Fingard, "Race and Respectability in Victorian Halifax," *Journal of Imperial and Commonwealth History* 20:2 (May 1992), 169, notes at 180–2, 185, that the Davises were well-established members of the Black elite in Halifax. For information on the racial segregation of barbershops and the niche that Black barbers established in Canada, see *

17. James Albert Davis managed the sizeable family real estate holdings of his own family and that of his wife until the Depression knocked the bottom out of the market. At that point, James Davis became the service manager of the Argyle Street Garage. He continued to cut hair for family and friends in his home throughout his life; Backhouse, "Interview with Wanda Robson; Backhouse, "Interview with Mrs S. A. (Emily) Clyke." Viola Desmond's grandfather secured a position as a letter carrier when he retired from barbering. Viola's uncle (and godfather), John Davis, also obtained employment in the Post Office Division in Halifax. On the rarity of Blacks achieving the status of civil-service or post-office employees, see correspondence from Beresford Augustus Husbands, President of the Colored Men's Conservative Social and Athletic Club, to the mayor of Halifax, 17 May 1937, protesting that "there is no representative of the colored race in any of the local civic departments": PANS RG35-102 (3B) v.7, no. 42; W. P. Oliver, "Cultural Progress of the Negro in Nova Scotia," *Dalhousie Review* 29:3 (1949), at 297–8, reprinted in George Elliott Clarke, ed., *Fire on the Water: An Anthology of Black Nova Scotian Writing*, vol. 1 (Lawrencetown Beach, N.S.: Pottersfield Press, 1991), at 129–33.

18. Henry Johnson was born in Richmond, Virginia. Full information concerning his parents is not available, although Wanda Robson was able to provide the following details: "His father was a white plantation owner … I can't tell you about his mother—I don't know. This is where the mixed race comes in. Henry Walter Johnson was maybe seven-eighths white—who is white, who is Black, I don't know. Henry was a Baptist minister in New Haven, Connecticut, and he also was at Cornwallis Street Baptist Church in Halifax for one year. While in New Haven, he worked as a businessman. He was a real estate entrepreneur who also sold antiques. He married Gwendolin's mother, Susan Smith, who was a white woman born in Connecticut. Henry bought property when living in Halifax. Gwendolin inherited those properties." See Backhouse, "Interview with Wanda Robson." For biographical details on Viola Desmond's parents, who married on 9 March 1908, see PANS Micro.: Churches: Halifax: Trinity Anglican: Baptisms no. 735, 736, 844; RG32 Marriages: Halifax County: 1908: no. 92, at p. 249; Notes of the researcher who assisted with the compilation of material for this chapter, Allen B. Robertson, "Interview with Pearleen Oliver," Halifax, July 1993.

19. Canadians appear to have accepted that any known Black ancestry resulted in a racial classification as "Black." for one example, see *Gordon v Adamson* (1920), 18 O.W.N., 191 at 192 (Ont. High Ct.), in which Judge Middleton describes the child of a "white" mother and a "negro" father as "coloured." Judith Fingard notes in "Race and Respectability in Victorian Halifax," at 170, that "regardless of skin colour," members of "the Afro-Nova Scotia community were universally identified as 'coloured.'" W. Burton Hurd, "Racial Origins and Nativity of the Canadian People," *Census of Canada 1931*, vol. 13 (Ottawa: Supply and Services, 1942), notes at p.vii that the instructions given to Canadian enumerators for the 1931 census were as follows: "The children begotten of marriages between white and black or yellow races will be recorded as Negro, Chinese, Japanese, Indians, etc., as the case may be." James W. St. G. Walker, *Race, Rights and the Law in the Supreme Court of Canada* (Waterloo: The Osgoode Society and Wilfrid Laurier University Press, 1997), notes at 18 that these instructions contradicted the provisions of the Indian Act at the time: see discussion of *Re Eskimos* in chapter 2. On the extensiveness of racial intermixing (some voluntary and some coercive) and the accepted rules of racial designation in the United States, see *

20. At the turn of the century, interracial marriages appear to have been on the decline: Fingard, "Race and Respectability in Victorian Halifax," at 179. Ruth I. McKenzie "Race Prejudice and the Negro," *Dalhousie Review*, vol. 20 (1940), notes at 201 that "intermarriage [of Blacks] with whites is not approved." Wanda Robson discusses Viola Desmond's racial identification in the following terms: "Would Viola have defined herself as 'mixed race'? Of course. Would you be wrong in describing her as Black? Not as far as I am concerned. I am of the generation that was raised to be proud of being Black. Viola is clearly Black. I know what I am, she is my sister." See Backhouse, "Interview with Wanda Robson." On the experience of claiming mixed-race heritage in Canada see Carol Camper, ed., *Miscegenation Blues: Voices of Mixed Race Women* (Toronto: Sister Vision, 1994). James and Gwendolin Davis produced twelve children. See PANS Micro.: Churches: Halifax: Trinity Anglican: Baptisms no. 735, 736, 844; Robertson, "Interview with Pearleen Oliver." Viola's obituary in the Halifax *Chronicle-Herald*, 10 February 1965, p. 26, lists nine surviving siblings. There were five sisters and one brother in Montreal: Gordon Davis, Emily (Mrs S. A. Clyke), Eugenie (Mrs F. L. Parris), Helen (Mrs B. W. Fline), Constance (Mrs W. Scott), Olive (Mrs A. Scott). There were two brothers and one sister in Halifax: John Davis, Allan Davis, Wanda (Mrs W. Neal). See also the obituary in Halifax *Mail Star*, 10 February 1965, p. 8.

21. During the depression, Viola worked after school as a mother's helper in order to make ends meet; Notes of the researcher who assisted with the compilation of material for this chapter, Allen B. Robertson, "Interview with Jack Desmond," Halifax, 16 June 1993 and 23 June 1993; Backhouse, "Interview with Wanda Robson"; Backhouse, "Interview with Mrs S. A. (Emily) Clyke." For details on the large number of Black women who chose teaching, and the expansion of occupational opportunities in hairdressing, see *

22. Viola's sister, Wanda Robson, recalls that Viola Desmond lived at the "Y" and worked part-time as a cigarette girl at Small's Paradise nightclub in Harlem to make ends meet. Viola Desmond took great pains to conceal her Harlem employment from her mother, because she knew her parents would not have approved. While in New York, she also worked as an agent for musicians, and obtained copyright for some lyrics for her clients. See notes of David Woods, who assisted with the compilation of material for this chapter, "Interview with Wanda Robson," North Sydney, October 1995; Backhouse, "Interview with Mrs S. A. (Emily) Clyke"; Robertson, "Interview with Jack Desmond"; Brigdlal Pachai, *Beneath the Clouds of the Promised Land: The Survival of Nova Scotia's Blacks* (Halifax: Lancelot Press for Black Educators Association of Nova Scotia, 1991), at 152–3, 297; Backhouse, "Interview with Wanda Robson." For details on the specific services that Black women sought from hairdressers and the spectacular career of Madame C. J. Walker, see *

23. Jack's father, Norman Mansfield Desmond, was a hack driver for John Church's Livery Stable and a founding deacon of the New Glasgow Black Baptist Church. Jack Desmond's mother, Annie Williams, worked as a domestic servant. Both Jack's parents were born into farming families in Tracadie in Antigonish County: Robertson, "Interview with Jack Desmond"; Pachai, *Beneath the Clouds*, at 152–4, 297; New Glasgow *Clarion* 1:1 (December 1946); *Halifax-Dartmouth City Directories* (Halifax: Might Directories Atlantic, 1938–46). On the emigration of Blacks to Nova Scotia, see *

24. Jack Desmond's sister, Amelia, married a Black barber, Sydney Jones, who initially offered Jack the opportunity to take up barbering. Wanda Robson recalls that Jack Desmond's customers were approximately 80 per cent Black and 20 per cent other races. She also notes that he was "easy-going" and not nearly as hard-working as Viola. Jack Desmond worked from his shop on Gottingen Street continuously until his retirement. When he closed his barbershop, he sold the site to Frank Sobey, who ultimately sold the store to Foodland groceries. Jack Desmond continued to work for both of the new owners, and to cut hair in people's homes for many years after: "Jack's Got All the Answers: King of Gottingen," Halifax *Mail-Star*, Saturday insert in *The Leader*, 31 May

1986, p. 13; Backhouse, "Interview with Wanda Robson"; Pachai, *Beneath the Clouds*, at 152–4; Robertson, "Interview with Jack Desmond." On the residence patterns of Black Haligonians and the importance of Gottingen Street to the Black community, see *

25. The precise opening date for Vi's Studio of Beauty Culture is unclear, with various sources suggesting 1937, 1940, and 1941. See Backhouse, "Interview with Wanda Robson"; Backhouse, "Interview with Mrs S. A. (Emily) Clyke"; Tanya Hudson, "Interview with Clara Adams," Halifax, 24 July 1995; Tanya Hudson, "Interview with Barbara Bowen," Halifax, 26 July 1995; Woods, "Interview with Pearleen Oliver"; Backhouse, "Interview with Mrs S. A. (Emily) Clyke."

26. Robertson, "Interview with Pearleen Oliver"; Constance Backhouse, "Interview with Gwen Jenkins," London, March 1995; Hudson, "Interview with Clara Adams"; "Takes Action," New Glasgow *Clarion* 1:1 (December 1946); advertisements for her business in New Glasgow *Clarion* 2:4 (28 February 1947) and 11:5 (15 March 1947); "Beauty School Graduation," Truro *Clarion* 2:9 (2 July 1947); Pachai, *Beneath the Clouds*, at 153; Robertson, "Interview with Jack Desmond"; *Halifax-Dartmouth City Directories*, 1938–46; Elaine McCluskey, "Long-Established Minority Still Excluded from Power," Halifax *Chronicle-Herald*, 16 March 1989, p. 41.

27. Backhouse, "Interview with Wanda Robson"; Robertson, "Interview with Pearleen Oliver." On the employment patterns of middle-class Black women and the resulting gender tensions, see *

28. Graduates of the school included: Nora Dill, Rose Gannon, Rachel Kane, Verna Skinner, Joyce Lucas, Helen Davis, Bernadine Bishop, Bernadine Hampden, Evelyn Paris, Vivian Jackson, Ruth Jackson, Maddie Grosse, Gene States, Patricia Knight, Mildred Jackson, and Barbara Bowen. Students were required to pay tuition of $40 a month, and to sign on for a minimum of six months' training. They were taught shampoo, press and curl, manicures, and hygiene: Backhouse, "Interview with Mrs S. A. (Emily) Clyke"; Hudson, "Interview with Barbara Bowen"; Hudson, "Interview with Clara Adams"; David Woods, "Interview with Rose Gannon-Dixon," Halifax, August 1995.

29. For details regarding Viola Desmond's reputation in Nova Scotia, see "Takes Action," New Glasgow *Clarion* 1:1 (December 1946). On the restricted business opportunities available to Black Nova Scotians, and the predominantly middle-class status of Blacks who contested racial segregation in Canadian courts, see * The issue of class designation is complex, especially when overlaid by race. Within the Black community, Viola Desmond would probably have been viewed as upper-class. From the vantage point of whites, a married woman who worked outside the home as a beautician would probably have been classified as working-class. Class definitions, when examined through distinct racial perspectives, can become as slippery as race definitions themselves. On the complex racial dynamics associated with the promulgation of and resistance to white middle-class culture within the African-American community, see Evelyn Brooks Higginbotham, *Righteous Discontent: The Women's Movement in the Black Baptist Church, 1880–1920* (Cambridge, Mass,: Harwood University Press, 1993).

30. See for example "Takes Action," New Glasgow *Clarion* 1:1 (December 1946); Pachai, *Beneath the Clouds*, at 152–5; McCluskey, "Long-Established Minority"; Robertson, "Interview with Pearleen Oliver"; Hudson, "Interview with Barbara Bowen"; Hudson, "Interview with Clara Adams"; Backhouse, "Interview with Wanda Robson." Although there were a number of cases brought by Black men earlier, and a few brought by Black couples (see further discussion in this chapter), Viola Desmond appears to have been the first Black woman in Canada to take legal action against racially segregated seating practices independently in her own right. This claim is based upon an appraisal of reported cases only. There may have been others whose cases were unreported, or whose cases do not reveal on the face of the documents that race was the issue. For details of similar challenges brought by Black women in the United States, see *

31. Evelyn Brooks Higginbotham, "African-American Women's History and the Metalanguage of Race," *Signs* 17:2 (Winter 1992), 251 at 254, 257, 261. For further analysis and references on the racialized configuration of gender, see *

32. McCluskey, "Long-Established Minority"; Pachai, *Beneath the Clouds*, at 154.

33. "Negress Alleges She Was Ejected from Theatre," Halifax *Chronicle*, 30 November 1946, p. 2.

34. Hudson, "Interview with Pearleen Oliver"; Ken Alexander and Avis Glaze, *Towards Freedom: The African-Canadian Experience* (Toronto: Umbrella Press, 1996), at 155. Prior to her marriage to Jack Desmond, Viola belonged to the racially mixed congregation of the Trinity Anglican Church. She switched affiliations to her husband's church upon marriage.

35. For biological details on Pearleen (Borden) Oliver, whose own attempts to enter the nursing profession were barred because of race, see Doris McCubbin, "The Women of Halifax," *Chatelaine*, June 1954, p. 16; Colin, A. Thomson, *Born with a Call: A Biography of Dr William Pearly Oliver, C.M.* (Dartmouth, N.S.: Black Culture Centre, 1986); George Elliott Clarke, ed., *Fire on the Water*, vol. 1 (Lawrencetown Beach, N.S.: Pottersfield Press, 1991), at 171; reference by Frances Early in her review of "Rethinking Canada: The Promise of Women's

History," *Resources for Feminist Research* 21 (Spring 1992), at 25, to oral interviews of Pearleen Oliver, held by Saint Mary's University Library, Halifax; Alexander and Glaze, *Towards Freedom*, at 155. For reference to Pearleen Oliver's public-speaking campaign in the 1940s to publicize cases of Black women refused admission to nursing schools see Agnes Calliste, "Women of 'Exceptional Merit': Immigration of Caribbean Nurses to Canada," *Canadian Journal of Women and the Law*, vol. 6 (1993), 85 at 92. For reference to Pearleen Oliver's interest in discrimination against Black women, see Clarke, ed., *Fire on the Water*, at 146, where he notes that Pearleen Oliver's *One of His Heralds* (Halifax: Pearleen Oliver, n.d.) discusses the situation of Agnes Gertrude Waring (1884–1951), whose attempt to receive ordination to preach at the Second Baptist Church in New Glasgow was refused by the Maritime Baptist Convention because she was female. For reference to the "Little Black Sambo" campaign, see correspondence from Beresford Augustus Husbands to the Mayor of Halifax, following Pearleen Oliver's address on 26 January 1944, in PANS. Helen Campbell Bennerman's *Story of Little Black Sambo*, first published in 1899, became a Canadian classic, according to Robin Winks, "still selling well in its sixteenth printing in 1969": Winks, *Blacks in Canada*, at 295.

36. Born in 1912, Rev. Oliver grew up in a predominantly white community in Wolfville, Nova Scotia, and graduated from Acadia University with a BA in 1934, and a Masters of Divinity in 1936. For biographical details on Rev. W. P. Oliver (who would later become the chair of the Black United Front) see Thomson, *Born with a Call*; "Halifax Cleric Elected," Halifax *Chronicle-Herald*, 3 September 1960, p. 13; Clarke, ed., *Fire on the Water*, vol. 1, at 171; Marjorie Major, "The Negroes in Nova Scotia," PANS Mg1, v. 1767, no. 42K; Oliver, "Cultural Progress of the Negro," at 134; W. P. Oliver, "Urban and Rural Life Committee of The African United Baptist Association of Nova Scotia," PANS Mg1, v. 1767 no. 42L; Winks, *Blacks in Canada*, at 350–2; Robin W. Winks, "Negroes in the Maritimes: An Introductory Survey," *Dalhousie Review* 48:4 (1969), 453 at 469; Nancy Lubka, "Ferment in Nova Scotia," *Queen's Quarterly* 76:2 (1969), at 213–28.

37. Viola Desmond sought medical treatment from a physician from the West Indies who resided in the same building as her parents and maintained an office on the corner of Gottingen and Gerrish streets. Being Black, this physician had no access to city hospitals and had to perform all procedures in his office: Robertson, "Interview with Pearleen Oliver." Wanda Robson believes the doctor's name may have been F. B. Holder, a British Guiana-born Black physician practising in Halifax at this time; Backhouse, "Interview with Wanda Robson."

38. Pearleen Oliver sought support from a number of other Black organizations: the Halifax Coloured Citizens Improvement League, the president of the Ladies' Auxiliary of the Cornwallis Street Baptist Church, and the president of the Missionaries' Society. She was disappointed how few people came to the meeting, and discouraged by the reluctance many expressed to "make trouble": Hudson, "Interview with Pearleen Oliver"; Robertson, "Interview with Pearleen Oliver." For the mission statement of the NSAACP, a list of its charter members, and information about predecessor organizations, see *

39. "Negress Alleges She Was Ejected from Theatre," Halifax *Chronicle*, 30 November 1946, p. 2. This position was supported by Mrs M. H. Spaulding, chair of the emergency committee for civil rights of the Civil Liberties League, whose views are quoted in "Ban All Jim Crow Rules Is Comment on N.S. Charge," Toronto *Daily Star*, 30 November 1946, p. 3: "'Jim Crow practices, such as segregating Negroes or any other group in certain sections of theatres, or in keeping them out of hotels, have no place in Canada and should be forbidden by law. There is no place for second-class citizenship in this country," said Mrs. Spaulding. She added there had been instances of the same sort of racial discrimination in other parts of Canada. The practice is that when Negroes try to buy a ticket at a theatre they are told the only seats available are in the balcony, she asserted. 'When Paul Robeson was in Toronto in "Othello" at the Royal Alexandra he said he would not appear if there was any discrimination against colored people, and they were seated in all parts of the house.'"

40. New Glasgow, N.S., *The Clarion* 1:1 (December 1946). For information on *The Clarion* and other Black newspapers in Canada, see *

41. "Editorial, Taking Inventory," New Glasgow, N.S., *The Clarion* 2:4 (28 February 1947), p. 2.

42. "Takes Action" and "Viola Desmond's Appeal," New Glasgow, N.S., *The Clarion* 1:1 (December 1946), p. 1; "Editorial: A New Year's Message," *The Clarion* 2:1 (January 1947). The latter article notes that "one of New Glasgow's leading business men" (race unspecified) donated ten dollars to the case, leading the editor to applaud him for his "courage and generosity." Pearleen Oliver recalls that money came in from all over the province, in amounts both large and small, with more white donors than Black: Robertson, "Interview with Pearleen Oliver." On the origins and meaning of the American phrase "Jim Crow," see *

43. PANS, SMI Division, CBC Radio, Collection Ar2265-2268 and 2279, Carrie Best Interview. Dr Carrie M. Best, whose birth name was Carrie Prevoe, was born in New Glasgow in 1903, and completed high school in New Glasgow. She married Albert Theophilus Best, a Barbadian-born Black porter for the Canadian National Railway, and had one son, J. Calbert Best. Carrie Best was an editor and publisher of several Black newspapers,

founding the *Clarion* in 1946, and publishing the nationally circulated *The Negro Citizen* in 1949. In 1956, she began to write columns in the Pictou *Advocate* on matters of human rights, and produced and narrated radio shows for five stations for twelve years. In 1970, she was awarded the Lloyd McInnes Memorial Award for her contribution to social betterment. She received the Order of Canada in 1974 and an honorary degree from St Francis Xavier University in 1975. Her son, Calbert Best, became national president of the Civil Service Association of Canada in Ottawa in 1960, and an assistant deputy minister for Manpower and Immigration in 1970. See Dr Carrie M. Best, *That Lonesome Road: The Autobiography of Carrie M. Best* (New Glasgow, N.S.: Clarion Publishing, 1977); Clarke, ed., *Fire on the Water*, vol. 1, at 171; Winks, *Blacks in Canada*, at 405, 408; "Albert Best Dies Sunday," New Glasgow *Evening News*, 5 August 1971; "The Gracious Activist," *The Novascotian*, 10 April 1982, cover story and pp. 3–4; "Nova Scotians Best, Buckler Honored," Halifax *Chronicle-Herald*, 21 December 1974; "St. FX Confers Honorary Degrees on Two N.S. Women, N.B. Lawyer," New Glasgow *Evening News*, 12 May 1975; "Three Honorary Doctorates to Be Awarded at Convocation," New Glasgow *Evening News*, 24 April 1975, p. 9; "Two to Receive Decorations in Order of Canada Tonight," New Glasgow *Evening News*, 16 April 1980; "J. C. Best Accepts New Post," Halifax *Chronicle-Herald*, 19 January 1966; "Cal Best Re-elected Civil Servants' Chief," Halifax *Chronicle-Herald*, 1 October 1960.

44. On 18 February 1942, Carrie Best issued a writ of summons against Norman W. Mason and the Roseland Theatre Co. Ltd, for ejecting her and her son, Calbert, from the theatre on 29 December 1941. The event was a deliberate, planned attack on the policy of racial segregation that the theatre began to impose in the 1940s, apparently at the request of some white patrons. Carrie Best wrote to Mason, the white owner of the theatre, challenging him on the policy and advising that she and her son intended to sit on the main floor on 29 December 1941. When she tried to do so that afternoon, she was asked to leave by the white assistant manager, Erskine Cumming, white police officer George S. Wright, and white police chief Elmo Langille. When she refused to leave, Officer Wright placed his hands under Mrs Best's arms and raised her from her seat. She apparently announced: "That's all I wanted you to do, put your hands on me. I will fix you for this." Then she and her son left the theatre. Carrie Best retained James Hinnigar Power, a white New Glasgow lawyer, and commenced litigation, claiming assault and battery and breach of contract. She sought $4 in repairs to her coat, $5,000 in general damages for the assault and battery, and $500 general damages for the wrongful revocation of the licence given to her to witness the performance. Trial was held on 12 May 1942, in the Pictou Court House, before Robert Henry Graham of the Supreme Court of Nova Scotia, the same judge who would later hear Viola Desmond's case. The white judge charged the all-white jury to answer the following questions, to which they responded:

1. Did the Defendant Company's ticket seller sell any tickets to the Plaintiff? No.
2. Did the Defendant ticket seller sell her a downstairs ticket? No.
3. Did the Plaintiff know the Defendant Company would not sell her a downstairs ticket? Yes.
4. Had the Plaintiff any reasonable grounds for thinking the ticket seller sold her a downstairs ticket? No.
5. Did the Plaintiff do as she did because she knew Defendant Company's ticket seller would not sell her a downstairs ticket? Yes.
6. Was any more force used to remove the plaintiff than was necessary? No.
7. What damage, if any, did the Plaintiff sustain? None.

Upon the return of these findings, Judge Graham dismissed Carrie Best's action, and charged her with the Defendant's bill of costs, which amounted to $156.07. See *Best v Mason and Roseland Theatre*, PANS RG39 "C" (PI) 1986-550/099, file A4013 (1942); "Case Dismissed against Mason and Roseland Theatre," New Glasgow *Evening News*, 15 May 1942; "Case Dismissed," New Glasgow *Eastern Chronicle*, 19 May 1942; "Two sentences Are Imposed in Supreme Court," Pictou *Advocate*, 21 May 1942; "Jury Dismisses Suit for Damages," Halifax *Herald*, 15 May 1942; "Colored Woman's Action Dismissed," Halifax *Chronicle*, 15 May 1942. For a fuller account, see Constance Backhouse, "'I was Unable to Identify with Topsy': Carrie M. Best's Struggle against Racial Segregation in Nova Scotia, 1942," *Atlantis* 22:2 (Spring 1998), at 16–26. I am indebted to Barry Cahill for bringing the archival file to my attention.

45. Best, *That Lonesome Road*, at 43–4. The Norfolk House, where Carrie's brother worked, had a history of refusing to support the practices of racial discrimination so common in the area. The Halifax *Eastern Chronicle*, 28 May 1885, noted that Mr H. Murray, a white man, refused to close his Norfolk hotel to the Fisk Jubilee Singers, a Black choir group. Members of the choir had earlier been refused admission to hotels in Pictou and Halifax.

46. Truro, which would earn itself the designation "the Alabama of Canada" and "Little Mississippi," also maintained a "Whites Only" waiting room in the railway station: Lubka, "Ferment in Nova Scotia," at 215; Winks, *Blacks in Canada*, at 319–25, 420; Winks, "Negroes in the Maritimes," at 466–7; Thomson, *Born with a Call*, at 467. On the activities of the KKK, see discussion of *R. v Phillips* in chapter 6.

47. Although similar legislation was not passed in provinces other than Ontario and Nova Scotia, New Brunswick's legislature enacted two statutes giving explicit recognition to the existence of Black schools. For details of the 1842 and 1843 New Brunswick provisions, and information about more informal segregation methods used in other provinces, see * For a comparison with the segregated schooling offered First Nations children, see discussion of *R. v Wanduta* in chapter 3.

48. For legislative details of the 1849, 1850, 1859, and 1886 provisions, see *

49. Winks, *Blacks in Canada*, at 365–76; Robin W. Winks, "Negro School Segregation in Ontario and Nova Scotia," *Canadian Historical Review* 50:2 (1969), 164 at 174, 176; Jason H. Silverman and Donna J. Gillie, "The pursuit of Knowledge under Difficulties: Education and the Fugitive Slave in Canada," *Ontario History*, vol. 74 (1982), at 95; Claudette Knight, "Black Parents Speak: Education in Mid-Nineteenth-Century Canada West," *Ontario History*, vol. 89 (1997), at 269. For some discussion of the resistance offered by Blacks to these practices see Peggy Bistow, "'Whatever you raise in the ground you can sell it in Chatham': Black Women in Buxton and Chatham, 1850–65," in Peggy Bristow et al., *"We're Rooted Here and They Can't Pull Us Up": Essays in African-Canadian Women's History* (Toronto: University of Toronto Press, 1994), 69 at 114–16; Afua P. Cooper, "Black Women and Work in Nineteenth-Century Canada West: Black Woman Teacher Mary Bibb," in Bristow et al., *We're Rooted Here*, at 148–68.

50. *Washington v The Trustees of Charlotteville* (1854), 11 U.C.Q.B. 569 (Ont. Q.B.), held that school authorities could not exclude Black children unless alternative facilities for "colored pupils" had been established, but *In re Dennis Hill v Schools Trustees of Camden and Zone* (1854), 11 U.C.Q.B. 573 (Ont. Q.B.), ruled that Black children could be forced to attend separate schools located miles away from their homes and outside of their school sections. *An Act to Amend the Act respecting Common Schools in Upper Canada*, S.O. 1868–69, c.44, s.9, provides "that no person shall be deemed a supporter of any separate school for coloured people, unless he resides within three miles in a direct line of the site of the school house for such separate school; and any coloured child residing farther than three miles in a direct line from the said school house shall be allowed to attend the common school of the section within the limits of which the said child shall reside." These provisions are continued by *An Act respecting Separate Schools*, R.S.O. 1877, c.206, s.2–5; *The Separate Schools Act*, R.S.O. 1897, c.294. After the amendment, several cases acknowledged that race should not be the sole ground for exclusion from common schools, but then accepted the testimony of school authorities regarding overcrowding and "'insufficient accommodation,'" using this to defeat the claims of Black parents to register their children in non-segregated schools: see *In re Hutchison and School Trustees of St. Catharines* (1871), 31 U.C.Q.B. 274 (Ont. Q.B.); *Dunn v Board of Education of Windsor* (1884), 6 O.R. 125 (Ontario Chancery Division). For two examples of cases where the efforts of education officials to bar Black children from common public schools were challenged successfully, see *Simmons and the Corporation of Chatham* (1861), 21 U.C.Q.B. 75 (Ont. Q.B.), quashing for uncertainty a by-law which purported to enlarge substantially the geographic catchment area of a separate school, and *Stewart and Schools Trustees of Sandwich* (1864), 23 U.C.Q.B. 634 (Ont. Q.B.), which accepted evidence that the separate school operated only intermittently as a reason to overrule the common school's refusal to register a Black female student. See also Winks, *Blacks in Canada*; Winks, "Negro School Segregation," at 175–82; Knight, "Black Parents Speak."

51. Winks, *Blacks in Canada*; Winks, "Negro School Segregation," at 182, 190.

52. For legislative details of the specific provisions relating to "coloured people" between 1887 and 1964, see *

53. Winks, "Negro School Segregation," at 177.

54. For legislative details of the 1865 and 1873 provisions, see *

55. For legislative details of the 1884 provision, see *

56. For legislative details of the provisions in force between 1900 and 1950, see *

57. In Lower Sackville, Mrs Pleasah Lavinia Caldwell, a Black Nova Scotian, responded by opening a "kitchen school" in her home, which educated Blacks in the area until her death in 1950: Helen Champion, "School in a Kitchen," unlabelled clipping dated 9 November 1949, PANS, Mg1, v.1767 no. 42a. In 1964, four such districts continued: Beechville, Hammond Plains, Lucasville, and Cherry Brook, all in Halifax County: Winks, *Blacks in Canada*, at 376–80. For details of the lack of funding and difficulties recruiting teachers and obtaining equipment, premises, and transportation in Nova Scotia see Winks, "Negro School Segregation," at 186–91.

58. Winks, *Blacks in Canada*, comments at 325 on the "formlessness of the racial barrier," noting at 326: "In the United States the Negro was somewhat more sure—sure of where he could and could not go, of when to be meek and when to be strong. In Canada he was uncertain."

59. Oliver, "Cultural Progress of the Negro," notes at 129–35 that most Black males could not find work except in the heaviest and most poorly paid jobs: agriculture, mining, lumbering, steel, railway, and shipping industries. In most cases, they were also barred from membership in unions. Business ventures were limited to barber-shops, beauty parlours, taxi business, trucking, shoe-making, a newspaper, and one co-operative store. See also James W. St. G. Walker, *Racial Discrimination in Canada: The Black Experience* (Ottawa: Canadian Historical Association, 1985), at 15, where he notes that, during the inter-war years, Black men were concentrated in the following jobs: waiters, janitors, barbers, and labourers. The elite among the men worked as railway waiters and porters: see Stanley G. Grizzle, *My Name's Not George: The Story of the Brotherhood of Sleeping Car Porters in Canada* (Toronto: Umbrella Press, 1998); Judith Fingard, "From Sea to Rail: Black Transportation Workers and Their Families in Halifax, c.1870–1916," *Acadiensis* 24:2 (Spring 1995), at 49–64; Agnes Calliste, "The Struggle for Employment Equity by Blacks on American and Canadian Railroads," *Journal of Black Studies* 25:3 (January 1995), at 297–317; Agnes Calliste, "Blacks on Canadian Railways," *Canadian Ethnic Studies* 20:2 (1988), at 36–52; Agnes Calliste, "Sleeping Car Porters in Canada: An Ethnically Submerged Split Labour Market," *Canadian Ethnic Studies* 19:1 (1987), at 1–20. Prior to the Second World War, Black females were limited to teaching school or domestic work. On the pervasive restriction to domestic work, Suzanne Morton, "Separate Spheres in a Separate World: African-Nova Scotian Women in late-19th-Century Halifax County," *Acadiensis* 22:2 (Spring 1993), 61, notes at 67: "African-Nova Scotian women had virtually no legal wage-earning oppor-tunities outside domestic service, taking in laundry, or sewing. Regardless of the status in the community, property holdings or occupation of the husband, married women and widows charred, and young women were servants." Dorothy W. Williams, *Blacks in Montreal, 1628–1986: An Urban Demography* (Cowansville, Que.: Yvon Blais, 1989), notes at 45 that the superintendent of nurses of the Montreal General Hospital admitted in the 1930s that Black nurses could not find employment in Montreal, "since there were not enough Black patients to care for in the hospitals (and White patients would not allow Black nurses to touch them)." See also "Girl Barred by Color from Nurses Training Course," New Glasgow, N.S., *The Clarion* 2:15 (6 October 1947), p.1, recounting race barriers against Black women throughout Ontario. The nursing field opened to women in Nova Scotia in 1949, when two Blacks graduated as registered nurses. See also Dionne Brand, *No Burden to Carry: Narratives of Black Working Women in Ontario, 1920s to 1950s* (Toronto: Women's Press, 1991), at 155, 184, 207. Williams notes at 45 that Blacks were barred from doing medical internships in Montreal between 1930 and 1947. The Faculty of Medicine at McGill University arranged instead for Blacks to serve their intern-ships with Howard University in Washington, D.C. Donald H. Clairmont and Dennis W. Magill, "Nova Scotia Blacks: Marginality in a Depressed Region," in W. E. Mann, ed., *Canada: A Sociological Profile* (Toronto: Copp Clark, 1971), 177 at 179, 183, quote P. E. MacKerrow, *A Brief History of the Colored Baptists of Nova Scotia* (Halifax, 1895): "the United States with her faults, which are many, has done much for the evaluation of the coloured race. Sad and sorry are we to say that is more than we can boast of here in Nova Scotia. Our young men as soon as they receive a common school education must flee away to the United States and seek employ-ment. Very few ever receive a trade from the large employers, even in the factories, on account of race preju-dices...." Rev. Adam S. Green, MS, *The Future of the Canadian Negro* (1904), PANS V/F v.144 no. 11, at 17, notes: "How many negroes do you find as clerks, book-keepers, or stenographers within the provinces? I know of but *one* ... Our people are excluded from such lucrative positions, not so much from disqualification, as from race-prejudice."
60. On the history of residential segregation by race across Canada, see *
61. Although there was no legislation explicitly barring Blacks from jury service, some legal officials took steps to eliminate their names in the empanelling of jury lists. Winks, *Blacks in Canada*, at 251, 284–6, notes that a challenge to Black jurors and jury foremen in Toronto in 1851 was unsuccessful, but that Blacks were excluded from jury service in Victoria between 1864 and 1872. James W. St. G. Walker, *The Black Identity in Nova Scotia: Community and Institutions in Historical Perspective* (Halifax: Black Cultural Centre for Nova Scotia, 1985), notes at 8 that Blacks "could not serve on juries or claim a jury trial." See also James M. Pilton, "Negro Settlement in British Columbia," MA thesis (University of Victoria, 1951); "Colored Men as Jurors," Victoria *Colonist*, 7 May 1872, p. 3; "Colored Jurors," Victoria *Colonist*, 21 March 1872, p. 3; "Have Them Right," New Westminister *Times*, 18 February 1860.
62. On the history of military segregation, see *
63. For a case documenting the resistance of a Black man to racial segregation on a Chatham steamer in the 1850s, see *
64. Winks, "Negroes in the Maritimes," at 466; Winks, *Blacks in Canada*, at 286, 325; Daniel G. Hill, *The Freedom-Seekers: Blacks in Early Canada* (Agincourt, Ont.: Book Society of Canada, 1981), at 104.
65. On the racial segregation of orphans and paupers in Nova Scotia, see *

66. On the denial of hospital services to Blacks in Halifax and Edmonton, see *

67. On segregated cemeteries, see *

68. Winks, *Blacks in Canada*, notes at 248, 283–4, 286, 325 that hotels in Hamilton, Windsor, Chatham, and London refused admission to Blacks in the mid-nineteenth century. In the 1860s in Victoria, the chief theatre refused Blacks access to the dress circle or to orchestra seats, the Bank Exchange Saloon refused service to Blacks, and they were also excluded from Queen Victoria's birthday ball and from the farewell banquet for Governor James Douglas. The colour line remained visible in British Columbia in restaurants and places of entertainment prior to the First World War. Blacks were not admitted to the boy scout troops or the YMCA in Windsor, and Black musicians had to establish their own orchestra in Owen Sound. Winks notes at 325–6, 388, 420, 457: "In 1924 the Edmonton City Commissioner barred Negroes from all public parks and swimming pools—and was overruled by the city council; in Colchester, Ontario, in 1930, police patrolled the parks and beaches to keep blacks from using them. In Saint John all restaurants and theatres closed their doors to Negroes in 1915; two years later the chief theatres of Hamilton also did so. […] In 1929, when the World Baptist Conference was held in Toronto, Negro delegates were denied hotel rooms. […] Only one hotel in Montreal could be depended upon not to turn Negroes away in 1941. […] Many dance pavilions, skating rinks and restaurants made it clear that they did not welcome blacks; and several pubs in Saskatchewan and British Columbia insisted that Negroes sit in corners reserved for them." Even into the 1960s, Black residents were virtually barred from community restaurants, and Windsor barkeepers designated separate "jungle rooms" for Blacks until 1951. See also "Hotels Refuse to Take Negroes," Vancouver *Province*, 13 August 1945, p. 2, recounting how Black members of the cast of *Carmen Jones* were denied hotel accommodation in Vancouver, and "Color Bar Said Drawn in Local Pub," Vancouver *Sun*, 30 July 1948, p. 1. Howard Lawrence, New Glasgow, N.S., *The Clarion* 2:2 (December 1946), urged the Black community to establish a community centre because "every place is closed to us." Anna-Maria Galante, "Ex-Mayor Lewis Broke New Ground," *Afro-Nova Scotian Portraits* (Halifax: Chronicle-Herald and Mail-Star, 19 February 1993), at P7, quotes Daurene Lewis stating that the dances in Annapolis Royal were always segregated (*circa* 1940s and 1950s) and attempts were made to segregate the movie house as well. McKenzie, "Race Prejudice and the Negro," notes at 201 that "[Negroes] are not always served in the best restaurants, nor admitted to high-class hotels. They are restricted, in cities, to the poorer residential districts, and are not accepted socially." See also Daniel G. Hill, "Black History in Early Ontario,." *Canadian Human Rights Yearbook* (Ottawa: Human Rights Research and Education Centre, University of Ottawa, 1984–5), at 265; Grizzle, *My Name's Not George*, at 54–5; Winks, "Negroes in the Maritimes," at 467; Winks, "Negro School Segregation," at 189; Allen P. Stouffer, *The Light of Nature and the Law of God: Antislavery in Ontario, 1833–1877* (Montreal and Kingston: McGill-Queen's University Press, 1992), at 200–1; Brand, *No Burden to Carry*, at 134, 149–50, 153, 210–11, 278. For reference to comparable treatment of First Nations peoples, see George Manuel and Michael Poslums, *The Fourth World: An Indian Reality* (Don Mills: Ontario: Collier-Macmillan Canada, 1974), at 101.

69. For legislative details regarding the 1947 and 1949 Saskatchewan provisions, and similar legislation enacted in Ontario in 1951 and 1954 on the heels of a concerted lobby campaign, see *

70. On the admission of Black lawyers (including James Robinson Johnston, Joseph Eaglan Griffith, Frederick Allan Hamilton, and George W. R. Davis) to the bar of Nova Scotia, to the bar of British Columbia (Joshua Howard), and to the bar of New Brunswick (Abraham Beverly Walker), see * For details concerning Ontario, see chapter 6.

71. Barry Cahill, "The 'Colored Barrister': The Short Life and Tragic Death of James Robinson Johnston, 1876–1915," *Dalhousie Law Journal*, vol. 15 (1992), 326, notes at 373 that Goffe was admitted to Gray's Inn in 1905, and called to the bar by Gray's Inn in 1908. He practised at the English bar for six years, and "was employed in various government departments" during and after the First World War. He died in 1962 in his ninetieth year.

72. For biographical details on F. W. Bissett, the son of Frederick W. Bissett and Ethel Gray (Smith) Bissett, see "Bissett, Frederick William, B.A., LL.B.," *Maritime Reference Book: Biographical and Pictorial Record of Prominent Men and Women of the Maritime Provinces* (Halifax: Royal Print, 1931), at 34; "Bench Vacancy Filled," Halifax *Chronicle-Herald*, 11 March 1961; "Mr. Justice F. W. Bissett," Halifax *Mail-Star*, 11 November 1978, p. 6; "Mr. Justice Bissett, 76, Dies in Halifax," Halifax *Mail-Star*, 10 November 1978, pp. 1–2; Tributes Paid to Mr. Justice F. W. Bissett," Halifax *Mail-Star*, 11 November 1978, pp. 1–2. Apart from Rev. Oliver's recommendation, it remains unclear why Viola Desmond selected F. W. Bissett. She seems to have been familiar with at least some other white members of the legal profession prior to this. Earlier, in November 1946, she retained Samuel B. Goodman, a white lawyer from Halifax, to issue a writ against Philip Kane, the white car dealer who sold her the 1940 Dodge, for overcharging her in violation of the Wartime Prices and Trade Board Order. See *Viola Desmond v Philip Kane*, PANS RG39 "C" Halifax v.936, no. S.C. 13304.

73. *Johnson v Sparrow* (1899), 15 Que. S.C. 104 (Quebec Superior Court), at 108. For details of Judge Archibald's decision, see * When the case went on appeal to the Quebec Court of Queen's Bench, Judge Bossé refused to equate a hotel and a theatre under the common-law rule, but upheld the $50 damage award based on the breach of contract. The court did not overturn Judge Archibald's explicit racial analysis, but stated that it was unnecessary to decide the question of whether Blacks were entitled to the same rights of admission as whites in this case; *Johnson v Sparrow* (1899), 8 Que. Q.B. 379. Walker, "Race," *Rights and the Law*, suggests at 146 that "in dismissing Justice Archibald's reasoning the appeal decision undermined any general application of the non-discriminatory principle." With respect, this is arguably an overreading of the appeal decision. Judge Bossé adverts to the legislation in the United States endorsing racial segregation, explicitly questions whether these enactments might be unconstitutional as violating the principle of equality, notes that similar legislation has not been enacted in Canada, and then concludes that the present dispute, which can be resolved on a purely contractual basis, does not require any further rulings on racial discrimination. This does not appear to be an overt rejection of Judge Archibald's analysis on racial equality, but a reluctance to rule on the matter in the present case. For further discussion of the common-law duty to serve, and another Ontario case that followed *Johnson v Sparrow*, see * Several earlier cases premised on an innkeeper's duty to serve the public were brought by Jacob Francis, an English-born Black saloon-keeper in Victoria. In the spring of 1860, Francis was refused service of two bottles of champagne in a billiard saloon at Yates and Government streets. On 20 April 1860, a civil jury heard his claim for forty shillings in damages in *Francis v Miletich*, Archives of British Columbia (hereinafter cited as ABC) C/AA/30.3D/2, Vancouver Island, Supreme Court of Civil Justice, Rule and order book, 1859–61, at 63, 69; C/AA/30.3P/5, Vancouver Island, Supreme Court of Civil Justice, at 118–19, 123; GR848, Vancouver Island, Charge Books; "Refusing a Drink to a Coloured Man," Victoria *Gazette*, 21 April 1860, p. 3. The jury held that Miletich was an innkeeper, that Francis was refused liquor but not received as a guest, and that Francis sustained no injury and was not entitled to damages. In 1862, Jacob Francis was refused service at the Bank Exchange Saloon in Victoria, and again sought legal relief. According to newspaper accounts, a white Victoria police magistrate, Augustus F. Pemberton, ruled that saloons that refused service to Black men would either not get a licence or would be fined and their licence not renewed when it expired. According to the charge book, the case was dismissed by Magistrate Pemberton on 4 July 1862. See *Jacob Francis v Joseph Lovett*, ABC GR848, Charge books, vol.3; "Wouldn't Let Him Drink," Victoria *Colonist*, 26 June 1862, p. 3; "Shall a Black Man Drink at a White Man's Bar?" Victoria *Colonist*, 28 June 1862, p. 3; "The Vexed Question Settled," Victoria *Colonist*, 5 July 1862, p. 3; "Shall a Coloured Man Drink at a White Man's Bar?" Victoria *British Colonist*, 5 July 1862, p. 3. For more details on Francis, who was earlier denied the right to take up an elected seat in the colonial Legislative Assembly because of his race, see Pilton, "Negro Settlement in British Columbia"; S. Stott, "Blacks in B.C.," ABC NW/016.325711/B631. For a similar case in 1913, see *Moses Rowden v J. B. Stevens, Prop., Stratford Hotel*, ABC GR1651, British Columbia County Court (Vancouver) Plaint and procedure books, 1886–1946 [B7314–B7376]; GR1651, British Columbia County Court (Vancouver), Indexes to plaint and procedure books, 1886–1946 [B7897–B7901]; GR1418, British Columbia County Court (Vancouver), Judgments 1893–1940 [B2611–B2643]; "Negro Sues Because Color Line Is Drawn," Vancouver *Province*, 4 October 1913, p. 15; "Hotel Bar Refused to Serve Negro," Vancouver *Province*, 10 July 1913, p. 17; "Enters Suit for Damages for Being Refused Drink," Vancouver *Sun*, 1 October 1913, p. 1. Rowden sought relief before the city's licence commissioners, who refused to intervene. He then claimed $500 damages on the basis that Stevens failed to meet his common-law obligation as an innkeeper to serve travellers. The outcome of the case is unclear from the surviving documentation.

74. *Barnswell v National Amusement Company, Limited* (1914), 21 B.C.R. 435, [1915] 31 W.L.R. 542 (B.C.C.A.). See also "Suit Against Theatre," Victoria *Times*, 30 May 1914, p. 18; "Damages Are Awarded," Victoria *Times*, 10 December 1914, p. 16; "Legal Intelligence," Victoria *Daily Colonist*, 10 December 1914, p. 3. For further details, see *

75. "Colored Patrons Must Pay Double," Regina *Leader*, 9 October 1911, p. 7, announces: "One of the city's restaurants has decided to draw the colored line and in future all colored patrons will pay just double what their white brothers are charged. This, of course, is not a money-making venture, but is a polite hint to these people that their patronage is not wanted. It is understood that the change is made at the urgent request of some of the most influential patrons, and not on the initiative of the management. It is an innovation in the running of hotels, cafes and restaurants of the city and the experiment will be watched with interest." The exact basis for the ruling, which is not reported in the published legal reports, is somewhat difficult to reconstruct from the press account in "May Charge Double Price," Regina *Leader*, 16 October 1911, p. 7. The newspaper specifies that the case was "a charge of obtaining money under false pretences" laid against W. B. Waddell by William Hawes. There was some factual dispute over whether Hawes had been notified of the double charge prior to

ordering, with Hawes claiming he had not, and Waddell claiming he had. White magistrates Lawson and Long concluded that Hawes had, and held that therefore there was no case of false pretences. The press seems to have been less convinced, claiming that the case stood for the proposition that "a restaurant keeper has the right to exclude colored patrons by charging double prices without, however, taking proper steps to make the charge known to those whom he proposes to exclude." The press report also hints that the claim may have been rooted in breach of contract, recounting that the plaintiff tried to show that Hawes "had no knowledge of [the double price] arrangement when he gave his order, and that the bill of fare from which he ordered constituted a contract … " The contract issues appear to have been ignored by the court. Counsel for Hawes, Mr Barr, sought leave to appeal, but this was denied. For another example of a case where Blacks were charged extra, see *R. v J. D. Carroll*, ABC GR419, B.C. Attorney General Documents, Box 1, file 21/1860, and "Police Court," Victoria *Colonist*, 14 January 1860, p. 3, where William Bastion, a Black man, charged J. D. Carroll, a white innkeeper, with extortion after he charged him $1.50 for three drinks he had already consumed on 10 January 1860. Charles Jackson and Arthur Wiggins, white men who were with Bastion at the time, testified that they had never been charged more than 12 1/2 cents per drink. Carroll was committed for trial by Magistrate Augustus Pemberton in Victoria Police Court on 12–13 January 1860, but the outcome of the case is not clear from the surviving records. The Victoria *Colonist*, 19 January 1860, suggests that the case was dismissed because Carroll was a spirit dealer and not an innkeeper; see Diba B. Majzub, "'A God Sent Land for the Colored People'? The Legal Treatment of Blacks in Victoria, 1858–1865," unpublished manuscript, at 23.

76. *Loew's Montreal Theatres Ltd. V Reynolds* (1919), 30 Que. K.B. 459 (Quebec King's Bench) per John-Edward Martin, J., at 466; Winks, "Negroes in the Maritimes," at 467; "Court Says Color Line Is Illegal; All Equal in Law," Montreal *Gazette*, 5 March 1919, p. 4. For details of the case, and a 1912 case in Edmonton that reached a more informal, but similar resolution, see *

77. *Franklin v Evans* (1924), 55 O.L.R. 349, 26 O.W.N. 65 (Ont. High Court). See also "Dismisses Suit of Colored Man," London *Evening Free Press*, 15 March 1924, which gives the name as W. K. Franklin. Strangely, neither *Johnson v Sparrow* nor *Barnwell* was cited in the legal decision, and Judge Haughton Lennox concluded that there were no authorities or decided cases in support of the plaintiff's contention. Most of the decisions centred on common-law rules requiring hotel-keepers to supply "accommodation of a certain character, within certain limits, and subject to recognized qualifications, to all who apply." Contrasting restaurants with innkeepers, Lennox held that the common-law obligations did not apply to the defendant. The white judge did, however, seem to have been ambivalent about the result he reached in this case. Disparaging the conduct of the white restaurant owner and his wife, whose attitude towards the plaintiff Lennox described as "unnecessarily harsh, humiliating, and offensive," Lennox contrasted their situation with that of the plaintiff: "The plaintiff is undoubtedly a thoroughly respectable man, of good address, and, I have no doubt, a good citizen, and I could not but be touched by the pathetic eloquence of his appeal for recognition as a human being, of common origin with ourselves." Lennox then expressly ducked the issue: "The theoretical consideration of this matter is a difficult and decidedly two-sided problem, extremely controversial, and entirely outside my sphere in the administration of law—law as it is." Lennox dismissed the action without costs. Curiously, the account in the local Black newspaper, *The Dawn of Tomorrow*, suggests that the plaintiff won: "W. V. Franklin Given Damages," London *Dawn of Tomorrow*, 2 February 1924, p. 1; "Mr. W. V. Franklin's Victory," London *Dawn of Tomorrow*, 16 February 1924, p. 2. This coverage appears erroneous in asserting that "the jury took only 20 minutes to decide that Mr. Franklin should be awarded damages," since the law report notes that there was no jury, and the claim was dismissed. However, the Black press, unlike the white press, did recount the plaintiff's testimony in valuable detail: "When Mr. Franklin was called to the witness box for the defence counsel [and asked], 'Have you any ground for damages?' Mr. Franklin's eloquent and polished reply was: "Not dollars and cents, but in humiliation and inhuman treatment at the hands of this fellow man, yes. Because I am a dark man, a condition over which I have no control, I did not receive the treatment I was entitled to as a human being. God chose to bring me into the world a colored man, and on this account, defendant placed me on a lower level than he is.'" Reference was also made in the Black press, on 16 February 1924, to the views of the Black community on the necessity of bringing the case: "In a recent article in our paper we stated that the colored people of London stood solidly behind Mr. Franklin. On the whole we did stand behind him but a few there were who doubted this wisdom of his procedure, believing, as they expressed it, that his case would cause ill feeling between the races. [… N]othing in respect is ever gained by cringing or by showing that we believe ourselves to be less than men. Nothing will ever be gained by submitting to treatment which is less than that due to any British subject." The financial cost of bringing such an action was acknowledged by the *Dawn of Tomorrow*, which made an express appeal to readers to contribute money to assist Mr Franklin in defraying the costs of the case, since "the monetary damages awarded him by the courts is far below the actual cost to him."

78. *Rogers v Clarence Hotel et al.*, [1940] 2 W.W.R. 545, (1940), 55 B.C.R. 214 (B.C.C.A.).

79. *Christie and Another v York Corporation* (1937), 75 Que. C.S. 136 (Que. Superior Court); rev'd *York Corporation v Christie* (1938), 65 Que. B.R. 104 (Que. K.B.); leave to appeal granted *Fred. Christie v The York Corporation*, [1939] 80 S.C.R. 50 (S.C.C.); upheld *Fred Christie v The York Corporation*, [1940] 81 S.C.R. 139 (S.C.C.). For a more detailed account of this case, see *

80. *Loew's Montreal Theatres Ltd. v Reynolds* (1919), 30 Que. K.B. 459 (Quebec King's Bench), at 462–3.

81. *Rogers v Clarence Hotel et al.*, [1940] 2 W.W.R. 545, (1940), 55 B.C.R. 214 (B.C.C.A.); ABC GR1570, British Columbia Supreme Court (Vancouver), Judgments, 1893–1947 [B6321] v.39, p. 257; GR1727, British Columbia Bench books, v.368, pp. 319–25; "Court Rules Beer Parlor Must Serve Colored Patron," Vancouver *Province*, 23 February 1940, p. 11; "Owner's Right: May Refuse to Serve Beer," 22 February 1940, Vancouver *Province*, p. 2; "Negro Suing Proprietor of Beer Parlor," Vancouver *Sun*, 22 February 1940, p. 1; "Negro Wins Right to Use Beer Parlor," Vancouver *Sun*, 23 February 1940, p. 17. For a more detailed account of the case, see *

82. *York Corporation v Christie* (1938), 65 Que. B.R. 104 (Que. K.B.), at 125–39.

83. *Fred Christie v The York Corporation*, [1940] S.C.R. 139 (S.C.C.), at 147, 152.

84. *Fred Christie v The York Corporation*, [1940] S.C.R. 139 (S.C.C.), at 152. On the significance of the many dissenting judges, see Frank R. Scott *Essays on the Constitution* (Toronto: University of Toronto Press, 1977), at 333.

85. Bora Laskin, "Tavern Refusing to Serve Negro—Discrimination," *Canadian Bar Review*, vol. 18 (1940), 314 at 316. See also Frank R. Scott, *The Canadian Constitution and Human Rights* (Toronto: Canadian Broadcasting Company, 1959), at 37.

86. None of the later cases mentioned *Barnswell v National Amusement Co.* The reluctance of Canadian judges to discuss matters of race explicitly may have had something to do with this. County Court Judge Lampman's trial decision in *Barnswell* was the only portion of the judgment that mentioned the plaintiff's race. In the report of the decision in the *Western Law Reporter*, Lampman's trial decision is not included, even in summary form. Since the appeal rulings make no express mention of race, a legal researcher would have been hard-pressed to conclude that the case was an anti-discrimination precedent. The report in the *British Columbia Reports*, however, does make the issue of race explicit. *Johnson v Sparrow* was mentioned briefly, in *Loew's Montreal Theatres Ltd. v Reynolds*, which distinguished it on two rather peculiar grounds: that the plaintiff in *Johnson* had already purchased a ticket prior to the refusal of entry while the plaintiff in *Reynolds* had not, and that the plaintiff in *Johnson* had been unaware of the colour bar, whereas the plaintiff in *Reynolds* was deliberately challenging the policy. Although the Quebec Court of King's Bench in *Christie v York Corporation* also cited *Johnson v Sparrow*, the Supreme Court ruling made no mention of the decision, nor did the other cases discussed above. The curious erasure of the earlier anti-discrimination rulings is underscored by the comments of Judge Lennox in *Franklin v Evans*, who noted that counsel for the Black plaintiff, Mr Buchner, "could find no decided case in support of his contention." A scholarly article written years later, Ian A. Hunter," Civil Actions for Discrimination," *Canadian Bar Review*, vol. 55 (1977), 106, also fails to mention the *Johnson v Sparrow* case or the *Barnswell v National Amusement Co.* case, although the author discusses the others in detail. See also D. A. Schmeiser, *Civil Liberties in Canada* (London: Oxford University Press, 1964), at 262–74, who erroneously refers to *Loew's Montreal Theatres* as "the earliest reported Canadian case in this area," ignores *Johnson v Sparrow* and *Barnswell v National Amusement Co.*, and then concludes: "The foregoing cases clearly indicate that the common law is particularly barren of remedies guaranteeing equality of treatment in public places or enterprises … "

87. *Johnson v Sparrow* (1899), 15 Que. S.C. 104 (Superior Court), at 107.

88. On the history of slavery under the French regime, see *

89. For reference to the clause in the 1763 Treaty of Paris, see *

90. For the 1790 English provision, see *

91. For details of the 1762 legislative provision, see *

92. For details of the 1781 legislative provision, which was repealed in 1825, see *

93. For details of the 1793 provisions and their re-enactment through 1897, see *

94. For details of the judicial cases, see *

95. For details of the 1833 English provision, see *

96. On the tenacity of slavery in Canada, see *

97. For details of the 1842 decision to permit the extradition of Nelson Hackett and the 1860–1 extradition of John Anderson, see *

98. *Re Drummond Wren*, [1945] O.R. 778 (Ont. Supreme Court), at 780–3, and quoting 7 Halsbury, 2d ed. 1932, at 153–4. See also *Essex Real Estate v Holmes* (1930), 37 O.W.N. 392 (Ont. High Court), in which the court took a narrow interpretation of the following restrictive covenant: "that the lands shall not be sold to or occupied by persons not of the Caucasian race nor to Europeans except such as are of English-speaking

countries and the French and the people of French descent," holding that a Syrian was not excluded by such a clause. See also *Re Bryers & Morris* (1931), 40 O.W.N. 572 (Ont. High Court). One year after the *Desmond* litigation, another set of white, Gentile judges would disagree with Judge Mackay's ruling. In *Re Noble and Wolf*, [1948] 4 D.L.R. 123, O.W.N. 546 (Ont. High Court), affirmed [1949] O.R. 503, O.W.N. 484, 4 D.L.R. 375 (Ont. C.A.), they explicitly upheld a restrictive covenant prohibiting the sale or lease of a summer resort property to "any person of the Jewish, Hebrew, Semitic, Negro or coloured race or blood." Fearful of "inventing new heads of public policy" that would impede "freedom of association," the judges espoused racial exclusivity as an obvious social right. Ontario Court of Appeal Chief justice Robert Spelman Robertson wrote: "It is common knowledge that, in the life usually led at such places, there is much inter-mingling, in an informal and social way, of the residents and their guests, especially at the beach. That the summer colony should be congenial is of the essence of a pleasant holiday in such circumstances. The purpose of [the restrictive covenant] here in question is obviously to assure, in some degree, that the residents are of a class who will get along well together. To magnify this innocent and modest effort to establish and maintain a place suitable for a pleasant summer residence into an enterprise that offends against some public policy, requires a stronger imagination than I possess. […] There is nothing criminal or immoral involved; the public interest is in no way concerned. These people have simply agreed among themselves upon a matter of their own personal concern that affects property of their own in which no one else has an interest." This ruling was later overturned, *Annie Maud Noble and Bernard Wolf v W. A. Alley et al.*, [1951] 92 S.C.R. 64, 1 D.L.R. 321 (S.C.C.). The Supreme Court justices made no explicit comment on the public policy reasoning of the earlier decisions. Instead they held the covenant void for uncertainty: "it is impossible to set such limits to the lines of race or blood as would enable a court to say in all cases whether a proposed purchaser is or is not within the ban." See also *Re McDougall and Waddell*, [1945] O.W.N. 272 (Ont. High Court), where the court considered a restrictive covenant that prohibited the sale or occupation of lands "by any person or persons other than Gentiles (non-semetic [sic]) of European or British or Irish or Scottish racial origin." The court held that such provisions did not violate the newly enacted Ontario Racial Discrimination Act, and that there were no legal restrictions to affect their implementation. For the first legislation to ban racially restrictive covenants on land, see *An Act to amend The Conveyancing and Law of Property Act*, S.O. 1950, c.11; *An Act to amend The Law of Property Act*, S.M. 1950, c.33....

99. The debate on the motion, which failed to lead to the incorporation of a Bill of Rights in the British North America Act is recorded in *Hansard Parliamentary Debates* 10 October 1945, at 900.

100. See *Viola Irene Desmond v Henry L. McNeil and Roseland Theatre Co. Ltd.*, PANS RG39 "C" Halifax, v.936-37, Supreme Court of Nova Scotia, no. 13299, filed 14 November 1946. On 12 December 1946, Bissett filed a notice of discontinuance against the Roseland Theatre Company Ltd, along with a writ alleging the same claim against the parent corporation: *Viola Irene Desmond v Odeon Theatres of Canada Ltd. and Garson Theatres Ltd.*, PANS RG39 "C" Halifax v.936-37, Supreme Court of Nova Scotia, no. 13334. For details concerning the law of "assault," "battery," "false imprisonment," "malicious prosecution," and the tort of "abuse of process," see * Under the latter cause of action, Bissett could have argued that MacNeil invoked summary criminal prosecution under The Theatres Act, a process not unlawful in itself, for the collateral and improper motive of enforcing racial segregation. The conviction would have become irrelevant, with the sole focus being whether racial segregation constituted an "unjustifiable" ulterior motive for the theatre manager's acts, which necessitated harm to others.

101. For details of the common law defence, see*

102. "Recognizance for Certiorari," 24 December 1946; "Notice of Motion," 27 December 1946; and "Affidavit of Viola Irene Desmond," PANS. The notice was served upon Rod G. MacKay and Harry MacNeil on 30 December 1946. Litigants were required to put up financial sureties before filing actions for judicial review.

103. For information on the availability of *certiorari* applications, see*

104. There is no published report of the case brought before Judge Archibald, and the press coverage contains no further details: see "Supreme Court Ruling Sought," Halifax *Herald*, 10 January 1947, p. 18. The "Notice of Motion" lists three grounds, although the vagueness of the claims permits little analysis: 1. That there is no evidence to support the aforesaid conviction. 2. That there is evidence to show that the aforesaid Viola Irene Desmond did not commit the offence hereinbefore recited. 3. That the information or evidence did not disclose any offence to have been committed within the jurisdiction of the convicting Magistrate. The report of the appeal of Judge Archibald's ruling, *The King v Desmond* (1947), 20 M.P.R. 297, at 298 and 300 (N.S.S.C.), suggests that Bissett also tried at first instance to make a technical argument that the prosecution failed to allege the location where the offence took place. Apparently he abandoned this claim when the original information, stipulating that the acts occurred "in the Town of New Glasgow," was located.

105. "Decision of Archibald, J.," 20 January 1947, PANS; *The King v Desmond* (1947), 20 M.P.R. 297 (N.S.S.C.), at 298–9. Judge Archibald was born in Manganese Mines, Colchester County, to John H. Archibald and Mary Alice (Clifford) Archibald. He was educated at public schools in Truro and received his LLB from Dalhousie in 1915. A Liberal in politics and United Church by religion, Judge Archibald lectured in Criminal and Statute Law at Dalhousie in the mid-1920s. He was appointed to the Supreme Court in 1937, and in 1948 he was appointed to the Exchequer Court of Canada, a post he held until his death in 1953. See "Archibald, The Hon. Maynard Brown," *Who's Who in Canada, 1945–46* (Toronto: International Press, 1946), at 1042; *Who's Who in Canada, 1951–52*, at 612; *Maritime Reference Book*, at 23–4; *Annals—North British Society: 1950–1968* (Kentville, N.S.: Kentville Publishing, 1969), at 58–9; and obituary, "Prominent Jurist Held Many Important Posts," Halifax *Chronicle-Herald*, 10 July 1953, pp. 1, 6.

106. "Decision of Archibald, J.," PANS, at p. 2; *The King v Desmond*, at 299.

107. For earlier Nova Scotia decisions see, for example, *The Queen v Walsh* (1897), 29 N.S.R. 521 (N.S.S.C.), at 527. See also *The Nova Scotia Summary Convictions Act*, S.N.S. 1940, c.3, s.58.

108. S.N.S. 1940, c.3, s.59, 60, 62, 66, as amended S.N.S. 1945, c.65.

109. "Notice of Appeal," 20 January 1947, and "Entry of Appeal," 21 February 1947, PANS. See also "Reserve Appeal Decision in Desmond Case," Halifax *Herald*, 14 March 1947, p. 18. For details of the appellant's and respondent's arguments, see *The King v Desmond* (1947), 20 M.P.R. 297 (N.S.S.C.), at 299–301.

110. Some cite the couple's disagreement over the case as the main source of the marital breakdown: Hudson, "Interview with Pearleen Oliver." Others suggest that there were long-standing, additional strains within the marriage caused by Jack Desmond's drinking and his distrust of Viola's ambitious business prospects: Woods, "Interview with Gannon-Dixon"; Backhouse, "Interview with Wanda Robson."

111. "Clarion Went A-Visiting!" New Glasgow, N.S., *The Clarion* 2:5 (15 March 1947), p. 2.

112. *The King v Desmond* (1947), 20 M.P.R. 297 (N.S.S.C.), at 307. Other reports of the case appear as (1947), 89 C.C.C. 278, 4 C.R. 200, [1947] 4 D.L.R. 81. For biographical details on Doull, who was born in New Glasgow on 1 November 1878, see Halifax *Chronicle-Herald*, 1 October 1960, p. 32; *Who's Who in Canada, 1945–46*, at 474.

113. Doull's comment is found at 309. Doull served as mayor of New Glasgow in 1925. Judge Robert Henry Graham noted at 304 that Bissett had argued a denial of natural justice, relying on *R. v Wandsworth*, [1942] 1 All E.R. 56, in which the court overturned the conviction of a defendant who had been denied the opportunity to defend himself. Judge Graham, however, made no reference to Viola Desmond's detailed affidavit alleging similar treatment and refused to find a denial of natural justice in the present case.

114. The son of a New Glasgow lawyer and politician Hon. Col. Edward Mortimer Macdonald, PC, Macdonald, Jr. was born in Pictou, called to the bar of Quebec in 1924, and the Nova Scotia bar in 1929. He practised with the law firm of Macdonald & MacQuarrie, with offices in Pictou and New Glasgow. He was a Liberal and a Presbyterian. See *Maritime Reference Book*, at 11; "Macdonald, E. M.: Death: Town Solicitor for New Glasgow Dies," PANS MG1, v. 2022 no. 20; Charles G.D. Roberts and Arthur J. Tunnell, *The Canadian Who's Who*, vol. 2 (1936–7) (Toronto: Murray Printing, 1936), at 660.

115. J. B. Milner, "Case and Comment," *Canadian Bar Review*, vol. 25 (1947), 925 at 915–22. Interestingly, Milner did not believe that the trial decision to convict Viola Desmond was incorrect, describing it at 919 as "technically perfect." For biographical details about Milner and further details concerning his article, see*

116. For Judge Graham's ruling, see *The King v Desmond* (1947), 20 M.P.R. 297 (N.S.S.C.), at 305, quoting in part Viscount Caldicott in *Rex v Nat Bell Liquors Limited*, [1922] 2 A.C. 128 (H.L.), at 151. For biographical details on Judge Graham, who was born in New Glasgow on 30 November 1871, the son of John George Graham and Jane (Marshall) Graham, see obituary, "Mr. Justice Graham Dies at Age 85," Halifax *Mail-Star*, 28 May 1956, pp. 1, 6; *Who's Who in Canada, 1945–46*, at 466; *The Canadian Who's Who*, vol. 4 (Toronto: Trans-Canada Press, 1948), at 380; *Catalogue of Portraits of the Judges of the Supreme Court of Nova Scotia and other Portraits* (Halifax: Law Courts, n.d.), PANS F93C28, at 110. Graham received a BA and LLB from Dalhousie, was called to the Nova Scotia bar in 1894, and named a KC in 1913. He served as town councillor in New Glasgow in 1898, mayor from 1899 to 1900, and represented Pictou County as a Liberal in the House of Assembly between 1916 and 1925. He served as stipendiary magistrate from 1906 to 1910, and was appointed puisne judge of the Supreme Court in 1925.

117. *The King v Desmond* (1947), 20 M.P.R. 297 (N.S.S.C.), at 305–7. Unlike Doull and Graham, Judge Carroll was not born in New Glasgow, but in Margaret Forks, Nova Scotia, on 11 June 1877. Educated at St Francis Xavier College in Antigonish and at Dalhousie University, he was called to the bar of Nova Scotia in 1905, serving several terms as a Liberal MP. For biographical details, see obituary, Halifax *Chronicle-Herald*, 26 August 1964, p. 16; *Who's Who in Canada, 1945–46*, at 666. The decision on file at the archives, "Decision

of Hall, J.," PANS, shows that the original typed version reads: "Had the matter reached the Court by some method other than *certiorari*, there might have been opportunity to right the wrong done this unfortunate woman, *convicted on insufficient evidence*" (emphasis added). The latter phrase was crossed out by pen, initialed by Judge Hall, and did not appear in the reported version of the decision. Judge Hall was born in Melvern Square, Annapolis County, in 1876 to Rev. William E. and Margaret (Barss) Hall. He was educated at Acadia and Dalhousie University and admitted to the bar in 1900. He practised law in Liverpool, N.S., from 1902 to 1918, and then became Halifax Crown Prosecutor. Active in the Conservative party, he was elected to the provincial legislature and served as attorney general in 1926. He was also an active worker for welfare organizations in Halifax. Judge Hall was appointed to the Nova Scotia Supreme Court in 1931. For biographical details see *Prominent People of the Maritime Provinces* (St. John: McMillan, 1922), at 77–8; obituary, "Veteran Jurist Dies at 81," Halifax *Mail-Star*, 27 May 1958, p. 3; PANS Biographical Card File, MG9, v. 41, p. 262; *Who's Who in Canada, 1945–46*, at 1494–5.

118. Backhouse, "Interview with Wanda Robson." Similar reactions were expressed by Ida B. Wells, the famous African-American campaigner against lynching, after she lost a lawsuit in Memphis, Tennessee, in the late nineteenth century, when she was denied accommodation in the "ladies only" (white) railway carriage. Ida B. Wells's diary entry reads: "I felt so disappointed because I had hoped such great things for my people generally. I have firmly believed all along that the law was on our side and would, when we appealed to it, give us justice. I feel shorn of that belief and utterly discouraged, and just now, if it were possible, would gather my race in my arms and fly away with them": Alfreda M. Duster, ed., *Crusade for Justice: An Autobiography of Ida B. Wells* (Chicago: University of Chicago Press, 1970), at p. xvii.

119. Milner, "Case and Comment," at 915–16, 922.

120. "The Desmond Case," Truro, N.S., *The Clarion* 2:15 (April 1947), p. 2, and "Dismisses Desmond Application," Truro, N.S., *The Clarion* 2:15 (April 1947), p. 4.

121. "The Desmond Case," Truro, N.S., *The Clarion* 2:15 (April 1947), p. 2. *The Clarion* would later reprint a 15 July 1947 (p. 1) editorial from *Maclean's* magazine, in which the *Desmond* case is described and critiqued: "In a free country one man is as good as another—any well-behaved person may enter any public place. In Nova Scotia a Negro woman tried to sit in the downstairs section of a theatre instead of the Jim Crow gallery. Not only was she ejected by force, but thereafter she, not the theatre owner, was charged and convicted of a misdemeanour. Most Canadians have been doing a fair amount of grumbling lately about the state of our fundamental freedoms. Maybe it's time we did more than grumble." See "Is This a Free Country?" Truro, N.S., *The Clarion* 2:12 (15 August 1947), p. 2.

122. On the allegations that Viola Desmond might have been trying to "pass," see Backhouse, "Interview with Wanda Robson." For Johnston's comments see "N.S. Negroes Libelled by Attack," Truro, N.S., *The Clarion* 3:8 (13 October 1948), p. 1.

123. "Toronto Leads the Way," Truro, N.S., *The Clarion* 2:12 (15 August 1947), p. 2. The same paper reports that the City of Toronto Board of Police Commissioners passed a regulation (inserted in a city by-law governing the licensing of public places) providing a penalty of licence cancellation for any hall, rink, theatre, or other place of amusement in the city which refused to admit anyone because of race, colour, or creed. See "Toronto Law Against Discrimination" and "Toronto Leads the Way," Truro, N.S., *The Clarion* 2:12 (15 August 1947), pp. 1–2.

124. "No Discrimination," Truro, N.S., *The Clarion* 2:12 (15 August 1947), p. 2. *Saturday Night* also draws a comparison with the United States, on 7 December 1946, p. 5: "Racial segregation is so deeply entrenched in what the American people are accustomed to call their way of life that the problems which it raises in a democracy (it raises none in a totalitarian state) will not be solved in the United States without a good deal of conflict. Canada is in a position to avoid most of that conflict if she avoids getting tied into the American way of life in that respect, and now is the time to take action to avoid it."

125. "American Artists Score Racial Discrimination," Halifax *Chronicle*, 15 September 1947, PANS Mg15, vol. 16. no. 18; "More Discrimination," Truro, N.S., *The Clarion* 2:14 (1 November 1947), p. 2. Selma Burke's female companion was A.F. Wilson, a noted American author of several books on race discrimination. *The Clarion* reports in 2:11 (1 August 1947), pp. 1–2, that a New Glasgow restaurant refused service to a young West Indian student working with the provincial Highways department. The same article notes that a Black couple, Mr and Mrs A. T. Best, was also refused seating in a small fruit store and fountain in New Glasgow.

126. Esmerelda Thornhill, "So Often Against Us: So Seldom for Us, Being Black and Living with the Canadian Justice System," Plenary Presentation to the IXth Biennial Conference of the Congress of Black Women of Canada, Halifax, 1989, at 3 (copy on file with the author).

127. "New Glasgow," Truro, N.S., *The Clarion* 3:6 (8 September 1948), p. 3....

128. Backhouse, "Interview with Wanda Robson."

129. Backhouse, "Interview with Wanda Robson"; Backhouse, "Interview with Mrs. S. A. (Emily) Clyke"; Obituaries in the Halifax *Chronicle-Herald*, 10 Feb. 1965, p. 26, and Halifax *Mail Star*, 10 February 1965, p. 8.

130. Robertson, "Interview with Pearleen Oliver." Paula Denice McClain, *Alienation and Resistance: The Political Behavior of Afro-Canadians* (Palo Alto: R. & E. Research Associates, 1979), notes at 59 that the NSAACP was responsible for integrating barbershops in Halifax and Dartmouth, sponsoring the first Blacks for employment in Halifax and Dartmouth stores, integrating the nurses' training and placement programs, persuading insurance companies to sell Blacks policies other than industrial insurance, and initiating a controversy that resulted in the Dartmouth school board hiring Blacks.

131. Thomson, *Born with a Call*, at 84.

Chapter Six

Affirmative Action and Employment Equity: Policy, Ideology, and Backlash in Canadian Context

Abigail B. Bakan and Audrey Kobayashi

Editors' Note: Abigail Bakan and Audrey Kobayashi address several important and contentious themes in their account of efforts to establish greater inclusiveness in Canadian workplaces as well as a concerted backlash against what were presented as progressive efforts. Ontario is used as a case-in-point for their analysis, complemented by examples from other jurisdictions. The authors discuss the impact of a Royal Commission report on Equality in Employment, released in the mid-1980s. Attention is paid to the decision to not use the somewhat loaded terminology of "affirmative action"; instead, Canadians have largely adopted the term "employment equity." As well, Bakan and Kobayashi review the U.S. Supreme Court's decision in 1978 in Bakke. In the article, the authors point to groups that have been subject to "measurable system discrimination"—women, visible minorities, Aboriginals, and "persons with disabilities." This chapter is useful in pointing out how the intent of legislation can be implemented in different ways: for example, not all provinces adopted the legislation and those that did, did so unevenly. The authors also explore the concept of political backlash," which they define as "a negative response to a progressive policy, campaign, or event."

Equality is thus a process—a process of constant and flexible examination, of vigilant introspection, and of aggressive open-mindedness.[1]

Employment equity became a significant public policy issue in Canada following the 1984 publication of *Equality in Employment: A Royal Commission Report*[2] under the direction of Commissioner Rosalie Abella. Abella consulted widely with individual advocates and representatives of social movements to capture the growing concern for equality and equity issues that had crystallized with the adoption of the *Charter of Rights and Freedoms*. The result was a unique, Canadian approach to equity and it guided the development of a public policy agenda in very significant ways. However, the significance was not only in the establishment of a political culture friendly to an ideology of inclusiveness in the country's workplaces; it also laid the ground for an acceptance of, and concessions to, certain aspects of political backlash.

The ideological foundations of policymaking or policy avoidance are difficult to trace, particularly in the Canadian context where there is little direct linkage between policy formulation and "think tanks."[3] We contend, however, that a discernable pattern can be identified in the debates surrounding employment equity policy in Canada. While there is direct backlash against any form of employment equity policy on the part of those ideologically opposed to the principle, there are also significant concessions, or accommodation, to such backlash from policymakers who nonetheless advocate for employment equity. Such concessions are often just as significant as direct backlash in weakening the policy, making it less effective and more subject to criticism. This article elaborates on this argument, suggesting a general analytical framework based on two case studies: the normative effects of the Abella Report's abandonment of the concept of

Source: Abigail B. Bakan and Audrey Kobayashi, "Affirmative Action and Employment Equity: Policy, Ideology, and Backlash in Canadian Context," *Studies in Political Economy*, No. 79, pp. 145–166. Reprinted with permission.

"affirmative action" in favour of "employment equity"; and the gradualism and timidity with which the Ontario NDP government implemented employment equity legislation in the 1990s.

From as early as the 1980s, Canadian discourse in defense of employment equity has been influenced by a strategy of yielding ground to the backlash. Initially reacting to the debate as it unfolded in the US context, the Abella report took an apparently contradictory and progressive approach, adopting fresh language to deflect adversaries while at the same time moving towards dramatic compromise. Abella argued that by avoiding the term "affirmative action," Canada would also avoid the ideological baggage that came with the term in the United States, and thus encounter less opposition. She made it clear that equity and quotas are not the same thing. Replacing the term "affirmative action" with "employment equity" may have deflected criticism, but it also failed to enshrine a proactive approach, seriously limiting the efficacy of the program. By avoiding the obligation to establish firm commitments to increasing numerical diversity in representation, the considerable effort and expense invested in employment equity during the 1980s failed to produce significant results by the end of the 1990s.[4]

A decade after the publication of the Abella Report, the province of Ontario's experience displays a similar pattern. At that time, the NDP government under Premier Bob Rae passed the Employment Equity Act and, although it was repealed less than a year later by the new Conservative government led by Mike Harris, it was the most comprehensive to date in any Canadian jurisdiction.[5] The retrospective story of the demise of employment equity legislation in Ontario, however, requires more than a simple narrative where the NDP introduced progressive legislation and the Conservatives reversed it.[6] A more in-depth analysis reveals a complex process in which the politics of frontal backlash and the politics of concession resulting from anticipated backlash coalesced. The result was a downward spiral of retreat on the part of employment equity advocates in the face of overt, and increasingly confident, ideological and political backlash.[7]

The fear of a US-style backlash against affirmative action and the experience of the rise and fall of employment equity legislation in Ontario continue to affect policy discourse among civil society stakeholders—both advocates and opponents and at both the provincial and federal levels—in Canada today. Understanding the politics of backlash has implications not only for interpreting historical events, but also for navigating policy debates in the present and future. Some of these implications are suggested in our conclusion.

CONSIDERING "BACKLASH"

"Backlash" is a phenomenon widely recognized to be significant in public policy development, but rarely defined or explained. Understood in the context of contemporary political debates, backlash is an ideological current or policy platform that is based on conservative premises, but is distinct from conservatism generally because of its specifically reactive character. Unlike ideological positions considered to be on the Right or far Right wing of the political spectrum—such as sexism, racism, or homophobia—backlash is a negative response to a progressive policy, campaign, or event. Backlash is therefore distinguishable from mere political opposition. Typically, it can be traced to a "trigger" or a "spark" that provokes a response considered otherwise to be nonexistent, or existent but dormant and lacking substantial influence.[8]

There is, then, an especially dynamic quality to backlash. It emerges as the second of two distinct but related phases of contested policy development. The first phase is the advance of a progressive ideological position or policy platform; this is understood to be a provocative element in shaping the second phase, backlash, where a reactionary and conservative force gains ascendance. Backlash arises as the result of a "boomerang" effect, where the desire to provoke progressive change unleashes a greater and more powerful regressive force.

Backlash develops, therefore, in specific contexts where there is sharply contested ground, and where traditional lines of ideological and partisan identity may be transgressed. Despite this polarization, however, those who adopt positions associated with backlash usually lay claim to political neutrality. Backlash defenders commonly insist that they are in a defensive posture, merely holding the terrain of the democratic centre. The politics of backlash have coincided comfortably with the rise of neoliberalism, and the links have been amply identified.[9] The general retreat of state support for social services, and the ideological insistence on the individual rather than the group as the basic unit of democracy, provides fertile ground for views that oppose any form of social intervention that might offset market forces or unhindered competition among individuals.[10] Backlash cannot be abstractly reduced to or equated with neoliberalism, however, as it can often challenge traditional ideological and partisan lines of adherence.

To this essentially "common sense" understanding of backlash, a new dimension needs to be added. The claim to represent a defense of the political centre, or neutrality, while at the same time unleashing extreme reactionary forces that challenge progressive measures, renders the politics of backlash variable and complex. On the part of those involved in developing progressive social policy, there may be, we maintain, a discursive and anticipated fear of backlash that can be instrumental in shaping the nature of any particular policy change or outcome. The fear of backlash has been central in shaping employment equity policy in Canada, and is the focus of the argument developed here.

Fear of backlash, particularly on the part of those who are at the leading edge of advancing progressive social policy, can be one of the most powerful and corrosive effects of the backlash agenda. Whether there is a direct frontal assault, or a refusal to advance social policy for fear of such an assault, the outcome is the same. Both result either in limiting debate or in silencing challenges to status quo conditions that may be discriminatory or biased. Both stifle proactive measures for redress.

Backlash can take a variety of forms, and needs to be considered within specific contexts and political cultures.[11] Recent debates in a number of Canadian jurisdictions show that, while the outcome of diminishing or eliminating employment equity policies and practices may be the same, the most effective patterns of backlash follow the contours of specific political circumstances. The Ontario case study that follows, therefore, depends upon an understanding of the specific ways in which political and ideological strategies played out in that province. Those events have reverberated through other jurisdictions, however; the Ontario case has been held up as an argument against using similar approaches in other places. As a result, employment equity policy throughout Canada has been shaped by anticipated or suspected backlash since the policy's inception because those who proclaim to support equity hesitate when it comes to actual implementation, citing the fear of "provoking a backlash." Fear of backlash as a form of backlash in itself has thus produced a self-limiting quality to employment equity advocacy throughout Canada.

The effectiveness of frontal backlash strategies therefore results in part in creating confusion and disorganization among the supporters of equity policies, leading them to offer ideological concessions to backlash in an effort to gain legitimacy.[12] As a pragmatic and strategic move, ideological ground is given up, ostensibly as a way to avoid conflict and in the hope of gaining or maintaining a policy foothold that will allow for greater advances in the future. But evidence drawn from employment equity outcomes suggests that such an incremental strategy does not lead to greater representation or more effective policy.[13] This brings us to the development of employment equity policy outlined in the Abella Report.

FROM BAKKE TO ABELLA: THE IMPACT OF BACKLASH IN THE MAKING OF FEDERAL EMPLOYMENT EQUITY POLICY

The term "employment equity" is commonly understood today according to concepts established in the Abella Report.[14] This is a two-pronged approach that addresses the societal conditions that affect access to employment, as well as the policies and practices that create or remove barriers to full and equal participation in the workforce for the four designated groups recognized in the Abella Report to suffer from measurable systemic discrimination in employment in the public service: women, Aboriginal peoples, members of visible minorities, and persons with disabilities.

The Abella Report deliberately distanced the concept of employment equity from that of affirmative action, which was seen as an American solution associated with quotas and government interference, creating a "protective wall through which reason cannot easily penetrate."[15] By employing the new language of "employment equity," Abella focused attention on the Canadian context, encouraging the kind of "aggressive open-mindedness" referred to above. In response, the federal government moved to establish an extensive policy and legislative framework based on the concept of employment equity that was soon viewed internationally as innovative and path-breaking.[16] It was subsequently adopted by most of the provinces, although unevenly and with considerably less enthusiasm.

Judge Rosalie Abella undertook extensive consultation and research in preparing the commission report. She sent letters to nearly 3,000 individuals and held 137 meetings attended by more than 1,000 people across Canada; she also commissioned 39 substantial research reports on topics including education, child care, racism, and pay equity.[17] The Abella Report maintained, in bold and unambiguous terms, that four identifiable groups were not being fairly represented in the Canadian public sector work force, despite demonstrated educational and skill capacity. Drawing on the recently enacted *Charter of Rights and Freedoms*, the Report established the constitutional legitimacy for a proactive approach to altering the historic bias in employment against women, visible minorities, Aboriginal peoples, and persons with a disability. On a normative level, the Report insisted that equality did not require equal treatment; on the contrary, differential treatment resulting from systemic discrimination requires the elimination of specific barriers:

> Equality under the Charter, then, is a right to integrate into the mainstream of Canadian society based on, and notwithstanding, differences. It is acknowledging and accommodating differences rather than ignoring or denying them. This is the paradox at the core of any quest for employment equity: because differences exist and must be respected, equality in the workplace does not, and cannot be allowed to, mean the same treatment for all. In recognition of the journey many have yet to complete before they achieve equality, and in recognition of how the duration of the journey has been and is being unfairly protracted by arbitrary barriers, section 15(2) permits laws, programs, or activities designed to eliminate these restraints.[18]

Notwithstanding this proactive statement, one of Abella's major findings based on the public presentations to the commission was that use of the term "affirmative action" creates an unnecessary association with the American concept and provokes confusing, emotional, and futile debates. Recognizing that the backlash against affirmative action in the United States had received considerable international support, she sought to clear a route for Canadian policy that would make a clean break with American discourses:

> The Commission was told again and again that the phrase "affirmative action" was ambiguous and confusing.... The Commission notes this in order to propose that a new term, "employment equity," be adopted to describe programs of positive remedy for discrimination in the Canadian workplace. No great principle is sacrificed in exchanging phrases of disputed definition for new ones that may be more accurate and less destructive to reasonable debate.... Ultimately, it matters little whether in Canada we call this process employment equity or affirmative action, so long as we understand that what we mean by both terms are employment practices designed to eliminate discriminatory barriers to provide in a meaningful way equitable opportunities for employment.[19]

At the core of the "disputed definition" of the term "affirmative action" in this period was the backlash argument developed in the US debate, where it was maintained that it constituted reverse discrimination and imposed quotas designed to ignore merit. In shifting the discursive ground to the removal of barriers, Abella caught the imagination of policymakers in Ottawa, who subsequently focused significant energy on creating a made-in-Canada approach. Proponents of the Canadian policy could claim that their approach was better because it did not use quotas (which, it was accepted, might compromise merit) and relied instead on changing the values of the workplace.

A lengthy analysis of trends in the United States related to the highly contested practice of affirmative action goes beyond the scope of this discussion. However, Susan Faludi's investigation of backlash in the United States, and the specific example of the Bakke case that advanced the notion of "reverse discrimination," are relevant to consideration of the debates surrounding employment equity in Canada.[20] Faludi has demonstrated that if the spectrum of opposition—whether passive or active—is wide enough, then even the strongest proponents of progressive measures may undermine their own efforts by giving ground in order to secure political gains.

Backlash against affirmative action in the United States consisted mainly of charges that it represented "reverse discrimination" against white, able-bodied men. Asserting a defense of the democratic centre, this claim challenged both the normative premise and the constitutionality of affirmative action, and marked the rise of a serious backlash against affirmative action that moved into the centre stage of US national politics, and gained extensive international attention when the case of Allan Bakke came before the US Supreme Court.[21] Bakke, a young white male and Vietnam war veteran, was declined admission to the University of California (UC), Davis campus, Medical School in 1973, while minority students with weaker academic records were accepted under the university's affirmative action program. The Medical School at UC Davis accepted 100 students per year, of whom a relatively small number, 16 placements per year, were set aside for African Americans, Chicanos and Chicanas, Asian Americans, and Native Americans. When Bakke's application was declined a second time in 1974, he filed a lawsuit against the university, arguing that he had been rejected solely on the basis of his race. Bakke sued for admission on the grounds that his rights under Title VI of the Civil Rights Act of 1964 had been violated. In 1978, the US Supreme Court ruled that Bakke should be admitted and he proceeded to complete his MD and pursue a medical career.[22] The Supreme Court also found, however, that affirmative action policies undertaken by universities and, by inference, employers, may consider race and ethnicity as one of a number of factors when offering admission or hiring—although students or employees could not be denied entrance or employment if race was the only factor considered. This ruling allowed both sides of the debate to claim victory.[23]

Returning to the Canadian case, the Abella Report considered the phrase "affirmative action" to be "ambiguous and confusing," but was "employment equity" less so? Abella's discursive strategy was effective in mobilizing an initial effort on the part of policymakers that won support more because of its disassociation from American-style affirmative action than because it provided a clear and effective way forward. Indeed, the scope of the policy actually shifted, and narrowed, considerably with the change in terminology. For example, whereas educational affirmative action had been one of the major areas of institutional policy in the United States, in Canada the federal government limited the concept to its application in the workplace. Further, only a limited number of workplaces were covered in the mandate: the federal public service (not initially covered under the Employment Equity Act, but under separate legislation), crown corporations, and federally regulated employers. While education, as well as childcare policies and practices, were addressed in the Abella Report as enabling factors that prepare individuals for the workplace, they are not addressed in subsequent policy or legislation. The narrowing of focus occurred partly because federal policy did not extend to those areas that were under provincial jurisdiction, but it was also a response to backlash against affirmative action. The notion of "equity" rather than "action" suggests a narrower lens, and thus a more palatable but less effective solution, for achieving equality.

The 1986 Employment Equity Act stood clear of numeric targets or "quotas," the issues at the centre of the Bakke dispute. Instead, those employers affected by the legislation were asked to file annual reports and plans, with virtually no obligation to follow up on those plans. In this way, despite the rhetoric of proactivity, ideological and practical concessions to the backlash were embedded in the Canadian policies from the outset. Tania Das Gupta states, referring to the federal Employment Equity Act:

> In effect, it is a voluntary program.... Some equity advocates have argued that the federal employment equity program has not been successful because it has been "top down" and not geared to "statistical improvement." It seems that most of the federally regulated employers are concentrating on removing biases from the outreach, screening and interview processes and concentrating less on actually increasing representation from target groups.[24]

The relevance of US debates was not lost on backlash ideologues in Canada. Author and conservative researcher William Gairdner, for example, in *The War Against the Family*, argued against what he called "The Feminist Mistake" that refused to recognize the inherent biological role of women as homemaker and mother. He praised Germaine Greer's *Sex and Destiny*, which celebrates women's role as child bearer and mother. This was an author, Gairdner maintained, who "had the courage to turn her back on her earlier inflammatory work, *The Female Eunuch*." Gairdner similarly praised Betty Friedan's "recanting book," *The Second Stage*, for its rejection of her earlier feminist perspectives.[25]

While a move towards overt "feminist revisionism," identified by Faludi as significant in the success of backlash in the United States, has certainly not been the standard in Canada, pragmatism and gradualism have claimed much of the same ground in the policy debates.[26] Timidity on the part of employment equity advocates has been based on a fear of provoking reactionary opponents, who have secured a number of concessions by remaining ready at the wait. Flora MacDonald, Minister of Employment and Immigration in 1984, reflected on the experience:

> My predecessor had appointed a one-person Royal Commission to look into limited aspects of equity in the public service. The commissioner, Rosalie Abella, came to me shortly after I was made minister and said, "I would like to have my mandate enlarged." I said, "Rosie, take the whole thing, whatever you want." It was on this basis that she wrote her report, using the term "employment equity." She did not want to follow what the Americans had done in affirmative action, which had greatly congested the courts.... Generally, there wasn't a great deal of support. The opposition came both from those who felt there should be nothing and those who felt there should be much more. I had a lot of difficulty with women's groups, who were saying, "Why haven't you done this, this, this and this?" To me, they didn't understand the reality of the House.... That has always been my way: If you can't get everything you want at the outset, get at least the basis that will allow you to build.... The greatest opposition came from those who were disabled. They didn't think the legislation went far enough.[27]

Although backlash in Canada has over the years found organized expression in various provincial contexts and in the political platform of the federal Reform/Alliance/Conservative party, employment equity policies enacted at the federal level have not explicitly generated the furor witnessed in the United States. Indeed, after making a quiet campaign promise to do so in 1993, the Liberal government under Jean Chrétien undertook a review of the legislation and introduced a revamped bill a few years later. For the most part, the legislation was "house-keeping," consolidating existing federal law.[28] A comprehensive audit system was also introduced, however, obliging employers to identify and eliminate barriers to employment for members of the designated groups, develop positive measures, and prepare employment equity plans, including both qualitative and numerical goals. Reports were to be filed annually with Human Resources Development Canada for federally regulated employers and with the Treasury Board for the Public Service.[29]

At the provincial level, backlash against employment equity has proceeded apace with significantly more vigour. While opponents of employment equity at the provincial level have been quick to take the ground of controversy, employment equity advocates have often hesitated to defend the policy when under direct challenge.[30] Some advocates maintain that even suggesting the need for legislation, rather than simply general policy, was detrimental to its effectiveness. The argument was that legislative debates would draw attention—and therefore resistance—on the part of both policymakers and a general public for whom equity remained a sensitive issue. The perception of backlash among advocates often appeared, however, to be greater than the actual strength or influence of anti-employment equity opinion.[31]

The Ontario context served as an important laboratory for backlash debates, not only in the explicit attacks by opponents of employment equity in policy and legislation, but also in the response of employment equity advocates. There are grounds to suggest that Canada's social democratic tradition has moderated the type of polarization that occurred in the United States by dulling the leading edge of the movement and accommodating the backlash even before the overt challenges had come fully into play. Nowhere have such politics of concession been more evident than in Ontario.

ONTARIO: NDP HESITANCY AND THE BACKLASH

The rise and fall of employment equity legislation in Ontario closely followed the rise and fall of the Ontario New Democratic Party (NDP) government in the 1990s and the subsequent election of the Ontario Progressive Conservatives. The Ontario NDP historically held a strong commitment to employment equity policy. During its single term in office (1990–95) under the premiership of Bob Rae, the NDP implemented the *Act to Provide for Employment Equity for Aboriginal People, People with Disabilities, Members of Racial Minorities and Women.*[32] Proclaimed in 1994, the legislation was repealed one year later in an atmosphere of extreme backlash, upon the election of Mike Harris and the Ontario Progressive Conservatives in 1995.

Elsewhere, we have pointed to the aggressive political and ideological assault carried on by the newly elected Harris Tory government against the Employment Equity Act in Ontario.[33] Here, we consider the factors in the NDP government's strategy that rendered the Act exceptionally vulnerable to challenge and ultimate repeal.[34]

In the early years of the Rae government, there was a broad base of public support for the employment equity initiative. Before the law was enacted, it was preceded by extensive public consultation. Although many employment equity advocates believed the legislation to be far too weak, the concern to maintain a united base of support across a spectrum of views was the stated goal of the NDP government's extensive consultation process.[35] The slow pace of development is now seen, however, to have cost the NDP dearly. The formal process began in November 1990 when, in the first Speech from the Throne, the newly elected NDP government identified employment equity as a provincial priority.[36] By March 1991, Juanita Westmoreland-Traoré was appointed as Ontario Employment Equity Commissioner. In the summer of the same year, the Commissioner established a Consultation Advisory Committee comprised of representatives of the four designated groups that would ultimately be identified in the title of the legislation, as well as business and labour representatives, and employment equity practitioners already active in the province. Between 25 June 1992 and 7 September 1993, more than 100 presentations and 184 written submissions were received. A clause-by-clause review by a designated standing committee concluded on 6 December 1993. The Office of the Employment Equity Commissioner established a Public Education Advisory Committee before Third Reading in December and passage in January 1994.

Winnie Ng was the Executive Assistant and Senior Policy Advisor to the Minister of Citizenship during the period of the Rae government. From her perspective, the long consultation process weakened the capacity of the legislation to withstand the later repeal under Harris:

> We went through a whole consultation process.... There may have been goodwill in trying to do the consultation. Trying to do it right was then being seen as part of an educational process. But one can also read it as a delaying tactic. There was hesitancy. And we ended up paying a major political price for it.... We never had full control within the Ministry, within the Minister's office, to push it. And there was great reluctance from the Premier's office. In retrospect, I think it took too long.... So by the time the Bill finally was proclaimed in 1994, there was really not much time to have the whole thing entrenched. That is why it was so easy for the Harris government, the Tories, to repeal the whole thing.[37]

Elaine Ziemba, former NDP government Minister of Citizenship with responsibilities for Human Rights, Seniors and Persons with Disabilities, identified an ambiguity in the process, as well as a delay that threatened its survival at the hands of the next government:

> I looked at what the federal government did and I saw that there was very little dialogue, or educational seminars. They kind of just did it. Our government was about being open, about dialogue. We were about making sure that people were in the picture and were being updated. I would like to have kept some of that openness. But I also think I would have liked to have just done it. I think we waited too long trying to get everybody on board.... I think on reflection, it's about timing. You know always in politics, it's timing.[38]

Rosario Marchese, former Ontario NDP Chair of the Standing Committee on the Administration of Justice, maintained that there should have been more emphasis on mass, general education and less on consultation with various stakeholders. In fact, his view was that the "consultation" process may have actually created more of a sense of fear and alarm, overexplaining rather than governing as if employment equity was a "business as usual" policy:

> Where we failed, in my view, is that unless you do the political preparation work to explain to people what you're doing, you're in trouble.... So while we dragged this issue through for a couple of years, we weren't really communicating to the public in a way that would explain what this bill is doing. Rather we were alarming the public.[39]

Marilyn Churley, former NDP Minister of Consumer and Commercial Relations and a strong advocate for employment equity legislation with the Cabinet, was even more definitive:

> I think a lesson learned is that you have to do these things more quickly. There is a happy medium—the Tories don't consult at all, or very selectively when they do. But I think that we over-consulted. I would propose that on some of these things that we believe in, we needed to get it done fast. At the end of the day, not everybody is going to be happy anyway. So we do the best we can and get the legislation passed in time, so that should there be another government, it is more entrenched. I think that is really important.[40]

Bob Rae, former Premier and ultimately responsible for the legislation and the process of enactment, however, defended the pace of development of the legislation:

> Basically, we started to proceed fairly early on in the government, recognizing that it was going to be politically difficult. We were determined to go ahead and get it done. We ran into all kinds of flak on our labour legislation, with major political opposition. There were huge billboards and we were accused of never consulting.... We decided that we really did have to try to generate as many incentives as we could. We had the parliamentary committee people who went out and listened. And Members throughout the committee came back and said "This is very tough and we are getting a lot of problems." There were negative reactions. So we had to listen and listen carefully. We went and did a lot of consultation and discussion and tried as much as possible to produce something like a consensus.[41]

When asked specifically about the argument that the consultation process was too lengthy and that earlier enactment of the employment equity legislation would have strengthened public support, Bob Rae responded:

> No. I don't think I agree with that. My own view is that if we hadn't had the consultation process, we wouldn't have had the benefit of what I felt was needed. I am speaking here as the Premier. I felt I constantly had to go back to the Ministry and say "I know you want to go with this." I mean people would want to go further. But people were also saying the legislation went too far. In fact, the legislation itself was a compromise. Some people were saying that it was better than nothing, but it didn't have this or it didn't have that. It didn't have all the bells and whistles that the advocacy groups had developed, sort of their model legislation. Frankly, I needed the consultation period to get the Legislature closer into line to what I thought was going to be politically manageable. I think if, in fact, had we passed it more quickly, the legislation would have been harder to administer.[42]

Notably, Bob Rae was unique among the respondents interviewed in suggesting that perhaps the lessons of history should be taken into account regarding the substantive content of the legislation. His commitment to legislating employment equity, in hindsight, had changed. He now identified the suggestions of Canadian Civil Liberties Association representative and human rights lawyer, Allan Borovoy,[43] as significant, emphasizing that if there was past discrimination reflected in workplace imbalances, current policies should not be called in to enact redress. According to Rae:

> Allan Borovoy made some tough presentations to the Standing Committee. His main arguments were from the perspective that you can't hold this generation responsible for what past generations have done. So his argument was that you had to construct the legislation in such a way that it would be anticipatory about going forward. But you can't sort of blame the past. In terms of targets and objectives which were said to be made, he said those targets and objectives would be too aggressive and would fail to take into account the fact that you're looking at making up for past wrongs. You can't make up for past wrongs—all you can do is basically move forward and make sure that the hiring is done from now on in such a way that you meet certain objectives.[44]

In effect, Borovoy was challenging the fundamental premise of employment equity policy, that patterns of workplace discrimination are systemic and not accidental. The aim of achieving numerical representation according to the availability of each designated group in the larger workforce population is central to this premise. Rae noted that, at the time, such an amendment would have been seen within the NDP government leadership as "watering it down too far."[45] He reflected, however, that when the final legislation was enacted, it still may have been too aggressive: "I think we probably built the bridge a little bit too far."[46]

In fact, the Ontario Employment Equity Act steered far away from even the initial expectations of NDP MPPs. It did not include quotas or statistical standards, instead calling upon employers to develop appropriate goals and flexible plans, with recognition of "different kinds of workplaces and workforces." It also allowed small businesses to be exempt. The legislation was enacted in part on the grounds that employment equity already existed in many sectors, and was defended as a means to consolidate existing policy. The Act therefore subsumed many other pieces of previously existing provincial legislation that brought equity policies in certain sectors under a single umbrella. When it was repealed, however, virtually all of the legislative infrastructure for equity issues that had been in place prior to the law was eliminated.

After the repeal, activists for employment equity attempted to reverse the backlash of the Harris Tories through a legal Charter challenge. Though it proved unsuccessful, the challenge did bring together a coalition of organizations that supported the continuation of a grassroots network of employment equity advocates: the Alliance for Employment Equity.[47] Winnie Ng's later reflections on her experience in this coalition contrast sharply with the sense of frustration expressed in the Ontario Parliament:

> The Coalition of Visible Minority Women got involved early on in the Alliance for Employment Equity. Sexism and racism are wings of the same bird of oppression. That was our key point to put on the Alliance agenda. It was a good process. There weren't tensions on race grounds in the Alliance. We were all in the same boat, and it was clear that we were after legislation and government response to address systemic barriers.[48]

In opposition after the 1995 election, the Ontario NDP no longer placed the same emphasis on employment equity policy that it had during the 1990s. NDP policy documents had included advocacy for employment equity as a general principle of workplace practices, but advocacy for employment equity law in Ontario was no longer pursued. By the late 1990s, the earlier commitment to legislative change and implementation "with teeth" had been replaced by a more moderate commitment.[49]

There is little to be gained, of course, in speculating about the fate of the employment equity legislation had political events in Ontario not taken the turn that they did. In retrospect, however, we can note that the story is much more complex than a simple policy about-face; the politics of concession to backlash are apparent in Ontario throughout the five-year period during which the NDP implemented the policy. The NDP in government developed a *modus operandi* of giving ground that, in the end, left no ground at all. Paradoxically, the "consultative process" itself left so much room for retreat that by the time the NDP mandate ended—having had no time in which to implement the controversial policy—it had achieved very little except to exacerbate hostility on a number of fronts, thus fuelling the subsequent backlash. Notably, federal employment equity legislation was not and has not been subject to a similar assault, from within Ontario or any other province.

CONCLUSION: THE PRICE OF ACCOMMODATION TO BACKLASH

Democratic theorists such as Iris Marion Young and Chantal Mouffe have argued that the paradox of democracy is that to achieve normative change that will enhance the common good requires that there is in fact a great deal in common.[50] If commonality is not to be based on exclusion of those not represented by the majority, whether defined by numbers or by access to power, then the liberal notion of human rights as purely individual rights becomes less and less feasible. In a plural society, there is a conflict between the democratic expression of normative values of the included majority and the achievement of rights for the excluded. Both Young and Mouffe have advocated more inclusive forms of democracy that depend upon broader consultation, participation, and representation. Debates regarding employment equity policy and legislation demonstrate that serious attempts to shift dominant values in a direction that is more inclusive encounter resistance from those who defend these values as entrenched norms. These debates suggest that encountering controversy over the meaning of democratic values is an inevitable feature of a shift from exclusion to inclusion. Such controversy, then, needs to be approached as an inevitable and necessary step towards increasing greater equity for those who have been systemically excluded or marginalized.

Steering advocates away from "controversy" was a key element in both the Abella Report's recommendation to avoid using the term "affirmative action," and in the hesitancy of Bob Rae's Ontario NDP majority government regarding employment equity legislation. In both examples, pragmatism was the overt motivating factor. We suggest, however, that the politics of concession to backlash were elemental and, despite the advocates' intentions, fed rather than forestalled backlash arguments.

The Abella Report and the Rae government's legislation are arguably the best case examples of political advocacy for employment equity in Canada, yet both have wielded a blunt sword in challenging systemic discrimination. Strategic accommodation has failed to advocate forcefully for accountable practices, or to achieve specific numeric targets. Members of the designated groups who are the victims of systemic discrimination have suffered the most from strategic accommodations. For them, it matters little whether that discrimination results from strategic accommodation or direct opposition.

There is a need to analyze employment equity's relative lack of advancement, therefore, in light of the effects of new forms of racism and sexism that wield tremendous discursive power. This may not entail explicit racist and sexist ideas or actions but, alternatively, the claim that racism and sexism no longer exist. In British Columbia, for example, the Liberal government has maintained that the provincial government no longer needs measures to advance employment equity because previous measures were so successful. In fact, previous employment equity practices were uneven and were applied more effectively for women and persons with a disability than for visible minorities and Aboriginal peoples. The discursive ideology, however, has hidden a profound attack on employment equity and other equity practices in British Columbia, in what we have termed a pattern of corrosive backlash.[51]

In the twenty-first century, such claims are much more persuasive than the previous arguments that members of designated groups are unqualified or essentially unsuited for equality. In future, therefore, strategies to resist and redress the effects of systemic discrimination need to consider the lessons of backlash, not only as they relate to employment equity but in the wider context challenging racism, sexism, and all forms of bigotry. In formulating such strategies, the risks of accommodation and concessions to backlash need to be considered with as much attentive care as is commonly applied to considerations of the consequences of failing to make such concessions.

QUESTIONS TO CONSIDER

1. John Porter's classic book, *The Vertical Mosaic* (1965), drew scholarly and public attention to the many ways that Canadian society was stratified along lines of social class, ethnicity, religion, and other variables. To what extent is contemporary Canada stratified along these lines? To what extent do we live in a meritocracy where people are rewarded based on their talents and efforts?

2. Do you agree with the authors' conclusion that many Canadian jurisdictions, including Ontario, adopt strategies of "gradualism and timidity" in promoting employment equity? Can you think of counterexamples? Be specific.

3. The authors draw on concepts of *progressive* and *reactionary* outlooks in the context of employment equity specifically and government policy generally. Do you agree with their terminology? What considerations do you have about governmental and private-sector initiatives to enhance equity in the workplace?

SUGGESTIONS FOR FURTHER READING

Ehrenreich, B. (2001). *Nickel and dimed: On (not) getting by in America.* New York: Henry Holt.

Faludi, S. (2006). *Backlash: The undeclared war against American women* (15th anniversary ed.). Three Rivers, MI: Three Rivers Press.

Hamilton, R. (2005). *Gendering the vertical mosaic: Feminist perspectives on Canadian society* (2nd ed.). Toronto: Pearson Prentice Hall.

Kellough, E. (2006). *Understanding affirmative action: Politics, discrimination, and the search for justice.* Washington, DC: Georgetown University Press.

Outshoorn, J., & Kantola, J. (Eds.). (2007). *Changing state feminism.* Houndsmills, UK: Palgrave Macmillan.

Porter, J. (1965). *The vertical mosaic: An analysis of social class and power in Canada.* Toronto: University of Toronto Press.

NOTES

1. Rosalie Silberman Abella, Commissioner, *Equality in Employment* (Ottawa: Minister of Supply and Services, October 1984). Hereafter referred to as the "Abella Report," p. 1.
2. This paper is part of a wider study on employment equity and the politics of backlash directed by the authors and funded by the Social Sciences and Humanities Research Council of Canada. We are very grateful to the expert research assistance of Hilary Janzen, Julie Devaney, Clara Ho, and Alberta Danso in the preparation of this paper, and to Judy Fudge, Donald Swartz, and the editorial collective *of Studies in Political Economy* for constructive comments on an earlier draft. This paper is equally and jointly written by the authors.

3. See Donald E. Abelson and Christine M. Carberry, "Following Suit or Falling Behind?: A Comparative Analysis of Think Tanks in Canada and the United States," *Canadian Journal of Political Science* XXXI/3 (September 1998), pp. 525–556.

4. Abigail B. Bakan and Audrey Kobayashi, *Employment Equity Policy in Canada: An Interprovincial Comparison* (Ottawa: Status of Women Canada, 2000).

5. The Ontario Tories had campaigned in the election of 1995 partly on the promise that they would rid the problem of "job quotas" legislation. See Abigail B. Bakan and Audrey Kobayashi, "Ontario: Lessons of the Rise and Fall of Employment Equity Legislation from the Perspective of Rights Advocacy," *Canadian Race Relations Foundation Reports* (March 2003), pp. 35–77.

6. Ironically, though the Ontario Employment Equity Act did not actually require quotas, opponents insisted on pinning this label on the legislation, a clear allusion to the US affirmative action program, despite the attempts of Abella and others to deflect such assumptions. In 2006, Right-wing critics of Bob Rae's campaign for leadership of the federal Liberal Party continued to emphasize the former premier's ostensibly poor record of governmental administration by highlighting "a workplace hiring law with the Orwellian moniker 'employment equity.'" Guy Giorno, "Don't Fall into a Rae Daze Looking for a Liberal Leader," *The Globe and Mail* (16 March 2006). Guy Giorno was Chief of Staff to Ontario Progressive Conservative Premier Mike Harris.

7. On the context of neoliberalism and the rise of racist discourse, see Yasmeen Abu-Laban and Christina Gabriel, *Selling Diversity: Immigration, Multiculturalism, Employment Equity and Globalization* (Peterborough: Broadview Press, 2002); Frances Henry and Carol Tator, *Discourses of Domination: Racial Bias in the Canadian English Language Press* (Toronto: University of Toronto Press, 2002); and Joseph Menseh, *Black Canadians: History, Experiences, Social Conditions* (Halifax: Fernwood Publishing, 2002). For perspectives consistent with the backlash against employment equity, see Neil Bisoondath, *Selling Illusions: The Cult of Multiculturalism in Canada* (Toronto: Penguin, 1994); Martin Loney, *The Pursuit of Division: Race, Gender and Preferential Hiring in Canada* (Montreal: McGill-Queen's University Press, 1998); Richard Gwyn, *Nationalism Without Borders: The Unbearable Lightness of Being Canadian* (Toronto: McClelland and Stewart, 1996); and William Gairdner, *The War Against the Family* (Toronto: Stoddart, 1992).

8. For example, it has been argued that the relative success of the post-apartheid regime in South Africa has triggered a backlash from the extreme Right. See Fred Khumalo, "White Backlash: The Fear that Mandela and de Klerk Will Eventually Reach Some Accommodation has Prompted a Massive Backlash by Extreme White Wing," *New African* (April 1992), pp. 12–13. For a review of the literature on "backlash," see Abigail B. Bakan and Audrey Kobayashi, "Employment Equity Legislation in Ontario: A Case Study in the Politics of Backlash," in Carol Agocs, (ed.), *Workplace Equality: International Perspectives on Legislation, Policy and Practice* (New York: Kluwer Law International, 2002).

9. See Lydia Chavez, *The Color Blind: California's Battle to End Affirmative Action* (California: University of California Press, 1998).

10. Cornel West, "Affirmative Action in Context," in George E. Curry, (ed.), *The Affirmative Action Debate* (New York: Addison-Wesley Publishing Inc, 1996), p. 31.

11. See Audrey Kobayashi and Abigail B. Bakan, "Nunavut: Lessons of an Equity Conversation for Anti-Racist Activists," *Canadian Race Relations Foundation Reports* (March, 2003), pp. 1–32.

12. This argument and the research upon which it is based can be found in Bakan and Kobayashi, *Employment Equity Policy in Canada*.

13. Carol Agocs, (ed.), *Workplace Equality: International Perspectives on Legislation, Policy and Practice* (New York: Kluwer Law International, 2002).

14. See for example, Lynne Pearson, Frederick Cuddington, and Deb Thorn, Commissioners, "Final Report and Recommendations of the Commission on Improving Work Opportunities for Saskatchewan Residents," Government of Saskatchewan (February 2006), <www.labour.gov.sk.ca>. This report identifies patterns maintained by "structural barriers that prevent Aboriginal peoples from entering the workplace," and recommends numeric targets for recruitment, hiring, and training of Aboriginal employees to ensure appropriate redress (p. 39, ff.).

15. Abella Report, p. 7.

16. However, in Quebec, New Brunswick, and Nova Scotia, the term "affirmative action" continues to be in use in public policy circles. Elsewhere, we have written about each of these provincial case studies in backlash against employment equity in detail. Ontario and BC have been the sites of particular and considerable backlash, the former in an overt manner, the latter more through gradual corrosive measures. The federal policy context, particularly at the level of legislation, continues to be more consistently favourable to employment equity than the provincial contexts. We have demonstrated that despite the now extensive list of policies that support employment equity, opposition remains strong and consists of new protective walls of discursive resistance. In a comparative study of employment equity in Canada's ten provinces, we found a recurrent pattern, where

those responsible for implementing the policies drew back from taking a proactive position for fear of backlash. Regarding Ontario, see Bakan and Kobayashi, "Employment Equity Legislation in Ontario": pp. 91–107; and "Ontario: Lessons of the Rise and Fall of Employment Equity Legislation from the Perspective of Rights Advocacy," *Canadian Race Relations Foundation Reports* (March 2003), pp. 35–77. Regarding BC, see "Backlash Against Employment Equity: The British Columbia Experience," *Atlantis* volume 29.1 (Fall, 2004), pp. 61–70. Also see Bakan and Kobayashi, *Employment Equity Policy in Canada*.

17. Bakan and Kobayashi, *Employment Equity Policy in Canada*, p. 13.
18. *Ibid*.
19. Abella Report, pp. 6–7.
20. Susan Faludi, *Backlash: The Undeclared War Against American Women* (New York: Crown Publishers, 1991).
21. "A Brief History of Civil Rights in the United States of America: The Bakke Case," <http://AfricanAmericans. com>.
22. Supreme Court Case 1978. US University of California Regents v. Bakke, 438 US 265 (1978), <http://caselaw. lp.findlaw.com/scripts/printer_friendly.pl?page=us/438/265.html>.
23. See for example, Allan P. Sindler, *Bakke, Defunis and Minority Admissions: The Quest for Equality* (New York: Longman, Inc., 1978); F. A. Blanchard and F. J. Crosby, *Affirmative Action in Perspective* (New York: Springer-Verlag and Society for Psychological Study of Social Issues, 1989); Russell Neili, (ed.), *Racial Preference and Racial Justice: The New Affirmative Action Controversy* (Lanham, Md.: Ethics and Public Policy Centre, 1991); Barbara Bergman, *In Defense of Affirmative Action* (New York: Harper Collins, 1996); George E. Curry, (ed.), *The Affirmative Action Debate* (New York: Addison-Wesley Publishing Inc., 1996); Lydia Chavez, *The Color Bind: California's Battle to End Affirmative Action* (Berkeley: University of California Press, 1998); M. Ali Raza, A. Janell Anderson, and Harry Glynn Custred, *The Ups and Downs of Affirmative Action* (Westport, Ct.: Praeger, 1999); John David Skrentny, (ed.), *Color Lines: Affirmative Action, Immigration and Civil Rights Options for America* (Chicago: University of Chicago Press, 2001); Jo Anne O. Robinson, *Affirmative Action: A Documentary History* (Westport Ct.: Greenwood Press, 2001); Steven M. Cahn, (ed.), *The Affirmative Action Debate* 2nd edition (New York: Routledge, 2002).
24. Tania Das Gupta, *Racism and Paid Work* (Canada: Garamond Press, 1996), p. 99.
25. Gairdner, *War Against the Family*. Gairdner was a senior advisor to the Reform Party in the early 1990s. See Paul Kellogg, "William Gairdner and the Trouble with Preston Manning," (February 2002), unpublished manuscript cited with permission. For an excellent summary of the role of the media in fuelling public opposition to the employment equity legislation in Ontario, see Henry and Tator, *Racist Discourse*, pp. 69–88.
26. See, for example, Bakan and Kobayashi, "Backlash Against Employment Equity: The British Columbia Experience"; and "Ontario: Lessons of the Rise and Fall of Employment Equity Legislation from the Perspective of Rights Advocacy."
27. Flora MacDonald, MP for Kingston and the Islands, 1972–1988, in "Closing the Wage Gap: Employment and Pay Equity," in Judy Rebick, *Ten Thousand Roses: The Making of a Feminist Revolution* (Toronto: Penguin Canada, 2005), pp. 203–204.
28. Critics had long maintained that because the federal public service was not covered under the original Employment Equity Act, the government was unwilling to abide by the standards it set for crown corporations and federally regulated employers. In fact, the parallel legislation was broadly similar, but by bringing the parties under one umbrella the federal government achieved a political advantage by quelling such criticism.
29. See Bakan and Kobayashi, *Employment Equity Policy in Canada*, pp. 20–22.
30. See Bakan and Kobayashi, *Employment Equity Policy in Canada*.
31. *Ibid*.
32. Hereafter referred to as the *Employment Equity Act*.
33. See Abigail B. Bakan and Audrey Kobayashi, "Employment Equity Legislation in Ontario."
34. This examination of the Ontario NDP's enactment of employment equity legislation, described below, is based largely on face-to-face interviews conducted in Toronto in 2001 with NDP legislators responsible for the Act. Those interviewed were selected on the basis of their involvement with the legislation as participants in the NDP government. The interviews were one to two hours long and loosely followed a schedule of questions focusing on the experience of the NDP government and the subsequent events surrounding the rise and fall of employment equity legislation. Based on a small sample, these findings are not presented as representative numerically, but rather as the qualitative interpretations and lessons gleaned from senior-ranking former members of the NDP government. A strategy of yielding concessions, principally advocated and directed by then Premier Bob Rae, and contested even among Rae's advisors in the government, is indicated. All of the interviews were taped and transcribed, and all of the interviewees provided written permission to be quoted in reference

to this research project. No portion of the quotations presented here may be quoted except as part of this study and with prior permission from the authors. Some of the findings from these interviews were presented in an earlier draft in Abigail Bakan and Audrey Kobayashi, "Employment Equity and the Ontario NDP: The Legacy of Defeat," Canadian Political Science Association (Quebec City: May 2001).

35. This was the view, for example, of the National Action Committee on the Status of Women at the time. See transcripts of the Legislative Assembly of Ontario, Standing Committee on Administration of Justice (30 August 1993), pp. J-508–12.

36. The main elements of this chronology are reported in Ontario Ministry of Citizenship, "The Employment Equity Consultation Process: A Backgrounder," (Toronto: Ontario Ministry of Citizenship, December 1993).

37. Winnie Ng, interview (Toronto: 5 April 2001).

38. Elaine Ziemba, interview (Toronto: 16 April 2001). This is a reference to the federal government's development of employment equity legislation.

39. Rosario Marchese, interview (Toronto: 5 April 2001).

40. Marilyn Churley, interview (Toronto: 29 March 2001).

41. Bob Rae, interview (Toronto: 24 April 2001).

42. *Ibid.*

43. See Allan Borovoy, Canadian Civil Liberties Association, transcripts of the Legislative Assembly of Ontario, Standing Committee on Administration of Justice (1 September 1993), pp. J-579–80.

44. Bob Rae, interview (Toronto: 24 April 2001).

45. *Ibid.*

46. *Ibid.*

47. See Abigail B. Bakan and Audrey Kobayashi, "Ontario: Lessons of the Rise and Fall of Employment Equity Legislation from the Perspective of Rights Advocacy," *Canadian Race Relations Foundation Reports* (March 2003), pp. 35–77.

48. Winnie Ng, Ontario Regional Director for the Canadian Labour Congress, in "It's Not Just About Identity: Women of Colour Organize," in Rebick, *Ten Thousand Roses*, p. 132.

49. See, for example, *General Policy Statement,* adopted by ONDP Biennial Convention (May 1998), "The Future of Work: Getting Control of Our Work, Our Work Time and Our Pensions," General Policy Statements adopted by Ontario NDP Biennial Convention (22–24 May 1998).

50. Iris Marion Young, *Inclusion and Democracy* (Oxford and New York: Oxford University Press, 2000); Chantal Mouffe, *The Democratic Paradox* (London and New York: Verso).

51. Bakan and Kobayashi, "Backlash Against Employment Equity: The British Columbia Experience."

Chapter Seven

First Nations of Canada and the Legal and Illegal Attacks on Their Existence

Laura Westra

Editors' Note: Laura Westra provides a thought-provoking, complex overview of government efforts to eliminate Indianness among Canada's First Nations and to entrench a policy of assimilation through such measures as residential schools. This is a thorough account of historical and ongoing examples of decisions that have exerted and continue to exert a profound impact on Aboriginal peoples and their ways of life. This chapter also provides a very critical outlook on some assumptions of lawmakers and lawyers surrounding ownership of land and individual rights in the Western tradition vis-à-vis collective rights as understood in many Aboriginal communities and nations.

Westra highlights environmental concerns expressed by First Nations communities and ways that biodiversity and ecological concerns can be undermined by resource development and legal decisions that support such corporate initiatives. She also introduces the concept of "environmental racism," drawing examples from African-Americans' experiences in the USA and those of other "vulnerable and often trapped minorities." Key points of an environmental justice perspective are discussed, including prevention of harm. The case study of Oka is presented to emphasize sharp conflicts between state authorities, such as the police, and members of the Mohawk confederacy.

Genocide is a new word for an old tragedy. The term, coined only in the twentieth century, describes the decimation of a people, of a nation … We most commonly think of genocide as synonymous with the Nazi Holocaust, the loss of six million or more lives, or in the context of the Chinese Communist extermination of eighteen to twenty million dissidents. The term also describes the North American Native experience. (Strickland, 1986)

FIRST NATIONS OF CANADA AND SOME LEGAL POLICIES OF ELIMINATION

It seems that North American indigenous peoples fare no better than those in developing countries in the face of Western conquest and economic interests. Strickland (1986) argues for another "conquest" long before the "second conquest" by transnational and multinational enterprises, and long after the violence vested by Spaniards and others on the hapless tribes of North America. He sees this conquest as one where the rule of law prevailed, but its aim was to deprive native peoples of their "Indianness," their pride and their culture. He cites Alexis de Tocqueville:

> The Spaniards were unable to exterminate the Indian race by those unparalleled atrocities which brand them with indelible shame, nor did they succeed even in wholly depriving it of its rights; but the Americans of the United States have accomplished this two fold purpose with singular felicity, tranquility, legally and philanthropically, without shedding blood and without violating a single great principle of morality in the eyes of the world. It is impossible to destroy men with more respect for the laws of humanity. (de Tocqueville, 1945 in Strickland, 1986)

Source: Laura Westra, "First Nations of Canada and the Legal and Illegal Attacks on Their Existence," from *Environmental Justice and the Rights of Indigenous Peoples*, Earthscan Ltd., 2007. Reproduced with permission of Earthscan Ltd. www.earthscan.co.uk.

One of the most disconcerting aspects of the legal forms of genocide of North America's aboriginal people is one that is not described in any of the instruments that specify what constitutes genocide; it is "genocide by assimilation" (LaVelle 2001). The main tools of assimilation, at least in Canada, were the "residential schools," where children were removed from their families and communities for the sole purpose of "eliminating their Indianness," or as the Report of the Royal Commission on Aboriginal Peoples[1] describes it:

> ... the children, effectively re-socialized, imbued with the values of European culture, would be the vanguard of a magnificent metamorphosis: the "savage" was to be "civilized," made fit to take up the privileges and responsibilities of citizenship.

In an atmosphere of general disrespect for the individual rights, their community, their tradition and history, these children were "educated" in surroundings that were "quite unfit for human habitation" for the most part. There was tuberculosis in the schools, and the conditions of heating, drainage, and ventilation were appalling. In addition, the food was of poor quality and limited quantity, so that their needs for a healthy and varied diet were not met. Neglect and harsh punishment were endemic (Westra, 2006). But although these would appear, *prima facie*, to be the sort of issues often found in poorly funded and supervised state institutions, there were certain aspects that were unique in this situation. General disinterest, even criminal negligence, although they are definitely crimes, do not rise to the level of genocide, as do these deliberate attacks on the very essence of what it is to be Indian. Thus there is the intent, openly stated in earlier times, to eliminate the essential features of their tradition and culture, a thing that made them a distinct people, even though there was no specific intent to kill individual Indian children. It seems that the defining conditions of cultural genocide*..., if nothing else, are present.

SUI GENERIS LAND-BASED RIGHTS

Aboriginal title encompasses the right to choose to what uses land can be put, subject to the ultimate limit that those uses cannot destroy the ability of the land to sustain future generations of Aboriginal peoples.[2]

The question of aboriginal title, and the difference between "ownership" and "possession" based on continued occupation and the use of traditional lands at the time of sovereignty, rather than the first time of contact,[3] clearly shows the centrality of land to the aboriginal way of life. It is ironical that, although that centrality to their survival as a people is acknowledged, their consent to any use of their land may "even" be required in some cases, and, when their title is infringed, "fair compensation will ordinarily be required."[4] But anything that is taking place in aboriginal people's traditional areas that affects their lands is more than likely to affect their present and future survival. In that case we are looking at incompensable harms, not harms that

*Editors' Note: This chapter is excerpted from Westra's book, *Environmental Justice and the Rights of Indigenous Peoples*. In an earlier chapter, she refers to cultural genocide as attempts to displace and even eradicate a people's culture. This involves "the absolute negation of 'cultural integrity'" (Westra, 2008, p. 171).

can be "fairly compensated." The special relationship between First Nations and the land is the topic of the next section, as I consider the historical background of the Canadian government's policies regarding their aboriginal peoples.

Historical and Traditional Background to Current First Nations Issues

Nations or Tribes of Indians ... should not be molested or disturbed in the possession of such Parts of our Dominions and Territories as not having been ceded to or purchased by Us, are reserved to them ... as their Hunting Grounds ... We do ... strictly enjoin and require, that no private Person do presume to make any purchase from the said Indians of any lands reserved to the said Indians ...; but that if, at any time any of the said Indians should be inclined to dispose of the said lands, the same shall be Purchased only by Us in our Name, at some public meeting or Assembly of the said Indians.[5]

After the Constitution Act of 1982, specifically after the adoption of section 35(1) of that act, aboriginal rights or title cannot be extinguished without the consent of aboriginal peoples (Ulgen, 2000), despite ongoing settlement treaties disputes (Asch and Zlotkin, 1997).

Prior to European occupation, and after the Treaty of Paris (1783), which ended the war between Britain and France regarding Canada, the aboriginal peoples did not sign treaties giving Europeans the power to decide their fate. In fact, as noted above, the Royal Proclamation of 1763 was intended to protect the land rights of aboriginal people in the region. However, before the Constitution Act of 1982 proclaimed that consent was needed before native rights could be extinguished, the situation was somewhat unclear. The Crown had a "fiduciary duty,"[6] so that its power regarding indigenous peoples was limited by its obligation to observe "the principles of recognition and reconciliation" (Ulgen, 2000; Hogg, 2005). The Crown had the obligation to ensure that there are limits to its sovereign power, in order to protect aboriginal peoples.[7] The aboriginal peoples once had sovereignty over the lands they occupied historically and the Crown did not avail itself of the categories of *terra nullius*, discovery or conquest, recognizing that these were organized native societies already present there (Ulgen, 2000).

As we will see, the 1990 case of *Sparrow v. The Queen* provides a clear statement of the obligation of the Crown regarding the protection of indigenous environmental rights. The case appears at first to be a fairly trivial one, as it deals with native fishing rights and the fact that "the net restriction in the Band's License violated Section 35" (Manus, 2006). The court pointed out that "An existing aboriginal right cannot be read so as to incorporate the specific manner in which it was regulated before 1982."[8]

Yet, while "the taking of Salmon was an integral part of their lives,"[9] and indeed the Indians of all bands had "a constitutionally protected, existing aboriginal right to fish" (Manus, 2006), there are, I believe, good and compelling reasons to view Sparrow's actions in a critical vein.

Questions raised by the court were many; among them, whether the new restrictions "reduced the Musqueam fish catch to levels below that needed for food and ceremonial purposes," and "whether the net length restriction caused the Musqueam to spend undue time and money per fish caught," both of which are not the most important consideration in the light of dwindling natural resources (Manus, 2006). The importance of *Sparrow* cannot be overestimated, both for what it says and for what emerges from the discussion.

The Significance of *Sparrow v. The Queen*

This case provided what was later termed the "Sparrow test," an approach that reappeared in any number of subsequent cases:

The first step in this test is to determine whether there was a prima facie infringement of an Aboriginal right. If an infringement is found, the Court would then determine whether it was justified. There are two steps to the justification determination in the Sparrow test. First, the Court would ask whether the objectives of the legislation were "compelling and substantial." If the[ir] answer is yes, the infringement moves to the second stage, where the Court asks whether the Crown has fulfilled its fiduciary duties to the First Nation, by implementing the legislation in a manner consistent with the honour of the Crown. (Imai, 2001; see also Hogg, 2005)

This test appears to be strong enough to withstand the attacks on First Nations' rights by corporate bodies intent on securing logging, fishing or other rights. Nevertheless other "rights" or objectives may be introduced into the argument, as providing equally compelling objectives, beyond the rights of aboriginal peoples. For example, these objectives might include "the economic and cultural needs of all people and communities in the Province."[10] Imai (2001) notes that recently the Supreme Court of Canada has been prepared to allow more and more "compelling and substantial" reasons for infringement, so that just about any "resource development activity" may be allowed to pass the test.[11] Unrestrained resource development on the part of either First Nations or corporate legal persons should be carefully examined from the ecological standpoint.

The problem is that the absolute importance of ecological integrity, of retaining lands in their natural state, has not been incorporated in the law of Canada (or any other country for that matter). But it is essential to maintain biodiversity in the region (Noss, 1992; Noss and Cooperrider, 1994), but also to ensure the continuance of its natural systemic processes, hence the presence of "nature's services" (Daily, 1997). This basic necessity applies to all humans, but its absence produces particularly severe results for First Nations and all aboriginal peoples who may not possess the temporary protection against environmental degradation that economically stronger groups possess, and that enables the wealthier groups to misunderstand the role and nature of such essential services to existence. First Nations are, in a sense, the "canaries" that show first and most clearly the results of the harms we are perpetrating on our habitat.

Their rights, like those of all indigenous peoples, are collective rights (Kapashesit and Klippenstein, 1991), and the right to social, cultural and economic survival are necessary, but not sufficient (… Scott, 2001b). Essentially, the most important right these groups have is the right to their lands in their natural condition, in perpetuity. Hence, when economic activities dictate the way "tracts taken up" are to be used, without any reference to ecological considerations, there will be "no appropriate approach to preserving First Nations resources" (Imai, 2001). Neither courts nor Canadian judges, not even First Nations' advocates can be relied upon to understand and respect the conditions required to maintain indigenous peoples' lands in the way that will ensure both the survival and the cultural needs of future generations. These are protected by treaty rights and, in the final analysis, by their constitutionally guaranteed rights supported by the "honour of the Crown."

But cases are tried singly by the courts, and it is impossible to fully understand the implications of the harms perpetrated by the infringements of those land rights. According to Imai (2001):

Unless there is a macro picture of the resources and territory needed, it would be very difficult to decide on a micro level whether a particular "taking up" would result in an infringement of a treaty right.

This is no longer a legal question; it is a scientific one that should be based on ecology. What is required then is the total respect for the integrity of the First Nations' traditional lands and even … an appropriately sized buffer zone around these lands, and a careful and thorough analysis of the ecological footprint of any and all commercial activities proposed. For First Nations, the basis for this conclusion is found, first, in the Great Law of Peace of the Haudenasaunee, and the widely accepted "seven generations rule"; but also, second, in the *sui generis* relation they have to their lands, the very foundation of the culture and lifestyle. Essentially then, aboriginal title manifests three basic differences from other forms of property under common law:

1. The title can only be surrendered to the Crown if that is the wish of the community; this may also happen if the people want to use their land in ways that are incompatible with their traditional ways;[12]
2. The title arises from the prior occupation of lands, namely, their "historical occupation before the assertion of British sovereignty"; the "occupancy requirement" is sufficient to demonstrate the connection to a specific parcel of land for their distinctive culture;
3. Aboriginal occupancy refers not only to the presence of aboriginal peoples in villages and to previously settled areas, *but also to the use of adjacent lands and even remote territories* used to preserve a traditional way.[13]

COLLECTIVE RIGHTS AND ABORIGINAL LAND MANAGEMENT: RESPECT FOR AND OBLIGATIONS TO NATURE

… For example, land used primarily as hunting grounds may not be used in such a way as to destroy its value by being used for strip-mining. If a group claims title by virtue of a special relationship to the land, the land may not be used in such a way to destroy this relationship, by turning it into a parking lot.[14]

Equity requires a *fortiori* that others should abide by the same policy that has been imposed on First Nations. If the First Nations must abide by environmental limitations to their right to self-determination, then commercial interests, eliminated *a priori* from dealing directly with First Nations for their lands (as only the Crown retains that privilege, should the First Nations so desire), have an even clearer, non-derogable obligation to abstain from using their lands in ways that clearly contradict both the Canadian Constitution and international agreements. For instance, United Nations Draft Declaration on the Rights of Indigenous Peoples (UNDD) (Article 25) states:

Indigenous peoples have the right to maintain and strengthen their distinctive spiritual and material relationship with the land territories, waters and coastal areas and other resources which they have traditionally owned or otherwise occupied or used, and to uphold their responsibilities to future generations in this regard. (emphasis added)

The concept of intergenerational equity is as entrenched in international law as that of intragenerational justice, for both environmental and ecological rights are foundational (Brown-Weiss, 1990; Westra, 2006). This double requirement renders the attacks on First Nations' children and their "Indianness" particularly heinous.

The environmental component of First Nations' rights is still being debated in the courts:[15]

And yet, the foremost factor in the survival of tribal cultures in nations with common law court systems may be the courts' willingness to accept as part of its judicial role a responsibility to both recognize and impose the sovereign obligation to understand, value and preserve the environmental interests of native populations. (Manus, 2006)

These obligations reflect more than the requirements of legal instruments and the constitution. They reflect the reality of aboriginal treatment and use of their lands. This is something technologically "advanced" societies have forgotten or ignored, resulting in the present global ecological situation.

First Nations Environmental Ethics and Their Collective Rights

> The Koyukon people are strongly influenced to harvest only as much as they can use and to use everything that they harvest. Among the Koyukon, reverence for nature, which is strongly manifested in both religion and personality, is unquestionably related to conscious limitation of use. (Nelson, 1982)

Governed by social custom, taboos, and strict regulations, most aboriginal peoples, such as the Cree for instance, "do not kill more than they need, for fun, or for self-aggrandizement, although they are fully aware of their ability to do so" (Kapashesit and Klippenstein, 1991; see also Feit, 1982). In general, aboriginal hunters are regulated through "rotational hunting" and by shifting the consumption from one animal to another, as well as other seasonal considerations to ensure sustainability (Feit, 1987). Their practices emphasize "reciprocity and balance" in their relation with the natural world, of which they deeply believe they are a part. Hence aboriginal environmental ethics are deeply embedded in their culture and in the social fabric of their community, and many environmental philosophers have noted this important fact, especially Callicott (1989b). But the best way to understand that connection starts with the famous work of forester Aldo Leopold (1949), who defines right conduct as that which "tends to preserve the ecological stability, *integrity* and beauty of the biotic community, and wrong as it tends otherwise."

First Nations and the Land: Our Forgotten Bond

It is not necessary for indigenous peoples living a traditional lifestyle to work out an explicit environmental ethic because their essential "Indianness" or the accumulated beliefs of their communal life incorporate precisely the outlook required for sane environmental policies, outlining the "principle of integrity" as the basis for an environmental ethic (Westra, 1994a). In addition, however, their tradition incorporates a spiritual role for nature that is unique, as it is not present in either environmental ethic literature or in ecological science (Kapashesit and Klippenstein, 1991). In fact, their approach represents the one way today's societies may still halt or at least moderate the environmental catastrophe that is upon us (see, for example, Gore, 2006) as:

> Aboriginal ecological management systems are distinct and largely independent from a modern Western state. Aboriginal ecological management systems are based on local knowledge and structures, and derive legitimacy from their traditional origin. (Kapashesit and Klippenstein, 1991)

From keeping track of the number and conditions of beaver lodges, to establishing "hunting bosses" charged with controlling where to hunt and how much could be taken, aboriginal practices manifest both scientific understanding of and respect for communal resources (Kapashesit and Klippenstein, 1991 ...). Had the affluent societies of the Western world been governed by such principles, we would not be facing what I have termed "the final enclosure movement," as the commons and even the common heritage of mankind, are almost entirely non-existent today (Beyerveld and Brownsword, 2001; Westra, 2004b).

The reciprocity with non-human animals and all of nature, and the intimate bond First Nations share with both, is something that modern liberal individuals have long since cast aside, as our economics are based on an impossible and unfair "growth" ethic. Ever-larger takings from nature, without any consideration for human and non-human life, and even less for the vulnerable people that try to cling to that nature, such as indigenous groups or future generations (Westra, 2006), manifest the violently oppressive aspects of our ecological footprint.

The neoliberal goals of an expansive economy and ever-increasing power are based on not recognizing limits to growth and to enrichment, no matter how unjust and at what cost. Ultimately, "appropriating" resources indiscriminately leads to a general biotic impoverishment that will affect first and most obviously the "canaries," or those who have neither the protection afforded by better economic conditions nor the luxury of being able to move elsewhere. Eventually, as epidemiology increasingly shows, we are all affected, albeit in different ways. Neither attackers nor victims can fully sever the natural bond we all have to the Earth. It might help us to learn from indigenous peoples, who are the only communities presently fighting to protect that bond.

THE PROBLEM OF "FROZEN RIGHTS" AND BORROWS' CRITIQUE OF THE ABORIGINAL RIGHTS TEST

In ways that we may not fully recognize or appreciate, native Canadians represent our society's only deep historical links to the land, consolidated over millennia. If their land is now our land as well, their relationship with that land is particularly worthy of our understanding and respect. (Slattery, 1987)

We must understand and respect First Nations' relations with the land, and those relationships must also be respected through entrenchment in the law for their protection. But some question this entrenchment and the effects that follow upon it. John Borrows (1997–1998) terms aboriginal rights based on their traditional relationship to the land "frozen rights." The Constitution Act, 1982, section 35(1) states that "The existing aboriginal and treaty rights of the aboriginal peoples of Canada are hereby recognized and affirmed." Tests for defining the import and scope of aboriginal rights may be found in *Van der Peet*,[16] under ten headings intended to specify what constitutes a "distinctive culture." Borrows (1997–1998) isolates the following:

1. "the perspective of aboriginal peoples themselves on the meaning of rights at stake";
2. "the tradition, custom or practice being relied upon to establish the right";
3. "the centrality of the practice to the group claiming the right";
4. the practice under consideration "integral to a distinctive culture" that has "continuity with activities which existed prior to the arrival of the Europeans in North America";[17]
5. the evidence offered should be accepted even if "it did not conform precisely with evidentiary standards in private litigation";
6. aboriginal rights are not "general and universal, but related to the specific history of the group claiming the right";
7. the practice contains "independent significance to the community";
8. aboriginal rights involve the "distinctive nature of the aboriginal practice";
9. "a distinctive practice does not derive solely as a response to European influences" and it "can arise separately from the aboriginal group's relation to the land";
10. the right may arise from the prior social organization and distinctive culture of aboriginal peoples.

Borrows (1997–1998) finds several aspects of the *Van der Peet* test problematic. His critique includes issues that seem to diminish rather than enhance the content of aboriginal rights in some way. The starting point ought to be the two principles that are internationally recognized to be basic to the protection of indigenous rights: "self-determination" and "cultural integrity," and the implication of those principles. The first thing to note is that these are two *equal* domains but they are interconnected, and both are collective in nature. Hence, for instance, individual self-determination is not part of the protected basis upon which aboriginal communities can rely. Several cases appear to bring into question individual choices: the right to fish using "contemporary implements" for instance, although fishing is certainly an activity that was practised since time immemorial. As Borrows (1997–1998) notes the Musqueam "always fished for reasons connected to their cultural and physical survival."

The court also acknowledged that those rights could be enjoyed equally by fishing in a more contemporary manner than by using more traditional ways. But the conflict between aboriginal activities "integral" or "distinctive" to the culture at the original time of first contact with Europeans, and one of the activities they seek to pursue in modern times, persists. For example, the establishment of casinos and gambling places is a fairly recent kind of activity, with no "continuity" with pre-contact culture (Borrows, 1997–1998). Nor is that practice "central" to any group's distinctive culture, or even part of any distinctive aboriginal national identity; "incidental practices, customs and traditions cannot qualify as aboriginal rights through a process of piggybacking on integral practices, customs and traditions."[18]

But it is modern-day aboriginal people who come before the courts with current problems and issues, hence it seems unfair to "freeze" any aboriginal rights to those present several centuries ago, from both substantive and procedural points of view. In other words, equity considerations suggest that both evidentiary rules and subject matter in each case ought to incorporate first and foremost the indigenous point of view today, and Borrows (1997–1998) emphasizes this approach.

Nevertheless it seems that not every aspect of the "essentialism" practised by the courts should be judged as inappropriate. The existence of land-based cultures of aboriginal peoples is not an outmoded "frozen" form of their rights but a basic and fundamental aspect of their existence as *a people*, totally aside from individual preferences or non-collective choices. Therefore, this is not only a "Western, non-aboriginal perspective," it is a basic foundation of their rights in international law, the best and strongest argument that aboriginal groups can advance for their own protection. The emphasis on different hunting or fishing techniques or equipment, or whether or not a casino on reserves is appropriate and should be permitted ought not to be judged solely from the standpoint of antiquated choices and lifestyles.

The Crown's Obligations: Local Issues or Fundamental Principles?

But, at the least, the following sorts of regulations would be valid: (1) regulations that operate to preserve or advance section 35 rights (as by conserving natural resources essential to the exercise of such rights); (2) regulations that prevent the exercise of section 35 rights from causing serious harm to the general populace or native peoples themselves (such as standard safety restrictions governing the use of fire-arms in hunting); and (3) regulations that implement state policies of overriding importance to the general welfare (as in time of war or emergency). (Slattery, 1987)

The most important point to keep in mind is emphasized by the wording of section 35(1) and the underlying principles dating back to the Royal Proclamation of 1763 and re-emphasized in *Delgamuukw, Sparrow* and other cases.[19] The Crown's fiduciary duty and the aboriginal peoples' right to their lands are based on *principles*, not on specific examples. They are universally valid, despite the attempts found in some cases to restrict and specify them as "distinctive" or specific to this or that national culture, as we noted in the *Van der Peet* test.

The cases deal with individual hunters or fishers, or others involved in specific forms of trade. The universally valid rights they all share represent the Crown's non-specific obligation: it is the *sui generis* land-based rights discussed above, rights to the land that will not impair "the ability of the land to sustain future generations of aboriginal peoples."[20] The Crown's fiduciary duty is not a temporary contract, as neither section 35(1) nor any other instrument dealing with these issues states time limits to those obligations, nor is the duty owed only to one or another nation. That duty, by its very nature, demands respect for the integrity of the land, in perpetuity. That in turn requires … protection of the land from both internal and external threats, starting with the addition/protection of a buffer zone to ensure the existence of bio/ecological integrity, on which alone future generations' rights can depend. In addition, that fiduciary duty should have strong *negative* as well as *positive* components. The negative protection should be exercised by denying firmly the individual economic rights of natural or legal persons who would pursue their own interests at the expense of the health, safety and integrity of indigenous peoples.

The question should not be, was a casino part of pre-confederation Indian lifestyles, but can the casino be built in a way that is less deleterious to the environment than other enterprises, and can it be built in a way that does not have an adverse impact on the health and integrity of aboriginal lands in the area? Conversely, a case involving land leased for a golf club[21] should involve more than the more obvious issues discussed in the case: lack of information, lack of consent by the band, and the concomitant breaches of fiduciary duty of the Crown, as well as breaches of trust and agency. The main issue should have been the presence of the "inherent limit" for aboriginal enterprise, no matter who approved the deal. Although this might be viewed as a paternalistic approach, it is instead one of respect for their uniqueness that depends on ecologically sound choices. Golf clubs are among the most hazardous areas on earth, as the amounts of pesticides, fungicides and other chemicals involved in keeping their "greens," sound the death knell for the area's integrity and multiply the cancers and other grave diseases of nearby inhabitants.

If the Crown has a fiduciary duty to protect the integrity of Indian lands and the supporting lifestyle these lands can provide for present and future generations, then that obligation cannot give priority to the interests of individuals or collectives inside, or even right outside Indian lands, without contradicting its own proclaimed intent. Hence any project or proposed activity within or outside the lands where aboriginal peoples reside, ought to be judged *first* from that point of view. If it is not, then the commitment to ensure the lands for *all* Indian generations is meaningless. The scientific research available in support of this argument is uncontroversial, and both lawyers and judges sitting in courts ought to be prepared to assess cases and situations in the light of that knowledge (Westra, 2006; WHO, 2002; Licari et al, 2005).

Returning for a moment to Slattery's (1987) summation of the Crown's obligations listed above, his first point supports the conclusions advanced here. The second point is equally important: the harms suffered by the proverbial "canary in the mine" are only the portent of what will befall the miners, unless they cease their activity immediately. The same is true in this case: the harms perpetrated on aboriginal populations by disregarding ecological and epidemiological evidence of the effects of hazardous industries, are more visible *first* in non-mobile populations that live directly on the land. But it is also a foregone conclusion that all humans will be adversely affected in some measure. Hence policies concerned with the general welfare (point three) could simply learn to comply with the basic tenet of the proclamation and of the Constitution Act. The duty of protection exists for all citizens (Westra, 2006), and the implied commitment to future generations of aboriginal people should support a reconsideration of all general welfare policies in order to protect all people in Canada.

ENVIRONMENTAL RACISM: A BRIEF INTRODUCTION

… the current environmental protection paradigm has institutionalized unequal enforcement, traded human health for profit, placed the burden of proof on the "victims" rather than on the polluting industry, legitimated human exposure to harmful substances, promoted "risky technologies" such as incinerators, exploited the vulnerability of economically and politically disenfranchised communities, subsidized ecological destruction, created an industry around risk assessment, delayed cleanup actions, and failed to develop pollution prevention as the over-arching determinant strategy. (Bullard, 2001)

Robert Bullard is arguably the best-known scientist and expert on environmental injustice regarding African American communities in the US. But the initial problems cited in the paragraph above, although aimed at the problems faced in urban minorities in his country, also represent a good introduction to the topic of traditional indigenous communities in Canada and elsewhere. In passing, it is worth noting that "environmental justice" is part of regularly taught courses at US universities.… In the US, the literature and research on environmental racism, or environmental justice, regarding African Americans is well established, and it emphasizes the multiple problems afflicting those citizens in various states, especially, but not exclusively, in the southern US. Repeatedly, the problems arise when corporate individuals pursue their interests and those of their shareholders at the expense of vulnerable, impoverished populations of colour. For the most part, the rationalizations offered by large companies assured African Americans and the general public that the siting decisions regarding hazardous facilities were purely motivated by economics, not race, from Chicago's "toxic doughnut" (Gaylord and Bell, 2001),[22] Titusville, Alabama and Browning-Ferris Industries (Westra and Lawson, 2001), "cancer alley," Louisiana (Wrigley and Shrader-Frechette, 2001), and Halifax, Canada (McCurdy, 2001). However, there is a vast difference between these citizens and the indigenous communities in Canada. Both are affected by decisions based on environmental racism, but the former would like nothing better than to be integrated within the general community, a very hard goal to achieve for a poor visible minority; the latter want to be respected and recognized in their difference and uniqueness instead, and "integration" in their case, is an existing and constant danger to their existence as a people.

Environmental racism refers to harms perpetrated in and through the environment, which affect disproportionately populations of colour. It includes both procedural and geographical inequities. Speaking of the problem in the US, Bullard (2001) argues that:

> The geographical distribution of both minorities and the poor has been found to be highly correlated to the distribution of air pollution, municipal landfills and incinerators, abandoned toxic waste dumps, lead poisoning in children and contaminated fish consumption.

Some of the categories emphasized in Bullard's writing fit equally well with indigenous traditional communities. There are serious lacunae in the regulatory framework regarding both of these communities, in Canada as well as in the US, which include problems of procedural equity, geographical equity and social equity (Bullard, 2001). According to Bullard (2001), the following are the five principles (without some of the details that pertain primarily to other populations) of environmental justice:

1. the right to protection;
2. the prevention of harm;
3. the need to shift the burden of proof;
4. laws should obviate the proof of intent; and
5. equities must be redressed.

Keeping in mind these principles, we can now return to the Canadian situation, first, to the "settlement" of a case that demonstrates why Bullard's analysis is also applicable to Canada: the Grassy Narrows and White Dog case. Finally I end this chapter with a somewhat dated case study that incorporates not only environmental racism, but also several other issues exclusively relevant to the Canadian indigenous peoples' scene, the 1990 *Oka* case (Wellington et al, 1997).

The Grassy Narrows and White Dog Reserves of Northern Ontario

... the settlement and the events leading up to it provide a striking example of the fragility of Canadians' environmental rights in the face of environmental wrongs. Access to justice has been difficult to achieve for victims of environmental catastrophes. The substantive, procedural and evidentiary rules in private environmental actions appear biased in favour of the polluter. (West, 1987)

The first point to note is that even a "mediated settlement" is, at best, a fought and won measure based on laws intended to *prevent* the occurrence of multiple harms. The case involves methyl mercury pollution, contaminating the English-Wabigoon River system downstream from Dryden, Ontario:

> Two pulp and paper plants in the area, the Dryden Paper Company Ltd., and Dryden Chemicals Ltd., both subsidiaries of Reed Paper Ltd., of England, used mercury cells in sodium chloride electrolysis to produce caustic soda and chlorine. (West, 1987)

The harm from mercury pollution is not a new discovery, as alternative technologies had already been discovered in the 19th century (Charlesbois, 1977); also, scientific evidence about the toxic effects of methyl mercury poisoning have been known since the early 1960s (West, 1987). In fact, the Ontario government had sent a team to the Japanese courts.[23]

[In another text,] I discuss the effects of various chemicals, especially pollution from oil production, not only on human physical health, but also on brain and character development and behaviour, in relation to the *Lubicon* case, as well as the Arctic area of Nunavut (the information for those cases comes from research by the WHO, as well as the November 2006 groundbreaking article by Grandjean and Landrigan in the *Lancet*). In this case, similar effects were observed in the Ojibway communities because the ravages of mercury pollution affect all aspects of the health and the life of the inhabitants. West (1987) lists some of the grave problems they encountered:

> ... in the years immediately preceding and following the pollution, the unemployment rate quadrupled from twenty percent to eighty percent.... Statistics indicated increases in violence, alcohol-related deaths caused by pneumonia, exposure, and suicide.

In addition, what emerged was "the link between mercury poisoning and the increase in deviant and violent behaviour" (West, 1987; see also Charlesbois, 1977; Troyer 1977). Nor is the mercury poisoning a thing of the past. Recent research[24] focuses on mercury poisoning occurring at Thunder Bay and elsewhere and is an example of current scientific information on this problem in Ontario (see table below):

Ontario Mercury Cell Chlor-Alkali Plants: Operation Dates and Release of Mercury

Location	Plant	Date mercury cells opened	Date mercury cells closed	Years in operation	Operational 1 Hg release in tonnes*
Sarnia	DowChemical Canada Inc.	1948	1973	25	317.73
Cornwall	ICI Ltd.	1935	1995	60	196.13
Sarnia	DowChemical Canada Inc. III	1970	1973	4	71.73
Marathon	American Can of Canada Ltd.	1952	1977	26	62.11
Hamilton	Canadian Industries Ltd.	1965	1973	8	51.47
Thunder Bay	DowChemical Canada Inc.	1966	1973	8	43.30

Note: *Does not include mercury released in solids
Source: After Tripp and Thorleifson (1998)

> 43.30 tonnes of mercury that was released by Dow Chlor-Alkali plant in Thunder Bay, right next to Fort Williams First Nation, puts into perspective [the Grassy Narrows case]: the Chlor-Alkali plant at Dryden (which mercury poisoned Grassy Narrows and White Dog people) only released 10 tonnes of mercury.

In addition, scientist Michael Gilbertson recently retired from the International Joint Commission and in 2006 submitted a PhD thesis entitled "Injury to health: A forensic audit of the Great Lakes Water Quality Agreement (1972–2005) with special reference to congenital minamata disease."

The scientific evidence has been available for years, yet in 1985 when the federal Department of Indian Affairs contacted Mr. Justice Emmett Hall (former Supreme Court of Canada Justice), who visited Grassy Narrows and studied a "211 pages legal brief prepared for the Indian Bands by Robert Sharpe, a University of Toronto professor and expert in such litigation" (West, 1987), what emerged persuaded him not to recommend going to trial. He believed that the results of the complex and time-consuming litigation would be uncertain, hence that the best interests of the Ojibways would be served by "a negotiated settlement outside the court system" (West, 1987).[25]

There is no question about the connection between mercury pollution and the diseases that follow upon that poisoning, yet Mr. Justice Hall was correct in stating the following, among his many concerns, in his affidavit:

> (vi) I was concerned about the Plaintiff's ability to establish their claim that mercury poisoning posed a potential hazard to the health of the unborn because of mercury induced genetic damage in one or both parents.
> (vii) In general, I was concerned about the likelihood of legally establishing the link between mercury pollution and health damages because the symptoms of mercury poisoning, such as tremor, ataxia, and sensory abnormality are also the symptoms of conditions such as alcoholism…[26]

Hence, to ensure some degree of success for the First Nations involved, Mr. Justice Hall decided to negotiate a settlement outside the court system. Because of the problems existing in the evidentiary and regulatory framework in environmental cases, "the Ojibway Bands really did not have an alternative to settlement," and the Can$14 million they received, helped them cope with the problems they were facing, although, to be sure, "no level of compensation exists which can ever redress the harms caused by the poisoning" (West, 1987).

The problem, as we have noted repeatedly, is not linked only to this case; it is a systemic problem, endemic to Canadian regulatory legislation. "Canadian plaintiffs must rely on inadequate common law remedies for a number of reasons" (West, 1987). These reasons include: first, the reliance on environmental law on English common law tort system, "a system geared to furthering the interests of industrial enterprises"; second, "group disputes and collective rights do not fit comfortably into the traditional framework of tort litigation"; third, "nuisance" action is incapable of accommodating modern scientific realities; fourth, "the Canadian Judiciary is reluctant to play an active role" to address environmental degradation and human rights; and fifth, the question of the "burden of proof borne by the victims in environmental tort litigation" is an "important insurmountable hurdle" (West, 1987).

Most of the problems listed here are clearly a part of the general difficulties faced by all cases involving environmental racism. West (1987) argues that the US judiciary is better equipped to accommodate environmental court cases but the analysis of the US situation in the work of Bullard (2001) points to the contrary, and ... cases tried in the US under ATCA are similarly affected. Both countries, as well as international law in general, have not accepted the direct causal link with health present in these cases:

> ... in environmental litigation a direct line for the health problems must be established, there is a tendency for some courts to confuse scientific and medical questions with legal questions, where they arise in a legal context. (West, 1987; see also Catrilli, 1984; Large and Mitchie, 1981)

In addition, I have argued that the whole concept of "torts" and compensation for environmental injuries is legally insufficient and morally inadequate (Westra, 2004a). The environmental attacks directed at vulnerable people should be considered crimes and proscribed accordingly. Aside from possible compensation to the victims, if harms occur they should be treated as the violations and homicide that they are. Further, the idea of closing cases with compensation may give some relief to the victims but does little or nothing to restrain the criminals who can easily pass the expense along to consumers, or claim it as a legitimate business expense.

Like other ongoing, economically driven issues, the whole idea of not addressing these grave problems through prevention but only *after* the fact, and only as torts, should be revised completely. One is reminded of the huge campaigns mounted everywhere to find the "cure" for cancer, despite the fact that Samuel Epstein published in 1978 a thorough indictment of that approach as he explained the role of the "dirty dozen" environmental practices that must be eliminated to achieve prevention of cancer instead (Epstein, 1978). Of course those who are presently ill must receive treatment, but the fact that treatment is available should not blind us to the fact that most cancers are extremely profitable for pharmaceutical companies and others, whereas prevention would be economically harmful to both pharmaceuticals and chemical companies (Grandjean and Landrigan, 2006; Tamburlini, 2002; WHO, 2002; Licari et al, 2005).

Hence, rather than compensating for the harms, strong environmental regulatory regimes would eliminate the suffering of countless people, such as those in the Grassy Narrows and White Dog in the "line of fire" from such operations.... For now, it seems that racism is alive and well in the cases we have considered, and that, in Canada, the indigenous peoples bear most of the brunt of it. The American experience demonstrates how often the use of "brownfields" and other apparent economic considerations, mask environmental racism. Such racism wears many masks, such as business requirements or economic rationality for decisions that are either based on it, or help to perpetuate it in the future, like the continuation of using polluted areas for more polluting businesses, thus perpetuating brownfields in areas where the lack of land value makes further hazardous sitings a "good" proposition, not only now but in the future. The next case describes and discusses several other related issues as well as environmental racism.

ENVIRONMENTAL RACISM AND STATE TERRORISM AT OKA: A CASE STUDY[27]

This is a case study about environmental racism, recently emerging as a "new" issue in the US and in countries in the South. Environmental racism is a form of discrimination against minority groups and countries in the South, practised in and through the environment. It involves such practices as the siting of hazardous or toxic waste dumps in areas inhabited primarily by people of colour, or hiring African Americans or Native Americans to work in hazardous industries, or even exporting toxic waste to impoverished countries (Westra and Lawson, 2001). However, the problem acquires a new "face" when it affects the aboriginal people of Canada. In their case, questions about environmental racism cannot be separated from issues of sovereignty and treaty rights, and this is clearly not the case for either urban or rural African Americans nor is it true of American Indian people. In the US, Native Americans are "regarded in law as 'domestic dependent nations' with some residual sovereign powers. In Canada the majority of First Nations people seek recognition under the Constitution of Canada of an inherent right to self-government."[28]

This difference is extremely significant as it injects an additional component of violence, repression and state terrorism that is largely absent from cases affecting visible minorities in the US, where even violence takes on quite different connotations and has no component of national self-defence (Westra and Lawson, 2001). This additional component of Canadian "difference" emerges clearly in the discussion of the Oka confrontation below.

Environmental racism is not a new phenomenon, but it is a new issue to some extent as it was targeted by the Clinton administration; Clinton signed an "Executive Order" on 11 February 1994 to make environmental justice for minorities a specific concern for the Environmental Protection Agency (Bullard, 2001).

The Mohawks at Kahnawake and Kanesatake, and the Confrontation at Oka, Quebec, Summer 1990

In order to understand the events culminating in the summer of 1990, several complex issues underlying the conflict must be understood. These are: first, the position of the Mohawks and their forms of government, as well as that of the Canadian government; second, the environmental issue and the demands of the township of Oka; and third, the chronology of the actual events and confrontations. All three issues are discussed in turn.

The Federal Government, the "Indian Act" and Mohawks' Governance

Mohawk communities in Canada total 39,263 persons, including Kanesatake, Kahnawake, Akwesasne and another four tribes. The Kanesatake community totals 1591 persons and the Department of Indian Affairs funds their total budget for education costs. Status Indians are eligible to attend both elementary and secondary schools off the reserve.[29] Nevertheless the "status of Kanesatake with respect to the land does not fit within the usual pattern of Indian reserve lands in Canada": they are Indians within the meaning of the term under the Indian Act, live on Crown Lands (since 1945) reserved for their use (within the meaning of section 91(24) of the Constitution Act of 1867), but they do not live on lands clearly having status as an Indian Act Reserve.[30]

The reason for this anomaly can be traced to the 1717 Land Grant by the King of France, and to seigneurial grant at Lac de Deux Montagnes given to the Ecclesiasticals of the Seminary of St. Sulpice. The Sulpicians' ⸺ te was "the purpose of protecting and instructing the indigenous ⸺ ⸺centrism and paternalism of that time)."[31] This led to con-
⸺at Kanesatake and the Sulpicians over land sales and
⸺ed France's king for a second land grant "to provide a
⸺s, too, was granted in 1735. The Indians were told that
⸺ly in the event that the Indians would decide to leave.
⸺sm quickly turned to tough-minded abuse. The Indians
⸺ps, but they could neither sell land nor wood or hay
⸺brought to trial for cutting wood for snowshoes, house
⸺repeated petitions to the King of France and, after his
⸺their miserable conditions and the exploitation of
⸺ans explained their position by saying that, without
⸺their "natural laziness" (Pindera and York, 1991).
⸺Methodist missionary, records many instances of
⸺s on the part of the priests. When Amand Parent
⸺h at Oka in 1872, the Sulpicians felt he taught the
⸺e too encountered ill-treatment and hostility. In
⸺der because it had been erected without permis-
⸺1887). In 1936, the Sulpicians, blatantly disre-
⸺h of the land to a rich Belgian, Baron Empain,

⸺uing disputes, which at times led to confronta-
⸺Council (then the highest court of appeal for
⸺s of any rights in respect to the lands "by virtue
⸺ed to sell off lands, the federal government
⸺urchasing the rest of the Sulpicians' lands in
⸺ds, however, were interspersed with "blocks"
⸺a (Begin et al, 1990).

⸺vance their claims on separate, but related,

⸺ ⸺om status as a sovereign nation;
⸺ rights;
3. the Royal Proclamation of 1763;
4. unextinguished aboriginal title under common law;
5. land rights flowing from the obligations imposed on the Sulpicians in the 18th century land grants by the King of France. (Pindera and York, 1991)

The federal government believed that the issues ere settled by the Privy Council Order of 1912, and that the claims were weakened by the fact that the Mohawks have not been continuously in possession of the land since time immemorial, as "land use by natives and non-natives is also recorded." These land users included some white settlers, as well as other native tribes. However, the federal department also described the Mohawks at Oka as descendents of some of these other groups who had been in possession, that is the Iroquois, Algonquians and Nipissings. In fact the federal government attempted to purchase additional land to give the Mohawks at Kanesatake a "unified land base," from 1985 up to the time of the Oka conflict.

Additionally, the Canadian government requires certain specific forms of Indian governments to order to recognize Indians' sovereign nation status. The Mohawks at Oka have a long history of debate about their own forms of governance. They belong to the Six Nations of the "Iroquois Confederacy" (the other five are Oneida, Onondaga, Cayuga, Seneca, and Tuscarora), and are governed by the "Great Law of Peace" (Kayanerakowa) or the "Longhouse System." But the Department of Indian Affairs (under the Indian Act), supports the act's election system of band councils. Instead, Chief Samson Gabriel wrote in 1967 that the Longhouse was the only form of legitimate Mohawk governance. As Chief Gabriel put it:

> We recognize no power to establish peacefully, or by the use of force or violence, a competitive political administration. Transactions of such groups in political and international affairs is very disturbing to the Six Nations "Iroquois Confederacy Chiefs." (Pindera and York, 1991)

In essence, there is a direct connection between any possible progress on land rights, native sovereignty or self-determination, and progress on the issue of Mohawk leadership or governance. The Department of Indian Affairs may permit the application of the Indian Act "on an interim basis," until some appropriate alternative local form of government policy can be established. If the Mohawks could not agree on the forms of leadership and governance appropriate to their tribe, then the Department of Indian Affairs could refuse to consider their claims because no local (native) governance policy was firmly established, as required.

The Environmental Issues and the Demands of the Oka Township in 1990

The previous section details the political and ideological controversies that led to the violence at Oka:

> The controversies included conflicts over divergent native ideologies about self-government and about the historical residence of other tribes in the disputed area, which was viewed by some to invalidate any native land claim on the part of the Mohawks. (Begin et al, 1990)

Before turning to a narrative of the events of the summer of 1990, it is necessary to show the role environmental issues played in the racism and the violence of the events that followed the dispute. The municipality of Oka "legally owns the clearing in the Pines and calls it a municipal park" (Begin et al, 1990), but the Mohawks argue that the land is theirs, and that they never sold it or gave it away, hence they do not recognize that ownership claim. The Pines have been part of the Kanesatake territory for over 270 years. About 100 years ago, the fine and sandy soil of the crest of the hill overlooking Oka was severely affected by deforestation and in danger of being washed away by the rains. The Mohawks, together with the Sulpician fathers, planted thousands of trees in the unstable sand. That area is now known as "the commons," at the very heart of the 800 hectares of Mohawk settlement. Thus the Mohawks' approach to dealing with the Pines was ecologically sound, and it is easy to understand their dismay at the later turn of events. They believed that the original "Lake of Two Mountains" seigneury (including the parish and the town of Oka), was their property. Yet they had to watch powerlessly as housing and recreational developments, including a golf course, continued to erode what they took to be Mohawk lands, in order to benefit the rich newcomers.

A small graveyard, the Pine Hill Cemetery, holds the bones of dead Mohawks at Kanesatake, the parents and grandparents of the warriors who were to fight for the Pines in 1990. It is placed between the Oka golf club's driveway and its parking lot. The Mohawks have cherished the Pines since they were planted, and they organize a careful clean-up of the area every year. But in March 1989, Oka's mayor, Jean Ouellette, unveiled his plans for the expansion of the golf club. A strip of 18 hectares of forest and swampland near the clearing in the Pines was to be bought and leased to the club in order to add nine holes to the golf course. The mayor did not consult the Mohawks as he believed he had the law on his side; the government had "consistently denied the Mohawk land claims for 150 years" (Pindera and York, 1991). When an angry citizen demanded to know why the township had been faced with a *fait accompli*, instead of being consulted before the fact, and why the Indians had not been consulted, Ouellette responded with a shrug and said, "You know you can't talk to the Indians" (Pindera and York, 1991). Many citizens were outraged by the mayor's attitude; 900 signed a petition opposing the project, which was perceived not to be in the interest of the general public as well as being environmentally unsound.

The Pines' soil is sandy, so erosion and shifting sands on the hillside would again become a continuing threat, if the painstakingly planted and nurtured trees were to be cut. At one time, in the 19th century, the sand had threatened to bury the town, and that formed the rationale for the planting of the pines themselves. Moreover, there are two additional environmental problems that are not even mentioned in the literature describing the Oka incident: first, the Indian "world view" about land and their respect for natural entities and laws; and second, the particularly hazardous nature of the envisioned project.

Native world views (basic to all Indian groups in North America) involve respect for nature and all the creatures with which we share a habitat. Disrespect and wasteful use of anything on Earth is unacceptable to Indians as a people, totally aside from personal preferences or even personal or group advantage (Sagoff, 1988). This represents a basic belief, a value akin to a religious one, and not to be confused with political beliefs about sovereignty or self-governance.

Further, even aside from the issue of shifting sands and deforestation, or of religious and traditional beliefs, the enterprise, namely a golf course, for which deforestation was planned, is often a significant source of environmental contamination, in spite of its benign green appearance (Pimentel, 1993). Lise Bacon, environmental minister at the time, could neither help nor intervene because the law did not require an environmental impact study for a recreational project in the municipality. But although golf courses are much in demand when they are adjacent to better housing developments, as well as for the sport for which they are created, their perfect manicured appearance depends heavily on fungicides, pesticides and other chemicals that are hazardous to wildlife, ecosystems and human health (Pimentel, 1991; 1992).

Hence, aside from the question of Mohawks' rights in regard to First Nations' sovereignty, the people of the Pines were correct in their opposition to the development, and so were the other objectors who protested on environmental grounds based on the value of life-support systems and the inappropriateness of siting a hazardous, chemically dependent operation near a fragile ecosystem on which the Mohawks depended (Westra, 1994a; 1994b). The Mohawks' lifestyle requires a healthy, unpolluted habitat, even more so than other Canadians, because their world view entails particularly close ties to the land, and their traditional reliance on hunting and fishing self-sufficiency demands it. As a people and as a separate nation, they have the right to live according to their religious beliefs, without being second-guessed or overruled by others. Even if they were not viewed as a separate nation and a separate people according to the Canadian Constitution, but simply as any other Canadians, they would have the right to live according to their own convictions. But the respect due and normally accorded separate ethno-cultural or religious groups was not accorded to the Mohawks. They were treated in a way which did not accord them either the respect due to them as free and equal citizens, or the respect due to citizens of a separate sovereign nation (that is, as people who were not subject to Canadian laws on their own territories). This lack of understanding and respect led to the ongoing hostility and the racism demonstrated through the events of the summer of 1990.

In this case, the racism was and is perpetrated in and through the land; it manifested itself in the careless attempt to impose environmental degradation and ecological disintegrity, hence it can be termed appropriately a form of environmental racism, but one which showed a unique, specifically Canadian "face."

The Chronology of the Events and the Confrontation at Oka

In early March 1990, the township council pressed for proceeding with plans for the golf club expansion, against a background of vacillations from Ottawa about appropriate forms of governance. The Mohawks, although disagreeing among themselves, were united in their opposition to the council and the mayor of Oka. In essence, although the Mohawks had always maintained that even the blocks that had been sold off to the township were part of their territory, there was a lot of disagreement on the question of compliance with the Indian Act. The Department of Indian Affairs demanded that "traditional or band custom councils" be used to pass band resolutions and to administer funds from Ottawa, and that some sort of democratic elections be used.

The Longhouse form of government was the Mohawks' traditional way, involving clan mothers whose role was "to listen to the people of their clans and counsel the Longhouse chiefs" (Pindera and York, 1991). When word spread about a possible early start to the project, a camp was set up in the clearing in the Pines to alert band members through an "early warning system"; this was the start of the occupation on 10 March 1990. As word spread through Kanasatake, more and more people came to see what was happening and then decided to stay. Signs were erected near the edge of the golf course in French and English, saying "Are you aware that this is Mohawk land?" (Pindera and York, 1991).

Although many Mohawks did not take the occupation seriously, others started to spend more time at the camp each day as they returned from work or from school, and some initiated a night shift armed with sticks, branches and axe handles for protection. After Earth Day on 22 April 1990, when the Mohawks traditionally cleaned up the forest area of garbage and debris, more and more Mohawks joined the camp. They were armed and erected the Warrior Flag and set up barricades of cement blocks a few metres back from Highway 344, and pushed a large fallen log across the northern entrance of the Pines (Pinder and York, 1991).

In May, the Akwesasne war chief, Francis Boots, made his first trip to the Pines in response to requests from a Longhouse chief's son for a patrol vehicle, a supply of two-way radios and money for gas and groceries (Pindera and York, 1991). Although not everybody was in favour of being armed, eventually a consensus was reached for resistance. On 7 May, a Mohawk representative was allowed to address the council of Oka citizens; he pleaded for peace rather than confrontation, but the mayor insisted there was no room for negotiations or discussions: the land belonged to the township. Premier Robert Bourassa and the Quebec public security minister were approached by the mayor, who asked them to send the police to dismantle the barricades. Bourassa responded: "I don't want to send anyone to play cowboy over the question of a golf course." The Provincial Minister of Aboriginal Affairs, John Ciaccia, was sent to negotiate, but he was not given the power to significantly affect the outcome of the discussions, beyond initiating a dialogue.

On 5 June, the municipality adopted a resolution: they proposed a moratorium on construction, but only if the barricades were lifted. The Mohawks refused, and Curtis Nelson of the Longhouse met with the Federal Minister of Indian Affairs, Tom Siddon, in Parliament in

Ottawa on 21 June. Nelson and other Mohawk representatives intended to press their land claims, but they hoped for some "limited jurisdiction" and hence they refused to discuss the barricades, and left.[33]

The municipality decided to seek an injunction against the Mohawks; at their meeting with Tom Siddon on 28 June, they compared the barricades to "a state of anarchy."[34] Further, when the municipality sought the help of the [Sûreté du Québec] 10 July, their request read, in part:

> … we ask you therefore to put a stop to the various criminal activities currently taking place … and arrest the authors of the crimes, so that we can proceed with establishing the recreational use of the occupied land.[35]

On 11 July, the police decided to intervene and, although before that date "the use of arms by First Nation people" was unprecedented, this time an armed conflict developed. The police had backed away from confrontation up to that time. When the police attacked and opened fire, the warriors, who had been quietly joining the resistance for the past several months retaliated and gunfire was exchanged. Corporal Marcel Lemay of the police was fatally wounded and rushed to hospital. To this day, it is unclear who hit him, as the recovered bullet could have come either from a police gun or from a warrior's gun. Eventually an inquest decided that it had been a Mohawk gun that had killed him but, since the only evidence submitted and accepted at the inquest was that of the police themselves, the result must remain uncertain (Pindera and York, 1991).

When a lawyer for the Kanesatake band in Montreal was told by the Mohawks that the police were getting ready to attack again, he made "forty-five calls in four hours" trying to reach someone with the power to stop the attacks. He finally reached Premier Bourassa, who, when told of the police officer's death, cancelled the second raid (Pindera and York, 1991).

From 13 July, a new strategy was initiated: the police would not permit supplies, food or medicine to enter the occupied lands, and even the Red Cross had to wait 24 hours before being permitted to enter. Indian women who attempted to go to the town to shop for groceries were jeered at and jostled. On one occasion, the police arrived barely in time to prevent a beating by an angry crowd. They had to leave without the food they had purchased. A Human Rights Commission official attempted to enter the roadblock to observe conditions at the camp, but he was refused, in glaring violation of the Quebec Charter of Rights and Freedoms. The Indians' survival was in fact dependent on the cooperation of other bands who brought in food and other necessities by canoe, under the cover of night and across the dense brush. Attempted negotiations continued to be stalled and the Mohawks issued a revised list of demands on 18 July. That list read:

> Title to the lands slated for the golf club expansion and the rest of the historic Commons; the withdrawal of all police forces from all Mohawk territories, including Ganienkeh in New York State and Akwesasne, on the Quebec, Ontario and New York borders; a forty-eight hours time period in which everyone leaving Kanesatake or Kahnawake would not be subject to search or arrest; and the referral of all disputes arising from the conflict to the World Court at the Hague. (Pindera and York, 1991)

Their demands also listed three "preconditions" before further negotiations: free access to food and other provisions; free access to clan mothers and spiritual advisors; and the "posting of independent international observers in Kanesatake and Kahnawake to monitor the actions of the police" (Pindera and York, 1991). Eventually talks were arranged in a Trappist monastery, la Trappe, at Oka, where the monks had been supportive of the Mohawks and had sent food and supplies for the warriors and their families. At this time, the Mohawks argued for their position on sovereignty. Loran Thompson, a Mohawk representative, showed his Iroquois Confederation passport, "complete with Canadian customs stamps from occasions when (he) had crossed the Canadian/American border," hence he had proof that Canadian officials had accepted them as a separate nation. The Mohawks also explained the major political principles that govern them: "The Two Row Wampum" Treaty (originally a treaty with the Dutch), and the "Great Law of Peace." The former supported peaceful but separate coexistence with non-Indians, as a canoe and a boat can both travel down the same river, provided each crew rowed their own boat only and did not attempt to straddle both. According to the treaty, any Mohawk who would submit to any other government would be treated as a traitor. The Great Law of Peace also supported separate sovereign status and non-submission, and it recommended not bearing arms and preferring peace.

Unfortunately, although the Mohawks were perceived as patriots whose cause was valid even by some of the soldiers who eventually replaced police at the barricades, their situation placed them in [a] "vicious circle." If they were not recognized as a separate nation, they could not bear arms in their own defence or in support of their territorial claims. But without arms, some argue, "they will not be able to affirm their rights as a nation" (Pindera and York, 1991) or to protect disputed territories until negotiations and peaceful talks could help rectify the problem.

At the Mohawks' request, international observers were allowed into the Pines, and it is very important to hear their comments:

> "The only persons who have treated me in a civilized way in this matter here in Canada are the Mohawks," said Finn Lying Hjem, a Norwegian Judge. "The army and the police do nothing. It's very degrading…degrading to us, and perhaps more degrading to the government who can't give us access." (Pindera and York, 1991)

When Premier Bourassa asked the international observers to leave, they warned Quebec and Canada of the "dangerous precedent" that had been set by arbitrarily breaking off talks. After many fruitless weeks of barricades and occupations, while the Mohawks' case became the cause for all First Nations people, no progress was made on any of their demands. Eventually the warriors, under pressure from the soldiers, decided to "disengage" and accept the word of the Canadian government that their land claims would be seriously considered. The warriors were taken off in police vehicles, each with several plastic handcuffs, as they showed they could easily break one handcuff with their bare hands. As a last gesture of defiance, a Mohawk warrior society flag was smuggled onto the bus and waved at onlookers as the police took them away.

This, unfortunately, was not the end of either violence or racism. Many of the warriors were badly beaten by the police during "interrogations." Some were roughed up as they were arrested and charged with "rioting and obstruction of justice." As well as Corporal Lemay, two Mohawks died. One, an elderly man, died of heart failure after a stone-throwing mob attacked him at the outskirts of town; the other was poisoned by tear gas and died later.

It is noteworthy that the Canadian Army (which eventually replaced the police) had only been used once before in Canadian history against domestic rebels (in the 1970 Quebec Liberation Front crisis). The crisis at Oka was described in the Canadian press as "the greatest ever witnessed in Quebec, Canada, even North America" (Pindera and York, 1991). Finally, more than ten months after the end of the conflict, disciplinary hearings were held "to examine the conduct of eight senior officers of the Quebec police, and of 31 junior officers, during the Oka crisis," (no information is available about the outcome of these hearings) and neither Quebec nor Canada showed any desire to improve relations with the people of the First Nations of Canada, even after the conflict, although the situation is substantially different today.

Environmental Racism, Environmental Justice and Terrorism: The Canadian Difference

In this section, I define and describe environmental racism in general, and relate the specific position of the Indians of Canada's First Nations to environmental racism so that the difference in their case becomes clear. I also discuss the interconnectedness of the land issue and the environmental questions in relation to territorial rights. I argue that the position of the First Nations required them to take a stand and even to take arms, and that the response of the provincial government could be fairly characterized as state terrorism.

Environmental Racism

Environmental racism can be defined as racism practised in and through the environment. It refers to environmental injustice whereby, for example, toxic and hazardous waste facilities are frequently located in or near poor non-white communities. Speaking of the US, Bullard (2001) says, "If a community is poor or inhabited largely by people of colour there is a good chance that it receives less protection than a community that is affluent or white." This is a recurring situation because in the US environmental policies "distribute the costs in a regressive pattern, while providing disproportionate benefits for the educated and the wealthy" (Bullard, 2001) in wealthy white neighbourhoods. This disparity has been institutionalized and has led to disregard for, and ultimately to ecological violence perpetrated against, people and communities of colour.

Furthermore, although both class and race appear to be significant indicators of the problems outlined, "the race correlation is even stronger than the class correlation" (Bryant and Mohai, 1990; Gelobter, 1988; United Church of Christ Commission for Racial Justice, 1987). What is particularly disturbing about this "trend," is that the ecological violence that is amply documented and which targets vulnerable and often trapped minorities, is not a random act perpetrated by a few profit-seeking operations that could perhaps be isolated and curtailed or eliminated, but that it is an accepted, institutionalized form of "doing business," taken for granted by most and ignored by all.

This institutionalized pattern of discrimination is an anomaly in a world that is committed to "political correctness," at least officially and in the so-called "free world" (Freedman and Narveson, 1994). For instance, both in Canada and the US, neither government institutions nor corporate bodies would deliberately promote or practise hiring in an openly discriminatory manner, or explicitly advocate segregation in housing or education. Although both women and minorities often feel that covertly discriminatory practices or "glass ceilings" exist both in business and government, which prevent them from achieving their full potential, still these difficulties are not openly fostered by institutions.

Yet the practice of placing hazardous business operations such as dump sites and other waste facilities in the "backyards" of minority groups is practiced regularly, with no apology. It is described as a purely economic decision with no consideration for the unjust burdens it may place on individuals and affected communities who are often too poor and weak to fight back (Gewirth, 1982; Rawls, 1999b). Similarly, when the US Environmental Protection Agency uses its "superfund" and other means to ameliorate acute problems in white neighbourhoods long before it even acknowledges or attempts to respond to environmental emergencies in black ones, then it appears that environmental racism is practised almost by rote, with little fear of retribution. Bullard (1994) argues that:

> The current environmental protection paradigm has institutionalized unequal enforcement; traded human health for profit, placed the burden of proof on the "victims" rather than on the polluting industry; legitimized human exposure to harmful substances; promoted "risky" technologies such as incinerators; exploited the vulnerability of communities of colour.

The same practice of ecological destruction happens overseas, by the countries of the North and the West in relation to the countries of the South and East. Toxic dumping and other unfair burdens are routinely imposed on countries whose leaders are often all too willing to trade off the safety of their uninformed and unconsenting disempowered citizens for Western hard currencies. Those who may respond that no racism is involved, as the hazardous transactions simply reflect economic advantage and "good business sense," ignore the fact that most often the perpetuation of brownfields is founded on various forms of earlier segregation and racism.

In the global marketplace, this approach has been termed the practice of "isolationist strategy" (Shrader-Frechette, 1991). In this case, the restraints and controls that businesses may employ in their home countries are not carried on in interactions with countries in the South. Relying on several arguments such as "the countervailing benefit argument," "the consent argument," "the social progress argument" and "the reasonable possibility argument," the isolationist strategy replicates many segregation arguments and thus cannot be acceptable from the moral standpoint (Shrader-Frechette, 1991).

Unfortunately, often poor communities cannot fight off the harm that threatens them insidiously through environmental contamination. When they actually try to do so, however, especially in present times and in the better-educated and better-organized countries of North America, they may reach a favourable outcome. For instance, in a recent case in Titusville, Alabama, a community group decided to fight Browning-Ferris Industries, who intended to site a waste-transfer station in their neighbourhood. The area was already legally the site of "heavy industry," but garbage was to be excluded, according to the ownership ordinance. It was also one of the few areas where African Americans had been able to buy property in the city of Birmingham, so that the whole community was and is one of colour. In this case, the community was exposed to a lengthy legal battle, and even police violence, as they demonstrated in the park between Birmingham's City Hall and its Civil Rights Institute. In the end, the city won against the company, and the infamous facility, already built, stood empty as late as November 1994, when I visited at the invitation of the community leader, Whitly Battle, and the lawyer, David Sullivan. In this case, the perpetuation of brownfields in one specific area indicates the institutionalized intent to burden disproportionately citizens of colour with society's hazards, without consent or compensation (Greenpeace, 1995; Westra and Lawson, 2001).

Examples of this kind of problem could be multiplied, although citizens' victories are rare indeed. From toxins in Altgeld Gardens in Chicago (Gaylord and Bell, 2001), to radioactive waste in Louisiana (Wigley and Shrader-Frechette, 2001) and predominantly in the southern US (Bullard, 1994), the story can be repeated again and again with slight variations, and with the black communities regularly the losers. But it is not only the urban minorities that are so targeted; their rural counterparts fare no better. "Geographic equity" does not exist in North America any more than it does in countries in the South.

Environmental Racism and First Nations: Human and Religious Rights to Self-defence

Recently there has been growing support for the defence of minority groups against the ecological violence perpetrated against them. The "First National People of Colour Environmental

Leadership Summit" was held in October 1991 in Washington DC. It united many grass-roots groups and inspired them to seek governmental and national support for strategies to eliminate the rampant environmental racism practised against them (Bullard, 1994–1995). In this section, I argue that the case of Canadian First Nations is quite different in several senses from what has been described above, although it remains environmental racism. Their case is unique because health and safety are not their only concern. Natives require high levels of environmental quality to meet both physical and spiritual needs. They need the land they inhabit to be free of toxic and chemical hazards so that various species of animal and fish, which are part of their traditional diet, do not suffer or disappear; but they also need spiritually to be able to live in a way that is consonant with their world view. This is grounded on respect for all living things with whom they share a habitat.

It can also be argued that the native traditional world view is so much a part of their deeply held values and beliefs that it can be considered a religion common to most Indians in North America. Quite aside from the issue of status as a separate nation discussed above, Mohawks' respect for their own ecologically inspired lifestyle should be treated as a constitutionally protected right to freedom of religion under the Canadian Charter of Rights and Freedoms. In fact, the "Great Law of Peace," which forms the basis for the Oka warriors' ideology, does not separate "church" and "state"; "it provides a complex combination of spiritual and political rules ... It is the rule book of an entire way of life ... it forms the thesis of a modern theocracy" (Pindera and York, 1991).

Hence the rights of the Mohawks to their traditional ways can be supported on the basis of freedom of religion, even before considering their separate national status. Unlike other minorities, these religious rights and freedoms are inseparable from environmental protection. Finally, this approach to ecological protection for large areas of wilderness is necessary for global sustainability, and the Indian traditional way is close to the mandate to "restore ecosystem integrity," which forms the basis of Environmental Canada's "vision" statement and a host of other regulations and mission statements around the globe (Westra, 1994a; 1995).

In sum, ecological concern is everyone's responsibility, but traditional American Indian "attitudes" towards nature appear to be particularly apt to support an environmental ethic (Callicot, 1989; Rabb, 1995). These attitudes also provide yet another reason why the Indians ought to have been permitted the peaceful enjoyment of their territory, and why their wishes in relation to the land ought to have been respected. The priests at St. Sulpice were twice granted lands on behalf of the Indians, with express instructions to administer them of their behalf. In fact their second request explicitly cited the Indians' needs and lifestyle as the basis for requesting larger areas from the King of France. The priests' needs or their economic advantage were never cited. Their role was not that of owners, but of caretakers and managers of the granted territories. Hence it would be unfair to penalize the Mohawks for the repeated sale of lands that were meant for their sole use and enjoyment. The lands were exploited, mismanaged, and sold inappropriately and illegally, and in clear violation of the mandate from either the King of France or that of England (Pindera and York, 1991).

Land, Environment, Territorial Rights and Native Identity

I have argued that the police of Quebec, federal government officials, and the residents and bureaucrats of Oka, can all be "charged" with environmental racism. To prove this, it is not necessary to demonstrate specific intent on the part of any one person or group, as environmental racism may be perpetrated through carelessness, self-interest or greed. It is sufficient to show that the practice is accepted and even institutionalized in a way that does ecological violence to a specific community or group of colour. I have also argued that in this case the Indians' historical and legal claim to independent nationhood, as well as their traditional lifestyle, culture and religious beliefs, all contribute significantly to their right to take a stance against environmental racism. The same combination of factors renders their resistance, their unshakable position and even their bearing arms potentially justifiable on moral grounds. Moreover, if their position is morally defensible, then their activities should not be viewed as crimes against the law, but as self-defence, conscientious objections, and affirmations of religious and cultural self-identity. That in turn makes the actions of both police and government in support of ecological violence and repression possible forms of state terrorism. It is this particular situation and combination that makes environmental racism distinctly Canadian in this case, as I argue below.

As the cultural self-identity argument is based on the understanding of the Indians as a people, one might ask, what makes a "people," other than law or custom? Do citizens involuntarily form associations, or is it their choice that makes them a community or a nation? Is it the case that common allegiance to a state constitutes a nation or people? On what grounds, then is national identity to be founded? According to Henry Sidgwick (1878), legitimate government rests on the consent of the governed, hence the "voluntarist" model of what constitutes a nation, "derives from the rights of individuals to associate politically as they choose" (Gilbert, 1994). But it is hard to understand what makes a specific association worthy of recognition, other than the exercise of the citizens' collective will, as people willingly form associations that may be less than worthy of respect (for example, the Ku Klux Klan). Another approach may be to appeal to a national character, emphasizing shared characteristics that might constitute a national identity. Gilbert (1994) terms this "the ethnic model of nationality." But to view nations as species of "natural kinds," is to subscribe to racist theory with the pitfalls we have all learned in Nazi and fascist times (Gilbert, 1994). But there are other, better ways of conceiving of national identity: "culturalism," for example, provides a useful model. This approach cannot rely exclusively on religion, which usually transcends national borders and hence language; common practices and aspirations, possibly even territory are required as well (Gilbert, 1994). Even someone's upbringing is constitutive of the national identity of individuals. Wil Kymlicka (1991) also discusses the parallel conception of "communitarianism," that is, viewing nations as groups living a common life in accordance with their own rules, hence this "community" view or "cultural view" (Gilbert, 1994), is also relevant to establish national identity. As Kymlicka (1991) points out, "cultural membership affects our very sense of personal identity and capacity."

First Nations people in general and Mohawks at Oka in particular can claim national identity, based on what Gilbert (1994) terms "culturalism," as well as their biological heritage. Kymlicka (1991) speaks of a "cultural heritage" for all Indians in Canada. This supports the Indians' claim that they are a "people," and that they can therefore demand to be treated as such:

> "All peoples have the right to self-determination" declares the first article of the United Nations International Covenant on human rights. That is to say, they have the right to independent statehood. (Gilbert, 1994)

If this is the case, then certain other rights follow from it, for example, "their right to throw off alien occupation, colonial status or absorption into some other state" (Gilbert, 1994). Furthermore, at Oka it seems that not only were the Mohawks treated unfairly, so that some suffered harm as the cost of increased benefits to others (an immoral position); they were also treated unjustly (an illegal action), because they were wronged through discrimination:

> Discrimination mistreats individuals because they are part of a certain group, so that the primary object of mistreatment is the group of which they are a part. (Gilbert, 1994)

But Gilbert's (1994) discussion, which is primarily about possible explanation and justification for terrorism in certain circumstances, is intended to deal with the situation between Israel and Palestine and that between Ireland and England. Hence, it cannot apply precisely to our case, although, as we have seen, many parallels can be drawn.

What is required then, is to understand the specific way in which racism and discrimination is practised against Indians in Canada that distinguishes their situation completely from that of African Americans in the US and minorities in countries in the South. As we argued earlier, the intent of the Executive Order by which President Clinton established an Office of Environmental Justice, was to eventually eliminate all practices that excluded black communities from the environmental protection and concern that favoured white communities, granting them not only defence against environmental threats, to some extent, but also redress in the case of problems or accidents, both of which were not equally available to communities of colour.

African Americans want to be included within the larger community. They want to avoid the *de facto* segregation to which exclusionary practices condemn them. They can argue that in housing, job seeking and schooling, segregation is not legally permitted at this time; thus, as I suggested earlier, environmental racism constitutes a "last frontier," or the only area within which racism is not only tolerated, but neither criticized nor discouraged or punished as such by the law.

The interest in avoiding this form of racism is equally as true for Indians as it is for blacks. But the forms of "discrimination," aside from those which involve the environment, are quite different for Canadian Indians; they are in fact opposite to those that affect blacks. Any "colour-blind" interpretations of the law are inappropriate for Indians; it is integration that is viewed as a "badge of inferiority" by Indians, not segregation.

Hence, simply granting Indians the same rights as all Canadians is not only insufficient, but essentially wrong. Kymlicka (1991) writes that "The viability of Indian communities depends on coercively restricting the mobility, residence, and political right of both Indians and non-Indians." It is therefore a necessary component of the Indians' rights and liberties to deny non-Indians the right to purchase or reside on Indian lands. A *fortiori* then, the right to adversely affect and pollute or otherwise ecologically affect these lands should be equally impermissible. Hence the activities of non-Indians in lands adjacent to Indian lands, must be consonant with a "buffer zone" (as it is for instance in Man and the Biosphere areas surrounding a wild "core" zone (see Westra, 1995).

In the concluding section, I defend the Mohawks' actions as morally defensible and discuss the government's interventions as motivated by environmental racism supported by terrorist attacks.

Conclusion: National Identity, Environmental Racism and State Terrorism

On the account presented in the last section, the cause of the Mohawks at Oka can be defended as just on moral grounds; environmentally and culturally they were clearly under attack. Those responsible for the circumstances in which they found themselves were guilty not only of racism but of environmental racism. The final question that must be asked at this point is whether the Mohawks were justified in taking up arms, and whether the police and the army were justified in the way they handled the warriors after the "disengagement." The Mohawks are not the first or even the only people who have resorted to civil resistance and even violence in defence of the environment. What makes their acts different and in fact unique, has been described above.

In contrast, those chaining themselves to trees at Clayoquot Sound in British Columbia came from all over Canada, and could have in fact come from anywhere in the world in defence of the common cause: protecting the environment. The Indians also shared this generalized concern, as I have shown, through their concern for the forest in relation to the township.

The Mohawks were also motivated by other, specific reasons. These were: first, the way their identity as a people is dependent on a certain place, so that any attack on either its size or its environmental quality and integrity must be construed as an attack on their identity; and second, the spiritual and religious components of their need for the land, which go beyond our own acknowledged need for wild places for various reasons (Westra, 1994a).

Hence, the Indians' defence goes beyond ecological concern in a general sense. It becomes a case of self-preservation. That makes bearing arms for that purpose more than a simple criminal act, as some claimed. The paradigm or model, according to which the Mohawks activities must be viewed, is not that of breaking the law or that of committing crimes. The closest model is that which fits other bi-national territorial disputes, such as those between Ireland and Britain, or between Israel and Palestine, where, as Gilbert (1994) has argued, border disputes are not open to democratic decisions based on votes. Neither Israelis nor Palestinians can democratically decide on the location of a specific border affecting their two nations. The only avenues open to these national groups, as to the Irish, in their territorial dispute, is either to declare war, or to attack or respond to violence through terrorist attacks outside a formal war situation.

Therefore these acts cannot be simply defined as "random violence" or as crime, because significant differences exist. The perpetrators announce their intention to stand their ground or to fight, and they publicize their political motives explicitly, in contrast with the hidden and furtive activities of criminals. Hence, the Mohawks' use of force must be viewed, and perhaps justified, in terms of terrorism, not random violence. It is important to note that they resisted and defended, but did not launch violent attacks beyond their own territories. In fact, all their interactions and negotiations with the representatives of the Canadian government or the township were characterized by reasoned arguments, the repetition of their claims and the reasons for those claims, coupled with the sincere desire to achieve and maintain peace. They bore arms for self-defence, not attack.

I have argued elsewhere (Westra, 1990) that often even terrorist aggressive violence may be defensible in principle, though not in its practical expression, and I have called defensible violence of this sort, a form of "whistle-blowing," as it calls attention to some grave injustice. The extent of the injustice and the discriminatory treatment, neither of which were random occurrences but rather formed a historical pattern on the part of the Canadians, has been discussed above. Their perpetration justifies, I believe, resistance on grounds of self-determination. Their resistance then becomes analogous to that intended to throw off foreign occupation (Gilbert, 1994).

The events may be described, using Gilbert's felicitous expression, as an "ethical revolution" (1994). Such a revolution is typically based on a "different conception of the state and the community"; it is an "inspirational aspect of violent change," which might be of two kinds: "ethically conservative," or "ethically radical" (Gilbert, 1994). The former appeals to values that the resisting group shares with the majority, including its opponents, but which are not properly implemented. The latter "makes its case on the basis of a change in the values themselves" (Gilbert, 1994), and is persuasive because it demands a change of values. The Mohawks' case seems to fit the second model. They can be seen as "ethical revolutionaries," as people who "seek to change the criteria for membership of the political community" (Gilbert, 1994).

They were criticized for not using democratic means to state their grievances and get redress, but their grievances were not of the sort that can easily be settled by democratic means. This is because the very core of their complaint was that the Mohawk nation was not viewed as an equal, viable political community, responsible for decisions affecting their people and their land. It is here that the parallel with terrorism becomes even clearer.

International terrorism is most often concerned with territory and political equality. But claims to self-determination should be "made within existing borders," an impossibility when the very extent of the territory within those borders is at issue (as argued earlier), and when the dissenting and protesting group is in a clear minority position. But in that case, the group seeking redress that is, as in this case, at the same time environmental, territorial and concerned with national independence, has no democratic recourse, no peaceful voice through which to make its claim other than perhaps attempting a "sit-in" to gain national and international attention. It seems as though it must resist, even while seeking peace. And if its arguments and claims are not heard and respected, its only recourse is to resist attack and bear arms. Note that they were indeed resisting peacefully, and only turned violent when violently attacked.

What is the state to do in response to such a position? Should it respond with force and attack? But then can we not charge it with hypocrisy and view its actions as open to a *tu quoque** (Gilbert, 1994)? It is not sufficient, as we have seen, to say that government force must intervene to "punish crime," as the Indians are not breaking a law to which they are legitimately subjected. On the contrary, their claim is that law is not their law, that state is not their state, and its values are not theirs. In this, the Canadian constitution appears to support their position. When weighing the forms of violence (that is the Indians' and the state's), there seems to be little cause to view the former as "wrong," the latter as "right," from the moral standpoint.

The stronger the moral case for the Mohawks, the weaker, morally, the case for the "legal" repression and violence they had to endure. While the reasons for supporting the Indians' position at Oka are many and defensible, only one possible reason can be given in support of the army's intervention (Gilbert, 1994). The state has the authority to enforce the law and to punish crimes. But is the state's violence against those who are not subject to its laws (or whose major claim for resistance is that they are not), morally better than their opponents' resistance? When we compare even terrorists' action "seeking to gain power, and those of the agents of the State in seeking to retain it," there may be no moral reason to term the former "criminal" and the latter "punishment of crime" (Gilbert, 1994). This is particularly the case, when there was no violent attack on the part of the Mohawks, and the main reason for their resistance was to protest the assumption that they were in fact subject to those laws.

It is also clear that the other alternative—that is, the presumption that while the Mohawks belonged to a separate, sovereign nation, Canada could bear arms against them as a form of warfare—is not appropriate. Rules of war demand that if violence is to be part of a just war, then the war should first be openly declared. This is the reason why terrorism is not precisely warfare, whether it is practised by dissenting groups or by the state itself. State terrorism, therefore, refers to violent responses to terrorism on the part of a government. It is often the alternative preferred to simply treating terrorists as criminals (that is, as innocent until proven guilty, using restraints but not violence against them, and so on). Although a violent response is often employed, this use of state power is hard to justify as anything other than retaliation.

State terrorism involves warlike intentions that are impeded by constraints from issuing an open war. These constraints are characteristically political rather than military, reflecting political inhibition from resorting to war (Gilbert, 1994). However Gilbert adds that normally "internal State terrorism" does not have the "warlike aims" of "acquisition and control of territory." It seems that the Oka situation instead manifested precisely this aim; perhaps then it represents an atypical form of state terrorism as it has the added component while manifesting many of the usual ones as well. As Gilbert outlines and defines state terrorism, the provincial government's intervention through the police and, particularly, through the army appears to fit under this heading. The state, of course, purports to be operating "within the framework of the

---

* *Tu quoque*, meaning "this also applies to you," refers to a logical fallacy where "a criticism or objection applies equally to the person making it" (Wikipedia, http://en.wikipedia.org/wiki/Tu_quoque).

law, which it presents itself as upholding" (Gilbert, 1994). But if its legal framework is "unable to resist terrorism," the state may simply "resort to the covertly warlike operations which constitute state terrorism" (Gilbert, 1994). Yet, lacking an openly declared war, "the ordinary rules of civil life" should guide the state's acceptable intervention. Armed attacks on dissenting citizens of another country (or even of one's own), or beatings as part of "interrogation" or "capture," are not the way the state ought to deal even with hardened criminals or serial killers, before or after sentencing. Hence the state denounced the Mohawks as criminals during the crisis but only belatedly treated them as such after their cases came to court. Throughout the crisis, a state of war appeared to prevail, giving additional credence to the Mohawks' claim to sovereignty and national independence, something that is already legally true in Canada for people of the First Nation in general.

It is clear that the federal government cannot have it both ways: either their attack on resisting Mohawks is war—in which case a proper declaration of war, the recognition of their independent nationhood and adherence to the rules of war are mandatory—or it is not. Further, over and above these formal requirements, from the moral standpoint only a war of self-defence (from an actual attack, not from dissent) may be viewed as a just war (Westra, 1990). Or we might accept the other alternative, that the state is viewing their resistance as criminal. It has been shown that this does not appropriately describe the government's response. Unless a criminal is actually attacking a police officer, for instance, drawing fire against him is not a permissible, legal response. As explained earlier, the Mohawks were standing their ground, not even fleeing from the law; and "if terrorists are denied due process of law, the same acts are criminal" (Gilbert, 1994).

To start shooting prior to trial and conviction of specific individuals, is to deny them due process. Had they even been convicted criminals or killers, retaliation in kind is not appropriate, particularly in a country with no capital punishment. And, it must be kept in mind, no one was ever found guilty of murder. Those who were considered the "worst offenders" were perhaps Ronald Cross (nicknamed "lasagna") and Gordon Lazore. Helene Sevigny (1993) reports on the actual sentencing:

> Sentence "Sa Majesté la Reine vs. Ronald Cross et Gordon Lazore" Province of Quebec, District of Terrebonne, No. 700-01-000009-913; Judge B.J. Greensberg, Superior Court, Criminal Division, St. Jerome, 19 February 1992. The two were found guilty of half of their charges, primarily attacks with "arms" such as baseball bats. The case was appealed on 20 February 1992. On 3 July 1992, the other 39 Mohawks that were originally taken from the barricades and detained, were acquitted. (author's translation)

The Mohawks' well-founded message and their fight against racism in all its forms, including its environmental aspect, [have] been around for a long time, as has the Indians' effort to have their cause and their reasons heard. Gilles Boileau's (1991) indictment of the "lords wearing cassocks" ("les seigneurs en soutane"), presents a detailed historical account of the difficulties the Mohawks had to endure:

> The "Messieurs" and all others must recognize that the Mohawks have a right to "their dignity and our respect," and it is high time that Oka should be recognized primarily as Indian land.

In conclusion, the Oka case combines several unique features specific to the Canadian political scene. It manifests aspects of environmental racism, as the ecologically inappropriate choices of a non-Indian majority were to be imposed on the Mohawks without regard for their traditional lifestyles. At the same time, the imposition infringed their right to self-determination and their constitutional status as First Nation. Finally, the case shows the inappropriate use of force and the employment of state terrorism in response to the Mohawks' position, which, I have argued, is defensible on moral, environmental and legal grounds.

It is clear that not everyone will readily agree to the strong, land-based obligation here proposed, but many do defend the ultimate importance of unextinguished aboriginal title (Asch and Zlotkin, 1997). The peoples in original Indian societies were strong on sharing, cooperation and good faith, all aspects missing from the dealings involving European newcomers.

Treaties that require the extinguishment of aboriginal rights cannot be based on: first, true collaboration; because, second, they are incompatible with the understanding of aboriginal rights in section 35 of the Constitution Act, 1982; third, they are incompatible with the Crown's fiduciary duty; fourth, they are incompatible with international human rights instruments and are not consistent with the prohibition against racial discrimination; fifth, asking aboriginal peoples to give up their rights would be "equivalent to asking Canadians to give up their Canadian citizenship"; and sixth, these policies can only be viewed as ethnocentric (Asch and Zlotkin, 1997).

Jim Antoine, Chief of Fort Simpson Dene Band, puts it well:

> We are a real part of the land. Our roots are connected into the land. But if you want to extinguish your aboriginal rights and title to it, then you are cutting off those roots. You are cutting us off from the land, and we are floating.[36]

This paragraph is consistent with the major premises of this work; that is, the primacy of the right to biological/ecological integrity of indigenous peoples and First Nations, and the role its absence plays in furthering the ongoing elimination of such people, as peoples, even without a clear genocidal intent on the part of the perpetrators.

CONCLUSIONS

Part Two discussed a number of representative cases, all of which support the main contention of this work: the basic need for the protection of both ecological and biological integrity, and the recognition of its lack as a crime resulting in genocide for the affected aboriginal communities. The contrast between the complaints (the "facts" in the court cases) of indigenous groups worldwide and the court decisions responding to those complaints repeats the argument of this work. In general, neither the quantitative nor the qualitative aspects of indigenous territories are respected, and the resulting biological and cultural harms to those communities are extensive.

The courts continue to ignore the full import of environmental harms to indigenous peoples despite the laudable 2002 initiative of Justice Arthur Chaskalson, of South Africa (and UNEP), to initiate the "Judges Portal," intended to promote environmental knowledge and understanding for all judges globally, so that they might better be able to decide on the cases brought before them.

Today, science in general, and public health and epidemiology in particular, have forged ahead of anything found in domestic or international instruments, upon which judges might depend for the cases they are asked to decide. When legal scholars of impeccable reputation are called as expert witnesses, they too are hampered by the limited array and reach of international environmental and human rights instruments. However, those who would be able to speak with an authoritative voice, and as totally independent, are the scientists of the WHO, and these experts are, unfortunately, never called to testify....

QUESTIONS TO CONSIDER

1. Westra offers a strong indictment of Western legal practices and cultural initiatives, such as assimilationist policy. Critically assess her examples and discuss whether quite different examples might provide a more positive elaboration of, or even appreciation of, non-Aboriginal peoples and their cultures.

2. How do variables of race, economics, gender, and politics intersect with respect to environmental protection measures and economic development? Use specific examples and consider whether Aboriginal people or other populations are at particularly high risk of injury through poisoning or other health harms.

3. Using outside readings, revisit the account of the Oka conflict articulated by Laura Westra. Where do you most strongly agree with her account? Where do you strongly disagree with some aspects of her account? Use specific examples from the Oka conflict or from other examples, such as the land dispute in Caledonia, Ontario, or other roadblocks to protest uranium mine development, tourism, or logging.

SUGGESTIONS FOR FURTHER READING

Backhouse, C. (1999). Bedecked in gaudy feathers: The legal prohibition of aboriginal dance: Wanduta's trial. In C. Backhouse, *Colour-coded: A legal history of racism in Canada, 1900–1950* (pp. 56–102). Toronto: University of Toronto Press.

Bell, C., & Napolean, V. (Eds.). (2008). *First Nations cultural heritage and law: Case studies, voices, and perspectives.* Vancouver: University of British Columbia Press.

Francis, D. (1992). *The imaginary Indian: The image of the Indian in Canadian culture.* Vancouver: Arsenal Pulp Press.

Slattery, B. (2007). The metamorphosis of Aboriginal title. *Canadian Bar Review, 85,* 256–286.

NOTES

1. *Report of the Royal Commission on Aboriginal Peoples: Looking Forward Looking Back* (Vol 1), 1996, RCAP, www.ainc-inac.gc.ca/ch/rcap/sg/sg28_e.html#99, "Residential Schools"
2. *Delgamuukw v. British Columbia* [1998] 1 CNLR 14, 11 December 1997, Lamer C. J. (Cory, MacLachlin and Major J. J. Concurring) para. 21.
3. ibid.
4. ibid.
5. Royal Proclamations, 7 October 1763, (1985 RSC Appendix II, No. 1, in part.
6. Reorganized in 1984 in *Guerin v. Canada* [1984] 2 SCR 335.
7. *Sparrow* [1990] SCR. See also Hogg (2005, pp. 621–621).
8. ibid.
9. ibid.
10. *Halfway River First Nation v. British Columbia* (Minister of Forests) (1999) 178 DLR (4th) 666 716; see Imai, 2001, p. 18.
11. *R. v. Gladstone* [1996] 2 SCR 723; *R. v. Van der Peet* [1996] 2 SCR 507.
12. *Delgamuukw v. British Columbia* [1998] 1 CNLR 14, 1997: Per La Forest and L'Heureux-Dube, J.J.: "Aboriginal title is based on the continuous occupation and use of the land as part of the Aboriginal peoples' traditional way of life."
13. ibid, emphasis added; however, in *R. v. Marshall* and *R. v. Bernard* (2005), The Supreme Court of Canada seems to pull back from this position.
14. ibid (*Delgamuukw v. British Columbia*).

15. *Marshall v. The Queen* [1993] 3 SCR 456; infra Part I A.2.c.

16. *R. v. Van der Peet*, 137 DLR 4th 289, 9 WWR1 (Can. 1996); *R. v. Gladstone*, 137 DLR 4th 648,9 WWR1 1996.

17. *Van der Peet*, 137 DLR 4th 289; see also *Pamajewon*, [1996] SCC.

18. *Van der Peet*, para. 40.

19. *Delgamuukw v. British Columbia* [1998] 1 CNLR 14, 11 December 1997; *R. v. Sparrow* [1990] 1 SCR 1075.

20. *Delgamuukw v. B.C.* [1998] 1 CNLR 14, para. 21.

21. *Guerin v. Canada* [1984] 2 SCR 335.

22. Clarice Gaylord was Bill Clinton's first appointee to the EPA office of Environmental Justice, by Executive Order No. 12898 in 1992, to redress inequities in the way EPA addressed environmental harms in white communities and communities of colour.

23. See the *Toyama Itai-Itai* case, 635 Hanji 17 (Toyama District Court, 30 June 1971); the *Niigata Minamaia* case, 642 Hanji (Niigata District Court, 29 September 1971); the *Yokkaichi Asthma* case, 672 Hanji 30 (Tsu District Court, Yokkaichi Branch, 24 July 1972); the *Kumamoto Minimata Disease* case, 696 Hanji 15 Kumamoto District Court, 20 March 1973; reprinted in J. Gresser, K. Fugikura and A. Morishima, *Environmental Law in Japan*, 1981.

24. Hummel, J. H. W. from links; see also the Madison Declaration on Mercury Pollution, www.unbc.ca/assets/ media/2007/03_march/madison_declarationon_mercury_pollution_with_non-techinical_summary.pdf

25. See also Mr. Justice Hall's "Affidavit" before the Supreme Court of Ontario, NO. 14716/77, no. 13.

26. ibid.

27. Adapted from Wellington et al (1997) with permission from Broadview Press, 1997.

28. *Fifth Report of the Standing Committee on Aboriginal Affairs, House of Commons,* Canada, May 1991.

29. ibid.

30. ibid.

31. ibid.

32. *Corinthe v. Seminary of St. Sulpice.*

33. ibid.

34. ibid.

35. ibid.

36. Transcript of the Public Hearing of the Royal Commission on Aboriginal Peoples, Fort Simpson, Northwest Territories, 26 May 1992.

Chapter Eight

Law, Homophobia, and Violence: Legislating against Hate

Douglas Victor Janoff

Editors' Note: Douglas Janoff explores hate legislation in Canada and how such provisions have been implemented. He begins with a detailed example drawn from an attack in and around a Vancouver nightclub, setting out not only the homophobic nature of the attacks on club patrons but also the rather lenient—in Janoff's view—dispositions for the men charged with assault. Janoff combines such accounts of cases of assault and prosecution with theoretical approaches to understanding homophobia in society at large and within the justice system specifically. A recurring theme is how violence against sexual minorities is ignored or treated with indifference. The advent of hate legislation in Canada is explored, using developments in the U.S. as a point of comparison to Canadian parliamentary debate and subsequent legislation. Douglas Janoff is wary of celebrating such legislation, given shortfalls in its implementation and the broader concern that legislation per se does not resolve many ongoing problems faced by sexual minorities. The author draws attention to allegations of a double standard in proceeding with cases involving gays and lesbians compared with heterosexual victims of violence. More informa-tion about Pink Blood and its author is available online at http://www.pinkblood.ca/home.php

---

Sociological and psychological theories do not tell the full story about homophobic violence. The missing link is the way homophobia is reproduced in law. It is bad enough that people form hateful thoughts about homosexuals and proceed to beat on them, but the real horror lies in the legal prac-tices that tend to downplay or excuse this violence. This chapter examines the way homophobia saturates the legal system; the system's limited ability to address homophobic violence; the move-ment to develop hate crime legislation; and legal remedies for victims of queer-bashing.

If a group of punks went on a rampage at a restaurant in Vancouver's Chinatown—yelling "Chinks," beating up patrons, and provoking a riot that shut down Pender Street—it would probably make the front page of the *Vancouver Sun*, and police would probably call a press con-ference to denounce the crime. But in 1994, when a group of thugs yelling "faggots" beat up customers at a crowded gay cafe on Davie Street, the story landed squarely on page two—and the police never mentioned it at their weekly press briefing.[1]

A minor quibble? I don't think so. The attack was an affront to the queer community, and the pathetic outcome—to which the mainstream media paid scant notice—was even worse: not one of the bashers served any jail time. I was in the courtroom the day the plea bargain was announced; there was no public outrage when the legal process sputtered to a halt. Perhaps Vancouverites had become inured—not just to the violence, but to its inevitable "resolution." I adduced many hidden facts about this case by interviewing "Brian," one of the victims.

LATE ONE NIGHT AT THE EDGE CAFÉ

On 5 May 1994, five drunk men leaving a Davie Street restaurant—located next door to the Edge Café, a gay nightspot—began screaming homophobic abuse at Brian, who was on his way

Source: Douglas Victor Janoff, "Law, Homophobia, and Violence: Legislating Against Hate," *Pink Blood: Homophobic Violence in Canada.* © 2005 University of Toronto Press Incorporated. Reprinted with permission.

home from a gay bar at 2:30 a.m. The men slammed him into the wall beside the cafe, which had a hundred patrons inside.[2] Brian estimated that one of the assailants weighed three hundred pounds.[3] The gang burst into the cafe and began attacking patrons and yelling anti-gay slogans.[4] The thugs were grabbing hot coffees and throwing them in people's faces, shouting "fucking faggots, we'll kill all of you."[5] One of the co-owners of the cafe was hit over the head with a wrought-iron stool; eleven stitches were required to close the wound. The customers inside fought back bravely, and two men—who managed to tackle and hold down two men trying to escape—suffered cracked ribs and a broken wrist.[6]

But Brian was the most unfortunate: one thug caught him in a bear hug, then smashed him against the sidewalk at full force. His thorax and two vertebrae were shattered, and his body was bruised for six months. Despite the severity of his injuries—and after arriving at the hospital in an ambulance—he was given a Demerol shot and told to either walk home by himself or pay for his own taxi. A year and a half later, Brian was on welfare, suffering from depression, and living in a rooming house on $285 a month after his rent was paid. Although he had received $6,500 in victim compensation, it had mainly gone toward debts accumulated during his ordeal. He was also suffering sinal pilonitis, an intestinal infection, and a skin infection—side effects from his daily medication: ASA, tetracycline, clonazepam, trazodone, penicillin, cloxacillin, ibuprofen, and lithium.[7]

Only three of the five men were charged. It took a year for a preliminary hearing, which was remanded five times.[8] The defence lawyer asked Brian if he was a friend of any of the other witnesses. He said no. The defence went on to describe the Edge Café as a "last-chance pick-up joint" for gays coming out of the bars at two a.m. The defence asked Brian three more times if he knew any of the witnesses. He said no. Then the defence asked him if he had ever *slept* with any of the witnesses. Brian yelled: "I object to this. You've asked me four times if I knew any of them, and I told you, 'No.' Now you're asking me if I slept with any of them? I told you: No!"

It was only at this point that the Crown objected. Later, the prosecutor was asked if it was normal for victims to be asked whether they had had sex with bystanders. The Crown replied: "Brian was asked questions that other witnesses would not have been asked because of his homosexuality." Dennis Dahl, a Vancouver lawyer, sees a double-standard at work: "We limit cross-examination of female victims about their sexual history, but most judges say that it's very relevant to talk about gay men's sexual history. The Crown definitely showed a lack of sensitivity."[9]

Three months later, Brian complained to Victim Services about the continued delays. (The trial, remanded three times, finally got going almost two years after the actual attack.) Apparently in the belief that Brian was going to commit suicide, a dozen police officers arrived with an ambulance. Brian said a policeman stormed into his apartment, swore at him, then slammed his back into a table and handcuffed him so tightly he had blue marks on his wrists for a week. Then they left him, unattended, at the office of a psychiatrist who had wandered off for lunch. "If I was such a threat to myself," Brian said later, "why did they leave me in an unlocked office?" After waiting for an hour, Brian gave up and walked home by himself.[10]

Two weeks into the trial—after seventeen witnesses had been called—a plea bargain was struck: only one man pleaded guilty to assault causing bodily harm. He received a suspended sentence.[11] He was ordered to publish an apology to one of the victims in *Angles*, a queer Vancouver newspaper that folded in the mid-1990s.[12]

LEGAL SCHOLARSHIP ON HOMOSEXUALITY

The Edge Café incident and its shameful aftermath exposed homophobic violence on three fronts: the actual physical violence inflicted on queer victims, the secondary victimization doled out by the criminal justice system, and the symbolic violence suffered by the entire community when such acts appear to go unpunished.

Some legal scholars have attempted to explain this mysterious and sometimes debilitating process. In discussing "the legal construction of heterosexual privilege," Ryder notes that the law is mainly silent on gay and lesbian existences, except when gay men are presented as "powerful victimizers, deserving weak victims, or as the perpetrators of unmentionable indecent acts." This silencing normalizes heterosexuality and discourages queers from expecting recognition and support.[13] According to Robson, "lesbian legal theory must put lesbians in the centre of its theoretical perspective," allowing lesbians to become "the centrifugal force around which all else is problematized."[14]

Stychin contends that students of common law are routinely taught to slot legal problems within specific, essentialized categories; "however, queer theory underscores the contingency and contestability of categories—that there is nothing natural about them."[15] He analyses the infamous British case *R v. Brown*. In 1993, five gay male adults involved in consensual sadomasochist acts in a private home were convicted of assault causing bodily harm, even though there had been no complaints to police and no permanent injuries had been suffered. The gay men's "uncontrolled and unregulated need for sexualised violence"[16] came out in the appeal. One judge referred to "legalised buggery, now a well-known vehicle for the transmission of AIDS."[17]

Stychin explains how Canada's Charter of Rights and Freedoms, when "viewed through the lens of postmodernism," allows new legal, political and cultural identities to broaden and deepen "along sexual lines." In contrast, in the United States, "distinctions in law based on sexual orientation in general have been upheld as 'rational' and not subjected to rigorous judicial examination."[18] Backer notes that in 1996 there were more than two hundred constitutional challenges to sodomy statutes in the United States. Twenty-three states continued to criminalize sodomy[19] until 2003, when the laws forbidding it were finally struck down by the U.S. Supreme Court.[20] *Bowers*[21]—an unsuccessful 1986 Supreme Court challenge of American sodomy laws—was supposed to be a cut-and-dried test case involving two adult men who had consensual sex in a private home. Instead, the Court was confronted with "images of predators and pedophiles, of whores and defilers."[22]

By 2003, Canadian queer activists were celebrating their recently won right to marry; however, many were unaware of the multitude of Canadian statutes that regulate homosexuality. Kinsman points out that Pierre Trudeau's famous line—"the state has no place in the bedrooms of the nation"—was "widely misunderstood as legalizing homosexual sex." The reforms of 1969 simply allowed two consenting adults over the age of twenty-one to have sex in private. In fact, gay sex actually began to be targeted more intensively, using some of the laws described by Kinsman and Cossman:

- Anal sex (Section 159 of the *Criminal Code*) is technically illegal in Canada for people under eighteen, even though the age of consent for penis–vagina sex is fourteen in most circumstances.[23] It's legal for three or more people to get together and have sex, "as long as there is no anal penetration." Although this discriminatory law was challenged in Ontario, "the law is still on the books and remains enforceable in other provinces."
- Indecent acts (Section 173 of the Code) are never defined, although courts have agreed that they are linked to a "community standard of tolerance." Cossman explains that this section has been used to control many different sex acts, including oral sex, anal sex, masturbation, exhibitionism, lap dancing, and sexual touching. These activities are not usually regulated in private homes, but what about strip clubs? In this grey zone, there is more ambiguity: owners and performers "are at risk of being charged with indecent acts or indecent theatrical performances," and bathhouse owners risk charges "if there's any hint of sex occurring outside of a locked cubicle."

- Owners of these clubs and bathhouses—where police have deemed that indecent acts occur on a regular basis—can be charged with running a common bawdy house (Sections 197 and 210 of the Code). Patrons can be charged with being found in a common bawdy house.[24]

Some heterosexuals believe there is a double-standard at work. Perhaps they are unaware of the extent to which queers have been regulated by these laws. In the late 1990s, Montreal undercover police, equipped with a hidden camera, arrested heterosexuals at a swingers' club. After his conviction, a club owner grumbled: "The gays, they do whatever they want. But hetero people, they can't do what they want? It's a joke."[25]

HOMOPHOBIC LEGAL PRACTICES IN CANADA

In the courtroom, queer issues can ruffle feathers. In Milton, Ontario, potential jurors were questioned about homosexuality prior to one trial; around 20 per cent admitted they wouldn't be able to view the case fairly.[26] An American survey of 1,012 potential jurors found that "gays and lesbians who are parties in a trial are at least three times as likely to face a biased jury as a person who is white, African-American, Hispanic or Asian."[27] During a California civil trial, a gay defendant's lawyers set up a mock trial that included jurors whose demographics matched the local jury pool. The mock jurors' deep-seated homophobia was rampant: they found against the defendant. Later, so did the trial jury.[28]

In 1993, an Ottawa jury consisting of one man and eleven women acquitted a man accused of killing Benoit Villeneuve, a male prostitute.[29] The *Ottawa Citizen* said the trial "provided a glimpse into the sordid subculture of homelessness, drug addiction and gay prostitution."[30] Villeneuve's body was found four months after his death, buried in a steamer trunk under his house.[31] The defence lawyer, congratulating himself after the victory, said he had tried for an all-woman jury: "Nothing is scientific," he said, "but because of the homosexual overtones in this case, women are less likely to be homophobic than men."[32]

Canadian queers face subtle forms of discrimination in the courtroom. Casswell points out that nearly twenty years ago, it was decided that evidence of the accused's homosexuality should only be raised if it has sufficient similarity to the circumstances of the evidence alleged.[33] However, lawyers have found other ways of labelling the defendant: Have you ever been married? Do you live with men? Do you think this boy is handsome?[34]

In Canada, judges and prosecutors have been known to downplay the homophobia inherent in some hate crimes. MacDougall notes that "the judge might even blame the target for his homosexuality causing the 'natural' reaction of a 'normal' person."[35] A classic case of blaming the victim occurred in 1997 at the Vancouver pride celebrations. "Sister C"—a beloved drag queen (alias Mr. Johnson), who wears a nun's habit—was assaulted on Denman Street. A group of gay men surrounded the suspect, named "Mr. Jolicoeur," until police arrived. The judge dismissed the charges, noting that

> there's also a misunderstanding perhaps on Mr. Johnson's part as to what Mr. Jolicoeur intended with his homophobic comments ... Mr. Jolicoeur was simply speaking in frustration ... It's clear that Mr. Johnson, in wearing a nun's robe, upset Mr. Jolicoeur ... so without any intention of doing that ... Mr. Johnson upset Mr. Jolicoeur and, I would guess probably upset a lot of other people ... I would have to say that Mr. Johnson was perhaps insensitive of the sexual proclivities of others and perhaps Mr. Jolicoeur was hypersensitive about that.[36]

The courts exhibit lenience in other ways. For example, a teenager who knifed three men in Ottawa was charged with attempted murder. The judge chose not to raise the youth to adult court, saying that he came from a good home—even though, as MacDougall notes, he had been "exposed to and participated in a variety of street crime and activities such as ... 'rolling queers' ... The profundity of the homophobia was ignored."[37]

In Toronto, Hugh Conroy, who was HIV-positive, brought Robert Moyer home from a pub. Moyer beat and robbed him. Conroy's sister said the victim "never regained his spirit and his health rapidly deteriorated." He died a year after the attack. The Crown seemed surprised: "We didn't know he wouldn't be around for the trial, so we did not ask him all the things we might have." Since there was nobody to contradict Moyer's version, the Crown agreed to a sixty-day sentence, to be served on weekends.[38]

If a wife-beater were sentenced to work at a battered women's shelter, a hue and cry would be heard from coast to coast. But in Saskatoon, when a man on the dance floor of a gay night-club punched a man whom he claimed had come onto him, his sentence was thirty hours of community work at the local gay and lesbian centre.[39] The activist I interviewed waxed philosophical. Instead of emphasizing the importance of maintaining spaces that are safe from queer-bashers, she felt the basher should be exposed to the queer community—so that his attitude toward us would change.

The question of community service also surfaced after a Ryerson student bashed a gay man on Church Street in 1991. Judge Harris wrote a thirty-nine-page judgment that compared gay-bashers to Nazis and Ku Klux Klan members. He also asked one of the victims what he thought the sentence should be. The victim said the basher should serve at the 519 Community Centre "to force him to see that gay men and lesbians aren't the great evil other the basher believed them to be." However, the policy of making bashers ... work at the centre was eventually reversed.[40]

In this vein, an activist for the 519 Community Centre said that jail time was not "going to teach people not to hate. We need a more creative restorative justice for queer-bashing."[41] In Port Dover, Ontario, a basher was fined $1,000, payable to "Family and Friends of Gays and Lesbians."[42] One Toronto basher was banned from living in the city.[43] However, restorative justice is sometimes ineffective. In 1996, a gay Toronto man was punched; the wound took sixteen stitches to close. The judge called the assault a "vicious and cowardly act" motivated by homophobia, but felt the two assailants were not "looking for gays to beat up." The two convicted bashers received an "alternative" sentence instead of jail time. Besides being fined more than $1,000, one was ordered to write an essay on a "famous homosexual," while the other was ordered to write about "a homosexual persecuted for his beliefs."[44]

In September 1993, three gay-bashings on a single night terrified Winnipeg residents. One of the accused incurred the wrath of the judge, who declared, "This is how Nazi Germany got started."[45] The assailant was sentenced to two years. However, Judge Huband reduced the term to seven months on appeal, writing that the accused was sorry and had dissociated himself from the others. MacDougall notes: "This is the school-of-quick-change-of-heart-on-homosexuality-come-time-for-sentencing."[46]

QUEER CRITICISMS OF THE CRIMINAL JUSTICE SYSTEM

In several cases, what first looks like lenience may simply reflect the inability of our system to address this type of violence. In one Vancouver incident, a gay man was assaulted. His friend said the police "basically told me to shut up ... I was to understand that someone could chase you down the street yelling 'fucking faggot' and as long as they did not touch you or say "I am going to physically harm you," they were not guilty of a crime."[47] The suspect was fingerprinted and released, but failed to appear in court.[48] When asked why the basher had been released, the Crown replied: "People with eight-page records are being released from this location every day."[49] One officer noted that if a separate hate-crime statute existed for hate-motivated assault, "and if we had seen that the offender had recently gay-bashed someone else, then we'd be able to keep him in."[50]

In 1994, a high-profile Toronto bashing ended in an acquittal. Ross Mulhearon and his partner Steve were outside the Second Cup cafe when a van containing six young men pulled up, followed by another car containing friends. Mulhearon said one passenger began yelling "fucking queers" from the fan, and smashed a beer bottle on the road. Mulhearon reacted: "What's your problem?" Four men jumped out and attacked the couple. Another man trying to defend them was smashed over the head with a beer bottle, and required twenty stitches. A week after the attack, 250 people gathered at the Second Cup, then marched down Yonge Street in protest.[51]

At trial, one of the accused suggested that Mulhearon had spat on the van, inciting the violence. With so many conflicting versions of the event, the accused was acquitted—which gave rise to cheering in the courtroom.[52] Mulhearon complained: "They were laughing and having fun—to them it was nothing." He wrote a play, described as "a gaybashing victim's revenge fantasy ... The attacker is kidnapped and restrained in a chair." He proposed putting on the play to raise funds for the 519, but the community group balked at the play's premise and chose not to participate.[53]

Police bend over backwards to warn communities when pedophiles arrive in town. Should the gay community be warned when a convicted basher is in their midst? Don Gunn was convicted of manslaughter for killing a gay man in 1986. In Hamilton in 1993, he assaulted another gay man at a donut shop. In a second Hamilton example, police noted that another basher, released in 1998, had "accosted and robbed a 72 year old male. Smith has 7 prior convictions for robbery, some of which were related to gay bashing type robberies."[54] In 2004, Toronto police issued a warning after a twenty-seven-year-old man failed to return to a Toronto halfway house. He was described as a predator known to frequent the Church-Wellesley area.[55]

A man with fifty convictions to his name used classified ads as his modus operandi. After moving in with gay men, he would rob them. He held a knife to the throat of a Toronto businessman, demanding cash. After his arrest, the man bragged to police about his victim. The judge commented: "He takes pride and justifies his criminal activities by replying ... that [the victim is] 'just a fag' ... and that type of thinking has to stop."[56] But what, if anything, did the criminal justice system do to prevent this violence from recurring?

KILLERS WHO GET OFF EASY

In certain trials, procedural issues emerged—either during the investigation or in court—that possibly allowed killers to either go free or plead down. In 1990, James Gee was charged with killing his apartment building manager, Gerald May, in a Vancouver suburb. Gee claimed that May had come onto him. The charges were stayed after the police breached Gee's rights. His girlfriend told an undercover officer she helped cover up Gee's involvement after Gee beat, stabbed, and robbed the victim.[57]

A killer in Ottawa also beat a murder charge. This killing occurred after Garth Balderston met Ian Anderson in a bar. Apparently they walked to a nearby park, where Balderston was beaten to death and robbed of his ring. Some friends said that Anderson bragged about beating a gay man in a park and showed them a stolen ring.[58] In all, Anderson hired and fired six lawyers. One lawyer told the judge that "the accused is admitting his acts caused the death," but this comment—which the jury never heard—was stricken from the record. Anderson was convicted of manslaughter.[59]

Did a procedural error allow a twenty-three-year old man in a Calgary restaurant to "get away with murder"? In 1994, Robert Carolan, who was extremely drunk, went to the washroom, where he claimed that a fifty-three-year-old man made a pass at him. The audio track on the in-store camera at the front of the restaurant recorded thirty-two blows being struck. The victim went into a coma. Carolan was later arrested on the street with blood on his boots.[60] When the Crown tried to introduce the videotape as evidence, the judge refused, stating that "any attempt to colour the events and inflame the court in this fashion is totally improper." I noticed in the case headnote that the victim had "subsequently died of respiratory failure."[61]

When I called the Crown's office to see whether the victim had indeed died, I was assured that the victim could *not* have died; otherwise, they would have raised the charge to manslaughter or murder. I then called the Calgary police to see whether anyone on the force was responsible for following up to see whether crime victims had died from their injuries. A deputy chief told me there was no particular person responsible for this task. This means that some assailants—and not just queer-bashers—may only face aggravated assault charges even after their victims die.[62] In a sad, ironic twist, Carolan's eight-year sentence for aggravated assault was probably more severe than he would have received for manslaughter.

A series of administrative errors may have actually caused the murder of Mario Desrosiers, who met Gregory Hanson in Montreal in the summer of 1994. "They were always together," a detective said afterwards.[63] Police seemed unaware that Hanson was wanted for violent crimes in California and British Columbia. One report said Hanson "engineered a daring escape from a BC prison on the back of a garbage truck" in May 1994.[64] He was arrested in Montreal two months later for assaulting a policewoman and possessing a gun used in a robbery. Montreal police apparently didn't realize they were dealing with an escaped convict—they let him out on $500 bail with an order to appear in court 23 August, 1994. By then, Hanson had met and killed Desrosiers.[65]

The two were in Gatineau, apparently planning an armed robbery. Hanson, afraid that Desrosiers would inform police, strangled him with a belt.[66] Hanson was arrested at Ottawa's airport on 18 August with Desrosiers's ID and possessions and a one-way ticket to Fiji. However, Hanson was in jail for two months before police eventually made a connection between him and Desrosiers. That was because friends didn't report Desrosiers missing for a few weeks. The victim's body was finally discovered, months later, buried behind the Hull police station.[67] Hanson pleaded guilty to second-degree murder, with no possibility of parole for thirteen years.[68]

KILLERS ON PAROLE

Many gay men have been killed by men who drifted into the gay community after being released from prison. In 1992, Terry Fitzsimmons married a Kingston woman while still in prison for killing a fellow prisoner. Within days of being released, he moved in with another woman, stole $10,000 in jewelry, and disappeared into Toronto's gay scene. He teamed up with "travel agent and sometime prostitute" Don Hebert, who became smitten. During a six-day crime spree in 1993 that spanned three cities, Fitzsimmons, twenty-nine, killed three men—including two gay men.

Hebert, who was HIV-positive, fancied himself and Fitzsimmons as the "first gay Bonnie and Clyde"—even though Fitzsimmons denied being gay. Both were coke addicts, and they held up the same Toronto bank twice to support their habit. The pair met up with Norman Rasky, sixty-two, a dentist with a crack habit,[69] who moved in with them[70] after being evicted for not paying rent.[71] While Fitzsimmons was high, he stabbed and bludgeoned Rasky repeatedly, with Hebert looking on. They left the body in the basement of the apartment building and fled to Montreal. They ran out of money, killed a taxi driver, then headed for Ottawa.[72]

After Rasky's body was found in Toronto, a homicide detective insisted that the killing of Rasky "had nothing to do with his sexual orientation. It wasn't gay bashing."[73] Toronto police appealed to the gay community to help them find the pair: "Mr. Fitzsimmons is described as 5-feet-7, 153 pounds, with numerous tattoos on both arms and chest. Mr. Hebert is 5-feet-10 with a dark mustache, a three-inch scar on the right side of his neck, and a tattoo of the Canadian flag on his right shoulder. Police believe the two men have shaved their heads to disguise their identity."[74]

On their last night of freedom, the two were seen wearing identical Blue Jays shirts at an Ottawa gay bar.[75] They ended up in an abandoned restaurant on Bank Street. Fitzsimmons said Hebert told him he couldn't bear the thought of going [to] jail for the previous murders. Fitzsimmons then strangled Hebert with a T-shirt, "injected two vials of his friend's tainted blood into his own veins," and "plunged a butcher blade through Hebert's heart." After calling 911, Fitzsimmons injected cocaine, then walked into a police station and told the receptionist: "It's got to stop. I'm tired of killing people."

Fitzsimmons claimed that he and Hebert had made a suicide pact: he didn't want Herbert "to rot away because of AIDS. It was almost like a brotherhood of the doomed."[76] Fitzsimmons said he wanted to die by Hebert's blood and spoke glowingly of "the best friend I ever had."[77] However, he wanted to correct "erroneous news reports about his relationship with Hebert" because "it makes a difference in the way you're treated in prison."[78] At sentencing, Fitzsimmons's lawyer argued that the death was the result of "spontaneous combustion, brought on by drugs, years of sensory deprivation in prison and an unsympathetic parole officer." The judge said the murder resulted from a "depraved mind" and sentenced him to sixteen years before the possibility of parole.[79] Fitzsimmons killed himself in 1995.[80]

Another killer on parole was Michael McGray, who grabbed headlines in 2000 after claiming to be Canada's worst serial killer. In 1991, he spent a homicidal weekend in Montreal while on a three-day Easter pass from a Quebec minimum-security prison. McGray said he was one of his father's "favorites" when it came to beatings, and that guards had sexually abused him at a boy's home in Nova Scotia.[81] He described "how hard it is to strangle a person, how he liked to kill when he was not drinking or using drugs, 'so he could enjoy it.'" He said he was not gay, but he observed: "It was just unbelievable how easy they tried to take you home, a total stranger."[82]

Police in Saint John linked McGray to the 1986 stabbing of a gay man, James Lloyd Beyea, nicknamed "Fluff."[83] He also pleaded guilty to first-degree murder in the 1991 killings of Robert Assaly, fifty-nine—a retired schoolteacher from the Lebanese Christian community—and Gaetan Ethier, forty-five, an unemployed salesman. In McGray's version of events, he met Assaly in the Gay Village over a few drinks and went back to Assaly's condo. McGray bludgeoned him with a lamp, stabbed him sixteen times, then left to find his next victim. Assaly's brother discovered the body a week later.

Back in the village, McGray then met Ethier, who also invited the killer back to his place. McGray recounted that after Ethier was asleep, he smashed a beer bottle over his head and stabbed him. McGray left Montreal and was arrested three weeks later—but only for further parole violations, not murder. It was nine years before he was linked to the Montreal murders. Robert Assaly's brother insisted that Robert was not gay, but simply working as a bartender in the village.[84] His perspective was understandable: I met a straight couple—close friends of Robert's, who taught with him—who went on lengthy overseas trips with him. They said there was never a hint that Robert was gay. And if he was, it saddened them to think that his sexual orientation was not something he felt comfortable sharing with them.

THE SOCIAL CONSTRUCTION OF HATE CRIME

Jenness points out that "legal reform is a dominant response to bias-motivated violence."[85] So far, I have demonstrated how the justice system's application of some laws—and its reluctance or failure to apply other laws—have created an environment in which homophobic violence can flourish. In this section, I focus on the movement that has constructed the term "hate crime" and created hate crime laws.

For Mason, hate crime is "a physical expression of the emotion of hate," which is "directed towards a person or persons on the basis, even if only in part, of a perceived group characteristic of that person." She recounts the story of an activist who shied away from queer-bashing because it was "not our kind of hate crime"—perhaps because the activist was not comfortable working with "queers, trannies and sex workers."[86]

Rosga deconstructs an infamous "hate crime" in Maryland known as the "burnt woman" case. She conducted interviews with the police to get the "media" version, then spoke to one of the "racist" and "misogynist" men who had committed "savagery" and "lynching." The man claimed he had many black friends and did not even realize his victim was black or a woman. He said he had been unfairly labelled a "hate-monger" by a Jewish judge whose wife had pushed through a state hate-crime law.[87]

Jacobs and Potter question the precept that hate crime is an "epidemic" in America, a precept that is "expressed over and over again by politicians, journalists, scholars." Gay and lesbian groups "have been among the most vocal proponents of the hate crime epidemic theory."[88] The authors heap scorn on Levin and McDevitt's overreliance on data obtained from advocacy groups[89] and question their central theory—that hate crimes are increasing due to "economic decline and attendant social-psychological malaise." Jacobs and Potter cite the lack of empirical evidence, "a theory in search of a problem."[90]

Jenness has authored and co-authored several analyses of hate crime legislation and the hate crime movement in the United States. She examines the Congressional hearings in the 1980s and 1990s that led to the passage of three federal hate-crime laws in the 1990s. She observes the ways in which social movement organizations "interact with policymakers' interpretive and discursive practices to give meaning to statutes as they develop and stabilize over time." Part of this process involves developing socially constructed definitions "that result in assigning victim status to some individuals and groups, but not to others."[91] The author delineates the following:

- The "claimsmakers" of each bill—"activists, politicians, social movement representatives, victims/survivors of violence."
- The "claims put forth in favor of and in opposition to" these bills.
- The way race, religion, ethnicity, sexual orientation, and gender are "characterized, described, implicated and negotiated in the process of making federal hate crime law."[92]

In the beginning, claims for race, religion, and ethnicity were made. But then "the domain of hate crime law began to expand," extending "the boundaries of the phenomenon deemed problematic." Gay and lesbian groups were "crucial in evoking and sustaining the expansion of the law." In part, they succeeded in this by comparing their violence with the hate violence that already enjoyed a certain legitimacy. Meanwhile, opponents dismissed the "militant homosexual agenda," refusing to equate homophobic violence with violence against other minorities.[93]

In another article, Jenness points out that before the term hate crime became popular, discrete minority movements politicized their own violence, albeit on a smaller scale. At the same time, an ever-growing crime victim's movement was beginning to demand "special assistance, support and rights *as crime victims.*" The conditions became ripe for the creation of an American anti-hate crime movement, which "invented the term hate crime, defined its initial properties, and demanded that lawmakers and other public policy officials recognize bias-motivated violence as a significant social problem."[94]

Three federal hate-crime laws have been passed by the U.S. Congress,[95] but these only cover hate crimes that occur on federal lands and properties:

- 1990: The Hate Crime Statistics Act.
- 1994: The Violence Against Women Act, which, although it has since been ruled unconstitutional, allocated over $1 billion for "education, rape crisis hotlines, training of justice personnel, victim services and police units."

- 1994: The Hate Crimes Sentencing Enhancement Act, which allowed judges to enhance penalties "of not less than three offence levels" for a list of eight specific offences, ranging from vandalism to murder.[96]

Jenness co-authored a book with Ryken Grattet, in which the two reflected on hate crime as "an age-old problem approached with a new conceptual lens and sense of urgency." What was once considered "ordinary crime has been parsed out, redefined, and condemned more harshly than before." Underlying this new trend is the desire to "transmit the symbolic message to society that criminal acts based on hatred will not be tolerated."[97]

The authors analyse hate crime as a "policy domain." Their focus, therefore, is less on the problem of hate crime itself, and more on the socially constructed "definitional and classification schemes." The first question of a policy domain is this: Which social actors, "for example, politicians, experts, agency officials, and interest groups ... have gained sufficient legitimacy to speak about or act upon a particular issue?" The second question: Which "cultural logics, theories, frameworks, and ideologies" are used to construct the problem and to determine the appropriate policy response?

The authors stress that policymaking is about more than just creating laws. Rather, policy "is renegotiated and redefined at multiple points." The policy domain can be traced through four overlapping phases:

- *Issue creation*, when the social problem "is recognized, named and deemed in need of a solution."
- *Solution choice*, which involves "the adoption of a particular policy solution from a range of alternatives."
- *Rule making*, at which time the exact meaning of the policy is "fleshed out."
- "*Real world*," when the rules are specified and applied by enforcement agencies.

In other words, the authors trace "how social movements constructed the problem of hate motivated violence, how politicians ... passed legislation defining the parameters of hate crime, how courts have elaborated the meaning of hate crime, and how law enforcement officials classify, investigate, and prosecute that behavior which is defined by statute as criminal."[98]

Note that the making of laws is not the final step: "Much of what constitutes a hate crime is determined by judges in the process of applying statutes to particular 'real world' situations. Over time ... they clarify precisely what the laws cover." Appellate courts play an especially crucial role; appellate judges "can elaborate or complicate the meaning of a statute, delimit its meaning and application, reject the language of particular statutes, validate or valorize others, work out deeper justifications ... and decide whether to widen the scope to include new actions." The authors analysed thirty-six constitutional challenges to hate crimes law and found that five main issues were disputed: vagueness; punishment of speech; overbreadth; speech regulation; denial of equal protection before the law.[99]

Jenness has argued elsewhere that in the courts, "equal" treatment tends to translate into "sameness"; the law cannot afford protection to one particular group without affording it to others. This is why hate crime laws do not spell out categories such as, "violence against blacks" or "violence against Jews," but instead use general terms like race and religion. As a result, a hate crime against a white person or a heterosexual is deemed to be just as serious as a crime against a Sikh or a transsexual. Although this appears to be the "right thing to do," the historical basis and meaning of hate crime is elided "by translating specific categories of persons ... into all-encompassing and seemingly neutral categories."

By clustering different varieties of hate crimes into one category, hate crime laws ensure "across-category sameness," so that "hate crimes against persons with disabilities are rendered equivalent to hate crimes against Muslims." Jenness contends that the social movements that originally galvanized these debates have been "muted." In fact, a "clear disconnect" has developed "between the origins of hate crime politics, the development of hate crime policy (i.e. the law), and the implementation of policy (i.e. law enforcement)."[100]

Jenness and Grattet found that through the process of judicial scrutiny, the "substantive meaning" of hate crime has evolved in two ways. The legal definition has become more nuanced, and courts "have consistently argued that states have a 'compelling interest' in curbing hate crime."[101] Moreover, the courts have elaborated on the extent to which the crime must be motivated by hate in order to be considered a hate crime. The tendency has been to consider bias as *a substantial factor* instead of *the sole factor*.[102]

To what extent have officials succeeded in prosecuting these crimes? The authors note that no statistics have been published because of "the newness of the criminal category." However, one way of measuring the "success" of a law is by measuring the total number of incidents reported that were actually prosecuted. Preliminary research in California indicates that the prosecution rates for hate crimes do not appear to vary wildly from overall prosecution rates.

The authors suggest another way to analyze prosecutorial success: "the proportion of hate crime filings that have led to convictions." In California, now that the system has successfully labelled certain incidents as hate crimes, the preliminary data suggest that "obtaining a conviction is no more difficult than in other crimes": "California prosecutors have increased the frequency with which they file hate crime complaints. Conviction rates and guilty pleas are increasing, which suggests that prosecutors are becoming more comfortable invoking and enforcing hate crime laws and criminal defense attorneys are less likely to effectively interfere with their doing so."[103]

HATE CRIME LEGISLATION AT HOME AND ABROAD

As I mentioned earlier, there has been an increasing tendency in the United States to criminalize hate. In Canada, however, there is still no law that makes hate-motivated violence a crime. In 2003, EGALE and other queer groups appealed to the community to support Svend Robinson's "hate-crime bill" in the House of Commons. There were several references to gay-bashing victims, leaving the public with the impression that the law would address homophobic violence. In fact, Robinson's private member's bill—Bill C-250—was created to rectify the hate propaganda law. As Roberts notes: "Some writers make no distinction between hate-motivated crime and hate propaganda."[104] Yet, the two issues are quite distinct.

Up until 2004, Sections 318 and 319 of the *Criminal Code* prohibited genocide and the spread of hatred toward other groups on the basis of their colour, race, religion, or ethnic origin—but not on the basis of their sexual orientation. For example, in 1995 a pamphlet was circulated in Winnipeg that called for the killing of homosexuals.[105] In 1997, an e-mail proclaimed: "Death to homosexuals; It's prescribed in the Bible! Better watch out next Gay Pride Week!!!" This one was signed, "Winnipeg's newly formed gay bashing patrol." The police were unable to press charges in these cases.[106]

In 1999, Robinson asked the justice minister to include sexual orientation. She said she would look into it. Two years later, she said she was still considering it. The proposed change was supported by the justice departments of all the provinces as well as by the Canadian Association of Police Boards. After Robinson introduced the bill, he complained that the religious right "flooded MPs with messages predicting apocalyptic results." He said one Alliance MP complained that "the bill could outlaw the Bible and Catholic catechism."[107] On 29 April 2004, the bill received Royal Assent.[108]

As a result of this debate, some Canadians have been left with the impression that the *Criminal Code* includes a specific statute that prohibits hate-motivated violence. In fact, it does not. The only place where the code addresses this issue is Section 718.2(a)(i), the sentencing-enhancement provisions, which give judges the option of making the penalty harsher when hate motivation can be proved beyond a reasonable doubt. There has been little discussion of the fact that these provisions are largely cosmetic and ineffective.

In his review of hate crime legislation in three countries, Roberts notes that there are three models for enhancing penalties for hate-motivated crimes. Mandatory sentencing statutes clearly spell out "a higher range, or minimum penalty for this kind of offending." Then there is appellate decision making, where appeal courts eventually determine appropriate sentences. Finally, there is the "statutory aggravating factor" model, adopted by Canada, which leaves the matter to the discretion of judges.[109] Generally speaking, the "most popular legislative response to hate crime involves … increasing the severity of the penalties imposed on offenders."[110]

In the United Kingdom, the Crime and Disorder Act (CDA) sets out a very narrow definition of hate crime. In defining racially motivated acts, for example, the CDA has created a whole new set of offences, such as racially aggravated assault and racially aggravated harassment. The CDA also "sets out a test for the court to apply." An offence is considered to be racially aggravated if "at the time of committing the offence, or immediately before or after doing so, the offender demonstrates towards the victim of the offence hostility based on the victim's membership (or presumed membership) of a racial group."

Roberts points out the advantages of this approach: the term "racially aggravated" is more nuanced than the term "racially motivated." In addition, the word "immediately" … establishes a temporal relationship" that "expands the scope of legislation beyond that which exists in other countries where the hatred must precede and precipitate the attack."[111]

The CDA clearly states that "any offence is to be punished more severely if it is found to have been racially motivated." In other words, discretion is taken out of the judges' hands. Once racial aggravation has been established beyond a reasonable doubt, the judge must factor this into his or her sentence, and furthermore, "shall state in open court that the offence is so aggravated." The CDA also spells out higher maximum penalties for racially aggravated crimes. For example, normally the maximum penalty for assault is six months. A racially motivated assault, on the other hand, could be punished by up to two years in prison.[112]

In the United States, the federal Hate Crime Statistics Act (HCSA) of 1990 had the advantage of establishing clear guidelines for the U.S. Attorney General regarding what does and does not constitute a hate crime. The HCSA's definition of a hate crime is broad; motivation can be "in whole" or "in part." As well, the HCSA sets out "a list of predicate or primary offences, including murder, non-negligent manslaughter; forcible rape; aggravated assault; simple assault; intimidation; arson; and destruction, damage or vandalism of property."[113]

The Hate Crime Sentencing Enhancement Act of 1994 specifies that "offenders convicted of hate crimes will have their offence categories 'bumped up' at least three levels." These "significantly harsher sentence lengths" are determined using a grid "in which the seriousness of the crime and the criminal history of the offender" are factored in.[114]

By 1999, more than forty American states had passed some form of hate crime legislation. Several states dole out more severe penalties by reclassifying hate-motivated crime; for example, "a felony of the second degree is punishable as if it were a felony of the first degree." In several states, hate motivation is considered "one of the aggravating circumstances which can result in the imposition of the death penalty instead of life imprisonment without parole."[115] For example, one Texas murderer was sentenced to death—instead of life in prison—after admitting that he killed his victim because he was gay.[116]

THE CANADIAN DEBATE ON HATE CRIME LEGISLATION

During the 1995 debate on Bill C-41—which introduced Section 718's sentencing enhancement provisions—Giese opined that "it doesn't actually do much to fight hate. It doesn't attack the root causes of prejudice, and it might even cause new human-rights abuses." She was alarmed at the queer community's call for blood during the trial of a basher: "Revenge—and punishment—provide a quick solution and temporary comfort to highly complex problems." Moreover, "joining the hate-crimes bandwagon has allowed the government to pretend that it's doing a lot more for minority rights than it really is."[117]

According to Jeffrey, although the media and activist groups depicted Bill C-41 as a sea change, in reality the provisions do "nothing to impair the wide discretion of judges to decide the weight to be attached to each factor when deciding sentencing." Whether the provisions have any impact whatsoever is unclear "since judges are not even obliged to cite the new provision when pronouncing sentence."[118]

There is surprisingly little academic debate in Canada about this issue. Shaffer wrote an article on the inadequacy of Bill C-41 just as it was being enacted. She argues forcefully for a separate hate-crime statute to recognize "that such violence constitutes a specific form of harm,"[119] since certain criminal laws play "a normative or symbolic role in instructing citizens about the types of conduct that give rise to social disapprobation." This separate hate-crime statute would allow for a more accurate statistical mapping of hate crimes since, at present, "in the course of plea bargaining the Crown and the defence sometimes agree to omit motive from the attention of the trial judge."[120]

Shaffer also asks why some governments are eager to adopt hate crime laws, an "easy way for the government to claim that it is addressing a social problem." Such a tack is relatively inexpensive and generates "considerable media attention, as do trials conducted under hate-crime provisions. The publicity provides the government with free political mileage"—in a way that less glamorous, grassroots education does not.[121]

Since criminal law reform does not usually create genuine social change, Shaffer believes the powers of the sentencing provisions are largely "illusory." Judges are under no obligation to use the sentencing guidelines. And even if they do, they do not have to explain the degree to which the sentence was increased because of aggravating hate factors.[122] On the whole, Shaffer feels that Canada would be better off adopting specific American-style hate crime laws.[123]

In my research, I analysed well over one hundred queer-bashing cases that had occurred since Canada's sentencing enhancement bill was enacted in 1995. None of the media reports describing these cases ever indicated that the enhancement guidelines had been applied.

Relative to the United States and Britain, Canada's sentencing enhancement provisions are quite vague: Section 718 specifies that the sentence should "reflect" the aggravating hate factors, but Roberts asks: "How much should this aggravate the severity of the sentence imposed? No direction is given, and the maximum penalty remains the same. The maximum penalty for assault (s. 266) is five years in prison, regardless of whether there was a component of hate motivation or not."[124] Roberts concludes that Section 718 reflects "a rather muted response from Canada … There is no evidence" that the section "has changed the way judges respond to persons convicted of hate-motivated crime."[125]

DOES ENHANCED SENTENCING REALLY WORK?

The head of the Toronto Police Service Hate Crime Unit seems to corroborate Roberts's assessment: he told me that in his experience, no gay-bashers had ever been handed a more severe sentence under Section 718. The only hate crime on his watch that garnered an enhanced sentence involved a skinhead who attacked a black victim on a streetcar, shouting, "White power!" He was arrested with a racist manifesto in his pocket; police discovered he was involved with hate websites. Instead of getting a conditional sentence, he got five months.[126]

In one woeful Toronto incident—the assaults on dentist Ed Pollak and his partner—the judge refused to call it a gay-bashing. In 1993, a car bore down on the couple in the gay ghetto;

after they jumped out of the way, four men bailed out of the car. Pollak's lip was split in four places, requiring stitches. He also lost a tooth and required two root canals.[127] His partner was kicked in the head fifteen times with boots.[128] Witnesses got the car's licence number, but police took forty-five minutes to arrive. They didn't ask whether it was a hate crime, and didn't even ask them if they needed an ambulance. "They couldn't wait to get out of there," Pollak said.[129]

Three young men from the Hamilton area eventually went on trial. One admitted to asking the victims what they were looking at, but he and another defendant said they were acting in "self-defence," while the third said he was trying to break things up. An independent witness testified he heard someone yell "Fags!" Yet the accused denied it was a gay-bashing.[130] Another independent witness was walking his dogs and "saw a man being punched and kicked, while huddled against a wall, protecting himself."[131]

Although the judge felt that "hate played a role" in the assault, he declined to call it a "gay bashing."[132] Only two of the men were convicted; each was sentenced to six months and two years' probation. However, the pair served only ten days in jail before being released on $10,000 bail. Both the Crown and the defence appealed the sentences. The Ontario Court of Appeal agreed that the assault was not motivated by the victim's sexual orientation. The sentences of the accused were reduced to six months conditional, with no probation.[133]

Pollak killed himself three months before the appeal was held. Shortly before his death, he admitted that "a portion of my freedom has been taken away for life … By speaking out about what happened, it's given me power."[134] But a former coordinator of Toronto's Anti-Violence Program complained: "Increased sentencing provisions don't work. The judges don't want to use it. I don't think the criminal justice system in any way meets the needs of bashing victims—they are not heard or acknowledged."[135]

LEGAL REMEDIES FOR VICTIMS

There are many different paths that queer-bashing victims can take in the pursuit of justice. Jeffery has written an important handbook that spells out clearly the many ways Canadian hate-crime victims can seek legal redress. For example, under section 737(3) of the *Criminal Code*, judges may order the offender to pay restitution as a parole condition, even though one survey showed that restitution was ordered only six times out of 4,294 appearances by offenders—that is, less than 0.1 per cent of the time.[136] Besides the more obvious charges (assault, sexual assault, attempted murder, and so on), there may be other applicable statutes:

- The *torture* provisions (s. 269.1) provide a penalty of up to fourteen years to persons "acting under the authority of a public official" who intentionally inflict "severe physical or mental pain or suffering, for the purposes of intimidating, coercing, punishing or extracting information from the victim or a third person."[137]
- Gangs who swarm their victims can be charged with *criminal harassment* (s. 264), *intimidation*, or *watching and besetting* (s. 423).
- Threats over the phone can result in charges involving *indecent or harassing phone calls* (s. 372) or *uttering threats* (s. 264.1).
- Harassing phone calls can also be pursued under Section 13 of the *Canadian Human Rights Act*.[138]
- Queer-bashers who demonstrate "a persistent pattern of sexually or physically violent behaviour" and who are "likely to cause death, physical injury or to inflict severe psychological damage on other persons in the future" may also be declared *dangerous offenders*.[139]

Unfortunately, queer victims cannot always rely on the state to investigate and prosecute these crimes. As I describe in the next chapter, dozens of Montreal police were recorded on camera beating queer protestors—but apparently nobody was convicted under the *Criminal Code*.

In some cases, private prosecutions may be the only way to achieve justice. Although the procedures require considerable legal expertise, time, and financial resources, they can have a huge impact, by bolstering subsequent litigation and creating public outrage.[140] For example, Jewish groups spearheaded a private prosecution against Ernst Zundel for "wilfully spreading false news." The state eventually took over the case and appealed it all the way to the Supreme Court of Canada. This generated a broad public debate about anti-Semitism in Canada.

Queer-bashing victims are eligible for compensation, which is administered by the provinces. Although compensation is relatively easy to apply for, there are many disadvantages to it. In 1998, Jeffery noted that the average award in Ontario was only $5,000. Lump sums were capped at $25,000, and at $1,000 for periodic payments. Applications had to be filed within a year of the crime, and the whole procedure could take up to three years to conclude. In addition, the payments affected welfare, insurance payouts, and disability pensions.[141]

Victims can file with quasi-independent police complaints commissions. In some provinces, including Ontario, these commissions have been abolished; police chiefs are now responsible for handling these complaints. In Brian Nolan's case, detailed in the previous chapter, the Newfoundland officers were eventually charged. However, all the police got was "a slap on the wrist … One got a 14-day suspension, while one got a ten-day suspension. But they wouldn't even offer an apology."[142]

Compensation handed out by human rights commissions generally has a low ceiling: "Often, defendants who recognize that there is little likelihood of being subject to a formal tribunal hearing will not make any genuine attempts at settlement in the hopes that the commission will simply abandon the case."[143] Provincial human rights commissions and their federal counterpart encourage both sides to resolve their disputes through mediation. Only a fraction of complaints are referred to a tribunal—the mechanism that has the power to order financial awards and other measures. The Canadian Human Rights Tribunal can order the respondent to pay a maximum of $20,000 for pain and suffering—although that respondent may also be ordered to pay for expenses incurred.[144]

Brian Nolan noted with some bitterness that the Newfoundland and Labrador Human Rights Commission is "very officious and bureaucratic, and decided that I had no case … Seven months after the incident, they phoned and said I hadn't filed the claim in time and so my claim was cancelled, even though I had walked in the door the Monday after the incident and gave them the information … It went back and forth and back and forth; after two years I was so frustrated. I thought, 'Why am I going through all this when they can't enforce anything?' … By this time I was exhausted by the whole thing. You can only do it for so long."[145]

According to Jeffery, litigation is "expensive, time-consuming and stressful to plaintiffs." Although many perpetrators of hate crimes are youths with limited financial resources, successful lawsuits can financially cripple or bankrupt perpetrators and organizations that would otherwise be untouched by the law. Since these are intentional torts, it is not necessary to prove physical harm: "The mere threat of harm is sufficient to constitute assault." These actions "empower the victim to direct and define the issues, the burden of proof is less onerous, and the plaintiff can receive compensatory damages and possibly punitive damages."[146]

In cases of assault, swarming, sexual assault, intimidation, and harassing phone calls, recognized grounds for civil action include the following: negligence, assault, battery, trespass to person, intentional infliction of mental suffering, and wrongful imprisonment.[147] However, substantial punitive-damage awards—in the event of harsh, vindictive, reprehensible, and malicious behaviour—are rare. As of 1996, there had only been four in excess of

$100,000 in Canadian legal history.[148] Moreover, to avoid the principle of double-punishment, punitive damages are not awarded when offenders have been sentenced in criminal court. However, this rule has been held not to apply where the defendant has received a conditional discharge.

Another option for queer-bashing victims is a class action, which is "a legal suit initiated by a representative on behalf of herself and other people who have suffered similar harm due to the same act or omission … They allow for a large number of victims to obtain redress in situations where no single individual could afford to sue on his or her own."[149]

Jeffrey notes: "Class actions remain poorly understood and under-used tools for achieving group restitution under appropriate circumstances." They are essentially "an alternative means of law enforcement and private compensation" because they promote deterrence. In addition, they level an economic penalty on people or organizations that would normally escape the law. Since preliminary procedures are costly and very time-consuming, only people with ready access to lawyers can consider this option. However, most provinces provide an advance to cover initial costs.

The legal remedies listed above provide all the more reason for a national organization to be established that would help victims take a stand against queer-bashers—and the laws, policies, and institutions that fail to protect us from them.[150]

SUMMARY

Homophobia is reproduced in a myriad of legal practices that minimize, rationalize, and even negate homophobic violence. Sometimes, in the case of procedural or administrative errors, the homophobia appears to be "unintentional." However, these errors have led to situations in which queers have been killed; killers have also gone free or had their charges reduced.

"Hate crime" is a relatively new social construct that reframes an ages-old problem. According to Jenness, hate crime legislation develops through a process whereby victim status is assigned to certain groups but not to others. Recent research examines which social actors "speak for" queer victims, and which discourses they use to frame the issues and develop policy positions.

Despite the proliferation of American hate-crime legislation and academic research, Canadian debate has been mainly limited to questions about the hate crime sentencing provisions and hate crime propaganda. Little evidence has emerged to indicate that the provisions have been effective. This book includes hundreds of examples of assaults and murders that occurred in Canada after 1995—the year the hate crime sentencing provisions came into effect. Yet I have found almost no reports confirming that judges have increased sentences for queer-bashers. This would seem to corroborate Shaffer's contention in 1995 that these provisions are ineffective and that a separate hate-crime statute is needed.

QUESTIONS TO CONSIDER

1. Outline some of the limitations discussed by Janoff when GLBTQ (gay, lesbian, bisexual, transgendered, questioning) individuals are assaulted, ostensibly based on their sexual orientation.

2. Discuss several specific areas identified by Janoff in which victims of hate crimes are denied their rights. Outline how Janoff wishes to remedy them. Also discuss the extent to which you agree or disagree with his arguments.

3. Critically assess whether interpersonal violence, as set out in this chapter, may be especially severe when it involves a gay or lesbian victim. What evidence is there for similar degrees of hatefulness and lethality for individuals who are not GLBTQ?

SUGGESTIONS FOR FURTHER READING/VIEWING

Daniels, D. (2009). *Polygendered and ponytailed: The dilemma of femininity and the female athlete*. Toronto: Canadian Scholars' Press and Women's Press.

Dauvergne, M., Scrim, K., & Brennan, S. (2008). *Hate crime in Canada, 2006*. Ottawa: Statistics Canada, Canadian Centre for Justice Statistics.

Sinclair, E. (Writer, Director), & Weis, N. (Producer). *Gloriously free*. (2004). [Documentary, 47 min.]. Canada: Filmblanc in association with Omni TV.

Lafferty, L. (2007). Religion, sexual orientation and the state: Can public officials refuse to perform same-sex marriage? *Canadian Bar Review, 85*, 287–316.

Moore, D., & Rennie, A. M. (2006). Hated identities: Queers and Canadian anti-hate legislation. *Canadian Journal of Criminology and Criminal Justice*, 823–836.

Smyth, M. A. (2006). Queers and provocateurs: Hegemony, ideology, and the 'homosexual advance' defense. *Law and Society Review, 40*(4), 903–930.

NOTES

1. Kevin Griffin, "Publicize Gay-Bashing, Activist Tells Police," *Vancouver Sun*, 14 May 1994, A7.
2. Kevin Griffin, "Gays Fight Back after Attack in Coffee Bar," *Vancouver Sun*, 11 May 1994, A2.
3. Douglas Victor Janoff, "Gay-bashing in Vancouver: A Case Study," (unpublished paper, 1995), 6.
4. Griffin, "Gays Fight Back."
5. Elizabeth Aird, "Queer Patrol Doesn't Have Limp Wrist, Only Needed Muscle," *Vancouver Sun*, 11 June 1994, A3.
6. Doug Barr, "Hate Season Kickoff," *Angles* (May 1994): 1.
7. Janoff, "Gay-bashing in Vancouver," 7–8.
8. Ibid., 6.
9. Ibid., 10–11.
10. Ibid., 8–9.
11. Raj Takhar, "Attack on Gays Draws Sentence," *West End Times*, 10 May 1996, 7.
12. Raj Takhar, "Basher Pleads Guilty," *Angles* (May 1996): 1.
13. Bruce Ryder, "Straight Talk: Male Heterosexual Privilege," *Queen's Law Journal* 16 (1991): 294–5.
14. Ruthann Robson, "Convictions: Theorizing Lesbians and Criminal Justice," Didi Herman and Carl Stychin, eds., *Legal Inversions: Lesbians, Gay Men and the Law* (Philadelphia: Temple University Press, 1995), 191.
15. Carl Stychin, *Law's Desire* (New York: Routledge, 1995), 148.
16. *R. v. Brown*, [1993] 2 All ER 75 (HL), cited in ibid., 129.
17. Ibid., 137.
18. Ibid., 102–3.
19. Larry Backer, "Constructing a 'Homosexual' for Constitutional Theory: Sodomy Narrative, Jurisprudence and Antipathy in the U.S. and Britain," *Tulane Law Review* 71 (Dec. 1996): 563–4.
20. Associated Press, "Gay Sex Ban Struck Down by US Supreme Court," *Globe and Mail* website. 26 June 2003. www.globeandmail.ca/servlet/story/RTGAM.20030626.wgsex0626/BNStory.html.
21. *Bowers v. Hardwick*, 478 U.S. 186 (1986).
22. Backer, "Constructing a 'Homosexual,'" 592.
23. Gary Kinsman, "History," *Capital Xtra*, 17 July 2003, 13. [The age of consent to sex in Canada was increased from 14 to 16 years, beginning May 1, 2008. This initiative was meant to protect children from sexual exploitation by adults who are several years older, including those who are "in a position of trust or authority towards the younger person". The legislation allows for a "close-in-age" provision such that youth who are close-in-age can consent to sexual relations under some circumstances. See Legal Information Society of Nova Scotia, http://www.legalinfo.org/news/latest/age-of-consent-to-sex-goes-up.html (Accessed online June 29, 2009).]
24. Brenda Cossman, "Sex Law," *Capital Xtra*, 19 June 2003, 15.
25. James Mennie, "Montreal Judge Rules Swingers Clubs Legal, but Not Orgies," *Ottawa Citizen*, 6 July 2003, G5.
26. Canadian Press, "Judge Lets Potential Jurors Be Queried on Gay Bias," *Canadian Press Newswire*, 11 Oct. 1996.

27. Peter Aronson, David E. Rovella, and Bob Van Voris, "Jurors: A Biased, Independent Lot." *National Law Journal*, 2 Nov. 1998, A1.

28. Drury Sherrod and Peter Nardi, "Homophobia in the Courtroom: An Assessment of Biases Against Gay Men and Lesbians in a Multiethnic Sample of Potential Jurors," In Gregory Herek, ed., *Stigma and Sexual Orientation: Understanding Prejudice against Lesbians, Gay Men and Bisexuals* (Thousand Oaks, CA: Sage 1998), 24–5.

29. Mike Blanchfield, "Murder Denials Just 'tall tales,'" *Ottawa Citizen*, 9 Dec. 1994, B7.

30. Mike Blanchfield, "Jury Surprises Court with Acquittal in Steamer Trunk Killing," *Ottawa Citizen*, 17 Dec. 1994, A1.

31. Mike Blanchfield, "Crown Claims 'Sex' Angle in Steamer Trunk Killing," *Ottawa Citizen*, 14 Dec. 1994, D11.

32. Mike Blanchfield, "Murder Denials," B7.

33. *R. v. Gendreau* (1980), 33 Man. R. (2d) 245 (CA), cited in Donald Casswell, *Lesbians, Gay Men and Canadian Law* (Toronto: Emond Montgomery, 1996), 616.

34. See *R. v. Wilson* (1990), 59 CCC (3d) 432 (BCCA), cited in ibid., 609.

35. Bruce MacDougall, *Queer Judgments: Homosexuality; Expression, and the Courts in Canada*, (Toronto: University of Toronto Press, 2000), 259–60.

36. *R. v. Jolicoeur* (1997), unreported, BC Prov. Cr., 7 Feb., cited in Garth Barriere, "Asking for Trouble?" *Xtra West*, 18 Sept. 1997, 17.

37. *R. v. M. (D.J.)*, [1990] OJ No. 514 (QL) (Prov. Ct.-Youth Off. Ct.); appeal dismissed, 61 CCC (3d) 129 (OCA), cited in MacDougall, *Queer Judgments*, 173.

38. Colin Leslie, "Life Cut Short?" *Xtra?* 17 April 1992, 11.

39. Interview with local activist, 13 July 1999.

40. MacDougall, *Queer Judgments*, 175; and Lara Bradley, "Educate the Enemy." *Xtra* 17 Dec. 1998, 11.

41. Interview, 26 May 1999.

42. Canadian Press, "Gay-Basher in Court," *Vancouver Province*, 15 Dec. 1999, A30.

43. Colin Leslie, "Tenant Accused in Second Bashing," *Xtra*. 3 April 1992, 1; Colin Leslie, "Accused Basher Banned," *Xtra*, 17 April 1992, 11.

44. Wendy Darroch, "Pair Who Beat Man Ordered to Write Essays on Gays," *Toronto Star*, 31 July 1996, A18; Alisa Craig, "A Bashing or a Simple Assault?" *Xtra!* 23 May 1996, 18.

45. Kevin Rollason, "High Court Reduces Gay-Bash Sentence," *Winnipeg Free Press*, 14 June 1994.

46. *R. v. Gallant* (1994), 95 Man. R. (2d) 296 (CA); MacDougall, *Queer Judgments*, 174.

47. Letter, 13 April 1999.

48. Interview with VPD officer, 13 May 1999.

49. Gareth Kirkby, "Police, Crown Give Run-Around," *Xtra West*. 12 Nov 1998, 10.

50. Interview with VPD officer, 13 May 1999.

51. Bruce DeMara, "Don't Be Afraid, Gay-Bashing Victims Say," *Toronto Star*, 23 Oct. 1994, A15.

52. Gretchen Drummie, "Man Acquitted in Gay Bashing," *Toronto Sun*, 28 Oct. 1995, 28.

53. Glenn Sumi, "Playing with the Truth," *Xtra!* 18 Aug. 1995, 32.

54. "History: Violence against the Gay/Lesbian/Transgendered Community" report prepared by the Community Relations Coordinator, Hamilton-Wentworth Regional Police, 28 May 1999.

55. Julia Garro, "Armed and Dangerous," *Xtra*, 22 Jan. 2004, 13.

56. *R. v. McDonald*, [1995] OJ No. 2137 (QL) (Ont. Prov. Ct. Gen. Div.); Sam Pazzano, "Robber Who Preyed on Gay Men Jailed," *Toronto Sun*, 10 Jan. 1995, 22.

57. Larry Still, "Burnaby Woman Given Unusual Accessory Conviction," *Vancouver Sun*, 31 May 1991, A1.

58. Sean Upton, "Reaction of Dead Man's Lover 'Odd,' Court Told," *Ottawa Citizen*, 26 March 1994, C5.

59. Mike Blanchfield, "Ottawa Man Convicted in Beating of Gay Man," *Ottawa Citizen*, 31 March 1994, B7.

60. *R. v. Carolan* (1995), 163 AR 238 (Alta. Prov Ct.) 239, at para. 8; interview with Crown attorney's office, Calgary, 29 June 1999.

61. *R. v. Carolan.*

62. Interview, 1 July 1999.

63. Tony Lofaro, "Gatineau Death Suspect Nabbed by Ottawa RCMP," *Ottawa Citizen*, 21 Oct. 1994, B8.

64. Mike Shahin, "Escaper Gets Life in Prison for Murder of Montreal Man," *Ottawa Citizen*, 18 Jan. 1995, B2.

65. Tony Lofaro, "Gatineau Death Suspect Nabbed by Ottawa RCMP," *Ottawa Citizen*, 21 Oct. 1994, B8.

66. Shahin, "Escaper Gets Life."

67. Lofaro, "Gatineau Death Suspect Nabbed."

68. Shahin, "Escaper Gets Life."

69. Eleanor Brown, "Suspects Arrested," *Xtra!* 20 Aug. 1993, 12; Cynthia Amsden, "Portrait of a Killer," *Ottawa Citizen*, 26 April 1995, B3.

70. Paul Moloney, "Gay Community Cautious after Two Men Beaten to Death," *Toronto Star*, 4 Aug. 1993, A6.

71. Cal Millar, "Police Delve into Mystery Behind 3 Stabbing Deaths," *Toronto Star*, 7 Aug. 1993, A10.

72. Amsden, "Portrait of a Killer."

73. Moloney, "Gay Community Cautious."

74. "Warrants Issued," *Globe and Mail*, 4 Aug. 1993, A10.

75. Millar, "Police Delve."

76. Mike Blanchfield, "Outcasts Formed Deadly Brotherhood of Doomed," *Ottawa Citizen*, 21 June 1994, A1.

77. Amsden, "Portrait of a Killer."

78. Bruce Ward, "Man, Charged in Second Death, Accused in Friend's Slaying Insists: 'I'm Not Gay,'" *Ottawa Citizen*, 7 Aug. 1993, C1.

79. Blanchfield, "Outcasts Formed Deadly Brotherhood."

80. Amsden, "Portrait of a Killer."

81. Graeme Hamilton, "The Torments That Sear the Soul of Michael McGray," *National Post*, 24 March 2000, A3.

82. Erin Anderssen, "I Got Very Good at It, Killer Says," *Globe and Mail*, 24 March 2000, A1, A8.

83. Rory MacDonald, "'Gay Men Easy Targets for Murder' Says Killer," *Capital Xtra*, 14 April 2000, 13.

84. Paul Cherry, "I'm Guilty of Gay Killings: McGray," *Montreal Gazette*, 26 April 2000, A1, A2.

85. Valene Jenness, "Managing Differences and Making Legislation: Social Movements, and the Racialization, Sexualization, and Gendering of Federal Hate Crime Law in the US," *Social Problems* 46, 4 (1999): 549.

86. Gail Mason, "Not Our Kind of Hate Crime," *Law and Critique* 12, 3 (2001): 255–60.

87. Annjanette Rosga, "Deadly Words: State Power and the Entanglement of Speech and Violence in Hate Crime," *Law and Critique* 12, 3 [2001]: 239–40.

88. James Jacobs and Kimberly Potter, *Hate Crimes: Criminal Law and Identity Politics* (New York: Oxford University Press, 1998), 45–6.

89. See Jack Levin and Jack McDevitt, *Hate Crimes: The Rising Tide of Bigotry and Bloodshed* (New York: Plenum Press, 1993).

90. Jacobs and Potter, *Hate Crimes*, 53.

91. Jenness, "Managing Differences," 559–61.

92. Ibid., 553.

93. Ibid., 557–9.

94. Valerie Jenness, "The Hate Crime Canon and Beyond: A Critical Assessment," *Law and Critique* 12, 3 (2001): 283–5.

95. See also Valerie Jenness and Ryken Grattet, "The Criminalization of Hate: A Comparison of Structural and Polity Influences in the Passage of 'Bias-Crime' Legislation in the United States," *Sociological Perspectives* 39, 1 (1996): 129–54.

96. Jenness, "The Hate Crime Canon," 286–7.

97. Valerie Jenness and Ryken Grattet (2001). *Making Hate a Crime: From Social Movement to Law Enforcement* (New York: Sage, 2001), 1–3.

98. Ibid., 6–7.

99. Ibid., 103–6.

100. Jenness. "The Hate Crime Canon," 293–4.

101. Jenness and Grattet, *Making Hate a Crime*, 112.

102. Ibid., 117.

103. Ibid., 147–51.

104. Julian Roberts, "Legislative Responses to Hate-Motivated Crime" (draft report for the Domain Seminar on Social Justice, Department of Canadian Heritage, 14–15 May 1999), 4.

105. "Kill Fags," *Xtra!* 9 June 1995, 18.

106. Doug Nairne, "Hate Mail Case Thrown Out," *Winnipeg Free Press*, 29 May 1997, A1.

107. Svend Robinson, "Svend Robinson," *Globe and Mail*, 27 May 2003. Downloaded from www.globeandmail.ca.

108. Egale Canada "Email Update," 11 May 2004.

109. Roberts, "Legislative Responses," 31.

110. Ibid., 18.

111. Ibid., 12–13.

112. Ibid., 19.

113. Ibid., 6–7.

114. Ibid., 24.

115. Ibid., 23.

116. See T. Maroney, "The Struggle against Hate Crime: Movement at a Crossroads," *New York University Law Review* 73 (1993): 564–620.

117. Rachel Giese, "Hating the Hate-Crime Bill," *This Magazine* (November, 1995): 7–9.

118. Bill Jeffery, Standing Up to Hate: Legal Remedies Available to Victims of Hate-Motivated Activity, Ottawa, Department of Canadian Heritage (1998), 21.

119. Martha Shaffer, "Criminal Responses to Hate-Motivated Violence," McGill Law Journal 41 (1995): 210.

120. Ibid., 213–14.

121. Ibid., 245–6.

122. Ibid., 203.

123. Ibid., 245–6.

124. Roberts, "Legislative Responses," 19.

125. Ibid., 32.

126. Interview, 28 Nov. 2002.

127. Eleanor Brown, "Victim Takes on Police," Xtra, 18 Feb. 1994, 15.

128. Gretchen Drummie, "Suspect in Gay Attack Denies Kicks," Toronto Sun, 11 Mar. 1995, 28.

129. Brown, "Victim Takes on Police."

130. Gretchen Drummie, "'Booze, Machismo, Hate': Prosecutor Explains Gay-Bashing," *Toronto Sun*, 16 March 1995, 43.

131. Alisa Craig, "Gaybashing Case Goes to Court," Xtra! 17 March 1995, 13.

132. Gretchen Drummie, "Attackers Get Jail," *Toronto Sun*, 13 May 1995, 17.

133. *R. v. Cvetan*, [1999] O.J. No. 250.

134. Eleanor Brown, "Death Won't Affect Trial," Xtra, 14 Jan. 1999, 13.

135. Interview with former coordinator, 26 May 1999.

136. Jeffery, *Standing Up to Hate*, 23.

137. Ibid., 25.

138. Ibid., 15.

139. Ibid., 25.

140. Ibid., 17–19.

141. Ibid., 28.

142. Interview, 7 July 1999.

143. Jeffery, *Standing Up to Hate*, 33.

144. Interview with CHRC official, 13 August 2003.

145. Interview, 7 July 1999.

146. Jeffery, Standing Up to Hate, 38–40.

147. Ibid., 13–16.

148. Cited in Ibid., 43.

149. Ibid., 43–4.

150. Ibid., 43–7.

Part Three

Women and the Law

The status of women in law is central to social activism and scholarly activity in Canada. Recognized as legal persons with respect to Senate eligibility only in 1929, women in Canada have challenged gender discrimination on many fronts. Increasingly, advocates of rights for women draw on women's experiences before the law and on broader, statistical evidence of gender discrimination. Even with advances in the status of women, many scholars point to ongoing studies of patterns of discrimination against women within the legal profession in North America as well as to documentation of gender discrimination in other occupations and other spheres.

The question remains, is law an effective means of remedying gender discrimination? Liberal-minded and more critical feminist scholars disagree over specific applications of law, with the former more inclined toward reform of existing legal and social structures, and the latter frankly skeptical of the power of law to move past its patriarchal roots. This section explores four key issues concerning women and law: legal and social policies on female partner abuse; the effect of allowing faith-based arbitrations in family-law deliberations; the Charter and equality rights; and legislation and policies in response to domestic violence.

The four chapters in Part Three touch on controversies identified by feminist scholars and allow the reader to weigh the extent to which legal structures can work toward women's equality before the law or toward other goals of the women's movement. These chapters should generate discussion about the degree to which social and legal relations are gendered and racialized and about the implication of relying on legal resources. The chapters help to illuminate trends in legal regulation and legal ideologies, and show the complexities of using legal powers to appreciate gendered differences in society and to reverse patterns of gender inequality.

Chapter Nine

Assessing Mutual Partner-Abuse Claims in Child Custody and Access Cases

Linda C. Neilson*[1]

Editors' Note: Linda Neilson's essay brings together key issues in Canadian family law, focusing on cases where both intimate partners allege domestic abuse. She presents litigation strategies commonly used by lawyers, investigates possibilities of gender bias in deciding such cases, and considers how allegations of violence might influence custody of, and access to, children. She acknowledges gender bias against some men in legal proceedings and post-separation arrangements but concludes that gender bias against women is much more prominent, including loss of custody to abusive partners and inadequate protection for children whose abusive fathers win visitation rights. She uses the best available literature to discuss the context of domestic violence, including subtle forms—"A whistle, a raised eyebrow, the use of a certain word . . . "—and more dramatic forms of injury, such as physical or sexual assault. She critiques ways of measuring violence and cautions that methodological approaches can produce differing results in understanding and defining violence and abuse. Specifically, she points out how many forms of intimidation and even terrorizing are not treated by lawyers and other professionals as assaults or tangible injuries. This downplaying of violence strengthens the mistaken assumption that family violence is confined to a small minority of separating and divorcing couples. Neilson enlivens her analysis through selected excerpts from the available literature and actual custody and access cases she researched, giving a forum for those most affected by court decisions.

Neilson reviews how mothers and fathers often experience settlement pressure, where one parent surrenders a claim for custody or access. Neilson argues that some commonsense arrangements for families can be reversed when abuse is present: "While researchers have demonstrated clearly that when abuse is absent, maximum contact with fathers and with mothers is usually the best option for children, different considerations apply in intimate-partner abuse cases." She also discusses how recent changes in rules of evidence allow Canadian court officials to consider established patterns of "past conduct and the power and control dynamics of the relationship."

INTRODUCTION

When parents decide to leave abusive relationships, they often[2] turn to the legal system for assistance with child custody, access, and safety matters. Lawyers and judges are uniquely positioned to enhance the health, safety, and well-being of family members in these cases. To do so, however, specialized understanding of the nature and dynamics of intimate-partner abuse[3] and its effects on children and victims, as well as some appreciation of how dynamics present themselves in professional-client interactions and in courtrooms, is necessary.[4] This article

Source: Linda C. Neilson, "Assessing Mutual Partner-Abuse Claims in Child Custody and Access Cases," *Family Court Review*, Vol. 42, No. 3, July 2004, pp. 411–438. © 2004 Association of Family and Conciliation Courts. Reprinted by permission of Blackwell Publishing Ltd.
*Linda Neilson BA (Hons), LLB, PhD. (law) (London, L.S.E.), Associate Professor, University of New Brunswick, Sociology and Law in Society. Fields of research and publication: domestic violence, conflict resolution (mediation) and family law. Current endeavours include the creation of a Canadian resource manual on intimate-partner abuse issues.

explores litigation and negotiation tactics commonly associated with custody and access cases involving allegations and counter-allegations of intimate-partner abuse. It offers a lens through which to assess or screen such cases. The article begins with a discussion of what is known, from socio-legal and domestic-violence research, about gender, children, and intimate-partner abuse in social and legal contexts. Material is drawn from published literature supplemented by illustrations from data collected during the "Spousal Abuse, Children and the Legal System" research study (1998–2001) conducted in association with the Muriel McQueen Fergusson Centre for Family Violence Research, University of New Brunswick, funded by the Canadian Bar Association, Law for the Futures Fund.[5] Italicized quotations are extracted from interview data collected during the course of the study unless otherwise specified.

Normally, lawyers and judges encounter family law cases after parents or partners decide to separate or divorce. Intimate-partner abuse[6] rates are considerably higher in this population than among couples in continuing relationships.[7] Domestic violence research indicates that 40 to 50 percent of separating and divorcing couples report abuse in the relationships they leave.[8] Younger couples disclose higher rates of abuse than older couples;[9] consequently, many intimate-partner abuse family law cases involve young children. Yet, research also indicates that mediators, therapists, evaluators, mental and medical health professionals,[10] and lawyers,[11] both tend to underestimate and to underdocument abuse of such clients.[12] It is likely that part of the problem is caused by limited use of assessment protocols specifically designed to identify intimate-partner-abusive violence[13] because research indicates that victims of intimate-partner abuse (and perpetrators)[14] fail to disclose abuse unless asked appropriate questions.[15]

Failure to consider intimate-partner abuse in child custody and access cases[16] is serious, because witnessing abuse can be as harmful to children as child abuse itself.[17] Moreover, abusive partners pose continuing risks both to children[18] and to victims[19] after separation or divorce. Patterns of hostility and conflict that developed during intact relationships tend to continue after separation.[20] Partner abuse is also relevant to decisions about children's future care because maximum contact with parents who abuse partners is said to impede child and victim recovery from abuse and places children at risk.[21] Jaffe, Zerwer, and Poisson, for example, report that in the intimate-partner abuse cases they studied, the longer children went without seeing the abusive parent, the better the children's adjustment.[22]

While researchers have demonstrated clearly that when abuse is absent, maximum contact with fathers and with mothers is usually the best option for children,[23] different considerations apply in intimate-partner abuse cases. While abused parents (most often mothers)[24] and domestic violence experts[25] agree that children should not be severed entirely from parents who have abused partners (unless safety, mental health, or child welfare considerations leave few alternatives) they also stress the need for specialized assessment, considerable caution, and meticulous consideration of child and victim health and safety issues.[26]

People who physically abuse partners commonly also physically abuse their children.[27] Bancroft and Silverman (2002)[28] discuss research indicating that between 49 and 70 percent of parents who physically abuse partners also physically abuse their children. The authors conclude that although there is little data relating exclusively to post-separation violence in intimate-partner abuse cases, it is unlikely that post-separation rates are lower.[29] Indeed, it is likely that continuing rates of emotional abuse are higher because patterns of emotional abuse are resistant to change.[30] Furthermore, separation may simply result in the replacement of partners with children as targets of abuse:

> **Mother:** *I lacked the skills to stand up for myself, which were my own issues. I have to learn how to set better boundaries. I left him because I had a good family upbringing and was able to recognize that this was an unhealthy situation. I am fearful that my children will not have the skills to defend themselves against it adequately. When I was in the household, I acted as the buffer, particularly between him and my oldest child. There was always a great deal of conflict between my oldest and my ex-husband because he attempted to control everything. And now I'm not there to be the buffer between them.[31]*

Batterers who regularly threaten, harass, demean, intimidate, and control partners and who have poor impulse control and little ability to accept responsibility are unlikely, without effective treatment,[32] to change such patterns when alone with children. Domestic violence experts Peter Jaffe, Lundy Bancroft, and others tell us that intimate-partner abuse is often associated with poorly developed parenting skills and limited ability to accept parental responsibility.[33] Indeed, failure to accept responsibility is characteristic of abuse perpetrators.[34] Post-separation parenting problems documented by researchers who have studied custody and access decisions in intimate-partner abuse cases include the following: continuing exposure of children to conflict and abuse directed at the nonabusing parent;[35] exposing children to additional patterns of intimate-partner abuse as new relationships are formed; teaching children intimate-partner abuse techniques; exposing children to criminal and addictive lifestyles; endangering children's safety; interfering with victim and child therapy; neglecting children's needs and interests; undermining the authority, health, and welfare of the custodial parent; involving children as allies in parental conflicts; and redirecting abuse at the children.[36] Studies have documented serious child safety and welfare concerns in partner abuse cases.[37] If women and children are to be protected by professionals and the legal system, it is imperative that evaluators, lawyers, and judges accurately assess allegations and counter-allegations of partner abuse in family law cases.

The body of this article is divided into four parts: (a) discussion of research relating to alleged gender bias in custody and access cases, with special emphasis on intimate-partner abuse cases; (b) discussion of statistics and research studies relating to intimate-partner violence and abuse; (c) discussion of abuser characteristics and litigation and negotiation tactics; and (d) discussion of assessment considerations that may help to promote accurate assessment.[38]

PART ONE: GENDER BIAS IN CUSTODY AND ACCESS CASES

Do mothers and children require, as many women claim, more legal protection in cases of domestic violence and abuse? Do women have far too much protection already? Is the legal system, as many men claim, biased against the continuing role of men as fathers? What does the research data say?

Male participants in the study on Spousal Abuse, Children and the Legal System[39] considered the legal system to be biased against fathers. Proof was offered in the form of professional and judicial "pressure" on fathers to abandon claims for joint or full custody. Fathers claimed that the legal system denies them their right to participate in the post-separation parenting of their children:

> **Father:** *The children have two parents, and deserve to be raised by both of them. The fact that mom and dad don't like each other any more is irrelevant. Giving all the power (sole custody) to either mom or dad only encourages the abuse of that power to control the other parent.*

Settlement data from court files and data from interviews with abused women tended to corroborate claims of settlement pressure. Both men and women reported having experienced pressure to accept "normal" or "usual" custody and access provisions: custody to the mother, unsupervised access to the father every second weekend from Friday to Sunday, with expanded access on holidays.[40] We do not know the extent to which such settlement pressure was directed against men and the extent to which it reflected professional and legal concerns about the best interest (health and safety) of children. (In connection with intimate-partner abuse cases such settlement patterns were a concern because intimate-partner abuse cases are not the same as "normal" or "usual" custody and access cases.)[41] Female participants also claimed that the legal system is biased—in favor of fathers. In support of this claim, mothers claimed that priority was being given to fathers' rights to have access to the children over considerations relating to the health and safety of victims or children. Considerable data from all sources (reported cases, court files in three jurisdictions, interview data from parents, survey data from lawyers) supported these assertions.[42] Let us examine these issues briefly in more detail.

In the vast majority of separation and divorce cases, children continue to reside primarily with mothers. Usually, however, this is the result of parental "agreement," not judicial order.[43] Would equality in the number of judicial custody orders granted to men and to women indicate lack of gender bias? The argument in support of the claim is that, in the absence of gender bias, the legal system should award custody of children as often to men as to women or that it should award custody equally or jointly to men and women. The argument is not supported by social science data. Although women in Canada report increased labor force participation, this has not, as Margrit Eichler and Susan Boyd document, been accompanied by substantial increases in men's contribution to child care and household management.[44] Although no one disputes that nurturing, caring fathers should be encouraged to be centrally involved in their children's lives, social science data continue to show that more mothers than fathers accept responsibility for children, particularly for young children. Moreover, the pattern holds when comparisons are limited to mothers and fathers who work outside the home.[45] If bonding, nurturing, and caregiving are important considerations, one would expect, in a gender-neutral environment, that decisions about custody would mirror child care social trends. If so, we should still expect mothers, including working mothers, to be awarded custody of children more often than fathers (assuming all other factors are equal).

What is the pattern now? It is difficult to pinpoint with certainty judicial child custody decisions by gender of parent. Reliable Canadian data are lacking.[46] Contested custody cases requiring judicial decisions are rare, because custody is usually settled by agreement. Most contested claims relate to access. Nonetheless, fathers who abuse their partners are more apt than other fathers to claim custody of children.[47] Court files in New Brunswick, Canada, for example, disclosed that fathers, alleged to have been abusive, claimed custody of children in at least 42 percent of the examined partner-abuse-court-file cases.[48] Parents settled a large number of these cases without trial. When settled cases were excluded, to consider only cases decided by judges, fathers who claimed custody and were alleged to have been abusive to partners[49] were awarded full or joint custody by a judge in 40 to 50 percent of cases, depending on the jurisdiction.[50] This finding is consistent with research data from other legal jurisdictions. Researchers are reporting, albeit with concern, that abusive partners are obtaining court-ordered or court-endorsed custody of children at least one-half of the time, and parents who abuse partners are almost always granted unsupervised access.[51] Moreover, data continue to show that victims of domestic violence are not receiving adequate legal protection in partner-abuse cases and that children are being placed at risk.[52]

In connection with gender bias, numerous evaluations of gender bias in various legal systems have been conducted throughout North America. Such studies do not document patterns of gender bias against men. On the contrary, most have concluded that systemic gender bias in the legal system, when it exists, is against women, particularly against women who are victims of abuse.[53] Although claims of injustice have been made by fathers in connection with individual cases, for example, claims reported in the Canadian Landon Pearson and Roger Galloway Report of the Special Joint Committee on Child Custody and Access (1988)[54] and certainly instances of injustice against individual men when these occur should not be ignored, the dominant pattern, verified by research data, continues to be bias against women and particularly against female victims involved in intimate-partner and sexual abuse cases.[55]

PART TWO: INTERPRETING STATISTICS AND RESEARCH RELATING TO INTIMATE-PARTNER ABUSE

Although the terms "domestic violence" and "domestic abuse" or the terms "intimate-partner violence" and "intimate-partner abuse" often are presented interchangeably, the concepts differ in fundamental ways. An appreciation of the differences is vital to an understanding of social science data relating to gender and intimate-partner violence, and to the assessment of claims of abuse.

Most research studies and statistical reports indicate that rates of violence against women in intimate relationships are higher than rates of violence against men, particularly once factors such as seriousness, pattern, frequency, and injury are considered.[56] Statistics from police forces and data from hospital records, court files, and service providers consistently and overwhelmingly document women as the targets of intimate-partner violence.[57] Yet, a number of large quantitative statistical studies indicate that women and men are equally violent.[58] Why? Why do many studies say that men are overwhelmingly the perpetrators of intimate-partner abuse and other studies say that men and women are equally violent?

The contradictions are largely the result of researchers asking different questions and using different methodologies to produce different answers. Some researchers study abusive relationships; others study violence in intimate relationships. Statistical studies purporting to show equality in male and female violence do not, for the most part, focus on abusive relationships.[59] Many, in fact most, collect information about violent acts (punching, hitting, slapping, shouting, name calling) from university students or from the general public. Students or members of the public are asked to answer questions about how they respond to conflicts with intimate partners or spouses.

A number of factors limit the usefulness of such studies if the goal is to understand male and female violence in abusive relationships. First, people who repeatedly abuse and victims who repeatedly suffer from abuse are unlikely to be represented in appreciable numbers in general population surveys.[60] Second, these studies assess relationships that are not necessarily abusive. It is unlikely that the interpersonal dynamics of violent action between men and women in nonabusive relationships during conflict are similar to those in abusive relationships.[61] Third, high-risk populations[62] are usually left out of general population surveys and certainly out of university student surveys.[63] Such omissions are not inconsequential.[64] Fourth, researchers have demonstrated that abusers minimize both the frequency and severity of their own violence when responding to data collection instruments such as Conflict Tactics Scales (CTS), which further calls into question the validity and applicability of such data to understanding gender in the context of abusive relationships.[65]

CTS collection instruments, or a variation thereof, are used in most quantitative statistical studies. They collect information about responses to conflict in intimate relationships. While they collect information about a broad range of violent acts, they have limited ability to control for the influence of long-term patterns of behavior, relationship, or social context; interpersonal vulnerability; or severity of injury.[66] As a result, domestic violence experts recommend against exclusive reliance on CTS[67] data if the goal is to understand intimate partner violence and abuse. For example, Walter DeKeseredy and Martin Schwartz comment,

The CTS was developed originally in the 1970s by University of New Hampshire Sociologist Murray Straus to study violence within families. By now the original or a modified CTS appears at the core of research reported in over 100 scientific journal articles and at least 10 North American books.... The instrument solicits information from both men and women about the "conflict tactics" used by both men and women.

The bulk of the research in this field has simply counted blows (who hit whom, and how often).

The survey still does not easily differentiate between a victim fighting back for her life, a survivor retaliating, and an instigator of violence without cause. All are considered violent. Even the more recent strategy of asking who struck the first blow [does not produce reliable results].[68] When a woman has been beaten 30 times in the past and knows from her husband's behavior that a beating is coming within minutes, and further knows that if she strikes first she will end up being hurt less, does that mean that the violence is the woman's fault?[69]

Researchers analyzing data from CTS scales risk inclusion of minor violent acts that are not necessarily threatening and/or are not part of a pattern of abuse. This, in part, leads to the erroneous conclusion that men and women are equally abusive.[70]

Assessing the frequency of abuse is complex. University students and members of the general public participating in large-scale quantitative statistical studies of intimate partner conflict, for example, are usually asked about violent acts within a particular time, say within the past year. Yet patterns of violent domination and control in an abusive relationship in the absence of a partner's violence,[71] survivors of long-term intimate-partner abuse do commonly report incidents of their own violence in abusive relationships,[72] including initiating violence, particularly once they make a decision to leave the relationship.[73] Sometimes these acts are defensive; sometimes they are retaliatory; sometimes they are acts of violent resistance. Other times they are a reflection of desperation or lack of concern for personal safety. Acts of violence by victims are often a reaction to or a product of past abuse. These acts can only be understood by looking at the dynamics of an abusive relationship over time.

Dobash, Dobash, Wilson and Daley explain:

> Wives' and husbands' uses of violence differ greatly, both quantitatively and qualitatively … …. exclusive focus on "acts" ignores the actors' interpretations, motivation, and intentions…. Only through a consideration of behaviors, intentions, and inter-subjective understandings associated with specific violent events will we come to a fuller understanding of violence between men and women. Studies employing more intensive interviews and detailed case reports addressing the contexts and motivations of marital violence help unravel the assertions of those who claim the widespread existence of beaten and battered husbands.[74]

Qualitative studies—studies that include fewer participants but explore complex issues in more depth—explain the meaning of data collected in larger quantitative statistical studies. They inform us that violent action is but one dimension of abuse. More important than individual acts of violence are patterns of control and domination and consequences of action over time. Once the context and the complexity of violent action are understood, it becomes clear that

> the serious violence experienced by some women is quantitatively different from the pushing, slapping and shoving that occurs with such regularity in many couples as to be considered "normal."[75]

Domestic violence expert Michael Johnson discusses the difference:

> The conflicts that are described by women entering shelters or filing Protection from Abuse Orders do not have the symmetrical feel of "incompatible goals." Instead, they seem to represent the single-minded commitment of one person to completely dominate and control another … …. I have argued that the characteristics of the heavily male type of violence are consistent with a general motive to control one's partner, a motive that is rooted in patriarchal ideas about relationships between men and women. The violence is used often because it needs to be, in order to subdue one's partner or to display one's power and control … …. The other type of violence, which is more gender-symmetric, is consistent with a more specific, narrowly-focused motive to get one's way in a particular conflict situation, within a relationship in which there is not a general pattern of power and control, but in which specific arguments sometimes escalate into violence.[76]

Richard Gelles, one of the social scientists whose own domestic violence research with Murray Straus[77] engendered the line of research purporting to demonstrate that men and women are equally violent, has tried, repeatedly, to explain:

> To even off the playing field it seems one piece of statistical evidence (that women and men hit one another in roughly equal numbers) is hauled out from my 1985 research—and distorted—to "prove" the position on violence against men.
>
> Research shows that nearly 90 percent of battering victims are women and only about ten percent are men.
>
> Indeed, men are hit by their wives, they are injured, and some are killed. But, are all men hit by women "battered?" No. Men who beat their wives, who use emotional abuse and blackmail to control their wives, and are then hit or even harmed, cannot be considered battered men.[78]

Minor non-threatening acts of violence during intimate-partner conflict in non-abusive relationships[79] (the type of violence commonly measured by quantitative studies) are qualitatively different from violence in abusive relationships. Abuse includes elements of domination, intimidation, degradation, and control. Abusive violence is both more dangerous and more likely to escalate than violence that is not part of a pattern of abuse.

One way to conceptualize the difference between incidents of violence during conflict and abusive violence against an intimate partner lies in the concept of "intimate terrorism":[80]

> The defining difference between these two types of violence is a difference of motives and the interpersonal dynamics that those motives produce across the many interactions that comprise a relationship. The defining characteristic of patriarchal terrorism is a general motive to control that activates a range of power and control tactics in addition to the use of violence.
>
> "Terrorism," with "patriarchal" in parentheses, refers to relationships in which only one of the spouses is violent and controlling, the other is not. In this data set, that violent and controlling spouse is the husband in 94 of the 97 cases, cases in which the term "patriarchal terrorism" is appropriate.
>
> The relationship between gender and these types of violence supports the hypothesis that "terrorism" is indeed an almost exclusively male phenomenon in heterosexual marital relationships, thus appropriately referred to as "patriarchal terrorism," while common couple violence is close to gender-symmetric.[81]

The similarities in technique and result between psychological torture employed by "professional" terrorists and terrorization in intimate partnerships are striking.[82] Jeri Martinez comments,

> Following numerous hostage-takings, the world has seen former hostages:
> • minimize their injuries,
> • refuse to participate in prosecuting terrorists,
> • raise money for defense counsel and
> • visit their captors in jail—even as long as 2 years after the incident—all the same things battered women do.

Abusers who terrorize partners do not have to use violence to terrorize; threats in the face of prior violence will suffice. As Joan Simalchik reports in connection with Canadian survivors of torture, "Torture is not intended to kill the body, but the soul. The physical scars heal more readily than the psychological ones."[83] Survivors of women abuse acquire similar scars.[84]

Thus, patterns of women abuse may continue in the absence of objective, observable violent action. As Mary Ann Dutton explains, women (and occasionally men) subjected to patterns of abusive violence by intimate partners learn to detect and respond to subtle signs of imminent danger. Thus, fear and perception of danger are more the result of past than of current behavior:

> Intimate partners generally learn to read the subtle nuances of each other's behavior more clearly than can others. Persons who are oppressed or victimized, such as prisoners of war or hostages, have a great incentive to read their oppressor's behavior accurately. This principle applies to battered women in their abusive relationships. That is, a battered woman's appraisal of the threat implicit in a batterer's behavior is based on his pattern of prior violence and abuse. Thus, the meaning of threatening behavior can best be understood in light of a woman's unique history and her knowledge of her partner's prior behavior.[85]

A whistle, a raised eyebrow, the use of a certain word may be abusive if understood in context—once it is understood that those behaviors preceded violent attacks in the past. Yet, presentation of such complaints is likely to encounter considerable opposition. In the absence of evidence about the historical patterns of a relationship, women who make such complaints might appear irrational or even vindictive. Yet, failure to take such complaints seriously has the effect of condoning continuing intimidation and abuse.

In sum, the concepts "violence" and "abuse" are related but different. Violence is behavior or action; abuse is a pattern of demeaning, controlling, intimidating action, including violence, within the context of evolving power and control dynamics of an intimate relationship causing psychological (and often physical) harm. Whereas it is useful to know something about violence among men and women generally and to acknowledge that women as well as men are capable of violence, it is important to recognize that abuse has additional dimensions and that the vast majority of people intimidated by intimate-partner abuse are women.

PART THREE: ABUSER CHARACTERISTICS AND LITIGATION TACTICS

As previously discussed, fathers who abuse [their] partners claim custody more often than fathers who do not. Study after study of partner-abuse cases has found that mediation, negotiation, litigation, and even supervised access centers[86] become "legitimized" tools abusive partners use to continue to dominate and maintain contact and control following separation.[87] Some have alleged that heightened litigation in these cases is a form of stalking,[88] whereby persistent litigation and insistence on frequent reports constitute continuing efforts to harass and control.[89] Certainly, in connection with the Spousal Abuse, Children, and the Legal System study, we found, as have others, high rates of continuing litigation in cases involving allegations of domestic violence.[90] Commonly, former partners or judges are blamed for such patterns. The argument is that fathers have little choice when mothers and courts fail to grant joint custody "rights":

Father: *My ex-partner has based her agenda on court unwillingness to order joint custody when conflict is high. This makes it possible to deny a child and father a normal parent-child relationship in violation of constitutional rights. In my opinion the conflict is indicative of her inability to put the children's interests above her own anger.*

Father: *I've been fighting for three years to get an even relationship with my kids. If I'm seeing the kids two weeks on and two off, to me that is joint custody and no reason for the money issues. That's fair.*

Men and women commonly make claims of partner abuse against each other during child custody and access litigation. Can research data shed light on the situation? In only 3 percent of the partner-abuse cases involving children, as reported in the Reports on Family Law between 1983 and 1997, did the father alone claim to have been abused; in 19 percent of the reported cases, there were allegations of abuse by both partners. The remaining cases mentioned partner-abuse allegations against the father only.[91] Turning to court files, allegations of abuse by each partner against the other were found in between 16 to 22 percent of the partner-abuse court files examined in three jurisdictions of New Brunswick.[92] In sum, whereas the majority of partner-abuse claims are made only by women, it appears that both parents frequently claim partner abuse in child custody and access cases.

What factors product mutual claims? Are the claims true? How should they be assessed? At present, there is no verifiable test of whether a person has been abusive to an intimate partner.[93] Batterers do not have a clearly identifiable psychological or socioeconomic profile. Many are relatively well-educated, affluent, successful professionals.[94]

> **Mother:** *It was not the non-payment that concerned me, it was the visitation. He would come into my apartment, demand entrance, search my apartment, take items. He kicked my door off the hinges once while holding my child. (Did you ever think about calling the police?) No—because he would lose his law career.*

Domestic violence experts are documenting a "complex diversity of psychological problems" rather than a single psychological profile.[95] Whereas a number of researchers have attempted to develop typologies or subcategories of abusers,[96] and certain psychological characteristics such as narcissism and "avoidance/dependence" are said to be common,[97] there is considerable debate about the validity and usefulness of existing categorizations.[98] Psychological testing alone, it appears, will not answer credibility or causality questions.[99]

Demeanor and presentation of self are also not reliable indicators. Many abusive partners are both manipulative and highly skilled at presenting positive public images of self:[100]

> **Mother:** *If you met him sitting here and didn't know he was abusive, you would not believe he could be so sweet. Old ladies loved him.*

Abusers commonly present themselves as warm, considerate, and caring partners. Victims may, as a result of damage caused by long-term victimization, seem confused, unreasonably fearful, or even aggressive.[101] Psychologists with domestic violence expertise warn that perpetrators will often perform better than victims on psychological testing unless testing is assessed through the lens of specialized knowledge about domestic violence.[102]

Indeed, perceptions based on demeanor are often simply wrong. By way of example, one of the women who participated in the Spousal Abuse, Children, and the Legal System study, a woman who had been subjected to years of physical violence, on occasion life-threatening violence and abuse:[103]

> **Mother:** *I went to the Doctor (after separation) and said "I'm falling apart." He said, "you have withdrawal from adrenalin," I never heard of that before but it was the result of abuse, not knowing what would happen next. He would try to run me off the road, he would beat me the second I got in the door, so the adrenalin was always pumping.*

When she was about to testify in court:

> *The Crown prosecutor and the police said, "You have to stand up for yourself because no one else will do it," I said, "I don't want to be here!" Then, when I came back out (into the court) I yelled out the answers.*

My husband said, "When I hit her, she hits me." He was jumping up calling me a liar. They even said I liked it. The judge said the children should have been taken out of our home. The judge gave him a year's probation. And the terrible thing was that he got my kids that night. I had to drop my kids off with him for the weekend.[104]

As a result of damage caused by the pattern of abuse in this relationship, this woman presented herself to the court as seemingly aggressive, lending a degree of false credibility to her husband's claim the abuse had been mutual.[105] The pattern is not uncommon in domestic violence cases.[106]

Abuse perpetrator attitudes and behavioral patterns in partner-abuse cases, as evidenced by litigation tactics, include the following: a sense of entitlement and superiority; patterns of attempting to dominate and control victim decisions and behavior; patterns of jealousy, monitoring, and negative dependency ("I can't live without her"); patterns of manipulation, projection, and externalization of blame; inability to accept responsibility; patterns of denial, minimization, and victim blaming.[107]

Domestic violence researchers document patterns among perpetrators of minimizing the nature, frequency, and severity of their own abusive behavior.[108] For example,

> **Father:** *Like the night that I put her out: we fell down the stairs. She was drunk and I was drinking a little bit. The next time I hear from her, she has black eyes and she is bruised and beaten and before that, she charged me with assault and she said I choked her. A friend of ours said she saw her later that evening and there were no marks on her but the next day, when she came to the police, she had fingerprints on her neck. I didn't put them there or they would have been there the night before. There was no trouble between her and I. No reason for either of us not to have visitation of the children. It's just that she says something and they believe her.*[109]

Bancroft and Silverman claim that perpetrators tend to admit to less serious acts of violence to increase credibility and to create an impression that women are exaggerating or are being "vindictive."[110] David Adams compares minimization patterns to denial patterns characteristic of alcoholics:

> The abuser's tendency to minimize problems is comparable to the denial patterns of alcohol and drug abusers. Problem drinkers minimize their drinking by favorably comparing their own consumption patterns to "worse case" alcoholics. Many battering husbands similarly minimize their violence by comparing it to "brutes who beat their wives every day."[111]

Abusive partners may truly believe the other partner is lying about the extent and frequency of the abuse. From the perpetrator's perspective, such actions are isolated incidents in a sea of good behavior. Perpetrators who dominate and demean, who exert excessive power and control, commonly present themselves as victims. This is to be expected. We create our own projections of the world through our own actions. Thus, those who victimize will, over time, come to interpret the behavior of others as if it were also victimization. Meanwhile, cumulative psychological damage to partners is ignored or poorly understood.[112]

When victims turn to the legal system for help, courts and professionals are actually at risk of becoming tools in the abuser's quest to dominate and control. Orders requiring victims to provide information to abusers about the education, health, and welfare of the children are readily turned into tools to harass, intimidate, monitor, and control.[113] Children's interests are better served when the perpetrator is required to make direct educational and medical enquiries of schools and doctors.

Another common litigation in partner-abuse cases is countering partner-abuse claims with allegations of child maltreatment. In partner-abuse cases, such claims may involve attempted manipulation of police or child protection agencies.[114]

> **Father:** *The night that I witnessed her, she pulled her [our daughter] out of the seat, dropped her off. I looked in the window and heard a screech come out of her. I even taped it. You can hear it. She had hauled her out of the chair by her two arms. There was also a question of weight loss and I had concerns about bruising on her. I phoned the RCMP and health and community services.*

Or, in another case,

Father: *I have a box full of pictures I prepared. She still has full custody of the children despite numerous incidents of medical neglect.*[115]

An associated trend is enlisting tactical help from paternal grandparents or from fathers' rights groups.[116] Although claims of child maltreatment or neglect should not be dismissed out of hand, since mistreatment of children can be associated with partner abuse,[117] we found little evidence in the New Brunswick partner-abuse court files to indicate that such claims warranted child protection proceedings.[118]

Another perpetrator litigation tactic is "setting up" the victim to make it appear that she acted immorally or illegally:

Mother: *About a month later I was talking to the police and they said, "Do you know that you have no insurance on that car?" He had cancelled it. That's illegal. The cops said, "He has already called to complain to us that you are driving without insurance."*

Associated with this tactic is initiating claims against the victim that actually reflect the perpetrator's own behavior:

Mother: *When she [our daughter] is there, he says it is his time and she has no right to call or to speak to me. [But] he has the [legal] right to call her here. When we've had to go away, we've left messages of times and dates when she can't be reached on her cell phone, leaving other numbers he can use to call. Instead, he goes down to the police station and gets them to call the cell phone. Then he applies to hold me in contempt (of court in another province). I sent in an affidavit with copies of my telephone bills but the judge just said I am denying him the right to be involved in his daughter's life.*

The tactic worked in this case. The mother was held in contempt of court and soundly criticized by the judge. The same mother commented, "He [the father] has convictions for death threats and one for assaulting his current wife." She reported her daughter's safety concerns relating to continuing abuse in the home and father's practice of driving while intoxicated. Despite these concerns, the mother reported having reached an agreement with the child that she would continue to visit the father until at least the age of twelve in order to avoid the risk of loss of custody to the father.

Bancroft calls this common litigation "tactic" in partner-abuse cases a "preemptive strike":

> The batterer accuses the victim of all of the things that he has done. If he has been denying her phone access to the children during their weekend visits with him, he will likely complain to the court that she is preventing *him* from calling the children during the week. These tactics can succeed in distracting attention from his pattern of abusiveness; in the midst of a cross-fire of accusations, court representatives are tempted to throw up their hands and declare the couple equally abusive and unreasonable.[119]

Yet other perpetrator tactics include manipulation of research data on the benefits of maximum contact for children. Refusal to concede to demands for joint custody "entitlements" or opposition to extensive unsupervised access is then reframed and presented as evidence of child abuse.[120] Child protection agencies and courts failing to act upon such allegations are said to be acting in opposition to the interests of the children. Retaliatory litigation and disciplinary complaints are also common in partner-abuse cases. These are initiated against those who appear to support the victim.[121] In New Brunswick, we found disciplinary complaints being pursued against victim's lawyers, formal complaints being made against judges, and professional complaints being initiated against evaluators and therapists. While a number of the complaints against evaluators and therapists were found warranted, more were not. Caution is required in partner-abuse cases to separate genuine from tactical claims.

Litigation tactics are often designed to discredit victim witnesses, such as claiming infidelity or promiscuity to deflect attention from abuse:

> **Mother:** *When we went to court he told everybody in town that I had an affair with my lawyer, a man from Canadian Tire, and a guy from the mine. My lawyer was a lady.*

Other forms of attack on credibility are made by attempting to discredit minute details of testimony, such as the color of a room or of a couch. In the New Brunswick study on Spousal Abuse, Children, and the Legal System, we found that responsible, caregiving parents, both male and female,[122] focused attention on responsibilities to children:

> **Father:** *primary caregiver: She wanted to get shared custody back. I did not have a problem sharing responsibility of the children, or authority of who does/says what, but along with authority comes responsibility and you can't have one without the other. That's a recipe for disaster.*

> **Mother:** *Children need both parents; that's so important! But they don't need a parent they can't depend on, that doesn't show up, that puts their life in danger. I think she would have been better off with no parent. That's so awful to say. She said today, "you know when I have kids, I'm not going to see dad. They're not going to be brought up in that situation." But she's one of the lucky ones.*

Parents alleged to have been highly abusive, on the other hand, tended to focus discussion on rights or entitlements.[123] Interviews with fathers, against whom the most serious allegations of abuse and violence had been made, tended to include little or no discussion of responsibilities or of activities with children. The focus was on the legal battle and the injustice of nonrecognition of perceived entitlements.[124]

Perpetrators of abuse are quick to allege or point out partner violence to justify or to excuse their own behavior:

> **Father:** *The first assault was just common assault. She tried to take the kids one night and I took the car keys from her. That was the first common assault. The police came out and gave me the summons for court and I said I'd like to have her charged because there were big handfuls of my hair all over the porch from when she was pulling on it.[125]*

We shall return to a discussion of allegations of mutual violence in Part Four ...

Another frequent claim during litigation in partner-abuse cases is "Parent alienation": "I believe my ex-partner intends to alienate me from my children." Before discussing alienation, let us first consider, briefly, children as potential witnesses in partner-abuse cases.

Children are not always reliable witnesses in partner-abuse cases.[126] Some children have ambivalent feelings about the abuse and about the abusive parent, loving yet fearing them,[127] others even side strongly with the abusive parent because, as a result of the abuse in the home, the abuser is viewed as powerful and competent. The victim parent may have been portrayed as incompetent or as deserving of abuse.[128] For example,

> **Mother:** *He (the father) did not (abuse the children). In fact, he was just the opposite. When he was beating me up, he was comforting them, saying "you can stay up late at night, you don't have to go to school tomorrow. Don't listen to your mother. She is an old slut, a pig. She's crazy." When I first left, my son called me all those names. He would beat me up but he doesn't now. Once in a while he will holler at me. I had to take him so many places to get him straightened out.*

Still other children develop negative feelings and ask not to see the perpetrating parent:[129]

Mother: *They were getting to an age where it was their choice. He didn't see them for months at a time, then he would call. The kids didn't trust him. They had no relationship with him—never did. They did go on the rare occasion.*

Mother: *They go up at 3:30 and they're home at 4. They don't want to be there. I'll be perfectly candid. He frightens them.*

When children respond negatively, as in the third set of examples above, parents may find it less painful (or more convenient) to blame the custodial parent for the children's reaction than to reflect upon how their own behavior might have contributed to the problem. This is in keeping with the pattern of entitlement and failure to accept responsibility all too often documented in the domestic violence literature. Thus, "parent alienation syndrome" and "malicious mother syndrome" become common complaints in partner-abuse cases.

Quoting from American data, child psychiatrist Lois Achimovich comments,

> In essentially every case in which courts have placed children with (alleged) abusers, despite substantial evidence of sexual abuse or domestic violence and no evidence of fabrication on the protecting parent's part, it is "parent alienation syndrome" that is used by the judge, the evaluator or the child's lawyer to ignore and discount the abuse evidence and to wrongfully construe all of the child's symptoms as evidence of alienation.[130]

A recent American award-winning documentary Small Justice: Little Justice in America's Family Courts[131] is attempting to raise public awareness and concern about the recent phenomenon of battered women losing custody of children to perpetrators of abuse as a result of "parent alienation syndrome" claims in American courts. Even Richard Gardner, the founder of the parent alienation concept, cautions,

> There is no doubt that some abusive-neglectful parents are using the PAS ["parent alienation syndrome"] explanation to explain the children's campaign of alienation as a cover-up and diversionary maneuver from exposure of their abuse-neglect.[132]

Although much has been written about "parent alienation syndrome,"[133] mental health and legal experts now contend that the concept lacks scientific validity and credibility. Consequently, legal and mental health experts are now questioning the admissibility of this diagnosis in custody and access cases.[134] In Canada, Justice E. A. Bennett recently commented on the lack of scientific validity of "parent alienation syndrome" assessments in A.J.C. v. R.C. 2003, BCSC 664. No verified, accepted research data has supported the notion that "parent alienation syndrome" explains claims of domestic violence. The concept, to the extent it is useful, can only come into play after it is known that abuse claims are both false and malicious.[135] When abuse claims are true, children have reasons other than "parent alienation" to be reluctant to see the abusing parent.[136] While evidence that a parent is denigrating the other parent to the children may be relevant to willingness to facilitate contact and thus to considerations associated with section 16 (10) of the Divorce Act R.S., 1985, c. 3, "parent alienation syndrome" is not a professionally accepted mental-health syndrome or state. In sum, while it is useful as a term to describe denigrating behavior, "parent alienation syndrome" does not explain the origin of such behavior.

Nor has there been academically, professionally accepted data to support the notion that it is necessarily in the best interests of children to remove them from the care of a custodial parent in order to place them with the allegedly "alienated" parent.[137] Lois Achimovich asserts that a number of children have actually committed suicide as a result of such practice.[138] Judges accused five of the women interviewed during the New Brunswick study of attempting to alienate their children when the mothers sought restrictions to protect their children from harm in partner abuse cases.[139] In none of these cases was there evidence in the court files or in the interview data to suggest that the mothers were denigrating the other parent to the children, although there was considerable evidence to suggest such behavior on the part of the allegedly "alienated" parent. In none of the cases was there evidence that false allegations of abuse had been made.[140] One is left to wonder why North American professionals and courts have been so reluctant to acquire knowledge about domestic violence, yet so quick to embrace a mere theory dismissing such evidence. The incredible speed with which courts and professionals have accepted "alienated parent syndrome" theory—with assertions that most of the perpetrators are women—may in and of itself indicate a continuing gender bias. It certainly illustrates the need for responsible professional and academic standards to ensure that professionals and evaluators presenting to courts make assessments based on academically sound and tested knowledge rather than on the latest trend or theory.

PART FOUR: ASSESSING MUTUAL CLAIMS OF ABUSE AND SUMMARY

In the face of mutual claims of violence and abuse how are professionals and courts to respond? Until very recently, Canadian courts tended not to respond at all when abuse claims were mutual:

> **[Did that go to court?] Mother:** *No, because he charged me and I charged him. They just looked at it, they threw it out. Anything he did before, who cares?*

Traditionally, victims of abuse who engaged in violent resistance tended to be left with little or no protection. In part this has been because victim violence and the dynamics of partner abuse have been poorly understood;[141] in part it has been because evidentiary rules seemed to preclude admission of evidence of prior bad conduct.[142] This made it difficult for courts to consider the nature and the meaning of violent action in the context of the power and control dynamics of the relationship. Yet as discussed earlier, abusive violence can only be understood in context. Now, however, two recent Canadian Court of Appeal decisions, R. v. F., D. S. 1999 ONCA 176: http://www.canlii.org/on/cas/onca/1999/1999onca176.html; and R. v. C. (D.A.R.), 2002 PESCAD 22: http://www.canlii.org/pe/cas/pescad/2002/2002pescad22.html have made it clear that courts may consider evidence of past conduct and the dynamics of the relationship in domestic violence cases. It is hoped that broadened access to information will enhance judicial assessments in partner-abuse cases.

Careful scrutiny of past conduct and the power and control dynamics of the relationship are critical to accurate assessment when intimate partners make allegations of abuse against each other. When male partners claim that female partners were also violent, this can be a reflection of several distinct realities. The first is that women and men do engage in acts of violence, usually relatively minor acts of violence, during conflict in non-abusive relationships. Such acts of violence tend to be far less dangerous than abusive violence.[143] While no violence can be condoned, the second reality, female victim violence within an abusive relationship, is more complicated and thus more difficult to understand. Women who are victims of intimate-partner abuse do engage in violence and violent self-defense, violent retaliation, violent reaction to abuse, violent resistance.[144] Victims of abuse may even initiate violence in an effort to get imminent violence over with or as a reaction to past abuse. Initiating violence by victims is particularly common once the decision has finally been made to separate.[145] Let us keep in mind the earlier discussion of the difference between abuse and nonabusive violence. The vast majority of victims of domestic violence are women. Abusive violence causes more psychological and physical damage, is more likely to escalate, and is far more dangerous than non-threatening, isolated[146] violence. Domination, intimidation and control are absent, it is questionable that what is being reported is abusive violence. It is more likely that what is being reported is a form of violence during conflict or one of the forms of victim violence mentioned earlier.[147] Although abuse victims can and do commit violent acts, the violence is not abusive. This is because, despite the victim's violence, it is the abuser, not the victim, who is dominating, intimidating, degrading, and controlling.

Consideration of these elements is critical to distinguishing the violence of victims in abusive relationships from the violence of perpetrators. Michael P. Johnson's research indicates that there are three types of abusive violence. Johnson uses the term "intimate-partner terrorism": terrorization where victims do not resist with violence (perpetrator-only domination and control with violence), … terrorization where victims resist with violence (perpetrator domination and control with violence and victim resistance with violence), and terrorization with equal domination and control (which the research indicates is rare, where both partners exert domination and control and both engage in violence). His research suggests that victim resistance violence, the second category, is relatively common in intimate-partner abuse cases.[148] It is also the case most likely to result in false identification of the victim as a perpetrator or as an equal participant. This is well illustrated by the following New Brunswick interview data:

> **Mother:** *I had my bags packed. I went and got supper, then he started on me. He slapped me across the face and knocked me on the floor. But he was so drunk. He said he was going to call the police. I was scared of the police because he had brainwashed me over the years to think that it was all my fault. I told him he was not calling the police and slammed the phone down. He dialed again. I punched him on the head. When he came to, he grabbed me and ripped my shirt and bra off and was strangling me. I was going for my last breath. His arm happened to be near my throat. I bit him, really hard. I tasted blood. He was bleeding bad but I knew if I let go, he would start again.*

The woman fought back when attacked. Nonetheless, if one looks at the history and dynamics of this case, it becomes clear that although she had a tendency to resist his violence with her own violence, the domination and control and timing of the violence, the terrorization in this relationship clearly resided with the male partner:

> *He hit me once (before marriage) and I thought it was my fault. I apologized. As the years went on, he beat me up really bad about every six months. The night I left, he had been beating me up about once a week for a couple of years. He was good at it. He never hit me in the face, until the last few months. Then I got black eyes. He locked me out of the room three years before I left. I was only allowed in if I was not arguing with him. If I cooked supper the way he wanted, if I had not talked back to him. I was not allowed to eat when he ate.*

The case also involved death threats, stalking, an assault on other family members, and considerable violence in front of children. Yet in the absence of information about the history of this relationship, and the dynamics of power and control, one might assume, from considering only evidence of the violence on the single occasion, as set out in the first quotation, that this was an instance of mutual violence. Indeed, this was the misunderstanding of the judge who heard the case. The end result was lack of protection for the woman and children.

Other New Brunswick abuse victims spoke of isolated instances of their own, sometimes serious, initiating violence at the point of separation. For example, one woman reported having struck her husband repeatedly over the head with a lampshade, resulting in his need for medical attention. Consideration of the incident alone would have made it appear that she was the perpetrator rather than the victim. Once the history and dynamics of the relationship were explored, however, it became clear that he had been in control of the relationship and that her violence at separation occurred after an earlier lengthy pattern of his violence, domination, and control.

The only way, therefore, to unravel mutual claims of intimate-partner's violence is by careful consideration of context. Context includes indicators of domination and control in the relationship in association with: patterns of violent action (including emotional abuse)[149] over time, social and cultural context, victim vulnerability, and psychological (as well as physical) impact. Victim fears and perceptions are particularly important.

Although most victims of intimate-partner abusive violence (intimate partner terrorization) and women, some are men. Consideration of context and particularly assessing evidence of violence through a lens of understanding patterns of domination and control in the relationship do not preclude recognition of men who are genuinely the victims of domestic abuse. The considerations do, however, enable professionals and courts to separate men who are genuinely victimized by abuse from men who point out their partners' violent acts to justify, explain, or excuse their own behavior. Genuine intimate-partner abuse victims, male and female, will report a pattern over time of being subjected to intimidation, abusive control, and domination, in addition to being subjected to violent acts. They will also report psychological and physical harm similar to that reported by abused women.[150] While, theoretically, it is still possible that a knowledgeable perpetrator could attempt to cast him or herself as the victim, this becomes difficult with careful consideration of the long-term history of the relationship. It is unlikely that perpetrators will be able to present evidence of a history of having been dominated and controlled. Indicators of control include:

- Control over decisions about associations with others, clothing and appearance, sex, eating habits, purchases, social activities
- Imposition of social isolation (from family and friends)
- Manipulation and control by provoking fear or destroying self-esteem through a pattern of degradation
- Expectation of servitude
- Cruelty to pets
- Expectations of entitlement
- Intense jealousy with monitoring[151]

Collection of evidence relating to power and control as well as the pattern of abuse requires the use of specialized information collection tools and interview protocols. These make significant differences in the number of abuse victims identified.[152] Included in this article's notes are Web links to intimate-partner abuse assessment tools and to discussions about assessment tools designed by domestic violence experts.[153] When considering mutual abuse claims of intimate partners, it behooves us to listen carefully, not only to descriptions of the violence but, more importantly, to information about who was exercising domination and control in the relationship. Failure to present and to consider such evidence[154] in domestic violence cases is the root of complaints that professionals and the legal system are continuing to fail to protect women and children in domestic violence cases. Consideration of such evidence is a first step toward holding perpetrators accountable while protecting victims and children. One hopes for the day when victims are no longer victimized, when children no longer learn violence from parents, when the cycle of passing violence from generation to generation is broken.

QUESTIONS TO CONSIDER

1. Marriage and partnerships are often viewed as a private world, a sanctuary that ought not be subject to outside scrutiny. However, when allegations of neglect, abuse, or violence are brought forward, do you believe that key decisions about adults and children should be left with mental health professionals and the courts? Under what circumstances, if any, might other family members or friends be involved in proceedings? Might a "restorative justice" approach be used to complement or replace current mediation strategies or adversarial litigation?

2. Discuss the extent to which "indicators of control" such as entitlement, jealousy, and imposing decisions on the other partner are actually gender-based in intimate relationships. How might lawyers, mediators, judges, or other professionals take such control indicators into account in resolving domestic conflicts?

3. In the last paragraph of her article, the author insists that professionals must carefully consider information of domestic abuse and violence. She argues that by not fully considering such information in context, many professionals "fail to protect women and children" in such conflicts. Collect and discuss evidence that the legitimate interests of *male* partners might also be jeopardized by current methods of assessing evidence; e.g., discounting violence from female partners, or child custody and access decisions.

SUGGESTIONS FOR FURTHER READING/VIEWING

Silverstein, M., & Spark, R. (2007). Social bridges falling down: Reconstructing a "troublesome population" of battered women through individual responsibilization strategies. *Critical Criminology, 15*(4), 327–342.

Khanum, S. (Dir.) (2005). *Love, honour and disobey.* 61 min. documentary about family violence responses in "ethnic minority communities" in Britain and about the work of the Southall Black Sisters. New York: Faction Films.

NOTES

1. Court file data collected during the "Spousal Abuse, Children and the Legal System" research study (1998–2001), Muriel McQueen Fergusson Centre for Family Violence Research, University of New Brunswick, funded by the Canadian Bar Association, Law for the Futures Fund. The author was principal investigator and team coordinator. Those who made major contributions to the study included students Judith Begley, Tina Oates, Kiran Pure, Korinda McLaine, Elaine Jones, Suzanne Blaney-Tremblay, Cathy Rogers, and Lynn Gunn; and research team members Susan Gavin, Timothy Gallagher, Alison Charley, and Michael Guravich.

2. Parents do not always turn to the legal system. We know, for example, that children from common-law unions are more apt than other children not to live with both parents and/or to experience their parents' separation. It is not uncommon for common-law parents to decide child custody and support matters on a de facto basis, without the help of lawyers, other professionals, or the legal system. For example, only 47.5 percent of separated parents in Canada and only 48.7 percent of separated parents in the Atlantic Provinces, report that they already had acquired or were in the process of obtaining a court order for custody. Sixty percent of separated parents who had not married reported not having submitted an application for a custody order to a court. Similarly, 51.2 percent of separated parents in the Atlantic Province, from nonmarital unions, and 42.2 percent in Canada, reported that they had no agreement, court or private, for child support. *See*, NICOLE MARCH-GRATTON & CÉLINE LE BOURDAIS, DEP'T OF JUST. CAN., CUSTODY, ACCESS AND CHILD SUPPORT: FINDINGS FROM THE NATIONAL LONGITUDINAL SURVEY OF CHILDREN AND YOUTH (1999).

3. Although I prefer the term "partner abuse" to the term "spousal abuse" for the reasons outlined in note 6 below, the project was called "Spousal Abuse, Children and the Legal System" so I shall continue to use that term when referring to the study to avoid confusion.

4. Although, theoretically, experts may provide such information to judges and lawyers, expert advice and testimony are reserved, in practice, to limited numbers of families with access to financial resources. *See*, Linda Neilson, *Partner Abuse, Children and Statutory Change: Women's Access to Justice*, 18 WINDSOR Y.B. ACCESS JUST. 115, 132–133 (2000).

5. Data for the study were collected from multiple sources: (1) a review of family-law cases reported to the *Canadian Reports on Family Law* across Canada between 1983 and 1997. A total of 5,170 cases were scanned in their entirety. Surprisingly, a mere 182 included dependent children and discussion of intimate-partner abuse. At first this was surprising, but evidentiary, procedural, and socioeconomic factors prevent evidence of intimate partner violence from reaching judges and thus from being mentioned in judgments. For discussion, see, Linda Neilson, *Spousal Abuse, Children and the Courts: The Case for Social Rather than Legal Change*, 12 CANADIAN J. of L. & Soc'y 101 (1997) [hereinafter Neilson, *Spousal Abuse*]; Linda C. Neilson, *A Comparative Analysis of Law in Theory and Law in Action in Partner Abuse Cases: What do the Data Tell Us?* 26 Stud. in L., Pol. & Soc'y 141 (2002) [hereinafter Neilson, *Comparative*]; and LINDA C. NEILSON, MURIEL MCQUEEN FERGUSSON CENTRE FOR FAMILY VIOLENCE RESEARCH, SPOUSAL ABUSE, CHILDREN AND THE LEGAL SYSTEM FINAL REPORT (2001) [hereinafter NEILSON, FINAL REPORT]. (2) In addition 2,138 Court of Queen's Bench, Family Division court files from three jurisdictions were examined, 289 of these involved dependent children and allegations of partner abuse. (3) One hundred forty-seven questionnaire responses from members of the Law Society of New Brunswick and (4) interviews with 74 fathers and mothers involved in high-conflict or intimate-partner abuse cases; of these, 54 were mothers, 20 were fathers. A coding system allowed us, in most cases, to compare interview and court file data.

6. The terms "abuse" and "violence" are not synonymous. Violence and abuse often but do not always occur together. Each can occur without the other. Abuse has a reciprocal, relationship dimension that is often different from mere violence. Further explanations are offered in Parts Two and Four of this article. I prefer use of the term "partner abuse" to the term "spousal abuse" because the term better reflects the variety of intimate partnerships in North American society. Moreover intimate-partner violence rates are higher among common-law than among married couples. Statistics Canada, *Family Violence in Canada: A Statistical Profile* (2003, 2002, 2001, 2000, 1999, 1998) at: http://www.statcan.ca/english/freepub/85-224-XIE/free.htm.

7. Debra Kalmuss & Judith A. Seltzer, *Continuity of Marital Behavior in Remarriage: The Case of Spousal Abuse*. J. of MARRIAGE & THE FAM., Feb. 1986, at 113. This may be a function in part of reluctance to acknowledge and to disclose abuse during a continuing relationship.

8. Statistics Canada, *Violence Against Women Survey*, at http://www.statcan.ca/english/IPS/Data/89M0012XTB.htm (last revised Mar. 21, 2004); HOLLY JOHNSON, DANGEROUS DOMAINS—VIOLENCE AGAINST WOMEN IN CANADA (1996); NICHOLAS M. C. BALA ET AL., STATUS OF WOMEN CAN., SPOUSAL VIOLENCE IN CUSTODY AND VISITATION DISPUTES: RECOMMENDATIONS FOR REFORM 5 (1998); D. Ellis, *Family Mediation Project Final Report* (1994); L. Neilson and C. James Richardson (1996) *Evaluation of the Domestic Legal Aid Program Report* p.42. See also, however M. P. Johnson's criticism of domestic violence figures. Michael P. Johnson, *Conflict and Control: Gender, Symmetry, and Asymmetry in Domestic Violence*, VIOLENCE AGAINST WOMEN (in press), at http://www.persona.psu. edu/faculty/m/p/mpj/02VAW.html (last visited Mar. 22, 2004). Basically Johnson's concern is that such figures may not adequately distinguish situational non-abusive couple violence from abusive violence.

9. Statistics Canada, *supra* note 6; JOHNSON, *supra* note 8.

10. PETER JAFFE ET AL., ACCESS DENIED: THE BARRIERS OF VIOLENCE AND POVERTY FOR ABUSED WOMEN AND THEIR CHILDREN'S SEARCH FOR JUSTICE AND FOR COMMUNITY SERVICES AFTER SEPARATION (London, Ontario: Centre for Children and Families in the Legal System, 2003); LUNDY BANCROFT & JAY G. SILVERMAN, THE BATTERER AS PARENT, ADDRESSING THE IMPACT OF DOMESTIC VIOLENCE FAMILY DYNAMICS 118–122 (2002); D. Garee, *Identifying Victims of Domestic Violence*, ON THE EDGE 7(3): 12–15; Randy H. Magen et al., *Domestic Violence in Child Welfare Preventative Services: Results From an Intake Screening Questionnaire*, at http://hosting.uaa.alaska.edu/afrhm1/wacan/PPRS.pdf (last visited Mar.22, 2004).

11. NEILSON, *Comparative*, *supra* note 5; NEILSON, *Final Report*, *supra* note 5; Nan Seuffert, *Lawyering for Women Survivors of Domestic Violence*, at http://www.walkato.ac.nz/law/wlr/special_1996/1_seuffert.html; Kathleen Waits, *Battered Women and Their Children: Lessons from One Woman's Story*, 35 HOUS, L. REV. 29 (1998) *available at*: http://www.omsys.com/fivers/waits_houston.htm.

12. See *supra* notes 10 and 11. See also BANCROFT & SILVERMAN, *supra* note 10.

13. GAREE, *supra* note 10; MAGEN ET AL., *supra* note 10.

14. Edward W. Gondolf, *Characteristics of Batterers in a Multi-Site Evaluation of Batterer Intervention Systems: A Preliminary Report*, at http://www.mincava.umn.edu/documents/gondolf/batchar/batchar.shtml (last visited Mar. 22, 2004).

15. *Supra* notes 10–14; MIRANDA KAYE ET AL., FAMILIES, LAW AND SOCIAL POLICY RESEARCH UNIT, GRIFFITH UNIVERSITY, NEGOTIATING CHILD RESIDENCE AND CONTACT ARRANGEMENTS AGAINST A BACKGROUND OF DOMESTIC VIOLENCE (2003).

16. Although, personally, I prefer the term "parenting responsibility" to "custody" or "access" I am using the terms "custody" and "access" throughout this article to reflect current legal terminology in Canada.

17. PETER JAFFE ET AL., CHILDREN OF BATTERED WOMEN 20 (1990) [hereinafter JAFFE, CHILDREN]; PETER JAFFE ET AL., CHILD CUSTODY AND DOMESTIC VIOLENCE: A CALL FOR SAFETY AND ACCOUNTABILITY (2003) [hereinafter JAFFE, CUSTODY]; A. STEWART ET AL., SEPARATING TOGETHER, HOW DIVORCE TRANSFORMS FAMILY (1997); ROBERT E. EMERY, MARRIAGE, DIVORCE AND CHILDREN'S ADJUSTMENT (1987); S. G. Kerr and P. Jaffe "Legal and Clinical Issues in Child Custody Disputes Involving Domestic Violence" 17 C. *F.L. Q.* 1-37; A. Hetherington, M. Cox, and R. Cox, *Family Interaction and the Social, Emotional, and Cognitive Development of Children Following Divorce*, in THE FAMILY: SETTING PRIORITIES (V. C. Vaughan and T. B. Brazelton eds., 1979); Gerald F. Jacobson & Doris S. Jacobson, *Impact of Marital Dissolution on Adults and Children: The Significance of Loss and Continuity*, in THE PSYCHOLOGY OF SEPARATION AND LOSS (Jonathan Bloom-Feshback and Sally Bloom Feshback eds., 1987); Janet R. Johnston et al., *Ongoing Post-divorce Conflict and Child Disturbance*, 15 J. OF ABNORMAL CHILD. PSYCHOL. 493 (1987); Janet R. Johnston et al., *Ongoing Post-divorce Conflict: Effects on Children of Joint Custody and Frequent Access*, in 59 AM. J. OF ORTHOPSYCHIATRY 576 (1989); MARLIES SUDERMANN ET AL., NATIONAL CLEARINGHOUSE ON FAMILY VIOLENCE, WIFE ABUSE—THE IMPACT ON CHILDREN (1991), *available at* http://www.hwc.ca/datahpsb/ncfv/nc-cn.htm (last revised Apr. 1996); Mildred Daley Pagelow, *Effects of Domestic Violence on Children and their Consequences for Custody and Visitation Agreement*, 7 MEDIATION Q. 347 (1990); Einat Peled, *The Experience of Living with Violence for Preadolescent Children of Battered Women*, 29 YOUTH & SOC'Y 395 (1998); Melanie Shepard, *Child Visiting and Domestic Abuse*, 71 CHILD. WELFARE 356 (1992).

18. BANCROFT & SILVERMAN, *supra* note 10; JAFFE, CUSTODY, *supra* note 17; JAFFE, CHILDREN, *supra* note 17; KAYE, *supra* note 15; NEILSON, FINAL REPORT, *supra* note 5; Linda C. Neilson, *Children and Partner Abuse in New Brunswick Law: How Responsibilities Get Lost in Rights* in UNDERSTANDING ABUSE: PARTNERING CHANGE Mary Lou Stirling ed., 2004).

19. Statistics Canada, *supra* note 6; Statistics Canada, *Family Violence: Impacts and Consequences of Spousal Violence* THE DAILY, June 26,2002, *available at*: http://www.statcan.ca/Daily/English/020626/d020626a.htm; Tina Hotton, *Spousal Violence after Marital Separation*, 21 JURISTAT, *available at* http://www.statcan.ca/english/IPS/Data/85-002-XPE2001007.htm; Jaffe et al., *supra* note 10; Jana L. Jasinski et al., *Partner Violence: A 20 Year Review and Synthesis, Executive Summary, available at*: http://www.agnr.und.edu/nnfr/research/pv/pv_execsumm.html (last visited Mar. 29, 2004); Chris O'Sullivan, *Estimating the Population at Risk for Violence During Child Visitation*, DOMESTIC VIOLENCE REP., June-July 2000.

20. JAFFE ET AL., *supra* note 20; Eleanor E. Maccoby et al., *Co-parenting in the Second Year After Divorce*, in JOINT CUSTODY AND SHARED PARENTING 132–152 (Jay Folberg, ed., 1991); R. Nelson, *Parental Hostility, Conflict and Communication in Joint and Sole Custody Families*, J. OF DIVORCE & REMARRIAGE, 1989; BANCROFT & SILVERMAN, *supra* note 10.

21. Bancroft & Silverman, *supra* note: 10; Jaffe et al., *supra* note 10.

22. Jaffe et al., *supra* note 10.

23. C. Bourdai, H. Juby and N. Marcil-Gratton *Keeping Contact with Children: Assessing the Father/Child Post-Separation* CE´LINE LE BOURDAIS ET AL., DEPT OF JUST. CAN., KEEPING CONTACT WITH CHILDREN: ASSESSING THE FATHER/CHILD POST-SEPARATION RELATIONSHIP FROM THE MALE PERSPECTIVE (2001); J. B. Grief (1979); M. E. Bowman and C. R. Ahrons, (1985); S. Bruch (1981); J. B. Grief (1979); R. D. Hess and K. Camara (1979); A. Hetherington, E. Cox and R.Cox (1976); F. Ilfeld, H. Ilfeld and J. Alexander Jr., (1982); M. B. Isaacs (1988); Ronald P. Rohner & Robert A.Veneziano, *The Importance of Father Love: History and Contemporary Evidence*, 5 REV OF GEN. PSYCHOL. 382, (2001); Joan Berlin Kelly, *Examining Resistance to Joint Custody*, in Joint Custody and Shared Parenting 43 (Jay Folberg, ed., 1991); Joan B. Kelly & Michael E. Lamb, *Using Child Development Research to Make Appropriate Custody and Access Decisions for Young Children*, 38 FAM & CONCILIATION CTS. REV. 297, (2000); D. Luepnitz (1982);

Maccoby et al., *supra* note 20; V. Shiller (1986) and one of the most influential books of the time: J. Wallerstein and J. Kelly (1980); Judith Wallerstein, *Children of Divorce: Report of a Ten-Year Follow-up of Early Latency-Age Children*, 57 AM.J. OF ORTHOPSYCHIATRY 281, (1987).

24. JAFFE ET AL., *supra* note 10; Neilson, Final Report, *supra* note 5.

25. Jaffe et al., *supra* note 10; Jaffe et al., Custody, *supra* note 17; Bancroft & Silverman, *supra* note 10; Einat Peled, *The Parenting of Men Who Abuse Women: Issues and Dilemmas*, Brit. J. of Soc. Work 25 (2000).

26. JAFFE ET AL., *supra* note 10; JAFFE ET AL., CUSTODY, *supra* note 17; CUSTODY, *supra* note 17; BANCROFT & SILVERMAN, *supra* note 10; Pauline O'Connor, Dep't of Just. Can., *Child Access in Canada: Legal Approaches and Program Supports* (2002) available at http://canada.justice.gc.ca/en/ps/pad/reports/2002-fcy-6.html (last updated Apr. 24, 2003).

27. Pagelow, *supra* note 17; Daniel Saunders, *Child Custody in Families Experiencing Women Abuse*, 39 SOC. WORK 51(1994); Evan Stark & Anne Flitcraft, *Woman-Battering, Child Abuse and Social Heredity: What is the Relationship?* in MARITAL VIOLENCE 147–165 (N. Johnson ed., 1985); Evan Stark & Anne Flitcraft, *Women and Children at Risk: A Feminist Perspective on Child Abuse*, 18 Intl. J. OF HEALTH SERVICES 97 (1988).

28. Bancroft & Silverman, *supra* note 10, 42–43.

29. *Ibid.* at 40–41.

30. *Ibid.* Numerous evaluations of treatment programs have documented that emotional or psychological abuse is far more resistant to change than physical abuse.

31. Victim of abuse participating in the Partner Abuse, Children and the Legal System study.

32. There is a considerable body of literature and research relating to effective and ineffective treatment programs. The findings from the evaluations are both contradictory and complex and will not be discussed here. It is known, however, that anger management and parent education programs are considered ineffective in domestic violence cases. For further information see, for example: Edward W. Gondolf, *Evaluating Batterer Counseling Programs: A Difficult Task Showing Some Effects and Implications*, AGGRESSION & VIOLENT BEHAVIOR (in press).

33. JAFFE ET AL., CUSTODY, *supra* note 17; P. JAFFE ET AL., *supra* note 10; MARLIES SUDERMANN & PETER JAFFE, A HANDBOOK FOR HEALTH AND SOCIAL SERVICES PROVIDERS AND EDUCATORS ON CHILDREN EXPOSED TO WOMAN ABUSE/FAMILY VIOLENCE (2000), *available at* http://www.hc-sc.gc.ca/hppb/familyviolence/html/femexpose_e.html (last visited Mar. 31, 2004); Bancroft & Silverman, *supra* note 10. BANCROFT AND SILVERMAN offer excellent guidance relating to custody and access considerations, assessments, and responses in domestic violence cases.

34. *Ibid.*

35. Access to children commonly becomes an opportunity for continuing abuse. For example, only 11.3 percent of lawyers responding to the Spousal Abuse survey indicated that access is not used to continue patterns of abuse and control; 28.2 percent said that this pattern occurs but is infrequent; 43.7 percent indicated that the occurrence is frequent; 16.9 percent said that the pattern occurs but declined an invitation to comment on frequency. Most mothers who participated in the study complained that exchanging children provided continuing opportunities for harassment, intimidation, abuse and control. For similar conclusions, see: Statistics Canada, *supra* note 6; Statistics Canada, *supra* note 19; Hotton, *supra* note 19; Jaffe et al., *supra* note 10; Jasinski et al., *supra* note 19; O'Sullivan, *supra* note 19; Kaye et al., *supra* note 15. This is a serious problem in terms of children's health, as it is well known that long-term exposure to parental conflict is damaging to children.

36. BANCROFT & SILVERMAN, *supra* note 10; JAFFE ET AL., CUSTODY, *supra* note 17; Jaffe et al., *supra* note 10; Key et al., *supra* note 15; NIELSON, FINAL REPORT, *supra* note 5; Neilson, *supra* note 18; Helen Rhoades et al, The Family Law Reform Act 1995: The First Three Years (2000), *available at* http://www. familycourt.gov. au/papers/html/fla1.html (last visited Mar. 31, 2004); see also Rosemary Aris et al., *Safety and Child Contact: An Analysis of the Role of Child Contact Centres in the Context of Domestic Violence and Child Welfare Concerns* (2002), *available at* http://www.dcs.gov.uk/research/2002/res02fr.htm#10_2002 last visited Mar. 31, 2004) in connection with safety concerns relating to access centres in domestic violence cases. For an illustration of such behavior in case law, see *Best v. McGraw* 2002 NBQB 349.

37. *Ibid.* See also Saunders, *supra* note 27.

38. The article focuses on assessing mutual claims. Not discussed in this article are risk and lethality assessment.

39. NEILSON, FINAL REPORT, *supra* note 5.

40. NEILSON, FINAL REPORT, *supra* note 5.

41. NEILSON, FINAL REPORT, *supra* note 5; Neilson, *Comparative supra* note 5. Safety concerns (for victims, children and interviewers) led us to exclude from the interview process fathers whose court files indicated dangerous levels of violence and abuse. Not every father who participated in the study was abusive. Data collected during the course of the study indicated that several fathers were more victims than perpetrators.

Two were primary caregivers of children. The research team endorsed the principles that (a) caring, responsible fathers should be encouraged to participate in children's lives; and (b) individual parents should not be judged solely on the basis of gender. In the words of one male caregiver, *Let's not say okay, this person happens to be female, this person happens to be male, so we are going to judge them that way. Possibly in 80% of families, the mother is the primary caregiver and if that is the case, probably she should get custody. But in situations where that is not the case, when things are a little bit off the socially accepted norms, [there is a need to] analyse the case and see what should be done for the children.*

42. Neilson, *Spousal Abuse, supra* note 5: NEILSON, FINAL REPORT, *supra* note 5. See also BALA ET AL. *supra* note 8; JAFFE ET AL., *supra* note 10.

43. SUSAN BOYD, CHILD CUSTODY, LAW AND WOMEN'S WORK (2002); Neilson, *supra* note 5; Department of Justice, Custody and Access: Public Discussion Paper (Ottawa: Minister of Justice 1993). Fathers do report, however, settlement pressure to agree. NEILSON, FINAL REPORT, *supra* note 5.

44. BOYD, *supra* note 43; MARGRIT EICHLER, FAMILY SHIFTS: FAMILIES, POLICIES AND GENDER EQUALITY (1997).

45. Cynthia Silver, *Being There: The Time Dual-Earner Couples Spend With Their Children,* CANADIAN SOC. TRENDS, Summer 2000.

46. NICHOLAS BALA, A REPORT FROM CANADA'S "GENDER WAR ZONE": REFORMING THE CHILD RELATED PROVISIONS OF THE DIVORCE ACT 6 (1999), at http://www.familylawcentre.com/ccbalad-ivpap.html (last visited Mar. 16, 2004); DEP'T OF JUST. CAN., SELECTED STATISTICS ON CANADIAN FAMILIES AND FAMILY LAW: SECOND EDITION 16 (2000) at http://canada.justice.gc.ca/en/ps/sup/index-stat.html (last visited Apr. 3, 2004).

47. BANCROFT AND SILVERMAN, *supra* note 10; AMERICAN PSYCHOLOGICAL ASSOCIATION, REPORT OF THE AMERICAN PSYCHOLOGICAL ASSOCIATION PRESIDENTIAL TASK FORCE ON VIOLENCE AND THE FAMILY (1996).

48. It is possible that additional claims were made during oral hearings that were not documented in the court files.

49. The court files included documentary information tending to corroborate such claims (in the form of affidavits of witnesses, information about criminal convictions, mental health evaluations, admissions) in approximately 70 percent of the cases.

50. I am referring here only to contested custody cases decided by a judge. I am including cases in which a judge ordered custody of the children to the abuser parent at some point in the file. In quite a few cases custody moved back and forth between parents several times over the years, sometimes by agreement, sometimes by judicial order. Judges will not always be fully aware of the particulars of intimate-partner violence or abuse when making orders in these cases because evidentiary matters, procedural settlement processes, and socioeconomic factors curtail presentation of intimate-partner abuse evidence to judges in practice.

51. AMERICAN JUDGES FOUNDATION, INC., DOMESTIC VIOLENCE & THE COURTROOM: UNDERSTANDING THE PROBLEM ... KNOWING THE VICTIM, at http://aja.ncsc.dmi.us/domviol/booklet.html (last visited Apr. 4, 2004); Nicholas Bala et al., *Spousal Violence in Custody and Access Disputes: Recommendations for Reform* (1998), at http://www.swc.cfc.gc.ca/pubs/spousal_violence/spousal_violence_e.html (last updated Nov. 17, 2003); Naomi R. Cahn, *Civil Images of Battered Women: The Impact of Domestic Violence on Child Custody Decisions,* 44 VAND. L. REV. 1041 (1991); MARGARET DENIKE ET AL., MYTHS AND REALITIES OF CUSTODY AND ACCESS (1998), at http://www.harbout.sfu.ca/freda/reports/myths.htm; SANDRA A.GOUNDRY, VANCOUVER ASS/N OF WOMEN & THE LAW., REPORT ON COURT-RELATED HARASSMENT AND FAMILY LAW "JUSTICE" (1998); Katie Kovacs, *Domestic Violence, Children and Family Law in Australia and New Zealand,* CHILD ABUSE PREVENTION NEWSLETTER (Nat'l Child Prot. Clearinghouse, Australia) ,Winter 2002, at 1–2, at http://www.aifs.org.au/nch/pubs/nl2002/winter.html (last visited Mar. 16, 2004); R. Langer "Male Domestic Abuse: The Continuing Contrast Between Women's Experiences and Judicial Responses" C.J.L.S 10(1)(1995) 65–90; Daniel G. Saunders, *Child Custody and Visitation Decisions in Domestic Violence Cases: Legal Trends, Research Findings, and Recommendations* (1998), at http://www.vaw.umn.edu/documents/vawnet/custody/custody.html (last modified Sept. 15, 2003); Waits, *supra* note 11.

52. BANCROFT & SILVERMAN, *supra* note 10; Battered Mothers Testimony Project (2002) Battered Women Speak Out: A Human Rights Report on Domestic Violence and Child Custody in the Massachusetts Family Courts (Wellesley Centres for Women); C. Bertoia & J. Drakich, *The Fathers' Rights Movement: Contradiction in Rhetoric and Practice,* 14 J. of FAM. ISSUES 592 (1993); CALIFORNIA NOW FAMILY COURT REPORT 2002, *available at* http://www.canow.org/fam.html (last revised Sept. 26, 2002); Barbara J. Hart, *Children of Domestic Violence: Risks and Remedies,* CHILD. PROTECTIVE SERVICES Q. Winter 2002, *available at*

http://www.mincava.umn.edu/documents/hart/risks.shtml (last visited Mar. 16, 2004); JAFFE ET AL., *supra* note 10; JAFFE ET AL., *supra* note 17; KAYEET AL., *supra* note 15; Kovacs, *supra* note 51; Neilson, *Spousal Abuse*, *supra* note 5; NEILSON, FINAL REPORT, *supra* note 5; Neilson, *supra* note 18; Rhoades et al., *supra* note 36; Saunders, *supra* note 51; Aris et al., *supra* note 36.

53. DEP'T OF JUST. CAN., research reports on justice and gender, see heading "Gender Issues" at: http://canada. justice.gc.ca/en/ps/rs/rep/202new2-e.html (last visited Mar. 17, 2004); Boyd, *supra* note 43; Marie Gordon, *What, Me Biased? Women and Gender Bias in Family Law*, 29 FAM. L. Q. 53 (2001); COMMISSION ON RACE & GENDER REL., IN. SUP. COURT., HONORED TO SERVE (2002), at http://www.in.gov/judiciary/fairness/ (last visited Mar. 16, 2004); JUDICIAL COUNCIL OF CA., ACHIEVING EQUAL JUSTICE FOR WOMEN AND MEN IN THE CALIFORNIA COURTS: FINAL REPORT (Gay Danforty & Bobbie L. Welling, eds., 1996) *at* http://www.courtinfo.ca.gov/programs/access/documents/f-report.pdf (last visited Apr. 5, 2004); GENDER BIAS STUDY IMPLEMENTATION COMMISSION, GENDER BIAS—THEN AND NOW: CONTINUING CHANGES IN THE LEGAL SYSTEM (1996), at http://www.flcourts.org/sct/sctdocs/library.html (last visited Apr. 6, 2004); Rhode Island Permanent Advisory Committee on Women in Courts. *Gender Bias in State Courts* (1998); GENDER BIAS STUDY COMMISSION, REPORT OF THE FLORIDA SUPREME COURT GENDER BIAS STUDY COMMISSION: EXECUTIVE SUMMARY (1998), *at* http://www.flcourts.org/sct/sctdocs/library.html (last visited Apr. 6, 2004); THE COMMITTEE FOR JUSTICE FOR WOMEN & THE ORANGE COUNTY WOMEN'S COALITION, CONTESTED CUSTODY CASES IN ORANGE COUNTY, NORTH CAROLINA, TRIAL COURTS, 1983–1987: GENDER BIAS, THE FAMILY AND THE LAW (1991); Nahid Roboubi & Sharon Bowles Federal, *Barriers to Justice: Ethnocultural Minority Women and Domestic Violence*, in THE CRIMINAL JUSTICE SYSTEM AND WOMEN: WOMEN OFFENDERS, VICTIMS, WORKERS, (Barbara Raffel Price & Natalie J. Sokoloff, eds., 1981), available at http://canada.justice.gc.ca/en/ps/rs/rep/tr95-3a-e.html; Norma Juliet Wikler & Lynn Hecht Schafran. *Learning from the New Jersey Supreme Court Task Force on Women and the Courts: Evaluation, Recommendations, and Implications for Other States*, 12 WOMEN'S RTS. L. REP 313 (1991); Trish Wilson, Domestic Violence in Maryland: More from the Gender Bias Report, *at* http://www.voiceofwomen.com/articles/violence.html

54. LONDON PEARSON & ROGER GALLAWAY, REPORT OF THE SPECIAL JOINT COMMITTEE ON CHILD CUSTODY AND ACCESS (1998), *at* http://www.parl.gc.ca/InfoComDoc/36/1/SJCA/Studies/Reports/sjcarp02-e.htm (last visited Mar. 16, 2004). This report is controversial; it has been strongly criticized in academic literature.

55. In addition to the sources cited above, see also, Leadership Council, Inc., *Are "Good Enough" Parents Losing Custody to Abusive Ex-Partners?* (2002) at http://www.leadershipcouncil.org/Research/PAS/PAS/DV/dv.html (last visited Apr. 6, 2004).

56. Statistics Canada, *supra* note 6; Statistics Canada, *supra* note 19; National Clearinghouse on domestic Violence, Woman Abuse, (2002), *at* http://www.hc-c.gc.ca/hppb/familyviolence/pdfs/woman%20abuse%20-%20e.pdf; Walter DeKeseredy, *Four Variations of Family Violence: A Review of Sociological Research* (1993), at http:// www.hc-sc.gc.ca/hppb/familyviolence/html/1variation.htm; Jasinski et al., *supra* note 19; Leslie Tutty, *Husband Abuse: An Overview of Research and Perspectives*, at 19–20 (1998), *available at* http://www.hese.gc.ca/hppb/familyviolence/pdfs/husbandenglish.pdf; Yasmin Jiwani, *1999 General Social Survey on Spousal Violence: An Analysis*, (2000), at http://www.harbour.sfu.ca/freda/reports/gss01.htm; Hotton, *supra* note 19. For similar findings in the United States, *see* Patricia Tjaden & Nancy Thoennes, *Prevalence and Consequences of Male-to-Female and Female-to-Male Intimate Partner Violence as Measured by the National Violence Against Women Survey, 6 Violence Against Women 000)*; PATRICIA TIADEN & NANCY THOENNES, NATIONAL INSTITUTE OF JUSTICE, EXTENT, NATURE AND CONSEQUENCES OF INTIMATE PARTNER VIOLENCE. FINDINGS FROM A NATIONAL VIOLENCE AGAINST WOMEN SURVEY (2000), *at* http://www.ncjrs.org/pdffiles1/nij/181867.pdf; Suzanne Swan & D. Snow, *Typology of Women's Use of Violence in Intimate Relationships*, 8 VIOLENCE AGAINST WOMEN 286 (2002); CALLIE MARIE RENNISON & SARAH WELCHANS, BUREAU OF JUSTICE STATISTICS SPECIAL REPORT, INTIMATE PARTNER VIOLENCE (2000), *at* http://www.prevlink.org/clearinghouse/catalog/crime_risky_behaviors/crime_violence/intimatepartnerviolence.pdf; CALLIE MARIE RENNISON, BUREAU OF JUSTICE STATISTICS SPECIAL REPORT, INTIMATE PARTNER VIOLENCE AND AGE OF THE VICTIM, 1993–99 (2001) *at* http://www.ojp.usdoj.gov/bjs/pub/pdf/ipva99.pdf; BUREAU OF JUSTICE STATISTICS, CRIME CHARACTERISTICS, TRENDS 1973–2001 (2001) *at* http://www.ojp.usdoj.gov/bjs/cvict_c.htm.

57. As one moves from statistics that include minor acts of violence to statistics on victims seeking help as result of injury caused by violence, to statistics on those victimized by patterns of intense violence, a smaller and smaller proportion of the number of victims are men. *See Tutty, supra* note 56; CANADA FIREARMS CENTRE, RESEARCH SUMMARY DOMESTIC VIOLENCE INVOLVING FIREARMS, *at* http://www.cfc.

ccaf.gc.ca/en/research/other_docs/factsheets/domestic (last updated Feb. 11, 2002); HOLLY JOHNSON, *supra* note 8; Walter DeKeseready, *In Defence of Self-Defence: Demystifying Female Violence Against Male Intimates, in* CROSSCURRENT DEBATES IN CANADIAN SOCIETY (R. Hinch ed., 1992); R. Emerson Dobash et al., *The Myth of Sexual Symmetry in Marital Violence,* 39 SOC. PROBLEMS 71 (1992); R. Emerson Dobash et al., *Separate and Intersecting Realities: A Comparison of Men's and Women's Accounts of Violence against Women,* 4 VIOLENCE AGAINST WOMEN 382 (1998); Robin Fitzgerald, *Spousal Violence,* JUST RESEARCH, Mar. 2001, at 7, *available at* http://canada.justice.gc.ca/en/ps/rs/rep/jr-mar01-e.pdf; Neilson (2001), *supra* note 5; Status of Women Canada, *Fact Sheet: Statistics on Violence Against Women in Canada, at* http://www.swc-cfc. gc.ca/dates/dec6/facts_e.html (last updated Nov. 13, 2003); Statistics Canada, *supra* note 6; RENNISON & WALCHANS, *supra* note 56; RENNISON, *supra* note 56; RHOADES ET AL., *supra* note 36.

58. See, e.g., TERRIE E. MOFFITT & AVSHALOM CASPI, NATIONAL INSTITUTE OF JUSTICE, FINDINGS ABOUT PARTNER VIOLENCE FROM THE DUNEDIN MULTIDISCIPLINARY HEALTH AND DEVELOPMENT STUDY, (1999), *available at* http://www.communitypolicing.org/eleclib/pdffiles/PartVi. pdf; Martin S. Fiebert, *References Examining Assaults by Women on Their Spouses or Male Partners: An Annotated Bibliography* (2001), *at* http://www.csulb.edu/mfieber/assault.htm.

59. See *supra* notes 8–10; *supra* notes 13–14.

60. *See, e.g.,* Steven Bittle, *Dating Violence Among Youth,* JUST RESEARCH, Mar. 2001, at 6, *available at* http://Canada.justice.gc.ca/en/ps/rs/rep/jr-mar01-e.pdf; Fitzgerald, *supra* note 57.

61. Michael P. Johnson, *Conflict and Control: Symmetry and Asymmetry in Domestic Violence, in* COUPLES IN CONFLICT (Alan Booth et al. eds., 2001), *available at* http://www.personal.psu.edu/faculty/m/p/mpj/dvpage.html.

62. High risk of intimate-partner-violence populations includes immigrant women whose language is not English or French, homeless women, women who are illiterate, women who have special mental or physical requirements (disabled).

63. *See, e.g.,* Jiwani, *supra* note 57.

64. Joan Zorza, *Woman Battering: A Major Cause of Homelessness.* 25 CLEARINGHOUSE REVIEW 421 (1991) (concluding that about one half of the homeless women and children she studied were homeless as a result of woman abuse).

65. Donald Dutton and K. J. Hemphill, *Patterns of Socially Desirable Responding Among Perpetrators and Victims of Wife Assault,* 7 VIOLENCE AND VICTIMS 29 (1992); Edward Gondolf, *Characteristics of Batterers in a Multi-Site Evaluation of Batterer Intervention Systems: A Preliminary Report* (Minnesota Center Against Violence and Abuse) (1995), *available at* http://www.mincava.umn.edu/documents/gondolf/batchar/batchar.shtml. See also, Indiana University of Pennsylvania, Mid-Atlantic Addiction Training Institute, *A Multi-site Evaluation of Batterer Intervention System: Abstracts on Research Design* (1997), at http://www.iup.edu/maati/publications/ designabstracts.shtm#design4; Kerri James et al., *"Using It" or "Losing It": Men's Construction of Their Violent Behavior Towards Female Partners* (Australia Domestic and Family Violence Clearinghouse) (2002), *at* http://www.austdvclearinghouse.unsw.edu.au/Occasional/James_et_al_researchpaper_final.pdf. Moreover, many alcoholic abusive men may actually not believe evidence of patterns of their own abusive behavior because, from their own perspective, they do not abuse their partners every day and thus tend not to view themselves as "usually abusive." See David Adams, *Identifying the Assaultive Husband in Court: You Be the Judge,* 33 BOSTON B. J. 23 (1989); BANCROFT & SILVERMAN *supra* note 10.

66. DeKeseredy, *supra* note 56; Walter DeKeseredy & Brian MacLean, *But Women Do It Too: The Context and Nature of Female-to-Male Violence in Canadian, Heterosexual Dating Relationships, in* UNSETTLING TRUTHS: BATTERED WOMEN, POLICY, POLITICS AND CONTEMPORARY RESEARCH IN CANADA (Kevin Bonnycastle & George Rigakos eds., 1998); Fitzgerald, *supra* note 57; JASINSKI ET AL., *supra* note 19; Walter DeKeseredy & Martin Schwartz, *Measuring the Extent of Woman Abuse in Intimate Heterosexual Relationships: A Critique of the Conflict Tactics Scales* (Minnesota: Violence Against Women On Line Resources Net) (1998), *at* http://www.vaw.umn.edu/documents/vawnet/ctscritique/ctscritique.html.

67. Conflict Tactics Scales provide dependable data on violence but limited information about abusive relationships. See DeDeseredy, *supra* note 56; JASINSKI ET AL., *supra* note 19; Jiwani, *supra* note 56; DeKeseredy & Schwartz, *supra* note 66; U.S. Department of Justice, Building Data Systems for Monitoring and Responding to Violence Against Women (Washington: Centre for Diseases Control and Prevention) (2001), *at* http://www.cdc.gov/mmwr/preview/mmwrhtml/rr4911a1.htm; Shamita Das Dasgupta, Towards an Understanding of Women's Use of Non-lethal Violence in Intimate Heterosexual Relationships, Applied Research Forum: Violence Against Women, *at* http://www.vaw.umn.edu/documents/vawnet/towards/towards.html: Johnson, *supra* note 8; WHAT CAUSES MEN'S VIOLENCE AGAINST WOMEN (J. O'Neil & M. Harway eds., 1999), bibliography on criticisms of Gender and Violence Literature, at http://www.ucc.uconn.edu/oneil/refere.htm.

68. The words in square brackets do not change the substance of DeKeseredy's comments but the words are my own.

69. DeKeseredy & Schwartz, *supra* note 66.

70. Johnson, *supra* note 61.

71. It is rare indeed to find claims of violence or abuse being made by men in child custody Source in the absence of claims of abuse or violence by female partners. In the Spousal Abuse, Children and the Legal System study, for example, we encountered allegations of intimate-partner violence or abuse by a male partner in only 1.4% of the court files and in only 3% of the intimate-partner abuse cases reported in the *Report on Family Law*. Mutual claims were more common at 9 to 13% of the cases, depending on the source of data. In the majority of cases, claims were made only by women (Neilson, 2000), *supra* note 4. See also, DeKeseredy, *supra* note 56; Dasgupta *supra* note 67.

72. DeKeseredy, *supra* note 56; Neilson, *Spousal Abuse*, *supra* note 5; Dasgupta *supra* note 67; M. A. Dutton as edited by M. Gordon, VALIDITY OF BATTERED WOMAN SYNDROME IN CRIMINAL CASES INVOLVING BATTERED WOMEN: THE VALIDITY AND USE OF EVIDENCE CONCERNING BATTERING AND ITS EFFECTS IN CRIMINAL TRIALS (Washington: U.S. Department of Justice and National Judicial Institute, 1996), *at* http://www.ncjrs.org/pdffiles/batter.pdf.

73. Women who participated in a New Brunswick study of legal responses in partner abuse cases involving women reported gaining the strength to fight back as a result of making the decision to separate and, or reported not caring any more whether they would be seriously injured or killed, see Neilson, *Spousal Abuse*, *supra* note 5.

74. See R. Dobash, et al., The Myth of Sexual Symmetry in Marital Violence, 39 SOCIAL PROBLEMS, 71–91 (1992).

75. Fitzgerald, *supra* note 57 at 8; See also Holly Johnson & Valerie Pottie Bunge, PREVALENCE AND CONSEQUENCES OF SPOUSAL ASSAULTS IN CANADA, 43 CAN J. OF CRIMINOLOGY 27 (2001); Patricia Tjaden & Nancy Thoennes, *Prevalence and Consequences of Male-to-Female and Female-to-Male Intimate Partner Violence as Measured by the National Violence Against Women Survey*; 6 VIOLENCE AGAINST WOMEN 142 (2000). *See* abstract, *at* http://www.ncjrs.org/rr/vol1_3/12.html.

76. Johnson, *supra* note 61.

77. See, e.g., MURRY ARNOLD STRAUS ET AL., BEHIND CLOSED DOORS: VIOLENCE IN THE AMERICAN FAMILY (Basic Books 1981).

78. Richard Gelles, *Domestic Violence: Not an Even Playing Field*, The Safety Zone Domestic Violence Resources Information on Woman Abuse, *at* http://www.serve.com/zone/everyone/gelles.html (last visited Apr. 19, 2004).

79. Michael P. Johnson, Patriarchal Terrorism and Common Couple Violence: Two Forms of Violence Against Women, 57 J. of MARRIAGE AND THE FAM 283 (1995); Johnson, *supra* note 8; Michael P. Johnson & Janel M. Leone, *The Differential Effects of Intimate Terrorism and Situational Couple Violence: Findings from the National Violence Against Women Survey*, J. of Fam. Issues (in press), *available at* http://www.personal.psu.edu/faculty/m/p/mpj/dvpage.html.

80. Johnson, *supra* note 61.

81. Jeri Martinez, *Hostages in the Home: Domestic Violence Seen Through its Parallel, the Stockholm Syndrome*, *at* http://www.mincava.umn.edu/documents/clergybook/clergyappendix2.doc (last visited Apr. 20, 2004).

82. Joan Simalchik, *The Politics of Torture: Dispelling the Myths and Understanding the Survivors*, *in* COMMUNITY SUPPORT FOR SURVIVORS OF TORTURE: A MANUAL (Kathy Price ed., 1995), *available at* http://www.icomm.ca/ccvt/simalchik.html. From a victim perspective, victimization by domestic abuse and victimization by terrorism are similar. To view other articles in the manual cited above, *at* http://www.icomm.ca/ccvt/ccvtpublications.html.

83. Lorraine E. Ferris et al., *Psychological Manifestations of Woman Abuse*, in A HANDBOOK FOR DEALING WITH WOMAN ABUSE AND THE CRIMINAL JUSTICE SYSTEM GUIDELINES FOR PHYSICIANS (2000), available at http://www.hc-sc.gc.ca/hppb/familyviolence/pdfs/physician-e.pdf; Elaine Grandin et al., *Couple Violence and Psychological Distress*, CAN J. OF PUB. HEALTH, Jan/Feb. 1998, at 43; Diane R. Follingstad et al., *The Role of Emotional Abuse in Physically Abusive Relationships*, 5J OF FAM VIOLENCE 107 (1990); LENORE E. WALKER, THE BATTERED WOMAN (1979); Laura Stevens, *What is Emotional Abuse?* (1996), *at* http://www.hc-sc.gc.ca/hppb/familyviolence/html/emotioneng.html. There is a difference, however. Domestic psychological torture tends to be longer term and occurs closer to home.

84. Dutton, *supra* note 72, at 8.

85. M. Sharon Maxwell & Karen Oehme, *Strategies to Improved Supervised Visitation Services in Domestic Violence Cases*, Violence Against Women Online Resources (Oct. 2001), *at* http://www.vaw.umn.edu/documents/commissioned/strategies/pdf.

86. Battered Mothers Testimony Project, *supra* note 52; Goundry et al., *supra* note 51; Kaye et al., *supra* note 18; Neilson (2001), *supra* note 5; NORTHWEST TRIBAL COURT JUDGES ASSOCIATION, VIOLENCE AGAINST WOMEN TRIBAL COURT BENCH BOOK FOR DOMESTIC VIOLENCE CASES (1999);

Rhoades et al., *supra* note 36; T.J. Sutherland, *High Conflict Divorce of Stalking by Way of Family Court? The Empowerment of a Wealthy Abuser in Family Court Litigation Linda v. Lyle—A Case Study, at* http://www.mincava. umn.edu/documents/linda/linda/shtml (last modified Apr. 17, 2003). During the Spousal Abuse, Children and the Legal System study, we found that abusive men who engaged in high rates of litigation against former partners usually blamed former partners for "forcing" extensive litigation upon them by refusing to agree to their joint custody "entitlements."

87. T. J. Sutherland, *supra* note 86.

88. *See also* Goundry et al., *supra* note 51.

89. Neilson (2001) *supra* note 5; Goundry, *supra* note 51; Rhoades et al., *supra* note 36. *See, e.g.,* Mitchell v. Mitchell, [1999] B.C.S.C. 10949; Broda v. Broda, [2001] A.B.C.A. 151; Broda v. Broda, [2002] A.B.C.A. 133.

90. Neilson, *supra* note 4.

91. *Ibid. See also* Neilson, *supra* note 5.

92. BANCROFT & SILVERMAN, *supra* note 10, at 21, 118; RICHARD J. GELLES & MURRAY A. STRAUS, INTIMATE VIOLENCE: THE CAUSES AND CONSEQUENCES OF ABUSE IN THE AMERICAN FAMILY (1988); Gondolf et al., *A Review of Quantitative Research on Men who Batter*, 5 J. of INTERPERSONAL VIOLENCE 87 (1990); Edward Gondolf, *"Do Batterer Programs Work?" A 15-month follow-up of a Multi-site Evaluation*, 3 DOMESTIC VIOLENCE REPORT 64 (1998); Edward Gondolf, Characteristics of Court-Mandated Batterers in Four Cities: Diversity and Dichotomies, 5 VIOLENCE AGAINST WOMEN 1277 (1999).

93. LIZ HART & WANDA JAMIESON, NATIONAL CLEARINGHOUSE OF FAMILY VIOLENCE, WOMAN ABUSE (2001), *at* http://www.hc-sc.gc.ca/hppb/familyviolence/pdf; Judicial Education Centre of New Mexico (JEC), *Domestic Violence Benchbook*, sections 1.5 to 1.6 *available at* http://jec.unm.edu/resources/benchbooks/dv/ (last visited Apr. 23, 2004); James et al., *supra* note 65; Gondolf et al. (1990), *supra* note 92; Adams, *supra* note 65.

94. Edward Gondolf, *MCMI Results for Batterer Program Participants in Four Cities: Less "Pathological" than Expected*, 14 J. OF FAM. VIOLENCE (1999); *See also* Mid-Atlantic Addiction Training Institute, Indiana University of Pennsylvania, Abstracts on Batterer Characteristics, *at* http://www.iup.edu/maati/publications/ BattererCharacteristics.shtm (last visited Apr. 21, 2004).

95. *Ibid.*; NEIL S. JACOBSON & JOHN GOTTMAN, WHEN MEN BATTER WOMEN (1998); Amy Holtzworth-Munroe & G. Stuart, *Typologies of Male Batterers in Four Cities: Diversity and Dichotomies*, 5 VIOLENCE AGAINST WOMEN 1277 (1994); Janet Johnston & Linda Campbell, *A Clinical Typology on Inter-personal Violence in Disputed Custody Decisions.* 63 AM. J. OF ORTHOPSYCHIATRY 190 (1993); JANET JOHNSTON & LINDA CAMPBELL, IMPASSES OF DIVORCE (1988); Janet Johnston, *Domestic Violence and Parent-Child Relationships in Families Disputing Custody* 9 AUSTRALIAN J. OF FAM. L. 12 (1995).

96. See e.g., Gondolf, *supra* note 94; see e.g., MID-ATLANTIC ADDICTION TRAINING INSTITUTE, *supra* note 94.

97. Jennifer Laughinrichsen-Rohling et al., *The Clinical Utility of Batterer Typologies*, 151 of Fam. Violence 37 (2000); *see also* Bancroft & Silverman, *supra* note 10 of Chapter 6 for a critical evaluation of J. Johnston and L. Campbell typologies.

98. Resources may not permit such assessments in every case.

99. JAFFE ET AL., *supra* note 17; CASEY GWINN, NATIONAL COLLEGE OF DISTRICT ATTORNEYS, PROSECUTING DOMESTIC VIOLENCE CASES WITHOUT VICTIM PARTICIPATION (2001), *at* http://www.sandiegodvunit.org/RenoProsecution.102901b.pdf; BANCROFT & SILVERMAN, *supra* note 10.

100. *Ibid.* P. Jaffe et al. note 18; Gwinn, National College of District Attorneys (2001) Prosecuting Domestic Violence Cases Without Victim Cooperation. Power Point presentation (San Diego City Attorney's Domestic Violence Unit): http://www.sandiegodvunit.org/RenoProsecution.102901b.pdf. L. Bancroft and J. Silverman (2002) note 10.

101. American Psychological Association, *supra* note 47; JAFFE ET AL., *supra* note 10; BANCROFT & SILVERMAN, *supra* note 10, *at* 18; Dutton, *supra* note 72.

102. American Psychological Association (1996) *Violence and the Family: Report of the American Psychological Association Presidential Task Force on Violence and the Family* (American Psychological Association); P. Jaffe et al. (2003) note 20; Bancroft and Silverman (2002) note 10 p. 118; M. A. Dutton note 44. Discussion of the effects of domestic violence on victims and how those effects affect both victim demeanor and psychological testing is beyond the scope of this article.

103. Interview data were corroborated by court file data as well as by subsequent events. Although the former husband was able for a time to mislead mediators, police, lawyers, and judges using various tactics, including presenting as a gentle, kind, considerate person trying to respond to his wife's angry disposition—because the historic pattern and context of the violence was not fully investigated—the true situation became increasingly apparent after the husband began to abuse violently subsequent partners.

104. Court file and interview data disclosed dangerous levels of abuse and violence including death threats and years of physical beating witnessed by the children. Nonetheless, this father was awarded access to the children by the family court.

105. M. A. Dutton, *The Validity of Evidence Concerning Battering and Its Effects in Criminal Trials*. (1996), at http://www.ojp.usdoj.gov/nik/vawprog/man04.htm; Adams, *supra* note 65; BANCROFT & SILVERMAN, *supra* note 10; C. Gwinn, *supra* note 99.

106. M. A. Dutton, *The Validity of Evidence Concerning Battering and Its Effects in Criminal Trials US Justice* (National Institute of Justice, 1996); http://www.ojp.usdoj.gov/nij/vawprog/man04.htm; D. Adams (1989) "Identifying the Assaultive Husband in Court: You Be the Judge" Boston Bar Journal July/August 1989: 23pp: L. Bancroft and J. Silverman (2002) *The Batterer as Parent Addressing the Impact of Domestic Violence on Family Dynamics* (Sage); C. Gwinn, National College of District Attorneys (2001) Prosecuting Domestic Violence Cases Without Victim Cooperation. Power Point presentation (San Diego City Attorney's Domestic Violence Unit) http://www.sandi-egodvunit.org/RenoProsecution.102901b.pdf

107. BANCROFT & SILVERMAN, *supra* note 10; Gondolf (1995), *supra* note 14; Gondolf (1998), *supra* note 92.

108. *See* Gwinn, *supra* note 99.

109. Bancroft & Silverman, *supra* note 10, at 123; Adams, *supra* note 105; Gondolf (1995), *supra* note 24; Gondolf & Bennett (1990), *supra* note 92; Gondolf (1998), *supra* note 92; James et al., *supra* note 65.

110. Adams (1989), *supra* note 65, at 24.

111. DONALD G. DUTTON, THE BATTERER: A PSYCHOLOGICAL PROFILE (1995); James et al., *supra* note 65.

112. Goundry (1998), *supra* note 51.

113. BANCROFT & SILVERMAN, *supra* note 10. *See also* [1999] N.S.C.A.113, *at* http://www.canlit.org/ns/cas/nsca/1999/1999nsca113.html.

114. *See e.g.*, *Best v. McGraw*, 2002 NBQB 349.

115. Jeffery Edleson, *Mothers and Children: Understanding the Links between Woman Battering and Child Abuse*, (1995), *at* http://www.mincava.umn.edu/papers/nij.htm; Michelle S. Jacobs, *Requiring Battered Women to Die: Murder Liability For Mothers Under Failure to Protect Statutes*, 88 J. L. CRIM. 579 (1998); Daniel Saunders, *Child Custody Decisions in Families Experiencing Women Abuse*, SOCIAL WORK, Jan. 1994, at 51–56; Evan Stark & Anne Flitcraft, *Woman-battering, Child Abuse and Social Heredity: What is the Relationship?*, in MARITAL VIOLENCE 147–165 (Norman Johnson ed., 1985); Barbara J. Hart, *Women and Children at Risk: A Feminist Perspective on Child Abuse*, 18 INTERNATIONAL J. OF HEALTH SERVICES 97–118 (1988).

116. For more complete discussion of the difficulties created by the tendency to consider partner abuse and child abuse distinct phenomenon, *see* Neilson, *supra* note 4, at 133–137. Excluded from this analysis are child protection cases initiated by the Province, Health and Community Services. Previously, in "Partner Abuse" it was reported that "twenty-two of the court files examined in New Brunswick involved interventions of child protection authorities as a result of abuse and violence between the parents. The affidavits filed with the court in these cases were framed in gender-neutral language, making the dynamics of the abuse between parents difficult, sometimes impossible, to interpret. Commonly the affidavits stated merely, "the parents deal violently with each other" or "there were more than 22 official reports of domestic violence, many with police involvement." Even so, documents in nine files made it clear that mothers lost, by agreement or judicial order, custody or guardianship of their children to the state as a result of their partner's violence. In two of these cases, the mothers agreed to grant guardianship of their children to the state because they feared for the children's safety upon the father's release from prison. In both cases the fathers had been imprisoned as a consequence of abuse of the mother. In seven of their cases women lost custody of their children to the state as a consequence of their partners' abuse; the reports did not include discussion of abuse by mothers. A similar pattern emerged in the reported cases and in court file cases in the other two jurisdictions.

117. R. LUNDY BANCROFT, RESOURCE CENTRE ON DOMESTIC VIOLENCE, UNDERSTANDING THE BATTERER IN CUSTODY AND VISITATION DISPUTES 5 (1996).

118. Partner abuse cases ought to be interpreted differently from nonabuse cases. Such claims may be a legitimate concern in some cases.

119. JUDICIAL EDUCATION CENTRE OF NEW MEXICO (JEC), *supra* note 93. *See also*, Collins-Mentis v. Mentis, [2000] N.S.S.C. 119, *available at* http://www.canlii.org/ns/cas/nssc/2000/2000nssc10119.html; *Broda v. Broda*, [2001] A.B.C.A.151, *available at* http://www.canlii.org/ab/cas/abca/2001/2001abca.151.html.

120. Several of the fathers interviewed during the study were not abusive. A few were primary caregivers.

121. Neilson (2000), *supra* note 4; Neilson (2001) *supra* note 5; Neilson (2003), *supra* note 18.

122. Safety considerations forced us to exclude from the study perpetrators whose profiles indicated a continuing danger to victims, children, or interviewers. The study was also relatively small, so the finding may not be transferable to other populations.

123. BANCROFT & SILVERMAN, *supra* note 10, at 51–52; Bala et al., *supra* note 8; Jaffe et al., *supra* note 17.

124. Peled, *supra* note 25.

125. Bala et al., *supra* note 8 (citing the Colin Thatcher case as one of Canada's best known public examples of children siding with the perpetrator).

126. Peled, *supra* note 25.

127. Lois Achimovich, *Parent Alienation Revisited*, presented at Child Sexual Abuse: Justice Response or Alternative Resolution conference (May 2003), *available at* http://www.aic.gov.au/conferences/2003-abuse/achimovich.html.

128. SMALL JUSTICE LITTLE JUSTICE IN AMERICA'S FAMILY COURTS, (Garland Walter 2003).

129. RICHARD A. GARDNER, THE PARENTAL ALIENATION SYNDROME (2nd ed. 1998); Richard A. Gardner, *Differentiating Between Parental Alienation Syndrome and Bona Fide Abuse-Neglect*, THE AM. J. OF FAM. THERAPY, Apr.-June 1999, at 97.

130. *See, e.g.*, Glenn F. Cartwright, *Expanding the Parameters of Parental Alienation Syndrome*, 21 THE AM J. OF FAM. THERAPY, 205–215 (1993); STANLEY S. CLAWAR & BRYNNE VALERIE RIVLIN, CHILDREN HELD HOSTAGE: DEALING WITH PROGRAMMED AND BRAINWASHED CHILDREN (1991); Gardner, *Ibid.*; JANET R. JOHNSTON & VIVENNE ROSEBY, IN THE NAME OF THE CHILD: A DEVELOPMENTAL APPROACH TO UNDERSTANDING AND HELPING CHILDREN OF CONFLICTED AND VIOLENT DIVORCE (1997); L. F. Lowenstein, *Parent Alienation Syndrome: Two Step Approach Toward A Solution*, 20 CONTEMP. FAM. THERAPY 505 (1997); Jayne A. Major, *Parents Who Have Successfully Fought Parental Alienation Syndrome* (2002), *available at* http://www.breakthroughparenting.com/PAS.htm; Anita Vestal, *Mediation and Parental Alienation Syndrome*, 376 FAM. & CONCILIATION CTS REV. 487 (Oct. 1999).

131. R. James Williams, *Should Judges Close the Gate on PAS and PA?*, 39 FAM. CT. REV. 267 (2001); Achimovich, *supra* note 128; Jerome Poliacroff et al., *Parent Alienation Syndrome: Frye v. Gardner in the Family Courts*, at http://expertpages.com/new/parental_alienation_syndrome.htm (last updated Apr. 23, 2004).

132. Carolyn Quadrio, *Parent Alienation in Family Court Disputes*, presented at the Child Sexual Abuse: Justice Response or Alternative Resolution Conference (May 2003), *available at* http://www.aic.gov.au/conferences/2003-abuse/quadrio.pdf.

133. *Supra* notes 128, 129, 132, 133.

134. *Infra* note 143; Quadrio, *supra* note 133; JAFFE ET AL., *supra* note 10 at 116.

135. Achimovich, *supra* note 128.

136. Neilson (2001), *supra* note 5, at 206–215.

137. Achimovich (2003) note 128.

138. Neilson (2001) 206–215.

139. *R. v. Handy*, [2002] S.C.R. 908; *R. v. D. (L.E.)*, [1989] 2 S.C.R. 111; *R.B.(C.R.)*, [1990] 1 S.C.R. 717.

140. *See e.g. Arlene May-Coroner's Inquest: Jury's Verdict and Recommendations* (1998), *at* http://www.owjn.org/archive/arlene3.htm; ARIZONA COALITION AGAINST DOMESTIC VIOLENCE, ARIZONA DOMESTIC VIOLENCE FATALITY REVIEW: A REVIEW OF 2000 & 2001 MURDER SUICIDES (2002), *available at* http://www.azcadv.org/PDFs/DVFatalityRevue.pdf; DOMESTIC VIOLENCE FATALITY REVIEW TEAM, 2003 ANNUAL REPORT EXECUTIVE SUMMARY (2003), *available at* http://www.fdle.state.fl.us/CitResCtr/Domestic_Violence/2003_DV_FRT.pdf.

141. BANCROFT & SILVERMAN, *supra* note 10; Johnson (1995), *supra* note 79; Johnson & Leone (in press) *supra* note 79; Johnson, *supra* note 8.

142. An important qualification is that even nonabusive violence when accompanied by a death threat or threatened suicide must be considered serious, particularly when accompanied with depression and expressions of intense dependency (I can't live without her/him), whether control and domination are factors in the relationship or not. Such threats are lethality indicators. *See, for example*: Arlene May Coroner's Inquest. Jury's Verdict and Recommendations: http://www.owjn.org/archive/arlene.htm; Arizona Domestic Violence Fatality Review: http://www.azcadv.org/PDGs/DVFatality-Revue.pdf; Florida DV Family Review: http//www.azcadv.org/PDGs/DVFatality-Revue.pdf; Florida DV Fatality Review: http://www.fdle.state.fl.us/CitResCtr/Domestic_Violence/2003_DV_FRT.pdf.

143. Bancroft and Silverman (2002) note, M. P. Johnson et al. (1995) (2003) note 79, (2001) note 76, (2000) note 80; M. P. Johnson (in press). "Conflict and control: Gender, symmetry, and asymmetry in domestic violence." *Violence Against Women* http://www.personal.psu.edu/faculty/m/p/mpj/02VAW.html.

144. *Ibid.* Women who participated in the New Brunswick study commented that they engaged in acts of violence once they decided to separate because they did not care about personal safety anymore, because they felt there was nothing left to lose, because they were at the end of their ability to tolerate abuse, or because the decision to separate had finally given them the psychological strength to fight back.

145. *See, e.g., supra* note 142.

146. *See* note 79.

147. Johnson (in press) *supra* note 142.

148. Emotional abuse includes financial abuse, such as withholding economic support, family resources, and necessaries of life from a partner or children.

149. LESLIE TUTTY, HEALTH CANADA, HUSBAND ABUSE AN OVERVIEW OF RESEARCH AND PERSPECTIVES 19–20 (1998), *available at* http://www.hc-sc.gc.ca/hppb/familyviolence/pdfs/husbandenglish. pdf, reports from a survey of service-providers that men who are truly victimized by abuse "told stories that were strikingly similar to women victims of husband abuse. They tended to minimize their partner's behavior, had low self-esteem, and admitted feeling both afraid of their parent's aggression and ashamed. They offered the same rationales for staying in the relationship as abused women. For example, some men did not wish to leave because they feared their children would be abused, or they stated that they loved their partners and simply want the abuse to stop." *See also*, Grandin et al., *supra* note 83; Dasgupta, *supra* note 67.

150. This list is not comprehensive. It merely identifies some common domination and control behaviors. Following are several links to abuse assessment tools with questions relating to domination and control. LAURA E. STEVENS, NATIONAL CLEARINGHOUSE ON FAMILY VIOLENCE, WHAT IS EMOTIONAL ABUSE (1996), *at* http://www.hc-sc.gc.ca/hppb/familyviolence/html/fvemotion_e.html; Kathryn Conroy & Randy Magen, *Training Child Welfare Workers on Domestic Violence: Trainer's Manual, at* http://hosting.uaa.alaska.edu/ afrhm1/wacan/Trainman4.html (last visited Apr. 21, 2004); Transition House Association of Nova Scotia, *Am I Being Abused, at* http://www.thans.ca/ami.html (last updated Apr. 13, 2001).

151. *See, e.g.,* Randy Magen & Kathryn Conroy, *Identifying Domestic Violence in Child Abuse and Neglect Investigations* (1995), *at* http://hosting.uaa.alaska.edu/afrhm1/wacan/FV_PAPER.html.

152. Julie K. Field, *Screening for Domestic Violence: Meeting the Challenge of Identifying Domestic Relations Cases Involving Domestic Violence and Developing Strategies for Those Cases.* COURT REVIEW, Summer 2002, at 8, *available at* http://aja.nesc.dni.us/courtrv/review.html; AMERICAN BAR ASSOCIATION COMMISSION ON DOMESTIC VIOLENCE, *Multidisciplinary Responses to Domestic Violence, at* http://www.abanet.org/ domviol/mrdv/identify.html (last visited Apr. 21, 2004); Transition Houses of Nova Scotia, *supra* note 148; Office on Violence Against Women United States Dep't of Justice, Legal Assistance for Victims Grant Recipients' Policy Guidebook 8 (2002), *at* http://www.ojp.usdoj.gov/vawo/docs/lavgbook02.pdf; HUMAN RESOURCES ADMINISTRATION CHILD WELFARE ADMINISTRATION, CPS DOMESTIC VIOLENCE PROTOCOL, *at* http://hosting.uaa.alaska.edu/afrhm1/wacan/CPSq.pdf (last visited Apr.21, 2004).

153. Procedural factors that prevent such evidence from reaching judges are discussed in Neilson (2000), *supra* note 5 and Neilson (2002), *supra* note 5.

154. Although, theoretically, it is still possible that a knowledgeable perpetrator could attempt to cast himself or herself as the victim, this becomes more difficult with careful consideration of the long-term history of the relationship. It is also unlikely that most perpetrators would be comfortable presenting themselves as having been dominated and controlled.

Chapter Ten

Religious Arbitration in Canada: Protecting Women by Protecting Them from Religion*

Natasha Bakht

Editors' Note: Natasha Bakht explores the controversy surrounding efforts to allow for faith-based arbitration as a facet of Family Law deliberations in Ontario. This article provides a detailed look at the politics and ethics of establishing such arbitration measures, including Bakht's own concerns about these measures. What follows is a detailed account of how social movements can be used to effect legal and policy change and, more broadly, considerations about entrenched stereotypes of Muslim peoples in Canada and, by extension, other minority groupings, such as Doukhobours, Sikhs, and Hutterites. These "familiar caricatures" of endangered Muslim women and threatening Muslim men resurfaced during the debate over sharia law in Ontario. This debate attracted considerable media attention and revealed the complexity of the Canadian Muslim community, with some members very supportive of arbitration through religious auspices, others more reserved in their support, and still others who opposed arbitration.

Bakht argues that the secular trajectory adopted by many feminists does not adequately take into account the protections and benefits that might accrue for women in such faith communities. Similarly, secularists who put their own faith in state agencies to promote women's equality may be myopic, given "colonialist and racist projects" that have sometimes been associated with state policies and powers. She suggests that a more sensitive approach requires us to reconsider simplistic dismissals of feminist activism vis-à-vis religious precepts and beliefs and to be cautious when presented with "the enticing narrative of secularism."

In Ontario, the issue of family law disputes being settled by religious arbitration has received much attention. Since 1991, the *Arbitration Act* has allowed people to authorize a third party to resolve their civil disputes using the legal framework of their choice.[1] Indeed, Jewish arbitrations have been functioning in this manner for many years without controversy. However, when a group of Muslims announced their intention to create similar tribunals, there was an unwarranted negative response from interest groups and the provincial government. Almost

Source: Natasha Bakjt, "Religious Arbitration in Canada: Protecting Women by Protecting Them from Religion," *Canadian Journal of Women and the Law*, 2007 (19), pp. 119–144. © University of Toronto Press Incorporated. Reprinted with permission from UTP Journals, www.utpjournals.com.

*Earlier versions of this article have appeared in conference proceedings at Emory Law School and in the *Ottawa Law Review*. See Natasha Bakht, "Religious Arbitration in Ontario: Protecting Women by Protecting Them from Religion" (paper presented to the Feminist Legal Theory Project's Workshop "All in the Family? Islam, Women and Human Rights," March 2006) [unpublished]; Natasha Bakht, "Were Muslim Barbarians Really Knocking on the Gates of Ontario? The Religious Arbitration Controversy—Another Perspective" (2006), Fortieth Anniversary Ottawa Law Review 67. I am grateful for the many conversations and insights provided by Baidar Bakht, Carmela Murdocca, Robert Leckey, the participants of Emory Law School's Feminist Legal Theory Workshop "All in the Family? Islam, Women and Human Rights," and the participants of the Feminist Methodologies Workshop sponsored by the UBC Centre for Feminist Legal Studies and the Arts and Humanities Research Council Centre for Law, Gender and Sexuality. I was also assisted by the excellent and thorough research of Colleen Bauman. Research funding for this article was made available by the Law Foundation of Ontario and the Ottawa Research Scholarship.

immediately, a flurry of damaging newspaper articles were published, unqualified campaigns against sharia courts were launched, and numerous politicians declared that religious arbitration would result in the government effectively sanctioning barbaric traditions and denigrating women's rights.[2]

Much of the deep anti-religious sentiment expressed in Ontario has been fuelled by the global phenomenon of imposing extraordinary measures of surveillance and control on Muslim communities in the name of gender equality following the events of 11 September 2001. This article examines the disconnect between the treatment of secular and religious arbitration agreements with a particular view to the way in which all things Islamic have been viewed as being necessarily oppressive to women. I point to the contradictions inherent in the strategy of prioritizing secular and/or recognizable ways of life particularly where Canadian common law provinces promote religious freedom and the private resolution of family law disputes. It is noteworthy that the religious arbitration debate only became a controversy when Muslims became visibly involved. While the Christian and Jewish faiths are more familiar to the Western psyche than is the apparently threatening faith of Islam, it is clear that the concern expressed over religious decision making in family law has less to do with religion generically and more to do with those religions that are less recognizable as being Canadian.

Using the prism of the "sharia debate" in Ontario, I explore the feminist strategy of proscribing religious arbitration as the only acceptable means of protecting vulnerable women.[3] This strategy has operated to the detriment of religious women who may want to live a faith-based life. This article also examines Ontario's *Family Statute Law Amendment Act*,[4] which is the government's response to the religious arbitration issue, in order to demonstrate the enormous influence of the anti-religion lobby. I consider the real impact that the new amendments will have on family arbitrations. Despite specific clauses that suggest that religious arbitration may be permissible in limited ways, the government has insisted on describing the amendments as an absolute proscription of legally enforceable religious decision making. The belief that religious arbitration has been banned appears to have given many Ontarians great reprieve. In fact, the new amendments may have inadvertently realized the only viable solution to this divisive issue—a balance between the concerns of gender equality and religious freedom.

FAMILIAR CARICATURES: "IMPERILED MUSLIM WOMEN AND DANGEROUS MUSLIM MEN"

On 11 September 2005, the premier of Ontario, Dalton McGuinty, announced that "sharia arbitration" in family law matters would be banned from the province.[5] He was referring to the controversial debate about the voluntary use of religious principles to resolve certain family law matters in the arbitral context that had consumed the province for over a year. The sharia debate, as it came to be known and as the name suggests, plays out many of the usual myths about Islam and Muslims. For many weeks, there was a prevalent misunderstanding, which continues to be repeated by both the media and the opponents of arbitration, that the government of Ontario surreptitiously colluded with a Muslim organization known as the Islamic Institute of Civil Justice to create a parallel legal system for Muslims, thereby depriving them of their legal rights under Ontario and Canadian law.[6] With this myth came the accompanying "moral panic"[7] that Muslim women in Canada would be stoned to death, that Muslim men would merely pronounce the words "talaq" three times for a divorce to be finalized, and that the custody and access of children would favour men since the righteous place of Muslim men is at the head of the household. The familiar caricature of the "imperiled Muslim woman" needing to be rescued from the "dangerous Muslim man" revealed itself in full force.[8] The prevalence of these caricatures are explained by Sherene Razack's contention that in describing patriarchal violence within Muslim migrant communities there tends to be an over-reliance on culturalist arguments—that is, explanations that depend on cultural deficit arguments that Muslims are uncivilized. I argue that a similar position was perpetuated in the religious arbitration controversy in Ontario.

Although in the contentious sharia debate, no "Muslim women's bodies" were being "confined, mutilated or murdered,"[9] as in the headscarf, female genital mutilation, and honour killing controversies, the discourse nonetheless resorted to the same sensationalized images that are so typical of Orientalist[10] structures. The onslaught of fear-mongering newspaper articles, opinion editorials, and television commentaries confirmed the view that the biggest threat in the world today is Islamic fundamentalism. For many months, the media pursued the notion that sharia would change the landscape of Canadian law and overlooked the fact that legally nothing had changed. The *Arbitration Act* had, since 1991, allowed parties to authorize a third person to resolve their civil disputes using the legal framework of their choice.[11] Indeed, Jewish tribunals or *beis din* had been operating in the province for years without similar alarm.[12] Nonetheless, the media cautioned that "Muslim barbarians [were] knocking on the gates of Ontario."[13] Representations of Islam as barbaric, as espousing values *other* than values that are democratically elected, and as being *outside* the Canadian mosaic were strengthened because many such descriptions came from members within the Muslim community itself.[14] Activist Homa Arjomand regularly referred to faith-based arbitration and its supporters as "backward"[15] and Québec member of the National Assembly Fatima Houda-Peppin led a unanimous motion opposing Islamic tribunals in the Québec National Assembly,[16] despite the fact that the *Civil Code of Québec* specifies that arbitration cannot be used to resolve family law disputes.[17]

According to Sharmeen Khan, the "stereotype of Muslim women—hidden behind the veil, barred from public participation unless given permission by their husbands—has captivated the imagination of some feminists in Canada and fuelled a commitment to 'save' the women behind the burqua."[18] While, for the most part, Canadian feminist mobilization on this issue has been careful not to portray patriarchy and violence as being unique to Islam,[19] Canadian feminist organizations[20] have nonetheless proposed prohibiting all religious arbitration as the solution to the sharia debate. This solution must be examined in light of Razack's criticism of the risk of feminist strategies being co-opted into colonialist and racist projects.[21]

There is no doubt that Ontario's 1991 *Arbitration Act* bore several deficiencies that the sharia debate exposed. Canadian feminist organizations were particularly valuable in uncovering many problematic features of an act that had been created primarily for commercial purposes yet that could be used in the area of family law, where history has shown many women to be vulnerable regardless of their culture/religion.

FEMINIST MOBILIZATION: LEGITIMATE CONCERNS WITH FAMILY ARBITRATION IN ONTARIO

Feminist criticism of the trend to privatize family law through the increasing use of alternative dispute resolution processes emanates from the fact that despite the theoretical choice to submit to arbitration, vulnerable people do not actually have free choice. Social inequities may be reproduced in privately ordered agreements and remain hidden from the public eye such that the status quo is maintained and women's inequality in relation to this "private sphere of the family is no longer a public concern."[22]

Family law raises unique concerns as a key site of oppression for women since far more of women's time and energy go into the preservation and maintenance of the private realm. Gender discrimination in family law has systemic effects on women's equality, given the substantive breadth of this law as well as its impact on women's ability to exercise specific rights.[23] Family law defines property relations between spouses and determines the economic and parental consequences of divorce. For women, these stakes are especially high, with separation and divorce typically resulting in the feminization of poverty.[24]

The arguments against alternative dispute resolution practices, which offer people a voluntary alternative to the increasingly lengthy and expensive cost of litigation under the traditional court system, have long been a part of the feminist initiative to ensure that the Canadian state takes responsibility for protecting women's interests. In the specific context of faith-based arbitration, the following additional concerns were raised by feminist organizations.

Ontario's old *Arbitration Act* did not require arbitrators to have any specialized legal training, yet the decision of these arbitrators could be filed with a court and have the force of law. Arbitrators were not required to give reasons for their decisions, creating a lack of transparency and difficulties in appealing errors of law. Parties to arbitration could contract out of their rights to appeal, thereby removing an important mechanism of judicial oversight.[25] The decision to arbitrate did not need to be made contemporaneously with the breakdown of the relationship. Thus, an arbitration agreement could be made in a marriage contract many years before the breakdown of a relationship and the actual decision to arbitrate was embarked upon. This time gap could be particularly problematic where a person may have changed her/his mind about wanting to submit a dispute to arbitration. In the context of arbitration using religious principles, the absence of a contemporaneous confirmation of the desire to arbitrate would pose problems for the individual whose religious beliefs had changed over the course of time. Thus, true consent in these circumstances would be illusory.

The act also failed to impose and fund independent legal advice prior to the signing of an arbitration agreement, removing a significant means of ensuring an informed decision. The act did not require arbitrators to keep records, thus preventing data collection and analyses on the impact of family arbitration on women. References to equality and fairness in the act were essentially procedural guarantees that had little impact on the substantive equality of arbitral awards.[26] And, most disappointingly, the old *Arbitration Act* permitted parties to resolve their family law disputes using any "rules of law."[27] Essentially, this section of the act allowed *any* conservative or extreme Right-wing standard to be used to resolve family law matters in Ontario despite the significant gains made for women in Canadian family jurisprudence over the past thirty years. Such a system of arbitration with very few substantive protections for equality did not protect vulnerable individuals, women in particular.[28]

The work of feminists in elucidating these severe deficiencies with the 1991 *Arbitration Act* was significant since the lack of records in arbitration prevented an empirical examination of discrimination against women in this context. Using the aforementioned analysis, feminists rightly speculated that the gender-based consequences of family arbitration with few limits would likely have intersecting class, (dis)ability, cultural, and religious implications.[29] For example, the head of the Islamic Institute of Civil Justice has been quoted as saying that since the *Arbitration Act* permits the use of sharia in civil law, Muslims in Ontario now have "no choice" but to submit to sharia arbitration.[30] Feminists (both Muslim and non-Muslim) feared that a devout Muslim woman could be susceptible to pressure to consent to sharia arbitration because of such a pronouncement by an *imam* or community leader.

In fighting for the protection of the interests of women, Canadian feminists brought to the forefront many complicated and detrimental shortcomings of the act that had somehow remained hidden from the public since 1991. Where feminists went astray was in their lobbying efforts to prohibit all religious arbitration. Canadian feminists resolved that the vulnerable interests of women—Muslim women, in particular—were best protected through the strict separation of law and religion.

LAW AND RELIGION: AN UNHEALTHY MIX?

The relationship between feminism and religion has historically been fraught with tension.[31] In the West, the mainstream of the women's movement has viewed religion as being "one of the chief enemies of its progress and well-being."[32] While in Canada, it is fair to speak of a system of law that generally attempts to separate religion and the state, one cannot ignore that the preamble of the *Canadian Charter of Rights and Freedoms*[33] begins by recognizing "the supremacy of God and the rule of law."[34] The degree of Canada's secularism is tempered by the fact that the *Charter* protects religious freedom, which is understood as "the right to declare one's religious beliefs openly and the right to manifest religious belief by worship, teaching, dissemination and religious practice."[35] Indeed, an absolute model of separation does not necessarily maximize religious freedom nor is it necessarily neutral.[36] Both fiercely secular states and theocratic states have been known to be equally oppressive to religious freedom.[37]

Where an issue is intrinsically religious in nature, Canadian courts have tended to decline to intervene, claiming that civil courts are inappropriate sites for deciding questions of religious doctrine.[38] However, Canadian judges will become involved in religion where necessary to prohibit practices that are harmful, that violate civil or property rights, or that infringe a person's constitutional rights.[39] Although there is no direct incorporation of Islamic or other foreign norms into Canadian law as new immigrants arrive and integrate into Canadian culture,[40] the accommodation of minority rights occurs regularly in both the legislative and judicial context and, indeed, is seen as a necessary component of living in a multicultural society.[41]

Religious communities such as the Sikhs, the Hutterites, and the Doukhobours have been granted certain exemptions from laws of general application in order to accommodate the specific needs of each community.[42] This model of differentiated citizenship is seen as levelling the playing field among various groups in order to destabilize the impact of the political, economic, social, and cultural hegemony of the majority.[43] While there is little doubt that the accommodation of minority groups is an indisputable virtue, what is equally important is the dilemma concerning the potentially injurious effects of accommodation policies on vulnerable individuals within such minority groups.[44] The creation of group rights cannot allow for the systemic maltreatment of individuals within the accommodated minority group—"an impact in some cases so severe that it nullifies the individual rights of citizens."[45]

A recent case, *Khan v. Khan*,[46] suggests that courts in Ontario are capable of drawing a distinction between group rights and individual protections. In *Khan*, a *nika namma* or valid marriage contract in Pakistan was upheld as being a valid domestic contract under Ontario's *Family Law Act*,[47] but the waiver of spousal support by the wife legitimated by the apparent bar on spousal support under Hanafi Islamic jurisprudence was deemed unconscionable. The court aptly noted that

> deference should be given to religious and cultural laws and traditions of groups living in Canada … [but] if cultural groups are given complete freedom to define family matters, they may tread on the rights of individuals within the group and discriminate in ways unacceptable to Canadian society.[48]

This decision appears deceptively simple but was impressive in its nuance. A Muslim marriage contract was not summarily denied enforcement in Canada merely because of its religious origins. The beliefs of the religious participants were respected in this way. Yet a term of the contract, the waiver of spousal support, which clearly would have produced unconscionable results, was rejected for its inconsistency with Ontario's family law. Canadian feminists could have used a similar logic in resolving the sharia debate in Ontario. Rather than proposing a blanket prohibition on all religious arbitration, a more nuanced approach that showed consideration for the religious rights *and* the equality rights of women would have been more useful.

In its submission to the government of Ontario, the Women's Legal Education and Action Fund (LEAF) originally proposed that the *Arbitration Act* be amended to provide that in arbitrations concerning family law matters Ontario family law apply. They argued that "[o]ther principles, such as religious precepts, may also be applied, but only to the extent that they do not conflict with Ontario family law."[49] LEAF was for some time the lone feminist voice making the logical argument that religious precepts are not objectionable per se but that the family law regime in Ontario, which reflects years of important reform in the area of women's rights and equality, cannot be undermined. LEAF's position recognized the multiple and conflicting voices of Muslim women on this issue and found a balance that would have guarded against possible oppression under the old act while recognizing that some Muslim women expressed support for the use of religious arbitration. After further consultation, LEAF modified its position, bringing it in line with most other feminist groups, to state: "[A]rbitration awards applying or concerning religious 'law,' practices, traditions, precepts or beliefs should never be enforceable under the *Arbitration Act, even if the religious issue does not conflict with the existing statutory regime*."[50]

In June 2005, the No Religious Arbitration Coalition was formed.[51] This coalition comprised over 100 organizations and individuals brought together by the Canadian Council of Muslim Women to actively oppose the use of religious laws in family law arbitration in Ontario. While certain members of the coalition opposed the use of any form of private arbitration in family law,[52] the group was united in focusing its efforts on ending religious arbitration, since this activity was seen as being particularly dangerous for vulnerable women and children, regardless of their religious beliefs.[53] The coalition included most Canadian feminist organizations and some Muslim organizations that identified themselves as moderate and/or secular/cultural Muslims.

The No Religious Arbitration Coalition was extremely effective in its lobbying efforts and eventually succeeded in convincing the government of the dangers of religious arbitration. This success was no doubt fuelled by the surrounding panic that had been generated in the name of Islam and Islamic fundamentalism.[54] Despite a report commissioned by the attorney general and the minister responsible for women's issues, which recommended the continued use of religious arbitration with certain safeguards,[55] the government was persuaded that allowing sharia "to get a foothold in Canada" would seriously jeopardize Canadian values. The broad-based support for this perspective[56] was not at all surprising given the dominant perception post-9/11 that Muslims are synonymous with terrorists and that the West must protect itself from barbaric Islam.[57] Indeed, the support for banning religious arbitration by some Muslims permitted ordinary Canadians and the government to feel safe in their position that the complete opposition to religion was for principled, and not prejudicial, purposes.[58]

A disturbing side effect of the government's ban on religious arbitration was the pitting of one religious group against another. Rabbi Reuven Tradburks, secretary of the Toronto Vaad Harabonim's Beit Din, stated: "Because sharia was at odds with modern values, they took it out on the Jews."[59] Rather than condemning the government's action regardless of its target, one noticed a disturbing trend of "religious misrecognition"—"I'm not a Muslim!"[60]

The blanket prohibition against religious arbitration assumes that reliance on religious precepts to resolve disputes is necessarily bad for women. It precludes any of the progressive possibilities that religious arbitration may entail for some women, undermining the work of many feminist religious scholars and reformers who have argued that their religion can, and, indeed, does, conform to women's rights. Increasingly, religious feminists are asserting that traditions can be modified. This understanding of religion is something that is shifting and being contested rather than fixed and static—something that contains a plurality of meanings and can be subject to various interpretations.[61] Importantly, Canadian judicial interpretation of religious freedom emphasizes the importance of an individual's sincere belief in a particular religious practice. One's sincere belief is given predominance over even the normative legal code of belief espoused by religious authorities or the community,[62] thus sustaining the idea that religious law is mutable and that custom and practice can assist in modifying religious traditions over time, "even within religious communities that insist on the immutability of the law as defined in religious texts held to be divinely inspired."[63]

Muslim feminists and Islamic reformers have asserted that the Qur'an and the example of the Prophet provide much support for the idea of expanded rights for women. Jewish women have also sought progressive, women-friendly interpretations of religious laws.[64] Contemporary Muslims such as Abdullahi An-Na'im and Fatima Mernissi have re-examined the sources and concluded that Islam calls for equal rights for men and women.[65] "Sharia is not simply an ancient code of rules. It is a process of analysis that must take into account more than just scripture, but also the context of the nation where it is applied."[66] Many Muslim countries have grappled with the tradition of sharia and the role that a modern nation-state plays in regulating rights. Tunisia, for example, prohibits polygamous marriages "relying on a Koranic verse stipulating that men can never be just to multiple women—justice being a requirement for polygamous marriages."[67] Indeed, sharia could incorporate principles of Canadian law and help arbitrators render decisions that are both Islamic *and* Canadian. The fact that Canadian law could also benefit from sharia might seem an unrealistic prospect, but there are illustrations of the influence of sharia in international law already—for example, the rules of war in the Geneva Conventions were derived in part from the Islamic rules of Holy War.[68] These narratives, which complicate the religious debate, were glaringly absent from both the media and feminist strategies to protect Muslim women. By promoting a ban of religious arbitration, feminists have supported the view that religion is bound to patriarchal tradition, unchangeable, and ultimately dangerous for women.

Some feminists that were active in the sharia debate have insisted that, while they were "believing"[69] women, they were simply of the view that a secular state required that religion be practised in private.[70] "Secularist insistence … … that religion be confined to the ever-diminishing 'private sphere'"[71]—that is, where the state does not regulate people's lives—might make sense in a minimalist state. However, such a claim is impracticable in a country such as Canada where the enforcement of hundreds of laws and regulations control virtually every aspect of peoples' existence including criminal law, family law, education, property, employment, and health care.

RELIGIOUS LIBERTIES IN THE CONTEXT OF "SECULARISM"

The Supreme Court of Canada has noted that religious liberties must be understood in the context of secularism:

> Religion is an integral part of people's lives and cannot be left at the boardroom door. What secularism does rule out, however, is any attempt to use the religious views of one part of the community to exclude from consideration the values of other members of that community. A requirement of secularism implies that, although the board is indeed free to address the religious concerns of the parents, it must be sure to do so in a manner that gives equal recognition and respect to other members of the community.[72]

Thus, to be secular, according to the Supreme Court of Canada, is to allow religion into public debate—in other words, to give equal recognition and respect to other members of the community but to limit religion's impact within the boundaries of tolerance and equality. Nayereh Tohidi has noted that "[s]ecularity works better for all when secularism means impartiality toward religion, not anti-religionism."[73]

The anti-religion position undertaken by feminist groups has shown no sympathy for the Muslim woman who might want to live a faith-based life.[74] Clearly, there are Muslim women in Ontario who did not support religious arbitration and others who preferred to have the option. Surely, a resolution that enhances women's choices[75] by accommodating both subgroups of women while protecting all women from equality rights violations is possible. Yet feminists have insisted upon secularism, understood as non-religious, as the obvious solution to gender inequality. Talal Asad, however, reminds us that secularism is also congruent with "repeated explosions of intolerance" in the world's history.[76] While secularism understood narrowly may be an appropriate and understandable strategy in certain contexts, in Canada, where the grasp of fundamentalism cannot be compared to such countries as Saudi Arabia or Iran, it is appropriate that our strategies for managing potential violations of individual rights based on religion might be different. Fareeda Shaheed of the network "Women Living under Muslim Laws" (WLUML) has stated:

> WLUML recognizes that living in different circumstances and situations, women will have different strategies and priorities. We believe that each woman knowing her own situation is best placed to decide what is the right strategy and choice for her.[77]

Abdullahi An-Na'im has wisely suggested that it should not be assumed that there is either an immediate compatibility or a permanent contradiction between gender equality and any religion.[78] Indeed, there must be willingness to question and challenge assumptions about both the relevant religion and the human rights or other paradigms that are applied. By setting up the secular against the religious, Canadian feminists have perpetuated the dichotomy between the modern, enlightened West and the pre-modern, backward Islam.[79] Also furthered was the notion of the irreconcilable "clash of civilizations"[80] between the West and Islam, wherein Islam possesses "neither a commitment to human rights, women's rights nor to democracy."[81] The idea that "sharia could be an operational system that allows for discretion, nuance and change is one that is nearly unthinkable in light of the current politically symbolic role [that] Islamic law is forced to play."[82] At the centre of the controversy surrounding religious arbitration stands Sherene Razack's notion of the "imperiled Muslim woman":

> We cannot forget for an instant the usefulness of her body in the contemporary making of white nations and citizens. Her imperiled body has provided a rationale for engaging in the surveillance and disciplining of the Muslim man and Muslim communities.[83]

During the sharia debate, feminists fell prey to the enticing narrative of secularism. They regarded secularism, as it is operated through the state, as the only progressive strategy capable of protecting Muslim women. Thus, the divide between the religious and the secular remained unexamined and uncomplicated, and, in the process, religious women were neglected. In a post-9/11 world where the surveillance and control of Muslims and those perceived as Muslims has been justified under the guise of national security, the feminist endorsement of an exclusively state-run apparatus has failed to understand the legitimate resistance to government policies that perpetuate punitive and stigmatizing measures against people of colour.[84]

ONE LAW FOR ALL CANADIANS?

Opponents of religious arbitration regularly relied on the slogan that there should be only one law for all Canadians. They invoked the idea of the rule of law wherein all Canadians regardless of status, colour, religion, or creed are subject to the same legal rights and responsibilities in accordance with written laws adopted democratically. Superficially, this slogan was an effective means of advocating that the prohibition of religious arbitration was just and fair. Certainly, the idea that personal characteristics ought to determine the law applicable to a group of people is repugnant to most.[85] Why should Muslim women, the argument went, not benefit from the democratic and judicial reforms that have been forged in the area of family law?[86] One commentator noted that

> [p]ermitting different religious interpretations and practices to extend their authority to the secular Canadian legal system jeopardizes the human rights of many Canadian citizens, particularly women. It also reinforces the notion of double-standard entitlement from some Canadians.[87]

In fact, it is disingenuous to speak of "one law for all" in the Canadian context for a number of reasons. As previously noted, part of Canada's commitment to all people is to ensure that they are treated equally. The commitment to equality is protected through non-discrimination clauses not only in several international instruments to which Canada is a signatory[88] but also, and more importantly, in section 15 of the *Canadian Charter of Rights and Freedoms*.

Section 15 jurisprudence has made clear that to treat people equally does not mean treating them in the same way. *Andrews v. Law Society of British Columbia* soundly rejected the formalism of the similarly situated test.[89] Thus, the many legal distinctions in the law based on, for example, sex and race are not considered measures that are discriminatory but, on the contrary, that promote substantive equality by emphasizing a consideration of the impact of laws on members of groups subject to stereotyping and historic disadvantage. This vision of equality is significant because it accounts for the cumulative effects of past discrimination. Thus, the sentencing provision in section 718.2(e) of the Canadian *Criminal Code*,[90] which directs judges to consider all alternatives to incarceration for Aboriginal offenders, is understood to be an equitable measure meant to address the extreme over-representation of Aboriginal peoples in Canada's prison population.[91] Under Canadian law, multiple standards are employed in order to treat individuals from all communities justly and with equality.

However, one need not look to specific equality-promoting measures in the law to explain why "one law for all Canadians" is an insincere maxim. In the context of Ontario's system of family law, parties to a marriage can agree to a resolution of their marital matters such as the division of matrimonial property, the provision of spousal support and child support, and any other matter in the settlement of their affairs.[92] While Ontario law provides a default statutory regime that equally divides the net matrimonial family property between married couples upon separation,[93] people are free to opt out of the Ontario design and resolve their marital affairs in another manner. Parties can, through negotiation, mediation, or arbitration, based on the right to contract freely, agree to almost any resolution of their marital affairs. Other than in matters involving children, such as custody and child support, where the courts will invoke their *parens patriae* jurisdiction[94] to approve agreements that are in the best interests of the children,[95] and in separation agreements that must meet the broad objectives of the Divorce Act,[96] couples' decisions to settle their family law affairs are generally left un-reviewed by the courts.[97] Consequently, a religious mediator such as an *imam* can be hired to help a couple resolve their family law issues using Islamic principles, and the final agreement can be filed in a court and enforced as an order. Incidentally, the use of religious negotiation and mediation will remain unaffected by the government of Ontario's recent amendments to the *Arbitration Act* and the *Family Law Act*.

Thus, it is not accurate to speak of only one family law for all Canadians, when most family law jurisdictions in Canada promote alternative dispute resolution mechanisms that permit parties to take "personal responsibility for their financial well-being upon the dissolution of their marriage."[98] In fact, "the current court infrastructure could not handle the volume of family cases if alternative resolution processes were not available and encouraged."[99] Given that ordinary Canadians can opt out of democratically formulated family law measures, it seems strange that religious Canadians should be prevented from taking similar ownership over their decisions.

Section 56(5) of the *Family Law Act*, which was enacted to assist Jewish women in obtaining a religious divorce or *ghet*, anticipates the possibility of religious influence on domestic agreements and the potential for conflict with Ontario law. The *Family Law Act* allows an agreement between couples to be set aside when faith-based barriers have been used as a factor against one spouse.[100] Moreover, the *Family Law Act* permits parties "to direct the education and moral training of their children."[101] Clearly, legislators contemplated that religious or other matters of conscience will arise in the resolution of certain family law matters. It is certainly plausible that sometimes Ontario's family law may not have anything to contribute on a specific matter of relevance to couples as they separate. Thus, parties must have the ability to agree to a course of conduct that is not at odds with justice and fairness as understood within the family law regime.

Family law in Ontario does not require that secular agreements be subject to *Charter* scrutiny.[102] Since family law is so fact-driven, the meaning of equality in a given set of circumstances is not always obvious. Secular arbitrations that seem inconsistent with the value of equality are sometimes even upheld by the courts. The Supreme Court of Canada in *Hartshorne v. Hartshorne* upheld a private agreement that it recognized to be unfair. Justice Michel Bastarache noted the Court's interest in upholding parties' private bargains:

> [I]n a framework within which private parties are permitted to take personal responsibility for their financial well-being upon the dissolution of marriage, courts should be reluctant to second-guess the arrangements on which they reasonably expected to rely. Individuals may choose to structure their affairs in a number of different ways, and it is their prerogative to do so.[103]

The plethora of secular arbitration cases suggests that the precise meaning of equality in the context of the dissolution of one's marriage will depend upon a variety of circumstances, including the length of the marriage, the roles that each person played in the marriage, the age of the parties, and whether there are children in the marriage. A fair resolution of the matters in question will be determined judicially with reference to a set of principles found in the various family law statutes and jurisprudence as well as principally with a view to the facts in each case. As previously mentioned, however, the parties are free to make their own arrangements. With equality in family law being so illusive, one wonders why some religious agreements are being over-policed? How are "breaches of equality" permitted in some contexts but not in others? Is it because we, as civilized Westerners, gain something from attempting to rescue "imperiled Muslim women from dangerous Muslim men?"[104] If there is really to be "one law for all Canadians," much more than just religious arbitration will be affected. It will mean a major change in the way family law currently operates.

THE GOVERNMENT'S SUPPOSED BAN OF RELIGIOUS ARBITRATION

Premier McGuinty announced that "he would not let his province become the first Western government to allow the use of Islamic law to settle family disputes and that the boundaries between church and state would become clearer by banning religious arbitration completely."[105] Relying on the entrenched Orientalist model that Islam and faith-based tribunals necessarily "threaten our common ground,"[106] the government of Ontario introduced the *Family Statute Law Amendment Act*,[107] which includes a number of amendments to the *Arbitration Act* and the *Family Law Act*. Many of the amendments take into account feminist criticism that the *Arbitration Act* has a gendered impact that threatens women's equality. Thus, several changes to the act have been proposed including, for the first time, the regulation of family law arbitrators,[108] the requirement that family law arbitration agreements be in writing and that each party receive independent legal advice,[109] the prohibition of advance agreements to arbitrate family law matters, and the prohibition on the waiver of one's right to appeal to a court of law.[110] Perhaps the most far-reaching amendment is that family law arbitrations will no longer permit a "choice of law" provision. Under the family law amendments, any family law arbitrations will be "conducted exclusively in accordance with the law of Ontario or of another Canadian jurisdiction."[111]

Despite the way in which the bill has been framed,[112] the package of legislative amendments does not in fact forbid religious arbitration. First, people can always settle their differences on any basis that they please, so long as both parties consent. However, with the new amendments, their decisions will not be binding in law—that is, they would not have the power of the state behind them.[113] Thus, the concern raised by feminist groups for Muslim women's rights in the family law context remains, particularly where women may still be vulnerable to the conscious or unconscious patriarchal practices of mediators (religious or otherwise).[114] Some commentators have noted that, with this change in law, we have lost an opportunity to prevent "back-alley arbitrations" through a "regime of government regulation that could have ensured a measure of transparency, accountability and competence in adjudication."[115]

A second way in which the amendments do not actually ban religious arbitration is that religious arbitrators can simply conform to the regulations regarding training and record keeping and then perform religious arbitrations that are consistent with Canadian family law. I believe that such an outcome is perfectly coherent with the concerns for gender equality that have been raised in this debate as well as the interest of religious freedom. The challenge for religious groups is to ensure that any of their practices are consistent with Canadian family law statutes and jurisprudence. Given the flexibility of Ontario's family law regime and the opinion of many religious scholars that Islam, for example, is perfectly compatible with human rights norms, this challenge should not be difficult to meet.

Perhaps for fear of reigniting some of the hysteria surrounding the sharia debate, which has temporarily been quelled, very little commentary has focused on the fact that the *Family Law Amendment Act* permits religious arbitrations that conform to Canadian family law.[116] Opponents of religious arbitration have been so vehemently anti-religion that the mere naming of a particular norm as religious seems to arouse an automatic and hostile opposition against the norm.[117] A systemic and blind refusal to accommodate believers is intrinsically problematic, particularly when the accommodations sought do not contradict a democratic society's most fundamental norms.[118] Indeed, the perceived "foreignness" of a norm or practice does not make it incompatible per se with constitutional rights. One would hope that a principle or norm is not rejected on the basis of simply having its origin in a religious belief, but, rather, because it is fundamentally incompatible with a valued Canadian principle or right such as equality. In seeking the equality rights of all women (including religious women), we may need to acknowledge the seemingly contradictory position that the state cannot be viewed as the only actor capable of promoting equality, while insisting that the state play a role in ensuring that vulnerable individuals opting for alternative mechanisms of equality are also protected.

The traditional legal system must continue to be reformed to be more culturally responsive. This accommodation must acknowledge the internal diversity and dissent among members of religious communities rather than treating religion as monolithic. As Madhavi Sunder has noted, law must not respond "to the pluralization of meaning within groups by exiling cultural dissenters in the hope of restoring cultural associations back to some glorious, homogenous past."[119] Where alternative mechanisms such as religious arbitration are employed, the state must intervene in internal religious matters to protect individual human rights. The common liberal approach of non-intervention in religious matters simply intervenes in favour of the stronger voices in the community and perpetuates the silencing of "other" voices.

The government's insistence on describing the new amendments as an application of only "one family law for all Ontarians"[120] is inaccurate. It can only be presumed that the reason for this description is to distance Ontario's progressive family laws from the potential influences of barbaric Islam. The fact that the government fell prey to the "moral panic" generated by the tremendous anti-religion lobby is disappointing. Despite its description, the amendments appear to find a balance between religious freedom and equality by permitting family arbitration with religious principles, so long as such principles do not conflict with Ontario's family law. In my mind, Ontario's family law is adaptable enough to allow the use of some religious principles while still protecting women from gross violations of their rights. Such an approach would mean that each religious norm or practice would be examined on its own merit. Courts must be prepared to accommodate a religious group "by interpreting open-textured positive norms in a manner that is both beneficial to the collective interests of that religious group and not detrimental to the fundamental norms applicable to the State."[121] This approach may also propel internal change from within the minority group,[122] which may legitimately create a "third space" for Muslim women between the patriarchy they may encounter within the minority group and the racism they may encounter outside of it.

Since individuals may perceive themselves as authors and subjects of more than one legal and cultural system,[123] it makes sense to approach the right to equality and religious freedom of religious women through a dual strategy of state accommodation/sensitivity to cultural practices and state intervention in private mechanisms. In framing strategies for reform, gender is a necessary lens through which such change must be affected. However, it cannot be the only lens. Feminists have often been too quick to assume that by addressing only gender concerns, all women will be protected, forgetting the feminist dialogue of the 1960s and 1970s about the race-specific struggles of African and Native women and "the lessons of history, be it colonialism, imperialism or even fascism."[124]

Legislators may have unwittingly found the only viable solution to this divisive issue, but, interestingly, the sigh of relief that has come over most Ontarians is the result of a false labelling of what the bill actually does. While Ontario's previous *Arbitration Act* left much to be desired in the way of safety measures for women, the revelation of these deficiencies suggests that religious arbitration need not be discarded altogether. The association of religion with unavoidably sinister means does nothing to further the cause of women's equality. More importantly, it leaves the future of religious women dismally bleak with no allies to turn to for support. Fortunately, the new amendments ensure basic safeguards of equality thanks to the work of many feminists. Importantly, the new amendments may also provide an opportunity for feminists to reconsider their relationship with religion.

QUESTIONS TO CONSIDER

1. Review the frequent impasse between feminist principles and practices and religiously based principles and practices. Use specific examples from Bakht's chapter and bring in more current examples drawn from Canada or elsewhere. What advantages do you see to maintaining this impasse or to easing it?

2. Do you agree with Bakht that there are deep-seated stereotypes, even caricatures, of people who are not Christian or Jewish? To what extent do you think that these more mainstream groupings are also liable to misunderstanding and even oppression? Give specific examples.

3. In what ways can family law arbitration in Ontario be seen as gender-neutral? Conversely, in what ways might such arbitration be gender-biased? Use specific examples to strengthen your approach.

SUGGESTIONS FOR FURTHER READING

Morris, M. with Bunjun, B. (2007, October). *Using intersectional feminist frameworks in research*. Ottawa: Canadian Research Institute for the Advancement of Women [CRIAW].

Stein, J., Cameron, D. R., Ibbitson, J., Kymlicka, W., Meisel, J., Siddiqui, H. et al. (Eds.). (2007). *Uneasy partners: Multiculturalism and rights in Canada*. Waterloo: Wilfrid Laurier University Press.

Tucker, J. (2008). *Women, family, and gender in Islamic law*. Cambridge: Cambridge University Press.

Wiles, E. (2007). Headscarves, human rights, and harmonious multicultural society: Implications of the French ban for interpretations of equality. *Law and Society Review, 41*(3), 699–735.

NOTES

1. *Arbitration Act*, S.O. 1991, c. 17 s. 32(1).
2. Ghammim Harris, "Sharia Is Not a Law by Canadian Standards," *Vancouver Sun* (15 December 2003) at A15; Sara Harkirpal Singh Sara, "Religious Law Undermines Loyalty to Canada," Letter to the Editor, *Vancouver Sun* (10 December 2003) at A23; and Gayl Veinotte, "A Legal Jihad: Islamic Groups Say They Don't Want Sharia Law to Apply Only to Muslims. They Want Everyone to Obey the Qur'an" *Western Standard* (31 October 2005) at 20.
3. I write this article both as a legal scholar and as someone who has been actively involved in the feminist discussions on this issue with such organizations as the National Association of Women and the Law, the Women's Legal Education and Action Fund (LEAF), and the Canadian Council of Muslim Women. While I am critical of the final recommendations made by many women's organizations concerning religious arbitration, I acknowledge that the debates that occurred among these women were vigorous and multi-faceted. I also acknowledge that my early research, which canvassed the potential risks associated with religious arbitration for women under the old *Arbitration Act*, may have helped to produce some of the feminist recommendations of which I am critical.
4. *Family Statute Law Amendment Act*, S.O. 2006, c. 1.
5. Lee Greenburg, "Ban on Religious Courts Draws Multi-Faith Attack: Jewish, Muslim Groups Say Hasty McGuinty Move Will Backfire, Hurt Women," *Ottawa Citizen* (13 September 2005) at A1. The irony of the date of the announcement combined with the excessive emphasis that Islam and sharia received in the religious arbitration debate in Ontario was not lost on most Muslims.
6. Marion Boyd, "Arbitration in Family Law: Difficult Choices" (2006) 18 Inroads 58 at 59.

7. Sherene Razack, "Imperiled Muslim Women, Dangerous Muslim Men and Civilized Europeans: Legal and Social Responses to Forced Marriages" (2004) 12 Feminist Legal Studies 129 at 151.

8. *Ibid.*

9. *Ibid.* at 130.

10. Orientalism as Edward Said has noted is "a style of thought based upon an ontological and epistemological distinction made between 'the Orient' and (most of the time) 'the Occident.'" Edward W. Said, *Orientalism: Western Conceptions of the Orient* (London: Penguin Group, 1995) at 2. The Orient exists for the West and is constructed by, and in relation to, the West. It is a mirror image of what is inferior and alien ("other") to the West and, thus, seen as separate, eccentric, backward, sensual, passive, and with a tendency towards despotism and away from progress.

11. *Arbitration Act, supra* note 1.

12. Lynne Cohen, "Inside the Beis Din," *Canadian Lawyer* (May 2000) at 27.

13. Haroon Siddiqui, "Sharia Is Gone but Fear and Hostility Remain," *Toronto Star* (15 September 2005) at A25. One newspaper headline warned of the impending doom of "legal jihad." Veinotte, *supra* note 2.

14. The author acknowledges the limitations of using the phrase "Muslim community," which tends to connote a singular, homogenous group with similar interests and goals. Muslims in Canada are, in fact, made up of people from a vast diversity of races, countries of origin, and beliefs. "Diversities are so pronounced that one has to ask whether the term 'the Muslim world' is at all meaningful if it refers to such an amorphous, divergent, shifting composition of individuals and societies who are not infrequently in conflict with one another." Fareeda Shaheed, "Asian Women in Muslim Societies: Perspectives and Struggle" (keynote address to the Asia-Pacific NGO Forum on B+10, July 2001, Bangkok), Women Living under Muslim Laws <http://www.wluml.org/english/newsfulltxt.shtml?cmd%5B157%5D=x-15759336%20&cmd%5B189%5D=x-189–59336>. Some of the deepest divisions concerning the sharia debate in Ontario occurred among Canadian Muslims, some of whom were in favour of religious arbitration under the old act, particularly where other religious communities had the option available to them, others who felt religious arbitration with some safeguards could be workable, and still others who were vehemently against it at all costs.

15. For example, Homa Arjomand stated: "[I]n backwards cultures, especially under Sharia or any other religion, there is no consequence for beating your wife or abusing your children." Quoted in Terry O'Neill "Homa Arjomand," *Western Standard* (19 September 2005) at 32.

16. Québec international relations minister, Monique Gagnon-Tremblay, stated: "Muslims who want to come to Quebec and who do not respect women's rights, or rights, whatever they may be, in our civil code … [should] stay in their country and not come to Quebec, because it's unacceptable." Quoted in Mike De Souza "Quebec Leaders Warn Ontario: Reject Sharia: Minister Wants Immigrants Who Support It Barred," *National Post* (11 March 2005) at A8.

17. *Civil Code of Québec*, S.Q. 1991, c. 64, Article 2639 provides: "Disputes over the status and capacity of persons, family matters or other matters of public order may not be submitted to arbitration."

18. Sharmeen Khan, "Racism, Feminism and the Sharia Debate" (2005) 34(7) Briarpatch 32.

19. The majority of the popular media coverage by contrast has resorted to typecasting Muslim women as victims.

20. In this article, my reference to Canadian feminist organizations includes such bodies as the Canadian Council of Muslim Women, the National Organization of Immigrant and Visible Minority Women Canada, and the Muslim Canadian Congress who joined with mainstream women's organizations such as the National Association of Women and the Law, the YWCA Canada, and LEAF in opposing the use of religious arbitration in Ontario.

21. Razack, *supra* note 7 at 134.

22. S. A. Goundry et al., *Family Mediation in Canada: Implications for Women's Equality* (Ottawa: Status of Women Canada, 1998); and R. Mandhane, *The Trend towards Mandatory Mediation in Ontario: A Critical Feminist Legal Perspective* (Ottawa: Ontario Women's Justice Network, 1999) at 34.

23. Natasha Bakht, "Arbitration, Religion and Family Law: Private Justice on the Backs of Women" (March 2005), National Association of Women and the Law <http://www.nawl.ca/ns/en/publications.html> at 40.

24. *Moge v. Moge*, [1992] 3 S.C.R. 813 at para. 55 (L'Heureux-Dubé J.).

25. Although, the Supreme Court of Canada cannot always be trusted to make decisions in favour of women, as the recent decision in *Newfoundland (Treasury Board) v. Newfoundland and Labrador Association of Public and Private Employees*, [2004] 3 S.C.R. 381, indicates, given the tremendous legal strides made in women's rights since the notorious case, *Murdoch v. Murdoch*, [1975] 1 S.C.R. 423, judicial oversight of the substantive content of an arbitral award remains nonetheless important. For a further explanation of the meaning of judicial oversight in the context of family arbitration means, see Bakht, *supra* note 23 at 12–16.

26. There is some case law to suggest that courts will interpret certain sections of the *Arbitration Act, supra* note 1, to include certain guarantees as to the substance of the arbitral award. See *Hercus v. Hercus,* [2001] O.J. 534 at paras. 96–7 (Sup. Ct. J.) [*Hercus*].

27. *Arbitration Act, supra* note 1 at s. 32(1).

28. Bakht, *supra* note 23 at 27–9.

29. *Ibid.* at 29.

30. Judy Van Rhijn, "First Steps Taken toward Sharia Law in Canada," *Law Times* (24 November 2003) at 10. Syed Mumtaz Ali was also quoted as saying "'to be a good Muslim' all Muslims must use these *sharia* courts.'" Cited in Margaret Wente, "Life under Sharia, in Canada?" *Globe and Mail* (29 May 2004) at A21.

31. Early feminist Elizabeth Cady Stanton rejected Christianity, believing that religion was at the root of women's oppression. Carmen Heider, "Suffrage, Self-Determination, and the Women's Christian Temperance Union in Nebraska, 1879–1882" (2005) 8 Rhetoric and Public Affairs 85 at 88. By contrast, Bronwyn Winter notes the resistance in feminist circles to the advocacy of atheism as a feminist stance. Bronwyn Winter, "Naming the Oppressor, Not Punishing the Oppressed: Atheism and Feminist Legitimacy" (2001) 13 Journal of Women's History 53 at 54.

32. Lois Lamya' al Faruqi, "Islamic Traditions and the Feminist Movement: Confrontation or Cooperation?" <http://www.jannah.org/sisters/feminism.html>.

33. *Canadian Charter of Rights and Freedoms*, Part I of the *Constitution Act, 1982*, being Schedule B to the *Canada Act 1982* (U.K.), 1982, c. 11 [*Charter*].

34. The preamble to the *Charter, ibid.*, states: "Whereas Canada is founded upon principles that recognize the supremacy of God and the rule of law."

35. *R. v. Big M. Drug Mart Ltd.*, [1985] 1 S.C.R. 295 at 336–7 [*Big M. Drug Mart*]. See also *Reference re Same-Sex Marriage,* [2004] 3 S.C.R. 698 at para. 57; and *Syndicat Northcrest v. Amselem,* [2004] 2 S.C.R. 551 [*Amselem*].

36. W. Cole Durham, "Perspectives on Religious Liberty: A Comparative Framework," in Vicki C. Jackson and Mark Tushnet, eds., *Comparative Constitutional Law* (New York: Foundation Press, 1999) at 1159.

37. The secular state of France and the theocratic state of Saudi Arabia have both been known for the deleterious effects that their policies have had on the ability to practise individual religious freedom.

38. *Levitts Kosher Foods Inc. v. Levin* (1999), 45 O.R. (3d) 147 (Sup. Ct. J.). See also *Markovitz v. Bruker* (2005), 259 D.L.R. (4th) 55 (Que. C.A.) (leave to appeal to the Supreme Court of Canada granted); and the prob-lematic interpretation in *Kaddoura v. Hammoud,* [1998] O.J. 5054 (Ct. J.), where the court refused to require payment of $30,000 in the form of the *mahr*, a Muslim marriage custom, because the contract had a religious purpose. See generally Pascale Fournier, "The Erasure of Islamic Difference in Canadian and American Family Law Adjudication" (2001) 10 Journal of Law and Policy 51 at 59–60.

39. *O'Sullivan v. Minister of National Revenue,* [1991] 45 F.T.R. 284 at para. 32.

40. In Germany and France, different aspects of state Muslim law have been transplanted into these Western legal nations through international private law rules that directly incorporate certain foreign norms. Pascale Fournier, "The Reception of Muslim Family Laws in Western Liberal States" (December 2005) Women Living under Muslim Laws Dossier 27. In Canada, unlike in France or Germany, it is the law of domicile and not the law of the parties' citizenship that is applicable in matters of family law.

41. Some feminists have echoed Susan Moller Okin's perspective that multiculturalism is detrimental to women's rights. Susan Moller Okin, "Is Multiculturalism Bad for Women?" in J. Cohen, M. Howard, and M. Nussbaum, eds., *Is Multiculturalism Bad for Women?* (Princeton: Princeton University Press, 1999), at 7. See, for example, Homa Arjomand's comments that "multiculturalism didn't help people integrate into the larger society. It made them more isolated, especially women …… [I]t became another tool to abuse women." Quoted in O'Neill, *supra* note 15 at 32.

42. Sikh men who wear turbans have successfully sought exemptions from motorcycle helmet laws and from the official dress codes of the Royal Canadian Mounted Police. See *Dhillon v. British Columbia (Ministry of Transportation and Highways, Motor Vehicle Branch)*, 1999 B.C.H.R.T.D. No. 25 (QL); and Will Kymlicka, *Multicultural Citizenship: A Liberal Theory of Minority Rights* (Oxford: Oxford University Press, 1995) at 31. The Supreme Court of Canada accepted the power of the Hutterite Church over its members and their property when two lifelong members of the community were expelled for apostasy and refused their share of the colony's assets, which they had helped to create with their labour. See *Hofer v. Interlake Colony of Hutterian Brethren,* [1970] S.C.R. 958; and *Lakeside Colony of Hutterian Brethren v. Hofer,* [1992] 3 S.C.R. 165. Canada provides exemptions regarding taxation, education, and military service to the Doukhobours, a Christian sect who emi-grated en masse from Russia in the late 1800s where they were being persecuted. See Kymlicka (at 42 and 216).

43. Kymlicka, *supra* note 42 at 153.

44. Ayelet Shachar, "The Puzzle of Interlocking Power Hierarchies: Sharing the Pieces of Jurisdictional Authority" (2000) 35 Harvard Civil Rights-Civil Liberties Review 385 at 385.

45. *Ibid.*

46. *Khan v. Khan*, [2005] O.J. 1923 (Ct. Just.).

47. *Family Law Act*, R.S.O. 1990, c. F.3, s. 52 [*FLA*].

48. *Khan v Khan*, *supra* note 46. at para. 52.

49. Women's Legal Education and Action Fund (LEAF), "Submission to Marion Boyd in Relation to Her Review of the Arbitration Act" (17 September 2004), LEAF <http://www.leafottawa.ca/news/archives/2004/11/media_release_leafs_submissions_to_marion_-boyd_in_relation_to_her_review_of_the_arbitration_act/index.php>.

50. Letter from Cynthia Wilkey, Co-Chair, LEAF National Legal Committee, to Michael Bryant, Attorney General of Ontario (30 May 2005) [emphasis added] [on file with author] [LEAF Letter].

51. The terms of reference for the No Religious Arbitration Coalition and steering committee can be found at YWCA Toronto, <http://www.ywcatoronto.org/advocate_change/arbitration_coalition.htm>.

52. See, for example, the National Association of Women and the Law's (NAWL) letter to the premier of Ontario, the attorney general, and the minister responsible for the status of women, urging them not to adopt Marion Boyd's recommendations (24 February 2005), NAWL <http://www.nawl.ca/Documents/BoydLetter.doc>. A similar position has been adopted by the Metropolitan Action Committee on Violence against Women and Children. See Ontario Women's Justice Network, "No Religious Arbitration Legislation Introduced" (16 November 2005), <http://www.owjn.org/issues/mediatio/legislation.htm>.

53. *Ibid.*

54. Protests against the use of sharia to settle family law disputes were held across Canada and Europe: "Attorney-General Michael Bryant and the Premier … were initially prepared to accept Marion Boyd's recommendations. But a backlash developed in the months that the government sat on the report." Murray Campbell, "McGuinty Still in the Line of Fire over Religious Tribunals," *Globe and Mail* (23 January 2006) at A11.

55. Marion Boyd, "Dispute Resolution in Family Law: Protecting Choice, Promoting Inclusion" (20 December 2004), Ministry of the Attorney General <http://www.attorney-general.jus.gov.on.ca/english/about/pubs/boyd/fullreport.pdf>. While many of the recommendations in Boyd's report attempted to correct some of the deficiencies in the *Arbitration Act*, on the whole, the report failed to find an appropriate balance between the rights of religious minorities and women. It unquestionably gave preference to religious freedom and demonstrated a clear refusal to assume responsibilities for the protection of vulnerable persons within minority groups, women in particular. For an analysis of the Boyd report, see Bakht, *supra* note 23 at 56–60.

56. According to a survey conducted by the Centre for Research and Information on Canada, "[s]ixty-three per cent of Canadians oppose giving any religious community the right to use faith-based arbitration to settle divorce, custody, inheritance and other family disputes." See Norma Greenaway, "Ontario Was Right to Reject Religious Arbitration: Survey," *Montreal Gazette* (31 October 2005) at A12.

57. Leti Volpp, "The Citizen and the Terrorist" (2002) 49 University of California Los Angeles Law Review 1575 at 1592.

58. Toronto Star columnist, Rosie DiManno, reminded Canadians that we should not be labelled racist for "daring to champion the secular over the infantilizing religious." Rosie DiManno, "Sharia Solution a Fair One, and Not Racist," *Toronto Star* (16 September 2005) at A2.

59. Ron Csillag, "New Ontario Bill Partially Strips Beit Din's Powers," *Canadian Jewish News* (24 November 2005) at 3. Similarly, Father Raymond J. de Souza argues that, instead of banning all religious arbitration, Premier McGuinty should have rejected only the use of sharia law. See Father Raymond J. de Sousa, "The Wrong Kind of Multiculturalism," *National Post* (15 September 2005) at A20.

60. This response is reminiscent of the actions of Chinese Americans who wore buttons in the Second World War that read "I'm Chinese, not Japanese," so that they would not be targeted for racial violence. See Volpp, *supra* note 57 at 1590–1.

61. Merav Shmueli, "The Power to Define Tradition: Feminist Challenges to Religion and the Israel Supreme Court" (S.J.D. thesis, Faculty of Law, University of Toronto, 2005) [unpublished, on file with author].

62. *Amselem*, *supra* note 35 at paras. 46–7. See also *Multani v. Commission scolaire Marguerite-Bourgeoys*, 2006 S.C.J. No. 6 (QL).

63. Donna Sullivan, "Gender Equality and Religious Freedom: Toward a Framework for Conflict Resolution" (1992) 24 New York University Journal of International Law and Policy. 795 at 813. While the inclusion of custom or sincerely held beliefs in the definition of religious law may entail the additional burden of engaging with offensive patriarchal practices where substantive safeguards for equality are put in place, such a risk can be curtailed.

64. See, for example, Judith Plaskow, *Standing Again at Sinai: Judaism from a Feminist Perspective* (New York: Harper San Francisco, 1991); Blu Greenberg, *On Women and Judaism: A View from Tradition* (Philadelphia: Jewish Publication Society of America, 1981); and Judith Hauptman, *Rereading the Rabbis: A Woman's Voice* (Boulder: Westview Press, 1998).

65. See Fatima Mernissi, *The Veil and the Male Elite: A Feminist Interpretation of Women's Rights in Islam* (Cambridge: Persus Books, 1991); Abdullahi An-Na'im, *Toward an Islamic Reformation: Civil Liberties, Human Rights and International Law* (Syracuse: Syracuse University Press, 1990). See also Amina Wadud, *Qur'an and Woman: Rereading the Sacred Text from a Woman's Perspective* (New York: Oxford University Press, 1999); and Amira Mashour, "Islamic Law and Gender Equality: Could There Be a Common Ground? A Study of Divorce and Polygamy in Sharia Law and Contemporary Legislation in Tunisia and Egypt" (2005) 27 Human Rights Quarterly 562.

66. Anver Emon, "Shades of Grey on Sharia: Counterpoint," *National Post* (29 July 2005) at A12.

67. *Ibid.* See also Mashour, *supra* note 65 at 577 and 585.

68. Anver Emon, cited in Peter McKnight, "Entrenching Sharia Law Would Help Muslim Women," *Vancouver Sun* (17 September 2005) at C5. Geneva Conventions, 7 December 1978, 1125 U.N.T.S. 3.

69. Challenging the notion of the monolithic "Muslim woman" also requires recognizing the differing levels of religiosity that different women may adhere to. Saba Mahmood's ethnographic method in her book *Politics of Piety* uses the accounts of Egyptian women of different ages, class backgrounds, and levels of religiosity to portray the participants of the mosque movement from a broad range of Muslim women's experiences. Mahmood shows that a "religious Muslim woman" cannot be defined in any particular way. Saba Mahmood, *Politics of Piety: The Islamic Revival and the Feminist Subject* (Princeton: Princeton University Press, 2005). Of course, Muslim women should not be viewed solely in religious terms. Shahnaz Khan articulates the "significance of Islam as a political, cultural, emotional and spiritual response to the de-legitimization experienced by Muslims." Shahnaz Khan, "Canadian Muslim Women and Shari'a Law: A Feminist Response to 'Oh Canada!'" (1993) 6 Canadian Journal of Women and the Law 1 at 52 and 56.

70. See, for example, the position adopted by the Canadian Council of Muslim Women discussed in Bakht, *supra* note 23 at 55–6.

71. Durham, *supra* note 36 at 1162.

72. *Chamberlain v. Surrey School District No. 36*, [2002] 4 S.C.R. 710 at para. 19. See also *Big M. Drug Mart*, *supra* note 35 at 346, where the Court stated: "The values that underlie our political and philosophic traditions demand that every individual be free to hold and to manifest whatever beliefs and opinions his or her conscience dictates, provided *inter alia* only that such manifestations do not injure his or her neighbours or their parallel rights to hold and manifest beliefs and opinions of their own."

73. Nayereh Tohidi, "'Islamic Feminism': Perils and Promises" (2002) 16 Mews Review 13, <http://www.amews.org/review/reviewarticles/tohidi.htm>.

74. "What many neo-secularists cannot grasp is the desire to cultivate a deep personal connection with God in daily life." Sheema Khan, "What Close-Minded Liberals Can Learn from a Rape Victim," *Globe and Mail* (12 November 2005) at A23.

75. I am conscious of the very poignant feminist critique of how "women's choices" reify women's inequality. D. Majury, "Women Are Themselves to Blame: Choice as a Justification for Unequal Treatment," in F. Faraday, M. Denike, and M.K. Stephenson, eds., *Making Equality Rights Real: Securing Substantive Equality under the Charter* (Toronto: Irwin Law, 2006).

76. Talal Asad, *Formations of the Secular* (Stanford, CA: Stanford University Press, 2003) at 7.

77. Shaheed, *supra* note 14.

78. Abdullahi An-Nai'im, "Human Rights and Scholarship for Social Change in Islamic Communities" (2005) 2(1) Muslim World Journal of Human Rights 2 at 2.

79. Razack, *supra* note 7 at 130.

80. Samuel P. Huntington, "The Clash of Civilizations?" (1993) 72 Foreign Affairs 22.

81. Razack, *supra* note 7 at 130.

82. Anver Emon, "Understanding Sharia Law: Further Education about Islamic History and Islamic Law Necessary" (2005) 59(6) Bulletin of the University of Toronto 20 at 20.

83. Razack, *supra* note 7 at 168–9.

84. Canada's *Anti-Terrorism Act*, S.C. 2001, c. 41, has codified extensive surveillance measures that have unduly targeted Muslims and those perceived to be Muslims.

85. Leti Volpp, commenting on the American situation, noted that before 11 September 2001 there was a strong belief that racial profiling was inefficient, ineffective, and most importantly, unfair. Since 11 September, and with the widespread publicity that all of the hijackers were Arabic, President Bush and other top officials have

characterized the war against terrorism as a battle of "civilizations." The practical effect has been a shift in public sentiment wherein racial profiling, at least when it comes to Arab Americans, is viewed as acceptable government practice. Volpp, *supra* note 57 at 1576.

86. Engaging in religious arbitration requires the voluntary consent of the parties involved. Muslim women would not be subject to sharia arbitration unless they agreed to it first. Feminists have noted the concerns regarding "real choice." Majury, *supra* note 75. By contrast, Homa Fahmy of the Federation of Muslim Women has stated: "The fact that I've been [characterized as being] unable to make a sound judgment in this matter, I find deeply offensive." Quoted in Melissa Leong, "Muslims Groups Promise Liberals a Fight on Sharia," *National Post* (15 September 2005) at A12.

87. Saeed Rahnema, "The Perils of Faith-Based Multiculturalism: The Case of Shar'a in Canada" (2006) 40(1) Canadian Dimension 21 at 21.

88. See *International Covenant on Civil and Political Rights*, 19 December 1966, 999 U.N.T.S. 171, Article 2; *Convention on the Elimination of All Forms of Discrimination against Women*, G.A. Res. 34/180, 34 UN GAOR Supp. No. 46 at 193, UN Doc. A/34/45 (1979); *International Convention on the Elimination of All Forms of Racial Discrimination*, 660 U.N.T.S. 195; *International Covenant on Economic, Social and Cultural Rights*, G.A. Res. 2200A (XXI), 21 UN GAOR Supp. No. 16 at 49, UN Doc. A/6316 (1966), Article 2; and the *Universal Declaration of Human Rights*, G.A. Res. 217 (III), UN GAOR, 3d Sess., Supp. No. 13, UN Doc. A/810 (1948), Article 2.

89. *Andrews v. Law Society of British Columbia*, [1989] 1 S.C.R. 143. See also Robert J. Sharpe and Katherine E. Swinton, *The Charter of Rights and Freedoms* (Toronto: Irwin Law, 1998) at 189.

90. *Criminal Code*, R.S.C. 1985, c. C-46.

91. *R. v. Gladue*, [1999] 1 S.C.R. 688 at para. 87.

92. *FLA*, *supra* note 47.

93. *Ibid*. at s. 5(1).

94. The courts' *parens patriae* jurisdiction refers traditionally to the role of the state as sovereign and guardian of persons under legal disability such as minors or the mentally unwell. See Bryan A. Garner, ed., *Black's Law Dictionary*, 7th edition (St. Paul, MN: West Group, 1999) at *s.v.* "*parens patriae*."

95. Section 56(1.1) of the *FLA*, *supra* note 47, additionally provides that a court may disregard any provision of a domestic contract where the child support provision is unreasonable having regard to the child support guidelines. Significantly, in *Duguay v. Thompson-Duguay*, 2000 O.J. No. 1541 (Sup. Ct. J.) (QL); and *Hercus*, *supra* note 26, the Court explicitly held that it retains its inherent *parens patriae* jurisdiction to intervene in arbitral awards where necessary in the "best interests of the children." See also *Children's Law Reform Act*, R.S.O. 1990, c. C.12 at s. 69.

96. *Miglin v. Miglin*, [2003] 1 S.C.R. 303 at para. 4. "The difference ... between separation agreements and prenuptial contracts is substantial. Separation agreements generally accept the default regime in the *Divorce Act*, R.S.C. 1985, c. 3 (2nd Supp.). One defends a separation agreement by arguing that it instantiates the legislative objectives, including equitable sharing of the consequences of marriage ... By contrast, a defender of a prenuptial agreement argues that it displaces the default norms." Robert Leckey, "Contracting Claims and Family Law Feuds" (2007) 57 University of Toronto Law Journal at 33.

97. Where the parties use an alternative means of dividing their property, a court's primary concern on appeal will be to examine whether the arbitration order failed to consider undisclosed significant assets, whether a party understood the nature or consequences of the arbitration agreement and any other matter in accordance with the law of contract. See *FLA*, *supra* note 47 at s. 56(4). Domestic contracts involving spousal support can be set aside by a court even where the parties expressly contract out of their right to appeal where (1) the provision for support or the waiver of the right to support results in unconscionable circumstances; (2) the provision/waiver for support is in favour of a dependant who qualifies for an allowance of support out of public money; or (3) if there is default in the payment of support under the contract at the time the application is made (at s. 33(4)).

98. *Hartshorne v. Hartshorne*, [2004] 1 S.C.R. 550 at para. 36 [*Hartshorne*].

99. Shelley McGill, "Religious Tribunals and the Ontario *Arbitration Act, 1991*: The Catalyst for Change" (2005) 20 Journal of Law and Social Policy 53 at 59.

100. Section 56(5) of the *FLA*, *supra* note 47, states: "The court may, on application, set aside all or part of a separation agreement or settlement, if the court is satisfied that the removal by one spouse of barriers that would prevent the other spouse's remarriage within that spouse's faith was a consideration in the making of the agreement or settlement."

101. *FLA*, *supra* note 47 at s. 52(1)(c).

102. For a discussion of the application of the *Charter* in the context of religious family arbitration, see Bakht, *supra* note 23 at 29–34.
103. *Hartshorne*, *supra* note 98 at para. 36.
104. Razack, *supra* note 7 at 129.
105. CTV.ca News Staff, "McGuinty Rules Out Use of Sharia Law in Ontario," *Canadian Television Network* (12 September 2005), CTV <http://www.ctv.ca/servelet/ArticleNews/story/CTVNews/1126472943217_26/?hub=TopStories>.
106. *Ibid.*
107. *Family Statute Law Amendment Act*, *supra* note 4.
108. Under the new amendments, family law arbitrators would be required by regulation to: (1) be members of a recognized professional dispute resolution organization; (2) undergo training including screening parties separately for power imbalances and domestic violence; (3) inquire into matters such as power imbalances and domestic violence; and (4) keep proper records and submit reports to be tracked by the Ministry of the Attorney General. Ontario Ministry of the Attorney General, "Backgrounder: The Family Statute Law Amendment Act, 2005" (15 November 2005), Ministry of the Attorney General <http://www.attorney-general.jus.gov.on.ca/english/news/2005/20051115-arbitration-bg-EN.pdf> at 2. See also clause 11 of the *Family Statute Law Amendment Act*, which permits the lieutenant governor in council to make certain regulations, *supra* note 4 at clause 11.
109. Although the requirement for independent legal advice has been met with approval by groups such as the No Religious Arbitration Coalition, they have noted that "currently legal aid does not apply in arbitration, which means that many women will not have the means to pay for legal advice." As a result, they advocated unsuccessfully for Bill 27 to be amended to make provision for legal aid funding for women in need in these circumstances. See Ontario, Legislative Assembly, Standing Committee on General Government, *Official Reports of Debates* (*Hansard*), G-11 (16 January 2006) at G-164 (Alia Hogben, No Religious Arbitration Coalition).
110. Many feminist groups supported the proscription of waiving one's right to appeal in order to have access to judicial oversight. The Ontario Bar Association has expressed concern that by not allowing couples to waive their right to appeal more cases will end up in the court system. See Canadian Broadcasting Corporation (CBC) News, "Arbitration Law Changes Could Send More Divorces to Court" (14 December 2005), CBC Ottawa <http://www.cbc.ca/ottawa/story/ot-arbitration20051214.html>. Indeed, the waiver of appeal is a complicated issue that could, in some instances, potentially leave women vulnerable to unending litigation and thus a significant drain on their financial and emotional resources by persistent male partners.
111. *Family Statute Law Amendment Act*, *supra* note 4 at clause 1.(1)(b).
112. "Ontario Prohibits Religious Tribunals in Family Disputes," (*Charlottetown*) *Guardian* (16 November 2005) at A9. See also Kerry Gillespie and Rob Ferguson, "New Law to Ban Religious Tribunals; Divorce Won't Be Settled by Sharia Same Law for All Ontarians: Bryant," *Toronto Star* (16 November 2005) at A9.
113. Peter Kormos, NDP MP for Niagara Centre, has stated: "Nothing in this bill will stop, has the power to stop, any two parties, any two spouses, from going to any religious authority of any faith and asking that religious authority to resolve their dispute by adjudicating, by hearing the respective sides and making a judgment. Bill 27 doesn't stop people from doing that." Ontario, Legislative Assembly, *Official Report of Debates* (*Hansard*), 22 (23 November 2005) at 1730 (Peter Kormos) [NDP position].
114. Religious influence in informal dispute resolution processes cannot be barred even in Québec where article 2639 prohibits arbitration in family law. *Civil Code of Québec*, *supra* note 17.
115. Professor Anver Emon asked "Would a regulated arbitration regime be perfect? Perhaps not. Would it have been better than the informal back alley Islamic mediations that are still in place? I suspect yes." Anver Emon, "A Mistake to Ban Sharia," *Globe and Mail* (13 September 2005) at A21.
116. NDP position, *supra* note 113.
117. LEAF Letter, *supra* note 50.
118. I am sympathetic to calls for resistance to religious arbitration when fundamentalist proclivities are suspected. The Islamic Institute of Civil Justice has certainly not garnered faith in its cause for a separate system of civil justice for Muslims. See Syed Mumtaz Ali, "The Review of the Ontario Civil Justice System: The Reconstruction of the Canadian Constitution and the Case of Muslim Personal/Family Law" (1994) Canadian Society of Muslims <http://muslim-canada.org/submission.pdf> at 3. However, I recognize the possibility that not all supporters of religious arbitration including Islamic arbitration have sinister aims.
119. Madhavi Sunder, "Cultural Dissent" (2001) 54 Stanford Law Review 495 at 502–3.
120. Ontario Ministry of the Attorney General, "News Release: McGuinty Government Declares One Law for All Ontarians" (15 November 2005), Ministry of the Attorney General <http://www.attorneygeneral.jus.gov.on.ca/english/news/2005/20051115-arbitration.asp> at 1.

121. Jean-François Gaudreault-DesBiens, "The Limits of Private Justice: The Problems of the State Recognition of Arbitral Awards in Family and Personal Status Disputes in Ontario" (2005) 16(1) World Arbitration and Mediation Reports 18 at 29.

122. Ayelet Shachar's model of transformative accommodation attempts to balance the interests of cultural groups with the interests of the state to uphold the liberties of its citizens. Shachar offers a "joint governance" approach to the paradox of multiculturalism wherein the institutional design aspires to engender interaction, even competition, between state and cultural group sources of jurisdiction. Ayelet Shachar, *Multicultural Jurisdictions: Cultural Differences and Women's Rights* (Cambridge: Cambridge University Press, 2001).

123. Shachar, *supra* note 44 at 425.

124. Azizah Al-Hibri, "Is Western Patriarchal Feminism Good for Third World/Minority Women?" in Cohen, Howard, and Nussbaum, eds., *supra* note 41 at 45.

Chapter Eleven

The *Charter*, Equality Rights, and Women:
Equivocation and Celebration

Diana Majury *

Editors' Note: Diana Majury covers various topics associated with the pursuit of equality rights under the Canadian Charter of Rights and Freedoms. In "The Charter, Equality Rights, and Women: Equivocation and Celebration," Majury shows how the Charter has been praised as a pragmatic way of advancing democracy in Canada but also how it has attracted sharp criticism for its role in perpetuating inequality due, in part, to costs and time for litigation. Building on dynamic theoretical approaches, including feminism, and also on specific cases, she illustrates how some Canadian activists, especially feminists, are equivocal about using the Charter to advance equality claims. Thus, for skeptics " … it is more likely that rights will be interpreted to reproduce power relations and protect the status quo than to challenge and redress inequities." Even so, many commentators credit Charter-based litigation with enhancing human rights protections and see the originators of the litigation as "pragmatists" who work progressively within the legal system rather than abandoning it altogether as a site of struggle.

Professor Majury's analysis establishes how heterosexism and inattention to social inequalities are often used in such cases. She concludes that "[t]he Charter is only as progressive as those applying it." Majury uses several cases-in-point to show how arguments are brought forward and then rejected or accepted by the Supreme Court of Canada. These examples include abortion and human reproduction; women's experiences of violence; family law issues; workplace and employment issues, including mandatory retirement; and "socioeconomic claims," including poverty and provision of social programs. She warns against sweeping analyses of a monolithic ideology among judges, claiming that female judges tend to be "more open and courageous" in approaching sex equity cases. Majury offers a wide-ranging, complex assessment of how legal struggles can be an "opening [rather] than a shortcoming."

I. INTRODUCTION

The *Charter*,[1] and particularly the equality rights provision,[2] has generated a proliferation of legal and social science scholarship; it has been the subject of innumerable conferences, symposia, and workshops. Much of this *Charter* writing and talking has been of the abstract, think-piece type of scholarship[3]—to which this article aspires to contribute. This attention alone tells us a great deal about the significance of the *Charter* and its impact—it has us talking, thinking, writing, and debating about the role of law, its possibilities and its limitations, its seductions and its portents. And, while the questions and the arguments relating to law more generally, as well as to specific attempts to use law to further social change, may basically be

Source: Diana Majury, "The *Charter*, Equality Rights, and Women: Equivocation and Celebration," *Osgoode Hall Law Journal*, Vol. 40, Nos. 3 & 4, pp. 297–336. © 2002, D. Majury. Reprinted by permission of the author.
*Associate Professor, Department of Law, Carleton University, Ottawa. The author wishes to thank her colleagues and friends on LEAF's National Legal Committee for great law/Law talks, pieces of which have found their way into this article; her writing buddy Daphne Gilbert, for wonderful lunch discussions, her support, and helpful comments on this article; and Constance Backhouse for the gladioli and all they represent.

the same as they were in pre-*Charter* days, the *Charter* has reinvigorated these debates such that they are very much alive and lively, informing and directing the more specific, focused *Charter* analysis. As someone who would describe herself as a *Charter* pragmatist,[4] I savour the questions and challenges that force me to think more deeply, more skeptically, more big-picturely, and, I hope, more radically, about *Charter* Work—its effectiveness, its limitations, its unintended consequences, and its larger political and social meanings. I think that we all need to be held accountable, and to account, for our thinking and for our activism; these intense *Charter* discussions and disagreements are an important part of that process of accountability.

In this article, I want to look at some of the major criticisms and concerns that left/feminist/marginalized groups have raised about the *Charter*, about rights, and about equality[5] and some of the more positive *Charter*/rights/equality expectations from among these same groups, looking for points of difference and commonality among these writers.[6] This background will help me look specifically at it and how these concerns and expectations have played out with respect to the *Charter*, equality rights, and women, which is the subject of this article, by looking at some of the sex equality cases that have come before the Supreme Court of Canada.

II. ACADEMIC WRITINGS

A. On the *Charter* Generally

The strongest and most vociferous critiques of rights discourse generally, and the *Charter* more specifically, have largely emanated from the white, male left, generally reflecting a Marxist or class-based perspective.[7] One of the primary issues that underlies the *Charter* critique for many on the left is the power the *Charter* cedes to the courts, that is, to elite, unelected judges who are largely unaccountable. According to Harry Glasbeek, "[n]o matter how little we think of our existing democratic institutions, they are intended to be democratic," while courts and judges " … [are] not, in any serious way, subject to the discipline of democratic politics…."[8] Glasbeek credits democracy—electoral mechanisms and public sphere activities—with the imposition of human rights obligations as a mechanism to force government and private sector actors " …. to deal more equitably in respect of differences," and then asks why we would "entrust our future to an appointed, electorally unaccountable institution such as the judiciary which has never produced any analogous results?"[9] But his question ignores the fact that much of the public sphere activity referred to actually took place in the courts. Frequently what has happened in the courts has forced our elected representatives to take action on the human rights front.[10] Legislative action acknowledging and supporting basic human rights has been painfully slow, often vigorously resisted, and sometimes enacted despite public opinion to the contrary. Minority rights and marginalized groups present a serious challenge to those who put their faith and hope in democracy, however flawed. Canada has a long history of sexist and racist legislation;[11] the courts have provided one forum in which to challenge and resist such majority dominance. There is something to be said for an independent judiciary with the power to make unpopular decisions, particularly in the context of human rights.

The *Charter* has become somewhat of a lightning rod in the larger debates about parliamentary supremacy and judicial activism and about legal, as opposed to political, engagement. Those commentators who are negative about the *Charter* tend to view the legal and the political as separate arenas, implying that intervention is an either or proposition. Those who are more sanguine about the *Charter* generally see the two arenas as highly interrelated and are often adept at playing one off against the other. The interplay between the courts and the legislatures opens up additional spaces for public participation and arguably strengthens the democratic process.

The concern of largely unfettered[12] judicial authority under the *Charter* relates to several critiques levelled against the *Charter*. The abstractness and indeterminacy of rights heighten concerns about judicial elitism and the lack of judicial constraints. Relatedly, the symmetrical and universal nature of the rights and protections are available to everyone and, because they are themselves without substantive content, they can be employed for almost any purpose. This problem is compounded by the perception of these rights as individualistic, exclusionary, and not amenable to group-based analysis or collective action. Given our judiciary and the absence of more specific direction from the *Charter*, it is more likely that rights will be interpreted to reproduce existing power relations and protect the status quo than to challenge and redress inequities.

Joel Bakan argues that the *Charter* is infused with the ideology of formal equality such that individuals are abstracted out of concrete social relations of inequality and portrayed as formal equals.[13] The ideology of formal equality masks and neutralizes inequality. In this context, disparate impact is constructed as natural and inevitable or as a product of choice or consent, and not as a function of discrimination. Marginalized claimants then have an uphill battle to prove inequality or discrimination, especially when that inequality is long-standing and deeply entrenched. Andrew Petter and Alan Hutchinson argue that rights provide a "veneer of consensus," the illusion of shared values and aspirations, that makes it more difficult to detect and respond to underlying disagreements and power struggles.[14]

By abstracting and individualizing, rights and rights discourse are seen to depoliticize issues of power and domination, making them more palatable and manageable, even rendering them invisible. The process of translating oppression and domination into the legal language of rights, discrimination, and equality is seen by *Charter* critics as necessarily conservative.[15] The arguments and analysis put before the courts are constrained and distorted so that even a victory can at best be only partial and inadequate, easily subverted and turned against the more vulnerable. The *Charter* creates the illusion of social change and the mirage of a better world that captures the imagination and energy of progressive people, who are then diverted into expensive and protracted legal battles that are conservatizing and counterproductive.

Charter critics view the anti-rights, anti-*Charter* backlash as reflecting negatively on the *Charter* and creating a more hostile and reactionary environment. The backlash is often framed in terms of formal equality that is being used to try to roll back earlier gains made by subordinated groups. *Charter* advocates, on the other hand, interpret the backlash as indicative of at least some successes under the *Charter* and point to the overtly political nature of the backlash as proof against the claim of *Charter* depoliticization. The formal versus substantive equality debate generated by the *Charter* is seen as significant, warranting serious public attention and involvement. The *Charter* has done much to foster public discussions about the meaning of equality in very concrete terms.

Given its exclusive application to government action, the *Charter* is criticized as inevitably reinforcing the segregation constructed between public and private, thereby enabling powerful private sector exploiters to evade social responsibility while portraying themselves as victims. Autonomous, "equal," private actors are seen as needing protection from the heavy-handed, interventionist state. The *Charter* reinforces the power imbalances, privilege, exploitation, and domination that permeate the private sphere. Private actors, including individuals, corporations, and institutions, are immune from having to adhere to *Charter* values in their own interactions but are encouraged to invoke the *Charter* when they believe the state is trenching on their private turf, reconfigured into rights through *Charter* discourse.

Even though they are general in nature, these criticisms of the *Charter* seem to focus primarily on the likely results in cases and on the negative uses that can and have been made of the *Charter*. Feminists, on the other hand, have tended to see the *Charter* as part of a bigger picture and a longer-term strategy.[16] While most feminists would, to a large extent, make these same criticisms, they tend to see them as cautions or concerns rather than as reasons to reject the *Charter*. The *Charter* is seen as providing a forum for raising issues, for developing more sophisticated analysis and argument for public, judicial, and political education; and for mobilizing and politicization.[17] From this perspective, the outcomes of individual cases are of less importance, and negative *Charter* arguments and decisions provide fodder for future action. Rather than masking disagreement and power differentials, the *Charter* is seen as offering an opportunity to bring these matters explicitly to the foreground.

Rather than falling into either the *Charter* optimist/enthusiast or the *Charter* pessimist/resister/skeptic categories that are often invoked, I would describe most feminists (including myself) who work in this area as *Charter* pragmatists who see the *Charter* as one among a limited number of potential tools to expose and to argue for the redress of women's and other marginalized groups' subordination. We have no illusions that *Charter* litigation is an easy undertaking; we know that it is fraught with dangers, both foreseen and unforeseen, and that whatever we do will have negative as well as positive repercussions. We know that when we invoke the *Charter* we take a calculated risk, and we try to make these calculations carefully and thoroughly. But we also know that to ignore the *Charter* is to ignore an opportunity, as well as to concede the equality terrain to those who would use it to justify and perpetuate inequality. This *Charter* pragmatism is consistent with the prevailing feminist attitude to law more generally—a strong critique of law, coupled with a recognition of the significance of law as a site of power and hence an arena for struggle, and of the practical impossibility of eschewing law altogether.[18]

From her perspective as an Aboriginal woman, Mary Ellen Turpel provides a much more fundamental critique of the rights paradigm and of the *Charter* than any criticism outlined above.[19] She calls into question the cultural authority of the *Charter*, pointing out that the *Charter* imposes a culturally and historically specific conceptual framework on people who do not share that culture or that history. Aboriginal people are put in the impossible position of having to assert cultural difference through the medium of an alien framework that is incapable of understanding or reflecting that difference. The fact that Aboriginal people have, in particular situations, chosen to rely on *Charter* rights is not an uncritical endorsement of the *Charter* but may simply be a concession to its dominance and a reflection of the urgency of, or lack of options with respect to, the specific issue.[20] Turpel does not attempt to resolve what is an unresolvable dilemma posed by " … problems of conceptual reference for which there is no common grounding or authoritative foothold."[21]

Equality rights present a similar dilemma for members of other subordinated groups who seek to invoke them. To varying degrees, they too will not share in the language or in the conceptual framework of the *Charter*. The challenge that Turpel describes for a judge adjudicating in a situation involving cultural difference may apply to other situations of "difference."

For a judge, a situation of cultural difference should be and must be a situation of not knowing which direction to go, a situation involving choices about reasoning that may not be defensible or acceptable. It involves episodes of undecidability, self-judgment, and uncertainty. It would involve acknowledging the imperative of admitting mistakes and recognizing ignorance.[22]

This imperative can be taken up by advocates who present equality claims that challenge underlying premises and taken-for-grantedisms. To try to use the *Charter* to its fullest, they need to take the risk of attempting to shift accepted truths and understandings and ways of knowing and to muster the confidence and courage to put forward arguments that may appear indefensible or unacceptable.[23]

B. On Equality

"Equality is thus a process—a process of constant and flexible examination, of vigilant introspection, and of aggressive openmindedness."[24]

Much of the academic writing examining the equality guarantee in the early days of the *Charter* referred to debates over the meaning of equality as largely a debate between formal and substantive equality. At that time, formal equality was the dominant understanding of what equality meant and required. Formal equality is premised on the understanding that equality means treating likes alike and posits same treatment as its defining feature. It focuses on procedures with the goal of ensuring equality of opportunity. Substantive equality recognizes that in order to further equality, policies and practices need to respond to historically and socially based differences. Substantive equality looks to the effects of a practice or policy to determine its equality impact, recognizing that in order to be treated equally, dominant and subordinated groups may need to be treated differently.

While feminists were unanimous in their rejection of the formal equality approach and their support for the substantive model of equality, they were dubious about the likelihood of Canadian courts adopting substantive equality as the guarantee provided by section 15. However, more recent equality writing accepts that substantive equality is the operative model in Canadian law.[25] This breakthrough came in the Andrews[26] case, the first decision by the Supreme Court of Canada on section 15. For all those who are not *Charter* resisters or *Charter* rejecters, the endorsement of substantive equality must be seen as a positive step. The feminist response to Andrews ranged from enthusiasm to cautious optimism. Among the cautiously optimistic were those who were skeptical about the courts' ability to make the transition from formal to substantive equality in more than name. Whatever we called it, the fear was that courts would inevitably and unconsciously continue to focus on likeness (to dominant groups) as the key to equality in terms of recognition and of remedy. This fear was magnified, not dissipated, in the years since Andrews. I increasingly hear the claim being made among social activists involved in *Charter* litigation that we (lawyers, activists, and judges) have not really moved beyond a formal equality analysis. This critique raises some very fundamental questions (for example, whether because it is a comparative concept, equality can ultimately only mean formal equality, albeit in forms more sophisticated than treating x and y identically) about what is meant by formal and substantive equality. The cases confirm that these continue to be difficult questions on which we have not progressed very far, if at all, beyond the judicial thinking in Andrews. Some of the most recent decisions of the Supreme Court of Canada raise the spectre that the Court is slipping backward in its understanding of and commitment to substantive equality.

Feminist legal scholars were engaging with these equality critiques long before the advent of the *Charter* and these debates continue. For some feminists, the problems inherent in equality as an analytical tool and as a goal render it of extremely limited utility for women and other subordinated groups. In taking this position, Radha Jhappan provides a strong and articulate critique of the concept of equality. She argues that " ... the discourse of legal equality as an overarching goal and strategy is an idea whose time may have passed."[27] One of her primary criticisms is the inherently comparative nature of equality, a criticism that anticipates the question raised above of whether an equality analysis can ever lead to anything more than variations on the formal equality theme. While I am sympathetic to this critique and share the concern, I am not convinced that other concepts, including the concept of justice that Jhappan prefers, are not also limited by an implicit need for comparators.[28]

The need for comparison gives rise to the related critique of essentialism—that equality posits women and men each as undifferentiated, undimensional groups. Differences among women, as among men, are ignored; other sites of oppression are treated as irrelevant. Further, the essentialism leads to assimilationist arguments, with white men as the standard to which all women are assumed to aspire and against which they are inevitably compared. Such an approach is incapable of understanding, not to mention addressing, the intersectional discrimination and disparate aspirations of those who are more than one identity removed from the dominant group. Here again the critique is of the formal model of equality and raises the question whether it is practically possible to use equality to move beyond that model to address the diverse needs and experiences of women. Jhappan thinks not: " ... the equality frame is simply too narrow to contain the complex intersectional analysis because it is by nature comparative (one group compared against another), essentialist and ... impossible."[29] These are pressing concerns, but it may be that whatever concept is adopted will be limited by prevailing assumptions and values and that the issue is less about finding the better concept and more about trying to make the concept at hand do what one wants it to.

In the *Charter*-lobbying days, feminists were not confident that an anti-discrimination equality provision would provide adequate protection to women. The perceived need for additional protection for women was grounded in the dismal history of sex discrimination complaints under the Canadian Bill of Rights,[30] U.S. jurisprudence under the U.S. Constitution[31] whereby sex discrimination allegations were subjected only to intermediate scrutiny rather than the more strict scrutiny accorded to some other forms of discrimination, as well as in fears generated by the inclusion of a perceived deference to multicultural rights in section 27 of the *Charter*.[32] For these reasons, section 28, the separate sex equality provision of the *Charter* that states, "Notwithstanding anything in this *Charter*, the rights and freedoms referred to in it are guaranteed equally to male and female persons," was considered of vital importance by those who were advocating on behalf of women's rights when the *Charter* was being drafted and going through the parliamentary process. While some critics saw section 28 as meaningless, arguing that it added nothing to the *Charter*,[33] much of the early feminist writing on the *Charter* saw great possibilities for the effective use of section 28. Colleen Sheppard saw this in relation to the enhancement of section 7 rights for women: "The radical potential of this section [28] becomes apparent if we contemplate the notion of equal liberty or security of the person for women and men."[34] Mary Eberts argued that section 28 "should ... lead a court to require a high level of justification [under section 1] for any sex-based distinction."[35] Similarly, Rosalie Abella postulated that section 28 "means that in interpreting the onus on a respondent to justify the reasonableness of a limit to an otherwise guaranteed right, gender equality is an immutable right."[36] According to Catharine MacKinnon, "Anti-subordination could be the distinctive guiding interpretive principle of section 28."[37] There was an impressive array of feminists anticipating a strong and meaningful section 28.

Despite these great hopes for section 28, it would seem that the critics were more accurate in their predictions of its impact. Section 28 is seldom alluded to in current *Charter* literature and cases. In my search, I was able to find only twelve Supreme Court of Canada cases in which section 28 was mentioned. The majority of these were sexual assault cases in which the reference to section 28 was found in the following frequently quoted passage from Justice Cory in Osolin: "The provisions of ss. 15 and 28 of the *Charter* guaranteeing equality to men and women, although not determinative should be taken into account in determining the reasonable limitations that should be placed upon the cross-examination of a complainant."[38] As in Osolin, the reference to section 28 is almost always in conjunction with section 15, confirming the critics' perception that section 28 added nothing beyond what was already provided by section 15. I found only three cases in which section 28 received any discussion separate and distinct from section 15. In NWAC, the only one of these cases in which the Court dealt at any length with section 28, Justice Sopinka, having dismissed the section 28 argument in relation to section 2(b) of the *Charter*, made the point that it would have been better characterized as a section 15 argument, which he then dismissed as failing on the same basis.[39] The other two references to section 28 alone were contained in single sentences of little substance.[40]

There has been no engagement in the decisions of the Supreme Court of Canada with the question of what, if anything, section 28 adds in terms of equality protection for women (or for men). It is interesting to speculate why this happened—whether section 28 was seldom invoked and accordingly has languished forgotten and untested; whether groups were unable to come up with a distinctive section 28 argument; whether it was eclipsed and made redundant by stronger section 15 jurisprudence than was anticipated; whether judicial discomfort and/or uncertainty about section 28 led to its abandonment; or whether women's groups developed discomfort about the apparent privileging of sex discrimination claims over other forms of discrimination.[41]

In the early days of the *Charter*, feminists who saw it as a potentially positive vehicle for raising and challenging issues of concern to women were fairly uniform in their descriptions of what they were looking for in section 15. Feminist academics promoted an interpretation of equality that focused on effect, inequality, and context, that was itself fluid and open,[42] and that understood equality as relational rather than comparative.[43] While cognizant of the risks involved, feminists tended to respond to the indeterminacy of equality as an opportunity for putting forward a radical vision of equality, rather than seeing it exclusively as a cloak for elitist self-perpetuation. Similarly, feminists' response to the critiques of abstractness, individualism, and false universals was to call for a contextual analysis that focused on particularized, group-based inequality. In other words, feminists generally seemed more interested in trying to make the *Charter* work than in wholesale rejection of it. McIntyre ascribes this more positive approach to the *Charter* to feminist activism and ongoing engagement in political struggle as part of feminists' daily lives, such that "declaring any dominant institution, including rights discourse and rights litigation, unambiguously off-limits is indefensible in theory as in practice."[44] As McIntyre asserts, this willingness to engage is always, and necessarily, accompanied by deep ambivalence and discomforting awareness of the risks of such involvement.

The critique of *Charter* rights as symmetrical and universal is particularly apropos with respect to section 15, given that it is intended to address issues involving asymmetrical power. In relation to this issue, Judy Fudge describes the situation of women having had to expend major time, energy, and money to defend against men's equality-based challenges to legislation that women had previously spent years fighting to attain as "the ultimate paradox of the *Charter*."[45] The concern with symmetry is that, with the exception of disability, the grounds are set out in neutral terms, that is, as Sheppard describes it:

> … in ways that obscure the historical and continuing realities of inequality facing the subordinated group or groups within each ground. Thus, in terms of the formal language of anti-discrimination law, discrimination on the basis of sex extends parallel, symmetrical protection to both men and women. Discrimination on the basis of race protects both minority and majority.[46]

Although I am not aware of the argument that section 15 should be applied exclusively to subordinated groups having been made explicitly,[47] feminists have certainly argued against the symmetrical application of the equality guarantee. Andrews, the first Supreme Court of Canada decision on section 15, with its contextualizing language of historical disadvantage, vulnerability, and lack of political power, went some way toward unbalancing the symmetry of section

15. Going beyond the individualized assessment, Lynn Smith has suggested the imposition of a different standard when the challenged provision worsens the situation of a disadvantaged person than when it is prejudicial to a member of an advantaged group.[48] Others have suggested that the symmetry problem could be overcome, or at least diminished, by a focus on groups rather than on the neutral grounds.

A further concern with the grounds set out in section 15 is whether they are capable of addressing situations of intersectional discrimination. The issue of intersectional discrimination was almost completely absent in the early feminist writings on the *Charter*. Since those days, intersectional discrimination as a critical component of any equality analysis has been powerfully brought to the foreground through the writings and advocacy of women of colour.[49] Antidiscrimination/equality law must be capable of responding effectively to the complex and intersectional discrimination that many people experience; to the extent that it fails to do so, the law itself is discriminatory. The concern has been raised that a grounds-based approach to discrimination may not be capable of addressing intersectional discrimination—that, at best, grounds of discrimination would allow one to argue the discrimination as sex plus race and/or disability and/or sexual orientation, that is multiple, not intersectional, discrimination. In response to this problem, Nitya Iyer has recommended a relational approach that addresses all of the potential grounds of discrimination, rather than focusing on the characteristics of the individual complainant.[50] Others have argued that a focus on specific groups, rather than on the more generalized grounds, would be more amenable to an intersectional analysis.[51] Justice Claire L'Heureux-Dubé unsuccessfully tried to persuade her fellow Supreme Court justices that an approach focusing on identifying the relevant subgroup(s) that have been subjected to exploitation was preferable to relying solely on the water-tight compartments of a grounds-based approach.[52] Dianne Pothier, in response to Justice L'Heureux-Dubé, has argued that we should not move away from grounds to groups, but rather should engage in a more sophisticated grounds-based analysis that recognizes grounds as historical markers of discrimination that raise suspicion when invoked.[53] As Pothier has commented, this is not a matter of oppositional approaches, but rather a question of how to make grounds and groups work together.

An assessment of women, equality rights, and the *Charter* must address questions relating to intersectional discrimination as a central concern. Tellingly, this is a bit difficult given the limited number of complainant groups that have come before the Supreme Court of Canada, as well as the limited ways in which their cases have been framed.

C. On the Decision Makers

One issue that many of the general discussions of the *Charter* largely ignore is the differences among the judges.[54] As discussed above, the power accorded unelected, unaccountable judges under the *Charter* is one of the principal critiques emanating from the male left. There is a tendency among these critics to lump all judges together as sharing a single judicial ideology that aligns them with the social and economic elite.[55] Feminists, however, have shown considerable interest and see considerable significance in gender differences among judges.[56] This is not surprising for a number of reasons. Advocating for more women/feminist judges, as well as male judges from other subordinated groups, has been a priority for many feminists. Women judges themselves have commented on the gendered dynamics of judging.[57] To date, the women judges on the Supreme Court have generally been more open and courageous in their equality analysis than their male colleagues. Women are recent entrants to the judicial arena, as they have been somewhat less recent entrants to the legal community and to academia. There are strong parallels among the subordinating experiences of feminist lawyers, feminist academics, and feminist judges that feminist scholars understand must have an impact on their judicial decision making.[58] And finally, as the cases discussed below demonstrate, there have been some striking gender splits in Supreme Court of Canada decisions, particularly on sex equality issues, that have certainly not escaped feminists' notice. While these women-only dissents are disappointing because they are dissents, they are at the same time affirming; they speak strongly to the importance of dissent judgments.[59]

There seems to be a commonly held view that unanimous decisions by the Supreme Court are the most desirable. According to Marc Gold, for example, "it would be bizarre and undesirable if efforts were not made to maximize those occasions where the Court could speak with one voice."[60] However, the costs exacted by forced unanimity can be high, as evidenced by the painstaking contortions and watering down of positions that seem to have gone into the creation of the Law[61] decision as a consensus of the Court. In some areas, the certainty and clarity that a unanimous Supreme Court decision can bring to bear on a fraught legal issue may well be a desirable goal, in the interests of both law and society. But this is not necessarily true with respect to a fundamental rights document, like the *Charter*, and particularly in relation to such an amorphous concept as equality rights, where consensus is likely to be either fleeting or case specific or to reflect a compromised vision and approach.

I think we should look more positively on split *Charter* decisions and dissents. I am often the most disappointed in and wary of unanimous decisions. The desire for unanimous decisions reflects a positivist understanding of law, the idea that the correct interpretation is lying in wait to be found. Such a desire is at odds with the more sophisticated and complex understandings of law generally held by social justice scholars and activists. Multiple judgments more fully reflect our plurality and usually provide a fuller and deeper canvassing of the issues and problems. Multiple judgments may provide better direction to legislatures required to implement the court's decision. According to Gold, "[t]o the extent that a further value of the *Charter* lies in the fact that it precipitates a dialogue between court and legislature, the divisions on the Court can be seen to contribute to a more realistic, flexible and less dogmatic dialogue on issues of rights."[62] Dissents provide hope for those whose rights have not been recognized by the majority. Gays and lesbians have, for example, drawn strength and determination from the strong dissents in cases like Mossop[63] and Egan, and, with that vision before them, they continued to push to have the discrimination that they face finally acknowledged by the majority in Vriend. In the slow incremental process that is law reform, it is often true that today's dissent is tomorrow's majority.[64] This may be particularly the case in areas like equality jurisprudence where we all have a huge amount to learn and integrate into our thinking. As much as I would prefer it if more of the decisions that I agree with were in the majority rather than the dissent, my sense is that a shift to greater consensus and unanimity among members of the Court would mean that the views and positions that I support would become increasingly muted and ultimately invisible.

If one accepts that the significance of *Charter* cases goes far beyond the specific outcome in the case, then multiple decisions provide much more fertile ground for public education, mobilizing, and political action. *Charter* decisions are about interpretation, values, and beliefs; it is no wonder that consensus is rare. As the diversity of the Supreme Court expands, we can anticipate greater diversity of perspective and analysis; we should look forward to greater and stronger disagreements and to more concurring and dissenting opinions. The benefits to be derived from academic debate about the *Charter* that I referred to at the beginning of this article apply similarly, in my view, to judicial debate about the *Charter*. While some argue that the rights in the *Charter* "mask fundamental social and political conflicts"[65] under an appearance of shared values and consensus, I think the opposite: that *Charter* rights provide the impetus and grounding to bring these conflicts out into the open—in the court room, in the legislatures, and in the streets. Rather than simply reflecting and reinforcing the established values of the legal system and legal elites, the *Charter* equality guarantee provides a basis from which to try to depose formal equality and individualism from their entrenched positions as dominant values.

III. THE CASES

I do not intend to discuss, or even refer to, all of the Supreme Court of Canada decisions in which the "sex" ground of section 15 was before the Court because they are not necessarily the most significant sex equality or *Charter* equality cases.[66] Despite the advent of section 15 of the *Charter*, a number of the most important Supreme Court of Canada cases for women over the past twenty years were not *Charter* cases[67]or, although *Charter* cases, were not brought or decided as equality cases.[68] This lack of centrality for section 15 can be seen either positively or negatively. It could be read as support for the argument that equality is an empty, meaningless concept and that section 15 is too abstract and open-ended to be of concrete assistance to women. Section 15 is not central in all of the cases and decisions of greatest significance to women, because equality is not central to the betterment of women's lives. On the other hand, it could be that the impact of the *Charter* and section 15 is much more diffuse and relational—that the Court's understanding of substantive equality for women is filtering into its judgments, lower courts' decisions, and the arguments and expectations of those who appear before the courts. The analysis of substantive equality is not contained by or within the *Charter* or even in the explicit language of equality. Given the similarities in wording and intent, human rights anti-discrimination provisions have, from the beginning, had a strong, interactive relationship with section 15 of the *Charter*. Initially, human rights jurisprudence was employed to steer the Court away from the formal equality model. At the same time, section 15 has presented opportunities to break out of some of the quagmire that was impeding the human rights provisions.[69] This dialectical relationship continues, largely to the benefit of both human rights and *Charter* analysis. This diffuse impact of section 15 may, to a limited extent and on a practical level, mitigate the restriction of the *Charter*'s application to state action; the *Charter* is, at least indirectly, affecting the private sector. But the fact that such impact is indirect and "private" may at the same time serve to reinforce the public/private dichotomy on the symbolic level.

I will discuss the cases under the following substantive headings: reproduction, violence against women, family, employment, and socio-economic claims, recognizing that these categories overlap significantly and do not account for all of the cases.

A. Reproduction

Abortion is one area in which our elected representatives and the institution of democracy have shown themselves remarkably undemocratic. Neither federal nor provincial governments under a range of leaderships were willing to introduce legislation to eliminate (federal) or circumvent (provincial) the *Criminal Code*[70] restrictions on abortion that were in effect until 1988. No government was willing to go out on the political limb of respecting and supporting a woman's right to choose abortion, despite the fact that the majority of Canadians support such a position. Politicians apparently feared taking sides on such a highly charged issue and risking the ire of voters for whom this would be a decisive factor. The fact that the federal government has only made a single, feeble attempt to reintroduce restrictions on abortion since the Supreme Court struck down the *Criminal Code* provision on abortion indicates that this fear, now operating in reverse, and not a principled position on the issue of abortion, was likely the inhibiting factor for a number of politicians. Before the advent of the *Charter*, pro-choice advocates were stalled by governments' unwillingness to act; the *Charter* opened the door for movement forward on this issue.

There have been at least three *Charter* cases dealing with abortion, all of which were among the early *Charter* cases to come before the Supreme Court of Canada.[71] Abortion is quintessentially a gender-specific issue. As such, and because its genesis is biological, abortion gives rise to the dangers of essentialist argument and decision making. Is it possible to ground the gender-specific argument in a social context that reflects the role played by biological difference without essentializing it? Is this a sex equality argument? Is it a section 15 argument? From an anti-choice perspective, the issue is solely the recognition of fetal rights; gender is irrelevant because the woman is irrelevant. From a fathers' rights perspective, often articulated in conjunction with the fetal rights position but actually in some ways contradictory to it, the issue is gender equality based on a formal equality model. This is a somewhat difficult argument to mount. Given the biological differences between a pregnant woman and a man who self-defines as a parent, it is difficult to see the likeness between the two on which the formal equality model could be imposed.

The decision in Morgentaler is, in terms of its outcome, a huge step forward for women. The decision struck down the *Criminal Code* prohibition of abortion and eliminated the humiliating, delaying, and inequitable process that women were required to undergo in order to obtain a legal abortion in Canada. The decision, however, is what Fudge describes as a "narrow … victory"[72] in that it did nothing to resolve any of the myriad problems that deny many women access to safe abortion in Canada. Given the procedural focus of the section 7 analysis, the case contains a great deal of discussion about access problems, but there is no reference to the socio-economic context of these access issues that have a disproportionate and negative impact on poor and low-income women. Morgentaler does lay some foundation for these arguments, and the decision is a necessary first step in ending the legislative stalemate so that the issue of the state's obligation to provide access to abortion services can be pursued on the political front, as well as possibly through litigation.

In terms of analyzing and recognizing women's equality rights, the case is disappointing, posits some problematic propositions, largely avoids the most difficult questions, and offers few rays of hope. It is narrowly focused; there is no discussion of the forced abortions to which young women, racialized women, women with disabilities, and poor women are frequently subjected. As one would expect, the Court was divided on both outcome and approach to the issue. There were four different judgments issued, with Justice Bertha Wilson, the lone woman on the Court, the only one to stand alone in her judgment. The case was decided on the basis of section 7 of the *Charter*—the right to life, liberty, and security of the person and the right not to be deprived of any of these except in accordance with principles of fundamental justice. The Crown's primary argument in support of the legislation was one of deference. All of the judges accepted that the state has an interest in the protection of the fetus but none felt obliged in the context of this particular case to fully investigate that interest or to determine what limits, if any, that interest might justify imposing upon a pregnant women's decision to terminate her pregnancy. Justice Wilson went the furthest in this discussion, proposing that the state's interest in protecting the fetus is greater at later stages of pregnancy.

Pro-choice supporters, understandably, have been concerned by this recognition of a state interest in protecting the fetus and fear the repercussions for women. So far, fetal rights arguments have been pursued in a number of different contexts but have not ultimately been successful.[73] I share these concerns. At the same time, feminist analyses of abortion have developed beyond a simplistic choice argument to recognize the complications of race, class, and disability and to acknowledge the difficult and painful dilemma that the abortion decision presents for most women. Differing views about the fetus are part of this dilemma and need to be incorporated into feminist abortion analysis. I am more concerned by the language in Morgentaler of balancing the state's interest in protecting the fetus against the rights of the pregnant woman. To see these rights as in conflict rather than as inextricably interrelated undermines the pregnant woman's bodily integrity and autonomy.

The section 15 argument that the *Criminal Code* prohibition of abortion, except in limited circumstances, infringed women's equality rights was summarily dismissed by the two dissenting judges in Morgentaler and not addressed by the other judges. Unavoidably, the language throughout refers to women and to pregnant women, but, with the exception of Justice Wilson, this was not enough to induce the Court to address abortion as a gendered issue and to inquire into the sex equality implications of the impugned law.[74] In a passage that has been extensively quoted by feminists and is hailed as a *Charter* high point by many, Justice Wilson provided a powerful discussion of the gendered nature of the abortion decision:

> This decision is one that will have profound psychological, economic and social consequences for the pregnant woman. The circumstances giving rise to it can be complex and varied and there may be, and usually are, powerful considerations militating in opposite directions. It is a decision that deeply reflects the way the woman thinks about herself and her relationship to others and to society at large. It is not just a medical decision; it is a profound social and ethical one as well. Her response to it will be the response of the whole person.
>
> It is probably impossible for a man to respond, even imaginatively, to such a dilemma not just because it is outside the realm of his personal experience (although this is, of course, the case) but because he can relate to it only by objectifying it, thereby eliminating the subjective elements of the female psyche which are at the heart of the dilemma.[75]

Justice Wilson directly places this discussion in the context of women's struggle for human rights, not as part of the earlier struggle to fit into the man's world, but as part of women's more recent struggle to recreate societal structures to include their needs and aspirations. In this context, "[t]he right to reproduce or not to reproduce … is one such [protected] right and is properly perceived as an integral part of modern woman's struggle to assert her dignity and worth as a human being."[76] In this discussion of abortion, Justice Wilson meets the difficult challenge of grounding the gender-specific argument in a social context that reflects the role played by biological difference without essentializing it. Although she does not engage in this discussion in relation to section 15 or 28, this is one of the best and strongest articulations of a substantive equality analysis that we have had from the Court to date. It is contextual, focused on inequality, and premised on women's experiences. The context is the human rights context of women's inequality and the history of women's struggle to be admitted as distinct persons within that context. There is no need for a comparator group; in fact, attempts to find a comparator group would undermine this analysis. Substantive equality is about recreating society and social structures to incorporate "differences," not to distort them, appropriate them, reject them through objectification or denial, merely "accommodate" them, or assess them against some presumably "undifferent" comparator group.

B. Violence Against Women

Violence against women is probably the area in which section 15 has been most frequently argued before the Supreme Court of Canada. From the early decision in *Hess*, challenging the constitutionality of the gender-specific absolute liability offence to sexual intercourse with a girl under fourteen, to the most recent decision in *Shearing*, relating to the cross-examination of a complainant in a sexual assault trial on her diary entries, there have been at least a dozen sexual assault cases in which sex equality has been referred to and has clearly informed the analysis.[77] Most of these cases involve the admissibility and use of confidential records relating to the complainant. If pornography is included as a form of violence against women, the number of Supreme Court *Charter* cases in this area rises to fifteen.[78]

Sexual assault is an area where there has been much interchange between the courts and Parliament, a situation that existed before the *Charter*[79] and has continued throughout the time of the *Charter*. The relationship has generally been one of Parliament providing some protection to women against the evidentiary abuses to which they have been subjected in sexual assault trials and the courts clawing back some of these protections in the name of the fair trial rights of the accused. Over time, Parliament has become more explicit in its equality rationale for these provisions. Amendments to the *Criminal Code* relating to sexual assault made in the last ten years have each contained a preamble that explains the gendered social context that gives rise to sexual assault and the gender issues that need to be taken into consideration in applying the new legislation.[80] Somewhat reluctantly, at least for some justices, the Supreme Court of Canada increasingly has been willing to explore the gendered assumptions and values underlying the evidentiary issues. This process culminated in the almost unanimous[81] decision in Mills in which the statutory protocols for the admission of confidential records pertaining to the complainant in a sexual assault trial were upheld. However, the more recent decision in Shearing represents a step backwards. The majority rules that the accused could not cross-examine the complainant on the absence of entries in her diary relating to the abuse in order to raise the presumption that if it was not recorded it must not have happened. Then, in a sleight of hand, the majority rules that the accused can cross-examine the complainant on the absence of entries in her diary in order to test the accuracy and completeness of her recollection of the events around the time that she was abused.[82]

It is impossible to know yet whether Shearing is an aberration or the beginning of a backslide into ignoring or downplaying women's equality interests in the context of sexual assault trials. I fear that the Court believes that it has now purged itself and the law of the erroneous and damaging assumptions, myths, and stereotypes about women's sexuality and women's reactions to having been raped that infused the rules of evidence and have continued to infect defence presentation and judicial decision making long after the rules were revised.[83] I fear that the Court will no longer feel the need to engage in a rigorous sex equality analysis in this area and will tune out these arguments when presented by counsel. I fear that the Court believes it has eliminated the sexual inequalities relating to sexual assault such that it can now revert to being dealt with as a gender neutral-offence. These fears are greatly exacerbated by the retirement of Justice L'Heureux Dubé, who has been a champion of women's equality rights. Her sexual assault judgments, often in dissent, are wonderfully affirming for feminist advocates who work on this issue. She gradually has pushed the Court to be able to understand and accept a gendered equality analysis in this area. Section 15 provided the foundation for a judge to publicly recognize, as did Justice L'Heureux-Dubé, that:

> Parliament exhibited a marked, and justifiedly so, distrust of the ability of the courts to promote and achieve a non-discriminatory application of the law in this area [sexual assault] … My attempt to illustrate the tenacity of these discriminatory beliefs and their acceptance at all levels of society clearly demonstrates that discretion in judges is antithetical to the goals of Parliament.[84]

Justice L'Heureux-Dubé has paid a huge price, in terms of vicious and personalized critique and public scorn, for her outspoken support for women's equality rights, particularly in the sexual assault context. With this kind of public controversy swirling around a sex-equality analysis in the context of rape, it is hard to credit the argument that the *Charter* depoliticizes the issues that come under its shadow.

C. Family Law

All family law cases are sex equality cases, including those arising between lesbians or gay men or involving bisexuals or transgendered persons. By this I mean that the family is a thoroughly gendered institution; it is premised on a gendered division of labour that permeates every aspect of family life. This is our inheritance—the family as fundamentally a gender construct from which it is very difficult to escape. The law has reflected and perpetuated the gendered family and only recently has there been a concerted effort, led by feminists, to introduce equality into the family and into family law. Ironically, those efforts have led to a gender-neutral approach to family law that belies its underlying gendered foundation, as well as the gender-based expectations and assumptions that inform our readings of the family. We are seeking to impose a gender-neutral solution on a gendered problem, all the while still trapped in our own gendered assumptions and judgments.

I am going to focus on my discussion of the *Charter* and family law almost exclusively on the opinions in M. v. H.[85] because they reflect an interesting and important debate over the gendered nature of family law that has potentially far-reaching implications for future sex equality-based claims. In this case, M. brought a section 15 challenge against the definition of "spouse" in Ontario's Family Law Act[86] that had the effect of extending the right to support upon relationship breakdown to members of opposite-sex couples but not to same-sex couples. The challenge, brought on the analogous ground of sexual orientation, was successful in over-turning the heterosexual definition of spouse.[87] Although the action was between two separated lesbian partners, the fact that the parties were both women was not a factor in the case.[88] Gender was, however, a major subtext. Gender enters into the case in the discussions of the purpose behind the state requiring that in some circumstances one party pay support to the other upon relationship breakdown. Justice Peter Cory, writing for a majority that included both women on the Court, made the following statement:

> It is true that women in common law relationships often tended to become financially dependent on their male partners because they raised their children and because of their unequal earning power. But the legislature drafted s. 29 [the definition of spouse at issue] to allow either a man or a woman to apply for support, thereby recognizing that financial dependence can arise in an intimate relationship in a context entirely unrelated either to child rearing or to any gender-based discrimination existing in our society.[89]

While Justice Cory's caveat is accurate, it does not detract from the fact that the need for spousal support flows primarily from the gendered division of labour within the family and from gender inequities outside the family.[90] There is no need to de-gender the analysis of support in order to extend the right of support to lesbians, just as, for example, there is no need to de-gender the analysis of sexual harassment in order to recognize that it can and does occur on a same-sex basis.[91]

Justice Frank Iacobucci, in his half of the majority judgment dealing with section 1 of the *Charter*, uses the family law reforms that feminists fought for to justify his contention that the support provisions are no longer premised on gender inequalities, that is, that the gender problem has been fixed.[92] This is a classic example of some progress on the issue masking the continuing existence of the problem. This position demonstrates the critique of the *Charter* as being infused with an ideology of formal equality that functions so as to neutralize ongoing inequalities. However, as Justice Iacobucci's discussion reflects, the critique is not unique to the *Charter* but is a function of the incremental progress itself. The same problem potentially arises with respect to any gains made to improve a subordinated group's situation such that the gain is seen as the equality solution rather than a small step toward equality. The more successful we are on the preliminary issues, the more difficult it will be to get at the more entrenched and systemic equality issues. This will be particularly true when the equality issues involve intersectional inequalities.

Justice Charles Gonthier takes the position opposite to that endorsed by the majority in M. v. H. and asserts that the purpose of the legislation is exclusively related to sex:

> The primary purpose of the *FLA* is to recognize the social function specific to opposite-sex couples and their position as a fundamental unit in society, and to address the dynamic of dependence unique to men and women in opposite-sex relationships. This dynamic of dependence stems from this specific social function, the roles regularly taken by one member of that relationship, the biological reality of the relationship, and the pre-existing economic disadvantage that is usually, but not exclusively, suffered by women.[93]

Almost all of the concerns raised by the *Charter* critics are present in this one judgment—biologism, essentialism, heterosexism, abstraction, a lack of gender analysis, and a lack of equality analysis. The *Charter* is only as progressive as those applying it. When judges are mired in stereotypes, they can only perpetuate those stereotypes, even in the name of equality.

Justice Michel Bastarache is the only judge to engage in a gender analysis of the purpose of the legislation and to acknowledge the glaring reality of gender inequality that the legislation was designed to address. He finds that "[t]he primary legislative purpose in extending support obligations outside the marriage bond was to address the subordinated position of women in non-marital relationships."[94] In this specific context, women's subordinated position relates to their generally more vulnerable economic situation, often worsened as a result of the relationship, leaving them economically disadvantaged after its breakdown. However, sex is not an absolute proxy for gender[95] and other inequalities may give rise to relationship-based economic dependencies. There is no justification for excluding others who might similarly find themselves in a situation of economic disadvantage related to the relationship upon its breakdown. When that exclusion is premised on a prohibited ground of discrimination, as in this case, the section 15 claim should be successful. Justice Bastarache found the middle ground of gender analysis between the extreme positions that gender is no longer relevant at one end of the spectrum and that sex is determinative at the other end. Family law may be particularly prone to these extreme interpretations and it may be difficult to find that middle gender ground. We need to be able to use the *Charter* to move beyond this dichotomy to recognize the centrality, but not exclusivity, of gender as mediated by other social factors.

It is disconcerting that the majority of the Court in M. v. H. felt the need to de-gender support. I am concerned about what this means for future analysis of family law issues. Family law desperately needs a comprehensive substantive equality analysis; it is an area in which such an analysis would no doubt be complex and contradictory. Yet family law is an area in which the applicability of the *Charter*, as well as its application, have been held to be uncertain[96] and thus where the critique that the *Charter* reinforces the private/public sphere dichotomy may be apt. Although we may not want the *Charter* to intervene at the microcosmic level of individual family disputes, we do need the *Charter* to apply to the legal rules and procedures that govern those breakups to ensure that gender inequities are addressed, not perpetuated or exacerbated. And this is one of the places where the public/private distinction breaks down. It is an area in which:

> [t]he private sphere has been, more often than not, an area where proxies for state power have been issued to designated actors whose status and role within the family privileges them as enforcers or conduits for social norms and values. Men, in their roles as heads of households— husbands and fathers—have historically employed and enjoyed reflected state power in this regard.[97]

The legal rules are not just the state-enacted laws; they are also the assumptions and presumptions that lie behind the interpretation and application of the law and that help create the law. These are the pieces that are extremely difficult to get at—because they are often not articulated, because they are so taken for granted and assumed to be true, because they can be difficult to argue against, and because they are "private." These are the pieces that a gender analysis needs to unpack and that the state/law "public" focus of the *Charter* may sometimes protect.

D. Employment

Employment is the flip side of the family—the public sphere where women have always been, but until recently, have been largely invisible. The workplace, long considered man's exclusive domain, has been modelled on the traditional male worker who, when he commences work as an adult, does so full-time and permanently. He does not take time out to bear or raise children, to accommodate a partner's work demands, or for any other reason. Women have had to fight hard to be recognized as legitimate and committed workers with perhaps different needs, aspirations, ways of working, and priorities than their stereotyped male counterparts.[98] Every victory that women have won in the employment context has been a begrudging accommodation of women's "differences"; there has been no revisioning of the workplace as a multi-gendered-abilitied-raced-aged-sexual-orientationed place. Section 15 of the *Charter* provides the grounding to make such revisioning arguments, but the potential here is severely restricted by the *Charter*'s limited application.

It is in relation to employment that the *Charter*'s restriction to state action is most problematic, where the myth of the public (as in state)/private (as in sector) divide most needs to be challenged in the interests of equality. In this era of globalization, corporations and organizations wield as much, and some would argue even greater, power as the state; they intervene and control people's lives and livelihoods in significant and pernicious ways.[99] The inability to use the *Charter* to directly challenge the entrenched inequalities on which this power is based and which it perpetuates is a serious shortcoming. McKinney v. University of Guelph,[100] addressing the issue of mandatory retirement in the university context, is a good example of the absurdity of this private/public distinction. Over half of this 110-page decision is taken up with detailed and convoluted discussions of whether universities constitute government for the purposes of *Charter* application when it seems patently clear that the issue of mandatory retirement is far from a "private" matter. It is a social issue of general concern, as is evidenced by the number of cases brought before the courts challenging mandatory retirement provisions, the extensive discussions engaged in by the courts on the question, and the types of arguments put forward in its defence and in the challenges to it.[101]

The *Charter*'s equality guarantee should be recognized as requiring consideration of potential impacts of mandatory retirement on the range of diverse employees. These issues were raised to a very limited extent by Justice L'Heureux-Dubé in McKinney. She rejected the all-too-frequently made argument that a practice should be preserved simply because it is deeply entrenched in our society, and that somehow, because of the longevity of a specific policy or practice, we should be precluded from inquiring into its discriminatory foundations and/or impact. Such a hands-off approach protects the most deeply systemic and insidious forms of inequalities by neutralizing and naturalizing them. From this point, L'Heureux-Dubé went on to address the disparate impact of mandatory retirement policies on poor people and on women in particular.

> The fact that "mandatory retirement has become part of the very fabric of the organization of the labour market in this country" is inapposite to the present analysis in so far as it ignores the promulgation of both the *Canadian Charter of Rights and Freedoms* and the *Human Rights Code, 1981* … The adverse effects of mandatory retirement are most painfully felt by the poor. The elderly often face staggering financial difficulties….
>
> [W]omen are particularly affected by this deficiency. Upon attaining the age of 65, women often have either lower or no pension income since a greater proportion of them are in jobs where they are less likely to be offered pension plan coverage. Women are more susceptible to interrupted work histories, partly as a result of childcare responsibilities, thereby losing potential pension coverage. Furthermore, women are prone to have lower lifetime earnings upon which pension benefits are based.[102]

Justice Wilson wrote her own reasons but expressed substantial agreement with Justice L'Heureux-Dubé with respect to her section 1 analysis. The two women judges were the two dissenters in this case and would have struck down the mandatory retirement provisions, at least in part because of their negative disparate impact on women and people with low incomes.

It should not be surprising, given the inability to employ the *Charter* to directly challenge the discriminatory employment practices of "private" employers or to compel them to address systemic inequalities in their workplaces, that there are very few section 15 sex equality employment cases and that, to date, the cases that have been brought mostly deal with employment insurance benefits.

In Schachter,[103] the Court held that the provision of unemployment insurance benefits to adoptive parents and not to "natural" parents constituted a breach of section 15 of the *Charter*. The choice to base the challenge on this distinction and not on the gender distinction related to the provision of maternity benefits in the absence of paternity benefits is interesting on a number of levels. If the section 15 claim had been based on sex, the arguments might have been more interesting and contentious because of the differences that exist between the biological mother and biological father that do not exist between adoptive parents and the biological father. While the risk of the Court opting to strike down maternity benefit, leaving women who have just borne a child vulnerable to the demands or decisions of their employers or union negotiators, might have been low, the consequences for women of such a decision would have been devastating.[104] The comparator group chosen in Schachter was the appropriate one, in this case, not despite but because it was the one that gave rise to a formal equality analysis. This case puts the lie to the notion that formal and substantive equality are in conflict and a formal equality analysis is always a problem and to be avoided.[105]

The focus of the Supreme Court of Canada in Schachter was on remedy. The Court's recognition of the inappropriateness of striking down an under-inclusive positive benefit provided by the state and of reading in as a legitimate *Charter* remedy was a very positive step, even while the limited nature of that remedy was a disappointment. The Court's unwillingness to extend state benefits was disheartening, at least for those of us less concerned about judicial activism. Parliament chose to amend the impugned legislation by reducing the benefits from fifteen to ten weeks and extending them to include natural as well as adoptive parents. Equality activists frequently argue that the equality measures we advocate will not mean a reduction for others but are aimed only at bringing those who have been kept behind up to the prevailing standard. That was clearly not the case in Schachter. Biological parents benefited but adoptive parents lost part of their benefits. This case illustrates the need for feminist advocates to address these issues directly and not pretend that they are cost-free. We need to provide the economic analysis of where the money should come from for the programs we advocate, not leave it to government to cut back on existing programs to finance *Charter*-required programs. In these times of tax and deficit reduction as fiscal priorities, there needs to be a countervailing voice arguing for higher taxes directed to social programs.

There are at least two section 15 *Charter* cases currently before the Federal Court of Appeal challenging different aspects of the Employment Insurance Act[106] on the ground of sex.[107] In these cases, the female plaintiffs are claiming that the unemployment benefits scheme is the mirror image of the male-based model of employment, premised on the same assumptions and values and thus giving rise to similar sex-discrimination problems. I think we can expect to see some of these cases coming before the Supreme Court in the not too distant future. Given government cutbacks and the impossible economic circumstances that so many women face, there will no doubt be increased *Charter* challenges relating to employment and to socio-economic issues more generally.

E. Socio-Economic Claims

While the courts have been doing poorly on socio-economic rights claims, the legislatures have been doing worse, forcing groups to go to the courts to seek redress against drastic government cutbacks and draconian revisions to social programs. The courts have largely failed in providing that redress. Poverty is one of the most glaring inequalities of Canadian contemporary society and is intimately interrelated with the other section 15 grounds. Assumptions and stereotypes about poor people abound and the disadvantages under which they have historically laboured are exacerbated at every turn. But the courts have, for the most part, refused to find socio-economic status or related economically situated inequalities to constitute analogous grounds under section 15.[108]

Socio-economic rights will prove to be the most significant and most difficult *Charter* battleground. They involve the assertion of positive rights, which the courts have been very reluctant to recognize. Refusal to fully engage with these claims is refusal to engage with the disparate impact of poverty that permeates so many other *Charter* equality claims. As Martha Jackman argues, the denial of such rights is itself a *Charter* infringement: "traditional distinctions between classical or negative rights, and social and economic or positive rights, and the willingness to provide for judicial enforcement of one, but not the other, operate in fact to discriminate against the poor."[109]

In the *Charter* context, claims to socio-economic rights by people who live in poverty are an assertion of social responsibility that, if successful, will cost society money. Although there have been situations in which the Court has granted a positive right and effectively required the payment of the benefit requested,[110] in the majority of such cases, the Court has refused the application. And public sentiment is very much in accord with the fiscal restraint, focusing on individualized self-protection, while distancing and blaming less privileged others. Contrary to the *Charter* critics, this is an area in which we need judges to be willing to be activist, to refuse to defer to right-wing parliamentary agendas so as to allow discriminatory programs to continue, and to take action themselves in the social services vacuum. Some provincial human rights codes do provide some protection against discrimination on a ground related to the receipt of social assistance.[111] The painfully tortured process of the recognition of sexual orientation as an analogous ground, based in part on its inclusion in human rights legislation, offers some hope for the eventual recognition of some grounds related to socio-economic status under the *Charter*. However, this hotly contested recognition would largely only be band-aid work to protect social programs relating to health, education, and social assistance that are being eroded or dismantled. The *Charter* cases brought to date have not argued for a more fundamental economic revisioning that would seriously challenge the huge disparities in income and wealth in this country. Some would argue that to use the *Charter* for such radical purposes that are so contrary to dominant economic attitudes would undermine the *Charter*'s credibility and therefore its utility in furthering more modest gains and protections; others would argue that this is the purpose of the *Charter* and its guarantee of equality, and if it cannot be employed to promote larger social justice goals, it is only shoring up a damaged and damaging system. To date, the claims have been very modest and the gains almost non-existent.

Symes[112] was a modest claim that nonetheless was unsuccessful. The Court found that the inability of a self-employed mother to deduct her full child care expenses as a business expense was not a violation of her section 15 equality rights. The two women judges sitting on the case dissented. This case has been critiqued by feminists as an example of privileged women trying to take advantage of a privileging tax system in a way that potentially undermines the interests of other, more disadvantaged women.[113] This criticism is consistent with the traditional left concerns with the *Charter*. But in some ways, these critiques have hampered the use of the case and the decisions themselves to critique a tax system that concerns itself only with horizontal equity and reinforces, and often exacerbates, vertical inequities. The criticisms have been misdirected to the claim and the claimant, instead of raising the larger and more fundamental critiques implicit in the claim. The majority and dissenting opinions clearly expose some of the inequalities of our tax system, relating to class as well as to gender. The case can be read as either a challenge to that system or a shoring up of that system. I prefer the former reading and, while the challenge was only partial, and unsuccessful even at that, it laid the groundwork for further and more extensive challenges.

A related criticism of Symes is that it was premised on a similarly situated analysis. While this is true, it is a function of the ongoing understanding that equality analysis requires a comparator group, a problem from which none of the section 15 cases have broken free. The concern that, despite the language of substantive equality, section 15 remains mired in a formal equality analysis is a legitimate one. To the extent that the majority of the Court can make statements like the following, that concern is painfully borne out: "[u]nfortunately proof that women pay social costs [of child care] is not sufficient proof that women pay child care expenses."[114] A substantive equality analysis would make the connection between social costs and financial outlay. However, those social costs and the realities of working mothers' lives were a significant part of the evidence put forward in the case and were there to be dealt with by the judges, as well as by case commentators and social activists; the basis for a substantive equality analysis was there.[115]

There are a number of important social assistance cases now coming before the Supreme Court of Canada. Gosselin,[116] an age-based challenge to the requirement under Quebec's social assistance regulations that single people under thirty deemed to be employable could only receive full regular benefits if they participated in employment and training programs, has been heard but the decision has not yet been released. Inability, seen as a refusal to participate in these programs, reduced social assistance benefits to $170 a month. Distinctions between the deserving poor and the undeserving poor are becomingly increasingly overt and the punitive measures taken against those perceived to be undeserving are chilling. The death of Kimberly Rogers while serving her prison sentence for welfare fraud in her own home and under a commuted lifetime ban from social assistance, is only one of the more extreme and highly public examples of the impact of these measures.[117]

Leave to appeal to the Supreme Court of Canada in Falkiner has been requested. The Ontario Court of Appeal in Falkiner struck down the "spouse in the house rule" that had been eliminated by the Ontario government in 1986 in response to a *Charter* challenge and then was reintroduced in 1995. The rule derives from the expansive definition of spouse that includes persons living together who have "a mutual agreement or arrangement regarding their financial affairs" and for whom "the social and familial aspects" of their relationship amount to cohabitation. The four applicants were all single mothers who had been living with a man in a "try-on" relationship for less than a year. The imposition of the "a man living in the house is defined as a spouse" rule had the effect of deeming the applicants to be in spousal relationships of presumed economic interdependence and, on this basis, reducing their benefits as sole support parents. The related appeal of Mr. Thomas, heard at the same time as the Falkiner appeal, involved a man with a disability losing his benefits as a permanently unemployable person under the same deemed spouse definition. Poverty provides the link between the inequalities associated with femaleness, single parenthood, and disability. Justice John Laskin, writing for a unanimous court, accepted the multiple-grounds approach and held that the definition of spouse imposed differential treatment on the applicants " ... on the combined grounds of sex, marital status and receipt of social assistance."[118] If this decision and approach are upheld by the Supreme Court, it would be a giant step forward in the recognition of socio-economic rights. The acceptance of receipt of social assistance as an analogous ground by the Supreme Court of Canada would be a major inroad into the position, supported by the Ontario Court of Appeal, that economic disadvantage, on its own, is not a basis for *Charter* protection.

Falkiner puts the issue of intersectional discrimination front and centre. While the Court accepted the applicants' characterization of themselves as being discriminated against on the basis that they are single mothers on social assistance, it could not continue to deal with them as unified, multi-identitied wholes. The discrimination had to be related back to grounds and distinct comparator groups had to be determined with respect to each ground. The structure of the equality analysis set out by the Supreme Court of Canada in its decision in Law requires this kind of dissection and the focus on comparator groups perpetuates the similarly situated analysis that is a defining feature of formal equality. The substantive equality of the *Charter* does not require identical treatment but, to date, it has required the comparison of likes. This comparative approach remains a limiting feature of the analysis and one that impedes the courts' ability to address situations of intersectional discrimination in their complex wholeness. Falkiner may be an indication that we are on the way to fuller and more sensitive treatment of intersectional discrimination, although it begs the question of the possibility of moving beyond the additive approach of discrimination to an integrated approach.

IV. CONCLUSION

> [O]utsiders, including feminists and people of color, have embraced legalisms as a tool of necessity, making legal consciousness their own in order to attack injustice … There are times to stand outside the courtroom door and say "this procedure is a farce, the legal system is corrupt, justice will never prevail in this land as long as privilege rules in the courtroom." There are times to stand inside the courtroom and say "this is a nation of laws, laws recognizing fundamental values of rights, equality and personhood." Sometimes, as Angela Davis did, there is a need to make both speeches in one day.[119]

This is the equivocal nature of the *Charter* and of equality, equivocation that I think is better seen as an opening than a shortcoming. Legal commentators tend to view themselves and others as either critics or supporters of the *Charter*, a demarcation that is seen to require the sacrifice of vision for action or vice versa. Embracing the contradiction of concurrent critique and invocation of the *Charter* may be one of the *Charter*'s gifts to us as social activists who have to learn how to do both, simultaneously.

The critics and the pragmatists have both been right. As the cases amply demonstrate, the *Charter* is full of problems, of analysis and of results. At the same time, there have been some positive decisions, some good equality analysis, and some statements that take my breath away coming from the top court in our country. But this should be no surprise—this is the nature of equality; it does not provide answers, not even much in the way of direction; it is complex and contradictory and so, necessarily, are the equality arguments and the equality decisions.

In terms of women and equality, in my assessment, the most clear-cut gains have been with respect to reproduction and violence against women, although even in these areas the victories have been only partial and feel insecure. Although the risks of essentialism and overprotection are high, these may be areas in which the gender analysis is more easily grasped and perceived as less systemically threatening. Family issues are mired in the tension between formal equality and substantive equality; the vision of independent ungendered "equal" participants and the reality of gendered dependencies, assumptions, and values clash. Deeper equality analysis and more creative responses are needed.

The concerns raised about the *Charter*'s inability, or the courts' unwillingness, to address socio-economic disparities and related issues are perhaps the most troubling. Given the current political climate and the ever-widening gap between rich and poor, as well as what appears to be increasing public tolerance for economic inequality, accompanied by increasing intolerance for "the poor," it may be that socio-economic rights are the most pressing equality issues for everyone, and particularly for women. The *Charter* has provided a grounding for challenging these inequalities, but these challenges have so far been largely unsuccessful, despite their limited and specific foci and modest demands. The *Charter* that precludes exposure of the "private" sector's role in poverty creation and perpetuation, and the veneer of formal equality coupled with liberal individualism that blame the most vulnerable and disadvantaged for the "choices" they are assumed to have made. The irony, however, is that many of these left critiques of the *Charter* are the arguments most strongly invoked against the *Charter*'s application to socio-economic rights such that the left critiques become a self-fulfilling prophecy in relation to one of the most significant areas of potential *Charter* application.[120] Rather than concede the critiques, these critiques need to be incorporated into *Charter* challenges.

Intersectional discrimination is only one among a large number of issues and shortcomings in the *Charter* that cry out for fundamental shifts in our compartmentalized thinking, for creative advocacy, for vision and revisioning, and for the kind of soul-searching, uncertainty, and risk taking that Turpel advocated.[121] It remains to be seen whether those arguing within the constraints of the *Charter* can forge a way out of these restraints to point the way, or a way, or ways, toward equality and social justice. The restraints of the *Charter* are no more than the restraints of the society in which we currently live—individualism, privilege, entrenched notions of formal equality, and commitment to neutrality are prevailing social values. They need to be challenged on all fronts. The *Charter* presents one avenue for public education, mobilization, politicization, [the] creation of alliances … and goals. The *Charter* presents the opportunity for equality and social justice advocates to critique and to dream at the same time and to pursue those dreams of concrete social change under a document that was not intended to accommodate fundamental social change. To me, these opportunities are at least as important as the question of whether those deciding *Charter* cases can be persuaded to embark on the social justice quest.

QUESTIONS TO CONSIDER

1. What financial and social barriers must be faced by those wishing to have a particular case reviewed by the Supreme Court of Canada? Discuss this question in general, and specifically in terms of barriers faced by Aboriginal people wishing to pursue the "rights paradigm" through *Charter* litigation.

2. As discussed in this chapter in Part III (C) on family law, the Supreme Court of Canada (in M. *v.* H.) interpreted Section 1 of the *Charter* to justify extending support payments to female common-law partners based on the rationale that "females in common-law relationships tend to become financially dependent on their male partners" due to child-care responsibilities and unequal earning power . Do you think that such a blanket assumption of inequality is warranted? Further, how might this logic apply to same-sex partners where no gender-based inequality exists?

3. Do you agree with the author that provincial governments and the federal government have been "remarkably undemocratic" in their approaches to the abortion debate? Using material in Part III (A), "Reproduction," and outside readings, draft an argument for changes in current law governing abortion in Canada. To what extent should race, gender, and social class be considered by legislators, the courts, and the general public?

SUGGESTIONS FOR FURTHER READING

Carter, M. (2008). "Debunking" parents' rights in the Canadian constitutional context. *Canadian Bar Review, 86,* 479–514.

Ehrenreich, N. (Ed.). (2008). *The reproductive rights reader: Law, medicine, and the construction of motherhood.* New York: New York University Press.

Young, M., Boyd, S., Brodsky, G., & Day, S. (Eds.). (2007). *Poverty: Rights, social citizenship, and legal activism.* Vancouver: University of British Columbia Press.

NOTES

1. *Canadian Charter of Rights and Freedoms, Part I of the Constitution Act, 1982,* being Schedule B to the Canada Act 1982 (U.K.), 1981, c. 11 [*Charter*].
2. Ibid., s. 15. The equivocation reflected in the title, that inheres in section 15 of the *Charter* and in feminist responses to it, arises even in relation to the creation of this special issue of the Osgoode Hall Law Journal

celebrating—or at least recognizing—the twentieth anniversary of the *Charter*. 2002 is not the twentieth anniversary of section 15 of the *Charter*; it did not come into effect until three years later, in 1985. In terms of celebration or recognition, this can be read two ways. One way is to see this as a continuing slight to section 15, the tag-along younger sister, who is included in the party but whose unique history, status and struggles are repudiated by that inclusion. Alternatively, or I prefer, simultaneously, one can see this as doubling the opportunities to mark the advent of section 15. She cannot be left out of the general *Charter* attention, but she will have her own exclusive party in three years' time. She is the difficult younger sister who demands more than her share of the attention because … she deserves it.

3. This is somewhat ironic, given that abstractness is a critique that many writing in this vein make of the *Charter* itself.

4. See infra, Part II. A., for discussion of what I mean by this term.

5. I am engaging here only with the critiques and discussions from among what might be termed "progressives." I am not looking at right-wing critiques, even though there are some interesting parallels and resonances among right and left critics. See Sheila McIntyre, "Feminist Movement in Law: Beyond Privileged and Privileging Theory" in Radha Jhappan, ed., *Women's Legal Strategies in Canada* (Toronto: University of Toronto Press, 2002) 42.

6. Despite my tendency to portray them as oppositional, I see these positions more as interrelated and overlapping, situated along a continuum.

7. I think it is important to try to identify who articulates various positions, that is who it is that is talking positively or negatively about the *Charter*, as a means of contextualizing and de-individualizing these discussions and providing additional political grounding for an analysis of what is being said. As one who believes that race, gender, etc., for example, matter to who we are, how we are treated, and relatedly then to how we think about the world, I think it is important to try to factor (as best one can) our multiple identities into the analysis of academics' work. The critique of the approach that I am advocating mirrors the more general critique of a grounds-based approach to discrimination. According to this critique, identity categories are artificial compartments that oversimplify and give rise to unwarranted assumptions and to the unreflective attributions of group characteristics. Given that the categories are the problem, relying on them inevitably reinforces the problem, that is one is actively engaging in the act one is critiquing when one categorizes people on these bases (race, gender, etc.). It is true that categorization is the source of discrimination; it is discrimination that makes the categories matter. But that is the very point, the Catch 22—discrimination does make the categories significant—the recognition that our experiences (of discrimination as well as of identity-based pride and connection) and our situation have an impact on our thinking. Group membership is not determinative, but it is a factor in forming one's perspective.

8. Harry J. Glasbeek, "From Constitutional Rights to 'Real' Rights—"R-i-g-hts Fo-or-wa-ard Ho!"?" (1990) 10 Windsor Y. B. Access Just. 468 at 469–70.

9. Ibid. at 470.

10. The history of Canadian sexual harassment law is one example and the inclusion of sexual orientation in Alberta's human rights legislation is another.

11. See Constance Backhouse, Petticoats and Prejudice: Women and Law in Nineteenth-Century Canada (Toronto: The Osgoode Society, 1991) and Constance Backhouse, Colour-Coded: A Legal History of Racism in Canada, 1900–1950 (Toronto: The Osgoode Society, 1999).

12. The question of the extent to which the judiciary is fettered is also subject to debate. Section 33 of the *Charter*, the "notwithstanding clause," leaves the final word to Parliament, if it has the courage to invoke it.

13. Joel Bakan, "Constitutional Interpretation and Social Change: You Can't Always Get What You Want (Nor What You Need)" (1991) 70 Can. Bar. Rev. 307.

14. Andrew Petter & Allan C. Hutchinson, "Rights in Conflict: The Dilemma of *Charter* Legitimacy" (1989) 23 U.B.C.L. Rev. 531.

15. William E. Conklin, "'Access to Justice' As Access to a Lawyer's Language" (1990) 10 Windsor Y. B. Access Just. 454.

16. This is not to say that all feminists support the *Charter*; feminists articulate the full range of perspectives on the *Charter*. My comments here are generalizations and suffer the over-inclusion problem of all generalizations. Nonetheless, I think that feminists tend to be drawn to the more pragmatic, it's-worth-a-try end of the *Charter* spectrum.

17. See McIntyre, *supra* note 5 and Didi Herman, *Rights of Passage: Struggles for Lesbian and Gay Legal Equality* (Toronto: University of Toronto Press, 1994).

18. See e.g. Sherene Razack, "Using Law for Social Change: Historical Perspectives" (1992) 17 Queen's L.J. 31; Carol Smart, *Feminism and the Power of Law* (London: Routledge, 1989).

19. Mary Ellen Turpel, "Aboriginal Peoples and the Canadian *Charter*: Interpretive Monopolies, Cultural Differences" in Richard F. Devlin, ed., *Canadian Perspectives on Legal Theory* (Toronto: Emond Montgomery, 1991) 503.

20. The complexities of this dilemma are readily apparent in the case of the *Native Women's Association of Canada v. Canada*, [1994] 3 S.C.R. 627 [NWAC] in which NWAC sought and was denied funding and rights to participate in the constitutional review process equal to the four national Aboriginal organizations included by the federal government. The intersectional discrimination of race and sex placed some Aboriginal women in an intolerable, bifurcated position that the Court did not address or even acknowledge in its decision in this case.

21. *Supra* note 19 at 508.

22. *Ibid*. at 527.

23. I see this as a particularly suitable role for intervenors whose job it is to bring a different perspective before the court and who are not constrained by the needs and interests of clients.

24. Rosalie Abella, "Limitations on the Right to Equality Before the Law" in Armand de Mestral *et al.*, eds., *The Limitation of Human Rights in Comparative Constitutional Law* (Cowansville, Qc.: Yvon Blais, 1986) 223 at 225.

25. See *e.g.* The Right Honorable Beverley McLachlin, "Equality: the Most Difficult Right" (2001) 14 Sup. Ct. L. Rev. (2d) 17. According to Chief Justice McLachlin, at 21, "[s]ubstantive equality is recognized worldwide as the governing legal paradigm."

26. *Law Society of British Columbia v. Andrews*, [1989] I S.C.R. 143 [*Andrews*].

27. Radha Jhappan, "The Equality Pit or the Rehabilitation of Justice?" (1998) 10 C.J.W.L. 60 at 63.

28. Jhappan argues that a justice approach would lead to the determination of a more appropriate reference group (*Ibid*. at 95). Thus, even with justice one faces the problem of finding the appropriate reference or comparator group. While this is an ongoing problem that can seriously hamper or defect the analysis of judges and litigators, I am not sure that there is anything inherent in either the justice concept or the equality concept that more, or less, effectively directs the comparative analysis.

29. *Supra* note 27 at 79.

30. *Canadian Bill of Rights*, S.C. 1960, c. 44, reprinted in R.S.C. 1985, App. 111.

31. U.S. Const. [*U.S. Constitution*].

32. Mary Eberts, "Sex-based Discrimination and the *Charter*" in Anne F. Bayefsky & Mary Eberts, eds., *Equality and the Canadian Charter of Rights and Freedoms* (Toronto: Carswell, 1985) 183; Katherine J. de Jong. "Sexual Equality: Interpreting Section 28" in Bayefsky & Eberts, *Ibid*. at 493; and Penny Kome, *The Taking of Twenty-Eight: Women Challenge the Constitution* (Toronto: Women's Press, 1983).

33. See *e.g.* Elmer A. Driedger, "The *Canadian Charter of Rights and Freedoms*" (1982) 14 Ottawa L. Rev. 366 at 373.

34. N. Colleen Sheppard, "Equality, Ideology and Oppression: Women and the *Canadian Charter of Rights and Freedoms*" (1986) 10 Dal. L.J. 195 at 222.

35. Eberts, *supra* note 32 at 216.

36. *Supra* note 24 at 232.

37. Catharine A. MacKinnon, "Making Sex Equality Real" in Lynn Smith, ed., *Righting the Balance: Canada's New Equality Rights* (Saskatoon: Canadian Human Rights Reporter, 1986) 37 at 41.

38. *R. v. Osolin*, [1993] 4 S.C.R. 595 at 669 [*Osolin*].

39. NWAC, *supra* note 20 at 665. The Federal Court of Appeal decision in this case providing a declaration that the federal government had restricted the freedom of expression of Aboriginal women, thus violating their section 2(b) and 28 *Charter* rights, is one of few decisions in which section 28 grounded an equality decision. This decision was overturned on appeal.

40. See *R. v. Hess*, [1990] 2 S.C.R. 906, Wilson J. [*Hess*] and *R. v. Seaboyer*, [1991] 2 S.C.R. 577, L'Heureux-Dubé J., dissenting [*Seaboyer*].

41. The question of the demise of section 28 is intriguing and worthy of a much fuller exploration but, sadly, I cannot dally with it any further in this article.

42. See e.g. Christine Boyle and Sheila Noonan, "Prostitution and Pornography: Beyond Formal Equality" (1986) 10 Dal. L.J. 225; Diana Majury, "Equality and Discrimination According to the Supreme Court of Canada" (1991) 4 C.J.W.L. 407; and Sheppard, *supra* note 34.

43. Dianne Pothier, "Connecting Grounds of Discrimination to Real People's Real Experiences" (2001) 13 C.J.W.L. 37; Nitya Iyer, "Categorical Denials: Equality Rights and the Shaping of Social Identity" (1993) 19 Queen's L.J. 179.

44. McIntyre, *supra* note 5 at 46.

45. Judy Fudge, "What Do We Mean by Law and Social Transformation?" (1990) 5 C.J.L.S. 47 at 58; see also Gwen Brodsky & Shelagh Day, *Canadian Charter Equality Rights for Women: One Step Forward or Two Steps Back?* (Ottawa: Canadian Advisory Council on Status of Women, 1989).

46. Colleen Sheppard, "Grounds of Discrimination: Towards an Inclusive and Contextual Approach" (2001) 80 Can. Bar Rev. 893 at 908.

47. One of the most obvious problems with such an approach is that it assumes that it is always clear which is the subordinated group. Such a clear-cut distinction between oppressed and oppressor is belied by our complex and multiple identities and issues of intersectional discrimination. The possibility of excluding the dominant group from section 15 protection in relation to the sex ground was explicitly rejected by Justice McLachlin in *Hess, supra* note 40 at 943–44: "There is no suggestion in that language [in *Turpin*] that men should be excluded from protection under s. 15 because they do not constitute a 'discrete and insular minority' disadvantaged independently of the legislation under consideration." She relied on section 28 to support this conclusion and proceeded to find a breach of section 15.

48. C. Lynn Smith, "Judicial Interpretation of Equality Rights under the *Canadian Charter of Rights and Freedoms*: Some Clear and Present Dangers" (1988) 23 U.B.C.L. Rev. 65 at 93–94.

49. See e.g. Kimberlé Crenshaw, "Demarginalizing the Intersection of Race and Sex: A Black Feminist Critique of Antidiscrimination Doctrine, Feminist Theory and Antiracist Politics" (1989) U. Chicago Legal F. 139; Iyer, *supra* note 43; Nitya Duclos, "Disappearing Women: Racial Minority Women in Human Rights Cases" (1993) 6 C.J.W.L. 25; and Carol A. Aylward, *Canadian Critical Race Theory: Racism and the Law* (Halifax: Fernwood 1999).

50. Duclos, *Ibid.*; see also Jennifer Nedesky & Craig Scott, "Constitutional Dialogue" in Joel Bakan & David Schneiderman, eds., *Social Justice and the Constitution: Perspectives on a Social Union for Canada* (Ottawa: Carleton University Press, 1992) 59.

51. See e.g. Anna Pellat's discussion of the group-based argument that the Women's Legal Education and Action Fund [LEAF] put forward in *Vriend v. Alberta*, [1998] I S.C.R. 493 [*Vriend*], in Anna S. Pellatt, "Equality Rights Litigation and Social Transformation: A Consideration of the Women's Legal Education and Action Fund's Intervention in *Vriend v. R.*" (2000) 12 C.J.W.L. 117.

52. See Justice L'Heureux-Dubé's dissent in *Egan v. Canada*, [1995] 2 S.C.R. 513 [*Egan*].

53. Pothier, *supra* note 43.

54. However, for an article that is all about differences among Supreme Court of Canada judges, see Marc Gold, "Of Rights and Roles: The Supreme Court and the *Charter*" (1989) 23 U.B.C. L. Rev. 507.

55. See e.g., *Bakan, supra* note 13 at 319. While there is no question that judges, almost by definition, are members of the social and economic elite in Canada, this does not preclude judges, like law professors, from having a class consciousness. Additionally, class is only one piece of multiple and complex identity and is not determinative of one's ideology.

56. There are as of yet so few Aboriginal and racialized judges that it is difficult to do anything more than speculate about the positive differences that these judges would bring and the personal cost to these judges. See e.g. *R. v. S.(R.D.)*, [1997] 3 S.C.R. 484.

57. See e.g. Madame Justice Bertha Wilson, "Will Women Judges Really Make a Difference?" (1990) 28 Osgoode Hall L.J. 507 and Justice Maryka Omatsu, "On Judicial Appointments: Does Gender Make a Difference?" in Joseph F. Fletcher, ed., *Ideas in Action: Essays on Politics and Law in Honour of Peter Russell* (Toronto: University of Toronto Press, 1999) 176.

58. See Constance Backhouse, "The Chilly Climate for Women Judges" (Paper presented to the "Adding Feminism to Law: The Contributions of Madame Justice L'Heureux-Dubé" workshop, Ottawa, September 2002) and Hester Lessard, "Farce or Tragedy?: Judicial Backlash and Justice McClung" (1999) 10 Const. Forum Const. 65.

59. See generally The Honourable Claire L'Heureux-Dubé, "The Dissenting Opinion: Voice of the Future?" (2000) 38 Osgoode Hall L.J. 495.

60. *Supra* note 54 at 508. This is an interesting statement from Gold given that his conclusions in this article espouse the contrary view and resonate with my views that split decisions and dissents in *Charter* cases are positive.

61. *Law v. Canada (Minister of Employment and Immigration)*, [1999] 1 S.C.R. 497 (*Law*) Beverley Baines, "*Law v. Canada*: Formatting Equality" (2000) 11 Const. Forum Const. 65 at 67, describes the consensus as " … a bland, pedantic portrayal of judicial unanimity," as compared to earlier (and later) " … robust factionalism … " While it lasted, the *Law* consensus led to problematic decisions like *Lovelace v. Ontario* (A.G.), [2000] 1 S.C.R. 950 and *Granovsky v. Canada (Minister of Employment and Immigration)*, [2000] 1 S.C.R. 703. However, the consensus was short-lived as evidenced by the split decision in *Lavoie v. Canada*, 2002 SCC 23 [*Lavoie*] that followed not long after.

62. *Supra* note 54 at 529.

63. *Canada (A.G.) v. Mossop*, [1993] 1 S.C.R. 554 [*Mossop*]; *Egan*, *supra* note 52; and *Vriend*, *supra* note 51.

64. Sadly, this may be more true than I would like to admit and we may see the positive *Charter* decisions of the last few years become dissents in future cases. For example, the Supreme Court's recent decision in *R. v. Shearing*, 2002 SCC 58 [*Shearing*], is, in my view, a troubling retreat from its earlier decision in *R. v. Mills*, [1999] 3 S.C.R 668 [*Mills*].

65. Potter & Hutchinson, *supra* note 14 at 536.

66. For a comprehensive examination of section 15 cases, see Sheilah Martin, "Balancing Individual Rights to Equality and Social Goals" (2001) 80 Can. Bar Rev. 299.

67. See e.g. *Brooks v. Canada Safeway Ltd.*, [1989] 1 S.C.R. 1219 (pregnancy discrimination) and *Janzen v. Platy Enterprises Ltd.*, [1989] 1 S.C.R. 1252 [*Janzen*] (sexual harassment). For a more recent case see *British Columbia (Public Service Employees Relations Commission) v. British Columbia Government and Service Employees' Union*, [1999] 3 S.C.R. 3 [BCGSEU] (aerobic standards for forest firefighters).

68. See e.g. *R. v Morgentaler*, [1988] 1 S.C.R. 30 [*Morgentaler*] (abortion) which was brought and decided as a section 7 *Charter* case, although section 15 was discussed. Section 28 was raised as part of the constitutional questions that were before the Court and was argued by LEAF in its intervenor's factum, but section 28 was not referred to in any one of the four separate judgments that were issued by the Court. See LEAF, *Equality and the Charter: Ten Years of Feminist Advocacy Before the Supreme Court of Canada* (Toronto: Emond Montgomery, 1996).

69. For example, the impossible distinction between direct and indirect discrimination that was finally dismantled in *BCGSEU*, *supra* note 67.

70. R.S.C. 1985, c. C-46, s. 251.

71. The other two Supreme Court decisions on abortion have not added to or revised the extensive discussion of the issues in *Morgentaler*. *Borowski v. Canada (A.G.)*, [1989] 1 S.C.R. 342, an action to strike down subsections of the *Criminal Code* abortion provision so as to leave only the prohibition of abortion standing, was found to be moot in light of the *Morgentaler* decision. *Tremblay v. Daigle*, [1989] 2 S.C.R. 530 raised the issue of the right of the would-be father of the fetus to be granted an injunction against the pregnant woman seeking an abortion. The father's claim was dismissed under Quebec's *Charter of Human Rights and Freedoms*, R.S.Q. c. C-12, and the federal *Charter* was held not to apply to a private claim. In addition, there have been other cases addressing reproductive issues. *R. v. Sullivan*, [1991] 1 S.C.R. 489 dealt with the status of a fetus in the context of criminal charges laid against midwives; *Winnipeg Child and Family Services (Northwest Area) v. D.F.G.*, [1997] 3 S.C.R. 925 dealt with the application of child protection provisions to a fetus.

72. *Fudge*, *supra* note 45 at 55.

73. See cases *supra* note 71.

74. This disturbing reluctance on the part of the Court to explicitly frame an issue as one of sex equality, even when a substantive sex equality is applied, runs throughout the *Charter* cases. For a recent example, see Shearing, *supra* note 64, where the issue is framed exclusively as one of privacy rather than one of sex equality.

75. *Morgentaler*, *supra* note 68 at 171.

76. *Ibid.* at 172.

77. It is perhaps self-serving to say this because I have been an active participant in the work of LEAF since its inception in 1985. But I think that the Court's positive movement over the course of these sexual assault cases and its greater, albeit hesitant and not unanimous understanding of the gendered nature of the problems that infect the law's handling of sexual assault are in large part due to the arguments LEAF has put forward in its interventions in these cases and its related advocacy work. It intervened before the Supreme Court in over half of the sexual assault cases and in two of the three pornography cases.

78. As there is a separate article on sexual assault and the *Charter* in this issue, I will make only a few general comments on the topic. See Lise Gotell, "The Ideal Victim, the Hysterical Complainant, and the Disclosure of Confidential Records: The Implications of the *Charter* for Sexual Assault Law" (2002) 40 Osgoode Hall L.J. 251.

79. See Christine Boyle, *Sexual Assault* (Toronto: Carswell, 1984).

80. See *An Act to amend the Criminal Code (sexual assault)*, S.C. 1992, c. 38; *An Act to amend the Criminal Code (self-induced intoxication)*, S.C. 1995, c. 32; and *An Act to amend the Criminal Code (production of records in sexual offence proceedings)*, S.C. 1997, c. 30. These lengthy preambles refer explicitly to the prevalence of sexual violence against women and children and to the particularly disadvantageous impact of violence on the equal participation of women and children in society and on the *Charter* rights of women and children, with specific mention of sections 7, 15, and 28.

81. Justice Lamer dissented in part.
82. Justices L'Heureux-Dubé and Gonthier dissented on this point.
83. Justice McClung's decision in *R. v. Ewanchuk*, [1998] 6 W.W.R. 8 (Alta. C.A.), and the responses it generated are glaring examples that these anti-woman views are still very much in operation among judges and among the public.
84. *Seaboyer*, *supra* note 40 at 707. See also Lessard, *supra* note 58 and Joanne Wright, "Consent and Sexual Violence in Canadian Public Discourse: Reflections on Ewanchuk" (2001) 16 C.J.L.S. 173.
85. *M. v. H.*, [1999] 2 S.C.R. 3 [*M. v. H.*].
86. R.S.O. 1990, c. F-3.
87. The decision is emphatically limited to this narrow ground. The frequency with which the Court insists that this case is not about the right to marry—that this appeal "has nothing to do with marriage per se," that marital rights and obligations "play no part in this analysis," that "there is no need to consider whether same-sex couples can marry," all statements made within a single page (at 48–49) and as part of the introduction to the section 15 analysis—is staggering. The decision clearly has implications for the right to marry and will be used to further the argument for that right. While this case does not decide that issue, it is not unrelated to it, as is clear from Justice Gonthier's dissent and his concern that "a constitutionally mandated expansion of the definition of spouse would open the door to a raft of other claims" (at 90) and from Justice Bastarache's comments relating to the possibility that the implications of the decision in this case may be greater than initially anticipated (at 157). The Court's discomfort with the homosexual marriage question is palpable and disconcerting, and is indicative of the entrenched position of the institution of heterosexual marriage. But the Court will have to deal with the right of gays and lesbians to marry and I sincerely hope that when it does, there is a gender analysis brought to bear on the question. The right to marry is a contentious issue among lesbian feminists because marriage has been, and arguably still is, an oppressive institution for women. From my perspective, a gendered analysis leads to the conclusion that it is not appropriate for the state to endorse marriage for anyone at all. This would leave the right to marry open to anyone but would divest it of legal significance. The state would continue to apportion rights and obligations incurred as a result of intimate and other relationships in which economic dependency may arise.
88. I think that this is appropriate—the fact that this was a lesbian couple, not a gay male couple, is irrelevant to the analysis. But I do think that the question of the potential relevance and impact on the suspect categories of discrimination should always be asked as an essential component of a substantive equality analysis.
89. *Supra* note 85 at 48.
90. Contrary to the implications of Justice Cory's statement, I expect that most men who are claiming spousal support are doing so because they have undertaken primary responsibility for the traditionally female tasks of child and home care.
91. This is something the Supreme Court recognized in Janzen, *supra* note 67.
92. *Supra* note 85 at 64–69. For a feminist critique of these reforms as exacerbating the more severe gender inequalities by furthering the property interests of middle- and upper-class women at the expense of the support needs of lower-income and poor women, see Martha Fineman, *The Illusion of Equality: The Rhetoric and Reality of Divorce Reform* (Chicago: University of Chicago Press, 1991), c. 3.
93. *Supra* note 85 at 104.
94. *Ibid.* at 189.
95. Sex is the biological division and gender is the socially constructed division. There is significant overlap but the terms are not synonymous.
96. See e.g. *P.(D.) v. S.(C.)*, [1993] 4 S.C.R. 141 and *Young v. Young*, [1993] 4 S.C.R. 3, which are confusing decisions relating to the application of the *Charter* to the "best interests of the child test" in which the majority decisions were that the *Charter* did not apply or that there was no *Charter* violation. The "best interests of the child test" is exactly the kind of positive-sounding family law rule that cries out for a thorough gender-equality analysis.
97. Martha Fineman, *The Neutered Mother, The Sexual Family and Other Twentieth Century Tragedies* (New York: Routledge, 1995) at 15.
98. Many men do not fit or do not want to fit the traditional male worker model either.
99. See e.g. Naomi Klein. *No Logo: Taking Aim at the Brand Bullies* (Toronto: Vintage Canada, 2000).
100. [1990] 3 S.C.R. 229 [*McKinney*].
101. See e.g. *Saskatchewan (H.R.C.) v. Saskatoon (City of)*, [1989] 2 S.C.R. 1297; *Douglas/Kwantlen Faculty Association v. Douglas College*, [1990] 3 S.C.R. 570; *Harrison v. University of British Columbia*, [1990] 3 S.C.R. 451; *Stoffman v. Vancouver General Hospital*, [1990] 3 S.C.R. 483; *Dickason v. University of Alberta*, [1992] 2 S.C.R. 1103.

102. *Supra* note 100 at 433–34 (footnotes omitted].

103. *Schachter v. Canada*, [1992] 2 S.C.R. 679 [*Schachter*].

104. Women in the United States have had a terrible time attaining maternity leave protection and paid benefits and the impact on mothers in the paid workforce has been devastating.

105. Possibly when there is an obvious comparator group, formal equality is the appropriate analytic approach, and a substantive equality analysis should be applied when there is no such readily apparent comparison and the comparative focus should be diffused or even abandoned.

106. S.C. 1996, c.23.

107. *Canada (A.G.) v. Lesiuk* (November 2002), A-281-01 (F.C.A.) (relating to part-time workers' eligibility for benefits) and *Miller v. Canada (A.G.)*, 2002 FCA 370 (relating to the impact of the receipt of maternity benefits on a woman's eligibility for regular benefits).

108. See Gwen Brodsky & Shelagh Day, "Beyond the Social and Economic Rights Debate: Substantive Equality Speaks to Poverty" (2002) 14 C.J.W.L. 185.

109. Martha Jackman, "What's Wrong with Social and Economic Rights?" (2000) 11 N.J.C.L. 235 at 243.

110. See e.g., *Schachter, supra* note 103 and *Eldridge v. British Columbia (A.G.)*, [1997] 3 S.C.R. 624.

111. See *Falkiner v. Ontario (Ministry of Community and Social Services)* (2002), 59 O.R. (3d) 481 (C.A.) [*Falkiner*].

112. *Symes v. Canada*, [1993] 4 S.C.R. 695 [*Symes*].

113. See Audrey Macklin, "*Symes v. M.N.R.*: Where Sex Meets Class" (1992) 5 C.J.W.L. 498.

114. *Symes, supra* note 112 at 765.

115. It is interesting in this regard to note that Justice L'Heureux-Dubé has referred to *Symes* as containing the first use of substantive equality in a Supreme Court decision. See The Honourable Claire L'Heureux-Dubé, "A Conversation About Equality" (2000) 29 Denv. J. Int'l L. & Pol'y 65 at 69, n. 20.

116. *Gosselin c. Quebec*, [1999] J.Q. No. 1365 (C.A.) (QL.).

117. For information on this case, see http://dawn.thot.net/Kimberly_Rogers.

118. *Falkiner, supra* note 111 at 514.

119. Mari J. Matsuda, "When the First Quail Calls: Multiple Consciousness as Jurisprudential Method" (1989) 11 Women's L. Rep. 7 at 8.

120. See McIntyre, *supra* note 5.

121. *Supra* note 19.

Chapter Twelve

Theorizing Civil Domestic Violence Legislation in the Context of Restructuring: A Tale of Two Provinces*

Jennifer Koshan and Wanda Wiegers

Editors' Note: By now, it is clear that legal changes and reforms to government policies and services cannot be understood without some reference to wider political, social, and economic forces. Koshan and Wiegers present a detailed analysis of recent legislation established in Alberta and Saskatchewan, provinces that manifest relatively high rates of domestic violence, including murder. This civil legislation, part of a general movement against domestic violence in Canada, is meant to protect women who have experienced spousal abuse. Much of our attention on law and abuse of women has centred on criminal sanctions. Interestingly, Koshan and Wiegers focus on civil legislation as part of their rounded approach to this topic. Koshan and Wiegers describe how ex parte orders can provide victims of domestic abuse continued access to their homes and how in some cases they may forbid contact between the alleged victim and assaulter. The authors critique neoliberal and neoconservative ideologies that support cuts in state funding, highlight individualism, reinforce heterosexism, and foster a "law and order" outlook on family conflicts. These ideologies serve to downplay structural forces that are associated with violence against women and other family members. They also raise concerns about how victims of violence can subsist on social assistance payments and barriers they may face in obtaining adequate housing, counselling services, and legal advice.

INTRODUCTION

… In the 1990s, provincial governments across Canada began to adopt legislation offering civil redress for victims of violence inflicted by cohabitants.[1] This type of initiative was generally represented as an effort to be more responsive to the needs of victims by providing more immediate and comprehensive remedies than were available under criminal or pre-existing civil law. Saskatchewan was the first province in Canada to implement civil legislation in 1995, and the *Victims of Domestic Violence Act (VDVA)*[2] has since served as a rough model for specialized legislation in other provinces and territories, including Alberta, where the *Protection against Family Violence Act (PAFVA)* was passed in 1999.[3]

Source: Jennifer Koshan and Wanda Wiegers, "Theorizing Civil Domestic Violence Legislation in the Context of Restructuring: A Tale of Two Provinces," *Canadian Journal of Women and the Law*, 2007 (19), pp. 145–178. © University of Toronto Press Incorporated. Reprinted with permission from UTP Journals, www.utpjournals.com. *We wish to thank Susan Boyd and the anonymous reviewers for their helpful comments, Ken Norman for his thoughts on administrative regimes, and Penny Andrews, Julie Goldscheid, and Emily Sack for assistance with our comparative analysis. This article is part of a larger five-year research project funded by a Community-University Research Alliance grant from SSHRC coordinated by RESOLVE (Research and Education for Solutions to Violence and Abuse), a cross-prairie research institute. The project involved comparisons of civil and criminal approaches to intimate violence in the three prairie provinces, based on data collection from court files and qualitative interviews with victims, justice personnel, and front-line community organizations. While the authors had access to this data, it was collected and analyzed by other researchers.

Across Canada, the most significant innovation introduced by civil domestic violence legislation has been the initial ex parte order. These orders, referred to as emergency intervention or protection orders in Saskatchewan and Alberta respectively, may be issued where necessary by reason of seriousness or urgency for the immediate protection of the victim. The legislation in both provinces provides that initial orders can be applied for without notice to the respondent at any time of day or night either in person or by telephone through designated agents. In Saskatchewan, the majority of orders are issued outside court hours, and all are applied for by telephone, most often from the home of the claimant. In both provinces, applications are often made by police on behalf of victims to justices of the peace or provincial court judges having some specialized training in the dynamics of domestic violence, and orders that are issued are subsequently reviewed by superior court judges.[4] Among other possibilities, emergency intervention or protection orders may grant exclusive possession of the family home and proscribe contact with the victim and children. Although the legislation does provide for additional remedies, our discussion focuses on the emergency intervention or protection orders. Other remedies have rarely been used, largely because they generally require formal court proceedings with legal counsel and notice to the respondent and, in large part, replicate existing family law remedies.[5]

Our objective in this article is to situate the emergence of civil legislation within the context of economic and political restructuring in Canada over the 1980s and 1990s and to analyze the extent to which it is consistent with broader policy directions. We draw on the different experiences in Saskatchewan and Alberta to illustrate distinctions between neo-liberal and neo-conservative approaches to social policy respectively. As Brenda Cossman notes in the context of family and social welfare law, the neo-liberal focus on individual self-reliance, which is evident in government policy generally, is also subject to the continuing influence of moral and social conservatism with its emphasis on the traditional hierarchical, gendered family.[6] This kind of contextual analysis can assist in identifying the benefits and limits of this particular approach to violence against women relative to other approaches and strategies and can also reveal nuances, contradictions, and tensions within and between neoliberal and neoconservative ideological positions.

Despite the policy silence around violence against women that others have documented over the past decade,[7] it remains a systemic problem of significant dimensions. While there is some evidence that rates of violence against women in intimate relationships have declined,[8] they still remain high. Alberta and Saskatchewan have among the highest rates of spousal violence against women in Canada,[9] and women in the prairie provinces and territories are at the highest risk of being killed by an intimate partner.[10] Aboriginal women, women of colour, immigrant and refugee women, young women, elderly women, poor women, lesbians, and women with disabilities may be especially vulnerable to intimate violence, or they may experience and respond to intimate violence in unique ways.[11] Although violence against men also occurs, women are far more likely than men to suffer physical injuries and require medical attention as a result of intimate violence and to experience multiple occurrences.[12] The vast majority of victims of intimate violence reported to police are women, and the alleged perpetrators are overwhelmingly male.[13]

We argue that civil legislation likely has both positive and negative effects in terms of preventing and redressing intimate violence against women. The legislation has the potential to increase the options and material resources available to individual women, particularly in relation to the exclusive possession of the family residence, and to make such relief more accessible and immediate. The legislation can also reinforce the view that violence within a "private" familial context is unacceptable. However, there are limitations as well, many of which reflect and reinforce central ideological features of neo-liberalism and, particularly in Alberta, those of neo-conservatism. The legislation has the effect of privatizing the immediate costs of violence by allocating them to an individual respondent. As with a criminal response, the focus is on crisis intervention and on acts of violence between individuals, reinforcing a dominant norm of individual responsibility and obscuring the social norms and structures that must be addressed in order to end violence against women. The legislation also participates in a degendering of woman abuse since the disproportionate incidence of violence against women, relative to other family members, is subsumed within general categories of domestic or family violence. In a social policy context of silence around woman abuse, this approach contributes to gender-neutral assumptions about violence in the home and tends to reify the family as the paramount site of social concern. Moreover, although the legislation provides civil not criminal relief, it can reinforce a simplistic law and order response to violence through its implementation. Police largely administer the legislation, especially in Saskatchewan, and pro-charging policies mean that criminal charges are a real risk whenever civil relief is invoked. Criminalization has been a significant policy instrument of both neo-liberal and neo-conservative regimes—one that has been criticized on many different grounds by feminists, particularly in relation to its impact on marginalized women.

In the next part of this article, we briefly canvass state reforms undertaken in relation to violence against women over the past two decades and position feminist advocacy in relation to these various initiatives. We then address how civil legislation reflects key aspects of neo-liberalism and neo-conservatism that obscure the persistent realities of substantive gender inequality and also suggest that resistance to feminist interventions on the part of men's rights groups has reinforced these outcomes. As part of this discussion, we examine the intersection between civil and criminal responses to intimate violence against women and address whether the civil response mitigates or reinforces the harms of criminalization. Since we recognize that the legislation is useful to some women, we do not advocate its repeal but, rather, explore reforms that could make it more attentive to the needs of women experiencing violence. In our conclusion, we briefly address how attention to neo-liberalism and neo-conservatism, while they cannot be treated as monolithic ideological positions, contributes to an understanding of the impact of legal reforms.

STATE REFORMS IN RELATION TO VIOLENCE AGAINST WOMEN

Civil legislation emerged in Canada in the mid-1990s, during a period of profound economic and social change that was driven by technological innovation, increased global integration, and state restructuring. The erosion of the Keynesian federal welfare state in favour of the contemporary neo-liberal state began in the mid-1970s but accelerated in the early 1990s, culminating in severe cuts and a restructuring of the federal funding of social programs in 1995.[14] During this period, state investments became increasingly targeted and strategic, shaped by the priorities of economic growth and enhanced competitiveness as well as a greater reliance on the market, the family, and the charitable sector in allocating resources and distributing benefits.[15]

Interestingly, during this same period of time, from the mid-1970s to the early 1990s, violence against women was increasingly cited by state actors as a significant problem requiring specific solutions, particularly at the federal level. During the 1980s and 1990s, the federal government funded a prominent commission on pornography and prostitution[16] and enacted sexual assault law reforms in consultation with women's and anti-violence groups.[17] In the wake of the Montreal Massacre on 6 December 1989, the federal government also announced a national day of remembrance, funded a national statistical survey, and established the Canadian Panel on Violence against Women in 1991 and five Family Violence Research Centres in 1992. According to a Health Canada survey in 1999, these initiatives moved the overall anti-violence agenda forward as a result of an increase in public awareness and an enhanced understanding of both the complexity of violence against women and the importance of prevention.[18]

Research initiatives may have promoted greater understanding of violence against women in some quarters, but, during the 1980s and 1990s, governments actively pursued only a limited range of solutions, primarily criminalization, while reducing or curtailing many types of social supports.[19] Between 1983 and 1986, most jurisdictions in Canada implemented pro-charging and pro-prosecution policies for spousal assault cases.[20] Although these policies differ somewhat between jurisdictions, they generally constrain the discretion of police officers and Crown prosecutors in domestic violence cases and require charging, where there are reasonable and probable grounds to believe an offence has been committed, and prosecution, where there is a reasonable likelihood of conviction. In the 1990s, some provinces also introduced specialized domestic violence courts,[21] and many established victim service offices as supports for the prosecution of criminal offences.

While these law reform efforts were clearly influenced by feminist anti-violence groups, this influence was seriously curtailed by the end of the millennium.[22] Responsibility for violence was increasingly institutionalized within government departments during the 1980s, and, by the late 1980s, advocacy groups experienced direct federal cuts.[23] Over the 1980s and 1990s, many groups and shelters experienced increasing pressure to redefine and present themselves as professional and bureaucratic social service agencies.[24] As a result of the shift to block funding in the 1995 federal budget, shelters became more reliant on precarious per diem funding from provincial and municipal governments[25] and, in some provinces, on charitable status and tax-deductible private donations.[26] Although shelters in Saskatchewan by and large escaped cuts and have generally been able to provide basic short-term emergency protection to those in need,[27] Alberta shelters were forced by budget cuts[28] to rely to a greater extent on volunteers, to limit stays, and to turn many women away due to insufficient space.[29]

In most provinces, including Saskatchewan and Alberta, provincial funding has been either inadequate or not consistently available for outreach services,[30] childcare and child counselling, public education, and second-stage housing.[31] In both Alberta and Saskatchewan, among other provinces, women fleeing abusive relationships have also experienced more restrictive eligibility criteria for social assistance, increased workfare requirements and surveillance, as well as abysmally low rates of assistance. According to an indepth study in 2004 of welfare reforms in Ontario, such changes had a seriously adverse effect on many women experiencing abuse and compromised their ability to live independently of abusive spouses.[32] As noted by Marina Morrow, Olena Hankovsky, and Colleen Varcoe, many of these policies disproportionately hurt marginalized populations, including "single women raising small children, women with psychiatric and/or physical disabilities, Aboriginal women and the homeless," most of whom experience disproportionately high rates of violence.[33]

As indicated, specialized domestic violence legislation was another popular law reform effort that emerged in Canada during the 1990s. Saskatchewan passed the first civil domestic violence statute, with five other provinces and the three territories following suit in the latter part of the decade and into the 2000s.[34] In introducing this legislation, policy makers were no doubt influenced by developments in the United States, since by the early 1990s every state had enacted similar legislation.[35]

Although civil legislation was a grassroots, or feminist-inspired, reform in the United States, the reform process in Canada was initiated and sustained by law reform commissions and justice officials.[36] According to Jan Turner, a senior policy analyst with the Saskatchewan Department of Justice at the time, the VDVA was intended to fill gaps in pre-existing civil and criminal responses to domestic violence.[37] It was designed to provide more immediate and comprehensive relief than was previously available, since applications could be made by telephone by designated agents at any time of the day or night and could focus more fully on the circumstances of the victim.[38] Alberta's legislation was also intended to provide additional, more expeditious remedies, in addition to the more symbolic goal of "recognizing the serious impact of family violence within our communities."[39] As we elaborate upon later in this article, however, the Alberta government also made it clear that while victims did require civil relief, there was also a need to "ensure that family members are not unjustly or frivolously accused."[40]

Frontline workers and advocates have generally viewed civil domestic violence legislation as a positive development. Interviews suggest that the legislation has helped to reinforce the message that domestic violence is unacceptable and has helped to remove an expectation that the victim will leave her home.[41] Remedies available under the statutes can shift responsibility for violence and its consequences away from victims and minimize disruption and the burdens of displacement in the wake of violence. Women claiming relief under the legislation have also been supportive.[42] Even though there are concerns that protective orders cannot guarantee safety and are poorly enforced, some studies suggest that women feel empowered and more in control with the orders in place.[43] Civil orders are posted on police computer systems and can improve subsequent responses in cases of escalating violence. Some evidence also suggests that the legislation itself deters subsequent violence,[44] although such evidence must be critically assessed in light of the inconclusiveness of similar studies on the impact of criminal remedies.[45]

This type of law reform effort is, however, subject to important limitations. Relief is short term in nature and vulnerable to potential constitutional challenges by respondents on the basis that it violates the *Canadian Charter of Rights and Freedoms*,[46] section 96 of the Constitution Act, 1867,[47] and the division of powers between the federal and provincial governments. In both Nova Scotia and Manitoba, these arguments have had some success as they relate to procedural fairness under the Charter.[48] Another significant constitutional limitation is that the civil remedy with the most potential to assist individual women—an order for exclusive possession of the family home— most likely does not apply to residences on First Nations reserves.[49] This limitation restricts the potential material benefits of civil legislation for Aboriginal women living on reserves, where the lack of shelters and the shortage of housing are notorious,[50] although no-contact orders may provide some protection.[51] Finally, usage of the legislation has varied in different parts of Canada and is affected by a host of local and cultural variables including low levels of police support and public awareness. Usage rates in Alberta are not high, and rates have been declining dramatically in Saskatchewan since 1997.[52]

Beyond these specific benefits and limitations, the general meaning and significance of the legislation can only be ascertained by examining it in relation to the political, economic, and ideological shifts occurring in Canada over the last two to three decades. In order to identify these overall effects, we turn to a more contextual examination of the ways in which civil legislation has been shaped or influenced by dominant ideologies and strategies of restructuring as well as a backlash against feminist anti-violence advocacy since the mid-1990s.

CIVIL DOMESTIC VIOLENCE LEGISLATION, RESTRUCTURING DISCOURSE, AND BACKLASH

Political and economic restructuring has been primarily identified with neo-liberalism, but neo-conservative approaches have been prominent in the United Kingdom and the United States and, with the emergence of the Canadian Alliance and the 2006 election of Stephen Harper's minority government, are also increasingly prominent in Canada. While there is likely a continuum or complex matrix of ideological positions,[53] neo-liberalism generally harkens back to the *laissez-faire* policies of the nineteenth century and a corresponding emphasis on the market as the primary mechanism for the production and distribution of goods and services.

Neo-liberal policies, hence, prioritize economic growth and efficiency and, ideologically, emphasize individual responsibility for meeting basic needs as opposed to collective provision. Neo-conservatism is distinguished by an emphasis on traditional, authoritarian structures and institutions and, thus, by a commitment to the traditional gendered family and to law and order campaigns in response to crime.[54]

While neo-liberalism generally emphasizes the individual and neo-conservatism highlights the family as the focus of responsibility, the two perspectives can reinforce each other. Most significantly, the neo-conservative emphasis on the natural support function of families can legitimize a neo-liberal privatizing agenda.[55] Brenda Cossman, however, also identifies contradictions that are particularly evident in contexts such as the recognition of gay and lesbian partnerships, where the neo-liberal commitment to private choice and responsibility is at odds with the neo-conservative promotion of a heterosexist, highly gendered family form.[56]

The neo-liberal focus on less state regulation would also appear to be inconsistent with a neo-conservative law and order approach to crime. In both orientations, however, criminalization is consistent with treating offenders as individually blameworthy and minimizing the structural causes of crime. Neo-liberal policies can also have the effect of increasing intolerance and greater punitiveness towards offenders. As David Garland and others have noted,[57] the increased dependence of individuals on the vagaries of the market in low tax and low welfare regimes inevitably undermines a sense of solidarity and community. Insecure employment, underfunded public institutions, the increasing social and economic marginalization of the poor, and a media culture that is focused on crime all generate widespread anxieties that can be mobilized to control dissent and reinforce privilege.[58] Since the 1980s, state policy in Canada has increasingly focused on policing, imprisonment, and risk management in response to crime rather than the rehabilitation of the offender.[59] Garland contends that neo-liberal policies on crime target certain groups and behaviours.[60] According to Nicholas Rose, the focus of the "risk gaze" is usually on excluded, marginalized populations.[61]

Janine Brodie has identified privatization, refamilialization (a revalorization of the family), and an increased reliance on criminal law and law enforcement agencies in achieving individual and collective security as dominant themes or policy trends within the rubric of restructuring discourse.[62] In her view, over the last two decades, these strategies have helped to transform our understandings of the model citizen, who is now the responsible and self-reliant individual. Together, they have helped to reduce expectations of what the state can do and to construct the ordinary citizen as someone who does not make claims on the state.[63]

In the following section, we evaluate each of these strategies in relation to civil domestic violence legislation in Saskatchewan and Alberta. Saskatchewan is identified historically with a social democratic tradition that can be traced to patterns of immigration, among other historically specific conditions,[64] but a pronounced shift towards neo-liberal policies has been evident, particularly in the area of welfare reform, over the last decade. Alberta, by contrast, has a long conservative tradition that has celebrated "family values" as well as what Nelson Wiseman describes as "rugged individualism" and "free enterprise."[65] However, as this case study itself reveals, neither Saskatchewan nor Alberta's policies in this context correspond precisely to a single ideological orientation.

A Privatized and Degendered Response

Although civil legislation itself represents a form of state action, its effect is to facilitate the privatization of the costs of violence. The relief authorized by the legislation is private and individualized, contingent on an individual application requesting possession of the home or other relief from an individual respondent. By shifting or reallocating the costs from victim or state to the individual abuser, the remedy is consistent with an increased emphasis on individual responsibility that can simultaneously obscure the social relations that produce and otherwise sustain violence. In relying upon action by the victim, it also fulfils the function of "helping citizens to help themselves."[66] However, the primary forms of relief available to victims—no contact orders or exclusive possession orders—tend to isolate women rather than facilitate connections between women or with women-centred services. In the absence of economic assistance and outreach services providing education in the dynamics of abuse as well as emotional support from other victims and workers, women may lack the financial, social, and psychological resources needed to end violent relationships. Finally, at least at the stage of initial orders, the process of seeking the remedies available under the legislation largely occurs in private, behind closed doors, rendering it difficult to monitor.

Civil legislation was also passed during a period identified as a "fiscal crisis," when most provincial governments faced mounting deficits arising from federal cuts to transfer payments, stringent monetarist policies (that spurred soaring interest rates), and increasing health costs. The overall cost to the state of civil legislation has been relatively small, limited largely to the training costs of designated agents,[67] justices of the peace (JPs), and judges. Since 1995 in Saskatchewan, JPs appointed exclusively to hear and determine applications under the VDVA have been paid only $25 per hour, and, in Alberta, existing JPs and provincial court judges have borne the added responsibilities, as have designated agents in both provinces. There is no evidence that the funding of shelters was reduced in the wake of this legislation, but its enactment may have relieved the strain on shelters somewhat and reduced the pressure for additional funding. The legislation is thus, by and large, consistent with the neo-liberal emphasis on strategic state initiatives that can privatize costs.

In this respect, Alberta and Saskatchewan's civil legislation is notably similar to other quasi-criminal reforms that have emerged since the 1990s and are grounded in neo-liberal and neo-conservative ideologies. For example, in 2000, Alberta enacted legislation allowing police and child welfare officials to apprehend and confine youth who are suspected of involvement in prostitution.[68] Steven Bittle argues that this legislation is a control strategy compatible with the "responsibilization" aspect of neo-liberalism, in that the causes and effects of youth prostitution are framed as the responsibility of individuals, their families, and communities rather than the state.[69] Civil domestic violence legislation similarly privatizes the causes and costs of violence. In both cases, responsibility is imposed regardless of the inadequacy of state supports for individuals, families, and communities.[70]

Civil legislation can also be seen as degendering the problem of violence against women, a strategy consistent with the broader federal response by the end of the 1990s. Although violence against women was highly evident in state discourse during the early 1990s, Lise Gotell argues that the problem of gender inequality tended to be reduced to violence by individual men, while women were generally presented as helpless victims in need of protection.[71] Lois Harder suggests that in Alberta the success of the shelter movement itself rested on its "common sense" view of women as weak and vulnerable.[72] As powerless victims of overt, physical violence, women could easily be situated within the narrow range of interests recognized as deserving of state intervention within neo-liberal theory. Beginning in the mid-1980s and through the 1990s, however, references to violence against women, wife assault, or woman abuse gradually disappeared in state discourse and were subsumed within general references to "victims," "family," or "domestic violence." By the late 1990s, as Gotell notes, there was a resounding silence surrounding violence against women in policy discourse—a silence that was reinforced by the background shift in the norms of citizenship towards the self-reliant citizen described by Janine Brodie.[73]

Differences in the way in which civil domestic violence legislation was introduced in Saskatchewan and Alberta illustrate to some degree this trend towards gender neutrality. The Saskatchewan New Democratic government introduced the VDVA on International Women's Day, 8 March 1994, and explicitly presented the bill in the legislative debates as a "significant step" towards achieving security and safety for women.[74] By contrast, Alberta's PAFVA, which was introduced four years later, was not grounded in a policy emphasis on violence against women. Although the Alberta Law Reform Institute noted the gendered nature of "domestic abuse" in its 1995 discussion report on the issue,[75] the Alberta government's report of its consultations in 1999 reveals an explicitly gender-neutral approach. In addition to framing draft legislation in gender-neutral terms, the government noted that it "contains measures intended to ensure that ... gender bias does not enter into the protection orders or the way the dispute is resolved."[76]

In both provinces, the legislation is gender neutral on its face. However, the overwhelming majority of claimants in Saskatchewan and Alberta—in excess of 90 per cent—have been women in spousal relationships.[77] To this extent, the legislation in both provinces participates in a reframing of violence against women as part of a generalized victim's rights discourse that is disconnected from women's economic and social inequality.[78] Since the "impact and incidence of violence are differentiated by gender,"[79] this distinctiveness should in some way be recognized by policy makers. Studies have consistently shown that the physical severity and the negative emotional and economic impact of violence are greater for women than for men.[80]

The reframing of violence against women as a gender-neutral problem of domestic violence, family violence, or intimate partner violence is consistent with a backlash or reaction against feminist advocacy around women abuse that was increasingly evident over the 1990s. Feminist advocacy was hobbled by government funding cuts, but it was also increasingly marginalized as the exaggerated, self-serving claims of a special interest group.[81] Even the Montreal Massacre, which was blatantly motivated by anti-feminism, generated an intense backlash against feminists,[82] who were perceived to be appropriating the tragedy and using it to further their own political agenda. Men's and fathers' rights groups also became more vocal during the 1990s and actively sought to discredit feminists through the use of the media, human rights complaints, and parliamentary hearings on child custody and access.[83] These groups appropriated studies of lesbian abuse and used decontextualized statistical studies to suggest that violence against men by women was a social problem of equal gravity.[84] By emphasizing that women were also capable of violence, their status as ideal powerless victims was rendered suspect and a formal vision of equality was reinforced. Walter DeKeseredy and Martin Schwartz argue that this anti-feminist backlash has influenced the gender-neutral approach to intimate violence against women taken by the government and by Statistics Canada in its reports on family violence.[85]

One of the groups participating in Alberta's consultations towards the enactment of the PAFVA, the Movement for the Establishment of Real Gender Equality (MERGE), later brought a human rights complaint against an Edmonton shelter, successfully arguing that its brochure discriminated against men in suggesting that intimate violence was a gendered problem.[86] In 1997 and 1998, the National Shared Parenting Association in Saskatchewan organized the lodging of several human rights complaints alleging in part that the VDVA discriminated against men since men were overwhelmingly the respondents in applications under the act. This outcome was said to be inconsistent with statistical studies allegedly showing that women were "just as capable of violence."[87] The reviewing investigator concluded that there was no sex discrimination within the act or in its administration.[88] However, anti-feminist ideals and fear of legal contestation or public controversy may continue to influence the implementation and usage of civil legislation and the likelihood of amendments.

Refamilialization

The state response to wife abuse has long been subject to tensions and contradictions. Before the late 1800s, the open subjection of wives to patriarchal discipline was one of the most obvious indicators of women's exclusion from the social contract. Since then, violence towards wives has been prohibited by the letter of the criminal law, reflecting recognition of an individual and formally equal right to protection from violence.[89] However, lax sentences, inconsistent enforcement, and indifference by law enforcement agencies have reflected not only sexist, racist, and classist assumptions but also, in significant measure, the continued valorization of the private, hierarchical, and highly gendered family.

While neo-liberalism relies on the family as one of the primary sources of economic support for individuals, neo-conservatism directly embraces the moral authority of the traditional family with its highly gendered roles, hierarchical, authoritarian structure, and a presumption of heterosexuality.[90] This neo-conservative vision of family is linked to a variety of issues such as opposition to abortion, daycare, relationships outside heterosexual marriage, and no fault divorce, as well as minimal government intervention into family and private life.[91] Neo-conservatives would not condone domestic violence because the family is envisaged and held out as a naturally happy and well functioning unit. However, violence within the family is often ignored in neo-conservative discourse.[92] Moreover, because hierarchy and gender differentiation are seen as being natural, violence can be minimized as aberrant and exceptional or explained in ways that both differentiate it from issues of structural or individual power and include significant elements of victim blaming.[93]

In most jurisdictions, civil legislation limits relief to those in familial relationships. In Saskatchewan and Alberta, relief is available to parents of children or to those who have cohabited in a spousal (heterosexual or same-sex) or other familial relationship. The legislation, therefore, allows for non-spousal claims including claims by children against parents and by elders against other family members but excludes those in dating relationships.[94] The distinctive dynamics of violence within families, particularly the intense emotional and economic dependencies experienced by family members, can justify distinctive legislative treatment of violence in this context. Moreover, it is obviously important to contest traditional ideologies of the family as a private realm. However, a singular state focus on domestic or family violence can also serve, at least in the longer run, as a way of reconstituting the family as the preferred site for caregiving and support.[95] In both provinces, attention to forms of violence outside familial relations has been largely focused on children, the ideal victims within neo-liberalism, rather than adult women.[96] Both the exclusion of dating relationships and a lack of attention to other forms of violence experienced by adult women tend to reify the family as the exclusive site of concern.

It is important to the neo-liberal agenda that the family be legitimized as an appropriate site of dependency given its enhanced functional role in any privatizing strategy.[97] Cossman notes, however, that the increased role the family is expected to play in terms of private support in both neo-liberal and neo-conservative visions is undermined not only by the way in which adult dependency has been pathologized in neo-liberal discourse but also by economic pressures arising from the "disappearance of the family wage."[98] There is no evidence that the significant changes in family life experienced since the mid-1970s have increased the incidence of domestic violence. However, such changes can generate social anxieties, and civil domestic violence legislation may play a role in responding to these anxieties both symbolically by appearing to support the family as a harmonious institution and by providing individualized remedies for victims where violence does occur.

In terms of neo-conservative support of the family, legislation authorizing the separation of family members would initially appear at odds with socially conservative values of family privacy and non-interference.[99] However, violence in emergency situations can easily be cast as an exception to a general rule of non-intervention.[100] Civil domestic violence legislation also permits only a temporary separation of family members and, unlike divorce, does not presuppose a permanent breakdown of the family or spousal relationship. In fact, as suggested earlier, state intervention in the short term may be seen as important to maintaining or preserving the family unit in the longer term.

In the context of civil legislation, the Alberta statute initially permitted courts to order counselling for victims as well as respondents under non-emergency orders, a provision that likely reflected a desire to maintain the family unit.[101] A preference for the heterosexual family was also evident in the Alberta government's refusal from 1999 to 2003 to include same-sex relationships as deserving of protection under its civil legislation.[102] Alberta's legislation is also unique in explicitly excluding violence committed in the context of disciplining children as worthy of relief, reflecting a hierarchical authoritarian form of family.[103] Further, the PAFVA reflects distrust of, or suspicion towards, accounts by victims (predominantly women) by including a prohibition against "frivolous or vexatious complaints made with malicious intent."[104] Together, these provisions reflect and reinforce as natural the traditional, ideal family of social conservatism. Their inclusion may have been influenced in part by the participation of pro-family and men's rights groups in the consultation process around the PAFVA.[105] Pro-family groups, in particular, have been said to have close ties to the Alberta government and to take a neo-conservative, anti-feminist stance in social policy debates.[106]

In November 2006, the Alberta government amended the PAFVA legislation to include stalking, to eliminate counselling orders for victims, and to clarify the criteria for granting emergency orders.[107] While the amendments are positive in many respects, the government emphasized that the changes were made to protect "vulnerable people" such as children and seniors, and its addition of stalking only applies between family members.[108] The changes thus reflect a continued focus on the family and a de-gendered approach to violence.

Criminalization

As previously indicated, criminalization is an increasingly significant policy instrument within neo-liberal and neo-conservative restructuring discourses. This section will explore critiques of the criminalization of domestic violence and examine whether the problems with an aggressive criminal response to violence can be mitigated by, or, alternatively, are reinforced by, civil legislation. We also interrogate the extent to which judicial interpretations of civil legislation serve to minimize the potential advantages that civil legislation might have over an aggressive criminal response.

Critiques of Criminalization

As noted earlier, neo-liberalism may converge with neo-conservatism in a law and order approach to crime, including increased support for law enforcement, punitive sentencing practices, exploitation of the public's anxiety over crime, and a focus on individual responsibility.[109] A more aggressive criminal response to domestic violence has also been spurred by feminist law reform efforts.[110] Women's groups have called for a "zero tolerance" policy on intimate violence against women, linking such a response to the potential for increased protection for women and their children as well as to concerns that criminal justice officials, particularly police, have not taken violence against women in the home as seriously as other forms of violence.[111] Feminists have also argued that the criminal law could fulfil important symbolic and material functions by reinforcing "the principle that everyone has the right to live free from violence" without regard to gender, sexual orientation, race, class, or abilities.[112] In addition to criminal reforms, however, women's groups have called for enhanced social supports to address the structural causes of violence against women.[113]

In spite of feminist demands for a multi-faceted approach to intimate violence against women, the Canadian state's response in the 1980s and 1990s centred largely on the criminal sphere, particularly pro-charging and pro-prosecution policies.[114] Locating the solution in the criminal justice system does help to identify domestic violence as a matter of public interest, but it also identifies the source of the problem as individual perpetrators, obscuring the links between violence and broader social, economic, and political inequalities. In particular, the escalation of criminal justice strategies in the midst of declining social supports reflects a tendency to explain wife battering in terms of individual pathologies.

An enhanced criminal response to intimate violence against women can appear to be in tension with other changes identified with restructuring. The process is costly relative to other support measures such as preventative services that help women leave violent men.[115] Further, criminalization can adversely affect the capacity of abusive partners to provide financial support for their families in the short term—an effect that is in tension with both the privatization agenda and the neo-conservative emphasis on preservation of the traditional family. However, in the longer term, criminalization (as with domestic violence legislation itself) may bolster the legitimacy of the family as a safe haven, providing reassurance that the state is dealing with the few aberrant individuals responsible for violence.[116]

Feminist critiques of the criminal justice response to domestic violence tend to fall within two broad strands. First, feminists have criticized the central focus on criminalization at the expense of more structural reforms. For example, Laureen Snider contends that the criminal law is not fundamentally transformative, particularly in light of its disproportionate impact on poor, racialized men.[117] Dianne Martin and Janet Mosher argue that the criminal law should be decentred "as the answer to wife abuse."[118] However, while these voices are critical of the ways in which feminist law reform efforts were appropriated by the state and used to further a law and order agenda,[119] they acknowledge that women still need some form of protection. More recently, Snider has also conceded that "a crucial cultural shift" around domestic violence was produced at least in part by the "symbolic stigma of criminal law."[120]

The second strand of the feminist critique points to problems with the pro-charging and pro-prosecution policies themselves, claiming that they do not provide the intended result of deterrence and that they have other unintended adverse effects on women and marginalized men. The decontextualized enforcement of pro-charging policies has, for example, led to the possibility of mutual arrests and charges, thereby criminalizing women who were seeking to defend themselves against violent partners.[121] Women have also been subjected to re-victimization through contempt of court proceedings or other criminal charges mounted in the face of their refusal to testify against their partners.[122] The possibility of retaliation by abusers may deter women from calling the police and also from testifying at the trial.[123]

Some consequences of aggressive criminalization are said to be uniquely and disproportionately experienced by vulnerable, marginalized groups of women and to inhibit their engagement with the criminal justice system. For example, lesbians may fear the implications both of coming out, which may result in homophobia and harassment from the justice system and women's shelters, and of ostracism from within lesbian communities.[124] Fear of child protection proceedings or custody battles have been noted as a factor deterring lesbians,[125] Aboriginal women,[126] and immigrant women[127] from contacting the police. Similarly, immigrant and refugee women may avoid criminal justice involvement because of the fear of deportation or other loss of status.[128] Marginalized and economically dependent women may also hesitate to engage with the criminal justice system because they fear the economic disadvantage that would follow if their partners were incarcerated and because of a lack of housing and other services.[129] Finally, racialized women may wish to avoid a justice system that has proven to be racist against both persons accused and victims of crime.[130] Snider notes that zero tolerance policies, under which some women have been subjected to assault laws for trying to defend themselves, have been enforced most stringently through arrests and charging of women who are "young, poor, and from minority groups."[131]

At the same time, another critique of the criminal reforms around domestic violence—and one that is made both by those who are supportive and those who are critical of pro-charging policies—relates to the lack of consistent enforcement by police and justice officials.[132] As noted by Martin and Mosher,[133] the fact that the policies are not consistently followed results in women being uncertain as to what the outcome of calling the police will be, often reinforcing their hesitancy to do so. Some women from marginalized communities who have articulated a desire for an aggressive criminal approach to intimate violence have also complained of inconsistent treatment.[134] Critics argue that police attitudes and charging practices are still governed by myths and stereotypes, and they contend that criminal policies have not resulted in fundamental or significant changes in the thinking of justice system officials regarding intimate violence nor in the protection or empowerment of battered women.[135] This critique, however, has not resulted in a widespread call to abandon pro-charging policies, which is likely due to fears that a return to absolute police discretion could increase the potential for indifferent and racist responses.[136]

The tensions among neo-liberal, neo-conservative, and feminist discourses may also explain some of the inconsistencies between the letter and application of the criminal law in relation to violence against women. They further raise the question of whether the civil response to domestic violence might mitigate some of the tensions within and between these discourses in the criminal domain or, alternatively, replicate and reinforce them.

Intersections between Criminal and Civil Responses to Violence against Women

Civil legislation holds potential advantages over the aggressive criminal charging and prosecution of domestic violence. Relative to the criminal law, civil legislation is not as potent a marker of individual responsibility nor as retributive a measure. In practical terms, the absence of a direct risk of incarceration or of a criminal record for respondents may translate into a reduced chance of stigma for the perpetrator, his partner, and their children as well as less jeopardy to their economic security. While it is not clear whether civil legislation itself adversely impacts marginalized women and men,[137] it seems reasonable to assume that at least some of the negative consequences of aggressive criminalization would be mitigated under a civil response. For example, mutual orders do not appear to be a significant problem under civil legislation in Alberta or Saskatchewan, which is likely because of the *ex parte* nature of applications.[138] There is also evidence that some women would prefer civil proceedings over a criminal response.[139] As noted by Jan Turner, "[t]his message was particularly clear from Aboriginal women" in Saskatchewan.[140] Other studies suggest that many women may simply want offenders to be removed from the home rather than be subjected to aggressive criminal justice intervention.[141]

In spite of these potential advantages, the way civil domestic violence legislation has been implemented in Saskatchewan and Alberta largely reflects a continuing emphasis on criminalization as the dominant response to domestic violence, with many of the same costs. Civil legislation did not emerge in response to the feminist critique of criminalization, and was never intended to supplant the criminal law or to provide an alternative option for women experiencing violence. Rather, the legislation was envisioned as a remedy that would supplement criminal proceedings. This policy choice reflects a privileging of criminal law as the primary means of dealing with violence against women[142] and was motivated, at least in part, by the fear of undermining a firm, consistent frontline response.[143]

Civil legislation is administered in large part by police, who remain subject to pro-charging policies. In Saskatchewan, although the legislation on its face allows for in person applications, in practice, specialized JPs can be accessed only through designated agents, who are most often police officers.[144] In Alberta, primary applicants are also police, at least outside of Calgary and Edmonton.[145] Even though the police do not often lay charges in such cases, charging remains a real risk.[146] If a decontextualized approach to "zero tolerance" is taken, the victim may be charged as well. In Alberta, child welfare workers are also empowered to apply for emergency protection orders, and, although such applications are rare, their powers may reinforce fears about child apprehensions, particularly among disadvantaged women, given the heightened scrutiny of their families. In both Alberta and Saskatchewan, police and other applicants are obligated by child welfare legislation or protocols to report instances of domestic violence to child welfare authorities whenever children are present at the time of the violence.[147] The involvement of police also suggests that the concerns of immigrant women regarding deportation will not be mitigated by the civil legislation.

There are advantages to police involvement under the civil legislation, particularly in the immediacy of orders through on-site applications, which can potentially reduce the frequency and escalation of violence.[148] However, the involvement of both the police and, in Alberta, child welfare workers may be reducing the numbers of women who would otherwise use the civil legislation. Interviews with justice personnel and community workers in Alberta and Saskatchewan suggest that immigrant and Aboriginal women, women with disabilities, and lesbians are not using the legislation as would be expected given their representation in the population.[149]

Such an outcome is potentially linked to avoidance of contact with the police, who are the main conduits for the civil system. In Saskatchewan and Alberta, there is also evidence that the police are not telling victims about the civil legislation and have indicated a continued preference for the criminal justice system.[150] This outcome is likely related to a lack of familiarity with the legislation on the part of some police officers, workload concerns, and a belief that the legislation provides no additional advantages to victims, particularly if a violent spouse is arrested and charged.[151] While women are free to make applications for emergency protection orders themselves in Alberta, a court appearance is required with attendant delays, expense, and access to justice issues, especially in rural and remote communities.[152]

A number of reforms could help to avoid or reduce some of these problems. The category of designated applicants could be expanded to include intermediaries other than, or in addition to, the police, such as shelter workers, immigrant workers, First Nations community workers, and legal aid/ community legal organizations.[153] This change would provide more flexibility and choice for victims, particularly those living in remote and isolated communities, and was specifically requested by Aboriginal women during consultations on Saskatchewan's legislation.[154] In this event, assurances that designated applicants would abide by the requirements of due process would be important.[155] In Saskatchewan, in-person applications should also be operationalized in order to give effect to the statutory right to make them.[156] Further, to the extent that police continue to be present on site for security reasons in both provinces, they should be required to inform victims of the legislation.[157] Increased funding and support for groups designated as applicants for emergency orders, as well as the provision of victim advocates to assist with in-person applications, should also be provided. Moreover, public education and awareness campaigns are necessary to ensure that women know about the existence and scope of civil remedies.[158]

Even if these proposals were implemented, however, a risk of charging could arise from the involvement of police in the service and enforcement of civil orders. Since the PAFVA and the VDVA do not contain offence provisions, breaches are dealt with under section 127 of the Criminal Code, which makes breach of a lawful court order an indictable criminal offence where a punishment is not expressly provided for by another law.[159] To the extent that breaches of civil orders are reported by women (or others) and enforced, abusers are thus subject to criminal sanctions. Some women may not want breaches of civil orders enforced precisely because this leads to criminal consequences for their (ex)-partners. Under the current system, the lack of enforcement of civil protection orders is a well-documented problem, perhaps because police are also reluctant to criminalize breaches.[160] The creation of an offence for breaches of civil orders within the legislation itself, coupled with powers of arrest in the event of a breach, might mitigate these concerns.[161] However, this approach requires further study in light of the fact that criminal charges under section 127 would no longer be possible and such a change might thereby fail to deal with some breaches in a sufficiently serious way.

Training for police on the dynamics of violence against women and women's inequality, as well as more targeted education to counteract racism, homophobia, and other forms of oppression of marginalized groups may also reduce problems with a lack of enforcement. Recommendations for such training have been made in the context of both criminal and civil remedies.[162] However, research on police culture suggests that there may be limits in the extent to which police training is effective with respect to these matters.[163] Finally, civil legislation should be monitored in terms of its usage, particularly by marginalized women, and in terms of the number of criminal charges laid and the enforcement of breaches. Monitoring would ensure that the private nature of civil proceedings does not obscure the impact of the legislation and is an important means of holding the state to account.

Constructions of Emergency and Remedial Powers

Narrow constructions of emergency and remedial powers by judges and JPs have also likely played a role in reducing the potential of civil legislation to respond to situations outside the ordinary reach of criminal law in Saskatchewan and Alberta.[164] As a result of the *ex parte* nature of the application and the possessory nature of the relief requested, reviewing courts have required a high threshold for meeting the criteria for emergency protection and intervention orders. JPs and judges have generally looked for a precipitating event that can be construed as creating a crisis or emergency, with an emphasis on the existence of discrete, isolated acts or threats of physical violence, rather than the cumulative impact of past violence or the ongoing coercive or controlling conduct that is typical of battering relationships.[165] This approach is also illustrative of what Colleen Varcoe and Lori Irwin describe as a tendency across formal systems, including criminal justice and child protection systems, "to deal with incidents of violence, rather than the patterns of ongoing abuse that characterize women's lives, and to deal with a narrow aspect of each situation."[166]

The practical effect of constructing an emergency in this way is that women attempting to escape violent relationships may have to wait for violence to reoccur before they can seek relief under the legislation. Reviewing courts have generally not considered the possibility that forcing a claimant to provide notice of her desire to separate could in fact increase her risk of being abused or assaulted.[167] Moreover, difficulties have arisen in meeting the element of urgency where women have temporarily taken refuge in a shelter and applied for relief even a short time after the violent incident[168] or where the police have failed to lay charges or apply for an order.[169] These constraints ignore the profound emotional effects of violence on women that can generate delays and the persistence of risk where there are longer-term cycles of violence.

Interestingly, Alberta has amended its legislation to deal with some of these obstacles. As of 1 November 2006, the PAFVA explicitly provides that certain circumstances should not preclude the granting of an emergency protection order, including the respondent's temporary absence from the residence at the time of the application, the claimant's temporary residence in an emergency shelter or other safe place, and the fact that criminal charges have been, or may be, laid against the respondent. Other amendments require that controlling behaviour by the respondent and the claimant's need for a safe environment be considered in determining whether to grant emergency relief under the legislation.[170] Other provinces, including Saskatchewan, have yet to introduce similar amendments to their legislation.

In making orders under the civil legislation, JPs and judges are also failing to focus sufficiently on the victim's needs and specific circumstances and thereby failing to provide relief substantially beyond what is available under the criminal process.[171] In Saskatchewan, JPs have the power to make exclusive possession orders but do not view themselves as empowered to make orders for the payment of rent or the transfer of car keys or bank cards, all of which are important to the household's ability to function independently of the abusive partner.[172] Further, orders recommending that the respondent obtain counselling are rarely made at the emergency stage in either province, again because of a perceived lack of authority to order or recommend treatment pursuant to emergency orders.[173] JPs and judges in Alberta also appear to avoid making orders relating to personal property and make exclusive possession orders less frequently than their counterparts in Saskatchewan.[174] Finally, even though the Saskatchewan act does not provide a maximum limit on the duration of orders, they are typically issued for only thirty days, requiring that a claimant either obtain a lawyer to pursue longer-term remedies or try to locate alternative accommodation.[175]

A more expansive definition of emergency, particularly in Saskatchewan, and of the remedial powers of JPs and judges could facilitate earlier intervention in long-term battering relationships and functional stability for the household over the duration of the order, which are both ways in which the criminal process often provides inadequate relief. Training and education have also been recommended for JPs and the judiciary in the civil context.[176]

CONCLUSION

While civil domestic violence legislation clearly has the potential to improve material resources available to women and has done so for some women, many of the drawbacks common to law reform efforts have also been identified. The potential of the legislation has first been limited in its interpretation and implementation by JPs, judges, and police. The rights granted to claimants have been substantially narrowed by the assertion of competing rights,[177] particularly the traditional judicial regard for due process and property rights. Applications have hence been subject to narrow interpretations of emergency and remedial powers and remain vulnerable to Charter challenges. Orders that have been granted have been short term, and concerns have been expressed regarding a lack of enforcement of orders by police.

The problem is not only that civil legislation will not end intimate violence against women. As Carol Smart notes, "[b]ecause the legal right can treat the woman and man involved only as adversaries,"[178] legal remedies also tend to obscure important elements of the relationship, including both economic and emotional dependencies. Material conditions, in particular, constrict the options of women, making it more difficult to leave or stay away. Civil legislation does not substantially reduce economic dependencies and may benefit marginalized women least in light of the fact that police are the major gatekeepers of the legislation. While there is no hard evidence that civil legislation itself adversely impacts racialized or other marginalized women, there are indications that it is not being used by them, likely because they seek to avoid police contact. Further, Aboriginal women receive limited benefits from the legislation on reserves because of issues related to the constitutional division of powers.

A more contextual analysis of the legislation in relation to restructuring and neo-liberal and neo-conservative ideologies assists in showing how this type of law reform effort relates to broader policy directions and ideological currents and helps to make more sense of the limits that are observed in a micro-analysis. Our focus on two provinces also suggests that it is important to analyze neo-liberalism and neo-conservatism within concrete historical, temporal, and political contexts in order to recognize the full range of potential responses and the factors that influence the extent to which, or the precise manner in which, the state responds. Such an approach reveals both the regional differences in political cultures and personnel as well as the contradictions and nuances in government responses. While the New Democratic government in Saskatchewan has in many respects followed the neo-liberal model in giving priority to deficit reduction, tax cuts, capital accumulation, and welfare reform, its resistance in other ways, notably through the funding of shelters, is more reflective of its social democratic traditions. Although the Alberta government's initial approach to the legislation was more reflective of neo-conservative tendencies, the government did amend its legislation in response to a report prepared by a feminist anti-violence research centre, which was commissioned by ministry officials committed to improving the response to domestic violence within the province.

Our analysis is therefore not intended to, nor should it, generate defeatist responses. The incremental changes to civil legislation that we have suggested can make a meaningful difference for some women. It is also worth considering whether a more highly developed administrative model could respond to violence against women in a more comprehensive and effective way. Such a model might be composed of a commission or "ombuds-like" position to undertake public education, along with a tribunal to hear applications for protection orders and both individual and systemic complaints. If provided with broad jurisdiction and constraints on judicial review, such a model might have a greater ability to contextualize, connect, and publicize the multifaceted aspects of violence and, potentially, to provide systemic remedies dealing with issues such as discriminatory enforcement and cuts to shelter funding. The success of such a model would be highly dependent on personnel and funding and could never be considered a panacea.[179] Nevertheless, an administrative model has the potential to improve outcomes relative to the current adjudicatory model and that of front-line departments by including appointees with acknowledged expertise, background, and sensitivity both to the dynamics of violence and the surrounding context of gender and other intersecting inequalities.

While this type of multi-faceted approach is needed, priority must always be given to ongoing efforts towards structural reforms. Contrary to the ideology of the self-reliant citizen, women's security, particularly that of poor, racialized, and other marginalized women, will only be achieved through increased access to social services and welfare benefits, educational opportunities, employment and pay equity, child and elder care, and housing. Adequate levels of funding for shelters and other grassroots women's organizations should also be maintained so that these groups can continue to advocate for structural reforms grounded in women's lived experiences.

QUESTIONS TO CONSIDER

1. Koshan and Wiegers argue that many remedies for abused women are short-term measures. Critically assess their approach. To what extent are these remedies helpful in reducing woman abuse? Draw on the examples in their chapter as well as on outside readings.

2. What differences in approach and services are identified between Alberta and Saskatchewan?

3. Do you agree with the authors' critique of the criminalization of domestic violence? What measures might be considered as an alternative to, or supplement to, the criminal justice system?

SUGGESTIONS FOR FURTHER READING

Johnson, M. P. (2008). *A typology of domestic violence: Intimate terrorism, violent resistance, and situational couple violence.* Boston: Northeastern University Press.

Richards, L., Letchford, S., & Stratton, S. (2008). *Policing domestic violence.* Oxford: Oxford University Press.

NOTES

1. We recognize the importance of using language that reflects the gendered nature of violence between intimate partners. However, the legislation we analyze in this article applies broadly to all victims of "family" or "domestic" violence, regardless of their gender and sexual orientation, and includes children and elders. For this reason, we use the terms "family" and "domestic violence" and "victims of violence" when discussing the legislation itself. Elsewhere we critique the governments' failure to recognize the gendered nature of such violence, and there we use terms that reflect this reality, such as "intimate violence against women."

2. *Victims of Domestic Violence Act*, S.S. 1994, c. V-6.02 [*VDVA*].

3. *Protection against Family Violence Act*, R.S.A. 2000, c. P-27 [*PAFVA*].

4. Superior court judges review emergency orders either through an automatic court hearing in Alberta or by way of a paper review and a hearing upon the application of either the respondent or the reviewing judge in Saskatchewan.

5. Howard Research, *Implementation and Impact of the Protection against Family Violence Act: Final Report* (Edmonton, AB: Government of Alberta, 2000) at 1–2; and Wanda Wiegers and Fiona Douglas, *Civil Domestic Violence Legislation in Saskatchewan: An Assessment of the First Decade* (Regina: Canadian Plains Research Centre, 2007) [forthcoming].

6. Brenda Cossman, "Family Feuds: Neo-Liberal and Neo-Conservative Visions of the Reprivatization Project," in Brenda Cossman and Judy Fudge, eds., *Privatization, Law, and the Challenge to Feminism* (Toronto: University of Toronto Press, 2002), 169 at 171.

7. See note 73 in this article and accompanying text.

8. See Statistics Canada, *Measuring Violence against Women: Statistical Trends 2006* (Ottawa: Minister of Industry, 2006) at 16–17 [*Measuring Violence*].

9. Karen Mihorean, "Trends in Self-Reported Spousal Violence," in Statistics Canada, Canadian Centre for Justice Statistics, *Family Violence in Canada: A Statistical Profile 2005* (Ottawa: Minister of Industry, 2005), 13 at 15, shows that Alberta had the highest rate of such violence over the past five years and Saskatchewan had the second highest rate. See also Federal-Provincial-Territorial Ministers Responsible for the Status of Women, *Assessing Violence against Women: A Statistical Profile* (Ottawa: Status of Women Canada, 2002) at 13 [*Assessing Violence*].

10. *Measuring Violence*, *supra* note 8 at 25. From 1975 to 2004, the average rate of homicide at the hands of an intimate partner in Canada was 1.0, per 100,000 spouses. In the prairies, the rates were: Manitoba: 1.5; Saskatchewan: 1.3; and Alberta: 1.2.

11. *Assessing Violence*, *supra* note 9 at 19, and 29; *Measuring Violence*, *supra* note 8 at 13–14; Statistics Canada, Canadian Centre for Justice Statistics, *Family Violence in Canada: A Statistical Profile 2004* (Ottawa: Minister of Industry, 2004) at 6 [*Family Violence*]; Canadian Panel on Violence against Women, *Changing the Landscape: Ending Violence—Achieving Equality* (Ottawa: Minister of Supply and Services, 1993) at 59.

12. See *Assessing Violence*, *supra* note 9 at 12, citing the General Social Survey (1999).

13. *Family Violence*, *supra* note 11 at 5; and *Ibid*. at 16.

14. See Janine Brodie, "Canadian Women, Changing State Forms, and Public Policy," in Janine Brodie, ed., *Women and Canadian Public Policy* (Toronto: Harcourt Brace, 1996), 1; Judy Fudge and Brenda Cossman, "Introduction: Privatization, Law, and the Challenge to Feminism," in Cossman and Fudge, eds., *supra* note 6, 3 at 3; Isabella Bakker, "Restructuring Discourse and Its Gendered Underpinnings: Toward a Macro-Analytical Framework," in Theodore H. Cohn, Stephen McBride, and John Wiseman, eds., *Power in the Global Era: Grounding Globalization* (London: MacMillan Press., 2000), at 24.

15. Although initially presented as an economic imperative arising largely from high government deficits, after achieving budgetary surpluses the federal government and provinces such as Saskatchewan and Alberta continued to prioritize economic expansion, tax cuts, and the reduction of debt over universal supports such as a national day care program or the provision of adequate income security policies. For a review of expenditures by the federal government during both deficit and surplus eras, see Armine Yalnizyan, *Canada's Commitment to Equality: A Gender Analysis of the Last Ten Federal Budgets (1995–2004)* (Ottawa: Canadian Feminist Alliance for International Action, 2005).

16. Paul Fraser and the Special Committee on Pornography and Prostitution, *Pornography and Prostitution in Canada: Report* (Ottawa: Minister of Supply and Services, 1985) [*Fraser Report*].

17. For discussions of these reforms and the role of women's and anti-violence groups, see Elizabeth Sheehy, "Legal Responses to Violence against Women in Canada" (1999) 19 Canadian Woman Studies 62; and Sheila McIntyre, "Feminist Movement in Law: Beyond Privileged and Privileging Theory," in Radha Jhappan, ed., *Women's Legal Strategies in Canada* (Toronto: University of Toronto Press, 2002), 42 at 68–82.

18. Donna Denham and Joan Gillespie, *Two Steps Forward ... One Step Back. An Overview of Canadian Initiatives and Resources to End Woman Abuse, 1989–1997* (Ottawa: Minister of Public Works and Government Services, 1999) at 8–9.

19. Sandra Burt and Christine Mitchell, "What's in a Name? From Sheltering Women to Protecting Communities," in Leslie A. Pal, ed., *How Ottawa Spends 1998–99; Balancing Act: The Post-Deficit Mandate* (Toronto: Oxford University Press, 1998), 271.

20. Trevor Brown, Charging and Prosecution Policies in Cases of Spousal Assault: A Synthesis of Research, Academic and Judicial Responses (Ottawa: Department of Justice Research and Statistics Division, 2000) at iii.

21. See, for example, Jane Ursel, "The Winnipeg Family Violence Court," in Mariana Valverde, Linda MacLeod, and Kirsten Johnson, eds., Wife Assault and the Canadian Criminal Justice System Issues and Policies (Toronto: University of Toronto, 1995), at 169.

22. See Burt and Mitchell, supra note 19.

23. Andrea Levan, "Violence against Women," in Brodie, ed., supra note 14, 319 at 329.

24. Zoe Hilton, "One in Ten: The Struggle and Disempowerment of the Battered Women's Movement" (1989) 7 Canadian Journal of Family Law 313 at 332. See generally Lee Lakeman for Canadian Association of Sexual Assault Centres (CASAC), Canada's Promises to Keep: The Charter and Violence against Women (Vancouver: CASAC, 2004); and Levan, supra note 23.

25. Marina Morrow, Olena Hankovsky, and Colleen Varcoe, "Women and Violence: The Effects of Dismantling the Welfare State" (2004) 24(3) Critical Social Policy 358 at 361.

26. Lois Harder, *State of Struggle: Feminism and Politics in Alberta* (Edmonton: University of Alberta Press, 2003) at 128–9; and Mandy Bonisteel and Linda Green, "Implications of the Shrinking Space for Feminist Anti-Violence Advocacy (paper presented at the Canadian Social Welfare Policy conference, *Forging Social Futures*, in Fredericton, New Brunswick, 2005) [unpublished; copy on file with authors].

27. Wiegers and Douglas, *supra* note 5.

28. Burt and Mitchell, *supra* note 19 at 288. See also Linda MacLeod, *Desperately Seeking Certainty: Assessing and Reducing the Risk of Harm for Women Who Are Abused* (Edmonton: Alberta Advisory Council on Women's Issues, 1995), which is a report commissioned by the Alberta Advisory Council on Women's Issues in the wake of these budget cuts.

29. Morrow, Hankovsky and Varcoe, *supra* note 25 at 367 and 371. See also William Hurlburt and Walder White, *A Coherent and Principled Response to Family Violence in Alberta: Recommendations for Action and Change* (Edmonton: Alberta Children's Services, 2003), available at <http://www.familyviolenceroundtable.gov.ab.ca/pdf/hurlburt_white.pdf>, who conclude that "too many women have to be turned away by ... shelters, particularly in large urban centres"

(at 57). The Alberta Council of Women's Shelters reports annual statistics on the number of women and children turned away from shelters. See <http://www.acws.ca/questions/stats.php>. See also *Assessing Violence, supra* note 9 at 35, which notes that on 17 April 2000, 9 per cent of women and children seeking admission to shelters across Canada were turned away, mostly because the shelters were full.

30. Mary R. Hampton, "The Power of Policy: Anti-Violence Workers Speak Their Peace," in Mary Rucklos Hampton and Nikki Gerrard, eds., *Intimate Partner Violence: Reflections on Experience, Theory, and Policy* (Toronto: Cormorant Books and RESOLVE, 2006), 144 at 156; and Amy Stensrud, *Toward a Better Understanding of the Needs of Shelter Users: A Consultation with Shelter Residents and Workers* (Regina: Provincial Association of Transition Houses and Services of Saskatchewan, 2005) at 22 and 25.

31. Denham and Gillespie, *supra* note 18 at 23; Hampton, *supra* note 30 at 157; Harder, *supra* note 26 at 128–9 and 156; and Stensrud, *supra* note 30 at 13–31.

32. Janet Mosher, Patricia Evans, and Margaret Little, Walking on Eggshells: Abused Women's Experiences of Ontario's Welfare System: Final Report of Research Findings from the Woman and Abuse Welfare Research Project (2004), <http://dawn.thot.net/walking-on-egg-shells.htm>; and see Jennie Abell, Structural Adjustment and the New Poor Laws: Gender, Poverty and Violence and Canada's International Commitments (Ottawa: Canadian Feminist Alliance for International Action, 2001) [on file with the authors].

33. Morrow, Hankovsky, and Varcoe, supra note 25 at 366.

34. PAFVA, *supra* note 3; Domestic Violence and Stalking Act, S.M. 1998, c. 41; Victims of Family Violence Act, R.S.P.E.I. 2002, c. 45; Family Violence Prevention Act, R.S.Y. 2002, c. 84; Domestic Violence Intervention Act, S.N.S. 2001, c. 29; Protection against Family Violence Act, S.N.W.T. 2003, c. 24; and Family Violence Protection Act, S.N.L. 2005, c. F-3.1. Ontario's legislation, the Domestic Violence Protection Act, S.O. 2000, c. 33, has not yet been proclaimed. In Nunavut, the Family Abuse Intervention Act (S. Nu. 2006, c. 18) received assent on 5 December 2006.

35. Emily J. Sack, "Battered Women and the State: The Struggle for the Future of Domestic Violence Policy" (2004) 6 Wisconsin Law Review 1657 at 1667.

36. For example, women's groups were only one of a broader range of community groups with which the government consulted in Alberta. See, for example, Alberta Law Reform Institute, *Protection against Domestic Abuse* (Report No. 74) (Edmonton, AB: Alberta Law Reform Institute, 1997), at Appendix D; Alberta Justice, *Protection against Family Violence Act: Consultation Report* (Edmonton, AB: Alberta Justice, 1998) at Appendix 2. By contrast, in the United States, demands for civil protection orders arose from within the battered women's movement itself and such legislation was one of the earliest and most commonly used interventions in the context of domestic violence. See Sack, *supra* note 35.

37. Jan Turner, "Saskatchewan Responds to Family Violence: *The Victims of Domestic Violence Act, 1995*," in Valverde, MacLeod, and Johnson, eds., *supra* note 21, 183.

38. The extent to which the legislation and its implementation in fact achieve these objectives is discussed in Wiegers and Douglas, *supra* note 5.

39. Alberta, Legislative Assembly, *Hansard* (2 March 1998) at 609 (Burgener).

40. Alberta Justice, *supra* note 36 at 9.

41. Wiegers and Douglas *supra* note 5; and Leslie Tutty, Jennifer Koshan, Deborah Jesso, and Kendra Nixon, *"Alberta's Protection against Family Violence Act: A Summative Evaluation* (Calgary: RESOLVE Alberta, 2005) at 80–2.

42. For a review of these studies, see Tutty et al., *supra* note 41 at 27–8.

43. *Ibid.*

44. *Ibid.* at 25–8.

45. Dianne Martin and Janet Mosher, "Unkept Promises: Experiences of Immigrant Women with the Neo-Criminalization of Wife Abuse" (1995) 8(1) Canadian Journal of Women and the Law 3 at 36–7. For a recent review of studies looking at the deterrent effect of mandatory arrest and prosecution policies in the United States, see Evan Stark, "Reconsidering State Intervention in Domestic Violence Cases" (2006) 5(1) Social Policy and Society 149. Stark notes that overall, the studies are inconclusive with respect to whether mandatory arrest leads to recidivism. See also Donna Coker, "Crime Control and Feminist Law Reform in Domestic Violence Law: A Critical Review" (2000–1) 4 Buffalo Criminal Law Review at 801.

46. *Canadian Charter of Rights and Freedoms*, Part 1 of the *Constitution Act, 1982*, being Schedule B to the *Canada Act 1982* (U.K.), 1982, 1982, c. 11 [*Charter*].

47. *Constitution Act, 1867*, (U.K.), 30 & 31 Vict., c. 3, reprinted in R.S.C. 1985, App. II, No. 5.

48. See A.L.G.C. *v. Prince Edward Island*, [1998] 160 Nfld. & P.E.I.R. 151 (S.C. (T.D.)) (QL) [*A.L.G.C.*]; and *Baril v. Obelnicki*, [2004] 183 Man. R. (2d) 118 (Q.B.), rev'd 2007 M.B.C.A. 40 (C.A.) (QL) [*Baril*]. In *A.L.G.C.*, P.E.I.'s *Victims of Family Violence Act* was found to unjustifiably violate section 7 of the *Charter*

because the respondent was not provided adequate notice or opportunity to be heard during the review process of the emergency order. In *Baril*, Manitoba's *Domestic Violence and Stalking Prevention, Protection and Compensation Act*, C.C.S.M. c. D93, was found to violate the respondent's rights under section 2(b) and 7 of the *Charter*. The court of appeal held that the section 2(b) violation could be justified under section 1 of the *Charter* and that the act could be interpreted such that the liberty violation in section 7 was not contrary to the principles of fundamental justice. Section 12(2) of the act, which placed a reverse onus on respondents "to demonstrate, on a balance of probabilities, that the protection order should be set aside," was read down so as to impose an evidentiary rather than legal burden of proof on respondents (at para. 121). In both cases, the courts rejected arguments that civil legislation was in pith and substance within Parliament's exclusive jurisdiction over criminal law under section 91(27) of the *Constitution Act, 1867*, and that the legislation improperly gave justices of the peace (JP) powers that were normally exercised by superior court judges contrary to section 96 of the *Constitution Act, 1867*.

49. See Tutty et al., *supra* note 41 at 41–2, citing *Derrickson v. Derrickson*, [1986] 1 S.C.R. 285 and *Paul v. Paul*, [1986] 1 S.C.R. 306. The same conclusion was reached by Wendy Cornet and Allison Lendor, *Discussion Paper: Matrimonial Real Property on Reserve* (Ottawa: Ministry of Indian Affairs and Northern Development, 2002) at 39. Aboriginal band by-laws have been used in some jurisdictions to resolve property issues; see Karen Busby, Jennifer Koshan, and Wanda Wiegers, "Civil Domestic Violence Legislation in the Prairie Provinces: A Comparative Legal Analysis," in Jane Ursel, Leslie Tutty, and Janice LeMaitre, eds., *What's Law Got to Do with It? The Law, Specialized Courts and Domestic Violence in Canada* (Toronto: Cormorant Books) [forthcoming].

50. For a broader discussion of the ramifications for Aboriginal women of matrimonial property issues on reserves, see Cornet and Lendor, *supra* note 49; Mary Eberts and Beverley Jacobs, "Matrimonial Property on Reserve," in Marylea MacDonald and Michelle Owen, eds., *On Building Solutions for Women's Equality: Matrimonial Property on Reserve, Community Development and Advisory Councils* (Ottawa: Canadian Research Institute for the Advancement of Women, 2004); and Mary Ellen Turpel, "Home/Land" (1991) 10(1) Canadian Journal of Family Law 17.

51. Nicholas Bala and Erika Ringseis, *Review of Yukon's Family Violence Prevention Act* (Whitehorse: Victim Services Office, Department of Justice, 2002) at 28.

52. In Saskatchewan, 395 emergency intervention orders (EIOs) were requested and 331 issued in 1997 compared to 187 requested and 159 issued in 2002, a drop of 53 per cent in the number of applications. Wiegers and Douglas, *supra* note 5. In 2002, there were 18.24 applications per 100,000 population in Saskatchewan, compared to only 9.8 in Alberta, where there was a total of 296 applications, 187 of those in Edmonton. See Busby, Koshan, and Wiegers, *supra* note 49. Numbers have increased in Calgary and Edmonton over time but have decreased in smaller urban centres (Red Deer and Lethbridge). The number of applications by police has also decreased over time in Alberta, from 35.8 per cent in 2002 to 21.3 per cent in 2004. See Tutty et al., *supra* note 41 at 43 and 48–9.

53. Pat O'Malley, "Globalizing Risk? Distinguishing Styles of 'Neo-liberal' Criminal Justice in Australia and the USA" (2002) 2(2) Criminal Justice 205; and Lorna Erwin, "Neoconservatism and the Canadian Pro-family Movement" (1993) 30(3) Canadian Review of Sociology and Anthropology 401.

54. Elizabeth Comack and Gillian Balfour, *The Power to Criminalize: Violence, Inequality and the Law* (Halifax: Fernwood, 2004) at 43–4.

55. *Ibid.* at 43.

56. Cossman, *supra* note 6 at 179.

57. David Garland, *The Culture of Control: Crime and Social Order in Contemporary Society* (New York: Oxford University Press, 2001) at 156–7.

58. Garland, *supra* note 57 at 157; Comack and Balfour, *supra* note 54 at 41. See also Dianne Martin, "Both Pitied and Scorned: Child Prostitution in an Era of Privatization," in Cossman and Fudge, eds., *supra* note 6, 355 at 362.

59. Comack and Balfour, *supra* note 54 at 42.

60. Garland, *supra* note 57 at 99.

61. Nicholas Rose, "Government and Control," in David Garland and Richard Sparks, eds., *Criminology and Social Theory* (New York: Oxford University Press, 2000), 183 at 198–9. See also Garland, *supra* note 57 at 99.

62. Brodie, *supra* note 14, and see Fudge and Cossman, *supra* note 14 at 20–3.

63. Janine Brodie, *Politics on the Margins: Restructuring and the Canadian Women's Movement* (Halifax: Fernwood, 1995).

64. Nelson Wiseman, "Social Democracy in a Neo-Conservative Age: The Politics of Manitoba and Saskatchewan," in Hamish Telford and Harvey Lazar, eds., *Canada: The State of the Federation 2001: Canadian Political Culture(s) in Transition* (Montreal: McGill-Queen's University Press, 2002), at 217.

65. *Ibid.* at 234–5. For a more nuanced account of Alberta's political context and the role of feminist claims makers in challenging conservative policies from the 1970s to the 2000s, see Harder, *supra* note 26.

66. Cossman, *supra* note 6 at 172.

67. Designated agents are those who are empowered to make applications under the civil legislation. In Alberta, police and child welfare workers can do so. See *Protection against Family Violence Regulation*, Alta. Reg. 80/1999, s. 3. In Saskatchewan, police, program coordinators of victim assistance programs, Aboriginal community case workers, and mobile crisis workers are designated agents. See *Victims of Domestic Violence Regulations*, R.R.S. c. V-6.02 Reg. 1, s. 3. As we will discuss, however, police are by far the most active designated agents.

68. See *Protection of Children Involved in Prostitution Act*, R.S.A. 2000, c. P-28. Similar links could be drawn with anti-panhandling laws, secure care and "safe communities" legislation, which individualize and criminalize poverty and drug addiction. See, for example, *Safer Communities and Neighbourhoods Act*, S.S. 2004, c. S-0.1. In *Baril*, *supra* note 48, the Manitoba Court of Appeal explicitly refers to the *Domestic Violence and Stalking Act* as "quasi-criminal" legislation (at para. 113).

69. Steven Bittle, "From Villain to Victim: Secure Care and Young Women in Prostitution," in Gillian Balfour and Elizabeth Comack, eds., *Criminalizing Women: Gender and (In)justice in Neoliberal Times* (Halifax: Fernwood, 2006), 195 at 202. See also Martin, *supra* note 58 at 399.

70. Bittle, *supra* note 69 at 202–3 and 205; and Martin, *supra* note 58 at 355. See also Jennifer Koshan, "Alberta (Dis)Advantage: The *Protection of Children Involved in Prostitution Act* and the Equality Rights of Young Women" (2003) 2 Journal of Law and Equality 210.

71. Lise Gotell, "A Critical Look at State Discourse on 'Violence against Women': Some Implications for Feminist Politics and Women's Citizenship," in Manon Tremblay and Caroline Andrew, eds., *Women and Political Representation in Canada* (Ottawa: University of Ottawa Press, 1998), 39. Note that in practice, and in the legal forum particularly, it has never been easy for women to present as ideal victims, since deserving and undeserving victims have been differentiated by race, class, occupation, conduct, and dress.

72. Harder, *supra* note 26 at 129.

73. Lise Gotell, "The Discursive Disappearance of Sexualized Violence: Feminist Law Reform, Judicial Resistance and Neo-liberal Sexual Citizenship," in Dorothy E. Chunn, Susan B. Boyd, and Hester Lessard, eds., *Reaction and Resistance: Feminism, Law, and Social Change* (Vancouver: UBC Press, 2007), 127.

74. Legislative Assembly, *Debates and Proceedings* (Hansard), 10 March 1994 at 24 (Attorney General Robert Mitchell), <http://www.legassembly.sk.ca/Hansard/.>.

75. Alberta Law Reform Institute, *Domestic Abuse: Toward an Effective Legal Response* (Edmonton: ALRI, 1995) at 9–14 and 56.

76. Alberta Justice, *supra* note 36 at 9.

77. In 2002, 94 per cent of claimants in Alberta and 93.2 per cent of recipients in Saskatchewan were women. Further, 90 per cent of applications (Alberta) and 90 per cent of orders granted (Saskatchewan) were made in the context of intimate relationships. In Saskatchewan, these were all spousal relationships. In Alberta, orders were also applied for in the context of (ex)-dating relationships even though the legislation does not protect such relationships, (perhaps) suggesting that JPs and judges are extending the scope of the legislation themselves. See Wiegers and Douglas, *supra* note 5; and Tutty et al., *supra* note 41.

78. See generally Gotell, *supra* note 71.

79. Burt and Mitchell, *supra* note 19 at 287.

80. See note 12 in this article.

81. See, for example, Harder, *supra* note 26 at 157–8.

82. Levan, *supra* note 23 at 334.

83. Susan B. Boyd, "Backlash against Feminism: Canadian Custody and Access Reform Debates of the Late Twentieth Century" (2004) 16(2) Canadian Journal of Women and the Law 255; Susan B. Boyd and Claire F.L. Young, "Feminism, Father's Rights, and Family Catastrophes: Parliamentary Discourses on Post-Separation Parenting, 1966–2003," in Chunn, Boyd, and Lessard, eds., *supra* note 73, 198.

84. Denham and Gillespie, *supra* note 18 at 46.

85. Walter S. DeKeseredy and Martin D. Schwartz, "Backlash and Whiplash: A Critique of Statistics Canada's 1999 General Social Survey on Victimization" (2005), <http://sisyphe.org/article.php3?id_article=1689>. Sack, *supra* note 35, argues that critiques of legal reforms from within the feminist anti-violence movement in the United States have created space for such backlash.

86. See Chris Cobb, "Violence Brochures Discriminate against Men, Rights Body Rules: Victory for Gender Equality Group," *National Post* (19 June 2000) at A1, <http://www.fact.on.ca/news/news0006/np000619.htm>. DeKeseredy and Schwartz, *supra* note 85, argue that MERGE "[had] the support of several prominent conservative federal politicians" as well.

87. Bill Rafoss, *Review of the Application of the Victims of Domestic Violence Act* (Saskatoon: Saskatchewan Human Rights Commission, 2000) at 14 [on file with the authors].

88. Kevin O'Connor, "Commission Upholds Domestic Violence Act," *Star Phoenix* (5 May 2000) at A9.

89. Diana Ginn, "Wife Assault, the Justice System and Professional Responsibility" (1994–5) 33(4) Alberta Law Review 908; and Anne McGillivray and Brenda Comaskey, *Black Eyes All of the Time: Intimate Violence, Aboriginal Women, and the Justice System* (Toronto: University of Toronto Press, 1999) at 88. The marital rape exemption was finally abolished in 1983 in Canada.

90. Katherine Teghtsoonian, "Neo-Conservative Ideology and Opposition to Federal Regulation of Child Care Services in the United States and Canada" (1993) 26 Canadian Journal of Political Science 97 at 102–3; Harder *supra* note 26 at 156 and 158; and Erwin, *supra* note 53.

91. See Erwin, *supra* note 53 at 401 and 408–10.

92. Pamela Abbott and Claire Wallace, *The Family and the New Right* (Boulder, CO: Pluto Press, 1992) at 12, 72, and 139.

93. In the United States, neo-conservatives are currently advocating marriage as a way of decreasing family violence among cohabiting couples. See Walter S. DeKeserdy, Shahid Alvi, and Martin D. Schwartz, "An Economic Exclusion/Male Peer Support Model Looks at 'Wedfare' and Woman Abuse" (2006) 14 Critical Criminology 23.

94. While Alberta recently added stalking to its legislation, relief is similarly limited to incidents of stalking between family members, see *Protection against Family Violence Amendment Act, 2006*, S.A. 2006, c. 8, s. 4. In contrast, see Manitoba's *Domestic Violence and Stalking Act*, *supra* note 34, which covers dating relationships and stalking between strangers.

95. Cossman, *supra* note 6 at 173–4.

96. See Burt and Mitchell, *supra* note 19, for a discussion of the emergence of a focus on violence against children in federal policy. The increased attention directed towards children in federal policy discourse and orientation is also critically examined in Wanda Wiegers, *The Framing of Poverty as Child Poverty and Its Implications for Women* (Ottawa: Status of Women, 2002). Kendra Nixon argues that relatively little attention has been paid in Alberta to other forms of violence against women such as sexual assault, pornography, and prostitution. "Alberta's Policy Response to Violence against Women" (2005) at 8 [unpublished, on file with the authors].

97. Cossman, *supra* note 6 at 172–80.

98. *Ibid.* at 175.

99. Teghtsoonian, *supra* note 90 at 103.

100. Frances Olsen, "The Myth of State Intervention in the Family" (1985) 18 University of Michigan Journal of Law Reform 835.

101. *PAFVA*, *supra* note 3 at s. 4(2)(k). As a result of recent amendments, only respondents and children can now be ordered to undertake counselling. In Saskatchewan, counselling can only be recommended, not ordered, and only recommended with respect to respondents in the context of longer term orders. See *VDVA*, *supra* note 2 at s. 7(1)(i).

102. The *PAFVA*, *supra* note 3, was amended by the *Adult Interdependent Relationships Act*, S.A. 2002, c. A-4.5 in June 2003 and now includes same-sex intimate relationships. The refusal to protect same-sex relationships under the legislation initially coincided with the Alberta government's failure to recognize sexual orientation in its human rights legislation, even after being ordered by the Supreme Court of Canada to do so. See *Vriend v. Alberta*, [1998] 1 S.C.R. 493. Alberta's human rights legislation continues to omit reference to sexual orientation as a protected ground of discrimination. See *Human Rights, Citizenship and Multiculturalism Act*, R.S.A. 2000, c. H-14.

103. *PAFVA*, *supra* note 3 at s. 1(e)(iv).

104. *Ibid.* at s. 13.

105. However, the Alberta Law Reform Institute's final report also supported the prohibition against frivolous and vexatious complaints *Alberta Law Reform Institute*, *supra* note 36 at 89, and this feature appears in civil legislation in PEI (*supra* note 34 at s. 16(b)) and Nova Scotia (*supra* note 34 at s. 18(b)) as well.

106. See Gillian Anderson and Tom Langford, "Pro-family Organizations in Calgary, 1998: Beliefs, Interconnections and Allies" (2001) 38(1) Canadian Review of Sociology and Anthropology 37; and Erwin, *supra* note 53. One influential pro-family group, the Alberta Federation of Women United for Families, participated in the *PAFVA* consultation process, along with a victim's rights group (CAVEAT) and several men's rights groups (Family of Men Support Society, MERGE, Men's Education Network, Men's Transition Centre, and National Alliance for the Advancement of Non-Custodial Parents).

107. See *Protection against Family Violence Amendment Act*, *supra* note 94.

108. Alberta Ministry of Children's Services, "New Law Better Protects Victims of Family Violence" (30 October 2006), <http://www.child.gov.ab.ca/whatwedo/fvp/page.cfm?pg=What%20the%20government%20is%20doing%20to%20help>.

109. Comack and Balfour, *supra* note 54 at 43; Ken Hatt, Tullio Caputo, and Barbara Perry, "Criminal Justice Policy Under Mulroney, 1984–90: Neo-Conservatism, Eh?" (1992) 18(3) Canadian Public Policy 245 at 248. See also George Rigakos, "New Right, New Left, New Challenges: Understanding and Responding to Neoconservatism in Contemporary Criminology" (1996) 7(2) Critical Criminology 75 at 83–4.

110. Comack and Balfour, *supra* note 54 at 148; Martin and Mosher, *supra* note 45 at 15–16; and Dawn Currie, "Battered Women and the State: From the Failure of Theory to a Theory of Failure" (1990) 1(2) Journal of Human Justice 77 at 89.

111. Currie, *supra* note 110 at 84–5.

112. Janice L. Ristock, "And Justice for All? … The Social Context of Legal Responses to Abuse in Lesbian Relationships" (1994) 7(2) Canadian Journal of Women and the Law 415 at 429. See also Emma LaRocque, "Violence in the Aboriginal Communities," in Valverde, MacLeod, and Johnson, eds., *supra* note 21, 104 at 108–9; and McGillivray and Comaskey, *supra* note 89.

113. Currie, *supra* note 110 at 84–5, citing Linda MacLeod, *Wife Battering in Canada: The Vicious Circle* (Ottawa: Minister of Supply and Services, 1980); Dianne Martin, "Retribution Revisited: A Reconsideration of Feminist Criminal Law Reform Strategies" (1998) 36 Osgoode Hall Law Journal 151 at 167.

114. Comack and Balfour, *supra* note 54 at 43; and Martin, *supra* note 113 at 185.

115. Morrow, Hankovsky, and Varcoe, *supra* note 25 at 368.

116. Martin and Mosher, *supra* note 45 at 10, citing Maeve Doggett, *Marriage, Wife-Beating and the Law in Victorian England* (London: Weidenfeld and Nicholson, 1992).

117. Laureen Snider, "Feminism, Punishment and the Potential of Empowerment" (1994) 9 Canadian Journal of Law and Society 75. See also Comack and Balfour, *supra* note 54 at 171.

118. Martin and Mosher, *supra* note 45 at 40, citing Carol Smart, *Feminism and the Power of Law* (London: Routledge, 1989) at 5.

119. Martin, *supra* note 113; Currie, *supra* note 110; and Comack and Balfour, *supra* note 54 at 43. Comack and Balfour note that the term "zero tolerance" is itself a creature of the neo-conservative war on drugs during the Reagan administration in the 1980s (at 148).

120. Laureen Snider, "Making Change in Neo-Liberal Times," in Balfour and Comack, eds., *supra* note 69, 323 at 340.

121. *Ibid.* at 334; and Comack and Balfour, *supra* note 54 at 170–1.

122. Snider, *supra* note 120 at 334.

123. See, for example, Martin and Mosher, *supra* note 45 at 31. Snider, *supra* note 117 at 87, argues that "the one documented effect of imprisonment is to make those subject to it more resentful, more dangerous … and more misogynous."

124. Ellen Faulkner, "Lesbian Abuse: The Social and Legal Realities" (1991) 16 Queen's Law Journal 261 at 265; and Ristock, *supra* note 112 at 419 and 425.

125. Faulkner, *supra* note 124; and Ristock, *supra* note 112 at 425.

126. Jennifer Koshan, "Sounds of Silence: The Public/Private Dichotomy, Violence, and Aboriginal Women," in Susan B. Boyd, ed., *Challenging the Public/Private Divide: Feminism, Law, and Public Policy* (Toronto: University of Toronto Press, 1997), 87 at 96.

127. Martin and Mosher, *supra* note 45 at 21 and 27.

128. *Ibid.* at 21 and 26. See also Colleen Sheppard, "Women as Wives: Immigration Law and Domestic Violence" (2000) 26 Queen's Law Journal 1.

129. Martin and Mosher, *supra* note 45 at 21 and 25; and Koshan, *supra* note 126 at 99.

130. Martin and Mosher, *supra* note 45 at 28–30; and Koshan, *supra* note 126 at 98.

131. Snider, *supra* note 120 at 334.

132. See, for example, Hilton, *supra* note 24 at 330–2. See also Coker, *supra* note 45.

133. Martin and Mosher, *supra* note 45 at 32 and 34.

134. See, for example, Sharon McIvor and Teressa Nahanee, "Aboriginal Women: Invisible Victims of Violence," in Kevin Bonnycastle and George Rigakos, eds., *Unsettling Truths: Battered Women, Policy, Politics, and Contemporary Research in Canada* (Vancouver: Collective Press, 1998), 63 at 67; McGillivray and Comaskey, *supra* note 89; and LaRocque, *supra* note 112.

135. Ginn, *supra* note 89 at 912 and 914; Snider, *supra* note 117; and Martin and Mosher, *supra* note 45 at 34–40. Judicial attitudes are also seen to be a continuing problem, resulting in the stereotyping and re-victimization of women.

136. See Sack, *supra* note 35; *Assessing Violence*, *supra* note 9 at 20; and Jane Ursel, "Over Policed and Under Protected: A Question of Justice for Aboriginal Women," in Hampton and Gerrard, eds., *supra* note 30, 80 at 91–2.

137. This matter requires further research. Currently, court files do not record information that would allow claimants and respondents under the civil legislation to be identified on the basis of their race, sexual orientation, income levels, and so on. For a recommendation that this information be gathered, see Tutty et al., *supra* note 41 at 92.

138. In Saskatchewan, one key stakeholder could recall only a single case of mutual orders having been issued by different JPs, and none was identified as a result of rehearing processes in 2002. See Wiegers and Douglas, *supra* note 5. In 2002, only three mutual orders were made in Alberta, all resulting from cross-applications made by respondents at the time of re-hearing. See Tutty et al., *supra* note 41 at 50. The fact that rehearings are mandatory within seven days of the issuance of the emergency order does increase the potential for mutual orders in Alberta. See, for example, *T.L.O. v. K.J.S.*, 2004 A.B.Q.B. 691 and *N.M.R. v. R.D.S.*, 2002 A.B.Q.B. 257, which suggest that mutual orders will be issued where the respondent denies the alleged conduct at the rehearing. However, in 2002, respondents made cross applications in only 1.3 per cent of cases, and these were denied in five of the eight cases from 2002 to 2004. See Tutty et al., *supra* note 41 at 50. The relatively private nature of applications for civil orders (as compared to criminal proceedings) could also in theory relieve the fear of disclosure of sexual orientation and immigration/refugee status. However, the mandatory hearing in Alberta and the fact that rehearings can be initiated by respondents or ordered by judges in Saskatchewan likely offsets this potential advantage.

139. See Mark Drumbl, "Civil, Constitutional and Criminal Justice Responses to Female Partner Abuse: Proposals for Reform (1994) 12 Canadian Journal of Family Law 115 at 159, citing Linda MacLeod, *Battered But Not Beaten: Preventing Wife Battering in Canada* (Ottawa: Canadian Advisory Council on the Status of Women, 1987). In interviews in Saskatchewan of ten women who made claims under the *Victims of Domestic Violence Act*, there was not significant support for charging their (ex)-partners. See Wiegers and Douglas, *supra* note 5.

140. Turner, *supra* note 37 at 190.

141. See, for example, Martin and Mosher, *supra* note 45 at 5; Koshan, *supra* note 126 at 97–8; Joanne Minaker, "Evaluating Criminal Justice Responses to Intimate Abuse through the Lens of Women's Needs" (2001) 13(1) Canadian Journal of Women and the Law 74; but see McGillivray and Comaskey, *supra* note 89, and Ursel, *supra* note 136. Hampton's interviews with shelter workers from the prairie provinces indicate that "women no longer call the police. They don't want to call the police; they don't want the police involved because they know the police will charge." Hampton, *supra* note 30 at 148.

142. There are parallels here with the operation of crime compensation systems in relation to the criminal process. Crime compensation systems are also more accessible than alternative remedies in tort and can be accessed without the participation of the abusive partner. However, the claimant must typically establish that she reported the crime to the police within a reasonable period of time. See Wanda Wiegers, "Compensation for Wife Abuse: Empowering Victims?" (1994) 28 University of British Columbia Law Review 247 at 278–9; and see Saskatchewan Justice, Victims Services, "Compensation," <www.saskjustice.-gov.sk.ca/victimservices/programs/compensation.shtml>.

143. Turner, *supra* note 37 at 188.

144. Wiegers and Douglas, *supra* note 5 at 26–8. Mobile crisis workers and victim service coordinators are also designated agents but apply for orders much less often than police.

145. Tutty et al., *supra* note 41 at 48–9. From 2002 to 2004, police applied for roughly 60 per cent of emergency protection orders (EPOs) in small urban centres and towns, while they only applied for 10 per cent of EPOs in large urban centres in Alberta.

146. In Saskatchewan, criminal charges were laid in 26 per cent of all cases where an emergency intervention order (EIO) was issued in 2002 and in 35 per cent of such cases in 1997: Wiegers and Douglas, *supra* note 5 at 35. Reasons for not charging were given in only 35 per cent of cases where an EIO was issued but charges were not laid. The primary reasons provided for not laying charges were that the victim did not wish to proceed or the investigation was still pending (*ibid.* at 54). In Alberta from 2002 to 2004, charges were laid in only 14 per cent of cases where applications for EPOs were made. Tutty et al., *supra* note 41 at 47. Reasons for not charging were recorded on 68.6 per cent of case files, and included: the police were not called (27.2 per cent), no criminal offence occurred (25.3 per cent), the investigation was pending (14.1 per cent), there was insufficient evidence to lay charges (13.5 per cent), or the victim did not want charges laid (9.8 per cent) (*ibid.* at 48).

147. Child welfare reporting is also an obligation of shelter workers whenever women use their services and as such raises broader concerns about the impact of child welfare legislation in the context of intimate violence against women.

148. See Ursel, *supra* note 136 at 97–8, who notes that police are uniquely positioned and trained to provide protection in high-risk situations on short notice.

149. Wiegers and Douglas, *supra* note 5; and Tutty et al., *supra* note 41 at 84–5. This under-usage occurs in spite of explicit support on the part of Aboriginal women for the legislation during consultations in Saskatchewan. See Turner, *supra* note 37 at 196.

150. Tutty et al., *supra* note 41 at 83; and Wiegers and Douglas, *supra* note 5.

151. Tutty et al., *supra* note 41 at 55–6 and 83; and Wiegers and Douglas, *supra* note 5.

152. Tutty et al., *supra* note 41 at 59.

153. In Alberta, First Nations police officers are empowered to make applications, but it is unclear how often they do so. See *Protection against Family Violence Regulation*, *supra* note 67 at s. 1(2)(a)(iii). First Nation court workers are designated under the regulations in Saskatchewan but do not in practice apply for orders. See *Victims of Domestic Violence Regulations*, *supra* note 67. Applicants with legal counsel may apply by telephone in the Northwest Territories (*Protection against Family Violence Regulations*, R-013–2005, s. 3(1)) and Manitoba (*Domestic Violence and Stalking Act*, *supra* note 34 at s. 4(2)). In Nova Scotia, applications may be made by victim services officers and transition house workers. See *Domestic Violence Intervention Regulations*, N.S. Reg. 75/2003, s. 3. Interestingly, victims may apply by telephone themselves in Nova Scotia, Prince Edward Island, and the Yukon. See Tutty et al., *supra* note 41 at 37.

154. Turner, *supra* note 37 at 190.

155. See Busby, Koshan, and Wiegers, *supra* note 49.

156. Given institutional arrangements, there may be difficulties in providing an accessible separate channel for in-person civil relief in some centres in Saskatchewan, but these difficulties should not be seen as insurmountable.

157. South Africa includes such an obligation in its domestic violence legislation. For an analysis of this legislation, see Penelope Andrews, "Violence against Women in South Africa: The Role of Culture and the Limitations of the Law" (1998–9) 8 Temple Political and Civil Rights Law Review 425.

158. Tutty et al., *supra* note 41 at 95–6; and Wiegers and Douglas, *supra* note 5.

159. *Criminal Code*, R.S.C. 1985, c. C-46.

160. In Alberta and Saskatchewan, interviews with community stakeholders and victims suggest that breaches of emergency intervention and protection orders were often not taken seriously by respondents, police, or judges. See Tutty et al, *supra* note 41 at 74 and 86; and Wiegers and Douglas, *supra* note 5.

161. Only the Nova Scotia (s. 18) and Prince Edward Island (s. 16) statutes (*supra* note 34) create offences for breaches of civil orders, and in both provinces, the legislation specifically sets out police powers of arrest in the event of a breach. In Alberta, the Law Reform Institute recommended that breaches be prosecuted under section 127 of the *Criminal Code* rather than though the *PAFVA* itself, citing Saskatchewan's successful experience with this model as a factor. See Alberta Law Reform Institute, *supra* note 36 at 89–90.

162. See, for example, Tutty et al., *supra* note 41 at 95.

163. See, for example, Kelly Hannah-Moffat, "To Charge or Not to Charge: Front Line Officers' Perceptions of Mandatory Charge Policies," in Valverde, MacLeod, and Johnson, eds., *supra* note 21, 35 at 45; George Rigakos, "Situational Determinants of Police Responses to Civil and Criminal Injunctions for Battered Women" (1997) 3(2) Violence against Women 204 at 208. Interestingly, the research comes to different conclusions about the resistance of police officers to change. Hannah-Moffat found that young officers were most resistant, while Rigakos found resistance to be more entrenched in senior officers. See also Rigakos, "Constructing the Symbolic Complainant: Police Subculture and the Nonenforcement of Protection Orders for Battered Women" (1995) 10(3) Violence and Victims 227. For an argument that police should be subject to a statutory duty to issue and enforce civil orders, see Drumbl, *supra* note 139.

164. For a more detailed account of this critique in terms of Saskatchewan cases, see Wiegers and Douglas, *supra* note 5.

165. See, for example, *Bella v. Bella*, [1995] 55 A.C.W.S. (3d) 582 (Sask. Q.B.) (QL); and *Dyck v. Dyck*, [2005] 141 A.C.W.S. (3d) 273 at para. 4 (Sask. C.A.) (QL). This outcome may be facilitated by the exclusion of emotional or financial abuse in the definition of domestic violence in the Alberta and Saskatchewan legislation. These forms of abuse are included in the legislation in some other jurisdictions, including Manitoba and Prince Edward Island. See Tutty et al., *supra* note 41 at 30.

166. Colleen Varcoe and Lori G. Irwin, "'If I Killed You, I'd Get the Kids': Women's Survival and Protection Work with Child Custody and Access in the Context of Woman Abuse" (2004) 27(1) Qualitative Sociology 77 at 92.

167. See Jennifer L. Hardesty and Jacquelyn C. Campbell, "Safety Planning for Abused Women and Their Children," in Peter J. Jaffe, Linda L. Baker, and Alison J. Cunningham, eds., *Protecting Children from Domestic Violence: Strategies for Community Intervention* (New York: Guilford Press, 2004), 89 at 91. In the 2004 general survey,

34 per cent of all women in violent relationships indicated that violence increased in severity or frequency after separation (Mihorean, *supra* note 9 at 16). There is a strong and positive association between separation and lethal violence in particular. See Rosemary Gartner, Myrna Dawson, and Maria Crawford, "Confronting Violence in Women's Lives," in Bonnie J. Fox, ed., *Family Patterns, Gender Relations* (Don Mills, ON: Oxford University Press, 2001), 473.

168. See *Dolgopol v. Dolgopol*, [1995] 53 A.C.W.S. (3d) 581 (Sask. Q.B.) (QL), where the claimant applied after having spent four days in a shelter; and *T.P. v. J.P.*, (2005), A.B.Q.B. 529 at paras. 36–40 (QL), where Justice Veit disbelieved the claimant's allegations of physical injury because of lack of confirming evidence, the fact that the complainant had "slept in close proximity" to the respondent for three nights while she had tried unsuccessfully during the days to find a shelter bed, and the delay of one week in making an application, having been put up by social services in a hotel for the remainder of the week.

169. *T.L.O. v. K.J.S.*, *supra* note 138 at para. 40, but see, for a contrary ruling, *K.K.O. v. O.K.O.*, (2005), A.B.Q.B. 50 (QL).

170. *PAFVA*, *supra* note 3 at s. 5(c). These amendments were made following an evaluation report submitted by RESOLVE Alberta, one of several anti-violence research centres established by the federal government in the 1990s. See Tutty et al., *supra* note 41.

171. No-contact and non-attendance orders are available upon arrest and release provisions of the *Criminal Code* pending a trial on charges or a hearing for a peace bond under s. 810. These orders often provide the same *de facto* protection as an exclusive possession order under civil legislation.

172. Wiegers and Douglas, *supra* note 5. These types of orders are specifically authorized only in the case of non-emergency or victim's assistance orders.

173. Both the Alberta and Saskatchewan statutes permit JPs to make any orders they consider necessary to provide for the immediate protection of the victim and thus arguably include the power to recommend counselling at the emergency order stage. Some key informants have cited the lack of treatment and follow up for respondents in the civil process as a source of concern. See Wiegers and Douglas, *supra* note 5. If criminal charges are laid in conjunction with or instead of civil remedies, the offender may be ordered to undergo treatment, particularly if the charges are heard in a specialized domestic violence court.

174. No evidence of orders relating to personal property is recorded in the empirical review of EPO files, and no counselling orders were made by JPs and judges in the first instance. See Tutty et al., *supra* note 41 at 51. Exclusive possession was granted in 57 per cent of EPOs in Alberta in 2002, compared to 93 per cent of EIOs in Saskatchewan that same year (Busby, Koshan and Wiegers, *supra* note 49).

175. Wiegers and Douglas, *supra* note 5. Orders are longer on average in Alberta (90 to 365 days), but this is likely a result of the automatic review by the Court of Queen's Bench. See Tutty et al., *supra* note 41 at 52.

176. Tutty et al., *supra* note 41 at 95–6.

177. Carol Smart, *Feminism and the Power of Law* (London: Routledge, 1989) at 145. See also Kathryn McCann, "Battered Women and the Law: The Limits of the Legislation," in Julia Brophy and Carol Smart, eds., *Women in Law: Explorations in Law, Family and Sexuality* (Boston: Routledge and Kegan Paul, 1985) 71, for an early analysis of the effects of civil domestic violence legislation in England.

178. Smart, *supra* note 177 at 144.

179. See Currie, *supra* note 110, who argues that the state often creates new institutions at the expense of more power in the hands of marginalized groups themselves. See also Coker, *supra* note 45 at 859, who has advocated for citizen review panels to monitor the police response to violence.

Part Four

Future Directions in Law and Society

We began this book by noting that legal conflict and legal debates have become increasingly common in contemporary Canadian society. The chapters included represent some of the most important examples of current debates occupying the attention of Canadian academics, politicians, and the media. Limitations of space made it impossible to include other important topics facing Canadian society, and we were forced to exclude many excellent articles and several important topics. In this concluding part, we highlight three topics that we feel will become increasingly important to the law and society field in Canada. This part opens with a chapter about homophobic bullying in schools that is not adequately challenged by teachers and school officials and closes with a chapter on environmental law. The middle chapter focuses on legislation aimed at anti-terrorism initiatives. Each of these chapters represents broader issues related to law and society in the Canadian context.

Canadian attitudes toward many once-revered moral values are changing rapidly because of several interrelated factors. The decline in the influence of religion as the primary moral order, combined with an increase in libertarian attitudes on both the left and the right, has led many Canadians to question long-held beliefs about right and wrong. From a left-wing perspective, these moral shifts can be seen in the growing acceptance of many previously disparaged moral choices, including same-sex relationships, abortion, and even euthanasia. However, there is evidence of growing pockets of intolerance that serve as reminders that the path to an equitable society does not always proceed smoothly. Haskell and Burtch's chapter on homophobic and transphobic bullying in schools serves as one example of this intolerance as well as counterexamples where antibullying measures take root. Clearly, the left needs to plan its strategies carefully in order to deal effectively with these residual elements.

On the other side of the spectrum, the right-wing shift in moral values is evidenced by the increasing public resentment toward beneficiaries of Canada's welfare state and a retreat from Canadians' traditional tolerance of official policies of bilingualism and multiculturalism. The tendency toward neo-liberal state policies has profound implications for "workers' safety provisions and environmental protection," a theme developed in David Boyd's analysis of environmental and public safety issues in Canada. Although seemingly contradictory, both of these shifts are consistent with the broad libertarian approach to individualism, in which individual autonomy is accepted as long as it does not impinge on the rights of others. Libertarians view welfare programs as infringements of the rights of taxpayers, who have to pay for the programs but who may not benefit directly from them. Such thinking has also changed the political landscape, as political parties attempt to capitalize on the growing distrust of big government and have begun to rethink the laws and social policies that have been considered an indispensable part of the Canadian social fabric.

The chapters in this part help to define new directions in law and society studies, relying on new theoretical and methodological approaches while exploring old, unsettled questions of law, social inequality, and social change. We can see a reflection of social values and conflicts in legal institutions and legal battles, including longstanding concerns over exclusion of certain groups through law and social conventions, and the difficult process of including more groups and individuals within the legal framework. We hope that these chapters, and discussions that accompany your reading of them, will prompt new ways of thinking and acting on the much-contested and elusive ideal of social justice.

Chapter Thirteen

"Teachers Don't Hear the Word 'Fag'": Homophobia and Transphobia in Canadian Schools

Rebecca Haskell and Brian Burtch

Editors' Note: Schools are places where youth acquire a formal education along with informal lessons through everyday interactions. The school curriculum and extracurricular events, such as clubs, athletics, and informal socializing, often promote certain values at the expense of others, leaving little room for alternative ideologies or identities that challenge mainstream gender and sexual norms. Drawing on a research study of 16 lesbian, gay, bisexual, trans, two-spirit,[1] and queer (LGBTTQ) youth who recently left B.C. high schools, the authors document how school curriculum can promote homophobic and transphobic harassment, and silence many queer youth. Implications of this silence are discussed, using Pierre Bourdieu's concept of symbolic violence. Drawing on changing legislation in Canada and on key legal cases related to sexual orientation, the authors review ways in which official and peer responses to homophobia or transphobia (HTP) in schools could advance social justice and human rights. This exploratory research might help to open the classroom closet, providing information and promoting discussion about homophobia and transphobia in Canadian high schools.

INTRODUCTION

... the reason why it happens in schools is because ... the administration and instructors in a lot of schools ... are kind of blind to it. [Teachers] don't hear the word 'fag' ... it's like they're in another world ... they choose to turn a blind eye to it basically, which just encourages the same behaviour to happen again and again.... (Participant 8).

The relationships I cultivated in high school were tenuous at best ... while I was outwardly surrounded by friends and acquaintances, I couldn't help feeling lonely. Despite the progress I had made, not much had changed since elementary school. But one thing had changed. The journey, even though not yet finished, had armed me with tools I would later use to defend myself (Stanton, 2006, p. 116).

Researchers and activists have become more interested in how individuals with alternative sexual and gender identities or expressions come to be seen as deviant by others and, sometimes, by themselves. This process can involve living in an oppressive high school environment and possibly incorporating oppression, even others' hatred, as a form of self-hatred, sometimes called "internalized oppression" (Burtch, 2007). We were aware of various research projects at Simon Fraser University (SFU) that explored abuses of power against sexual minorities, especially gay bashing (Samis, 1995; Janoff, 2005). Our concern centred on instances of homophobic behaviour in high schools as well as on antibullying initiatives and the wider legal framework involving

Source: Rebecca Haskell and Brian Burtch, *"Teachers Don't Hear the Word 'Fag'": Homophobia and Transphobia in Canadian Schools*. Reprinted by permission of the authors.

legislation, the courts, and human rights tribunals. Our work is part of ongoing efforts to study how we learn acceptable expressions of sexuality or gender, particularly through formal educational experiences. Here, we focus on bullying[2] motivated by homophobia[3] or transphobia[4] (HTP) after becoming more aware of the prevalence of such behaviours, particularly in high schools, and the difficulties in developing a practical means to address them.

The rights of gays and lesbians have been increasingly recognized in the past few decades. Beginning in the 1980s, provinces in Canada began to include, or read, sexual orientation into their human rights codes. In 2005 Canada became the fourth country to legalize same-sex marriage, joining the Netherlands, Belgium, and Spain. More recently, South Africa, Norway and Sweden have legalized same-sex marriage and several American States allow for such marriages (Stritf and Stritf, 2009; www.samesexmarriage.ca). Despite this progressive legislation, a number of queer youth are still unable to safely hold hands with their partners while in or around their high schools. In fact, while we were completing this chapter, the lead story in a Vancouver paper, *XTRA! WEST*, focused on an alleged assault on two gay men holding hands in Vancouver (Perelle, 2009). Douglas Sanders (2006, 2007) contends that even as gains are made in terms of formal equality in Canada, issues of "social inclusion" remain.

Considering the multicultural climate of Canada, it is also wise to consider how lesbian, gay, bisexual, trans, two-spirit, and queer (LGBTTQ) people are viewed around the world. Canada is home to people of various nationalities and cultures, who hold varied beliefs and values. According to Citizenship and Immigration of Canada (2007), more permanent residents, temporary foreign workers, and foreign students entered Canada in 2007 than ever before. Some immigrants travel from countries where same-sex sexual behaviours are against the law. As such, being outed or coming out can be truly dangerous (see Scagliotti, 2003). One commentator cautions that we are far from a Golden Age of tolerance for alternative forms of sexual expression:

> … the twentieth century was … the most violently homophobic period in history: deportation to concentration camps under the Nazi regime, gulags in the Soviet Union, and blackmail and persecution in the United States during the Joseph McCarthy anti-communist era. For some, particularly in the western world, much of this seems very much part of the past. But … [h]omosexuality seems to be discriminated against everywhere: in at least seventy nations, homosexual acts are still illegal (e.g. Algeria, Cameroon, Ethiopia, Kuwait, Lebanon, and Senegal) and in a good many of these, punishment can last more than ten years (India, Jamaica, Libya, Malaysia, Nigeria, and Syria). Sometimes the law dictates life imprisonment (Guyana and Uganda), and, in a dozen or so nations, the death penalty may be applied (Iran, Mauritania, Saudi Arabia, and Sudan). (Tin, 2008, p. 11)

In a recent article, Bryers (2008) noted that two Iranians were executed in 2007 for homosexuality. Clearly, the conditions Tin speaks of are not merely remnants of unenforced laws that have yet to be repealed.

Trans people worldwide face even greater discrimination. Many assume that rights and protections awarded to gays, lesbians, and bisexuals are automatically extended to trans people as well. Some trans people identify with a LGBQ sexuality and are legally protected from discrimination based on sexual orientation; however, gender identity itself is not included in our federal Human Rights legislation. In fact, the Northwest Territories is the only region in Canada with legislation against discrimination based on gender identity, although some jurisdictions allow complaints under the general "gender" or "sex" category of human rights codes (Luhtanen, 2005). Aside from legal protections, schools seem like a logical starting place to educate people about the natural occurrence of homosexuality and gender variance in our society. To date, school administrators and officials seem to balk at such suggestions. Why is this so?

The exploratory study outlined in this paper was designed to explore this question. We conducted focus groups and interviews with 16 young LGBTTQ people who experienced homophobic and/or transphobic (HTP) bullying while in a British Columbia (B.C.) high school. Here, we focus on a key theme: the deep silence about homosexuality and gender variance in schools, a silence that our sample believed contributed to the homophobia and transphobia they experienced.

BACKGROUND AND LITERATURE REVIEW

Many people assume that high schools comprise students who are heterosexual and who readily fit into the dichotomy of male or female. Although these assumptions prevail, they have been challenged. In B.C., several Human Rights Tribunal decisions have held members of school boards and public servants in the Ministry of Education responsible for providing an educational environment that reflects and respects the diversity of the Canadian population.

In 1997, the most publicized queer "book banning" in a Canadian school occurred in Surrey, B.C. (Warner, 2002, p. 339). James Chamberlain, an elementary schoolteacher, requested permission from the Surrey School District 36 to use three books depicting same-sex families to teach his kindergarten and grade one students about diversity and tolerance. Under pressure from parents and various groups, school board members refused this request, instigating a lengthy Human Rights complaint that culminated at the Supreme Court of Canada. There, all but two judges found the book banning "unreasonable" and directed the members of the school board to reconsider their decision to ban the books, taking into consideration the guiding principles of "tolerance and non-sectarianism underlying the *School Act*, R.S.B.C. 1996, c. 412" (*Pegura et al. v. School District No. 36*, 2003, ¶3).

In 1999, Peter and Murray Corren filed a complaint with the British Columbia Human Rights Tribunal (BCHRT), accusing the Ministry of Education of systemic discrimination against "non-heterosexual students and their parents." They claimed that same-sex parents, sexual orientation, and gender identity were excluded from the curriculum (*Corren and Corren v. B.C.*, 2005, p. 2). The Correns argued that the silence surrounding same-sex relationships in the curriculum bred an atmosphere of ignorance and intolerance toward sexual minorities ("School system accused," 2005) and that schools were ill-equipped to deal with the homophobic and transphobic bullying that results from such oversights (*Corren and Corren v. B.C.*, 2005, p. 2).

Before the 2006 trial began, the Correns reached an agreement (often called "the Corren agreement") with the provincial government whereby authorities agreed to review the current curriculum for inclusiveness. The agreement also gave the couple an "unprecedented right to have direct input into the content of the whole of the British Columbia school curriculum so as to make it more inclusive of and responsive to the queer community and its history and culture" (Murray and Peter Corren Foundation, n.d., n.p.). Following up on the agreement, in June 2006 the B.C. Attorney General announced an elective course for grade 12 students focusing on social justice issues, including sexual orientation. Three years later, controversy about "Social Justice 12" persists as at least one district has opted not to offer the course in its schools and representatives of various faith communities find fault with the Corren agreement.

Concerns about homophobic bullying in school came to the forefront in 2003, when Azmi Jubran placed a complaint with the Human Rights Commission in British Columbia. Jubran was subjected to constant taunting and bullying behaviours throughout his time in a North Vancouver high school, including being called a "fag." In a decision that eventually went to the Supreme Court of B.C., Justice Stewart found that the homophobic harassment was harmful and violated the *Charter* because it was directed at someone perceived to be gay (Jubran did not identify as gay) (GALE BC, n.d.). Justice Stewart found that Jubran's dignity and full participation in school were denied, and he placed blame on the North Vancouver school board for the discrimination through its failure to provide a harassment-free environment. This landmark case sent a strong message to educational administrators that merely reprimanding students for discriminatory actions was inadequate. Justice Stewart demanded that the school board provide a clear statement of conduct regarding homophobic bullying and ensure that it be communicated to all students. He also ruled that school staff should be provided with appropriate training and resources to prevent discrimination and harassment from occurring (The Continuing Legal Education Society of British Columbia, 2005).

These court and tribunal decisions illustrate a growing concern on behalf of LGBTTQ advocates and judiciaries to promote inclusiveness of, respect for, and safety of queer people in schools. These examples also illustrate the increasing recognition of the legal, and perhaps moral, responsibility of school officials to address homophobic and transphobic harassment in schools. Legal and financial ramifications provide school administrators with an impetus to at least appear as though they are taking action, even if many of their constituents disagree with anti-homophobia and anti-transphobia efforts. Recently, there have been several initiatives in Canadian educational systems to provide a safer environment for queer youth, and many of these have been in B.C.

In 2003, the British Columbia Safe School Task Force released a report regarding bullying, harassment, and intimidation in schools. In the report, bullying based on one's sexual orientation—or perceived sexual orientation—was recognized as a significant problem in British Columbia schools. The task force urged school board officials to adopt policies and programs congruent with "values and categories" detailed in the B.C. *Human Rights Code* and the *Charter of Rights and Freedoms* (Mayencourt, Locke, & McMahon, 2003).

Sexual orientation and gender identity do not explicitly appear in the *Charter of Rights and Freedoms*. Nevertheless, in the 1995 case of *Egan and Nesbit v Canada*, a judge decided that sexual orientation was an "analogous ground to other characteristics of persons" covered in s. 15 (Grace, 2005, n.p.). In other words, sexual orientation and, arguably, gender identity should be read into the existing legislation. In addition, the B.C. *Human Rights Code* specifically outlines the rights to protections against discrimination that should be afforded to sexual minorities (*Human Rights Code*, 1996). Since the "Safe School" report, school boards in the Southeast Kootenays, and in Victoria, Vancouver, the Gulf Islands, North Vancouver, Prince Rupert, and Revelstoke have adopted policies that prohibit discrimination on the basis of sexual orientation or gender identity (GALE BC, n.d.). These policies, however, have been adopted despite a lack of research on homophobia and transphobia in Canadian high schools.

While research and literature on homosexuality has grown in the past 50 years, research documenting the lives of queer youth has only become more common in the past two decades. In 2008, advocates with Egale Canada, a national organization promoting the rights of LGBTTQ people and their families (www.egale.ca), along with Dr. Catherine Taylor at the University of Winnipeg launched the first National Climate Survey on homophobia in Canadian high schools (see www.climatesurvey.ca). With a total sample of 1200 youth thus far, results from the first phase of the Egale study show that over two-thirds of queer youth feel unsafe in their schools, compared to one in five straight students who reported similar feelings (Egale Canada, 2008). Almost half of queer youth in that sample reported having been verbally harassed because of their sexual orientation; over one-quarter had been physically assaulted (Egale Canada, 2008).

Regionally, a small amount of quantitative data has been generated. Researchers at the University of British Columbia have published results from a study looking at experiences of lesbian, gay, bisexual, and questioning (or unsure) youth in 18 B.C. high schools. Lesbian and gay youth reported significantly higher levels of verbal, physical, and social harassment than did their heterosexual peers (Darwich, 2008). The McCreary Centre Society in B.C. has published several studies on queer, high school–aged youth. In the most recent B.C. Adolescent Health Survey, over 60 percent of high school–aged youth who identified as gay or lesbian reported verbal harassment from their peers and more than half experienced purposeful exclusion (Saewyc et al., 2007). Similarly, in his pioneering exploration of the extent and nature of anti-lesbian/gay violence in the Greater Vancouver area, Samis found that 61 percent of the 327 queer people who responded to the specific question pertaining to verbal harassment said they had experienced homophobic slurs while at school (Samis, 1995, p. 80).

In Saskatchewan, Cochrane and Morrison (2008) found that 52 percent of the 54 high school–aged youth in their sample reported frequently hearing words like *fag*, *dyke*, *homo*, or *lezzie* in their schools. In Ontario-based studies of young gay men (Smith, 1998) and lesbians (Khayatt, 1994), participants reported that homophobic speech was a common occurrence in their high schools. Smith (1998, p. 320) reported that a number of gay, male youth frequently encountered homophobic graffiti, such as "kill the faggot." Arsenault (2000) reported that the three lesbians she spoke with in Nova Scotia believed they had to make themselves invisible to ensure their safety. In that study, Arsenault (2000, p. 1) asserted, "… silence has surrounded the experiences of lesbians in the public school system. The presence of homophobia and heterosexism in this system has strengthened the silence, rendering lesbians invisible." In the U.S., participants in the Gay, Lesbian, and Straight Education Network (GLSEN) produce reports documenting the experiences of students from grades kindergarten to 12. In the most recent study, researchers found that 9 out of 10 youth reported hearing *gay* used in a negative context and that the majority of them said that they were bothered by such use (Kosciw, Diaz, & Greytak, 2008).

As Smith (1998, p. 320) asserts, the "logical conclusion" of more subtle forms of antigay abuse is violence, and research indicates that physical forms of homophobic harassment persist. Compared to their heterosexual counterparts, twice as many bisexual males (13 percent vs. 28 percent) and four times as many bisexual females and lesbians (5 percent vs. 20 percent and 19 percent, respectively) in the latest McCreary Centre sample said that peers at school had physically assaulted them in the year preceding the survey (Saewyc et al., 2007). Also in Canada, Samis (1995) found that approximately 20 percent of the lesbians and gay men in his sample were physically attacked at school (22.4 percent of 303 respondents).

Perhaps because of Canada's reputation for tolerance or simply because of a lack of research in the area here, studies conducted in the U.S. indicate that physical forms of high school bullying motivated by gender or sexual identity are more prevalent than levels reported by Canadian researchers. In their nationwide U.S. study for GLSEN, Kosciw, Diaz, and Greytak (2008, p. 20) found that almost half of the youth in their sample were physically harassed (pushed or shoved) due to their sexual orientation and that 22 percent were punched, kicked, or injured with a weapon. It is no wonder, then, that more than 60 percent of the youth in their sample felt unsafe at school because of their sexual orientation (Kosciw, Diaz, & Greytak, 2008, p. 25).

While there have been a number of quantitative studies dedicated to homophobic bullying in schools, very little qualitative research has been dedicated to understanding the effects that homophobic or transphobic harassment has on students, especially in a Canadian context. Moreover, only recently have protective factors been examined (Darwich, 2008). The literature that we have, then, provides a heartbreaking glimpse at the negative outcomes of some youth who fail to pass.[5]

Due to the pervasiveness of homophobia and transphobia, many youth internalize negative attitudes toward gay men, lesbians, bisexuals, two-spirit, and transgender individuals before they begin to appreciate their own sexuality. This internalization can gravely affect their self-worth. Flowers and Buston (2001) claim that most adolescents who are minorities (for example, ethnic minorities) can reduce distress through support from their families and peers. The minority status of LGBTTQ youth is not so obvious and is often not shared with family or friends. In fact, queer youth who choose to identify themselves as LGBTTQ may be shunned by the people closest to them. Consequently, youth harassed because of their real or perceived sexual identities frequently remain silent, failing to report the harassment they experience and its effects.

Dorias and Lajeunesse (2004, p. 87) contend that some LGBTTQ youth who have strong social support and who are "inclined to challenge the established social order and related beliefs may find the motivation to fight when faced with discriminations and related injustices." Bullied youth, however, are more likely to socially withdraw and report feelings of isolation (Bochenek & Widney, 2001). In addition, feeling unsafe in their school environment leads some queer youth to perform poorly academically and sometimes to stop attending school activities (Bochenek & Widney, 2001). In 2008, GLSEN reported that more than 30 percent of the queer youth they surveyed had skipped school in the prior month because they felt unsafe in the school environment compared to only 5 percent of heterosexual youth (Kosciw et al., 2008, p. 26). Negative effects, like poor academic performance, can worsen the already stigmatized identities of LGBTTQ youth and increase the likelihood that they will suffer from depression and low self-esteem (Sawyc et al., 2007; Wyss, 2004).

Queer youth adopt various means of dealing with insecurities brought on by experiencing HTP. They may engage in a number of harmful and risk-taking behaviours, including substance abuse,[6] (Buston & Hart, 2001; Henning-Stout et al., 2000) and unsafe sexual practices that lead to sexually transmitted infections (STIs), including the human immunodeficiency virus (HIV) and acquired immune deficiency syndrome (AIDS) (Healthy People, 2001; Bochenek & Widney, 2001). Other consequences of HTP harassment may include denial of one's sexual identity, and contempt for other minorities (including other LGBTTQ individuals) and for oneself.

DiPlacido (1998, p. 147) says that many queer youth internalize negative messages about queer people and, once they realize they differ from social norms, internalize HTP. Internalized homophobia and transphobia, DiPlacido (1998, p. 147) argues, "can range from self-doubt to overt self-hatred" and can lead to depression, self-mutilation, eating disorders, and attempts at taking one's own life (see Dorais & Lajeunesse, 2004, for a synopsis of existing literature on young gay men and suicide). Given the shame and silence that have often accompanied transgressive sexualities, it is not surprising that many outings of queer youths have resulted in their being outcast and have even led to a number of suicides, as with the 1920 investigation into alleged homosexual activities at Harvard University (Wright, 2005).

Suicide is the second leading cause of death among young people in Canada (Saewyc et al., 2007), and queer youth are overrepresented among those who attempt to and those who successfully take their own lives. In a recent province-wide study in B.C., Saewyc et al. (2007, p. 31) reported that LGB youth in their sample were "significantly more likely to report suicidal thoughts in the past year compared to heterosexual peers." Queer youth in that sample attempted suicide at a rate of up to five times as often as heterosexual youth (Saewyc et al., 2007). In an earlier study, researchers at The McCreary Centre Society found that nearly half of the 77 lesbian and gay youth they surveyed in B.C. had attempted suicide, with the average age of attempt being 13 (The McCreary Centre Society, 1999). Media reports and academic discussions of the suicides of Jamie Lazarre, an 18-year-old student from Prince George, and Hamed Nastoh, a 14-year-old grade 8 student in Surrey, depict homophobic bullying as influential in their decisions to end their lives.

Some researchers have found, however, that youth who have social support are significantly less likely to think about suicide (Rutter, 2007), echoing an assertion made by Durkheim more than a century ago. In his groundbreaking book, first published in 1897, Durkheim (1951) found that people who were not well integrated into society were at a higher risk of suicide than those who had support and guidance. Thus, in regard to queer youth who are *not* supported, O'Connor declares the following:

> The voices of [LGBTTQ] adolescents may have been silenced, but these youth are screaming out in other ways to be heard, notably through suicide. It is a situation that cannot be tolerated, and it is time to open the door to the "classroom closet" and begin to debate in earnest. (O'Connor, 1995, p. 8)

RESEARCH METHODS

We spoke with queer youth—19 years of age and older, who had left high school in the past five years—about their retrospective experiences with harassment based on sexual or gender identity in the school setting.[7] Discussions were held in groups so participants could compare and contrast experiences with HTP. GLBTTQ volunteers were recruited and selected using purposive sampling. Advertisements were posted in spaces established for queer individuals in the Greater Vancouver Area, at drop-in centres, and online. Additionally, handbills were handed out at the 2007 Vancouver Pride Festival.[8] In total, we spoke with 16 LGBTTQ youth about their experiences with homophobia and transphobia in high schools. Table 13.1 displays the gender identity and sexual orientation of each of the participants.

We developed open-ended questions to explore contextual factors of HTP (i.e., types of bullying, frequency, who is involved, location) and the effects the harassment had on the participants. Participants were asked to hypothesize about possible causes of homophobic and transphobic bullying and to suggest ways to prevent incidents motivated by these phobias from happening in high school. We also asked volunteers to share *positive* experiences. Participants were given the opportunity to share information privately through follow-up questionnaires. After transcription of the taped discussions, The Research Ethics Board at Simon Fraser University approved the research and deemed it to be "minimal risk."

Table 13.1: Demographics of Participants (N=16)

Gender Identity	
Female	3
Male	8
Gay/Androgynous	3
Left Blank	2
Sexual Orientation	
Queer/Lesbian, Queer/Gay, Queer, Pansexual	6
Gay	7
Bisexual	2
Left Blank	1

FINDINGS

After discussing which forms of homophobia and transphobia were most frequently experienced by our volunteers and how they were affected by them, we now relay participants' beliefs why HTP persists in Canadian high schools.

Subtle Messages: Forms of Homophobia and Transphobia

Walton (2006, p. 17) likens discourse around bullying, including media reports, to Foucault's (1977) "society of the spectacle," in which sensational and violent incidents appear normative. While this may be true of the discourse, it is not the case for the bullying behaviours themselves. For study members, physical violence was one of the *least* frequent forms of HTP they encountered. Homophobic and transphobic name-calling, avoidance, exclusion, and heterosexist or gender-limiting environments were more common than physical forms of harassment. The potential for costly legal battles along with pressure from child advocates and queer activists have created an impetus to curb physical abuse in schools. School board officials have developed policies, and teachers have begun to intervene in situations where physical harm is a possibility. According to participants, then, students most often engage in HTP bullying tactics that are least likely to draw the fire of school administrators. For example, one participant said this:

> … *high school for me wasn't really typified by bullying really. I mean although I was bullied on some occasions because people perceived that I was queer it wasn't like really severe, you know, beatings or like that kind of thing. (P1, queer/gay, queer)*

The focus groups challenged participants to think about how they defined bullying, especially as more subtle experiences with homophobia and transphobia emerged. For instance, P2 said the following:

> *Now that I think about it … I just think there were small little things, like we tried to set up a GSA [Gay Straight Alliance] and we put posters around, and like a week later people had tore them down and we had to put them back up. Or like writing over what we wrote and then we had to take them down and put up new ones. (P3, gay, gay)*

In general, the youth were eventually able to express how nonphysically violent forms of harassment affected them; however, their narratives illustrate that students and teachers may tacitly accept these forms because of perceptions that subtle forms of HTP are "not that bad." Given the tendency of school administrators, academics, and the media to focus on spectacular forms of bullying at the expense of subtle, there is a danger that we may assume that homophobic and transphobic bullying in schools is a nonissue. According to the participants, HTP harassment persists in more subtle yet effective ways.

Silencing Homosexualities: The Effects of HTP on Youth in High School

Participants identified *gender variance*[9] as a precipitating factor that often resulted in homophobic and transphobic accusations and accosting, and other researchers have drawn similar conclusions (Mahan et al., 2006). In our study, youth believed that even subtle forms of HTP induce students to regulate their gender expressions so they will not be perceived as queer and consequently "picked on" (a term most participants used). One person believed that what some saw as a too-masculine appearance triggered insults like "lezbo." To avoid HTP harassment, P1 said they were self-conscious of their appearance and the signals they gave off:

> … *it was terrible because … whenever I saw something I wanted to wear I had to interrogate myself and I'd be like "Why do you want to wear this?" You know? Or like "What will people think if you wear this?" I remember buying a pair of shoes, and we got them home and I had to take them back because I was like, "Oh my god!" you know, this is like … [signal of sexuality/gender identity] and they were just, they were shoes right? And they weren't like big … dykey motorcycle boots [laughs] or anything. (P1, queer, queer)*

P2, on the other hand, said he had to be careful about how he spoke because of the tendency for people to associate soft or higher-pitched voices with effeminacy and, consequently, homosexuality. He spoke candidly of how this affected him:

> … *that was really tough for me. And overcoming that was tough because it's almost like it was silencing 'cause I didn't want to say anything. 'Cause people would try and identify [his sexuality] just the way I spoke. So … it's taken me a long time, even public speaking or anything like that just from that, from those incidents, so … That sucked. (P2, gay, male)*

Participant 6 may not have been silenced entirely but she described "hiding" to avoid encounters with HTP harassment:

> *By the end [of high school] I just kind of hid. I was just like "I don't want to deal with it." So I just stayed in my drama room. (P6, lesbian/queer, female)*

Participant 5, whose story was especially moving, expressed how queer youth may be doubly silenced by HTP bullying. To avoid being identified as LGBTTQ and subjected to HTP harassment, queer high school students may become introverted, silent, and uninvolved in their schools. Silenced, or "closeted," often these queer youth are unable to confide in others about the negative effects of HTP. P5, whose high school girlfriend committed suicide, was unable to turn to others for support because they were "in the closet" at that time. Asked what experiences came to mind after reading an advertisement for the study, P5 remembered as follows:

> … *my ex-girlfriend … committed suicide…. I remember being in high school and not being able to tell anyone because no one there knew and even now I'm not sure if anyone knows…. (P5, queer/gay, *)*

In general, participants expressed the feeling that HTP tainted their high school experiences, creating an environment where they could not be themselves or be involved as much as they would have liked to be.

Teaching Homophobia and Transphobia: Why HTP Persists in High Schools

According to our participants, subtle forms of HTP persist in British Columbia high schools and can have a negative impact on young people. We asked our volunteers why they believe HTP continues, and three major themes emerged. First, there remains a lack of queer curriculum; second, they believed that HTP bullying would continue as long as no one intervened; finally, some thought that schools were microcosms of the discriminatory systems operating in larger society.

"There's a complete absence of queer people": Lack of a Queer Curriculum

Participants in this study believed that educators, especially in rural and socially conservative schools, were hesitant to discuss issues affecting queer people:

> … *there's a complete absence of queer people in social studies…. That would be a start. Like even saying that you guys are a part of history too, right? (P4, gay, male)*

To raise visibility of queer people and awareness about issues that affect them, the young people suggested changes to the curriculum. For example, P2 talked about the potential positive impact of the Corren Agreement, which has lead to the creation of a Grade 12 class on social justice issues, including homophobia:

* Denotes a field that the participant left blank, used above and on subsequent pages

I also think the Corren agreement … it would be really great if that went through … just to have that in the class, in the schools and then just to know those ideas are there, whether you take them or not, it's a pretty powerful force I think … to counter that kind of homophobia. (P2, gay, male)

Some participants even shared experiences where teachers *had* included queer people in their lessons and described those in a positive light:

… [one teacher] just happened to mention that a guy in there was queer, like one of the guys who had made something (inaudible) I don't remember which one it was, but it was just kind of random, came out of nowhere, but then she just kept going, and … it made it so natural. (P5, queer/gay, *)

I was in sex ed class … we got a sheet and the sheet had definitions of different words…. I still remember them, they were homosexual, bisexual, and transgendered … And it was not an atmosphere where you were supposed to be making fun of it, or cracking jokes, it was like you're learning something, just like you would learn anything else in this class…. I remember seeing that list and it was like a light bulb over my head. It was like, "ding!" [makes hand motion of light turning on over head] I fit somewhere! Right on that sheet! [laughs] (P7, queer, androgynous)

The volunteers, however, cautioned that piecemeal efforts to raise awareness about HTP in schools were ineffective (if not insincere) and advocated a more comprehensive approach to representing and supporting queer people in high school. When asked how they thought schools could be better for queer youth, participants in one group said the following:

… they're just trying to do like the usual slap on the wrist or get the guest speaker, what-not, and just hopefully that gets through their head, you know. Same thing with drunk driving, or drug abuse or whatever. (P9, *, female)

The token guest speaker that everyone's going to laugh about the second they walk out of the assembly. (P12, gay male)

Yeah. So I just think that they just need to figure out a new approach for how to handle it. Because I know like in CAP, or whatever they call it now, they did like a section of like safe sex, drug abuse … all that kind of crap. And then they did like a thing on homosexuality, but it was like, you know, one class. You know, and you get to watch some movie from 1987 talking about, you know, "Are you gay?" [all laugh] (P9, *, female)

The young people we spoke with believed that silence about LGBTTQ people and issues affecting them extended beyond the formal curriculum. According to the youth, school staff members were silent when it came to addressing homophobia and transphobia as well.

"Bullying that was acceptable": Lack of Intervention and Support for Queer Youth

According to the youth we spoke with, few teachers seemed to appreciate the damage done through homophobic and transphobic slights and exclusion:

[T]hey'd say "Oh, I'm going to do something about it," … occasionally they'd even just tell us to tell them to … fuck off or whatever, but, that's not going to help. That's just going to make it worse. [laughs] (P16, gay, male)

And that was I think the clearest and easiest way to get at someone was to call someone a fag or something like that. Because it was almost accepted. Teachers wouldn't do anything about it. It was the bullying that was acceptable … that you could get away with. (P2, gay male)

At least two people suggested teachers need to intervene in specific ways. One recommended that reactions should be quick and consistent:

But I find it's better, when they tend to act out and right away someone says that's wrong. Like the teachers that stand up … they know that they can't tolerate it in the class so nobody's going to say anything because they don't want to get kicked out for something stupid, right? Or they'll still get kicked out anyways, they just don't care. But at least they're gone. (P12, gay, male)

Another argued that teachers need to address the language being used. Failing to do so, P1 believed, contributes to the perception that terms like gay and queer are "bad" words.

The administration and teachers would rarely admonish people for calling others fag or whatever, and if they did they would react the same way as if one was calling someone an asshole the implication was that these were bad words. Fag, gay, homo, lesbian, transsexual, etc. … do not have to be bad words. It would be nice if teachers and students, when intervening in homophobic and/or transphobic bullying, could essentially get across "your comments were obviously mean-spirited and when your words have harmful motives they are unacceptable" instead of "don't say fag. It is a bad word." (P1, queer/gay, queer)

Some participants gratefully acknowledged teachers who *did* intervene when students used HTP language. In one discussion group, youth who attended the same high school praised a supportive teacher, saying:

… my [History] teacher, she was amazing! … she had big posters on the front of her door that were like, "That's so gay" with a big X through it. [others laugh] And she was like, you don't call anyone, "faggot" or anything in this classroom or you get out. (P8, gay, male)

So many people got out of her classroom for that. (P11, bisexual, male)

She was the best for that kind of stuff…. (P8)

She would send you home! Just be like leave! (P11)

Others found instances where teachers intervened especially memorable and shared them when asked to think of positive experiences in high school. These experiences appear below:

… there was one, I don't know if he was out … But, he was … a dancer and he danced quite a bit at shows and stuff and people would actually boo him while he was on stage…. And one teacher was really supportive of him … he tried to stop it … he'd get right into the seats and shush people and just be like "Be quiet" and "Don't do that." (P2, gay, male)

I think at my schools, teachers were really good about it. My … teacher, I'm not sure what [the students] comment was, something about gay lifestyle… and then [the teacher] said, "would you choose to be persecuted?" or "Why would you choose a harder life?" I thought that was pretty good. (P4, gay, male)

The former students were clearly appreciative of teacher interventions. In instances where this happened, queer students felt supported and cared for. By addressing HTP behaviours of one student, the youth felt, staff curbed similar behaviours from others. Why, then, was intervention not more frequent? For the most part, participants did not feel teachers were choosing not to intervene out of malice toward queer youth. Many of their school staff were unaware of how harmful HTP can be or were unsure of how to deal with it when it happened. For example, one participant condemned some educators for "turning a blind eye":

… they choose to turn a blind eye to it basically, which just encourages the same behaviour to happen again and again…. They're choosing not to see it or they're choosing not to deal with it. Like, "whatever! I'm going to go hang out in my teachers' lounge and drink my coffee and hide in here." (P7, queer, androgynous)

But soon after, P7 surmised that teachers may not understand the impact HTP language has on queer youth:

I think they're aware of it, but they just don't understand the weight behind it. I think they don't understand how much it can negatively impact someone's life in the long term ... especially if they're not gay. (P7, queer, androgynous)

Most volunteers attributed teachers' and counsellors' ignorance or discomfort when it came to addressing HTP harassment to a lack of training or resources. They stressed the importance of providing training about issues that affect LGBTTQ youth, either once hired or during the course of teacher education programs.

... if teachers were given ... more training of accepting diversity in the classrooms, I think that would be really helpful. Like stopping that kind of homophobia when it happens in the classroom or even in the hallways, just taking a more proactive stance on it. (P2, gay, male)

If that was actually a part of teacher training and administrator training. If that was something that they learned in school or learned in the training process, or in a workshop, or something, you know. Like, this exists, we need to address it, and here's how you do it, and here's what's going on. (P7, queer, androgynous)

The youth believed that students, teachers, and counsellors were not educated about homosexuality or gender variance and that, often, HTP stemmed from such ignorance. Some people, however, believed that teachers should not intervene in HTP bullying. These participants thought counsellors, school safety officials, and students needed to take on more responsibility when it came to providing a safe school. In one focus group, volunteers questioned whether teachers should be responsible for handling *any* kind of harassment and said that counsellors needed to take a more active role to raise awareness about homophobia and transphobia in high schools. P8 exclaimed the following:

... it may sound crude, but [the teacher's] job is not to rescue little Johnny who just got picked on because he got called a faggot. That's what counsellors are for, that's what student safety administrators are for ... it shouldn't be laid on the teachers so much. (P8, gay, male)

Volunteers said counsellors should take a more active role in HTP. They also believed counsellors need to be more approachable and make it known they are open to talking to queer youth. Explaining why he did not report the harassment he experienced in high school to school counsellors, P10 said this:

They need to be more approachable. There's that whole stigma! I mean, when everyone was coming up and asking me [if he was gay], I didn't feel like I could go to the counsellors. I didn't feel like I could just go into the office and be like "they keep asking me this, and I don't know why." I never felt like I could go in and ask that sort of question. (P10, gay/homosexual, male)

Participant 14 believed his experience with a school counsellor illustrated the positive impact they could have on queer youth in high school:

I used to have a school counsellor ... even though I wasn't part of the school anymore, she'd sit down and talk to me about my situations I'm in. If there were more counsellors like that, I swear, every school would be a little bit better. Like, you don't have to deal with the bullies, but if you can at least help the student get it off their chest, or talk to them about it, you know, give them some sort of support, I think, things would be a lot better in schools. (P14, gay, male)

Other young people said that students should speak up and challenge the homophobia and transphobia that exists in schools. For example, when asked why he thought HTP persists in high school, P12 said students should take the harassment more seriously and recognize the potential impact their words could have:

I think that a lot of people think that homophobia is a joke … they don't realize how serious it really is…. Like if someone was to walk around the halls and start calling you nigger … everybody in the hall would probably smash them [laughs] and throw them into a locker. But someone calls you a faggot, and nobody says anything. (P12, gay, male)

Participant 8 believed that it was partly his (and other students') responsibility to do something about the HTP in his high school:

I say "Ok, well if my school's not gay friendly, I'm going to make it gay friendly. And I'm going to do everything I can, in my power, to get there…." I went to my counsellor … and said, "Have you guys heard of [gay youth group], have you guys heard of all these places?" And they were like "No, no, no" and I said "Ok, well here's the phone numbers [acts like he's giving something], here's the addresses, call them, get information, and put that information out in the lobby for LGBT, transgender, whatever, to come and look at it. Because otherwise it's not going to get done." (P8, gay, male)

Other researchers have urged young people to demand and develop means of addressing the harassment they face (Kenway & Fitzclarence, 1997). In Kenway and Fitzclarence's (1997, p. 124) opinion, students should be treated as "agents rather than passive recipients of anti-violence reform." Participants in this study seemed to agree.

"They just see it as something that's completely foreign": Silence in Larger Society

Finally, some young people thought schools only exacerbate the silence or negative messages about HTP people that emanate from larger society. One participant (P8) noted the historical maltreatment of LGBTTQ people by the state through law. Issues surrounding sexuality and gender are very complex, and even the assumption that heterosexuals are invariably more privileged than LGBTTQ people has been questioned. Jane Rule, for example, argues that social arrangements do not automatically favour heterosexuals and that heterosexual parents in particular carry a heavy weight of responsibility:

What amazes me is that most people really do seem to think that government and business support heterosexuality. If they really did, we'd have decent child care for every child, pay for work done at home, and free education through university … So where do we get the notion that heterosexuality is such a big privilege? It's very simple really, and it's not about rewards at all … If you're heterosexual you're normal. (Rule 2008, p. 145)

Another person (P5, gay, male) implicated the media for portraying heterosexuality as the norm, a factor that he saw as increasingly influential today as children's time in front of television (and now on the Internet) rivals time spent with working parents. Participant 4 agreed that the media often fails to portray homosexuality and gender variance:

… when we were first getting started with the GSA we passed around this survey … I remember reading one of them, [they] said it's just something that … isn't very common, isn't as portrayed as much [in the media] and that's why people are scared of it, they're scared of … difference … and they just see it as something that's completely foreign. (P2, gay, gay) [10]

Others spoke of the role of social conservatism and religion on their high school climate. Social conservatism and religiousness are not always related;[11] participants mentioned these factors, however, sometimes as a two-fold force contributing to HTP and as a lack of initiative to address behaviours motivated by those phobias in their high schools.

Everyone goes to Church [in the area she was in]. And if they don't go to Church, their Grandma goes to Church. [laughs] … I think it happens because of the parents. The parents don't accept it [being gay], they take that down to you, put it down onto you, so you're not going to accept it, you're not going to understand it, you're going to be scared and you're going to take it out [on other people]. (P6, lesbian/queer, female)

These messages from larger society have an impact, not only on queer youth, but on others who learn that LGBTTQ people do not deserve to be treated as normal, respectable citizens. The next section discusses implications of the persistence of subtle forms of HTP for young people. Regardless of their roots, subtle manifestations of HTP harassment are less noticeable; consequently, these forms may be more effective techniques of normalization because students and staff rarely recognize, let alone intervene, when they happen.[12] Certainly, the people we spoke with said they were affected by the subtle forms of HTP they experienced in high school and in society in general.

CONCLUSION

The lesbian, gay, bisexual, trans, two-spirit, and queer youth who participated in this study conveyed the belief that the formal and informal education they received in high school failed to include positive and accurate information about LGBTTQ people. This absence constitutes a form of homophobia or transphobia in and of itself; however, it also breeds an environment where other, more overt forms of HTP persist. The young people identified a lack of information and exposure to queer people and to issues affecting them as a significant factor leading to the homophobia and transphobia they experienced in high school. In the experiences of many of the youth, LGBTTQ people were referred to only in negative contexts, and homophobic comments or stereotypes were not addressed by teachers.

These subtle forms of HTP create the perception that LGBTTQ identities and the appearances or behaviours often associated with them are unnatural and unacceptable, constituting a form of what Bourdieu (1991) terms symbolic violence. Bourdieu and Passeron (1990, p. 4) say that symbolic violence constitutes a form of violence precisely because it "generates the illusion that it is not violence." Speaking of this illusion, Bourdieu (2001, p. 1) describes symbolic violence as "a gentle violence, imperceptible and invisible even to its victims." Subtle, constant techniques of discipline are more effective and more likely legitimized precisely because they go unrecognized as forms of power.

Homophobia and transphobia as forms of power and discipline function as lessons (often referred to as the hidden curriculum), teaching us which behaviours and associated identities are valued and which are not. To avoid negative responses (or HTP harassment), youth learn to enact those behaviours and adopt those identities that *are* valued. In this study, the queer youth felt uncomfortable and sometimes unsafe in their high schools. They stifled behaviours and appearances often associated with homosexuality and did what they could to get through most of high school unnoticed. Consequently, educational institutions, often perceived as apolitical fields, may be carrying out a form of symbolic violence (and condoning other forms of aggression) as they quietly reinforce dominant worldviews (Bourdieu & Passeron, 1990).

One important finding of this study is that more attention needs to be given to "gentle" forms of HTP violence; surely, more extreme forms of homophobia and transphobia will flourish as long as more subtle manifestations persist. Participants discussed the role of teachers, teachers' training, counsellors, and students themselves in intervening and raising awareness about subtle HTP in B.C. high schools. The most resonant theme of all of these recommendations, however, was that *someone* needs to intervene.

According to Bourdieu, revealing power relations and providing a starting point for resistance to them requires increased awareness and reflexivity in our everyday thinking and sociological thought. Similarly, participants saw the need for reflexivity in educational institutions. They recommended school staff encourage reflection on the social categories we often take for granted (and in turn that teacher trainers should do the same). Increasing awareness about the range of sexual and gender identities that exist could help reduce the perception that LGBTTQ identities are unnatural, wrong, and deserving of punishment. Challenging those conceptions requires, first, that LGBTTQ be represented in schools and, second, that they be portrayed in a positive light.

> As Youdell (2004) states, identities are fragile constructions that come about through discourse or language. Gains in legal arenas are helpful in bringing issues to the surface and, arguably, in securing rights for sexual minorities. Such gains do not in themselves help to protect or even celebrate sexual diversity, as much of the groundwork needs to be outside of courts, tribunals, and legislatures. Open discussion of sexual minorities provides a means of, at the very least, acknowledging the existence, and legitimacy of queer identities (Youdell, 2004). Through this acknowledgement, school administrators gain access to discourses about sexual minorities and with that, the "symbolic power" to reconstruct the sullied identity conferred upon them. (Bourdieu, 1991)

QUESTIONS TO CONSIDER

1. Critically assess the argument that Canada has become very tolerant of sexual expression. Review public opinion surveys and other sources that track public sentiment toward, for example, same-sex marriage initiatives and other issues that might fall under the heading of gay and lesbian rights.

2. In what ways do high schools serve as a venue for homophobic and transphobic acts? How might initiatives such as a Gay-Straight Alliance (GSA) affect such acts? Do you believe that the Corren Agreement in B.C. is a progressive step? Explain why or why not.

3. Review how legislative change might serve to make schools more inclusive, especially as this relates to LGBTTQ students, staff, and teachers. To what extent can new laws affect our values and behaviours? To what extent do you believe that social change hinges on the wider society, not on legislatures, courts, and tribunals? Use specific examples in supporting your answer.

SUGGESTIONS FOR FURTHER READING

Kimmel, M., & Mahler, M. (2003). Adolescent masculinity, homophobia and violence. *American Behavioural Scientist, 46*(10), 1439–1458.

Messerschmidt, J. (2004). *Flesh & blood: Adolescent gender diversity & violence.* Lanham, MD: Rowman & Littlefield Publishers.

Meyer, E. (2009). *Gender, bullying, and harassment: Strategies to end sexism and homophobia in schools.* New York, NY: Teachers College Press.

Morrison, B. (2007). *Restoring safe school communities: A whole school response to bullying and alienation.* Annandale, N.S.W.: Federation Press.

NOTES

1. *Two-spirit* is a term originally "used by North American Aboriginal societies to describe what Europeans now call Gay, Lesbian, Bisexual, Transgendered and Transsexual people" (Lerat, 2004, p. 6).
2. Olweus (1993, p. 9) defines bullying as repeated negative action toward a student or students. Negative actions include intentionally inflicting or attempting to inflict harm verbally or physically, or through social exclusion (Olweus, 1993, p. 9). In this paper, the terms *bully* and *harass* are used synonymously.

3. Homophobia is "prejudice and discrimination against lesbians, gays, and bisexuals" or queer-identified people (Blumenfeld & Raymond, 1993, p. 219).

4. Transphobia is "a reaction of fear, loathing and discriminatory treatment of people whose gender identity or gender presentation (or perceived gender or gender identity) does not match in the socially accepted way, the sex they were assigned at birth. Transgendered people, intersexuals, lesbians, gay men and bisexuals are typically the targets of transphobia" (Trans Accessibility Project, n.d., section titled "Transphobia").

5. *Passing* is a term that can be used to describe members of a group (i.e., sexual or gender identity) who attempt to present themselves as another (Monette, 2004) (originally published in 1992).

6. Lampinen, McGhee, and Martin (2006, p. 25) reported that gay and bisexual youth they surveyed in Vancouver and Victoria were "at a greatly increased risk for reporting use of crystal methamphetamine, ecstasy, and ketamine…. "

7. For more specific information on the study methodology, including sampling and ethical safeguards, see Haskell's M.A. thesis, A Gentle Violence? (2009).

8. The authors acknowledge the support of the Vancouver Pride Society for this project.

9. A synonym for *transgender*, used to describe people outside of the male/female framework.

10. Speaking about cinema originating from Hollywood and Hong Kong, Helen Leung (2008, p. 50) asserts that LGBTTQ people are virtually invisible in film and argues, "… when queer characters are on screen, they largely occupy marginal roles—as neighbour, best friend, victim, or killer—and (until quite recently) are rarely protagonists."

11. For research on homophobia in Canadian Catholic schools, see Callaghan (2007).

12. Holli and Kantola (2007, p. 95), writing about the Finnish experience of furthering human rights and gender equality, conclude that there is a considerable shortfall in that country's provision of effective monitoring and effective mechanisms, partly because specific bureaus are not designed to explore intersections of race and sexuality, for instance.

REFERENCES

Arsenault, L.A. (2000). High school confidential: Lesbian students speak of public high school experiences in Nova Scotia. Unpublished M.A. thesis, Faculty of Education, Acadian University, Wolfville, NS. Blumenfeld, W., & Raymond, D. (1993). Looking at gay and lesbian life: Updated and expanded edition. Boston: Beacon Press.

Bochenek, M., & Widney, A. (2001). Hatred in the hallways: Violence and discrimination against lesbian, gay, bisexual, and transgender students in U.S. Schools. New York, NY: Human Rights Watch. Retrieved November 15, 2007, from http:// www.hrw.org/reports/2001/uslgbt

Bourdieu, P. (1990). *The logic of practice*. (R. Nice, Trans.). Cambridge, UK: Polity Press. (Original work published 1980).

Bourdieu, P. (1991). *Language and symbolic power*. (J. Thomson, Ed.). (G. Raymond, Trans.). Cambridge, MA: Polity in Association with Basil Blackwell.

Bourdieu, P. (2000). *Pascalian meditations*. (R. Nice, Trans.). Cambridge, UK: Polity Press. (Original work published 1997).

Bourdieu, P. (2001). *Masculine domination*. (R. Nice, Trans.). Cambridge, UK: Polity Press. (Original work published in 1998).

Bourdieu, P., & Passeron, J. C. (1990). *Reproduction in education, society, and culture*. (R. Nice, Trans.). London; Newbury Park, CA: Sage. (Original work published in 1970).

Bryers, M. (2008, August 21–28). Canada isn't rushing to defend human rights. *The Georgia Straight*, p. 23.

Burtch, B. (2007). Oppression. In Flood, M., Kegan Gardiner, J., Pease, B., & Ringle, K. (Eds.) *Routledge international encyclopedia on men and masculinities*. London and New York: Routledge, in press.

Buston, K., & Hart, G. (2001). Heterosexism and homophobia in Scottish school sex education: Exploring the nature of the problem. *Journal of Adolescence, 24*(1), pp. 95–109.

Callaghan, T. (2007). That's so gay!: Homophobia in Canadian Catholic schools. Germany: VDM Verlag Dr. Mueller e.K.

Citizenship and Immigration Canada. (2007). Immigration overview: Permanent residents and temporary foreign workers and students. Retrieved August 24, 2008, from http://www.cic.gc.ca/english/resources/statistics/facts2007/foreword.asp

Cochrane, D., & Morrison, M. (2008). How safe and welcoming are Saskatchewan secondary schools for LGBTTQ youth? A preliminary report on student perceptions. Presentation at *Breaking the Silence*, University of Saskatchewan.

The Continuing Legal Education Society of British Columbia. (2005). *BCCA: North Vancouver school board liable for homophobic harassment of student*. Retrieved February 12, 2006, from http://www.cle.bc.ca/CLE/Stay+Current/Collection/2005/4/05-bcca-jubran?practiceAreaMessage=true&practiceArea=Administrative%20Law

Corren and Corren v. B.C. (Ministry of Education) (No. 2) 2005 BCHRT 497

Darwich, L. (2008). Lesbian, gay, bisexual, and questioning adolescents: Their social experiences and the role of supportive adults in high school. Unpublished M.A. thesis, Faculty of Education, University of British Columbia, Vancouver, BC.

DiPlacido, J. (1998). Minority stress among lesbians, gay men, and bisexuals: A consequence of heterosexism, homophobia, and stigmatization. In G. Herek (Ed.), *Stigma and sexual orientation: Understanding prejudice against lesbians, gay men, and bisexuals* (pp. 138–159). Thousand Oaks, CA: Sage Publications.

Dorias, M., & Lajeunesse, S. (2004). *Dead boys can't dance: Sexual orientation, masculinity, and suicide.* (P. Tremblay, Trans.). Montreal, QC: McGill-Queen's University Press.

Durkheim, E. (1951). *Suicide.* New York, NY: Free Press. (Originally published in 1897.)

Egale Canada. (2008). *Backgrounder: Egale Canada first national survey on homophobia in Canadian schools phase one results.* Retrieved September 19, 2008, from http://www.egale.ca/extra%5C1393-Homophobia-Backgrounder.pdf

Flowers, P., & Buston, K. (2001). "I was terrified of being different": Exploring gay men's accounts of growing-up in a heterosexist society. *Journal of Adolescence, 24*(1), 51–65.

Foucault, M. (1977). *Discipline and punish: The birth of the prison.* (A. Sheridan, Trans.). New York, NY: Pantheon Books. (Original work published 1975).

GALE BC. (n.d.). *About gale.* Retrieved February 7, 2006, from http://www.galebc.org/main.htm

Grace, A. (2005). Lesbian, Gay, Bisexual, and Trans-identified (LGBT) Teachers and Students and the Post-Charter Quest for Ethical and Just Treatment in Canadian Schools. (Paper presented at the 'Building Inclusive Schools: A Search for Solutions', a national conference sponsored by the Canadian Teachers' Federation in Ottawa, Ontario, November 2005).

Haskell, R. (2008). A "gentle violence"?: Former students' experiences of homophobia and transphobia in British Columbia high schools. Unpublished M.A. Thesis. School of Criminology, Simon Fraser University, Burnaby, B.C.

Healthy People 2010 Companion Document for Lesbian, Gay, Bisexual, and Transgender (LGBT) Health. (2001). San Francisco, CA: Gay and Lesbian Medical Association.

Henning-Stout, M., James, S., & Macintosh, S. (2000). Reducing harassment of lesbian, gay, bisexual, transgender, and questioning youth in schools. *School Psychology Review, 29*(2), 180–191.

Holli, A. M. and J. Kantola. (2007). State feminism Finnish style: Strong policies clash with implementation problems In J. Outshoorn and J. Kantola (Eds.), *Changing State Feminism* (pp. 82–101). Houndmills, UK: Palgrave Macmillan.

Human Rights Code, RSBC 1996 U.S.C. Chapter 210 (1996). Retrieved February 12, 2006, http://www.qp.gov.bc.ca/statreg/Stat/H/96210_01.htm

Janoff, D.V. (2005). *Pink blood: Homophobic violence in Canada.* Toronto, ON: University of Toronto Press.

Kenway, J., & Fitzclarence, L. (1997). Masculinity, violence and schooling: Challenging "poisonous pedagogies." *Gender & Education, 9*(1), pp. 117–134.

Khayatt, D. (1994). Surviving school as a lesbian. *Gender & Education, 6*(1), pp. 47–62.

Kosciw, J., Diaz, E., & Greytak, E. (2008). The 2007 National School Climate Survey: The experiences of lesbian, gay, bisexual and transgender youth in our nation's schools. New York: Gay, Lesbian, and Straight Education Network [GLSEN].

Lampinen, T., McGhee, D., & Martin, I. (2006). Increased use of "club drugs" among gay and bisexual high school students in British Columbia. *Journal of Adolescent Health, 38*(4), pp. 458–461.

Lerat, G. (2004). Two-spirit youth speak out!: Analysis of the needs assessment tool. Urban Native Youth Association. Retrieved May 22, 2009, from http://www.unya.bc.ca/resources

Leung, H. (2008). *Undercurrents: Queer culture and postcolonial Hong Kong.* Vancouver, BC: UBC Press.

Luhtanen, M. (2005). *Challenging equality: human rights for trans-identified communities.* LawNow. Retrieved August 25, 2008, from http://findarticles.com/p/articles/mi_m0OJX/is_1_30/ai_n25121531

Mahan, W., Varjas, K., Dew, B., Meyers, J., Singh, A., & Marshall, M., et al. (2006). School and community services providers' perspectives on gay, lesbian, and questioning bullying. *Journal of LGBT Issues in Counseling, 1*(2), 45–66.

Mayencourt, L., Locke, B., & McMahon, W. (2003). *Facing our fear—accepting responsibility: A report of the safe schools task force.* Safe Schools Task Force, Victoria, BC: Government of British Columbia.

The McCreary Centre Society. (1999). Being out—Lesbian, gay, bisexual, and transgender youth in B.C.: An adolescent health survey. Vancouver, BC: The McCreary Centre Society.

Murray and Peter Corren Foundation. (n.d.). History on the establishment of the foundation. Retrieved September 18, 2008, from www.corren.ca

O'Connor, A. (1995). Breaking the silence: Writing about gay, lesbian, and bisexual teenagers. In G. Unks (Ed.), *The gay teen: Educational practice and theory for lesbian, gay, and bisexual adolescents* (pp. 13–16). NY, New York: Routledge.

Olweus, D. (1993). Bullying at school: What we know and what we can do. Cambridge, MA: Blackwell Publishers.

Pegura et al. v. School District No. 36, 2003 BCHRT 53

Perelle, R. (2009, February 12). No other word for it: it was a gaybashing: Smith. *Xtra! West,* pp. 13–15.

Rule, J. (2008). "You be normal, or else … " In J. Rule, *Loving the Difficult (pp. 144–149).* Sidney, BC: Hedgerow Press.

Rutter, P. (2007). Young adult suicide and sexual orientation: What should counselors know? *Journal of LGBT Issues in Counseling, 1*(3), 33–48.

Saewyc, E.M., Poon, C., Wang, N., Homma, Y., Smith, A., & the McCreary Centre Society. (2007). *Not yet equal: The health of lesbian, gay & bisexual youth in BC.* Vancouver, BC: McCreary Centre Society, pp. 84–85.

Samis, S. (1995). "An injury to one is an injury to all": Heterosexism, homophobia, and anti-gay/lesbian violence in Greater Vancouver. Unpublished M.A. thesis, Department of Sociology and Anthropology, Simon Fraser University.

Sanders, D. (2006). Constructing lesbian and gay rights. In B. Burtch and N. Larsen (Eds.), *Law in society: Canadian readings* (2nd edition) (pp. 185–220). Toronto: Nelson.

Scagliotti, J. (Director). (2003). *Dangerous living: Coming out in the developing world* [documentary film]. United States: First Run Features.

School system accused of same-sex discrimination. (2005, July 11). *CBCNews.ca.* Retrieved February 27, 2008, from http://www.cbc.ca/canada/british-columbia/story/2005/07/11/bc_same-sex-teachers20050711.html

Smith, G. (1998). The ideology of "fag": The school experience of gay students. *The Sociological Quarterly, 39*(2), pp. 309–355.

Spencer, L., Ritchie, J., & O'Connor, W. (2003). Carrying out qualitative analysis. In J. Lewis & J. Ritchie (Eds.), *Qualitative research practice: A guide for social science students and researchers* (pp. 199–218). London/Thousand Oaks/New Delhi: SAGE Publications.

Stanton, T. (2006). A fairy's tale. In D. Levithan and B. Merrell (Eds.), *The full spectrum: A new generation of writing about gay, lesbian, bisexual, transfer, questioning and other identities* (pp. 108–120). New York: Alfred A. Knopf.

Stritof, S. and B. Stritof (2009) Same-Sex Marriages FAQ—Gender-Neutral Marriage Laws. Retrieved July 6, 2009, from http://marriage.about.com/cs/samesexmarriage/a/samesex.htm).

Tin, L.G. (Ed.). (2008). *The dictionary of homophobia: A global history of gay & lesbian experience.* (M. Redburn, A. Micahud., & K. Mathers, Trans.). Vancouver, BC: Arsenal Pulp Press. (Original published in 2003.)

Trans Accessibility Project. (n.d.). *Transphobia and discrimination.* Retrieved November 6, 2008, from http://www.queensu.ca/humanrights/tap/3discrimination.htm

Walton, G. (2006). "no fags allowed": An examination of bullying as a problematic and implications for educational policy. Unpublished Ph.D. dissertation. Faculty of Education, Queen's University, Kingston, ON.

Warner, T. (2002). *Never going back: A history of queer activism in Canada.* Toronto, ON: University of Toronto Press.

Wright, W. (2005). *Harvard's secret court: The savage purge of campus homosexuals.* New York: St. Martin's Press.

Wyss, S. (2004). "This was my hell": The violence experienced by gender non-conforming youth in US high schools. *International Journal of Qualitative Studies in Education, 17*(5), pp. 709–730.

Youdell, D. (2004). Wounds and reinscriptions: Schools, sexualities, and performative subjects. *Discourse: Studies in the Cultural Politics of Education, 25*(4), pp. 477–493.

Chapter Fourteen

Keeping Up with the Neighbours? Canadian Responses to 9/11 in Historical and Comparative Context

*Reg Whitaker**

Editors' Note: In "Keeping Up with the Neighbours," Professor Whitaker draws on three key examples: the terrorist attacks of September 11, 2001, and subsequent anti-terrorist initiatives; the 1940s' Cold War; and the October Crisis in 1970 between the Canadian state and Le Front de Libération du Québec (FLQ). He outlines the massive pressure on Canadian authorities to harmonize our national efforts with U.S. policies, a situation eased only partly by ideologies favouring Canadian sovereignty vis-à-vis American civil liberties and anti-terrorism legislation. Professor Whitaker provides many examples of Canadian government efforts to confront actual or imagined threats to the security and safety of its citizens and its political sovereignty. He draws on contemporary incidents and laws as well as those from the mid-twentieth century. Specifically, efforts during the Cold War, beginning in the 1940s, have been criticized for being undemocratic, including stifling dissent and scapegoating those allied with communistic beliefs. Nevertheless, Reg Whitaker argues that this priority of social order and state authority was a catalyst for "the strengthening of democratic accountability and greater concern for the protection of rights." Moving to the 1970s era, he reviews some aspects of the October Crisis, a phenomenon he considers the "worst internal security crisis" in Canadian history. Practices under the October Crisis attracted great criticism, exemplified by concerns over an atmosphere of half-truths and lies by government agencies or by then prime minister Pierre Trudeau's famous response, "Just watch me," when asked what he might do in the face of terrorism. Critics opposed widespread arrests of supposed suspects and policies that threatened or removed civil liberties in Canada. As Whitaker puts it, powers of security and police forces took the form of "blank cheques" that were widely used, sometimes illegally.

The post-9/11 scenario builds on these historical precedents, but this time moving the focus to a transnational level, with both support for American anti-terrorist initiatives and enduring opposition to some U.S. policies, especially the overseas war against terrorism. For instance, Whitaker acknowledges that Canadian authorities weakened our own privacy law in providing "personal data on passengers" destined for the U.S., but points out that without such a concession Canadian airline companies would forfeit "landing rights." He discusses the ongoing clash in the United States between (a) high-security approaches, such as indefinite detention without trial of suspected terrorists or their sympathizers, and (b) a rule-of-law approach favoured by civil libertarians and others whereby such detention—"without legal representation and without judicial review"—is seen as unconstitutional. Professor Whitaker contrasts some American enactments and decisions with the Canadian context, arguing that Canadian authorities are less prone to racial profiling, particularly of Muslims, even though our authorities do implement a more restrained form of profiling. This chapter offers an incisive look at similarities and differences in political cultures, especially Canadian and American, and an analysis of overlaps and differences in legal responses including the Canadian Anti-Terrorism Act in 2001.

Source: ©2003, R. Whitaker. Reprinted by permission of the author.
*Distinguished Research Professor Emeritus, York University. Adjunct Professor of Political Science, University of Victoria.

To assess the impact of 9/11 on Canada, historical and comparative perspectives are helpful. This article offers two historical precedents in Canada, followed by some comparative context for Canada's post-9/11 actions in the experience of Canada's closest neighbours, the United States and the United Kingdom.[1]

When Canada joined the war on terrorism after the attacks of September 11, 2001, the decision was not without historical precedents in the post-war world. The Cold War, especially in its initial stages from 1945 to the early 1950s, and the October 1970 Crisis in Quebec offer two intriguing parallels to the present situation, providing a number of useful lessons.

I. THE COLD WAR

In the late 1940s, Canada went to a so-called Cold War, against Soviet Communism. Just as Canadian troops have found themselves fighting terrorists on the front lines in Afghanistan, Canadian soldiers in the Cold War found themselves battling Communists in Korea. Both wars included a home front and the identification of enemies within. Both wars involved Canada in ever closer integration with the Americans, through the generals directing the conflicts. Both wars, especially in their initial, anxious stages, raise issues of individual and group rights in contrast to the demands of the community for security.

9/11 was, as many have pointed out, America's 21st century Pearl Harbor. As such, it has compelled an immediate and aggressive American response. The Cold War turned out to be an American-led and American-directed conflict, but in its earliest stages it did not follow the script of December 1941. In fact, the first public notice that the wartime alliance was about to break down into inter-bloc rivalry and hostility came in Ottawa. How this small, dull, rather provincial capital became the focal point for great power conflict in 1945–1946 is part of Canadian mythology. Igor Gouzenko, the first important Soviet defector, exposed a spy ring operated by Canada's ostensible wartime ally, the USSR, exploiting the willingness of Canadians sympathetic to Communism to betray their own country on behalf of a higher loyalty to the Socialist motherland. Canada, it was said, experienced a sudden wake-up call, communicated this to its allies, and then settled in for a prolonged struggle on many fronts with the new enemy once its senior partner, America, had taken overall charge.

The struggle lasted four decades and, for most of this time, Canada was a very junior partner. It toiled in alliance obscurity. It very occasionally raised a cautious criticism, only to be quickly cuffed for its temerity. But it is important to understand that when the Gouzenko spy scandal broke, first in secret in September 1945, and then publicly in February 1946, Canada was, in important ways, on its own, without clear models to guide it. It consulted and received advice from its close allies, but it had to work out the details for itself. Its response stamped a distinctive made-in-Canada look on Canadian Cold War security policy.[2]

Once the extent of Soviet espionage and Canadian complicity had become apparent from the documents and information Gouzenko brought with him, the government of Canada acted with what might be called the firm smack of Prussian command. There was a secret Order in Council, known only to three Cabinet ministers, under the authority of the *War Measures Act*,[3] even though the war had been over a few weeks before Gouzenko defected; it empowered the government to act against the suspected spies with little or no regard for civil liberties, outside the normal processes of the legal system. Armed with this power, the government bided its time, consulted its allies, studied the evidence, watched the suspects, and waited for the right moment to strike in light of the international scene.

When it did strike, in mid-February 1946, it was with a series of dawn raids by blackleather-jacketed members of the drug squad of the Royal Canadian Mounted Police (RCMP), who entered Ottawa homes and apartments without specific warrants, detained a dozen people (more followed in the days and weeks ahead), and seized papers and documents. The detainees were transported to the RCMP barracks, where they were interrogated for weeks on end. The detainees were not arrested under criminal charges, and were unrepresented by counsel; *habeas corpus* was ignored. Then they were brought before a secret tribunal—a Royal Commission of Inquiry, a formidable establishment body, headed by two Supreme Court justices—with Commission counsel being the President of the Canadian Bar Association. They were still without legal representation. They were told they had no choice but to answer all questions put to them, and they were deliberately not informed that they had the right of protection against self-incrimination; they were bullied and harried by the Commission counsel.

The Kafkaesque overtones are captured in an exchange between one detainee, Israel Halperin (who was in fact almost certainly innocent of espionage) and the Commissioners. When brought into the hearing room and told he must be sworn in, he fired back: "Before you swear me, would you mind telling me who you are?" "Well," answered one of the Commissioners, "we are the Royal Commission appointed by the government to investigate certain matters." "Are you empowered to use physical intimidation?" he persisted. "Not physical intimidation, but we have the power to punish you if you do not answer." The witness then turned and tried to leave the room, but was forcibly returned to the witness box.[4]

At the end of these proceedings, the Commission published a lengthy and widely read report in which it named some two dozen persons as spies and traitors to their country.[5] The detainees were then turned over to the courts. Charges were brought against them under various statutes, particularly the draconian *Official Secrets Act*,[6] which made communication of classified information to a foreign power a serious offence, but did not distinguish between information that might be damaging and information that was harmless. This statute also laid the burden of proof upon the accused. Despite what appeared to be a stacked deck, only about half of the two dozen eventually charged with criminal offences as a result of the inquiry were ever convicted. Those who had incriminated themselves before the Commission were mainly acquitted. Nevertheless, with one exception, all those acquitted were denied further employment with the government.

At the time, there was not a great deal of criticism of the government's methods. Public opinion (by and large) approved the actions taken. Important sections of elite opinion, especially within the legal community, seemed unperturbed. In retrospect, critics have described the treatment of the suspects as abusive of their rights and as a serious violation of liberal democratic norms. Some have even compared Canadian behaviour unfavourably with that of the United States. Even in the dark days of McCarthyism, the Americans did not round up suspects before dawn, hold and interrogate them incommunicado, and haul them before secret tribunals which would later officially name them as traitors without legal recourse.

These criticisms are important—I have made many of them myself—but they do not get at the rationale for the government's methods. Contextually, this was a pre-*Charter* (and pre-*Bill of Rights*) era, and it followed immediately upon a war in which extraordinary state action against dissidents—detention without trial, search and seizure, censorship, even the forcible relocation of the entire Japanese-Canadian community from the west coast to camps in the interior, and the confiscation of their property—had been not only tolerated, but sanctioned by the highest authorities in the land. It is not surprising that in this context, faced with clear evidence of espionage and betrayal of trust, the government should have reached for the most expedient administrative method for protecting national security. Not surprising, but unfortunate, in that a precedent was being set for a relatively low priority on civil liberties in peacetime, albeit the twilight peacetime of the Cold War.

There was more to the government's response than context alone. There was a consistent pattern that ran through all of its planning and execution with regard to how to handle the explosive spy affair. The government wished to maintain maximum control over the story—to frame it in the most appropriate manner—and its effects, both internal and external. In terms familiar to today's world, the government wanted to manage the spin. There were good reasons for this. Externally, Canada found itself in a highly exposed position *vis-à-vis* the spy affair. At a time when the wartime alliance had not yet broken down publicly, a wrong move by Canada might precipitate grave consequences for East-West relations. Prime Minister Mackenzie King wanted no part of such a critical international situation. That would be left to the big battalions of the Americans and the British. Thus the Soviet angle of the affair was systematically down-played in the Commission report. Others might draw strongly anti-Soviet lessons, but Canada would not. (Ironically, and for similar reasons, the Soviets vented their wrath over the affair at Canada, an altogether safer target than the United States or the United Kingdom.)

The other reason for government control of spin was domestic, and here the wisdom of the government became apparent only later. In downplaying the Soviet role, the government also chose to highlight the role of Communism in subverting the loyalties of Canadians. There was genuine shock and dismay at the evidence that some Canadians held a higher loyalty to a for-eign power, and were willing to serve that power, over their own country. The Commission report was an attempt at public education and public warning about the dangers of dabbling in extreme left-wing ideas. It could also be seen as an exercise in *political policing*, or setting author-itative boundaries on permissible limits of dissent. But this could itself be a dangerous process, spinning out of control as rivals to the party in power sought to exploit the politics of loyalty. Without strict limits, and outside direct supervision by the Crown, the politics of loyalty could become divisive and socially and politically destructive.

Indeed, shortly after the Gouzenko affair had been resolved, anti-Communism in the U.S. threatened just this sort of anarchy. In 1947, the House Committee on Un-American Activities began its Hollywood witch hunt, and by 1950 Senator Joe McCarthy was launching his dema-gogic anti-Communist smear campaign that gave the English language a dark epithet: 'McCarthyism.' Before McCarthyism had run its course by 1954, the integrity of such institu-tions as the U.S. Presidency and the Army was threatened. In 1946, the Canadian government did not foresee these developments, but by strictly controlling the Gouzenko story and its effects, they did pre-empt the emergence of potential Canadian McCarthys, one of whom was no less than the leader of the opposition by 1948, George Drew, who tried but failed to forge a demagogic anti-Communist role for himself.

There was a direct link between the Gouzenko affair and the government of Canada's Cold War internal security policies. In its aftermath, the security screening system was set in place for civil servants, immigrants, refugees, and citizenship applicants. The screening system was also extended to defence industries and even to shipping on the Great Lakes. In all cases, the process was kept as secret as possible, with security never being advanced as a reason for limiting a person's employment or their admission to Canada or to citizenship. For many years, there was no appeal process for persons denied security clearance.

There were American pressures to step up security. The Americans were evangelical in their Cold War crusade, and from time to time thought it necessary to nudge, or push, their allies to shape up to appropriate (i.e., American) standards. Sometimes they were particularly insistent upon doing something that the Canadians deemed silly or excessive, and usually the Canadians complied, with weary resignation, on the principle that it would be more costly to provoke them. Yet, by and large, Cold War security policies were made in Canada. Canadians set their own rules for security screening and always sharply distinguished themselves from the United States by pointedly not referring to loyalty or disloyalty, but only to *risk*. What distin-guished the two approaches was the secrecy in which the Canadian policy was administered, and its strict monopolization by the executive branch of the federal government. With the exception of Quebec under Maurice Duplessis—a distinct society before the phrase was invented, where provincial anti-Communist laws like the Padlock law, and provincial Red Squads operated outside federal control—it was Ottawa that prosecuted the Cold War on the home front, and Ottawa kept its cards well hidden. When opposition voices were raised to demand information, Ottawa tended to respond serenely (or smugly) that it was taking care of matters and that details were the business of the proper authorities. The operative principle was trust us.

Witch hunts wracked McCarthy-era America at all levels of government and throughout civil society. But not in Canada—at least, not publicly. In point of fact, there were purges and victims. There was a witch hunt at the National Film Board (NFB): scores of people lost their jobs and saw their careers suffer. But unlike the witch hunt in Hollywood, there were few headlines and no names bandied about in the media. The government even denied there was a purge, insisting officially that only three persons had been removed. Behind the scenes, they gave the Security Service and a new, purged, NFB management a blank cheque to remove persons on suspicion. By the end, some thirty-five permanent or contract employees were terminated or encouraged to depart before they were targeted, although the total number could only be confirmed by documents released under *Access to Information* requests many decades later. The position of Canadian officials was that the politicization of security issues inherently risked illiberalism, and they could point to the U.S. example as confirmation. Some of the victims of these silent purges have different views in retrospect. The Hollywood witch hunt resulted in blacklists and blighted careers, but finally in the public vindication of those purged, who have been transformed from villains in the 1950s to virtual folk heroes decades later. For better or for worse, that was not the Canadian way.

Security screening of immigrant/refugee and citizenship applicants involved Canada in extensive and persistent application of a double standard with regard to potential new Canadians.[7] Applicants with left-wing backgrounds or associations were security risks, while those with right-wing backgrounds were generally welcomed as anti-Communists. This had unfortunate implications for lax treatment of Nazi war criminals and collaborators; this issue was later subject to a Royal Commission of Inquiry and a special section of the Justice Department that was designated for retroactively tracking down war criminals and criminal collaborators who had passed through the security screen. It also meant that Canada put out the welcome mat for refugees from Communism (Hungary in 1956–1957; Southeast Asia in the late 1970s), while making it difficult for those fleeing right-wing violence (Chile in the 1970s, central America in the 1980s). Apart from double political standards, Cold War immigration security firmly established a precedent of highly state-centred procedures. Immigration was deemed a privilege, not a right. Risk was determined by the state, and doubt must be resolved in favour of the state, not the individual. Moreover, procedurally, the deck was highly stacked in favour of the Crown, with non-disclosure of evidence and *ex parte* proceedings the norm in deportation cases.

Security screening has been an important tool for the political policing of Canadian society. The Security Service, first the RCMP and later the Canadian Security Intelligence Service (CSIS), has routinely used screening as an effective instrument for establishing sources within suspect organizations: the threat of lost employment or, worse, of deportation is an effective persuader for co-operation. As an offshoot of this, and of its preparation of threat assessments for the government, the security service amassed a remarkable volume of dossiers on Canadians and Canadian civil society. When the McDonald Commission of Inquiry investigated RCMP wrongdoing in the late 1970s, it discovered that the security service held files on no less than 800,000 individuals and organizations—a proportion of the population watched by the secret police that would have done credit to some less savoury regimes abroad.[8] This kind of excess drew so much criticism that the government of Brian Mulroney in the late 1980s ordered the closure of the Counter Subversion branch of CSIS, with most of its files to be destroyed or transferred to the National Archives.

There are some general points to be made about Canada's Cold War experience. First, when directly provoked, Canada could act with impressive firmness and resolution. Second, while Americans might be leading the Cold War charge, Canada was quite capable of setting and enforcing its own stiff standards for security. Even when pushed further in particulars than they might prefer by the Americans, Canadian Cold War policy was essentially made-in-Canada, according to Canadian imperatives; in the end, it was not significantly different from the Americans in content, although it did differ in style. What was most distinctive about Canadian Cold War security policy was its strict control by the executive branch of the federal government, and the zeal with which the federal government guarded its prerogatives. The federal government had responsibility for external relations and for peace, order, and good government within Canada. The differential, and sometimes invidious, effects of national security on individuals and groups in Canadian society were unfortunate by-products, but the security of the state and order in the community normally took precedence over individual and group rights. Yet ironically, the long-term consequences were the strengthening of democratic accountability and greater concern for the protection of rights.

II. THE OCTOBER 1970 CRISIS

When Canada faced the aftermath of the horrific attacks of 9/11, and the requirement to join in a new global war on terrorism, it was not altogether lacking in historical experience in dealing with terrorists. In October 1970, Canada faced its worst internal security crisis, when cells of the violent separatist group, *Le Front de Libération du Québec* (FLQ) kidnapped the British Trade Commissioner, James Cross, and kidnapped and later murdered the Quebec Minister of Labour, Pierre Laporte. Canada was thrust at this time into a harsh global spotlight amid a rising tide of anxiety and uncertainty at home; there were conflicting calls for negotiating with the terrorists or for staring them down. To make matters more difficult for the federal government, this was primarily a domestic terrorist crisis (in spite of ineffectual attempts to link the FLQ to wider terrorist networks or even to Communism), with potentially serious consequences for Canada-Quebec relations. Faced with this mushrooming crisis, Canada acted swiftly and forcefully with no regard for civil liberties. Invoking the *War Measures Act* under a putative, and unproven, apprehended insurrection, the federal government placed Quebec under what amounted to a state of martial law. Extensive use was made of the power to detain and interrogate without charge, without counsel, and without *habeas corpus*. The media were censored and the FLQ declared a banned organization, association with which could land someone in prison; further, association was considered retroactively. In the aftermath of the crisis proper, the resources of the RCMP Security Service and the Quebec and Montreal police were mobilized to counter and negate by virtually any means, fair or foul, the FLQ or its successors. In filling out the blank cheques issued them, the security and police forces so exceeded their lawful roles that their activities were subject to a series of federal and provincial Commissions of Inquiry.

However controversial the methods employed, the result was clear and unequivocal: the FLQ and, with it, the entire terrorist tendency of the sovereignty movement in Quebec, was eradicated. From the early 1970s onwards, the sovereignty field was left entirely to the legitimate, lawful, and peaceful form of the Parti Québécois (PQ), and the contestation of federalism to democratic elections and referenda. Indeed, in surveying the contemporary history of terrorist movements around the world, the Canadian experience in stopping terrorism dead in its track and diverting the political energies that had helped drive the movement into constitutional channels, stands out as a quite remarkable success story. Timing was obviously important: the terrorist movement was crushed at an early enough stage that its repression did not elicit any popular upsurge in support—as for instance with the Irish Republican Army (IRA) among the Catholic population of Northern Ireland. Maximum force can work at preliminary stages of the development of an insurrectionary terrorist movement; at later stages, it may well be counter-productive, as in the current morass of death and retribution in which Israel finds itself enmeshed with the Palestinians. The FLQ also self-destructed with its wanton murder of Laporte, a senseless act that disgusted Quebecers. Above all, there were alternative, peaceful means of expression available for sovereignist sentiment. The PQ had just entered the National Assembly in Quebec elections earlier the same year. Force could be used successfully against illegitimate force when legitimate channels existed.

Does the successful outcome of the affair offer retroactive justification to a government that in effect put liberal freedoms on hold and declared that the end justified the means? There are perhaps two answers to this question, and each has significance for how we understand the response of the government of Canada to 9/11.

First, it must be clearly stated that the Trudeau government during and after October 1970 was less than frank in its justification of its actions before Parliament and the public.[9] There was no apprehended insurrection: the failure of the government to follow up with supporting evidence for its claim in invoking wartime emergency powers was telling, for there was no such evidence, or at least nothing compelling. Moreover, the advice of the RCMP would have been against using emergency powers—if its officials had been consulted, which they were not. The government's retroactive justification leaned heavily on the alleged shortcomings of the intelligence on the terrorist groups provided by the security service that supposedly left them no choice but to round up all the usual suspects and sort them later. This official rationale was revealed to be seriously distorted when documents on intelligence reports on the FLQ and other separatist groups were declassified later.[10] The distortions are unfair to the RCMP, which had in fact done a competent job of penetrating and reporting on violent separatist groups. They also constitute a reprehensible example of blaming the servants for the masters' misdeeds. The RCMP had even delivered a very clear warning in the summer of 1970 that the FLQ had adopted kidnappings as their priority tactic, and even specified diplomats and Cabinet ministers as their likely targets. Yet the warnings were ignored, and potential targets left unprotected at the tragic cost of Laporte's life. The lesson here is one often repeated in modern history: intelligence failures are as often failures of governments to listen to their intelligence as of intelligence professionals failing to provide.

The RCMP believed that the crisis was essentially a criminal matter, to be solved by good, careful, patient police work. That was how, in the end, James Cross was liberated, and it might have saved Laporte's life. Instead, the government, or at least the Prime Minister and his close Cabinet associates from Quebec (who in every instance of debate in Cabinet proved to be the hawks), disingenuously citing an exaggerated threat they know to be false, chose to perform a *coup de théâtre*, a striking demonstration of the power of the federal government and the futility of violent resistance to it. From a liberal standpoint, the October Crisis offers a salutary warning about how the state can lie and use pretexts to aggrandize its power and crush opposition. From a Machiavellian standpoint, Trudeau skillfully manipulated a crisis not of his making to effect an end that was in the national interest.

Choosing between these alternative assessments is not easy. It is difficult to justify the Trudeau government's actions in misrepresenting facts and in shifting blame. On the other hand, a terrorist avenue that might have turned Quebec into an Ulster-style battleground was avoided and the constitutional avenue for the sovereignty movement opened. Moreover, despite dire predictions at the time that the fabric of liberal democracy had suffered irreparable harm from the arbitrary actions taken in 1970, the evidence suggests otherwise. As a long term result of the crisis and its aftermath, the *War Measures Act* was later repealed and replaced with an emergency powers statute[11] that is much more measured and balanced. As a direct consequence of the post-crisis countering of the violent separatists by unlawful and improper means, the McDonald Commission recommendations led to the removal of the Security Service from the RCMP and the creation of a civilian agency; CSIS has a specific legal mandate for what it is authorized and not authorized to do, and elaborate mechanisms of accountability, oversight, and review attached to its operations. These are very positive gains for liberal democracy, which derive, paradoxically, from the violations of liberal democracy practised during the crisis. History, it should be remembered, does not always move in straight lines.

III. KEEPING UP WITH THE NEIGHBOURS? AFTER 9/11

The war on terrorism differs from the two historical precedents in a number of particulars, despite certain déja vu elements. Most significantly, 9/11 constituted a violent attack on American civil society, indeed the attacks appear to have been designed to spread fear throughout all levels of American life. Moreover, the targets have been publicly designated in Al-Qaeda pronouncements as *any* and *all* Americans, not limited to state officials, military/security personnel, or corporate executives, as was the case with some earlier terrorist groups. The Cold War was only weakly felt as constituting a threat to the personal security of ordinary North Americans in their homes and families. The *subversive* threat of the Communist enemy within was largely a constructed abstraction that waxed briefly in the early, anxious days of the Cold War, and then waned by the middle of the 1950s, when an uneasy stability took hold in East-West relations. The material threat to ordinary people in the Cold War was the spectre of nuclear holocaust, but this actually turned out to be a powerful factor pushing governments toward negotiating differences with the enemy and reducing the possibility of war. The diffuse threat of post-9/11 terrorism, on the other hand, works decisively in the opposite direction, putting popular pressure on government to defeat and eliminate the terrorists, at whatever cost.

The war on terrorism is thus a more popular struggle than the Cold War, which was always primarily a matter of concern to states and state elites. The danger of populist authoritarianism is very real to vulnerable minorities—in this case, the Muslim and Arab communities—and to the fabric of liberal democracy. States will no doubt always attempt to seize the opportunities offered by major security crises to enhance their coercive powers at the expense of individual and group rights. When they have deep and enduring popular support in exploiting such opportunities, the long-term result promises to be bleaker from a civil libertarian point of view.

9/11 was, however, not just an attack on civil society, but in the first instance, an attack on *American* civil society. As a liberal, capitalist, 'infidel' democracy allied closely to the United States, Canada is obviously implicated as a target of radical Islamist terror. The apparently authentic statement issued by Osama bin Laden in the fall of 2002 specifically threatened Canada along with other Western states associated with the United States. As primary targets are hardened by tough security measures, it is always possible that softer targets will be sought by the terrorists, even in other countries. Nonetheless, it was evident from 9/11 that America is the primary focus of terrorist wrath, and Canada is at best a secondary, peripheral target. The attacks on the twin towers of global capitalism and the headquarters of U.S. military might were brilliantly chosen for the spectacular symbolism encoded in the acts. Attacks on the CN Tower and the Defence headquarters in Ottawa would send an indecipherable message to the world.

Canadians instinctively sympathized with Americans, shared their pain and anger, and continue to support the idea of a war on terrorism.[12] Despite the successful coalition-building activity of the U.S. administration around the invasion of Afghanistan, and the rather less enthusiastically received efforts around a projected war on Iraq, Canadians have tended to see the war on terrorism as primarily an American, rather than a multilateral, struggle. President Bush's pointed omission of Canada from his otherwise exhaustive list of countries officially thanked, and his offhand dismissal of the need to offer any apology for the four Canadian soldiers killed by American friendly fire in Afghanistan, were widely perceived in Canada as insults. They also confirmed the specifically American nature of the war on terrorism, and Canada's distinctly auxiliary role in the conflict. Public opinion analysis suggests that Canadians, like much of the rest of the world, have actually grown more distant from the United States, and more critical of American leadership, since 9/11.[13]

Analysis of the policy response of the Canadian government to 9/11 suggests that Canada has actually been fighting a war on two fronts. One front is the public face of the war on terrorism: Canada fulfills its obligations as an ally in the broad coalition against terrorist movements and reassures its own citizens that it is doing what it can to protect their safety. The second front, less publicly acknowledged, is essentially damage limitation: not in relation to terrorist acts, but in relation to the potential collateral economic harm to Canadian interests caused by the U.S. interpretation of national security on its northern border. U.S. homeland security will be protected, either at the Canada-U.S. border or around a wider North American perimeter. If security is imposed along the border, it will be at an economic cost unacceptable to Canada, which sends more than eighty-five per cent of its exports to the United States. The costs would also be high to the United States, but loom proportionately less on the American side; moreover, the Bush administration is willing to pay very high economic costs for security, including the $158 billion U.S. federal deficit incurred in 2002.

Faced with a formidable big business lobby insistent on reopening the border for unimpeded commerce, at whatever political cost,[14] the Canadian government confronted an unsettling policy alternative: a North American security perimeter in which Canadian sovereignty would be seriously threatened by pressures to harmonize its rules on entry—given the balance of power between the two countries, this would inevitably mean wholesale adoption of American standards. The Canadian policy dilemma on the second front has been how to reassure the United States sufficiently on border security so that commercial traffic can be maintained, while not surrendering a critical degree of Canadian sovereignty in the process.

The two fronts are interrelated. Everything that Canada contributes to the war on terrorism, and to maintain strong security against terrorism within Canada, tends to relieve U.S. pressure on the border. The Canadian first front response has involved: more resources for security and intelligence; a streamlined security decision-making structure within the federal government at both the political and bureaucratic levels; new and expanded legal powers for anti-terrorist law enforcement and investigation; and closer coordination and sharing of information with allies.[15] All of these have helped maintain Canadian economic security by reassuring the U.S. that Canada is enforcing adequate security standards on its own. However, they have not been enough.

Parallel to this track, Canada has taken another series of initiatives under the rubric of the Smart Border agreements.[16] These initiatives involve a series of ongoing negotiations with the United States on such matters as pre-clearance of container traffic at the point of origin; fast-tracking of safe persons and goods; collection and retention of a wide range of data on persons travelling by air across the border; the application of high-tech surveillance equipment along the border; expansion of Integrated Border Enforcement Teams; and, controversially, a "safe third country" agreement to reduce the flow of refugees across the border. Despite some inevitable glitches, these negotiations have so far been largely successful, in the view of U.S. Homeland Security secretary Tom Ridge, who has warmly stressed the usefulness of their further expansion. Critics in Canada, from those on the political right who have characterized these measures as too little, too late, to those on the nationalist left who have tended to see them as sellouts of sovereignty, have unanimously missed the point of the Canadian strategy. The Canadian government has tried to avoid being trapped into sweeping negotiations on a mega-agreement over a Fortress North America—such as the perimeter security project proffered by Paul Cellucci, the United States Ambassador to Canada, just after 9/11 (and endorsed by a number of provincial premiers, the Official Opposition in Ottawa, and the influential Council of Canadian Chief Executives). Instead, the Canadian government has engaged the Americans in a series of incremental negotiations, segmented but linked, the successful outcome of which has had the cumulative effect of mollifying American security concerns, while keeping the flow of cross-border commerce more or less intact. Absorbed in the specifics, the U.S. negotiators have lost sight of the larger picture, which is exactly to the taste of the Canadian negotiators who wished to minimize the larger loss of sovereignty necessarily entailed in any grander, macro-level integration and harmonization project.

Although the Canadian federal government has shown considerable skill and adroitness in managing the second front of this two-front war, it is a volatile process subject to unpredictable upsets. Certain politicians and journalists in the United States allude frequently to the alleged security risk to America posed by lax Canadian security policies and a lamentably undefended northern border. An imagined Canadian connection to 9/11 was doggedly investigated, but all leads came up empty. In fact, the U.S. State Department in its official report tracking global terrorist trends for the year 2001 explicitly denied any Canadian connection and went on to describe Canadian co-operation in anti-terrorism as a model the U.S. would like to see practised with its other allies.[17] Yet as late as January 2003, five mysterious "Arabs" who had allegedly entered the United States from Canada were the subject of an all-points terrorist alarm, endorsed by no less than President Bush. Within a few days, the story collapsed, revealed as a hoax. Nonetheless, despite an angry demand from Canadian Immigration minister Denis Coderre, New York Senator Hilary Clinton refused to apologize for her claim that the non-existent suspects had entered the United States via Canada.[18] The Canadian connection stories have proved to have about the same credibility as the episode of the TV series *The West Wing*, in which the White House was alerted to a terrorist who had infiltrated across the Ontario-Vermont border. Although no responsible official of the U.S. government has ever given credence to this mythology, anti-Canadian suspicions form a political background to American perceptions of Canada that Canadian officials are persistently forced to confront.

In fact, there is very little evidence that Canadian security is any less vigilant than that of America. Canadian and American authorities share common databases on the bad guys; exchange intelligence on a regular, indeed institutionalized, basis; and cooperate closely on cross-border enforcement.[19] If there was any performance gap in the past, it was in enforcement and was attributable not to lower Canadian standards, but simply to fewer resources available to the Canadians relative to their U.S. counterparts. That gap was closing even prior to 9/11. Certainly, it has been reduced since the national security budget in early 2002, which allocated $49 million of new funding to immigration and border enforcement and over $110 million to security and intelligence agencies.

Despite these facts, there are influential forces in Canada always ready to reinforce American suspicions: the Canadian Alliance and its successive leaders; some provincial ministers; the *National Post*, Southam Press, Global and CTV News; and certain so-called terrorist experts. They have all relentlessly endorsed the idea that Canada is a haven for terrorists, where feeble security enforcement and loose social liberalism combine to provide a haven and base for terrorists threatening the United States. The existence of a cadre of serial confessors eager to assert Canadian responsibility for American security and intelligence failures is a curious feature of the Canadian political culture, even a subject for satire by a columnist in the principal offending newspaper, the *National Post*.[20] It has not made the task of the government any easier in managing an already delicate two-front campaign.

A more serious challenge to Canadian sovereignty is the widespread and influential support voiced by business lobbies, think tanks, and even the parliamentary committee on foreign affairs and international trade,[21] that Canada should seize the opportunity offered by 9/11 to think big and negotiate a much wider ranging arrangement for North American economic integration (including all, or some, of a customs union, a common labour market, adoption of the American currency). Opinion on this is divided between advocates who see a window of opportunity in the 9/11 security crisis, and opponents, some of whom are opposed in principle to integration, but all of whom see more dangers than opportunities in any deals made with an American administration in a highly unilateralist and nationalistic mood post 9/11. For a Liberal government preoccupied with managing Canadian-American relations on a range of touchy security issues, including military contributions to a war with Iraq, the prospect of entering onto the mine-laden field of comprehensive negotiations for a NAFTA Plus, can hardly seem appealing. Whether it can be avoided is another matter.

The prospect is mentioned here only to demonstrate that 9/11's impact on Canada is by no means straightforward. Nor was the impact of the Cold War. Indeed, on the matter of Canadian sovereignty in North America, there is considerable continuity between the Cold War and the war on terrorism. Both crises extend quickly from the security sphere to the economic sphere, and from there to the political and cultural dimensions of Canadian nationhood. In neither case, however, does a purely nationalist reading make much sense. It is not a question of U.S. hegemony versus Canadian resistance. Rather, the lines are drawn within Canada, as they were during the Cold War, between those advocating greater integration with the United States and greater support for the American international position, and those wishing to limit that support and insisting on skepticism toward greater integration as a by-product of security co-operation. The latter camp must come to terms with the reality that there is underlying public support for the general stance of Canadian-American co-operation. During the Cold War, Canadians generally agreed that the Communist bloc represented the chief security threat and accepted American leadership in contesting Communism as appropriate. In the current crisis, Canadian opinion accepts that terrorism is the major security threat and supports Canadian participation, under American leadership, in confronting terrorism. Neither then nor now does this mean Canadian support for all aspects of American leadership, or a willingness to follow the United States down any path—especially one entered upon in a unilateral fashion that ignores the United Nations and multilateral relationships. Yet underlying support, along with the inescapable economic realities of the existing degree of economic integration, limits the scope of open criticism of U.S. leadership and places Canadian governments in the position of negotiating degrees of integration, rather than allowing the liberty of asking whether greater integration ought to take place.

In 1965, George Grant published *Lament for a Nation*, in which he blamed the Liberal elites of the day for the demise of Canada, while nonetheless insisting on the inevitability of the end of nationhood. In the early 21st century, with another war replacing the Cold War that was Grant's despair, the role of the Liberal elites remains ambiguous and subject to varying interpretations, although this time there is more criticism of them as anti-American than as pro-American. The contradiction in Grant points to a paradox in both instances: in the face of powerful structural forces favouring integration and the decline of sovereignty, the Liberal elites are neither integrationist nor nationalist, rather they are negotiators of a persistently difficult passageway between pressures to go too far and pressures to go not far enough.

Critics of government security policy after 9/11 have charged that the anti-terrorist legislative changes brought before Parliament are largely a result of pressures to keep up with the neighbours. Indeed, among these critics is the former Director of CSIS, Reid Morden.[22] Yet on closer examination, there is rather less than meets the eye in this charge. Canada was indeed forced to legislate specifically in response to an American policy decision, in the case of federal aviation regulations demanding advance production of a range of personal data on passengers arriving from abroad at U.S. airports. Canada had no choice in this matter, short of losing landing rights for Canadian carriers, even though this American policy did necessitate overriding Canadian privacy law.

Beyond this instance, direct response to American pressure is more difficult to pin down. Certainly some indirect pressure may have been applied on Canada to comply with a generally more stringent anti-terrorist regime that was falling into place after 9/11. In its centerpiece *Anti-Terrorism Act*,[23] Canada felt compelled to join in the multilateral anti-terrorist campaign by, for instance, developing a legal definition of terrorism that conformed to definitions in various international texts, and in defining terrorist entities under Canadian law and listing them for the purposes of blocking the financing of terrorism, in conformity with international efforts sanctioned by the UN. With regard to stepped-up electronic surveillance powers—a key feature of American anti-terrorist legislation—the *Anti-Terrorism Act* is silent, except for an accompanying promise that Canada would develop legislation in conformity with the *European Convention on Cyber Crime*.[24] This promise is now in the process of enactment with the Justice Department's public consultation on lawful access.[25] Analysis of the *Anti-Terrorism Act*, as well as the proposed *Public Safety Act*, discloses little that can be seen as directly responding to specifically American demands, as such, or reflecting American provisions and practices.

Upon reflection, it is not difficult to discern why the relationship between American and Canadian legislative initiatives is relatively weak. While the terrorist threat may be similar in all Western countries, each country has its own unique set of political institutions and processes, its own legal traditions, and its own specific political forces in play.

The United Kingdom, with a long history of confronting Irish Republican terrorism in Britain, already had a very strong, in cases draconian, security legislation in place, in the form of successive *Prevention of Terrorism Acts*. Interestingly, one new power sought by the UK government was the deportation of persons suspected of terrorist associations to their places of origin, even in cases where this might entail returning a refugee to the country of their persecution, thus violating the UN Convention on Refugees.[26] This power was not sought by the Canadian government, and was specifically brought into question post-9/11 by the Supreme Court in the case of *Suresh*.[27]

The most striking divergence in practice, although not clearly in law, between Canada and the United States and United Kingdom post-9/11, has been the indefinite detention in the latter two countries of non-citizens on suspicion of terrorist associations. The Court of Appeal in the United Kingdom has agreed that foreign terror suspects can be held in the United Kingdom jails indefinitely without trial. There was an initial round of detentions in the United States just after 9/11, numbering somewhat over 1,000 (the exact figures have never been released), and sporadic detentions have taken place subsequently. The *USA PATRIOT Act*[28] as drafted by the Justice Department originally called for the power of indefinite detention of non-citizens on suspicion. This power proved controversial, however, and Congress insisted upon time limits on detention of seven days before cause had to be shown. The executive, relying on loopholes in the legislation, has detained non-citizens indefinitely, without legal representation. Various devices have been invoked, including the holding of suspects as material witnesses, normally used with regard to grand jury investigations, but in these cases leaving the question "material witnesses to *what?*" unanswered. This behaviour appears to demonstrate contempt for Congress, yet has elicited remarkably little criticism from that body. Nor has the issue of the constitutionality of the executive's actions been effectively challenged in the courts, although various challenges have yet to arrive at the final level of appeal in the Supreme Court. The issue of the treatment of non-citizens in the United States has been skewed by the administration's decision to treat foreign terrorists as enemy combatants, subject to military law outside the normal Geneva Convention rules for the treatment of prisoners of war. In two cases, the same treatment has been accorded U.S. citizens suspected of Al-Qaeda activities. To this point, the courts have upheld the administration's right to hold citizens indefinitely without legal representation and without judicial review.[29] In this instance, there are grave consequences for the constitutional rights of American citizens, a situation that has drawn strong criticism from at least some legal and journalistic quarters.

In Canada, indefinite detention on suspicion is not practised. Non-citizens subject to removal on security grounds are sometimes detained, a practice that predates 9/11. However, these persons are not denied representation and the Crown must show cause in court. The 1984 Supreme Court of Canada decision in the case of *Singh* would appear to raise an effective barrier against a general practice of differential treatment of non-citizens as falling outside the protection of the *Charter*.[30] If the United States had been insistent upon harmonization of North American immigration security rules, or if Canada had believed it necessary to conform to American practice on detentions in order to keep cross-border commerce flowing, the federal government might have been faced with having to invoke the notwithstanding clause to override the effect of *Singh*. Although such an action would no doubt have been approved by the same lobby that has been pushing in Canada for a more integrated perimeter security arrangement, the government has never even hinted that such an action was being contemplated. In short, U.S. pressure has been negligible on this issue.

During the passage of the *Anti-Terrorism Act*, considerable controversy was generated by provisions for preventive arrest and investigative hearings; both were ultimately subjected to a sunset clause. Preventive arrest is strictly limited to forty-eight hours, although refusal to comply with terms of recognizance could result in imprisonment. At all times, however, a person held under preventive arrest is fully represented. Investigative hearings appear to be modeled to a degree on the U.S. grand jury system, but even where a person brought before such a hearing could be compelled to testify against others, *Charter* protection against self-incrimination is explicitly recognized. Under questioning by a parliamentary committee in June, 2002, a senior Justice Department official acknowledged that neither of these extraordinary powers had by that date actually been invoked,[31] and there have been no subsequent reports of their use.

If this pattern persists, it will echo a precedent set ... during the early Cold War, when a series of amendments were made adding offences and stiffening penalties in the *Criminal Code* for treason, sabotage, and sedition—all of which are linked to the Cold War threat of Communism. Critics at the time suggested, without evidence, that these changes had been initiated by American pressures. If so, pressure had been fruitless: no Communist or Communist sympathizer was ever charged under the amended provisions, which lay dormant for almost two decades, until the October 1970 Crisis, when a seditious conspiracy provision was dusted off and used against five people accused of being associated with the FLQ, newly banned under the *War Measures Act*. All such charges failed in court.[32] There is thus some precedent for tough sounding legislative actions that prove to be more symbolic than substantive in intention.

The main reason for downplaying American pressures as a basis of Canadian legislation is that a great deal of the *Anti-Terrorism Act* is not directly related to 9/11 at all, but answers to wider and deeper issues surrounding the legal and institutional framework for national security policy. Among the non-9/11 related elements of the *Anti-Terrorism Act*:

- The *Official Secrets Act* is replaced by a new *Security of Information Act*, including new offences such as economic espionage;
- The Communications Security Establishment (CSE), the electronic eavesdropping agency, is for the first time given a statutory mandate, with its powers and limitations spelled out, and with an important additional power to retain Canadian communications related to terrorism (this is 9/11 related);
- Serious limitations are imposed on the *Access to Information, Privacy,* and *Personal Information Protection and Electronic Documents Acts* with regard to disclosure and retention of information relating to national security; and
- Provisions regarding non-disclosure of sensitive national security evidence serve mainly to *Charter*-proof existing evidence provisions following the *Stinchcombe* decision of the Supreme Court of Canada.[33]

Taken together with the Canadian Security Intelligence Service Act[34] and the Security Offences Act[35] of 1984 (the latter now augmented by An Act to Amend the Foreign Missions and International Organizations Act)[36] and the Immigration and Refugee Protection Act,[37] the last two passed just prior to 9/11 and the latter itself amended by C-36, the Anti-Terrorism Act constitutes the basis for comprehensive Canadian national security legislation, which will be further augmented when the Public Safety Act finally becomes law. The opportunity offered by 9/11 was alertly seized by the Canadian security and intelligence community, which has ended up with much more than it would likely have achieved had 9/11 not happened. But most of these ideas for change were already in the pipeline in Ottawa, sometimes for years, awaiting the political push that would bring them to the front of the policy agenda. The push came from Al-Qaeda, not from the United States. The specifics of Canada's national security policy regime owes little to the model of the U.S. system; indeed, on many important points, it differs sharply from their American neighbours.[38]

Nor does Canada show enthusiasm for emulating the Americans in another particular: the targeting of the Muslim minority as a threat to security. Both governments began shortly after 9/11 by saying all the right things that would steer the majority away from the kind of ethnic victimization of the Japanese communities that occurred in both countries during World War II. In both countries, the objective effect of security policies has amounted to ethnic profiling of Muslims in practice. From a policing and security perspective, the targeting of high risk people simply represents the effective direction of resources; from the perspective of those flagged for particular attention, the policy represents ethnic and religious victimization. In the US, apparent anti-Muslim bias in government policy is becoming increasingly public. Although targeting has focused on non-citizens, the line between aliens and Muslim-Americans is increasingly blurred, or so it is perceived to be by Muslim-Americans. The requirements for all aliens from listed Muslim countries to register with the Immigration and Naturalization Service has sent a deep chill through the entire Muslim-American community.[39]

The targeting of people born in certain so-called high-risk Muslim countries attempting to enter the United States—and their subsequent special treatment, including interrogation and fingerprinting—has raised official protests from Canada regarding Canadian citizens whose treatment on arrival at American entry points seems to be discrimination on the basis of their country of birth.[40] Canada does practise effective ethnic profiling in its own antiterrorist security measures, but it typically does so in a more guarded, less public manner than the Americans. This is a parallel to the McCarthy era in the United States during the early Cold War, when

Canadians somewhat smugly congratulated themselves on avoiding the excesses of Communist witch hunting in the United States, while at the same time doing some of the same things behind closed doors. Yet it is the very public singling out of Muslims that sets off alarm bells among minority communities at risk in the United States, while these same groups tend to feel less threatened in Canada. In an eerie parallel to the Cold War, when threatened leftists, especially in academe, fled across the border to find safer havens in Canada, there were reports in early 2003 of Muslims from the United States seeking refuge in Canada.[41]

IV. CONCLUDING REFLECTIONS

Canada's response to 9/11 does indicate that keeping up with the neighbours is, to a degree, an important guide to public policy. Like the Cold War, the war on terrorism is a multilateral effort under American leadership. As a participant in the alliance, Canada has to do many things to keep up its part. However, most of these things it would have done on its own, both to assure an anxious public concerned about threats to their security, and to pre-empt the Americans from taking more drastic measures that would directly threaten Canadian sovereignty. Ottawa recognizes that important, and influential, sections of the Canadian business, political, and media elites constantly push for greater integration with the United States and greater harmonization of Canadian policies with U.S. policies, and that these pressures are more influential than usual during times of international crisis and high insecurity. At the same time, Canadian public opinion demands some distance from the appearance that Canadian policy is being dictated from Washington. This latter tendency is heightened when the U.S. leadership is perceived by many in Canada as immoderate and potentially dangerous, which seems to be the case today.

As historical precedents, the Cold War and the October 1970 Crisis demonstrate that Canada is capable of acting forcefully, and with relatively few restraints, in dealing with a perceived threat from within linked to a threat from without. The anti-terrorism legislation and the shift in resources towards national security enforcement in the wake of 9/11 come as no surprise. Yet the historical precedents are double-edged. If they suggest a capacity for repressive and illiberal actions in the name of national security, it is also the case that the long-term result of both of these crises was to strengthen liberal democracy and the protection of civil liberties, as a direct consequence of revulsion generated by repressive and unaccountable state actions. This too is part of the historical background to the present crisis. Canadians have learned from experience about the consequences of overreaction. There is a space between the Canadian and American responses, partly generated by the direction of the terrorist threat primarily against the United States, and partly generated by differences in the political cultures. This space allows Canadians some critical distance, some room to develop made-in-Canada policies, and some capacity to resist American pressures—especially when these pressures come in the form of unilateralist, America First, imperatives. Canada is always more comfortable keeping up with the neighbours when this is a multilateral enterprise.

QUESTIONS TO CONSIDER

1. Given the tendency among officials to deny legal recourse to those suspected of treason or terrorism, under what circumstances should we tolerate denying legal rights to such suspects? What lessons from the Cold War era and the October Crisis might be brought forward in assessing law and policy decisions by the Canadian and U.S. governments after 9/11? Use specific examples to strengthen your position.

2. To what extent are the principles of democracy, human rights, and the rule of law eroded by economic factors such as cross-border trade? How might the issue of globalization be introduced in any analysis of national security measures against alleged terrorists?

3. To what extent has Canada behaved autonomously in the face of American security policies and pressures to "keep up with the neighbours"? Review Professor Whitaker's examples and draw on outside sources in building your argument for ways in which Canada can "stand tall" beside (or against) other countries combating terrorism.

SUGGESTIONS FOR FURTHER READING

Canada. Standing Committee on Public Safety and National Security. (2007). *Rights, limits, security: A comprehensive review of the anti-terrorism act and related issues.* Ottawa: SCPSNS.

Diab, R. (2008). *Guantánamo north: Terrorism and the administration of justice in Canada.* Black Point, NS: Fernwood Publications.

Moeller, S. (2009). *Packaging terrorism: Co-opting the news for politics and profit.* Malden, MA: Wiley-Blackwell.

NOTES

1. The historical sections of this paper draw freely from my article "Before September 11—Some History Lessons" in Canadian Institute for the Administration of Justice, *Terrorism, Law & Democracy: How Is Canada Changing Following September11?* (Montreal: les Editions Thémis, 2002) 39–54.
2. Reg Whitaker & Gary Marcuse, *Cold War Canada: The Making of a National Insecurity State, 1945–1957* (Toronto: University of Toronto Press, 1994) [Cold War Canada].
3. Repealed, R.S.C., 1985, c. 22 (4th Supp.) s.80.
4. *Supra* note 1.
5. *The Report of the Royal Commission Appointed Under Order in Council P.C. 411 of February 5, 1946* (Ottawa: King's Printer, 1946).
6. *Security of Information Act*, R.S.C., 1985, c. O-5, s 1; 2001, c. 41, s. 25.
7. Reg Whitaker, *Double Standard: The Secret History of Canadian Immigration* (Toronto: Lester & Orpen Dennys, 1987).
8. Canada, *Commission of Inquiry Concerning Certain Activities of the RCMP, Second Report: Freedom and Security Under the Law*, vol. 1 (Ottawa: Minister of Supply & Services, 1981) at 518. According to the 1971 census, the total population of Canada was 21,568,000: 800,000 files represent information on more than one out of every twenty-seven Canadians.
9. Leading figures, even in retrospect, were evasive in their justifications. Immediately after the crisis, a prominent Quebec minister in the Trudeau government, Gérard Pelletier, published a memoir, *Le Crise d'Octobre* (Montreal: Editions du Jour, 1971). In Mr. Trudeau's own memoirs, his account of the affair raises many questions of both fact and interpretation: Pierre Elliott Trudeau, *Memoirs* (Toronto: McClelland & Stewart, 1993) at 128–52.
10. Reg Whitaker, "Apprehended Insurrection? RCMP Intelligence and the October Crisis" (1993) 100:2 Queen's Quarterly 383.
11. *Emergencies Act*, R.S.C., 1985, c. 22 (4th Supp.).
12. There are a number of polls that have shown that Canadian support for the war on terrorism, and the Afghan intervention, has remained strong. For instance, EKOS reported in August 2002 that three out of five Canadians supported Canadian military participation in Afghanistan, while only one in five were opposed. See "September 11th in Hindsight, Recovery and Resolve" online: *EKOS Research Associates* <http://www. ekos.com/admin/articles/9sept2002.pdf> at 22, 23 (date accessed: 18 May 2003). Gallup reported in September 2002 that sixty-one per cent of Canadians approved of the U.S. conduct of the war on terrorism. An invasion of Iraq was received much less enthusiastically. In January 2003, Ipsos-Reid found that only fifteen per cent of Canadians

would support Canadian participation in an Iraq war without UN sanction, less than the eighteen per cent who were opposed to any war, with or without UN sanctions. See "A Special Report: Attacking Iraq" online: *Ipsos-Reid* <http://www.ipsos-reid.com/media/dsp_displaypr.prnt.cfm?D_to_view = 1711> (date accessed: 28 May 2003).

13. A year after 9/11, CRIC (Centre for Research and Information on Canada) reported a dramatic turnaround: thirty-five per cent of the population wanted Canadian ties to the United States to be "more distant," an increase of twenty-two points over October 2001; twenty-eight per cent of the population wanted closer ties to the United States, a decrease of five points over October 2001. See "More Canadians Distance Themselves From U.S. Neighbours" online: *Centre for Research and Information on Canada* <http://www.cric.ca/pdf/ cric_poll/borderlines_ca_us/borderlines_pressneighbours sept2002.pdf> (date accessed:18 May 2003).

14. Coalition for Secure & Trade-Efficient Borders, *Rethinking our Borders: A Plan for Action* (3 December 2001); Presentation of Thomas D'Aquino, President and Chief Executive (January 14, 2003) "Security and Prosperity: The Dynamics of a New Canada-United States Partnership in North America," to the Annual General Meeting of the Canadian Council of Chief Executives, Toronto, online: <http://www.ceocouncil.ca/English/ Publications/ reports/jan14-03.pdf> (date accessed: 18 May 2003).

15. Reg Whitaker, "More or Less Than Meets the Eye? The New National Security Agenda," in Bruce Doern, ed., *How Ottawa Spends 2003/04* [forthcoming 2003].

16. Department of Foreign Affairs and International Trade ("dfait"). *The Canada-U.S. Smart Border Declaration*, online: *DFAIT* <http://www.dfait-maeci.gc.ca/anti-terrorism/declaration-e.asp> (date accessed: 18 May 2003). DFAIT News Release, "Manley and Ridge Release Program Report on the Smart Border Declaration and Action Plan" (28 June 2002), online: *DFAIT* <http://webapps.dfait-maeci.gc.ca/minpub/Publication.asp?FileSpec=/ Min_Pub_Docs/105343.htm&bPrint=False& Year> (date accessed: 18 May 2003).

17. The pre-9/11 case most cited by critics is that of Ahmed Ressam, apprehended in late 1999 attempting to enter the United States at Port Angeles, Washington, on his way to play a part in a planned millennium terror attack on the L.A. Airport. Yet in 2001, U.S. Attorney General John Ashcroft brushed off critics of Canadian security by insisting that in this case the United States had acted on information provided by Canadian authorities, with whom cooperation was "outstanding"; interview of John Ashcroft (4 December 2001) on CTV News, CTV Television.

18. Sheldon Alberts, "Clinton refuses Ottawa's call for apology" *The National Post*, January 10, 2003.

19. Reg Whitaker, "Refugee Policy After September 11: Not Much New" (2001) 20:4 Refuge 29.

20. Paul Wells, "Thousands die—blame Canada" *The National Post* (18 December, 2001) A6.

21. House of Commons, *Partners in North America: Advancing Canada's Relations with the United States and Mexico*, Report of the Standing Committee on Foreign Affairs and International Trade (December 2002), online: <http://www.parl.gc.ca/InfoComDoc/37/2/FAIT/PressReleases/FAITpr2-e.htm> (date accessed: 18 May 2003).

22. Reid Morden, "Finding the right balance" (2002) 23:06 Policy Options 45–8.

23. S.C. 2001, c. 41. Even before its final passage, this legislative package received extraordinary academic attention in a book of essays, most of which were critical: Ronald J. Daniels, Patrick Macklem, & Kent Roach, eds., *The Security of Freedom: Essays on Canada's Anti-Terrorism Bill* (Toronto: University of Toronto Press, 2001). See also Erroll P. Mendes & Debra M. McAllister, eds., *Between Crime and War: Terrorism, Democracy and the Constitution,* (2002) 14:1 N.J.C.L.

24. ETS No. 185, Budapest, November 23, 2001.

25. Department of Justice Canada, Lawful Access—Consultation Document (25 August 2002): online: *Department of Justice Canada* <http://www.canada.justice.gc.ca/en/cons/la_al/> (date accessed: 18 May 2003).

26. *Anti-Terrorism, Crime and Security, Act 2001* (U.K.), 2001, c. 24, ss. 21–22.

27. Audrey Macklin, "Mr. Suresh and the Evil Twin" (2002) 20:4 Refuge 15.

28. Pub. L. No. 107–56, 115 Stat. 272 (2001). Uniting and Strengthening America by Providing Appropriate Tools required to Intercept and Obstruct Terrorism (*USA Patriot Act*).

29. These are the cases of Yasser Esam Hamdi, one of the enemy combatants captured in Afghanistan who turned out to have been American-born, and José Padilla, the so-called dirty bomb suspect. Both cases continue through the legal appeal process, but in the case of Hamdi a federal appeals court ruled in early 2003 that in wartime the state can indefinitely detain a United States citizen captured as an enemy combatant on the battlefield and deny that person access to a lawyer. Neil A. Lewis, "US Is Allowed to Hold Citizen as Combatant" *New York Times* (January 9, 2003).

30. *Singh et al. v. Canada* (Minister of Employment and Immigration), [1985] S.C.R. 177.

31. Testimony of Richard Mosley, Assistant Deputy Minister, Criminal Law Policy, Department of Justice (June 10, 2002), to the House of Commons Sub-Committee on National Security, online: <http://www.parl. gc.ca/InfoComDoc/37/1/SNAS/Meetings/Evidence/snasev05-e-htm#Int-278274> (date accessed: 18 May 2003).

32. M. L. Friedland, *National Security: the Legal Dimensions*, study prepared for the Royal Commission of Inquiry Concerning Certain Activities of the RCMP (Ottawa: 1979) 22–30, *Cold War Canada, supra* note 2 at 197– 204.

33. *R. v. Stinchcombe*, [1991] 3 S.C.R. 326, ordered the production in court of criminal intelligence relevant to the defence. *Stinchcombe* was a criminal case and its relevance to national security cases was unclear. The evidence provisions in C-36 are in the spirit of better safe than sorry.

34. R.S.C. 1985, c. 23 (note: pending amendment not in force, S.C. 2001, c 27,ss 223–226).

35. R.S.C. 1985, s. S-7.

36. S.C. 2002, c. 12.

37. S.C. 2002, c. 27.

38. A notable example of institutional difference is the debate that has opened in Washington since 9/11 about the desirability of splitting the FBI into a counter-terrorist intelligence agency and an institutional separate criminal law enforcement body. In Canada, this was done in 1984 with the CSIS Act separating the security service from the RCMP.

39. American Civil Liberties Union, Press release: "Immigrant Registration Program Pretext for Mass Detentions" (December 19, 2002).

40. David Ljunggren, "Upset Canada Issues Rare Caution on Travel to U.S." *Reuters* (October 30, 2002).

41. Michael Powell, "Pakistanis Flee to Canada and Uncertainty: Families Uprooted By INS Deadline" *The Washington Post* (January 18, 2003) A01.

Chapter Fifteen

Excerpts from *Unnatural Law*: *Rethinking Canadian Environmental Law and Policy*

David R. Boyd

Editors' Note: The final chapter in this book deals with government policies, self-regulation in the private sector, and federal and legislative responses concerning the environment. This chapter consists of excerpts from two chapters in David Boyd's comprehensive book, Unnatural Law: Rethinking Canadian Environmental Law and Policy *(2003). He points out how Canada's track record of environmental protection often falls short of government and private-sector rhetoric and promises.*

Systemic obstacles include (1) a sub-par performance on several environmental measures compared with other developed countries; (2) inordinate discretionary power of governmental officials whereby they have "no duty" to exercise their powers; (3) absence of key legislation, including nation-wide laws and comprehensive laws; (4) the repeated failure to incorporate scientific findings or to establish policies based on conservation biology; (5) substantial barriers to public input and influence in devising environmental legislation and specific policies; and (6) a limited range of legal measures and public policies, worsened by the failure to explore new approaches beyond the traditional polarization of either strict control or deregulation and reliance on voluntary measures from industry and other private-sector stakeholders.

In exploring the nature of environmental protection and public safety in Canada, Boyd outlines more hopeful initiatives that could be implemented to improve governance in environmental matters. His research helps to advance long-established work in support of environmental protection as well as emerging critical perspectives within Criminology.

Systemic Weaknesses

Despite significant advances in Canada, including some progress in terms of the rehabilitation of particular sites and ecosystems, there can be no illusion about general success in bringing severe threats of continuing environmental risk under control.

—*Professor Jamie Benidickson, Environmental Law*

While it is encouraging to recognize that Canada has made progress in some aspects of environmental protection, the reality is that on most environmental issues Canada is performing poorly. On seventeen of twenty-five environmental indicators, Canada is among the five worst nations in the OECD [Organization for Economic Development]. The future of Canadian environmental laws and policies results, in large part, from six systemic weaknesses. First, Canada still lacks a number of important environmental laws that are commonplace in other industrialized nations. Second, existing Canadian laws and regulations are undermined

---

Source: David Boyd, *Unnatural Law: Rethinking Canadian Environmental Law and Policy*, UBC Press, 2003, pp. 228–250 for Chapter 8, "Systemic Weaknesses"; pp. 251–272 for Chapter 9, "Obstacles to Further Progress." Reprinted by permission of UBC Press.

by excessive discretion. Third, environmental laws and policies fail to reflect contemporary scientific knowledge and principles. Fourth, Canadian environmental law suffers from inadequate resources for implementation and enforcement. Weak implementation and enforcement are exacerbated by budget cuts, the downloading of environmental responsibilities (from the federal government to the provinces, and from provinces to municipalities), and excessive reliance on voluntary initiatives. Fifth, the public has insufficient opportunities to participate meaningfully in developing and enforcing environmental laws. Sixth, Canadian governments rely on an unduly narrow range of law and policy options in their efforts to protect the environment.

MISSING LAWS

Some of the most basic, rudimentary environmental laws enacted by other nations are still absent in Canada. The most obvious comparison is between Canada and the United States. For example, at the federal level Canada has

- no enforceable national air quality standards
- no enforceable national water quality standards
- no national law guaranteeing safe drinking water
- no national law requiring the clean-up of contaminated sites
- no national law to protect wilderness areas outside of national parks
- no law to protect wild and scenic rivers
- no law guaranteeing citizens access to information about all of the types and sources of toxic pollution in their communities
- no comprehensive law to protect whales and other marine mammals
- no national law to protect wetlands
- no national hazardous waste law
- no law requiring sustainable fishing practices
- no law to address the threat of invasive exotic species
- no national forest management law.

In contrast, at the federal level the United States has, respectively, the Clean Air Act, the Clean Water Act, the Safe Drinking Water Act, the Comprehensive Environmental Response, Compensation and Liability Act, the Wilderness Act, the Wild and Scenic River Act, the Emergency Planning and Community Right-to-Know Act, the Marine Mammal Protective Act, the Emergency Wetland Resources Act, the Resource Conservation and Recovery Act, the Sustainable Fisheries Act, the National Invasive Species Act, and the National Forest Management Act. While Canada has policies such as the National Ambient Air Quality Objectives, the Canadian Heritage Rivers program, and the Guidelines for Canadian Drinking Water Quality, none of these policies has any legal effect. These nonbinding policy mechanisms are clearly less effective than enforceable national legislation, regulations, and standards.[1]

This comparison is not meant to suggest that by merely passing a long list of laws Canada will solve its environmental woes, nor that the United States is an ecological utopia. Nor is this comparison intended to suggest that the federal government bears full responsibility for environmental protection; Canada's Constitution places more power in provincial hands than the US Constitution gives to the states. Yet none of the gaps in Canada's federal environmental law identified above are adequately addressed by provincial laws. Some provinces have endangered species legislation while other provinces do not. Some provinces have safe drinking water laws while others do not. Some provinces have air quality standards while others do not. And so on. The result of these inconsistencies is that environmental standards vary widely among Canadian provinces and territories. The patchwork of provincial laws and policies is widely regarded as "a stumbling block to coordinate national action."[2] American states have more consistent environmental law regimes than Canadian provinces because they are responsible for meeting national standards established by federal environmental laws, and because the US government provides extensive funding to states for the purpose of environmental protection, which does not happen in Canada.

From time to time there have been unsuccessful efforts to fill some of the gaps in Canadian environmental law. Detailed proposals have been published by the Canadian Bar Association, the Law Reform Commission of Canada, academics, think tanks, and public interest environmental law organizations. In response, governments have promised laws but never introduced them, introduced laws but never passed them, and passed laws but never proclaimed them. Instead of moving forward, some provincial governments have begun to eliminate environmental laws and regulations.[3] In short, as an international assessment of environmental laws around the world concluded, in Canada "there is no coherent or comprehensive legislative and regulatory scheme" to protect the environment.[4]

Filling the Gaps

To suggest that more laws and regulations are required to protect the environment runs counter to the prevailing political atmosphere in much of Canada, which is antagonistic to regulations. The situation in Canada is part of a global trend, as "regulators are in retreat, reluctant to argue for new or tougher regulations for fear of alienating either their political masters or influential business lobbies who are never reticent to suggest that such regulations will make them less competitive, or hasten their move to another jurisdiction."[5] This anti-regulatory attitude can have serious environmental consequences. The report of the Walkerton Inquiry identified the Ontario government's hostility toward regulation as a contributing factor in the contaminated water disaster.[6]

Canadian businesses complain about the allegedly onerous burden of environmental regulation, arguing that the market should be allowed to take the place of "regulatory red tape."[7] Although provincial governments in Alberta, Ontario, and British Columbia aggressively eliminated environmental regulations in response to these concerns, evidence suggests that the problem is illusory. A study conducted in 1999 revealed that Canada has the lowest business costs of all the countries in the G7. A seventy-five-country study by the World Bank concluded that Canada "throws up less red tape" than any other nation it examined.[8] Industries in Canada face fewer regulatory obstacles in the environmental field than their competitors in the United States.[9]

In any case, studies have not found that environmental policy reduces business competitiveness.[10] Strong, well-designed regulations can inspire technological innovation and enhance international competitiveness. The OECD and other economic experts agree that "environmental legislation can be a driver spurring technological changes that lead to efficiency and competitive advantages."[11] Strong air pollution standards helped make Germany a world leader in air pollution technology, while British environmental technology exports fell when Britain's standards lagged under Margaret Thatcher.[12] Canada's former finance minister, Paul Martin, supports the strategy of using environmental regulations to promote industrial competitiveness.[13] Numerous American studies have found that the states with the strongest environmental laws and policies enjoy the highest levels of economic growth and job creation.[14]

It seems that "couching the debate in terms of either regulation or deregulation kindles a spurious and sterile ideological divide, which inhibits attempts to find solutions containing the best of both approaches."[15] For some environmental problems, regulation has been very effective…. For other environmental problems, different law and policy solutions are required. The choice between more government and less government is a false choice. What Canada really needs is better governance, which will probably require more government intervention (including, though not necessarily limited to, more regulation) to achieve superior environmental protection.

Positive Signs

Despite industry opposition, Canada has recently shown signs that it may finally address some of the longstanding lacunae in its array of environmental laws. Federally, the long-awaited enactment of the *Species at Risk Act* and changes to the *Pest Control Products Act* in 2002, and the designation of major air pollutants as toxic substances under the *Canadian Environmental Protection Act, 1999*, represent steps in the right direction. At the provincial level, several provinces strengthened regulations for drinking water safety in response to the Walkerton disaster, efforts to limit acid rain through stronger regulations continue, and most provinces now prohibit bulk water exports.

There are still many holes to be filled before Canada's legal system can be said to comprehensively address threats to the environment. Moreover, whether new or existing laws and regulations passed by Canadian governments will be effective remains in doubt, as the following section explains.

EXCESSIVE DISCRETION

The second systemic weakness in Canadian environmental law is that the vast majority of laws and regulations are undermined by their broadly discretionary nature. Environmental laws are almost always drafted in such a way as to give Canadian governments the power to take action or meet specified standards but no duty to take action or meet those standards. Discretion is one of the defining characteristics of Canadian environmental law, as it pervades almost every law, regulation, and policy.[16] Seemingly insignificant differences in wording, such as using "may" instead of "must," transform potentially effective laws and regulations into paper tigers.

A prime example of the problem caused by discretionary powers in environmental law is provided by federal statutes that enable, but do not require, Ottawa to address cross-border issues where provincial actions are insufficient to address a problem. Such provisions are found in the *Canada Water Act*, *Canada Wildlife Act*, *Canadian Environmental Assessment Act*, and the *Canadian Environmental Protection Act, 1999*. These provisions have never been used, although they have existed for up to thirty years. The federal government has never used its discretionary power to require an environmental assessment of a project with international impacts, interprovincial impacts, or impacts on Aboriginal people. Nor has Ottawa ever used its discretionary power to address the sources of transboundary air or water pollution, or to protect wildlife at risk.[17]

There are many more examples of problematic discretion at the federal level. Under the *Canadian Environmental Assessment Act*, the federal government retains the discretion to approve a project even when experts determine that the project will have "significant adverse environmental effects." Over 99.9 percent of projects subject to federal environmental assessment are approved. The *Species at Risk Act* authorizes but does not require the federal government to establish a national safety net to protect endangered species and their habitat on provincial and private lands. Enforcement of environmental laws is also entirely discretionary, and not subject to judicial review.[18] In other words, the government cannot be forced to enforce the law. According to Professor George Hoberg, environmental laws in Canada "do not contain sufficient nondiscretionary action-forcing language to justify judicial intervention."[19]

Provincial laws rendered ineffective by excessive discretion include endangered species legislation that enables but does not require the designation of species at risk, the protection of habitat, or the preparation of recovery plans. Because these provisions are discretionary, provincial laws do not protect most known endangered species, habitat is rarely protected, and recovery plans are rarely prepared. Provincial forest management laws give bureaucrats the discretion to approve logging beside streams, on steep slopes, and in areas that are important for drinking water or wildlife. As a result, logging commonly occurs right up to the banks of fish streams, on steep slopes subject to erosion, in community watersheds, and in critical wildlife habitat. Provincial drinking water laws give officials the power to protect drinking water sources but do not require the exercise of those powers. As a result, few sources of drinking water are protected. Provincial pollution laws allow discretion to be exercised in granting permits to pollute, resulting in unsafe air emissions and effluent discharges.

In its discretionary nature, the Canadian legal system differs markedly from the American legal system: Canadian environmental laws are "far more discretionary than comparable U.S. statutes."[20] For example, the US *Endangered Species Act* states that where there is scientific evidence that a species is endangered, the species must be listed under the *Act*. If government refuses to act, US citizens can use a variety of administrative and legal means to force government to comply with the law.[21] Accountability is built into the system, and is reinforced by the courts. In Canada, the listing of species is usually left to government discretion, so few species receive legal protection. If governments choose not to exercise their discretion, that is the end of the matter, because governments cannot be legally compelled to do so.[22] Excessive discretion thus profoundly limits the utility and efficacy of environmental legislation in Canada. The discretionary nature of Canadian environmental law dramatically reduces political accountability and undermines the judicial system's ability to act as a check on the exercise of bureaucratic decision making.

Beacons of Hope

The predominance of discretion in Canadian environmental laws may be starting to diminish. Some important provisions in recently enacted Canadian environmental legislation are mandatory rather than discretionary. For example, federal and provincial laws governing ozone-depleting chemicals and energy-efficient appliances use mandatory language. The *Canadian Environmental Protection Act, 1999* imposes a mandatory obligation on the federal government to enact regulations to address the threats posed by substances designated as toxic. Changes to the *Pest Control Products Act* require regular reevaluation of pesticides. The new *Canada National Parks Act* mandates the protection of ecological integrity and the designation of wilderness areas identified in park management plans. Saskatchewan's *Forest Resources Management Act* requires mandatory environmental assessment and auditing of forest management plans. However, the majority of Canadian environmental laws are still largely discretionary.

THE FAILURE TO REFLECT CONTEMPORARY SCIENCE

The third systemic flaw running through Canadian environmental law and policy is the failure to incorporate contemporary scientific knowledge and principles. For example, laws governing endangered species, protected areas, and marine biodiversity do not reflect principles of conservation biology. The new *Species at Risk Act* protects "residences" rather than critical habitat. Laws governing parks and protected areas allow activities that are incompatible with the conservation of biodiversity, despite the role that these areas are intended to play in conserving nature. The new *National Marine Conservation Areas Act* allows fishing in marine protected

areas, although fishing is the main threat to marine biodiversity. Increasing scientific awareness of the critical importance of the ecological services provided by water, forests, and other
ecosystems is not yet reflected in environmental laws or policies.[23]

One of the most important scientific advances, ironically, is the recognition of how little
humans understand about ecosystems, ecological processes, the relationship between chemicals
and health, and other critical environmental issues. Only half of the species believed to live in
Canada have been identified. The rate and severity of climate change, the rate of healing of the
ozone layer, and the long-term health and environmental impacts of chemicals that disrupt
endocrine systems are vital issues for which science offers no definitive answers. As a result,
environmental law and policy must confront pervasive uncertainty. Two important scientific
concepts—the precautionary principle and adaptive management—have emerged to respond
to this uncertainty. However, neither of these concepts has been incorporated in a meaningful
way into Canadian environmental laws and policies.

The Precautionary Principle

The precautionary principle requires that "where there are threats of serious or irreversible
damage, lack of full scientific certainty should not be used as a reason for postponing measures to prevent environmental degradation." This principle is quickly becoming an established
norm of international law.[24] Canadian environmental law is generally based on the opposite of
the precautionary principle, in that conclusive scientific evidence of harm is necessary before
steps will be taken to limit an activity or restrict the use of a particular substance.[25]

However, many notoriously dangerous chemicals were once deemed safe.[26] Paul Hermann
Müller received the Nobel Prize in 1948 for his discovery that DDT is an efficient insecticide.
Not until decades later was DDT banned in Canada after scientists identified the disastrous
ecological effects of using DDT in agriculture. Other examples of past failures include chloro-
fluorocarbons (CFCs), regarded as wonder chemicals until scientists discovered their destructive impact on the ozone layer, and PCBs, used extensively in electrical applications before
their harmful health and environmental effects became apparent. Back in the 1920s, Ethyl
Corporation argued that there was no conclusive scientific proof that putting lead in gasoline
would cause health impacts, although medical experts at the time expressed concern.[27] Decades
passed before the scientific evidence and public outcry convinced governments to ban leaded
gasoline. A precautionary approach could have prevented the tragic damage caused by these
substances.

The stories of DDT, CFCs, PCBs, and lead cannot be dismissed as past mistakes that will
not be repeated. In 2002 American scientists revealed that one of the most widely used pesticides in Canada and the United States, atrazine, has unexpected and devastating impacts on
frogs at very low levels of exposure. Although exposed to atrazine at levels lower than existing
standards for drinking water, frogs in lab tests and in the wild exhibited hermaphroditic characteristics—possessing both male and female sexual organs.[28] The implications of these findings for human health are unknown.

Canadian regulation of pesticides and toxic chemicals demonstrates the law's failure to
apply the precautionary principle. All Canadians are living science experiments, with hundreds
of synthetic chemicals present in our bodies.[29] More than 110,000 chemicals are in use globally,
and approximately 1,000 new chemicals are added annually. Yet for most chemicals there are
no long-term studies of their health and environmental impacts, no studies of the ways that
they might interact in combination with other chemicals in the environment, and no studies of
their cumulative impacts in addition to other environmental stressors. Despite these known
knowledge gaps, Canada attempts to regulate single chemicals rather than the combination of

chemicals that characterize actual exposures. Because of industry pressure, Canada takes a reductionist approach whereby "every regulatory proposal is studied and contested for years until it theoretically provides acceptable public health protection from one chemical and one route of exposure."[30] Scientists argue that the "complexity of underlying biological and physical systems precludes a reductionist approach to management."[31]

The current approach of studying chemicals in isolation in an effort to find conclusive evidence of harm to health or the environment is expensive, difficult, and slow. Canada has fully evaluated only one hundred or so chemicals and designated only fifty-two substances as toxic under the *Canadian Environmental Protection Act, 1999*. The reevaluation process for pesticides continues to crawl along under the *Pest Control Products Act*. Although the total *volume* of releases of toxic chemicals in Canada appears to be stabilizing or declining, the *toxicity* of waste streams is increasing.[32] The overall goal of a precautionary approach should be to reduce risks to human health and the environment through pollution prevention.[33]

The controversy surrounding genetically modified organisms provides another example of Canada's failure to apply the precautionary principle.[34] Canada is one of the world's largest producers and exporters of genetically modified crops despite widespread public concern about the potential impacts.[35] Biotechnology in Canada is regulated under a tangled array of federal laws including the *Food and Drug Act, Fertilizers Act, Feeds Act, Seeds Act, Pest Control Products Act, Health of Animals Act, Fisheries Act*, and the *Canadian Environmental Protection Act, 1999*. The *Canadian Environmental Protection Act, 1999*, which is alone among these laws in incorporating the precautionary principle, applies only to biotechnology products not covered by the other laws. Lawyers warn that "it is questionable whether the current legislative and regulatory scheme is capable of preventing or mitigating any large-scale ecological disaster."[36] Government is supposed to be an "honest broker" but has been an "aggressive promoter" of plant biotechnology.[37] In short, the precautionary principle is not being used in Canada's regulatory approach to biotechnology.[38]

To make matters worse, Canada has argued against the precautionary principle in international forums, such as the World Trade Organization (WTO) and negotiations on the *Cartagena Protocol in Biosafety*.[39] When France banned asbestos imports because of health concerns, Canada challenged the French law in proceedings before the WTO. Although the WTO upheld the French ban, Canada continues to aggressively challenge other nations that attempt to ban asbestos, such as Chile.[40] Canada succeeded in persuading the WTO to overturn a European ban on Canadian beef produced with growth hormones, despite Europe's argument that its ban was a precautionary measure.[41]

Adaptive Management

Adaptive management recognizes the intrinsic variability of natural systems and the pervasive uncertainty inherent in regulating environmental issues.[42] Scientists are urging government and industry to practice adaptive management because it makes practical and effective links among science, policy, and law. In the legal context, adaptive management means adjusting laws and policies to reflect new knowledge and changing conditions. Canada's failure to incorporate the principles of adaptive management into the development of environmental laws and policies results in legislation that remains inflexible, even in light of ecological collapse.

Most areas of environmental law and policy would benefit greatly from adopting adaptive management. For example, the rate of logging in Canada should decline, in order to reflect our better understanding of the global and ecological values of forests. The designation of new protected areas should reflect improvements in our understanding of the size and representation required for marine areas, grasslands, old-growth forests, and large wilderness areas. Instead, relevant laws are not amended, bottom-dragging continues in sensitive ocean habitats despite evidence of habitat damage, pesticides are used in Canada that have been banned for health and environmental reasons in other nations, and point sources of pollution are emphasized when nonpoint sources now constitute the bulk of the problem. Adaptive management offers policy and law makers a framework that recognizes, simultaneously, that natural resource use is necessary but must be sustainable.

Signs of Hope

Some Canadian laws are beginning to reflect contemporary scientific principles. For example, the *Canada National Parks Act* and the *National Marine Conservation Areas Act* emphasize the importance of maintaining ecological integrity. More statutes are recognizing the meaning and value of biodiversity.[43] Several recently enacted or amended environmental laws in Canada tentatively incorporate the precautionary principle.[44] For example, the precautionary principle is specifically referred to in the *Species at Risk Act, Pest Control Products Act, Oceans Act, Canadian Environmental Protection Act, 1999*, New Brunswick's *Clean Air Act*, and Nova Scotia's *Environment Act*. In its 2001 decision confirming that municipalities have the power to regulate pesticides, the Supreme Court of Canada embraced the precautionary principle. Federal and provincial laws governing the use of ozone-depleting chemicals reflect both the precautionary principle (laws were passed before the science of ozone depletion was certain) and adaptive management (laws were repeatedly strengthened in response to new scientific knowledge).

Despite modest progress, many challenges remain in redesigning Canadian environmental laws and policies to incorporate the precautionary principle, adaptive management, and other scientific knowledge.[45] Science in Canada suffers from a chronic shortage of financial support. The National Round Table on the Environment and the Economy urged the federal government to invest heavily in research and "drastically increase government scientific capacity."[46] On the other hand, government control and manipulation of science can result in bad law and policy decisions, perhaps best illustrated by a series of fisheries management fiascoes.[47] Canada would be wise to make better use of the expertise of the Royal Society of Canada in shaping public policy on complex environmental issues, as the United States relies on the independent National Academy of Sciences.[48]

INADEQUATE IMPLEMENTATION AND ENFORCEMENT

It shall be unlawful, at any season, to hunt or kill buffalo for the mere motive of amusement or wanton destruction, or solely to secure their tongues, choice cuts or peltries.

—*An Ordinance for the Protection of the Buffalo, 1877, Northwest Territories*

The fourth systemic weakness afflicting Canadian environmental law and policy is a failure to effectively implement and enforce the law, dating back to the nineteenth-century slaughter of the buffalo. On paper, Canada has many seemingly impressive environmental laws. In practice, key elements of these laws are rarely, if ever, implemented. For example, Canada has yet to develop a single ocean management plan under the *Oceans Act*. Until 2003 no marine protected areas had been formally designated under the *Canada National Parks Act, Oceans Act, Canada Wildlife Act*, or the *National Marine Conservation Areas Act*.[49] Provisions of the *Forest Practices Code* intended to protect biodiversity are not implemented, years after the law came into force. Environmental policies announced and promoted with great fanfare, such as

Canada's *Green Plan*, the Canadian Biodiversity Strategy, and various climate change action plans, are never fully implemented.

Although the federal government candidly admits that "legislation and regulation are only as good as their enforcement," criticism of Canada's ongoing failure to enforce its environmental laws is widespread.[50] The OECD has repeatedly chided Canada for its lax environmental enforcement regime. In 1998 Parliament's Standing Committee on Environment and Sustainable Development concluded, "Environment Canada and indeed some provinces are not enforcing environmental laws when they could and should. This failure to act is of deep concern."[51] The environmental group Friends of the Earth released a scathing report detailing ten years of "minimalist" enforcement by Environment Canada. In 1999 the *Globe and Mail* described Canada as the "promised land" for polluters because of a 78 percent drop in prosecution rates between 1992 and 1999. An audit by the commissioner of the environment and sustainable development concluded that "within existing budgets, departments are struggling to meet legislated responsibilities, policy commitments, and international obligations and, in many cases, are failing to do so."[52] Environment Canada itself admits that overall enforcement efforts are "falling short of fulfilling departmental responsibility, and ... not providing adequate protection to the public, the environment or wildlife."[53]

The following points illustrate the decline in the enforcement of environmental laws in Canada:

- Government reports acknowledge that hundreds of companies and municipalities regularly break environmental laws without being prosecuted.[54]
- Environment Canada identified over three thousand documented violations of federal laws by eastern Canadian pulp mills in recent years but conducted only seven prosecutions.[55]
- According to Ontario Ministry of Environment figures, in 2000 there were 1,900 violations of water pollution laws by two hundred corporations and municipalities, but only four charges laid.[56]
- The number of inspections carried out annually under the *Canadian Environmental Protection Act, 1999* fell during the 1990s from two thousand to seven hundred.[57]

Across Canada, major industrial polluters often break the law with impunity. During the 1990s large corporations like Alcan, Weyerhaeuser, Inco, Skeena Cellulose, Petro-Canada, and Ethyl Canada appeared repeatedly on provincial lists of companies in violation of pollution laws, yet were rarely prosecuted. All too often, governments interpret noncompliance "not as a sign that the company was breaking a law and that enforcement action was required but that the standards were too strict and accordingly should be renegotiated."[58] Law enforcement agencies are more likely to prosecute small companies or individuals despite the fact that their levels of pollution pale in comparison to major industrial polluters.[59]

American law professor Daniel Farber writes that "in all areas of law there are gaps between the 'law on the books' and the 'law in action' but in environmental law the gap is sometimes a chasm."[60] If there is a chasm between environmental laws and their enforcement in the United States, then in Canada there is a Grand Canyon. In 1998 the US Environmental Protection Agency (EPA) used administrative actions to force companies to spend US\$3.6 billion for environmental cleanups and pollution control equipment. That year the EPA's civil and criminal enforcement actions resulted in US\$236.8 million in fines and 208 years of prison time.[61] In comparison, a decade (1989-99) of enforcing Canada's main pollution laws resulted in fines totalling \$8,696,149.[62] In just one year, the EPA obtained more fines and jail sentences than authorities responsible for environmental enforcement in Canada have obtained in their entire history.[63] Three of the main reasons for Canada's failure to adequately implement and enforce environmental laws and policies have been budget cuts, the downloading of enforcement responsibilities to provinces (under the guise of harmonization), and excessive reliance on voluntary initiatives.

Cutbacks to Federal Environmental Budgets

The link is obvious between budget cutbacks in environmental departments and a declining ability to implement and enforce environmental laws. Governments in Canada engaged in an unprecedented downsizing of environmental departments in the 1990s, led by the federal government. In 1988 Environment Canada had a budget of $800 million, and the 1990 *Green Plan* promised to inject an additional $3 billion over five years. However, in part because of the recession in the early 1990s, more than 70 percent of the *Green Plan* money was never allocated to the environment.[64] By 1998 the budget for Environment Canada had fallen 30 percent to $550 million, more than $200 million of which was earmarked for weather forecasting.[65] In terms of personnel, in 1988 Environment Canada was the seventh-largest federal department; by 1998 it was the smallest.[66] Nationwide, Environment Canada had fewer than seventy enforcement officials in 1998. There was one Environment Canada enforcement officer in New Brunswick, a province with 750,000 people, a resource-based economy, numerous pulp and paper mills, and other heavy industry. The Pacific and Yukon region saw its operations and maintenance budget drop 72 percent in 1998 when temporary funding under the *Green Plan* expired.[67]

Other federal departments with environmental responsibilities suffered the same magnitude of cuts as Environment Canada. Between 1994-5 and 1998-9, the Department of Fisheries and Oceans budget was sliced by one-third, from $1.4 billion to $950 million, while staff cuts were roughly 40 percent.[68] The internationally renowned Great Lakes Laboratory for Fisheries and Aquatic Science, which studies the impacts of toxic substances on fish, suffered cuts ranging from 40 to 70 percent.[69] Parks Canada's budget and staff were cut by more than 40 percent. The Canadian Forest Service was cut by 57 percent.

In contrast, American spending and staffing levels for environmental protection have risen steadily since the 1970s.[70] The EPA's 2001 budget was US$8.3 billion, with US$400 million earmarked for enforcement.[71] The National Parks Service budgeted US$2.1 billion for 2000, the National Oceanic and Atmospheric Administration budget was US$2.6 billion, the Forest Service budget was US$3.5 billion, and the Fish and Wildlife Service budget was US$1.6 billion.[72] Compared to Canada, the United States spends at least twice as much per citizen on environmental protection. Unlike Canada's "kid gloves approach" to environmental crime, enforcement in the United States is getting tougher, with fines and jail sentences steadily rising over the past twenty years.[73]

To the federal government's credit, it has begun to rebuild Environment Canada, with the department's 2001 budget rising to $650 million.[74] Federal budgets from 2000 to 2003 began the process of reinvesting in environmental protection, with significant expenditures on climate change, clean air, and municipal infrastructure. The number of enforcement officers increased from fewer than 70 in 1998 to 93 in 2003. The 2003 budget, which Environment Minister David Anderson described as the "greenest budget in Canadian history," promised almost $3 billion in new spending over five years, primarily to address climate change.[75] However, there is still a long way to go before federal environmental departments have the resources needed to implement and enforce existing laws, let alone the new, stronger laws and policies required in many areas.

Provincial Cutbacks

The provinces followed the federal government's "leadership" in chopping environment departments. Newfoundland and Quebec led the way with cuts of 65 percent between 1994 and 1998: in Newfoundland the environment budget fell to $3.6 million from $10.6 million; the Quebec environment department's budget fell to $53 million from $151 million.[76] Spending on environmental protection in New Brunswick and Alberta fell by more than 30 percent in the same period, with Alberta's budget declining to $296 million from $405 million.[77] In Ontario, the Ministry of Environment budget fell to $165 million in 1998 from $290 million in 1995, a drop of 43 percent.[78] The BC Ministry of Environment budget was slashed by 35 percent between 1995 and 2000 and again by 30 to 35 percent in 2002.[79]

Ontario provides a compelling example of the tangible human and environmental costs of cutbacks in environmental spending and regulation. The Conservative government under Premier Mike Harris engaged in a dramatic campaign of deregulation, downsizing, privatization, and downloading of environmental responsibilities to municipalities. Ontario cut programs for reducing hazardous waste, funding public transit, promoting recycling, encouraging green industries, and enforcing wildlife conservation rules. The province weakened environmental laws governing pesticides, energy, wildlife, environmental assessment, and land-use planning. Ontario also eliminated mining and forestry regulations, privatized sewage treatment, and discontinued the Ontario Round Table on the Environment and the Economy, the Advisory Committee on Environmental Standards, the Environmental Assessment Advisory Committee, and the Municipal-Industrial Strategy for Pollution Abatement Advisory Committee.[80] In the words of the Canadian Environmental Law Association, "Moving very quickly and with very little consultation the government dismantled thirty years' worth of safeguards to protect the environment and conserve natural resources."[81]

In detailed annual reports, Ontario's independent environmental commissioner harshly criticized the Harris government's changes.[82] In 1996 the provincial auditor criticized the Ministry of Environment for inadequate tracking of hazardous waste, antiquated air pollution controls, and deficient monitoring of groundwater resources.[83] In 1998 the environmental commissioner urged the Ontario government to change its focus "from one of granting regulatory relief for polluters to improving its commitment to the environmental health of its residents and the natural environment." The next year, the environmental commissioner issued a three-hundred-page analysis concluding that "evidence of the deterioration of the province's environmental protection standards is widespread" and warning that laws and policies governing groundwater were inadequate.[84] In 2000 the provincial auditor concluded that the Ministry of Environment did not have satisfactory systems and procedures in place to administer approvals and enforce compliance with environmental legislation.[85]

As a result of budget cuts to environmental ministries and the weakening of regulations, Ontario is the most heavily polluted province, endured the Walkerton tragedy, and suffers significant health and environmental problems because of air pollution. Placing Ontario's forest companies in the position of policing themselves has resulted in far fewer violations being detected, as government audits find five times as many violations as the companies report. Despite the problems that have plagued Ontario, governments in British Columbia, Alberta, and other provinces are implementing similar environmental policies. It seems likely that the financial savings resulting from environmental cutbacks will be more than offset by increased health care, legal, and environmental costs.[86]

Harmonization Agreements

A second factor contributing to inadequate enforcement of Canadian environmental laws during the 1990s was the negotiation of so-called harmonization agreements between the federal and provincial governments. These agreements were ostensibly intended to reduce the overlap between environmental laws and policies at the two levels of government. In reality, harmonization was a euphemism for the devolution, or downloading, of responsibility from the federal government to provincial governments. Some provinces, such as Ontario and BC, in turn downloaded environmental responsibilities onto local governments and municipalities. Nationwide harmonization efforts in the 1990s grew out of a series of bilateral agreements between Ottawa and individual provinces dating back to the 1970s. These earlier agreements were sharply criticized by environmental lawyers as "a virtual abdication" of federal responsibility for environmental protection.[87]

Prior to the signing of the Canada-Wide Accord on Environmental Harmonization in 1998, Parliament's Standing Committee on Environment and Sustainable Development held hearings seeking evidence of overlap and duplication of federal and provincial environmental laws and regulations.[88] Despite extensive inquiries, the Committee could find *no evidence* of either duplication or overlap, and recommended that the federal government delay signing the Harmonization Accord until the Accord's implications could be more fully studied and evaluated. A 1995 report prepared for the Canadian Council of Ministers of the Environment examined the rationale for harmonization and concluded that "most overlap and duplication which existed has been addressed."[89] A study prepared for the Alberta government, a vocal advocate of harmonization, also failed to produce any evidence of costs associated with regulatory overlap or duplication.[90]

According to environmentalists, harmonization weakens environmental protection by reducing the federal role, tying Ottawa's hands, and leading to "lowest common denominator" outcomes.[91] Former Canadian environment minister Tom McMillan argued that "the record of provincial governments in this country in the environmental field is appalling when the federal government has devolved or delegated some of its authority."[92] The Canadian Bar Association also concluded that if harmonization proceeded, environmental protection would suffer.[93] Internal federal government documents confirmed that these concerns about harmonization were valid.[94]

Despite the warnings, the federal and provincial governments, with the exception of Quebec, moved forward with signing and implementing the harmonization agreements. A legal challenge brought by the Canadian Environmental Law Association, arguing that the federal government was unlawfully delegating authority to the provinces, was unsuccessful.[95] In 1999 the federal commissioner of the environment and sustainable development evaluated federal-provincial agreements regarding environmental protection. The commissioner found extensive problems common to all of the harmonization agreements, including:

- limited reference to environmental protection as an objective
- limited federal access to provincial information on enforcement
- no analysis of reductions in duplication
- no evaluation of the agreements' impact on environmental performance
- no audit provisions in the agreements
- no accounting for federal funds transferred to the provinces.

In conclusion, the commissioner warned that "if Environment Canada does not take corrective action, there is a risk that the environment could suffer as a result of deficiencies in both existing and future bilateral environmental agreements."[96]

Some of the predictions of harm arising from harmonization have already been compellingly borne out. After the federal government and Quebec signed a harmonization agreement assigning enforcement responsibilities to the provincial government, there were no prosecutions of pulp mills in Quebec despite 1,700 documented violations of the *Fisheries Act*. Similarly, Canada's auditor general observed lower levels of compliance with the *Fisheries Act* by industry when monitoring and enforcement of fish habitat provisions were downloaded to the provinces.[97]

In theory, reducing overlap and duplication between federal and provincial environmental laws is a laudable goal. Harmonization should be a process dedicated to negotiating, implementing, and enforcing mandatory national standards in all aspects of environmental protection. However, harmonization in Canada has been a subterfuge, because there is no evidence of duplication. The hidden agenda behind harmonization involved saving money and placating the provinces, with the result that the Canadian environment suffered.

Excessive Reliance on Voluntary Initiatives

The third factor implicated in the lack of adequate enforcement of Canadian environmental laws is that governments rely heavily on voluntary programs and industry self-regulation.[98] For example, instead of passing laws or regulations to govern greenhouse gas emissions, reduce smog, increase motor vehicle fuel efficiency, or require energy-efficient buildings, the federal government made voluntary agreements with industry. Advocates of voluntary agreements claim that they are more flexible and can achieve progress faster and more efficiently than regulations.[99] Critics argue that voluntary initiatives lack transparency and accountability, encourage free riders, undermine the role of government, maintain the status quo, have high administrative costs, and preempt more effective measures to protect the environment.[100]

Despite their promise, voluntary agreements in Canada have largely failed. Greenhouse gas emissions continue to rise despite the Voluntary Challenge and Registry Program. Smog alerts are more frequent despite voluntary efforts undertaken pursuant to the 1990 joint federal-provincial management plan. Overall motor vehicle fuel efficiency is getting worse, not better, despite a voluntary agreement between Ottawa and vehicle manufacturers. Only a tiny fraction of new homes are energy efficient despite the voluntary R-2000 standard. Reductions in toxic releases, which some industries have ascribed to voluntary programs, have in fact been compelled by regulations.[101] As the OECD concluded in 2000, Canadian "voluntary agreements have not proved up to the task of dealing with resource and environmental challenges."[102]

Numerous studies have examined the effectiveness of voluntary programs in achieving environmental objectives. A study conducted in 1996 surveyed 1,547 large corporations and institutions about factors motivating them to take action on environmental issues. Compliance with regulations was identified by 92 percent of corporations surveyed as an "important motivating factor." In second place, at 69 percent, was director and officer liability for environmental offences. Down at fifteenth place, with only 16 percent of corporations surveyed identifying them as an important motivating factor, were voluntary programs.[103] A report prepared by Environment Canada in 1998 also provides compelling evidence of the inadequacy of voluntary measures. The study looked at nineteen industrial sectors and found that sectors relying on voluntary measures and self-monitoring had a compliance rating of 60 percent, whereas industries subject to regulations, consistent inspections, and enforcement had a compliance rating of 94 percent. The study concluded, "Reliance on voluntary compliance was demonstrated to be ineffective in achieving even a marginally acceptable level of compliance."[104]

An audit of voluntary initiatives by the commissioner of the environment and sustainable development approved of these programs in theory but found them flawed in practice. Voluntary programs audited by the commissioner lacked clear goals and targets, standardized performance measures, clearly defined roles and responsibilities, consequences if objectives were not met, adequate reporting, and independent verification.[105] Canadian studies indicate that industry claims about the effectiveness of voluntary programs are exaggerated.[106] The evidence from the United States also suggests that voluntary initiatives produce little tangible environmental protection unless supported by legislation. As several American law professors point out, "Purely voluntary compliance cannot be expected within our social and economic institutions."[107]

Voluntary initiatives do have the *potential* to produce environmental results that go beyond regulatory requirements with less cost and less conflict. A group of Canadian business executives and environmentalists agreed in 1997 that in order to be successful and credible, voluntary programs should be developed in an open and participatory manner; be transparent in design and operation; be performance-based with specified goals, measurable objectives, and milestones; clearly specify rewards for good performance and the consequences of not meeting the goals; encourage flexibility and innovation in meeting goals; have prescribed monitoring and reporting requirements; include mechanisms for verifying performance; and encourage continual improvement.[108] If these ambitious requirements could be met, the concerns about the effectiveness of voluntary measures would largely be addressed.

The bottom line is that voluntary agreements should be used to supplement, not replace, regulations. As Professor Robert Gibson concludes in his book *Voluntary Initiatives*, "If designed carefully and adopted as contributing parts in a larger whole, [voluntary initiatives] could fill neglected niches and add to the diversity and integrity of a strong overall approach to environmental improvement."[109] However, others point out that "when a government is intent on deregulation, the policy instrument of voluntarism is inherently incapable of achieving its objectives."[110] In the current Canadian context, the increased reliance on voluntary measures is inappropriate, because the regulatory framework provides inadequate incentives in the form of either carrots or sticks.

LACK OF MEANINGFUL OPPORTUNITIES FOR PUBLIC PARTICIPATION OR ENFORCEMENT

The fifth fundamental flaw of Canadian environmental law and policy is the lack of meaningful opportunities for public participation, including effective mechanisms for enforcement by the public. In 1990 the Canadian Bar Association (CBA) observed that greater public participation in environmental decision making would produce "fairer decision-making and better decisions" but that citizens are "either excluded from the process or treated as second-class citizens."[111] The CBA made nine recommendations to ensure greater democratization of environmental decision making, but none have been implemented.[112] Canadian environmental policy making is still described as "secretive and opaque, organized around negotiations that involve only a limited number of parties and are insulated from public scrutiny."[113] While access to information has increased in recent years, the public's role is still largely restricted to being notified of government decisions and provided with an opportunity to comment upon proposed decisions. This kind of limited input does not meet public expectations.[114] Even in the rare situations where the public has a more extensive role, as in public hearings either under the *Canadian Environmental Act* or before Parliament's Standing Committee on Environment and Sustainable Development, governments often ignore the public's input. For example, after public hearings about the *Species at Risk Act* and amendments to the *Canadian Environmental Protection Act*, the Standing Committee made extensive changes to the bills to reflect the concerns and expert evidence presented at the hearings. In both cases, the government reversed the majority of the changes made by the Standing Committee.

Professors Tony Dorcey and Timothy McDaniels observe that "relatively little progress has been made in enshrining public rights to participation in law in Canada (in contrast to the U.S.)." There were some interesting experiments during the 1990s, including Ontario's *Environmental Bill of Rights*, British Columbia's Commission on Resources and the Environment, and the Fraser Basin Council. However, "Enthusiasm across Canada for the new citizen involvement initiatives waned in the mid-nineties as governments at all levels became doubtful about their worth and as concerns about economic issues came to dominate their agendas."[115] A number of new public participation tools appear to have been designed to fail, in that the hurdles involved in using these tools render them toothless. For example, British Columbia's *Recall and Initiative Act* allows citizens to put forward proposals for provincial legislation if a sufficient number of voters' signatures are obtained, but high thresholds, short time periods, and complex rules make the legislation unworkable.[116] Overall, on the spectrum of public involvement ranging from nonparticipation to citizen control, the majority of environmental decision-making processes in Canada can still be characterized as allowing only token partici-pation from the public.

An increasingly important exception to the rule of limited public participation in Canadian environmental policy making involves Aboriginal people. Recognition of their constitutional rights is forcing governments to engage in meaningful consultation or face legal challenges.[117] The trend in parts of the country, particularly in the northern territories, is to move toward comanagement of natural resources.[118] Comanagement means sharing the responsibility for decision making between government and Aboriginal people. Aboriginal involvement is expected to result in more sustainable decisions, because of traditional values and knowledge about local ecosystems. In the Supreme Court of Canada's landmark *Delgamuukw* decision, the Court stated that because of the special relationship between Aboriginal people and the land, there is an "inherent limit" on the kinds of activities that can take place on lands subject to Aboriginal title.[119] The Court used strip mining in a tra-ditional hunting area and paving a burial site as examples of activities prohibited by the unique nature of Aboriginal title. At a minimum, comanagement systems represent an opportunity to innovate and diversify the range of institutions and approaches involved in environmental management in Canada.[120]

Citizen Enforcement Efforts

Another aspect of the lack of opportunities for meaningful public participation involves the dif-ficulty faced by citizens and environmental groups seeking to enforce environmental laws when governments refuse to do so. Courts will not compel the government to enforce the law.[121] However, in a tradition of the legal system Canada inherited from England, individual citizens have the power to lay charges against a person or corporation that breaks the law. This type of legal proceeding is known as a private prosecution. The process is straightforward, but is subject to the supervision of the provincial attorney general, who can either allow such a prosecution to proceed or can intervene and take it over. If the attorney general takes over a private prosecu-tion, he or she can either proceed with the case or drop the charges.[122]

The effectiveness of private prosecutions varies from province to province, depending on the provincial government's policy. The Ontario government has allowed numerous private prosecutions to proceed in recent years. For example, Kingston resident Janet Fletcher, assisted by lawyers from the Sierra Legal Defence Fund, successfully prosecuted the city of Kingston for violating the *Fisheries Act*, resulting in a fine of $120,000.[123] A private prosecution against the city of Hamilton resulted in a guilty plea and fines of $450,000 under the *Ontario Water Resources Act* and the federal *Fisheries Act*.[124]

In contrast, Alberta, British Columbia, and Newfoundland have stonewalled citizen efforts to enforce the law. In Alberta, environmental activist Martha Kostuch laid a series of charges relating to the construction of the controversial Oldman Dam. In BC, lawyers with the Sierra Legal Defence Fund have laid numerous charges against forest companies and municipalities for violating the *Fisheries Act*. The provincial attorneys general took over *all* of these private prosecutions and dropped *all* of the charges before the cases went to trial.[125] Public efforts to enforce environment laws in Newfoundland when construction of a new hydroelectric project caused extensive damage were also unsuccessful.[126] Courts are extremely reluctant to review the reasons why an attorney general takes over a case and then drops the charges, leading to a dead-end for law enforcement. The government refuses to enforce the law and then blocks the public from enforcing the law. As author Jack Glenn observes, "The unfettered power of attorneys general, which the courts are not prepared to challenge and Parliament is not prepared to diminish, allows governments to sidestep their own laws."[127] Calls to reform the system so that private prosecutions function more effectively have been ignored.[128]

Because private prosecutions in Canada are undermined by the unconstrained ability of attorneys general to derail them, a new tool for public enforcement has been introduced. Several recently enacted environmental laws contain what are known as citizen suit provisions.[129] These provisions explicitly recognize the right of citizens to take law breakers to court in situations where the government refuses to enforce the law. Citizen suits have been successful in the United States in supplementing government enforcement action and in providing concerned citizens with a means of defending the environment.[130] A major advantage of citizen suits is that the standard of proof is based on the balance of probabilities, a much less onerous standard than beyond a reasonable doubt (which is the standard used in criminal and regulatory prosecutions).

Unfortunately, in Canada citizen suits are surrounded by a large degree of suspicion. Industry lobbyists warn of frivolous litigation, threats to corporate reputations, and economic chaos. When the federal government proposed including citizen suit provisions in its endangered species legislation, lawyers for the Canadian Pulp and Paper Association warned of a "flood of lawsuits," "rampant judicial second-guessing of federal ministers," and "potentially disastrous consequences."[131] These industry arguments are largely groundless. Procedural safeguards enshrined in the judicial system, such as cost rules and motions for summary judgment, provide adequate checks and balances to avoid frivolous cases or harassment. Citizen suits will result in fines or other penalties *only* if a citizen can prove that an environmental law has been broken. For law-abiding individuals and businesses, citizen suits should be no concern.

Despite the weak arguments against citizen suits, Canadian governments continue to capitulate to industry objections. Citizen suit provisions were dropped from the federal *Species at Risk Act*, even though Environment Minister Sergio Marchi assured the BC Forest Alliance (a timber industry lobby group) that these citizen suit provisions would be harmless. Marchi pointed out that citizen suit provisions in existing laws have "seldom, if ever, been exercised."[132] In fact, existing citizen suit provisions in Canadian environmental laws are so complex as to be unworkable. Citizens must jump through a series of hoops before being able to take court action. As a result, the citizen suit provisions that do exist, in Ontario, Quebec, the Yukon, the Northwest Territories, and in the *Canadian Environmental Protection Act, 1999* have *never* been used successfully.[133] Given the obstacles to private prosecutions and limited, unworkable citizen suit mechanisms, the public has no means of ensuring that environmental laws in Canada are enforced.

CANADA'S NARROW APPROACH TO SOLVING ENVIRONMENTAL PROBLEMS

The sixth systemic weakness in Canadian environmental law and policy is an excessively narrow approach to solving problems. Canada is paralyzed by a long-standing and intractable debate between two polar extremes: strict command-and-control environmental laws on one hand, and deregulation accompanied by voluntary measures on the other hand. Environmentalists advocate the former model while industry prefers the latter. This polarization breeds mistrust and sabotages efforts to create and implement more innovative laws and policies. Innovative tools such as economic instruments, [which] produce responsibility programs, or environmental rights are rarely used. Canada continues to involve a limited number of parties (primarily government and industry) in developing and implementing environmental laws and policies, and uses policy tools in isolation rather than in combination. A one-size-fits-all philosophy continues to dominate, although the complexity of environmental challenges and the diversity of the regulated community demand a more nuanced approach.[134] Canada has been slow to react to changing circumstances and to learn from past experience.

Regulations may not always be the most efficient means of reaching environmental quality goals. ... [R]egulations have been effective in achieving progress on a number of issues, particularly with respect to some industrial sources of air and water pollution. However, other environmental challenges, such as nonpoint source pollution and the protection of drinking water sources, have proven immune to conventional regulatory solutions. Certain areas where Canada's record is particularly poor, such as water and energy consumption, also do not lend themselves well to command-and-control regulation and have proven resistant to voluntary measures. To make progress on these issues, governments in Canada must employ a wider range of laws, regulations, programs, policies, and parties than they have to date. As Professors Gunningham, Grabosky, and Sinclair conclude in their book *Smart Regulation*, "Command and control regulation is not well-equipped to deal with diffuse, non-point and multi-media sources of pollution or with ever more complex and systemic environmental problems such as climate change and the loss of biodiversity, that demand far more sophisticated policy responses."[135]

Economic instruments and policies such as tax shifting, incentives, the removal of subsidies, and emissions trading can provide powerful incentives to change industry and individual behaviour.[136] Other economic instruments include taxes, charges, financial incentives, green loans, rebates, fee-bates, revolving loans, subsidies, full cost pricing, demand-side management (e.g., low-interest loans for energy-efficient building retrofits), buybacks of old, inefficient cars or appliances, liability instruments (e.g., financial responsibility for the rehabilitation of contaminated sites), and performance bonds.[137] These tools could be applied to redesigning the economic system so that incentives and disincentives are in the right places and capable of responding to changing circumstances.[138] Canada lags far behind most countries in using economic instruments to protect the environment.

For twenty-five years, reports and recommendations by Canadian academics, lawyers, and economists have extolled the potential virtues of economic instruments.[139] Yet as one academic observes, "For all practical purposes, nothing has been done. How many more reports will be commissioned, laboured over, submitted, and praised, only to be shelved by policy makers?"[140] The OECD also agrees that in Canada "there is a need to increase the use of economic instruments (for instance, charges on toxic emissions and waste, and disposal fees for products containing toxic substances) to reinforce the polluter-pays principle."[141]...

Implementing Broader Approaches

After years of delay, Canadian governments are beginning to experiment with a wider range of policy instruments. The *Canadian Environmental Protection Act, 1999*, and several provincial laws explicitly authorize the use of economic instruments.[142] Environment Canada is using a cap-and-trade system to phase out methyl bromide, an ozone-depleting chemical. The federal government has endowed a number of funds with money to be used in research, climate change programs, and funding green municipal infrastructure.[143] The Toronto Atmospheric Fund is a municipal example of economic innovation. An endowment established in 1991 is used to finance projects that reduce greenhouse gas emissions, such as energy-efficiency upgrades to municipal buildings. BC has taken some tentative steps toward implementing programs to make producers responsible for a number of hazardous household items, from paint to batteries. Tax laws have been amended to encourage donations of ecologically sensitive land. Partnerships between environmental organizations and private landowners are being used to protect endangered species and their habitat. These examples suggest that Canada is belatedly beginning to adapt successful environmental law and policy tools from other countries to Canadian circumstances. Much more remains to be done.

CONCLUSION

This chapter identifies six critical weaknesses in Canadian environmental law and policy. Disturbingly, these systemic problems have been known for decades. Back in 1969 federal water quality laws were described as "a patchwork quilt" characterized by extensive "leeway" in granting permits to pollute.[144] In 1973 a book called *Canada's Environment: The Law on Trial* chronicled some of the same shortcomings of Canadian environmental law and policy described in this chapter.[145] In his 1980 book, *Environmental Regulation in Canada*, Andrew Thompson wrote that environmental law in Canada was hampered by a "lack of clearly stated goals and objectives and of will to obtain those that are stated, inadequate funding and staffing, inconsistent enforcement policies, and failure to inform or involve the public."[146] In 1990 environmental law in Canada was described as having a "history of regulations written and violated, of deadlines missed and rescheduled, of postponement and delay and exception."[147] These criticisms were echoed in 1990 reports from the Law Reform Commission of Canada and the Canadian Bar Association, and a report prepared for the National Round Table on the Environment and the Economy in 1992.[148] The problems persist today.

To remedy the systemic weaknesses in Canadian environmental law and policy outlined in this chapter is a daunting challenge. Considerable energy, resources, and ingenuity will be needed to enact new environmental laws and regulations, ensure the use of mandatory, binding language, incorporate contemporary scientific concepts like the precautionary principle and adaptive management, enforce laws vigorously, engage the public in decision making, and diversify the approach to solving environmental problems. Remedying these systemic weaknesses is made more difficult by a number of underlying institutional obstacles, which are explored in ... [the following section, "Obstacles to Further Progress," also an excerpt from *Unnatural Law*].

Obstacles to Further Progress

I'm tired of hearing about trees.

—Mr. Justice Law, BC Supreme Court, 1993

For more than three decades, environmental problems have been a major concern for Canadians. Significant efforts have been made at every level—individual, community, corporate, and government—to improve Canada's environmental record. And yet, despite improvements in some areas, Canada's overall performance remains poor. As described in the preceding chapter ["Systemic Weaknesses"], Canada's legal system is still plagued by systemic weaknesses. Why do these weaknesses persist?

The answer is that there are structural obstacles to further environmental progress, including most importantly, the continued predominance of economic interests over environmental protection, international trade liberalization, unresolved constitutional problems, the lack of separation of powers between the legislative and executive branches of government, the extraordinary concentration of power in the prime minister's and premiers' offices, and barriers to an effective role for the courts. These obstacles impede efforts to strengthen Canadian environmental law and policy and, ultimately, to improve Canada's environmental record.

THE DOMINANCE OF ECONOMIC INTERESTS

Short-term economic considerations such as profits, competiveness, and jobs are the main reasons that Canada is missing key environmental laws, that existing laws are flawed, and that laws are neither implemented nor enforced to the extent required to ensure environmental protection. Economic factors explain why many provincial laws allow industrial activities in parks and protected areas, why air pollution is tolerated at levels that cause thousands of premature deaths annually, why fishing is allowed in marine protected areas, why overcutting and clear-cutting are still prevalent in Canada's forests, why no laws have passed to reduce greenhouse gas emissions, why the clean-up of contaminated sites is not required by law, why pesticides banned in other countries continue to be used in Canada, why environmental assessment laws favour development over sustainability, why laws do not protect the sources of Canadians' drinking water, why the habitat of endangered species lacks legal protection, and why laws are not enforced against known polluters.

The last two decades have seen a shift to the right in Canadian policies as governments have prioritized debt and deficit reduction, deregulation, privatization, downsizing, and free trade. Canadian governments, both federal and provincial, consider economic issues more important than environmental concerns, despite opinion polls suggesting that most Canadians would place environmental protection ahead of economic growth. The federal government's main concerns during the 1990s were eliminating the budget deficit, reducing the national debt, creating jobs, and maintaining national unity. This agenda, dominated by economic concerns, "resulted in major cuts to federal environmental science and regulatory capacity, a reluctance to challenge industry on environmental issues, and a desire to devolve as much activity to the provinces as possible."[1] At both federal and provincial levels of government, finance ministers have far greater influence than environment ministers. Economic portfolios dominate cabinets.[2]

Despite much ado about the "new economy," Canada still relies heavily on exports of natural resources, from softwood lumber, grain, and fish, to metals, minerals, natural gas, and petroleum products. Canada's eight largest exports are natural resource commodities.[3] The extraction of these natural resources accounts for a substantial proportion of the environmental damage in Canada. Economists have long warned that Canada is suffering both economically and environmentally because of excessive reliance on unprocessed exports of natural resources.[4] Studies indicate that governments will allow high levels of environmental degradation "in situations where the economic future of a community dependent on a particular resource industry is at stake."[5]

Over 80 percent of Canadian exports go to the United States. Indeed, Americans consume more Canadian forest products, more Canadian oil and gas, and more Canadian metals and minerals than do Canadians.[6] Because of the close economic relationship between the two countries, Canada is reluctant to implement environmental laws and policies that are perceived as potentially affecting Canadian industry's competitiveness vis-à-vis the United States. This reluctance is misguided for several reasons. According to the OECD, "The cost of compliance with environmental regulations has had little or no impact on the overall competitiveness of countries."[7] In fact, American industries generally face stricter environmental laws and policies than their Canadian counterparts. Weaker environmental regulations in Canada may limit Canadian access to American markets, as the softwood lumber dispute suggests.[8]

Industry's Influence on Environmental Law and Policy

Environmental regulation is described as "a classic case of diffuse benefits and concentrated costs."[9] In other words, the entire public reaps benefits from environmental protection, but regulated corporations and individuals bear the costs. The concentration of costs creates a defined group with a common interest in opposing the enactment, implementation, and enforcement of new or stronger environmental laws. Industry has far greater resources and power than environmental advocacy organizations.[10] Businesses own most media outlets and buy the lion's share of advertising. Industry can offer direct benefits to politicians in the form of campaign contributions, and indirect benefits by creating jobs and paying taxes. As a result, the majority of environmental laws and regulations in Canada are produced by negotiations between government and business in which the latter tends to have the upper hand.[11]

Industry has blocked and weakened many important environmental law and policy initiatives. For instance, objections from industry resulted in the watering down of the regulation for the *Canadian Environmental Assessment Act*.[12] Industry lobbying managed to delay the implementation of new standards for sulphur levels in gasoline.[13] One of the main reasons for the federal government's reluctance to make long-overdue changes to Canada's pesticide law was that the chemical industry opposed stricter regulation.[14] In effect, the government consistently puts the economic concerns of the private sector ahead of the need for public health protection.

Pressure applied by Canadian Pacific Hotels on the prime minister and the minister of Canadian heritage in 1996 resulted in the approval of a convention centre at Lake Louise despite public opposition, legal questions, and concerns over the environmental impact of additional commercial expansion in Banff National Park.[15] The forest industry played a major role in the weakening and eventual death of the proposed *Canada Endangered Species Protection Act* in 1997. According to an assessment of the history of the *Species at Risk Act*, the federal government's actions demonstrated a consistent bias in favour of business.[16] These examples are the tip of the iceberg. Every time government proposes a new or improved environmental law or policy, those with a vested interest in maintaining the status quo raise economic objections.

The Canadian Council of Chief Executives

The organization in Canada that plays the most powerful role in environmental law and policy development at the national level is not Greenpeace, but rather the Canadian Council of Chief Executives (CCCE, formerly the Business Council on National Issues). The CCCE is composed of 150 CEOs from Canada's largest corporations, is patterned after the US Business Roundtable, and is intended to protect corporations from public criticism and government intervention.[17] The member corporations of the CCCE have 1.3 million employees in Canada and over $2 trillion in assets. Because of this economic importance, the CCCE enjoys unparalleled access to, and influence with, the prime minister and federal cabinet ministers. Professor David Langille describes the CCCE as "a virtual shadow Cabinet."[18] The CCCE uses its political power to shape environmental laws and policies by opposing strict laws or regulations, opposing economic instruments such as energy or pollution taxes, and promoting voluntary initiatives as a panacea for solving environmental problems.

The Canadian Council of Chief Executives was responsible for the last-minute weakening of Bill C-32, the revised *Canadian Environmental Protection Act, 1999*. After Parliament's Standing Committee on Environment and Sustainable Development had strengthened Bill C-32, lobbying by the CCCE and other corporations led the government to overturn most of the Standing Committee's improvements.[19] The CEO of Alcan Aluminum wrote to Prime Minister Chrétien warning that the proposed law could result in the closure of all of Canada's aluminum smelters, including a smelter in the prime minister's Shawinigan riding.[20] This form of economic blackmail is a typical industry tactic. The chair of the Standing Committee, Liberal MP Charles Caccia, charged that the government had weakened the bill to please the chemical industry.[21]

The Canadian Council of Chief Executives also leads the lobbying efforts of Canadian corporations trying to dissuade the federal government from any effective steps to address climate change. To discourage government action, the CCCE warned that fulfilling Canada's promises to reduce greenhouse gas emissions under *Kyoto* would require either an end to Canadian agriculture and turning off the heat in 25 percent of Canadian homes, or taking all cars and 80 percent of commercial vehicles off the roads.[22] To date the CCCE has successfully persuaded the federal government to rely on voluntary programs to address climate change, programs that have failed to stop the Canadian growth in greenhouse gas emissions.

Further evidence of the extent of the influence of the CCCE, and industry generally, on environmental law and policy is that soon after his appointment of Canada's environment minister in August 1999, David Anderson telephoned at least ten major industry associations including the CCCE, the Canadian Chemical Producers' Association, the Mining Association of Canada, and the Canadian Pulp and Paper Association.[23] Within a week of his appointment, Anderson met with the CCCE. Briefing notes explain that one of Anderson's purposes for the meeting was to reassure the CCCE that, despite media coverage suggesting his appointment signalled a higher priority for environmental issues, "productivity continues to be the government's predominant theme."[24] The CCCE frequently meets with cabinet ministers and senior Environment Canada bureaucrats in order to push its agenda promoting voluntary programs and opposing regulation and economic instruments. In effect, the CCCE is lobbying for an environmental law and policy approach with a track record of failure, while blocking the use of laws and policies that have proven effective in protecting the environment.

Industry's Influence on Provincial Environmental Law and Policy

The predominance of economic considerations over environmental concerns is stronger at the provincial level. Provincial governments have jurisdiction over most natural resources and often rely heavily upon these industries for revenue and regional economic development. Professor Robert Paehlke argues that powerful resource industries, such as the oil and gas industry in Alberta, the forest industry in BC, and fisheries in the Maritimes, dominate provincial governments.[25] The BC forest industry's ability to minimize the on-the-ground impacts of government policy changes purporting to deliver sustainable forestry is well documented.[26] Resource industries and provincial governments enjoy a "symbiotic relationship," meaning that laws and policies favourable to industry are generally perceived as benefiting provinces as well.[27] Paehlke and other experts fear that provinces may engage in a "race to the bottom," lowering environmental standards in order to attract investment.[28] This theory is supported by the agenda of regulatory rollbacks, extensive cuts to environmental protection budgets, and the ensuing decrease in enforcement implemented by provincial governments in Alberta, Ontario, and British Columbia.

Labour Union Influence in Environmental Law and Policy

Industry is not always alone in blocking environmental initiatives. The economic interests of labour unions may also trump environmental concerns. The powerful loggers' union in British Columbia successfully derailed the provincial government's attempt to pass endangered species legislation and an environmental bill of rights in the mid-1990s.[29] Although drafted, published, and circulated for public comment, the proposed laws were never enacted. In a confidential letter, Environment Minister Moe Sihota informed the president of the loggers' union that, contrary to the government's public position, because of the concerns expressed by the union the government had no plans to enact endangered species legislation.[30] The loggers' union also contributed to the policy decisions that undermined the environmental protection potential of BC's *Forest Practices Code*.[31] On the other hand, unions deserve credit for supporting many environmental law initiatives, particularly those related to toxic substances and pollution.

Bureaucratic Inertia and Regulatory Capture

Another important reflection of the dominance of economic concerns involves the government agencies that are responsible for managing natural resources and regulating industry. Government departments that manage natural resources were originally established to ensure their orderly exploitation, which was perceived as vital to the economic growth that government values.[32] Environmental protection is a relatively recent government priority and to some extent is still treated as an afterthought. Senior bureaucrats support the status quo and resist change, and bureaucratic inertia is a well-documented impediment to environmental protection.[33] Moreover, many senior environment bureaucrats are more concerned about protecting the government from environmental issues than protecting the environment. For example, deputy ministers of Environment Canada are appointed by, and report to, the prime minister. One of their primary duties is "blame avoidance," meaning minimizing the risk of backlash from the creation, implementation, or enforcement of environmental laws and policies.[34]

Government departments are also subject to regulatory capture, meaning that the corporations and individuals subject to environmental regulation become "clients" whose interests prevail over the broader public interest that the government is supposed to defend.[35] For example, the Department of Fisheries and Oceans, the agency in charge of protecting and restoring marine biodiversity, is also charged with maintaining an economically thriving fishing industry. The federal auditor general highlighted the conflict of interest between DFO's duty to protect and restore depleted wild salmon populations and DFO's active support for salmon farming, which threatens wild salmon.[36] Similarly, as one academic observes, "The instinct of Natural Resources Canada, urged on by Alberta and other key energy provinces, is to defend the oil and gas industry."[37] The Standing Committee on Environment and Sustainable Development found that enforcement officials with Environment Canada are "subject to undue managerial influence, particularly in so-called 'sensitive' situations, that is, where action is taken or being considered against influential economic entities."[38] The Standing Committee described the federal Pest Management Regulatory Agency as a captive agency, subservient to the pesticide and agriculture industries. The uncomfortably close relationship between the Canadian nuclear industry and its regulatory body (the Atomic Energy Control Board) also illustrates this problem.[39] Provincial resource and regulatory bodies, such as forest ministries, are also plagued by regulatory capture.

Economics Dominates International Environmental Negotiations

In the international environmental arena, where Canada was once a global leader, the 1990s saw a dramatic shift in the Canadian approach to environmental protection. Under Brian Mulroney, Canada led the development of international agreements such as the *Montreal Protocol on Substances That Deplete the Ozone Layer* and the *Convention on Biological Diversity*. With the election of the Chrétien government in 1993, Canada's domestic economic interests began to dominate.[40] Canada's negotiating stance on environmental issues now must be "consistent with Canada's competitive and trade goals."[41] Negotiations about greenhouse gas emissions exemplify the change in Canada's role from environmental leader to environmental laggard. As well, Canada's position in international talks about the *Cartagena Protocol* on genetically modified organisms was largely dictated by the Canadian agriculture industry.[42] Canada, along with the United States and Australia, has become one of the leading opponents of meaningful international agreements to address environmental issues.[43]

INTERNATIONAL TRADE LIBERALIZATION

Another important aspect of the dominance of economic over environmental concerns involves international trade liberalization. Since the late 1980s, successive Canadian governments have aggressively pursued a series of trade and investment agreements that undermine existing environmental laws and policies. More ominously, these agreements limit prospects for new or improved environmental laws in the future.[44] As a report by the US Congress concluded, because of trade agreements "it is no longer possible for a country to create an appropriate environmental policy entirely on its own."[45] Of particular concern are NAFTA, the World Trade Organization, the Multilateral Agreement on Investment, the Free Trade Agreement of the Americas, and the General Agreement on Trade in Services.

The North American Free Trade Agreement

NAFTA came into force 1 January 1994, going well beyond the Canada-US Free Trade Agreement signed in 1988.[46] NAFTA's most environmentally problematic provision is Chapter 11, the investor-state dispute resolution mechanism.... Under Chapter 11, foreign corporations based in other NAFTA nations can sue governments for passing environmental laws that allegedly affect their investments through expropriation or actions "tantamount to expropriation." NAFTA thus gives foreign corporations unprecedented rights under international law— rights that were previously available only to nations.[47] Professor Luc Juillet describes NAFTA's Chapter 11 as "exceedingly generous to corporations."[48]

NAFTA is worded so broadly that it includes "virtual" expropriation: a corporation can claim that a law affects not property (the usual prerequisite for an expropriation claim), but the company's future profitability or opportunities for growth. Expropriation under NAFTA includes expropriation in its usual sense, "but also covert or incidental interference with the use of property which has the effect of depriving the owner, in whole or in significant part, of the use or reasonably-to-be expected economic benefit of property."[49] Thus, an American logging company could seek compensation for new regulations that limit logging in a provincial park or restrict the use of clear-cutting. A study prepared by trade lawyer Howard Mann for the International Institute for Sustainable Development concluded that Chapter 11 of NAFTA goes far beyond what Canadian law considers expropriation that legally warrants compensation.[50] The fact that a law may be justified on environmental grounds makes no difference under NAFTA; the law can stand but the company is still entitled to compensation. As trade law expert Barry Appleton notes, "Governments make big mistakes. They make policies for reasons that are based on public governance—very legitimate—but they don't know what their international obligations are. As a result, when they run afoul of them, they are in a position where they have to pay compensation."[51]

The most notorious challenge to date under NAFTA's Chapter 11 involved the Canadian government's efforts to ban MMT, a gasoline additive containing the heavy metal manganese. There are health and environmental concerns about MMT, but no scientific consensus that MMT poses a significant health risk.[52] In 1997 Canada passed a law banning the import or interprovincial trade of MMT.[53] Because Health Canada concluded the health risks associated with MMT were negligible, the federal government could not ban MMT as a toxic substance under the Canadian *Environmental Protection Act,* but was forced to resort to using its power to regulate interprovincial trade. The American manufacturer of MMT, Ethyl Corp., filed a NAFTA lawsuit seeking C$250 million in compensation for harm to its business and reputation. Corporate lawsuits under NAFTA proceed in secret, and efforts by nongovernment organizations to intervene in the Ethyl case were rejected. In 1998 the government of Canada negotiated a settlement with Ethyl. Environment Minister Christine Stewart and Industry Minister John Manley apologized to Ethyl, promised that the ban on MMT would be lifted, stated that Health Canada found MMT poses no health risk, and agreed to pay Ethyl almost $20 million in compensation.[54] The safety of MMT, which is now legally used in Canada, continues to be debated.

Canada lost a second Chapter 11 case brought by an American corporation after the federal government banned PCB exports.[55] In another ongoing NAFTA case, an American chemical company is seeking US$100 million in compensation from Canada because the federal government banned some uses of lindane, a pesticide banned in other nations because of health and environmental concerns.[56]

Although the provinces did not sign NAFTA, their laws are also subject to the agreement, as illustrated by Sun Belt Water's challenge of British Columbia's ban on water exports and a controversial case involving an American corporation called Metalclad. Metalclad sued Mexico because the state of San Luis Potosi refused to approve a landfill. Local authorities were concerned that the dump would pollute the local water supply. A NAFTA tribunal, interpreting expropriation very broadly, found that Metaclad's investment had been expropriated and ordered Mexico to pay Metalclad US$16,685,000.[57] A Canadian court upheld the decision, although it took note of the NAFTA tribunal's "extremely broad" interpretation of expropriation.[58]

The Chapter 11 lawsuits concluded thus far confirm earlier fears that NAFTA would be bad for the environment. The majority of the lawsuits filed by corporations under NAFTA's Chapter 11 investor protection provisions between 1994 and 2001 targeted environmental laws.[59] The uncertainty surrounding the scope of Chapter 11 has a chilling effect on new environmental laws, regulations, and policies. In other words, governments hesitate to enact new environmental laws because of fears that the laws *may* run afoul of NAFTA, resulting in expensive compensation claims by foreign corporations.

NAFTA also contributed to an unexpected 400 percent increase in hazardous waste imports from the United States into Canada. The CEC describes this jump as "a vivid example of what happens when domestic environmental policies are weakened at precisely the time that liberalization and open markets occur."[60] Most of the American hazardous waste was shipped to Ontario and Quebec, where loose regulations were eventually tightened.[61]

The World Trade Organization

The World Trade Organization (WTO) is an international trade body that enforces the General Agreement on Tariffs and Trade, the main global treaty governing trade between nations. Under WTO rules, environmental laws must be drafted so as to restrict trade as little as possible. The WTO has broad powers, and has repeatedly ruled against environmental laws that were alleged to interfere with free trade. Although the WTO does not have the power to actually strike down laws, it can effectively do so by requiring countries to pay large sums of compensation to other countries that suffer economic damage as a result of an impugned environmental law. Unlike NAFTA, the WTO dispute resolution mechanism is open only to nations, not corporations. Like NAFTA, the WTO process is conducted in complete secrecy with no opportunities for public involvement.[62]

With only one exception, in each complaint to date targeting a nation's environmental laws, the WTO has ruled in favour of free trade and against environmental protection. For example, after a complaint from Mexico, an American law requiring tuna sold in the United States to be caught in dolphin-friendly nets was found to violate WTO rules.[63] In a case brought by Asian nations, an American law intended to protect endangered turtles being killed by shrimp fishing was found to violate WTO rules.[64] An American regulation under the *Clean Air Act* was successfully challenged by Venezuela and Brazil on the basis that it discriminated against foreign gasoline producers. The United States was ordered to pay US$150 million in compensation.[65]

Canada has used the WTO twice to attack the environmental laws of other countries. In an effort to promote Canadian beef exports, Canada challenged a European ban on hormone-fed beef.[66] Europeans are understandably cautious about beef in light of the mad cow epidemic that swept Great Britain. Canada also used the WTO to challenge a French ban on asbestos imports. In both of these cases, Canada argued *against* the precautionary principle, claiming that hormone-fed beef and asbestos should be considered safe until conclusive evidence proved them to be unsafe. In 1998 the WTO upheld Canada's challenge of the European beef ban. In 2000, for the first time, the WTO upheld a law intended to protect health and the environment by endorsing the French ban on asbestos.[67] Like NAFTA, the WTO not only has direct impacts on environmental laws, it also has a chilling effect on environmental laws not yet passed.

The Multilateral Agreement on Investment

Negotiated in secret during the late 1990s, the Multilateral Agreement on Investment (MAI) would have given multinational corporations the ability to challenge regulations in a broad range of sectors including the environment, culture, health care, and education. As details of the MAI emerged, concerned citizens, municipalities, Aboriginal organizations, and provincial governments fought to derail the negotiations. Although the government of Canada supported the MAI, Canadians played a leading role in opposing the deal, particularly the nonprofit Council of Canadians, led by Maude Barlow. Barry Appleton, the lawyer who represented Ethyl Corp. in its NAFTA case against Canada, admitted that his clients "like these agreements" but criticized the MAI as "very problematic" and "broader than NAFTA."[68] Ultimately, as a result of vocal protests from civil society, France withdrew from the negotiations and the MAI was scrapped.[69]

Ongoing Trade Liberalization Efforts

Despite the MAI's defeat and the unprecedented protests at the WTO meeting in Seattle in 1999, Canada continues to press for further trade liberalization. Canada is participating in ongoing negotiations for the Free Trade Agreement of the Americas and a global General Agreement on Trade in Services. Both of these prospective agreements are expected to further limit the ability of governments to take steps to protect the environment.[70]

CONSTITUTIONAL PROBLEMS

The Canadian Constitution's lack of clarity on environmental matters is often blamed for creating confusion about which level of government is primarily responsible for environmental protection. The Constitution provides "ample opportunities for ambiguity, redundancy, conflict, and evasion of responsibility."[71] Both provincial and federal governments use the Constitution's ambiguity to justify their reluctance to act, when the reality is that environmental authority overlaps.[72] For example, Ontario, with the worst pollution record in Canada, blames the federal government for refusing "to commit to tough national air quality and climate change standards for all provinces and territories."[73] The federal government in turn blames Ontario for not doing enough to reduce air pollution.[74] Provincial and federal governments have also clashed over constitutional responsibility for bulk water exports, environmental assessments, energy exports, endangered species, and climate change.

Although uncertainties do persist, the extent of the constitutional confusion is overstated. Experts in constitutional law, including Dale Gibson, Belzberg Fellow of Constitutional Studies at the University of Alberta, and retired Supreme Court of Canada justice Gerard La Forest, agree that the federal government has more power to protect the environment than it has exercised to date.[75] The Supreme Court of Canada has repeatedly supported a strong federal role in environmental protection.[76] Supreme Court decisions have identified marine pollution and the preservation of green space around Ottawa as issues of national concern and therefore subject to federal regulation.[77] As a federal report on protecting the ozone layer states, "The federal government is generally responsible for issues deemed to be in the national interest, and as such is responsible for implementing the provisions of the *Montreal Protocol*."[78] If marine pollution, green space around Ottawa, and ozone depletion are matters of national concern that justify federal regulation, then climate change, the loss of biological diversity, and safe drinking water could also be subject to federal laws. According to Professor Kathryn Harrison, "Constitutional uncertainty persists primarily because the federal government has taken a narrow view of its own powers."[79]

The Influence of Quebec

A major reason for the federal government's constitutional deference to the provinces is the fear of exacerbating federal-provincial tensions during a critical period for national unity.[80] Québécois nationalism and environmentalism emerged as political movements at around the same time: the FLQ crisis was simultaneous with the first Earth Day, and the proliferation of American environmental legislation in the 1970s coincided with the rise of René Lévesque and the separatist Parti Québécois. Since the ascendance of the sovereignty movement in Quebec, the federal government has been reluctant to assert its powers to protect the environment for fear that this would add fuel to the separatists' fire.

The prospect of Quebec separating from Canada has profoundly influenced environmental law in Canada for more than three decades. Quebec's fierce opposition to the *Canadian Environment Protection Act* in 1987 led the federal government to incorporate the concept of equivalency, so that federal regulations would not apply in provinces with equal or stricter standards.[81] During debates about amendments to the *Canadian Environmental Protection Act* in 1998, Bloc Québécois MP Bernard Bigras attacked the federal government for "denying the right of the Quebec people to decide their own fate."[82] The federal government responded by adding mandatory consultation with the provinces before the federal government can take certain actions under the *Act*.

Industries in Quebec are particularly difficult for the federal government to regulate, for political and economic reasons. For example, "The power of the asbestos industry, and the close ties between the industry and the Quebec and Canadian governments, has created formidable obstacles to those favouring more stringent asbestos regulations."[83] As a result, US standards for asbestos are five times more stringent than Canadian standards, and Canada is the world's second-largest producer of asbestos.[84] The federal government is also reluctant to enforce federal environmental laws in Quebec, as demonstrated by the 1,700 recorded violations of the *Fisheries Act* by Quebec pulp and paper mills that failed to result in a single prosecution.

The Influence of Other Provinces

Pressure from other provincial governments urging Ottawa to decentralize powers also constrains the federal government's enthusiasm for environmental protection. Most provinces vehemently oppose the so-called threat of federal interference in the management of natural resources, fearing that a federal environmental law and policy role could limit economic activities. The pressure for decentralization is strengthened by a strong strain of political conservatism in western Canada that seeks to minimize Ottawa's role in all areas of government.[85] Provincial opposition contributes to the watering down of federal environmental laws and to the absence of legally binding national standards. Many provinces opposed the enactment of federal laws such as the *Canadian Environmental Protection Act*, *Canadian Environmental Assessment Act*, and the *Species at Risk Act*. A lawyer for the federal government candidly admitted that the narrow scope of the *Species at Risk Act* is a direct result of concern about alienating the provinces.[86]

The contentious environmental harmonization agreements are the product of three convergent forces: the possibility of Quebec separating, provincial pressure on the federal government to reduce its role in natural resource management, and the federal government's efforts to reduce the deficit. Harmonization was fast-tracked by Prime Minister Chrétien after the narrow federalist victory in the 1995 Quebec referendum. Numerous scholars and lawyers describe harmonization as a process through which the federal government has "abdicated" its environmental responsibilities.[87] In some areas that are clearly a federal responsibility, such as aquaculture or inland fisheries, it is difficult for Ottawa to refute this accusation.

At the end of the day, the Constitution provides a convenient smokescreen for both federal and provincial politicians seeking to avoid enacting, implementing, and enforcing environmental laws and policies. This constitutional buck-passing contributes to the spotty patchwork of laws, regulations, and policies ostensibly intended to protect Canadian air, water, land, and biodiversity. David Schindler accurately identifies the "tiresome, juvenile turf war between federal and provincial politicians" as a leading cause of environmental degradation.[88] Addressing Canada's environmental challenges will, as the Supreme Court of Canada recognizes, require a concerted effort by *all* levels of government.

THE LACK OF SEPARATION OF POWERS IN CANADA

[The preceding excerpt from *Unnatural Law*, "Systemic Weaknesses"] explained in detail how Canadian environmental laws are characterized by discretion, enabling but not requiring governments to take actions that protect the environment. In contrast, in the United States, environmental laws are mandatory in nature, requiring governments to take specified actions and meet specified standards. This fundamental difference can be traced to the lack of separation of powers between the legislative and executive branches of government in Canada.

In the United States, power is divided between Congress (the legislative branch of government), which makes the laws, and the administration (i.e., the executive), which implements the laws. In practice, different political parties often rule the Congress and the administration. As a result of this separation of power, congress writes and enacts laws that are mandatory, rather than discretionary, so that the administration is forced to obey congressional intent.

For example, pollution laws enacted by Congress, such as the *Clean Air Act, Clean Water Act,* and *Safe Drinking Water Act,* create legally binding standards that the administration must meet. If these standards are not met, the government can be held accountable through the judicial system.

In Canada, both federally and provincially, there is no separation of powers. The cabinet effectively controls both the legislative and executive functions of government. As a result, Canadian environmental laws are drafted to provide maximum flexibility and a minimum of mandatory duties. In contrast to the US, with its legally enforceable standards for clean air, clean water, and safe drinking water, Canada has *flexible* national goals embodied by the National Ambient Act Quality Objectives, Guidelines for Canadian Drinking Water Quality, and the misnamed Canada-Wide Standards. There is no legal obligation upon either the federal or provincial governments to achieve these objectives, guidelines, and standards.

Advocates of the Canadian system argue that discretion allows the legal system to be more flexible. While this is true in theory, in practice Canada's overall environmental record shows that flexibility is almost invariably exercised to the detriment of the environment. The separation of powers results in uneven, inconsistent legal protection on vital issues like clean air, safe drinking water, and the protection of endangered species. Yet surely Canadians deserve equal environmental protection regardless of where they live. To achieve this equality will require overcoming the barrier posed by the separation of powers and implementing legally enforceable national standards on a range of environmental issues.

THE CONCENTRATION OF POWER IN THE PRIME MINISTER AND PREMIERS

Every four years we elect a dictatorship.

—*Professor Chris Levy, University of Calgary Faculty of Law*

The problems caused by the lack of separation of powers between branches of government in Canada are exacerbated by another flaw in the Canadian political system. As Professor Wesley Pue of the University of British Columbia observes, "An increasing concentration of power is transforming all 'Westminster-style democracies' into one-person prime-ministerial shows."[89] This trend is particularly strong in Canada. According to academics and journalists, more power is concentrated in the Canadian prime minister's office than in the leader of any other western democracy.[90] The reasons for the dramatic extent of this phenomenon in Canada are as follows:

- The Canadian political system lacks the checks and balances of the US system.
- Canada lacks the effective Parliamentary and party systems of Britain.
- Unlike Australia, Canada has no elected and independent second chamber.

As explained in the previous section, there is no separation of powers between the legislative and executive branches of government in Canada: the prime minister is the head of the civil service as well as the House of Commons. As a result, the prime minister is ultimately responsible for both the enactment and the administration or implementation of laws and policies. This is in marked contrast to the American system, where an independent, law-making Congress balances the president's executive power. The Canadian Senate, which is appointed by the prime minister rather than elected, generally does not provide effective oversight of the House of Commons.[91]

The prime minister appoints members of cabinet, judges, the governor general, the leaders of Crown corporations, senators, and ambassadors. Even Canada's ethics counsellor is appointed by, and reports to, the prime minister. As one lawyer and academic describes the situation, "The Prime Minister, in some respects at least, controls all three branches of government."[92] The prime minister's own website states, "The Prime Minister used to be described as 'the first among equals' in the Cabinet ... That is no longer so. He is now incomparably more powerful than any colleague."[93] Remarkably, even cabinet decisions are not necessarily determined by majority vote because "a strong prime minister, having listened to everyone's opinion, may simply announce that his view is the policy of the government, even if most, or all, the other ministers are opposed."[94] Another aspect of this concentration of power is that the prime minister's close advisors, although they are not elected and have low public profiles, wield tremendous influence. Author Jeffrey Simpson and former Liberal MP John Nunziata both suggest that Prime Minister Chrétien's advisors [were] more powerful than any cabinet minister.[95] Deputy ministers in all federal departments are also chosen by, and effectively work for, the prime minister.[96]

Moreover, a prime minister with a majority government wields total control over Parliament. Canada has a very strong tradition of party discipline, in part because any vote in the House of Commons may be viewed as a nonconfidence motion. Members of Parliament put loyalty to the party ahead of the opinions of their constituents, whereas members of the US Congress serve their electorate first and their party second. Backbenchers and maverick members of Parliament who refuse to follow the party line face harsh disciplinary action, including expulsion. For example, MP John Nunziata was expelled from the Liberal caucus in 1996 for voting against his party.

These observations apply equally to provincial politics and the role of premiers. There are no checks and balances, party discipline is strictly enforced, and there are no provincial senates. Like the prime minister, premiers control cabinet, the caucus, the legislature, and the civil service, as well as hundreds of appointments to provincial agencies, boards of Crown corporations, and other provincial bodies. In Ontario and Alberta under Premiers Mike Harris and Ralph Klein, large increases in the budget of the premiers' offices reflect increasing centralization of power.[97]

The Impacts of the Concentration of Power on Environmental Law and Policy

The concentration of power in the offices of the prime minister and provincial premiers affects environmental law and policy in three main ways. First, it is difficult for environmental issues to get priority because of the wide range of economic and social challenges confronting political leaders. Despite the heightened degree of environmental awareness in Canadian society, Canadians consistently base their votes on other issues (e.g., the economy and health care). Politicians understand that support for environmental protection is "a mile wide and an inch deep."[98] Prime ministers and premiers are acutely aware that their continued political success is far more likely to depend on the state of the economy than the state of the environment. Second, environmental initiatives are viewed by some politicians as lose-lose propositions.[99] Because environmental issues almost always involve vocal advocates on both sides, whatever action is taken will be loudly criticized. Third, access to prime ministers, premiers, and their top advisors is limited to very powerful members of society, who are usually opponents rather than proponents of environmental protection.[100]

Because so much power is concentrated in the prime minister and premiers, and because environmental laws and policies raise significant economic questions, the prime minister and premiers control the environmental law agenda. In 1997 and again in 2003, Prime Minister Chrétien called early federal elections, and important environmental laws died on the order paper when Parliament was dissolved. In 1997 the environmental laws that were abandoned were the

Canada Endangered Species Protection Act, the revised *Canadian Environmental Protection Act*, the revised *Fisheries Act*, Bill C-96 implementing the *United Nations Convention on the Law of the Sea*, the *Nunavut Water Resources Act*, and the *Drinking Water Materials Safety Act*. Most of these laws have never been reintroduced. In 2000 the environmental laws that died on the order paper were the *Species at Risk Act*, the *National Marine Conservation Areas Act*, *An Act to Amend the International Boundary Treaty Waters Act*, and the *Foundation for Sustainable Development Technology Act*.

Prime Minister Chrétien pushed through the Canada-Wide Accord on Environmental Harmonization in 1998 despite opposition from his own environment minister, backbench MPs, the Standing Committee on Environment and Sustainable Development, environmental groups, and the Canadian Bar Association.[101] Despite similar opposition, the prime minister placated industry by forcing last-minute changes to weaken the *Canadian Environmental Protection Act, 1999* and the *Species at Risk Act*. In Alberta, Ontario, and more recently British Columbia, Premiers Klein, Harris, and Campbell have led dramatic reductions in environmental regulation and enforcement. The lack of effective checks and balances in the Canadian political system makes it difficult to effectively oppose decreases in environmental protection.

Occasionally the power of the prime minister or premiers works in favour of environmental protection. For example, in 1997 Prime Minister Chrétien was publicly embarrassed at the five-year follow-up meeting to the Rio Earth Summit. As a result, Chrétien ordered that Canada take a stronger stance than the United States during the negotiation of the *Kyoto Protocol*.[102] Canada's *Kyoto* commitment, to reduce greenhouse gas emissions by 6 percent between 1990 and 2010, is modestly better than the US commitment of a 5 percent reduction. Chrétien then used his power to ensure that Canada ratified *Kyoto* in 2002. Prime Minister Chrétien also deserves credit for the 2002 passage of the *Species at Risk Act*, *National Marine Conservation Act*, and *Pest Control Products Act*, in addition to significant funding increases for environmental priorities. These actions, in the final year of his mandate, represent a remarkable reversal of Chrétien's earlier record. In BC, Premier Mike Harcourt's personal commitment to environmental protection contributed to significant provincial law and policy improvements during the early 1990s. BC passed new laws including the *Environmental Assessment Act, Forest Practices Code of British Columbia Act, Water Protection Act*, contaminated sites legislation, tougher pulp and paper mill regulations, and regulations governing motor vehicle emissions and cleaner fuels. Harcourt's government also added millions of hectares of new protected areas, cancelled the ill-advised Kemano Completion Project, and created an environmental watchdog known as the Commission on Resources and the Environment.[103]

The OECD observes that for sustainable development to succeed, a strong political commitment "must come from the highest levels of government and be embraced by prime ministers as well as ministers of finance."[104] This strong political commitment is not yet consistent in Canada.

BARRIERS TO AN EFFECTIVE ROLE FOR THE COURTS

Because of flaws in Canada's political system such as the lack of separation of powers and an ineffective Senate, the Canadian judicial system has a particularly important role in holding governments accountable. It is up to the courts to fill the void left by the Canadian political system's lack of effective checks and balances. Unfortunately, the judicial system's contribution to environmental protection in Canada is undermined by several factors, including a historical bias toward private rather than public interests, the absence of constitutional environmental rights, a lack of access to the courts, the high costs of litigation, judicial deference to government decision makers, and low penalties for environmental offences. Progress has been made on some of these issues in recent years, but major barriers remain.

Private Rights versus the Public Interest

The Canadian legal system is based mainly on the English common law system, which focuses on the *private* rights of parties. The emergence of a judicial role in protecting the *public* interest, sometimes at the expense of private interests, is a recent phenomenon.[105] Judicial recognition of the public interest in environmental protection was slow to develop in Canada but increased considerably in the 1990s. In 1973 an Ontario judge criticized environmental lawsuits by citizens as "ill-founded actions for the sake of using the courts as a vehicle for expounding philosophy."[106] In the 1980s a judge presiding over an environmental private prosecution in Ontario admitted a desire "to be back with my burglars and murderers."[107] In 1993 a judge involved in sentencing individuals for protesting at Clayoquot Sound in BC said, "I'm tired of hearing about trees."[108] One of [the] clearest situations in which private and public interests clash is injunction applications by environmental groups to stop specific activities, such as the logging of a particular area or the building of a road. Courts must weigh the private interest in lost profits, economic impacts, and possible job losses against the public interest in environmental protection. Although judges have historically been reluctant to grant injunctions in these circumstances, the trend in recent years is toward environmental protection, in recognition of the irreparable nature of ecological damage.[109] Canadian courts, led by the Supreme Court of Canada, have become increasingly cognizant of the legitima[cy] and importance of public interest environmental legislation.

Environmental Rights

Constitutional recognition for rights is the strongest form of protection available under the Canadian legal system. Although citizens in many other countries, from Azerbaijan to Vanuatu, enjoy constitutional protection for environmental rights, Canadians do not. Canada's *Charter of Rights and Freedoms* contains no provision recognizing the right of Canadians to a clean, safe, and healthy environment. The closest provision is section 7 of the *Charter*, which protects Canadians' "right to life, liberty, and security of the person." Attempts to persuade courts to interpret this provision broadly, so as to include some form of environmental right, have not been successful.[110] A BC judge rejected arguments made by lawyers for a group of concerned residents that Canadians enjoy a right to safe drinking water.[111]

Residents of Ontario, Quebec, the Yukon, the Northwest Territories, and Nunavut enjoy limited statutory environmental rights because of recently enacted laws.[112] These environmental rights for the most part are procedural, not substantive. Statutory environmental rights are much weaker than constitutionally protected environmental rights. Apart from ensuring access to information and requiring public notification of changes to environmental laws and regulations, these laws have had minimal practical impact on environmental protection in Canada. For example, despite the *Environmental Bill of Rights* passed in 1993, Ontario is still Canada's most polluted province, the site of the Walkerton disaster, and a jurisdiction subject to dramatic reductions in environmental protection.

Access to Courts

[The preceding excerpt from *Unnatural Law*, "Systemic Weaknesses"] detailed the ineffectiveness of private prosecutions and citizen suits in protecting Canada's environment. Citizens can also go to court in an effort to overturn government decisions, a process known as judicial review. The first obstacle to judicial review is called standing, or the legal right to bring a case to court. Traditionally, a person needed a direct personal or property interest in order to gain standing. In recent years, however, courts have established a concept called public interest standing that allows citizens, environmental groups, and other organizations to bring lawsuits challenging government decisions.[113] As long as a citizen or group can demonstrate a genuine interest in a problem, raise a serious issue of law, and convince a judge that the issue would not otherwise be brought to court, then public interest standing will be granted.[114] Only in rare cases is public interest standing denied.[115] In some provinces, however, such as Alberta, standing is limited by some environmental laws to individuals who are "directly affected" by a project or activity.[116] This greatly restricts the public's ability to use the judicial system to hold governments accountable.

The High Costs of Litigation

The accessibility of the justice system under the concept of public interest standing is in danger of being undermined by the high cost of litigation. Although there are now a number of non-profit organizations offering free legal services (e.g., Sierra Legal Defence Fund, Canadian Environmental Law Association, Environmental Defence Canada, West Coast Environmental Law Association) and an increasing number of lawyers willing to work on a pro bono basis, demand still exceeds supply. A larger problem is that courts generally award costs against unsuccessful litigants, meaning the losing party in a lawsuit pays a portion of the winner's legal costs. These cost awards can be more than $100,000, making litigation prohibitively expensive for local citizens and smaller environmental groups.[117] Class actions, lawsuits brought on behalf of a group of individuals allegedly suffering similar damages, can also result in huge cost awards against unsuccessful plaintiffs, as two recent Ontario cases demonstrated.[118] Recent changes to the *Federal Court Rules* increased the likelihood that unsuccessful public interest litigants will be forced to pay costs.[119] There are compelling arguments that courts should create an exception to the costs rule for precedent-setting cases brought to advance the public interest, just as courts created an exception to the traditional rules of standing to enable public interest litigation.[120] To date, however, Canadian courts have refused to create an exception to the general costs rule for public interest litigants.

Judicial Reluctance to Engage in Substantive Review

Judicial review cases are based on two main considerations: did decision makers act "within their jurisdiction" (i.e., the parameters set out in the relevant law), and was their decision "reasonable"? Canadian courts are very deferential toward government decision makers, generally refusing to overturn decisions unless there is an "error of law" or the decision is "patently unreasonable." In practice, the doctrine of judicial deference can produce absurd results, as in a 1990 lawsuit intended to protect Atlantic cod where the court refused to critically examine federal fisheries management.[121] In the field of environmental law, Canadian courts focus on procedural matters, and are extremely reluctant to scrutinize the substantive factual issues. The consensus among legal experts is that "substantive review of legislative and administrative performance is highly atypical of the judiciary in Canada."[122]

Often courts will be satisfied if minimal procedural requirements are met by government decision makers, regardless of the extent or quality of substantive evidence to support the decision. In the late 1980s and early 1990s, Canadian courts made a series of relatively bold decisions forcing the federal government to conduct environmental assessments of major projects with impacts in federal areas of jurisdiction. However, since that time "courts have demonstrated reluctance ... to scrutinize those assessments with a high degree of intensity."[123] In a recent environmental assessment case, the Federal Court decided, "If there has been some consideration [of a factor, such as cumulative effects], it is irrelevant that there could have been further and better consideration."[124] Canadian courts are particularly reluctant to delve into the complex scientific questions raised in environmental cases. The same Federal Court decision stated, "It is not the function of this Court to identify and correct poor science." This is a familiar judicial position in environmental cases, yet in criminal cases courts are able to decipher expert evidence on complex scientific issues such as DNA testing, and in corporate cases courts untangle complicated business transactions.[125]

Low Penalties for Environmental Offences

Another problem is that, historically, penalties for environmental offences in Canada were extremely low. Several corporations convicted of violating the *Fisheries Act* for unlawfully discharging toxic effluent were fined $1.[126] According to author Michael Harris, among Canadian commercial fishers in the 1980s and early 1990s, "Fines had become so minimal, they were a standing joke in the industry, a minor cost of doing business."[127] Many federal and provincial environmental laws were amended at that time to provide stronger penalties. Stiff fines and jail sentences were intended to send a clear message that environmental offences will not be tolerated by Canadian society.[128] However, as ["Systemic Weaknesses"] makes clear, environmental laws in Canada are not being rigorously enforced. Larger potential penalties have little deterrent effect where a law is not being enforced.[129]

Judicial awareness of the significance of environmental offences is increasing. During the 1990s, a Quebec company was fined $4 million for pollution offences, while a pulp and paper mill in Newfoundland was fined $750,000.[130] Some judges are making stronger pronouncements in environmental prosecutions, such as:

> Every act of degradation of the environment is cumulative and has to be addressed that way.[131]
>
> The message has got to go out there that infractions of the environmental legislation are not going to be tolerated.[132]
>
> Pollution prevention "requires not only a change in technology but a change in mindset."[133]

Fines and jail sentences given to corporate directors and business leaders send a message to corporate Canada that violating environmental laws could have serious repercussions.[134] However, only a handful of individuals have ever received jail sentences in Canada for environmental offences.[135] Far more Canadians have been jailed for attempting to protect the environment than for damaging it. In the summer of 1993 alone over eight hundred people were arrested in the rainforest at Clayoquot Sound on Vancouver Island. Using mass trials, the courts handed out surprisingly harsh sentences ranging up to six months.[136] A grandmother, Betty Krawczyk, spent many months in jail for her part in various logging protests.[137] In contrast, four loggers who assaulted a group of environmentalists in British Columbia and deliberately destroyed evidence of the attack received no jail time but were sentenced to perform community service and take anger management courses.[138]

On a positive note, courts are beginning to use the creative sentencing provisions found in many modern environmental laws. These provisions enable courts to make a wide range of orders against parties convicted of environmental offences. Examples of creative sentences include orders to restore damaged habitat, contribute funds to universities for research, or undertake prescribed activities to prevent future pollution.

The Role of the Courts in the United States

In the United States, many of the barriers to an effective role for the courts have been lowered. Professors Kathryn Harrison and George Hoberg conclude that in the context of environmental law and policy, "Perhaps the most significant difference in the regulatory frameworks of the two countries is the pivotal role of the judiciary in the United States."[139] The United States has a more complete array of environmental laws, legally enforceable national standards, extensive opportunities for public involvement in decision making, and a judiciary with a history of activism. American courts are willing to evaluate the substantive merit of government decisions, even if it means delving into complex scientific evidence.[140] Courts in the United States have creatively modified ancient legal concepts, such as the public trust doctrine, to protect the environment.[141] Citizen suit provisions in almost all major American environmental statutes allow the public to assist government in enforcing environmental laws and are seen as "a critical aspect of democratization."[142] And finally, American courts impose very large sentences, both in terms of fines and jail time, on those who violate environmental laws.

The barriers to an effective role for the courts in Canada, combined with the absence of key laws, the lack of enforceable national standards, and the pervasiveness of discretion, make environmental litigation far less common in Canada than in the United States, and far less effective.[143] Environmental lawyers Elizabeth Swanson and Elaine Hughes conclude, "Litigation with the primary and immediate purpose of bringing a halt to unwanted development activity has not, for the most part, succeeded."[144] The systemic problems in Canada's environmental law system caused another author to bemoan the "absolute futility of looking to the courts to defend the environment from governments that wish to exploit its economic potential."[145] The bottom line is that in Canada, courts are unlikely to overturn government decisions in the area of environmental law and policy.[146]

CONCLUSION

This chapter describes a number of imposing obstacles that must be overcome to strengthen Canada's environmental laws and policies and improve Canada's environmental performance. First and foremost, economic considerations continue to dominate the enactment, implementation, and enforcement of environmental law and policy. Other hurdles to strengthening environmental law in Canada include constitutional problems, the ongoing threat of Quebec separation, the lack of separation of powers between the legislative and executive branches of government, the concentration of power in the prime minister and premiers, and barriers to an effective role for the courts. However, even if these hurdles could be successfully cleared, what would be the impact on Canada's environmental record?

QUESTIONS TO CONSIDER

1. Discuss the author's outline of weaknesses in environmental protection policies and laws in Canada. What measures could be taken as part of "better governance," according to Boyd? Which specific measures do you regard as most useful in enhancing our environment?

2. To what extent should the precautionary principle be implemented as part of environmental safety policies? Address the role of scientific investigations into a specific environmental issue, for example, air pollution, water pollution, or genetically modified organisms (GMOs).

3. Despite some advances in environmental matters, Boyd lists several obstacles to environmental protection and public safety. To what extent do you think we should be pessimistic or optimistic about further progress in this area? Will political and economic interests undermine environmental efforts in Canada? Use specific examples from his chapter as well as outside readings.

SUGGESTIONS FOR FURTHER READING/VIEWING

Benidickson, J. (2008). *Environmental law*. Toronto: Irwin Law.

Gibney. A. (Director). (2008). *Taxi to the dark side*. [Documentary]. United States: Jigsaw Productions. (Academy Award winner, Best Documentary, 2008).

Hogg, P. (2008). *A question of parliamentary power: Criminal law and the control of greenhouse gas emissions*. Toronto: C.D. Howe Institute.

NOTES FOR "SYSTEMIC WEAKNESSES"

1. O'Connor (2002a); Harrison (2000b; 2001a).
2. VanNijnatten and Lambright (2001, 253).
3. For example, *Intervenor Funding Project Act*, R.S.O. 1990, c. I-13; *Commissioner on Resources and the Environment Act*, S.B.C. 1996, c. 59; *Public Participation Act*, S.B.C. 2001, c. 19, repealed by *Miscellaneous Statutes Amendment Act*, S.B.C. 2001, c. 32.
4. Handy and Hamilton (1996, 9).
5. Gunningham, Grabosky, and Sinclair (1998, 8).
6. O'Connor (2002a, 33).
7. Dewees (1993).
8. Scoffield (1999a); Dixon (2000).
9. Wolf (2001).
10. Hitchens (1999).
11. OECD (1993, 118). See also Porter and van der Linde (1995).
12. Porter (1990, 168).
13. Martin (1992).
14. Power and Barrett (2001). See also Gillies (1994); Kromm and Ernst (2000).
15. Gunningham, Grabosky, and Sinclair (1998, 9).
16. Schrecker (2001, 54); Hoberg (1997; 2001b, 176); Harrison and Hoberg (1994); Benidickson (1997, 5); Tilleman (1995, 397); Ross (1995, 90).
17. *Canadian Environmental Assessment Act*, S.C. 1992, c. 37, ss. 46-8; *Canadian Environmental Protection Act, 1999*, S.C. 1999, c. 33, ss. 166, 175; *Canada Wildlife Act*, R.S.C. 1985, c. W-9, s. 8.
18. Swanson and Hughes (1995, 111).
19. Hoberg (1994, 115).
20. Harrison (2001a, 140).
21. See *Seattle Audubon Society v. Evans*; *Seattle Audubon Society v. Mosely*; *Northern Spotted Owl et al. v. Hodel*; *Northern Spotted Owl v. Lujan*; *Administrative Procedures Act*, 5 U.S.C. 702.
22. Jones and de Villars (1999, 570–1).
23. Daily and Ellison (2002).
24. McIntyre and Mosedale (1997); Cameron and Abouchar (1996).
25. M'Gonigle, et al. (1995).
26. European Environment Agency (2001).
27. Schettler et al. (1999).
28. Hayes et al. (2002).
29. Schettler et al. (1999); Thornton (2000).
30. Schettler et al. (1999, 308).

31. Ludwig, Hilborn, and Walters (1993).
32. Harrison and Antweiler (2001).
33. Leiss (2001, 199).
34. Leiss and Tyshenko (2001); Johnson (1996, 34).
35. Royal Society of Canada (2001); Commissioner of the Environment and Sustainable Development (2000, 6–24); US National Research Council (2002).
36. Mandrusiak (1999, 261).
37. Leiss (2001, ch. 2).
38. Barrett (2002); Royal Society of Canada (2001).
39. Shrybman (1999a, 84–5); Barrett (2002); Winfield (2000); Swenarchuk (2000).
40. Shrybman (1999a); Schiller (2001).
41. WTO Panel Report (1997); WTO Appellate Body Report (1998).
42. Walters (1986); Parson (2001).
43. See *Environment Act*, S.N.S. 1994–95, c. 1; *Endangered Species Act*, S.N.S. 1998, c. 11; *Wilderness Areas Protection Act*, S.N.S. 1998, c. 27; *Wilderness and Ecological Reserves Act*, R.S.N. 1990, c. W-9.
44. Abouchar (2001).
45. Moffet (1997); Freestone and Hey (1996); VanderZwaag (1998); Raffensperger and Tickner (1999).
46. National Round Table on the Environment and the Economy (2001a, 14); see also Science Council of Canada (1988, 18).
47. Leiss (2001, 180); Hutchings, Walters, and Haedrich (1997).
48. Schrecker (2001).
49. Canada announced the first MPA under the *Oceans Act* in March 2003. See *Endeavour Hydrothermal Vents Marine Protected Areas Regulations*, SOR/2003-87.
50. Environment Canada (1990a, 156).
51. OECD (2000a; 1995a); Standing Committee on Environment and Sustainable Development (1998, para. 114).
52. Friends of the Earth Canada (2001); Mittlestaedt (1999a; 1999b); Commissioner of the Environment and Sustainable Development (1999, 3–18).
53. Environment Canada (1999d).
54. For repeat offenders in British Columbia, see the annual "Non-compliance list" published by the Ministry of Water, Land and Air Protection, <http://wlapwww.gov.bc.ca/epd/epdnon>. For repeat offenders in Ontario, see Sierra Legal Defence Fund (2002f; 2001a; 2000; 1999).
55. Christie (2000).
56. Sierra Legal Defence Fund (2001a).
57. Benidickson (1997, 123).
58. Macdonald (1991, 181).
59. VanderZwaag (1995, 315–16).
60. Farber (1999).
61. US Environmental Protection Agency (1999).
62. Friends of the Earth Canada (2001).
63. Berger (1994, Sentencing tables).
64. Environment Canada (1990a, 22); Stefanick and Wells (1998).
65. Toner (1996).
66. Leiss (2001, 169).
67. Standing Committee on Environment and Sustainable Development (1998).
68. Harris (1998, 214).
69. Commissioner of the Environment and Sustainable Development (1999, 3–21).
70. US Office of Management and Budget (1998).
71. Natural Resources Defence Council (2001).
72. Fact sheets from US government websites: National Parks Service, <http://www.nps.gov>; National Oceanic and Atmospheric Administration, <http://www.noaa.gov>; Forest Service, <http://www.fs.fed.us>; Fish and Wildlife Service, <http://www.fws.gov>.
73. US Environmental Protection Agency (1999).
74. Government of Canada (2001).
75. Anderson (2003, 1).
76. McKay (1997); Canadian Institute for Business and Environment (1997).
77. McKay (1997).

78. Muldoon and Nadarajah (1999, 54).
79. Boyd (1998; 2002a).
80. Clark and Yacoumidis (2000); Muldoon and Nadarajah (1999).
81. Cooper (1999b, 9).
82. Environmental Commissioner of Ontario (2000a; 1999; 1998; 1997; 1996).
83. Ontario Provincial Auditor (1996, ch. 3.09).
84. Environmental Commissioner of Ontario (1998, 4; 1999, 4, 35).
85. Ontario Provincial Auditor (2000, ch. 3).
86. West Coast Environmental Law Association (2002), Sierra Legal Defence Fund (2002c).
87. Huestis (1984).
88. Standing Committee on Environment and Sustainable Development (1997).
89. Canadian Institute for Environmental Law and Policy (1996).
90. Kennett, McKoy, and Yarranton (1996).
91. Ogan (2000).
92. McMillan quoted in Standing Committee on Environment and Sustainable Development (1993, 256).
93. National Environmental Law Section of the CBA (1996).
94. McIlroy (1997b).
95. *Canadian Environmental Law Association v. Canada* (Minister of Environment) (2000).
96. Commissioner of the Environment and Sustainable Development (1999, 5–22).
97. Auditor General of Canada (1999c, para. 28.79).
98. OECD (1999f, 93).
99. Moffet and Saxe (1998).
100. Harrison and Andrews (1998).
101. Harrison and Antweiler (2001); Harrison (2000a).
102. OECD (2000a, 17).
103. KPMG Chartered Accountant (1996).
104. Krahn (1998, 22).
105. Commissioner of the Environment and Sustainable Development (1999, ch. 4).
106. Harrison (2001b).
107. Menell and Stewart (1994, 531); see also US General Accounting Office (1997); Davies and Mazurek (1996).
108. New Directions Group (1997).
109. Gibson (1999, 239); see also Gunningham, Grabosky, and Sinclair (1998, 52).
110. Chang, MacDonald, and Wolfson (1998).
111. Gertler, Muldoon, and Valiante (1990, 79).
112. Andrews (2000).
113. Schrecker (2001, 32).
114. Shillington and Burns Consultants (1999).
115. Dorcey and McDaniels (2001, 264, 261).
116. *Initiative Petition Administration Regulation*, B.C. Reg. 70/95.
117. *Delgamuukw v. British Columbia*, [1997] R. v. Marshall, [1999] and [1999], *Council of the Haida Nation v. British Columbia* (2002). See Doyle-Bedwell and Cohen (2001).
118. *Mackenzie Valley Resource Management Act*, S.C. 1998, c. 25, and the *Nunavut Land Claims Agreement Act*, S.C. 1993, c. 28. See also Egan et al. (2001, 45–50).
119. *Delgamuukw v. British Columbia*, (1997).
120. For two innovative proposals based on Aboriginal comanagement, see Burda, Collier, and Evans (1999) and M'Gonigle et al. (2001).
121. Swanson and Hughes (1995, 111).
122. Duncan (1990a).
123. The conviction was overturned on appeal but is still before the courts, see *Fletcher v. Kingston* (1998).
124. Hamilton (City), 18 September 2000 (unreported) described in Berger (1994).
125. For example, *Kostuch v. Kowalski* (1990); *Kostuch v. Kowalski* (1991); *Kostuch v. Kowalski* (1991); *Kostuch v. Alberta* (1992); *Kostuch v. Alberta* [1996].
126. *Mitchell v. Canada* (Attorney General), [1999].
127. Glenn (1999, 251).
128. Law Reform Commission of Canada (1986).

129. Canadian Environmental Protection Act, 1999 S.C. 1999, c. 33; Environmental Bill of Rights, 1993, S.O. 1993. c. 28; Environmental Quality Act, S.Q. 1994, c. Q-2; Environment Act, S.Y. 1991, c. 5; Environment Rights Act, R.S.N.W.T. 1988 (Supp.) c. 83.
130. Morelli (1997).
131. A. Keith Mitchell, Farris, Vaughan, Wills & Murphy, letter to Jean-Pierre Martel, Canadian Pulp and Paper Association, 7 April 1997. On file with the author.
132. Sergio Marchi, letter to Jack Munro, chairman, Forest Alliance of BC, 21 March 1997. On file with the author.
133. VanNijnatten and Boardman (2001).
134. Gallon (1999, 250); Gunningham, Grabosky, and Sinclair (1998).
135. Gunningham, Grabosky, and Sinclair (1998, 7); see also Benidickson (1999).
136. Doernand Conway (1994); Nemetz (1986).
137. Panayatou (1994).
138. Wiener (1999).
139. Jutlah (1998); Rolfe and Nowlan (1993); Task Force on Economic Instruments (1994).
140. Leiss (2001, 172).
141. OECD (1995a, 17).
142. *Canadian Environmental Protection Act, 1999*, S.C. 1999, c. 33, ss.322-7, *Environment Act*, S.N.S. 1994–95, c. 1, s. 15; 143. *Environmental Protection and Enhancement Act*, R.S.A. 2000, c. E-12, s. 13.
143. *Canada Foundation for Sustainable Development Technology Act*, S.C. 2001, c. 23.
144. Systems Research Group (1969).
145. Morley (1973).
146. Thompson (1980, 5).
147. Dewees (1990, 145).
148. Webb (1990); Canadian Bar Association (1990); Doering et al. (1992).

NOTES FOR "OBSTACLES TO FURTHER PROGRESS"

1. Juillet and Toner (1997, 194).
2. Doern (2001, 116); Harrison (1995, 172).
3. Canadian Global Almanac (2001).
4. Porter (1991).
5. Schrecker (2001, 36).
6. Hoberg (2001b, 173); Natural Resources Canada (2001c; 2001b; 2001d).
7. OECD (1993,7).
8. Bernstein and Cashore (2001a).
9. Harrison (1996, 14).
10. Hessing and Howlett (1997, 220); Schrecker (1989).
11. Macdonald (2001, 66); Howlett (2001d, 34).
12. Harrison (1996, 157).
13. Sierra Legal Defence Fund (2002a).
14. Castrilli and Vigod (1987, 131).
15. Robert S. Demone, chairman, president and CEO of Canadian Pacific Hotels, letter to Sheila Copps, Minister of Canadian Heritage, 25 June 1996. On file with the author.
16. Amos, Harrison, and Hoberg (2001, 161).
17. Brooks and Stritch (1991, 211).
18. Langille (1987, 41).
19. Macdonald (2001,81); Winsor (1999).
20. Jacobs (1999).
21. Eggerston (1999).
22. Gwyn Morgan, speech at the APEC CEO Summit, Vancouver, 21–4 November 1997.
23. Environment Canada, "Minister's Introductory Calls on Industry Associations," Briefing note, 5 August 1999. On file with the author.
24. Environment Canada, "Minister's meeting with Tom d'Aquino, Business Council on National Issues," Briefing note, 1. On file with the author.
25. Paehlke (2001, 86).

26. Cashore et al. (2001).

27. Harrison (1996, 176).

28. Paehlke (2001, 111–14).

29. Pifer (1997).

30. Moe Sihota, BC minister of environment, letter to Gerry Stoney; president IWA Canada. 13 February 1996. On file with the author.

31. Cashore et al. (2001).

32. Dale (2001, 98); Schrecker (2001, 40).

33. Rabe (1997); Doern and Conway (1994); Cashore et al. (2001).

34. Harrison (1996).

35. OECD (1999f, 31–7).

36. Auditor General of Canada (2000b).

37. Doern (2001, 116).

38. Standing Committee on Environment and Sustainable Development (1998, para. 96).

39. Leiss (2001, ch. 5).

40. Dwivedi et al. (2001, 216).

41. Boardman (2001, 225).

42. Winfield (2000); International Institute for Sustainable Development (2000a); Boardman (2001, 222).

43. Greenpeace International (2002).

44. Parson (2001, 359).

45. US Office of Technology Assessment (1994, 24).

46. Johnson and Beaulieu (1996).

47. Appleton (1994).

48. Juillet (2001, 141).

49. International Centre for Settlement of Investment Disputes (2000, para. 103).

50. Mann (2001).

51. Appleton (1998, 40).

52. Leiss (2001, 66–101); Schettler (1999).

53. *Manganese-based Fuel Additives Act*, S.C. 1997, c. 11.

54. Leiss (2001, 66–101).

55. Canada is appealing the tribunal decision, which determined Canada's ban on PCB exports violated NAFTA. See the NAFTA dispute resolution page. <http://www.dfait-maeci.gc.ca>.

56. Chase (2001).

57. International Centre for Settlement of Investment Disputes (2000).

58. *United Mexican States v. Metalclad* (2001).

59. Mann (2001). See <http://www.naftaclaims.com>.

60. Commission for Environmental Cooperation (2002a, 14).

61. Castrilli (2002).

62. Shrybman (1999a).

63. World Trade Organization (1996). United States—Restrictions on Import of Tuna, GATT Doc. DS21/R, BISD (39th Supp.).

64. World Trade Organization (1998). United States—Import Prohibition of Certain Shrimp and Shrimp Products.

65. World Trade Organization (1996). United States—Standards for Reformulated and Conventional Gasoline.

66. World Trade Organization (1998). EC Measures Concerning Meat and Meat Products (Hormones).

67. World Trade Organization (2001). EC Measures Affecting Asbestos and Asbestos Containing Products.

68. Appleton (1998, 26, 37, 39).

69. Lalumière and Landau (1998); Drohan (1998).

70. Sinclair and Grieshaber-Otto (2002); Swenarchuk (2002); McCarthy (2001).

71. Parson (2001, 5).

72. Harrison (2001a, 125).

73. Ontario Ministry of Environment (2001).

74. VanNijnatten and Lambright (2001).

75. La Forest and Gibson (2000a; 2000b).

76. *Friends of the Oldman River v. Canada*, [1992], *R. v. Hydro-Quebec*, [1997]; Valiante (2001, 19).

77. *R. v. Crown Zellerbach*, [1988] *Munro v. National Capital Commission*, [1966].

78. Environment Canada (1997a, 13).

79. Harrison (1996, 54).

80. Juillet and Toner (1997, 180).

81. Harrison (1995, 129).

82. Bernard Bigras, *Hansard*, House of Commons Debates, 24 April 1998.

83. Harrison and Hoberg (1994, 149).

84. Hoberg (1991).

85. Paehlke (2001, 75).

86. Dawson (2001).

87. Harrison (1995, 175).

88. Schindler (2001, 21).

89. Pue (2000, 11).

90. Savoie (1999); Simpson (2001).

91. Hoy (1999).

92. Tilleman (1995, 394).

93. See the "Role of the Prime Minister" page, Prime Minister of Canada's website, <http://www.pm.gc.ca>.

94. Forsey (1991).

95. Simpson (2001); Cosh (1996).

96. Schrecker (2001, 39).

97. Taft (1997); Ralph, Regimbald, and St-Amand (1997).

98. Schrecker (2001, 35).

99. Harrison (1996).

100. Brooks and Stritch (1991).

101. Harrison (2001a, 131).

102. Stefanick and Wells (1998, 263).

103. Many of these advances have been weakened by subsequent governments.

104. OECD (2001e, 120).

105. Estrin and Swaigen (1993, 7).

106. *Green v. The Queen*, [1973].

107. Swaigen (1992, 204).

108. MacIsaac and Champagne (1994, 158).

109. Boyd (2001b).

110. *Operation Dismantle v. R.*, [1985]; *Energy Probe v. Canada* (1989).

111. *Red Mountain Residents v. B.C.* (2000).

112. *Environmental Bill of Rights 1993*, S.O. 1993, c. 28; *Environmental Quality Act*, S.Q. 1994, c. Q-2; *Environment Act*, S.Y. 1991, c. 5; *Environmental Rights Act*, R.S.N.W.T. 1988 (Supp.), c. 83.

113. Elgie (1993).

114. *Finlay v. Canada*, [1986].

115. For a recent discussion of the principles of public interest standing, see *Sierra Club of Canada v. Minister of Finance*, [1999]. Examples of cases where public interest standing was denied include *Shiell v. Amok Ltd.* (1988) and *Shiell v. Canada* (1995).

116. *Kostuch v. Environmental Appeal Board* (1996).

117. *Palmer v. Stora Kopparbergs* (1983); *Reese v. Alberta* (1992); *Manitoba Future Forest Alliance v. Canada* (1999); *Inverhuron and District Ratepayers Association v. Canada* (2000).

118. *Pearson v. Inco* (2002); *Gariepy v. Shell Oil* (2002).

119. Under previous *Federal Court Rules* (C.R.C. 1978, c. 663), Rule 1618 limited cost awards in judicial review proceedings to cases where there were unusual circumstances, such as frivolous or vexatious proceedings. Under the new *Federal Court Rules* (SOR/98-106), Rule 400 gives courts complete discretion to award costs. Rule 400(3)(h) identifies one factor in the determination of cost awards as being "whether the public interest in having the proceeding litigated justifies a particular award of costs."

120. Tollefson (1995).

121. *National Inshore Fisherman Association v. Canada*, [1990].

122. Wood (2000, 197); see also Hessing and Howlett (1997, 208); Hoberg (2000).

123. Benidickson (1997, 187).

124. *Inverhuron and District Ratepayers Association v. Canada* (2000).

125. "It is not the role of the Court to become an academy of science to arbitrate conflicting scientific predictions" (J. Strayer, in *Vancouver Island Peace Society v. Canada*, [1992], 51). See also *Palmer v. Stora Kopparbergs* (1983).

126. *R. v. Cyanimid Canada Inc.* (1981); R. v. McCain (1984). McCain was actually fined $1 on each of eight separate counts upon which it was convicted, for a total fine of $8.
127. Harris (1998, 134).
128. Saxe (1990).
129. Ironically, after cutting back staff and funding for environmental enforcement, the Ontario government passed a law with potential fines of up to $6 million per day on a corporation's first offence and $10 million per day on subsequent offences (Toughest Environmental Penalties Act, 2000, S.O. 2000, c. 22).
130. *R. v. Tioxide Canada Inc.* (1993); *R. v. Corner Brook Pulp and Paper* (1997).
131. *R. v. Beaulieu* (2000), 103.
132. *R. v. Brunswick Electric Power Commission* (1991), 191.
133. *R. v. Canadian Pacific Forest Products Limited* (1991), 3.
134. *R. v. Bata Industries Ltd.* (1992), (1992).
135. Berger (1994).
136. *MacMillan Bloedel v. Sheila Simpson et al.* (1993).
137. *Interfor v. Paine and Krawczyk* (2001); Krawczyk (2002).
138. Canadian Press (2001c).
139. Harrison and Hoberg (1994, 13).
140. Hoberg (2000, 39–44).
141. Sierra Club v. Department of Interior (1974); Sierra Club v. Department of Interior (1975).
142. Wilkinson (1997, 659).
143. Hoberg (2001b, 176); Elgie (1993).
144. Swanson and Hughes (1995, 114).
145. Glenn (1999, 254).
146. Howlett (2001d, 34).

REFERENCES FOR "SYSTEMIC WEAKNESSES" AND "OBSTACLES TO FURTHER PROGRESS"

Abouchar, Julie. 2001. "Implementation of the Precautionary Principle in Canada." In Tim O'Riordan, James Cameron, and Andrew Jordan, eds., *Reinterpreting the Precautionary Principle*, 235–67. London: Cameron May.

Amos, William, Kathryn Harrison, and George Hoberg. 2001. "In Search of a Minimum Winning Coalition: The Politics of Species at Risk Legislation in Canada." In Karen Beazley and Robert Boardman, eds., *The Politics of the Wild: Canada and Endangered Species*. Don Mills, ON: Oxford University Press.

Anderson, David. 2003. Budget Speech 2003, House of Commons. (Speaking Notes). 26 February 2003. Ottawa.

Andrews, William J. 2000. "Public Access to Environmental Justice: A Comment Ten Years After." In Leonard J. Griffiths and Patricia Houlihan, eds., *Sustainable Development in Canada: Into the Next Millennium*. Ottawa: Canadian Bar Association.

Appleton, Barry. 1998. "Testimony." In BC Special Committee on the Multilateral Agreement on Investment. *Report of Proceedings (Hansard)* 29 September.

———1994. Navigating NAFTA: A Concise User's Guide to the North American Free Trade Agreement. Toronto: Carswell.

Auditor General of Canada. 2000b. "Fisheries and Oceans: The Effects of Salmon Farming in B.C. on the Management of Wild Salmon Stocks." Chapter 30 in Report to Parliament. Ottawa: Minister of Supply and Services. <http://www.oag-bvg.gc.ca>.

———1999c. "Pacific Salmon: Sustainability of the Fisheries." Chapter 20 in Report to Parliament. Ottawa: Minister of Supply and Services.

Barrett, Katherine. 2002. "Food Fights: Canadian Regulators Are Under Pressure to Face the Uncertainties of Genetically Modified Food." Alternatives Journal 28(1): 28–33.

Benidickson, Jamie. 2002. Environmental Law. 2d ed. Toronto: Irwin Law.

———1999. "Sustaining Old-growth Pineland in Ontario: Pathways to Reform." 9 Journal of Environmental Law and Practice 199.

———1997. *Environmental Law*. Toronto: Irwin Law.

Berger, Emily A. 2000. "Standing at the Edge of a New Millenium: Ending a Decade of Erosion of the Citizen Suit Provision of the Clean Water Act." Maryland Law Review 59(4): 1371.

Berger, Stanley D. 1994. *The Protection and Defence of Environmental Offenses*. 2 vols. Toronto: Emond Montgomery.

Bernstein, Steven, and Benjamin Cashore. 2001a. "Globalization, Internationalization, and Liberal Environmentalism: Exploring Non-Domestic Sources of Influence on Canadian Environmental Policy." In Debora L. VanNijnatten and Robert Boardman, eds., *Canadian Environmental Policy: Context and Cases*, 212–232. 2d ed. Oxford: Oxford University Press.

Boardman, Rogert. 2001. "Milk and Potatoes Environmentalism: Canada and the Turbulent World of International Law." In Debora L. VanNijnatten and Robert Boardman, eds., *Canadian Environmental Policy: Context and Cases*, 190–211. 2d ed. Oxford: Oxford University Press.

Boyd, D., David R. 2002a. "Beautiful B.C. Will Be Scarred by Cuts." Victoria Times-Colonist, 21 January, A9.

———1998. *Betraying Our Trust: A Citizen's Guide to Environmental Rollbacks*. Vancouver. Sierra Legal Defence Fund.

Boyd, David R., and S. Wallace. 2001. *Sea Change: Strengthening Bill C-5, the Species at Risk Act, to Protect Marine Biodiversity*. Victoria: Eco-Research Chair in Environmental Law and Policy.

Brooks, Stephen, and Andrew Stritch. 1991. *Business and Government in Canada*. Scarborough, ON: Prentice Hall.

Burda, C., R. Collier, and B. Evans. 1999. *The Gitxsan Model: An Alternative to the Destruction of Forests, Salmon and the Gitxsan Land*. Victoria: University of Victoria Eco-Research Chair in Environmental Law and Policy.

Cameron, James, and Julie Abouchar. 1996. "The Status of the Precautionary Principle in International Law." In David Freestone and Ellen Hey, eds., *The Precautionary Principle and International Law*. The Hague: Kluwer Law International.

Canadian Bar Association. 1990. *Report of the CBA Committee on Sustainable Development Options for Law Reform*. Ottawa.

Canadian Global Almanac. 2001. Toronto: Global Press.

Canadian Institute for Business and the Environment. 1997. Gallon Environment Letter, 11 November.

———1996. *The Environmental Management Framework Agreement—A Model for Dysfunctional Federalism?* Toronto.

Canadian Press. 2001c "Loggers Who Trashed Camp Get Probation." Victoria Times-Colonist, 5 January. A5.

Cashore, Benjamin, George Hoberg, Michael Howlett, et al., 2001. *In Search of Sustainability: British Columbia Forest Policy in the 1990s*. Vancouver: UBC Press.

Castrilli, J. F. 2002. "The New Ontario Hazardous Waste Regulations of 2000: Waste Identification and Protection of the Environment." 11 *Journal of Environmental Law and Practice* 285.

Castrilli, J. F., and Toby Vigod. 1987. *Pesticides in Canada: An Examination of Federal Law and Policy*. Ottawa: Law Reform Commission of Canada.

Chang, E., D. MacDonald, and J. Wolfson. 1998. "Who Killed CIPSI?" *Alternatives Journal* 24(2): 20–25.

Chase, Steven. 2001. "Ottawa Faces Suit over Banned Pesticide." *Globe and Mail*, 11 December, B1, B6.

Christie, Elizabeth. 2000. *Pulping the Law: How Pulp Mills Are Ruining Canadian Waters with Impunity*. Toronto: Sierra Legal Defence Fund.

Clark, Karen, and James Yacoumidis. 2000. *Ontario's Environment and the Common Sense Revolution: A Fifth Year Report*. Toronto: Canadian Institute of Environmental Law and Policy. <http://www.cielap.org>.

Commission for Environmental Cooperation 2002a. "Free Trade and Environment: The Picture Becomes Clearer." <http://www.cec.org>.

Commissioner of the Environment and Sustainable Development. 2000. *Report to the House of Commons*. Ottawa: Minister of Public Works and Government Services.

———1999. *Report to the House of Commons*. Ottawa: Minister of Public Works and Government Services.

Cooper, K. 1999b. "An Updated Chronology of Changes in Ontario's Environmental Policy." *Intervenor* (Canadian Environmental Law Association) 24(1): 9–16.

Cosh, Colby. 1996. "The Elected Dictatorship: Can Parliament Be Made an Adequate Instrument of Democracy?" *Alberta Report*, 16 December.

Daily, Gretchen, and Katherine Ellison. 2002. *The New Economy of Nature*. Washington, DC: Island Press.

Dale, Ann, 2001. *At the Edge: Sustainable Development in the 21st Century*. Vancouver: UBC Press.

Davies, J. C., and J. Mazurek. 1998. *Pollution Control in the U.S.: Evaluating the System*. Washington, DC: Resources for the Future.

Dawson, Mary. 2001. *Evidence, Standing Committee on Environment and Sustainable Development. Hearings on Bill C-5. The Species at Risk Act*, 6 June. <http://www.parl.gc.ca>

Dewees, Don. 1993. *Reducing the Burden of Environmental Regulation*. Discussion Paper 93-07. Kingston: Queen's University School of Policy Studies.

———1990. "The Regulation of Sulphur Dioxide in Ontario." In G. Bruce Doern, ed., *Getting it Green: Case Studies in Canadian Environmental Regulation*. Toronto: C.D. Howe Institute.

Dixon, Guy. 2000. "Canada Tops for Least Amount of Red Tape: Study." *Globe and Mail*, 14 November, B9.

Doering, R., F. Bregha, D. Roberts et al. 1992. *Environmental Regulations and the Pulp and Paper Industry*. Ottawa: National Round Table on the Environment and the Economy.

Doern, G. Bruce. 2001. "Environment Canada as a Networked Institution." In Debora L. VanNijnatten and Robert Boardman, eds., *Canadian Environmental Policy: Context and Cases*. 2d ed Oxford: Oxford University Press.

Doern, G. Bruce, and T. Conway. 1994. *The Greening of Canada: Federal Institutions and Decisions*. Toronto: University of Toronto Press.

Dorcey, Anthony H. J., and Timothy McDaniels. 2001. "Great Expectations, Mixed Results: Trends in Citizen Involvement in Canadian Environmental Governance." In Edward A. Parson, ed., *Governing the Environment: Persistent Challenges, Uncertain Innovations*. Toronto: University of Toronto Press.

Doyle-Bedwell, P., and F.G. Cohen. 2001. "Aboriginal Peoples in Canada: Their Role in Shaping Environmental Trends in the Twenty-first Century." In Edward A. Parson, ed., *Governing the Environment: Persistent Challenges, Uncertain Innovations*, 169–206. Toronto: University of Toronto Press.

Duncan, Linda. 1990a. *Enforcing Environmental Law: A Guide to Private Prosecutions*. Edmonton: Environmental Law Centre.

Dwivedi, O.P., Patrick Kyba, Peter J. Stoett et al. 2001. *Sustainable Development and Canada: National and International Perspectives*. Peterborough, ON: Broadview Press.

Egan, Brian, Lisa Ambus, Bryan, Evans et al. 2001. *Where There's a Way, There's a Will. Report 2, Models of Community-Based Natural Resource Management*. Victoria: Eco-Research Chair in Environmental Law and Policy.

Eggerston, Laura. 1999. "Controversial Environment Bill Passed by House." *Toronto Star*, 2 June. News section.

Elgie, Stewart. 1993. "Environmental Groups and the Courts: 1970–1992." In G. Thompson, M.L. McConnell, and L. Huestis, eds., *Environmental Law and Business in Canada*, 185–224. Toronto: Canada Law Book.

Environment Canada. 1999d. National Enforcement Program Business Case. Ottawa.

———1997a. The Right Choice at the Right Time: Highlights of the Global Benefits and Costs of the Montreal Protocol on Substances That Deplete the Ozone Layer. Ottawa.

———1990a. Canada's Green Plan for a Healthy Environment. Ottawa: Minister of Supply and Services.

Environmental Commissioner of Ontario. 2000a. Changing Perspectives: Annual Report 1999-2000. Toronto.

———1999. 1998–99 Annual Report. Toronto.

———1998. Open Doors: Annual Report. Toronto.

———1997. Open Doors: Annual Report. Toronto.

———1996. Open Doors: Annual Report. Toronto.

Estrin, David, and John Swaigen. 1993. Environment on Trial: A Guide to Ontario Environmental Law and Policy. Toronto: Emond Montgomery.

European Environment Agency. 2001. Late Lessons from Early Warnings: The Precautionary Principle, 1896–2000. Copenhagen.

Farber, Daniel A. 1999. "Taking Slippage Seriously: Noncompliance and Creative Compliance in Environmental Law." 23 Harvard Environmental Law Review: 297.

Forsey, Eugene A. 1991. How Canadians Govern Themselves. Ottawa: Minister of Canadian Heritage and the Minister of Public Works and Government Services Canada.

Freestone, D., and E. Hey, eds. 1996. The Precautionary Principle and International Law: The Challenge of Implementation. London: Kluwer Law International.

Friends of the Earth Canada. 2001. Primary Environmental Care: An Assessment of Environment Canada's Delivery. Vol.2, Ten Year Record of Environmental Prosecution, 1989–1999. Ottawa.

Gallon, Gary. 1999. "A Five-Tier Approach to Effective Environmental Initiatives." In Robert B. Gibson, ed., *Voluntary Initiatives: The New Politics of Corporate Greening*. Peterborough, ON: Broadview Press.

Gertler, Franklin, Paul Muldoon, and Marcia Valiante. 1990. "Public Access to Environmental Justice." In Canadian Bar Association Committee on Sustainable Development, ed., *Sustainable Development: Options for Law Reform*. Ottawa: Canadian Bar Association.

Gibson, Robert B. 1999. "Voluntary Initiatives, Regulations, and Beyond." In Robert B. Gibson, ed., *Voluntary Initiatives: The New Politics of Corporate Greening*, 239–257. Peterborough, ON: Broadview Press.

Gilles, A. M. 1994. The Greening of Government Taxes and Subsidies, Where to Start: An Action Plan for Protecting the Environment and Reducing the Deficit. Winnipeg: International Institute for Sustainable Development.

Glenn, Jack. 1999. Once upon an Oldman: Special Interest Politics and the Oldman River Dam. Vancouver: UBC Press.

Government of Canada. 2001. Public Accounts of Canada, 2000–2001. Vol. 1. Ottawa: Minister of Public Works and Government Services.

Greenpeace International. 2002. Who to Blame Ten Years After Rio? The Role of the USA, Canada, and Australia in Undermining the Rio Agreements. Amsterdam: Greenpeace International.

Gunningham, Neil, Peter Grabosky, and Darren Sinclair. 1998. Smart Regulation: Designing Environmental Policy. Oxford: Clarendon Press.

Handy, Francis J. F., and Douglas T. Hamilton. 1996. "Environmental Law of Canada." In Nicholas A. Robinson, ed., *Comparative Environmental Law and Regulation*. New York: Oceana Publications.

Harris, Michael. 1998. *Lament for an Ocean, the Collapse of the Atlantic Cod Fishery: A True Crime Story*. Toronto: McClelland and Stewart.

Harrison, Kathryn. 2001a. "Federal-Provincial Relations and the Environment Unilateralism, Collaboration and Rationalization." In Debora L. VanNijnatten and Robert Boardman, eds., *Canadian Environmental Policy: Context and Cases*, 123–44. 2d ed. Oxford: Oxford University Press.

———2001b. "Voluntarism and Environmental Governance." In Edward A. Parson, ed., *Governing the Environment: Persistent Challenges, Uncertain Innovations*, 207–46. Toronto: University of Toronto Press.

———2000a. Challenges in Evaluating Voluntary Environmental Programs. Paper prepared for National Academy of Sciences/National Research Council Workshop on Education, Information and Voluntary Measures in Environmental Protection. Washington, DC. 29–30 November.

———2000b. "The Origins of National Standards: Comparing Federal Government Involvement in Environmental Policy in Canada." In Patrick C. Fafard and Kathryn Harrison, eds., *Managing the Environmental Union: Intergovernmental Relations and Environmental Policy in Canada*. Montreal: McGill-Queen's University Press.

———1995. *Passing the Buck: Federalism and Canadian Environmental Policy*. Vancouver: UBC Press.

Harrison, Kathryn, and Richard N. L. Andrews. 1998. "Environmental Regulation and Business Self-Regulation." *Policy Sciences* 31: 177–97.

Harrison, Kathryn, and W. Antweiler. 2001. "Environmental Regulation vs. Environmental Information: A View from Canada's National Pollutant Release Inventory." <http://www.policy.ca>

Harrison, Kathryn, and George Hoberg. 1994. *Risk, Science and Politics: Regulating Toxic Substances in Canada and the United States*. Montreal: McGill-Queen's University Press.

Hayes, T.B ., et al. 2002. "Hermaphroditic, Demasculinized Frogs after Exposure to the Herbicide, Atrazine, at Low Ecologically Relevant Doses." *Proceedings of the National Academy of Sciences* (U.S.) 99: 5476–80.

Hessing, Melody, and Michael Howlett. 1997. *Canadian Natural Resource and Environmental Policy: Political Economy and Public Policy*. Vancouver: UBC Press.

Hitchens, D. 1999. "The Influence of Environmental Regulation on Company Competitiveness: A Review of the Literature and Some Case Study Evidence." In D. Hitchens, J. Clausen, and K. Fichter, eds., *International Environmental Management Benchmarks: Best Practice Experiences from America, Japan, and Europe*, 39–53. Berlin: Springer.

Hoberg, George. 2001a. "The British Columbia Forest Practices Code: Formalization and Its Effects." In Michael Howlett, ed., *Canadian Forest Policy: Adapting to Change*. Toronto: University of Toronto Press.

———2001b. "Canadian-American Environmental Relations: A Strategic Framework." In Debora L. VanNijnatten and Robert Boardman, eds., *Canadian Environmental Policy: Context and Cases*. 2d ed. Oxford: Oxford University Press.

———2000. "How the Way We Make Policy Governs the Policy We Make." In Debra J. Salazar and Donald K. Alper, eds., *Sustaining the Forests of the Pacific Coast: Forging Traces in the War in the Woods*, 26–53. Vancouver: UBC Press.

———1997. "Governing the Environment: Comparing Canada and the United States." In K. Banting et al. eds., *Degrees of Freedom: Canada and the United States in a Changing World*. Montreal: McGill-Queen's University Press.

———1994. *Regulating Forestry: A Comparison of British Columbia and the U.S. Pacific Northwest*. Kingston: Queen's University School of Policy Studies.

Howlett, Michael, ed. 2001d. "Policy Instruments and Implementation Styles: The Evolution of Instrument Choice in Canadian Environmental Policy." In Debora L. VanNijnatten and Robert Boardman, eds., *Canadian Environmental Policy: Content and Cases*. 2d ed. Oxford: Oxford University Press.

Hoy, Claire. 1999. *Nice Work: The Continuing Scandal of Canada's Senate*. Toronto: McClelland and Stewart.

Huestis, Lynn. 1984. *Policing Pollution: The Prosecution of Environmental Offenses*. Ottawa: Law Reform Commission of Canada.

Hutchings, J.A., C. Walters, and R.L. Haedrich. 1997. "Is Scientific Inquiry Incompatible with Government Information Control?" *Canadian Journal of Fisheries and Aquatic Sciences* 54: 1198–210.

International Institute for Sustainable Development. 2000a. *The Cartagena Protocol on Biosafety: An Analysis of Results*. Winnipeg.

Jacobs, Donna. 1999. "How Industry Beat the Environmental Protection Act." *Ottawa Citizen*, 7 September A1.

Johnson, L. 1996. "Naked Lunch: Canada's Dismal Biotech Regs Are as Full of Holes as Swiss Cheese." 29 *This Magazine* 34.

Johnson, P.M., and A. Beaulieu. 1996. *The Environment and NAFTA. Understanding and Implementing the New Continental Law*. Washington: Island Press.

Jones, D.P., and A.S. de Villars. 1999. *Principles of Administrative Law*. 3d ed. Scarborough, ON: Carswell.

Juillet, Luc. 2001. "Regional Models of Environmental Governance." In Edward A. Parson, ed., *Governing the Environment: Persistent Challenges, Uncertain Innovations*. Toronto: University of Toronto Press.

Juillet, Luc, and Glen Toner. 1997. "From Great Leaps to Baby Steps: Environment and Sustainable Development Policy under the Liberals." In Gene Swimmer, ed., *How Ottawa Spends, 1997–98*, 179–209. Toronto: Oxford University Press.

Jutlah, Russell J. 1998. "Economic Instruments and Environmental Policy in Canada." 8 *Journal of Environmental Law and Practice* 323.

KPMG Chartered Accountants. 1996. *Canadian Environmental Management Survey*. Toronto: KPMG.

Krahn, Peter K. 1998. *Enforcement vs. Voluntary Compliance: An Examination of the Strategic Enforcement Initiatives Implemented by the Pacific and Yukon Regional Office of Environment Canada, 1983 to 1998*. Vancouver: Environment Canada.

Kromm, Chris, and Keith Ernst. 2000. *Green and Gold 2000*. Durham, NC: Institute for Southern Studies.

La Forest, Gerard, and Dale Gibson. 2000a. *Constitutional Authority for Federal Protection of Migratory Birds, Other Cross-border Species and their Habitat in Endangered Species Legislation*. Vancouver: Sierra Legal Defence Fund.

Lalumière, C., and Jean-Pierre Landau. 1998. *Report on the Multilateral Agreement on Investment*. Paris. Ministry of the Economy: Finance and Industry.

Langille, David. 1987. "The BCNI and the Canadian State." *Studies in Political Economy* 24: 41–85.

Law Reform Commission of Canada. 1986. *Private Prosecutions*. Criminal Law Working Paper No. 52. Ottawa.

Leiss, William. 2001. *In the Chamber of Risks: Understanding Risk Controversies*. Montreal: McGill-Queen's University Press.

Leiss, William, and Michael Tyshenko. 2001. "Some Aspects of the 'New Biotechnology' and Its Regulation in Canada." In Debora L . VanNijnatten and Robert Boardman, eds., *Canadian Environmental Policy: Context and Cases*, 321–44, 2d ed. Oxford: Oxford University Press.

Ludwig, Donald, Ray Hilborn, and Carl Walters. 1993. "Uncertainty: Resource Exploitation, and Conservation: Lessons from History." 260 *Science 17*.

Macdonald, Douglas. 2001. "The Business Response to Environmentalism." In Debora L. VanNijnatten and Robert Boardman, eds., *Canadian Environmental Policy: Context and Cases*. 2d ed. Oxford: Oxford University Press.

———1991. *The Politics of Pollution: Why Canadians Are Failing Their Environment*. Toronto: McClelland and Stewart.

McIlroy, Anne. 1997b. "Ottawa's Environmental Joy Ride." *Globe and Mail*, 4 October, D1–2.

McIntyre, O., and T. Mosedale 1997. "The Precautionary Principle as a Norm of Customary International Law." 9 *Journal of Environmental Law* 221.

MacIsaac, Ron, and Anne Champagne. 1994. *Clayoquot Mass Trials: Defending the Rainforest*. Philadelphia: New Society Publishers.

McKay, Paul. 1997, "Environment Canada Told to Cut Staff, Spending: Impact Compounded by Provincial Cuts and Harmonization." *Ottawa Citizen*, 4 October, A1.

Mandrusiak, Bradley. 1999. "Playing with Fire: The Premature Release of Genetically Engineered Plants into the Canadian Environment." 9 *Journal of Environmental Law and Practice:* 259.

Mann, Howard. 2001. *Private Rights, Public Problems: A Guide to NAFTA's Chapter on Investor Rights*. Winnipeg: International Institute for Sustainable Development.

Martin, Paul. 1992. *L'environnement: L'optique du Parti Liberal-Document de Travail*. Ottawa: Liberal Party of Canada.

Menell, Peter S., and Richard B. Stewart. 1994. *Environmental Law and Policy*. Boston: Little, Brown.

M'Gonigle, M., et al. 1995. "Taking Uncertainty Seriously: From Permissive Regulation to Preventative Design in Environmental Decision-Making." 32 *Osgoode Hall Law Journal:* 99.

M'Gonigle, Michael, Brian Egan Lisa, Ambus et al. 2001. *Where There's a Way, There's a Will*. Report 1, *Developing Sustainability through the Community Ecosystem Trust*. Victoria: Eco-Research Chair in Environmental Law and Policy.

Mittelstaedt, Martin. 1999a. "Criminal Polluters Finding Canada the Promised Land." *Globe and Mail*, 23 March, A7.

———1999b. "Water Polluters Escaping Prosecution." *Globe and Mail*, 1 March, A1.

Morelli, Lisa J. 1997. "Citizen Suit Enforcement of Environmental Laws in the United States: An Overview." *Environmental Liability* 5: 19–29.

Morley, C.G., ed. 1973. *Canada's Environment: The Law on Trial—Proceedings of an Environmental Law Conference*. Winnipeg: Manitoba Institute of Continuing Legal Education.

Muldoon, Paul, and Ramani Nadarajah. 1999. "A Sober Second Look." In Robert B. Gibson, ed., *Voluntary Initiatives: The New Politics of Corporate Greening*. Peterborough, ON: Broadview Press.

National Environmental Law Section of the Canadian Bar Association. 1996. *Commentary on the Draft Environmental Management Framework Agreement*. Ottawa: Canadian Bar Association.

———2001a. *Managing Potentially Toxic Substances in Canada: A State of the Debate Report*. Ottawa.

Natural Resources Canada. 2001b. *The State of Canada's Forests 2000–2001, Sustainable Forestry: A Reality in Canada*. Ottawa.

———2001c. Statistics and Facts on Energy. Ottawa.

———2001d. Statistics and Facts on Minerals and Metals. Ottawa.

Natural Resources Defence Council. 2001. The Bush Environmental Budget: Building a Bridge to the 19th Century. Washington, DC.

Nemetz, P.N. 1986. "Federal Environmental Regulation in Canada." Natural Resources Journal. 26: 551–608.

New Directions Group. 1997. "Criteria and Principles for the Use of Voluntary or Non-regulatory Initiatives to Achieve Environmental Policy Objectives." In Robert B. Gibson, ed., Voluntary Initiatives: The New politics of Corporate Greening, 229–38. Peterborough, ON: Broadview Press.

O'Connor, Dennis R. 2002a. Report of the Walkerton Inquiry. Part 2, The Events of May 2000 and Related Issues. Toronto: Queen's Printer.

OECD (Organization for Economic Cooperation and Development). 2001e. Policies to Enhance Sustainable Development. Paris.

———2000a. Economic Survey of Canada. Paris.

———1995a. Environmental Performance Review: Canada. Paris.

———1993. Environmental Policies and Industrial Competitiveness. Paris.

Ogan, Marshall. 2000. "An Evaluation of the Environmental Harmonization Initiative of the Canadian Council of Ministers of the Environment." 10 J.E.L.P. 15.

Ontario Ministry of Environment. 2001. "Leading the Climate Change Challenge." Media backgrounder. 26 January <http://www.ene.gov.on.ca>.

Ontario Provincial Auditor. 2000. Special Report: Accountability and Value for Money. Toronto.

———1996. Annual Report. Toronto.

Paehlke, Robert. 2001. "Spatial Proportionality: Right-Sizing Environmental Decision-Making." In Edward A. Parson, ed., Governing the Environment: Persistent Challenges, Uncertain Innovations. Toronto: University of Toronto Press.

Panayatou, T. 1994. Economic Instruments for Environmental Management and Sustainable Development. Nairobi: United Nations Environment Program.

Parson, Edward. A. 2001. "Environmental Trends: A Challenge to Canadian Governance." In Edward A. Parson, ed., *Governing the Environment: Persistent Challenges, Uncertain Innovations*. Toronto: University of Toronto Press.

Parsons, Tim. 2001. "Survival, by Sea: An Eminent Scientist Ponders the Neglect with Which Humanity Treats a Resource Vital to Life on Earth." *Vancouver Sun*, 2 March, A19.

Pifer, J. 1997. "Loggers Are an Endangered Species: Union Advice Thwarted NDP Plans for a Job-Killing Eco-bill." *British Columbia Report*, 16 June, 19.

Porter, Michael E. 1991. *Canada at the Crossroads: The Reality of a New Competitive Environment*. Ottawa: Business Council on National Issues and Government of Canada.

———1990. *The Competitive Advantage of Nations*. London: Macmillan Press.

Porter, Michael E., and C. van der Linde. 1995. "Green and Competitive: Ending the Stalemate." *Harvard Business Review*, Sept.-Oct.: 120–34.

Power, Thomas, M. and Richard N. Barrett. 2001. *Post-Cowboy Economics: Pay and Prosperity in the New American West*. Washington, DC: Island Press.

Pue, W. Wesley, ed. 2000. *Pepper in Our eyes: The APEC Affair*. Vancouver: UBC Press.

Rabe, Barry. 1997. "The Politics of Sustainable Development Impediments to Pollution Prevention and Policy Integration in Canada." *Canadian Public Administration* 40(3): 415–35.

Raffensperger, Carolyn, and Joel Tickner, eds. 1999. Protecting Public Health and the Environment: Implementing the Precautionary Principle. Washington, DC: Island Press.

Rolfe, Chris, and L. Nowlan. 1993. Economic Instruments and the Environment: Selected Legal Issues. Vancouver: West Coast Environmental Law Research Foundation.

Ross, Monique. 1995. Forest Management in Canada. Calgary: Canadian Institute for Resource Law.

Royal Society of Canada. 2001. Elements of Precaution: Recommendations for the Regulation of Food Biotechnology in Canada. Ottawa.

Savoie, Donald. 1999. Governing from the Centre: The Concentration of Power in Canadian Politics. Toronto: University of Toronto Press.

Saxe, Dianne. 1990. Environmental Offences: Corporate Responsibility and Executive Liability. Aurora, ON: Canada Law Book.

Schettler, Ted, et al. 1999. Generations at Risk: Reproductive Health and the Environment. Cambridge, MA: MIT Press.

Schiller, Bill. 2001. "Chilean Ban to Boost Asbestos Woes." *Toronto Star*, 8 July, 9.

Schindler, David W. 2001. "The Cumulative Effects of Climate Warming and Other Human Stresses on Canadian Freshwaters in the New Millennium" *Canadian Journal of Fisheries and Aquatic Science* 58: 18–29.

Schrecker, Ted. 2001. "Using Science in Environmental Policy: Can Canada Do Better?" In Edward A. Parson, ed., *Governing the Environment: Persistent Challenges, Uncertain Innovations.* Toronto: University of Toronto Press.

Science Council of Canada. 1988. *Environmental Peacekeepers: Science, Technology, and Sustainable Development in Canada.* Ottawa: Minister of Supply and Services.

Scoffield, Heather. 2001. "Federal Spending Will Jump by 9.4 Percent." *Globe and Mail*, 11 December, A1.

———1999a. "Canada Lowest of G7 in Business Costs." *Globe and Mail*, 11 March, B5.

Shillington and Burns Consultants. 1999. *Background Study on Public Participation in Screening and Comprehensive Studies.* Ottawa: Canadian Environmental Assessment Agency.

Shrybman, Steven. 1999a. *A Citizen's Guide to the World Trade Organization.* Ottawa: Canadian Centre for Policy Alternatives.

Sierra Legal Defence Fund. 2002c. *False Economy: The Hidden Future Costs of Cuts in Regulatory Services.* Vancouver.

Sierra Legal Defence Fund and Wildlands League. 2001. *Improving Practices, Reducing Harm: A Forestry Field Audit in the Lower Spanish Forest.* Toronto: SLDF.

Simpson, Jeffrey. 2001. *The Friendly Dictatorship.* Toronto: McClelland and Stewart.

Sinclair, Scott, and Jim Grieshaber-Otto. 2002. *Facing the Facts: A Guide the GATS Debate.* Ottawa: Canadian Centre for Policy Alternatives.

Standing Committee on Environment and Sustainable Development. 1998. *Enforcing Canada's Pollution Laws: The Public Interest Must Come First.* Ottawa: House of Commons.

———1997. *Harmonization and Environmental Protection: An Analysis of the Harmonization Initiative of the Canadian Council of Ministers of the Environment.* Ottawa: House of Commons.

Stefanick, Lorna, and Kathleen Wells. 1998. "Staying the Course or Saving Face: Federal Environmental Policy Post-Rio." In Leslie A. Pal, ed., *How Ottawa Spends, 1998–99. Balancing Act: The Post-Deficit Mandate.* Toronto: Oxford University Press.

Swaigen, John. 1992. "The Role of Civil Courts in Resolving Risk and Uncertainty in Environmental Law." 2 *J.E.L.P*: 199.

Swanson, Elizabeth, and Elaine L. Hughes. 1995. *The Price of Pollution: Environmental Litigation in Canada.* Edmonton: Environmental Law Centre.

Swenarchuk, M. 2000. *The Cartagena Biosafety Protocol: Opportunities and Limitations.* Toronto: Canadian Environmental Law Association.

Systems Research Group. 1969. Canadian Legislation Relating to Environmental Quality Management. Toronto.

Taft, Kevin. 1977. *Shredding the Public Interest: Ralph Klein and 25 Years of One-Party Government.* Edmonton: University of Alberta Press.

Task Force on Economic Instruments and Disincentives to Sound Environmental Practices. 1994. *Economic Instruments and Disincentives to Sound Environmental Practices: Final Report.* Ottawa: Department of Finance and Environment Canada.

Thompson, Andrew R. 1980. *Environmental Regulation in Canada.* Vancouver: Westwater Research Centre.

Thornton, Joe. 2000. *Pandora's Poison: Chlorine, Health and a New Environmental Strategy.* Cambridge, MA: MIT Press, Appendix A.

Tilleman, William A. 1955. "Public Participation in the Environmental Assessment Process: A Comparative Study of Impact Assessment in Canada, the United States, and the European Community." 33 *Columbia Journal of Transnational Law*: 337.

Tollefson, Chris. 1995. "When the Public Interest Loses: The Liability of Public Interest Litigants for Adverse Cost Awards." 29 *UBC Law Review*: 303.

Toner, Glen. 1996. "Environment Canada's Continuing Roller Coaster Ride." In Gene Swimmer, ed., *How Ottawa Spends 1996–97: Life under the Knife*, 99–132. Ottawa: Carleton University Press.

US Environmental Protection Agency. 1999. Annual Report on Enforcement and Compliance Assurance Accomplishments in 1999. Washington, DC.

US General Accounting Office. 1997. *Global Warming: Information on the Results of Four of the EPA's Voluntary Climate Change Programs*. Washington, DC.

US National Research Council. 2002. *Environmental Effects of Transgenic Plants: The Scope and Adequacy of Regulation*. Washington, DC: National Academy Press.

US Office of Management and Budget. 1998. *Historical Tables, United States Government, Fiscal Year 1999*. Washington, DC: Government Printing Office.

US Office of Technology Assessment. 1994. *Trade and Environment: Conflicts and Opportunities*. Washington, DC: Government Printing Office.

VanderZwaag, David. 1998. "The Precautionary Principle in Environmental Law and Policy: Elusive Rhetoric and First Embraces." 8 *J.E.L.P.* 355.

———1995. *Canada and Marine Environmental Protection: Charting a Legal Course toward Sustainable Development*. London: Kluwer Law International.

VanNijnatten, Debora L., and Robert Boardman, eds. 2001. *Canadian Environmental Policy: Context and Cases*. 2d ed. Oxford: Oxford University Press.

Van Nijnatten, Debora L., and W. Henry Lambright. 2001. "Canadian Smog Policy in a Continental Context: Looking South for Stringency." In Debora L. VanNijnatten and Robert Boardman, eds., *Canadian Environmental Policy: Context and Cases*, 253–73. 2d ed. Oxford: Oxford University Press.

Walters, Carl. 1986. *Adaptive Management of Renewable Resources*. New York: Wiley.

Webb, Kernaghan. 1990. *Pollution Control in Canada: The Regulatory Approach in the 1990s*. Ottawa: Law Reform Commission of Canada.

West Coast Environmental Law Association. 2002. *The B.C. Government: A One Year Environmental Review*. Vancouver. <http://www.wcel.org>.

Wiener, J. B. 1999. "Global Environmental Regulation: Instrument Choice in Legal Context." 108 *Yale Law Journal* 677.

Wilkinson, Charles F. 1997. "The National Forest Management Act: The Twenty Years Behind, The Twenty Years Ahead." 68 *University of Colorado Law Review*: 659.

Winfield, Mark S. 2000. *Reflections on the Biosafety Protocol Negotiations in Montreal*. Toronto: Canadian Institute for Environmental Law and Policy.

Winsor, Hugh. 1999. "Ex-Liberal Spearheads Industry's Campaign against Bill." *Globe and Mail*, 26 April, A4.

Wolf, Michael Allan. 2000. "Environmental Law Slogans for the New Millennium." 30 *Environmental Law Reporter*: 10283.

Wood, Paul M. 2000. *Biodiversity and Democracy: Rethinking Nature and Society*. Vancouver: UBC Press.

FEDERAL LAWS AND REGULATIONS

Canada Foundation for Sustainable Development Technology Act, S.C. 2001, c. 23.

Canada Wildlife Act, R.S.C. 1985, c. W-9, amended by S.C. 1994, c. 23.

Canadian Environmental Assessment Act. S.C. 1992, c. 37.

Comprehensive Study List Regulations, SOR/94-229.
Exclusion List Regulations, SOR/94-3 16.
Inclusion List Regulations, SOR/94-164.
Law List Regulations, SOR/94-163.

Canadian Environmental Protection Act, 1999. S.C. 1999, c. 33.

> Asbestos Mines and Mills Release Regulations, SOR/90-341.
> Benzene in Gasoline Regulations, SOR/97-493.
> Chlor-Alkali Mercury Release Regulations, SOR/90- 13 0.
> Contaminated Fuel Regulations, SOR/91-486.
> Diesel Fuel Regulations, SOR/97-1 10.
> Leaded Gasoline Regulations, C.R.C. 409.
> Lead-free Gasoline Regulations, C.R.C. 408.
> Ozone Depleting Substances Regulations, SOR/99-7.
> Persistence and Bioaccumulation Regulations, SOR/2000-107.
> Phosphorous Concentration Regulations, SOR/89-501.
> Pulp and Paper Mill Defoamer and Wood Chip Regulations, SOR/92-282.
> Pulp and Paper Mill Effluent Chlorinated Dioxins and Furans Regulations, SOR/92-267.
> Secondary Lead Smelter Release Regulations, SOR/91-155.
> Sulphur in Gasoline Regulations, SOR/99-236.
> Tetrachloroethylene Regulations, SOR/2003-79.
> Vinyl Chloride Release Regulations, SOR/92-63 1.

Mackenzie Valley Resource Management Act, S.C. 1998, c. 25.

Manganese-based Fuel Additives Act, S.C. 1997, c. 11.

Nunavut Land Claims Agreement Act, S.C. 1993. c. 28.

Oceans Act, S.C. 1996, c. 31.

> Endeavour Hydrothermal Vents Marine Protected Areas Regulations, SOR/2003-87.

PROVINCIAL AND TERRITORIAL LAWS AND REGULATIONS
Alberta

Environmental Protection and Enhancement Act, R.S.A. 2000, c. E-12.

> Environmental Assessment (Mandatory and Exempted Activities) Regulation, Alta. Reg. 11/93.
> Ozone Depleting Substances and Halocarbon Regulation, Alta. Reg. 18 1/00.
> Pesticide Sales, Handling, Use, and Application Regulation, Alta. Reg. 24/97.

Manitoba

Endangered Species Act, C.C.S.M. E-11 1.

Environment Act, C.C.S.M. E-125.

> Livestock Manure and Mortalities Management Regulation, Man. Reg. 42/98.
> Manitoba Classes of Development Regulation, Man. Reg. 164/88.
> Sensitive Areas Regulation, Man. Reg. 126/88.

Newfoundland and Labrador

Wilderness and Ecological Reserves Act, R.S.N.L. 1990, c. W-9.

Northwest Territories

Environmental Rights Act, R.S.N.W.T. 1988 (Supp.) c. 83.

Nova Scotia

Environment Act, S.N.S. 1994-95, c. 1.

Wilderness Areas Protection Act, S.N.S. 1998, c. 27.

Ontario

Environmental Bill of Rights, 1993, S.O. 1993, c. 28.

Quebec

Environmental Quality Act, R.S.Q., c. Q-2.

> Agricultural Operations Regulation, O.C. 695-2002.
>
> Regulation respecting environmental impact assessment and review, R.R.Q. 1981, c. Q-2, r. 9.
>
> Regulation respecting ozone depleting substances, O.C. 812-93.
>
> Regulation respecting the quality of drinking water, R.R.Q., c. Q-2, r. 4.1.

Yukon

Environment Act, S.Y. 1991, c. 5.

> Yukon's Ozone Depleting Substances and other Halocarbons Regulations, O.I.C. 2000/12 7.

INTERNATIONAL LAW

World Trade Organization. 2001. European Communities—Measures Affecting Asbestos and Asbestos Containing Products, WT/DS135/AB/R, 12 March 2001. <http://www.wto.org>

World Trade Organization. 1998. EC Measures Concerning Meat and Meat Products (Hormones) Complaint by Canada. WT/DS48/R/Can and WT/DS48/AB/R/1 998.

World Trade Organization. 1998. United States—Import Prohibition of Certain Shrimp and Shrimp Products, WT/DS58/AB/R.

World Trade Organization. 1996. United States—Standards for Reformulated and Conventional Gasoline, WTO Doc. WT/DSR/R, 29 January 1996, 35 I.L.M. 274.

World Trade Organization. 1996. United States—Restrictions on Import of Tuna, GATT Doc. DS21/R, BISD (39th Supp.).

WTO Appellate Body Report. 1998. EC Measures Concerning Meat and Meat Products, WT/DS26/AB/R.

WTO Panel Report. 1997. EC Measures Concerning Meat and Meat Products, WT/DS26/R/USA.

CASES

Canadian Environmental Law Association v. Canada (Minister of the Environment) (2000), C.E.L.R. (N.S.) 159 (F.C.A.).

Council of the Haida Nation v. B.C. Minister of Forests and Weyerhaeuser (22 February 2002), 0147 (B.C.C.A.).

Delgamuukw v. British Columbia, [1997]3 S.C.R. 1010.

Finlay v. Canada (Minister of Finance), [1986] 2 S.C.R. 607.

Fletcher v. Kingston (City) (1998), 28 C.E.L.R. (N.S.) 299 (Ont. Ct. Prov. Div.).

Friends of the Oldman River Society v. Minister of Transport et al., [1992] 1 S.C.R. 3.

Green v. The Queen in Right of the Province of Ontario, [1973] 2 O.R. 396 (Ont. H.C.).

Interfor v. Paine and Krawczyk (25 January 2001), B.C.C.A. 48, C.A. 027708.

Inverhuron and District Ratepayers Association v. Canada (Minister of Environment) (2000), 34 C.E.L.R. (N.S.) 1 (F.C.T.D.), affirmed (2001), 39 C.E.L.R. (N.S.) 161 (F.C.A.).

Kostuch v. Alberta (Attorney General) (1992), 125 A.R. 214 (C.A.).

Kostuch v. Alberta (Attorney General), [1996] 1 W.W.R. 292 (Alta. C.A.).

Kostuch v. Environmental Appeal Board (1996), 21 C.E.L.R. (N.S.) 257 (Alta. Q.B.). *Kostuch v. Kowalski* (1990), 75 Alta. L.R. (2d) 110 (Prov. Ct.).

Kostuch v. Kowalski (1991), 78 Alta. L.R. (2d) 131 (Prov. Ct.).

Kostuch v. Kowalski (1991), 81 Alta. L.R. (2d) 214 (Q.B.).

MacMillan Bloedel v. Sheila Simpson et al. (1993), 84 C.C.C. (3d) 559 (B.C.C.A.).

Mitchell v. Canada (Attorney General), [1999] Newfoundland Supreme Court, Trial Division, 9 April 1999, Roberts J.

National Inshore Fisherman Association v. Canada (Minister of the Environment), [1990] 37 F.T.R. 230 (F.C.T.D.).

Operation Dismantle v. R., [1985] 1 S.C.R. 441.

Palmer v. Stora Kopparbergs [1983], 12 C.E.L.R. 157 (N.S.S.C. T.D.).

Pearson v. Inco (9 September 2002), (Ont. S.C.) [unreported], Nordheimer J.

R. v. Bata Industries Ltd. (1992), 14 O.R. (3d) 354 (Ont. Ct. Gen. Div.).

R. v. Bata Industries Ltd. (1992), 70 C.C.C. (3d) 394 (Ont. Ct. Prov. Div.).

R. v. Beaulieu (2000), 34 C.E.L.R. (N.S.) 100.

R. v. Brunswick Electric Power Commission (1991), 10 C.E.L.R. (N.S.) 184 (N.B. Prov. Ct.).

R. v. Canadian Pacific Forest Products Limited (12 June 1991), (B.C. Prov. Ct.) [unreported].

R. v. Crown Zellerbach Canada Ltd., [1988] 1 S.C.R. 401.

R .v. Cyanimid Canada Inc. (1981), 3 F.P.R. 151 (Ont. Prov. Ct.).

R. v. Marshall, [1999] 3 S.C.R. 456.

R. v. Marshall, [1999] 3 S.C.R. 533.

R. v. Tioxide Canada Inc. (31 May 1993), File 765-72-000060-528 (Que. Crim. Ct.).

Red Mountain Residents and Property Owner's Association v. B.C. (Ministry of Forests) (2000), 35 C.E.L.R. (N.S.) 127 (B.C.S.C.).

Seattle Audubon Society v. Evans, 771 F. Supp. 1081 (W.D. Wash., 1991), affirmed 952 F. 2d. 297 (9th Cir., 1991).

Shell v. Amok Ltd. (1988), 27 Admon. L.R. 1 (Sask. Q.B.).

Shell v. Canada (Atomic Energy Control Board) (1995), 33 Admin. L.R. (2d) 122 (F.C.T.D.).

Sierra Club v. Department of Interior, 376 F. Supp. 90 (U.S. Dist. Ct., 1974).

Sierra Club v. Department of Interior, 398 F. Supp. 284 (U.S. Dist. Ct., 1975).

United Mexican States v. Metalclad Corporation (2001), 38 C.E.L.R. (N.S.) 284 (B.C.S.C.).